A History of
MEDIEVAL SPAIN

A History of
MEDIEVAL SPAIN

Joseph F. O'Callaghan

CORNELL UNIVERSITY PRESS

Ithaca and London

First published 1975 by Cornell University Press.
Published in the United Kingdom by Cornell University Press Ltd.,
2–4 Brook Street, London W1Y 1AA.

International Standard Book Number 0-8014-0880-6
Library of Congress Catalog Card Number 74-7698

Printed in the United States of America by York Composition Co., Inc.

For

Anne, Billy, Cathy, Annie, and Joe

Espanna sobre todas es engennosa, atreuuda et mucho esforçada en lid, ligera en affan, leal al sennor, affincada en estudio, palaciana en palabra, complida de todo bien. . . . Espanna sobre todas es adelantada en grandez et mas que todas preciada por lealdad. Ay, Espanna! Non a lengua nin engenno que pueda contar tu bien!

More than all other lands Spain is shrewd, bold and vigorous in struggle, nimble in action, loyal to her lord, eager for study, courtly in speech, filled with every good thing. . . . Spain is set above all other lands in greatness and is more precious than all for loyalty. O Spain! there is neither tongue nor talent that can recount your worth!

Alfonso X, Primera Crónica General, 558

Contents

8   Contents

Illustrations

Maps

Preface

I began writing this book in the belief that a narrative history of the Hispanic Middle Ages, based upon the research and investigations of the best contemporary historians, would be useful to English readers. Until recently American and most northern European scholars have paid scant attention to the history of the Iberian peninsula in the Middle Ages and have often been content with superficial judgments founded upon antiquated and inaccurate works or on opinions clouded by the prejudices accumulated over the past four hundred years. If this book contributes to a clearer understanding of the formation of medieval Spain it will have served a valuable purpose. As the field of medieval Spanish and Portuguese history is still relatively unexplored, I hope that readers will be encouraged to pursue more intensive investigation into many of the subjects dealt with.

Chronologically this book extends from the coming of the Visigoths in the fifth century until the conquest of Granada and the discovery of America in 1492; geographically it embraces the entire peninsula, including both modern Spain and Portugal.

Consistency in the spelling of personal and place names is difficult to achieve, but I have tried to be consistent in my fashion. For the Roman and Visigothic periods I generally employ anglicized forms of personal names. There is no reason why they should be put in Castilian, and though Latin might be appropriate, "Reccesvinth" seems to me preferable to "Reccesvinthus." For Arabic names I usually adopt a simplified spelling based upon the forms used in the *Encyclopedia of Islam* (1960). I retain Romance names, except in such very familiar cases as Henry the Navigator and Ferdinand and Isabella, and I make use of the Castilian and Portuguese forms, for example, Alfonso, Afonso, Juan, João. Where there are several kings with those names ruling simultaneously, the different spellings will help to identify them more clearly. Names of rulers in the crown of Aragon pose a problem. I use Catalan spelling for persons distinctly Catalan, such as the counts of Barcelona and the kings of Majorca; but I use the Aragonese form for the kings of Aragon who also ruled Catalonia, for example, Alfonso, Pedro, Jaime, rather than Alfons, Pere, or Jaume. Similarly, when referring to the parliament in the Catalan-speaking areas, I use the form *corts*; elsewhere in the peninsula this is spelled *cortes*. For most place names I use the anglicized forms; however, I use Duero and Miño instead of the Portuguese Douro and Minho, but this should cause no difficulty.

All translations appearing in the text are my own, unless otherwise indicated.

In preparing this volume I was aided by a fellowship from the National Endowment for the Humanities in the summer of 1971, a faculty research grant from Fordham University for the same period, and faculty fellowships from the University for the summer and fall of 1966 and the fall and spring of 1961–1962. I am indeed grateful to Fordham and to the Endowment for their essential financial support. I also wish to record my debt of long standing to the Institute of International Education for having first given me the opportunity to do research in Spain in 1955–1956 and to the Fulbright Commission for a fellowship for study in Spain in 1961–1962.

My thanks are due also to Rev. Robert I. Burns and Archibald Lewis, who read the manuscript and offered many helpful suggestions; to my friends C. J. Bishko, the dean of American Hispanists, for his kindness and encouragement; Bernard F. Reilly, for his counsel on many specific points; James F. Powers, for reading the text and offering me many of his photographs for use as illustrations; Betty and John Finkbiner, for their care in preparing the maps; and to my teachers who initiated me into the realm of medieval history: Jeremiah F. O'Sullivan, Gerhart B. Ladner, and James S. Donnelly.

My deepest gratitude is owed to my parents, now deceased, who long ago encouraged me in my studies. I can only hope that this book would be a source of joy to them. My most faithful ally has been my wife, Anne, who always lent support and intelligent interest at crucial times. To her and to our children I dedicate this volume.

JOSEPH F. O'CALLAGHAN

St. Patrick's Day, 1973
Fordham University

Abbreviations for Citations

CC: *Cancionero castellano del siglo XV.* Ed. R. Foulché-Delbosc. 2 vols. Madrid, 1912–1915.

CHDE: Alfonso García Gallo. *Curso de Historia del Derecho español.* 2 vols. Madrid, 1958.

CLC: *Cortes de los antiguos Reinos de León y Castilla.* 5 vols. Madrid, 1861–1903.

CMCH: José Saénz de Aguirre. *Collectio maxima Conciliorum omnium Hispaniae.* 4 vols. Rome, 1693–1694.

DP: Demetrio Mansilla. *La Documentación pontificia hasta Inocencio III (965–1216).* Rome, 1955.

ES: Enrique Flórez. *España Sagrada.* 51 vols. Madrid, 1754–1759.

LCA: Joaquín Molas and Josep Romeu. *Literatura Catalana Antiga.* 4 vols. Barcelona, 1961–1964.

MHDE: Alfonso García Gallo. *Manual de Historia del Derecho español.* 3d ed. 2 vols. Madrid, 1967.

PL: J. P. Migne. *Patrologia Latina.* 222 vols. Paris, 1844–1864.

UKS: Richard Scholz. *Unbekannte kirchenpolitische Streitschriften aus der Zeit Ludwigs des Bayern (1327–1354).* 2 vols. Rome, 1914.

A History of
MEDIEVAL SPAIN

Hispania universa terrarum situ trigona est et circumfusione Oceani Tyrrheni-
que pelagi pene insula efficitur.

By the disposition of the land, Spain as a whole is a triangle and, surrounded
as it is by the Ocean and the Tyrrhenian Sea, is almost an island.

Paul Orosius, Historiarum Libri Septem, I, 2

Hispania

The Problem of Hispanic History

Within the thousand years from the coming of the Visigoths in the fifth century to the reign of Ferdinand and Isabella in the fifteenth, the character of Hispanic civilization was shaped and molded in significant ways. In the struggle for existence in an often inhospitable environment the Hispanic peoples developed those distinctive traits cited by Ramón Menéndez Pidal: austerity, stoicism, individualism, bravery to the point of rashness, and the desire for fame—the imperishable fame that comes through remembrance in history. While historians agree that the medieval centuries were important in the making of Hispanic civilization, they are divided in their estimates of the relative influence of ethnic, religious, and cultural elements.

Spanish historians especially have explored their past in an attempt to explain those apparent faults of character they see as causing Spain's decadence in modern times or the retardation of her political and cultural development when compared to that of other European countries. The debate among them is colored by ideological considerations, such as the traditional Castilian ambition to dominate the entire peninsula and the contrary desires of Basque and Catalan nationalists to preserve their identity and to recover their independence. The Portuguese, having maintained their independence of Spain and of Castilian hegemony, have taken less interest in a controversy that seems not to affect them.

José Ortega y Gasset (d. 1956), the great philosopher of our century, expressed the view in his *España invertebrada* that neither the ancient Iberians nor the Romans nor the Arabs provided the determining elements in the development of the essential Spanish character. For

17

him the Visigoths were decisive. Intoxicated by Roman civilization, they were no longer noble savages bursting with vitality, as were the Franks, their neighbors in Gaul, and so were incapable of uplifting and reinvigorating the decadent Hispano-Roman civilization. Thus, he reasoned, the advent of the Visigoths was the source of all the calamities that have befallen Spain over the centuries. This interpretation has been dismissed as superficial and simplistic by Claudio Sánchez Albornoz, the principal historian of medieval Spanish institutions, whose special interest has been to elucidate the role of the Visigoths in Hispanic history.

For some years now Sánchez Albornoz has been engaged in a fiery polemic with Américo Castro (d. 1972) concerning the nature of the Spanish character. A philologist and philosopher, Castro expounded his thesis in a book that appeared in several versions and in English translation as *The Spaniards: An Introduction to Their History*. At the outset he took strong exception to the idea, commonly expressed by Spanish writers, that the Spanish personality or spirit was permanent and unchanging over the centuries. The ancient Iberians, Romans, and Visigoths, he declared, were not Spaniards and had little to do with the eventual development of the Spanish people; it is folly, therefore, to speak of Seneca and other figures of the Roman world as though they were Spaniards in the same sense as Ferdinand and Isabella, as many modern patriotic writers have been wont to do.

Castro believed that the causative factor in the formation of Spain and of the Spanish people was the coexistence in the peninsula from the eighth to the fifteenth centuries of Christians, Muslims, and Jews, who were conscious of their identity primarily as members of separate religious groups. From their interaction, the fundamentally religious nature of the Spanish personality received definitive form. This, he believed, is the key to an understanding of Spanish history and the unique character of Spain in western Europe.

Castro was quite right in challenging the concept of an eternal and immutable Spain and Spanish character, but his own vision tends to be static and does not give sufficient importance to the gradual nature of the historical process. There were real differences in the ideas and attitudes of the men of the tenth, the twelfth, and the fifteenth centuries, but these are not made clear. While properly emphasizing the impact of Muslims and Jews upon Hispanic Christianity, the examples used to illustrate his argument are often quite tenuous. For example, the suggestion that the Christians borrowed the Muslim concept of the holy war fails to reckon with Christian traditions and ideas concerning the legitimacy of warfare. His argument that the Jews conducted all significant business activity in Christian Spain does not square with the facts; and the idea that Jews converted to Christianity were primarily responsible for the inquisition, the persecution, and eventual expulsion of their coreligionists is debatable.

While Castro's opinions have attracted great interest and acceptance, they have been strongly opposed and rejected in almost every instance by Sánchez Albornoz. In his *España, un enigma histórico*, Sánchez Albornoz stresses the fundamental continuity of history and, against Castro, argues that the Iberians, Romans, and Visigoths, as well as the medieval Christians, Muslims and Jews, in their several distinctive ways, made substantial contributions to the formation of the Hispanic personality. He believes that there are common aspects of the Hispanic character discernible over the centuries, but he recognizes that there were very real differences among the people of Roman times and those who lived in the centuries of the reconquest or of the Golden Age. He repudiates the idea that the character of the Spanish people was immutably fixed or determined in any period of history, as Castro seems to imply. As a Castilian, Sánchez Albornoz inclines to emphasize unity rather than diversity and regionalism, and he takes particular pains to point out those traits which Castilians, Portuguese, Basques, and Catalans, as Hispanic peoples, have in common.

Sánchez Albornoz criticizes Castro for neglecting the study of institutions and law where Roman and Germanic influence was especially vigorous and persistent; of exaggerating the impact of Islam and Judaism out of all proportion and of failing to realize that it was uneven and hardly touched some peninsular regions; of not acknowledging indigenous Hispanic, rather than Arabic or oriental, influences in Muslim Spain; and of ignoring the very strong influence of northern Europe upon Christian Spain, particularly from the eleventh century onward, precisely when Christians and Muslims were coming into closer and more continuous contact along the frontiers. The impassioned tone of Sánchez Albornoz's critique, however, often detracts from the justice of his arguments.

The Catalan historian Jaime Vicens Vives (d. 1960), in his *Approaches to the History of Spain*, stated that the polemic between Castro and Sánchez Albornoz could only result in a sounder interpretation of Spanish history, but he suggested that the methodology of both men was now somewhat dated. Fully aware of the hazards of entering the lists against them, he insisted that one must put aside ideological preconceptions and avoid excessive reliance upon literary texts or law codes as accurate reflections of what people at any given moment were thinking or doing. In order to achieve a fuller understanding of peninsular history, in all its complexity and diversity, he argued that one must come down from the world of abstraction and theory and look at the practicalities of life as documents recording daily activities reveal them to us. Admittedly, documents of this kind are not always available to the historian.

One of the aims of the present book is to provide a necessary foundation for a proper comprehension and evaluation of these various theories. I conceive of the history of medieval Spain as the history of *Hispania*, the Iberian peninsula in its totality, embracing the modern states of Spain and Portugal, and all the peoples who inhabited the area from the fifth through the fifteenth century. The peninsula was known to the ancient Greeks as *Iberia*, but the Romans called it *Hispania*; in the medieval Romance tongue this became *España*, whence our *Spain*. In explaining the scope of his *Primera Crónica General* (972), Alfonso X of Castile remarked: "In this our general history, we have spoken of all the kings of Spain and of all the events that happened in times past . . . with respect to both Moors and Christians and also the Jews. . . ." In the same way, the concern of this book is with Christians, Muslims, Jews, Castilians, Portuguese, Basques, Catalans, Aragonese, Andalusians; in other words, with all the peninsular peoples of medieval times.

Though one may look at their ideas, institutions, laws, customs, languages, and religious beliefs and see naught but diversity, they had much more in common than mere geographical propinquity. As descendants of families long settled in the peninsula, they were, in varying degrees, heirs to a common tradition, and at any given period of medieval history they shared a common historical experience. During the centuries of the reconquest there existed in Christian Spain a religious and cultural community that transcended purely local or regional concerns. Just as the Christian peoples, despite linguistic and other differences, borrowed ideas and institutions from one another, so too were they open to influences from Muslim Spain where a similar community of interests and traditions persisted, in spite of the political fragmentation that often prevailed in that area. This book seeks to illustrate the life of the Hispanic community in all its variety and complexity, pointing up what was common to many, while giving full recognition to their differences.

The Quest for Unity

Reflecting upon the history of medieval Spain, one can perceive as the recurrent theme the persistence with which men strove to unify the peninsula. The task was fraught with difficulties arising not only from the internal physical characteristics of the country, but also from the diversity of peoples within its borders. The Romans first established a uniform authority over the peninsula in the first century before Christ. By incorporating Spain into their empire they gave it a cultural foundation that subsisted in large measure through the vicissitudes of later centuries. The Germanic tribes who crossed the Pyrenees in the fifth century A.D. disrupted the imperial administration, and two centuries elapsed before the Visigoths were able to extend their rule over the entire peninsula. The course of peninsular history during that time was comparable to that of the other barbarian kingdoms of western Europe, but to a greater degree than elsewhere the Visigoths bowed to the superior civilization of Rome and adopted as their own the Latin language, the orthodox Christian religion, and much of the substance of Roman law.

In the eighth century Muslim conquerors, Arabs and Berbers, destroyed the unity of the Visigothic kingdom and interjected new religious and cultural elements into peninsular life. From that point the history of medieval Spain took on a unique character that distinguished it from the other western European states. Muslim influence upon Hispanic civilization was profound and is attested even today by architectural remains, the presence of numerous Arabic words in the Hispanic languages, and more subtly, by patterns of thought and behavior. But Spain was not Orientalized, Arabized, Islamized, or Africanized. The links with the past were not obliterated, nor did Muslim influence overwhelm or wholly displace the Roman, Germanic, and Christian contributions to peninsular development. As a bridge between Europe and Africa, between West and East, between the worlds of Christianity and Islam, Spain experienced in the medieval centuries a continual tension created by the shifting balance of religious and cultural influences. In the end the balance was tipped decisively in favor of the Christian and western European world.

Muslim failure to occupy permanently the regions of the far north-west and northeast gave the Christian population an opportunity to establish an independent basis from which to initiate the long and arduous task of reconquering the land they believed to be rightfully theirs. Several Christian states, namely Asturias, León, Castile, Navarre, Aragon, Catalonia, and Portugal, emerged in the centuries following the collapse of the Visigothic kingdom, and each evolved distinctive qualities, customs, and language. Despite these differences the Christian people were conscious of their joint responsibility for the reconquest. In the early centuries the rulers of Asturias and León presented themselves as heirs of the Visigoths and hoped to recover all the territory of the Visigothic kingdom. As J. A. Maravall pointed out in his *El Concepto de España en la edad media,* the word *Hispania* itself became for many medieval men the summons to the reconquest, the symbolic expression of the potential unity of the peninsula. From the tenth to the mid-twelfth century this concept was expressed in terms of an Hispanic empire seated in the kingdom of León, but it never achieved lasting juridical reality. Yet even as the Christian states grew steadily stronger from the late twelfth century, and pursued their own aims, without regard for Leonese claims to supremacy, the reconquest remained their common enterprise, a task to be carried to its inexorable conclusion. Though their ambitions might differ, the Christian rulers were united in this, as their collaboration against their common foe and their treaties for the partition of Muslim territory make manifest. Throughout these long centuries the reconquest was the common purpose and the cohesive principle of the Christian states.

The reconquest may be described as a holy war in the sense that it was a conflict prompted by religious hostility. But it was something more than that. By proclaiming oneself a Christian, a Muslim, or a Jew, one espoused specific religious doctrines and also accepted a whole system of cultural values that affected one's daily life, one's habits, traditions, laws, and even language. The difficulty, if not the impossibility, of reconciling or assimilating these different religious and cultural points of view was at the root of the struggle. Both sides came to recognize that it could only end with the complete triumph of one over the other.

It is one of the ironies of history that in Spain, a land widely known in modern times for religious intolerance, Christians, Muslims, and Jews often lived peacefully with one another in the medieval centuries. Religious minorities in general were tolerated in both Christian and Muslim kingdoms. This does not mean that they were loved or revered, but simply that they were permitted to exist and within certain limits to practice their religion and to be governed by their own laws and by their own judges. Periods of tolerance alternated, however, with persecution, and as the Middle Ages drew to a close the trend toward persecution grew stronger. This was partly a natural consequence of the successful progress of the reconquest which had reduced Muslim territory to the small kingdom of Granada. But the generally unsettled political and economic conditions prevailing in the late fourteenth and fifteenth centuries also stirred resentment against the Jews. Thus when Ferdinand and Isabella completed the reconquest in 1492, they decided that religious diversity was no longer acceptable; they expelled the Jews and began efforts to convert the Muslims who remained in the peninsula. Even though the Muslims accepted Christianity at least outwardly, they were never wholly trusted and were expelled finally in the seventeenth century. Religious uniformity and intolerance were thus consecrated as public policy.

Besides religious differences, a complexity of laws, customs, and languages developed in medieval times, and as the centuries wore on these dissimilarities served to strengthen and encourage regionalism. Roman law was incorporated in very large degree in the Visigothic Code, which remained in vigor during the centuries of the reconquest, but custom, derived principally from the Germanic tradition, challenged the supremacy of the written law. The *fueros* of León, Castile, Aragon, Navarre, and Portugal, and the *Usages of Barcelona* embodied the ancient customs by which the Christian people governed themselves for centuries. Royal attempts in the twelfth and thirteenth centuries to bring about legal uniformity by imposing Roman law met with strong popular resistance. In Muslim Spain the law was closely bound up with religion, and consequently its influence upon the Christian states was limited.

Among the different linguistic forms* in the peninsula the Basque language survived from prehistoric times in Navarre and the adjacent provinces. While few traces of Visigothic forms have come down to us, Latin eventually gave birth to several Romance languages, such as Gal-

---

* Spelling of personal and place names is explained in the Preface.

lego-Portuguese in Galicia and Portugal; Castilian, born in the central *meseta* and eventually spreading through the reconquered regions of Extremadura and Andalusia; Catalan, reaching from the French border down through Valencia and also to the Balearic Islands. In Muslim Spain, Arabic was the official language, but in daily affairs Berbers and Jews used their languages, and the Christians there developed a form of Romance. These linguistic differences were not an insuperable barrier to political union in the medieval era, but they have assumed great importance in modern times and have given impetus to Basque and Catalan demands for autonomy or independence.

The unification of Spain was achieved in part by the marriage of Ferdinand and Isabella, whose respective kingdoms, Aragon and Castile, the largest in the peninsula, were brought under their joint rule. The fall of the last Muslim outpost, the kingdom of Granada, in 1492, completed the reconquest and added a significant segment to their dominions. Political union was unfinished, however, because Portugal remained independent and successfully resisted all efforts to be absorbed or united with her larger neighbor. Moreover, Ferdinand and Isabella and their successors learned that the cultural and psychological differences developed during the medieval centuries were not easily resolved and that political union could not assure the spiritual cohesion of the people.

The achievement of a united Spain, incomplete as it was, was the consequence of fortuitous circumstances; in no way was it assured or foreordained. Indeed, if the accidents of history had been otherwise, Spain might be today what it was for so long in the Middle Ages, a congeries of states, both Christian and Muslim. Even so, the quest for unity, whether achieved or not, is the characteristic theme of medieval Hispanic history.

The Geographical Foundations

The physical structure of the peninsula has had much to do with its political and cultural development and its regional diversity. One of the most clearly delimited geographical entities on the European continent, its external appearance is deceptive in that it has always encouraged men to attempt to rule it as a whole. Separated from northern Europe by the Pyrenees mountains, it is bounded on three and one-half sides by the Mediterranean, the straits of Gibraltar, the Atlantic Ocean, and the Bay of Biscay.

For centuries the Pyrenees have served as a barrier, though by no means an impenetrable one, to communication between Spain and France. Two good passes through the mountains, Roncesvalles on the west and Le Perthus on the east, have enabled Celts, Visigoths, Franks, Frenchmen, and others to enter Spain. Throughout the medieval era communication was constant between Catalonia in the northeast and Languedoc and Provence in southern France. The oft-quoted phrase, "Africa begins with the Pyrenees" is a superficial judgment which neglects to take into account the diffusion of European ideas and institutions throughout the peninsula. Despite the Pyrenees, Spain remained an integral part of Europe.

To the south the straits of Gibraltar have never hampered communication between Spain and Africa, but have often afforded a facile passage for invaders such as the Arabs and Berbers in the eighth century, the Almoravids and Almohads in the eleventh and twelfth centuries, the Marinids in the thirteenth and fourteenth. As the Christians brought the conquest of Andalusia near completion, they endeavored to close the ports of Gibraltar and Algeciras to future invaders and contemplated the occupation of North Africa itself.

Although the peninsula appears as a self-contained geographical unit, its natural internal divisions have impeded the achievement of political unity and have encouraged separatism. The central nucleus of the peninsula is composed of a rather desolate *meseta,* a vast plateau which Madariaga called "the citadel of the Spanish castle." The rulers of the *meseta* (the future kingdom of León-Castile) strove to impose their authority upon the peripheral areas, but mountains rising sharply from the sea made access to the coastal regions difficult and sheltered rebels against a central power.

The great mountain ranges intersect the peninsula in an east-west direction. In the northeast the Pyrenees, the highest and broadest of these, separate Spain from France. The Cantabrian mountains, extending through Asturias into Galicia, border the *meseta* on the northwest. Crossing the center of the peninsula and dividing the *meseta* into northern and southern sections are the Serra da Estrela, the Sierra de Gredos, and the Sierra de Guadarrama. The Iberian mountains of Soria and Teruel form the eastern limit of the *meseta,* and the Sierra Morena its southern limit. Running through Andalusia south of the Guadalquivir is the Cordillera Bética, of which the Sierra Nevada is the highest range. The mountains and the *meseta* give the peninsula the second highest altitude in Europe, after Switzerland.

Of the principal rivers, only the Ebro runs in an easterly direction to the Mediterranean. From its source in the province of Santander it makes its way over 465 miles through Aragon and its capital, Zaragoza, and empties into the sea at Tortosa. The other great rivers move westward to the Atlantic. Rising in Galicia, the Miño (Minho) travels a distance of 212 miles, passing through Orense and Túy, forming the northern boundary of modern Portugal. From the province of Soria, the Duero (Douro) flows 485 miles through Old Castile, León, and Portugal, touches Valladolid and Zamora, reaching the Atlantic at Porto (Oporto). The Tagus has its source in the province of Guadalajara and flows westward for 565 miles through Toledo to Lisbon. The Guadiana originates in the province of Ciudad Real and courses 510 miles through Mérida and Badajoz, where it turns southward, forming part of the Portuguese frontier and emptying into the Gulf of Cádiz at Ayamonte. The Guadalquivir, the great river of Andalusia, rises in the province of Jaén and passes through Córdoba and Seville where it turns southward to the Atlantic, covering a distance of 512 miles. The rivers of Spain, though hardly comparable to the great rivers found in other parts of Europe, played an important role in the medieval history of the peninsula, for the reconquest can be seen as a gradual advance from one river frontier to the next. The particular disposition of the rivers flowing east-west rather than north-south has also been seen by Vicens Vives as a deterrent to political unity.

The peninsula has always been known for the harshness of its climate and the aridity of much of its soil. Extremes of heat and cold are common, especially in the *meseta;* rainfall is scanty, and the land is rude and poor. The regions of Andalusia, the Levant, Galicia, and Cantabria are much more fertile than the greater part of the Castilian and Aragonese lands of the central plateau. As a consequence, man has always had to struggle with the land to gain from it sufficient to sustain himself. Perhaps this constant struggle for survival has contributed to the strong individualism that is often suggested as typical of the Spanish character.

Roman Spain

Over the many centuries Spain, standing at the extremities of Europe and Africa, has served as a natural crossroads and has been populated by many diverse peoples. Here there is no need to discuss the complicated theories concerning prehistoric settlers, of whom the Basques remain as a unique element, whose language is of unknown origin or relationship to any other known to man. Ancient historians spoke of the Iberians, a people who came from Africa and constituted the basic Mediterranean element in the population. The Celts, an Indo-European people, crossed the Pyrenees and settled in the northern and western reaches of the peninsula between 900–600 B.C. and by their wide use of iron weapons, horses, and chariots were able to dominate the earlier arrivals. Intermarriage between these groups led the geographers and historians to refer to the peninsula as Celtiberia.

Attracted by reports of mineral wealth, the peoples of the eastern Mediterranean established colonies on the eastern and southern coasts; around 800 B.C. the Phoenicians founded Gades or Cádiz, and from the seventh century onward the Greeks began to found colonies, like Emporion (Ampurias) on the Catalan coast. In the sixth century B.C. the Carthaginians penetrated the peninsula and overthrew the Tartessians, a people of African origin who had created a powerful kingdom in Andalusia. As Carthage developed a commercial empire in Sicily and southern Spain, she provoked the rivalry of the Roman city state, and a struggle for supremacy in the western Mediterranean ensued.

The contending powers tested their strength in the First Punic War (264–242 B.C.), with Rome emerging as the victor. To repair Carthaginian fortunes Hamilcar Barca, his son-in-law Hasdrubal, and his son Hannibal began to transform Spain into a major military base. Hannibal's sack of Saguntum (219), a peninsular town in alliance with Rome, opened the Second Punic War (218–201 B.C.). While Hannibal crossed into Gaul and Italy to carry the fight to the portals of Rome itself, Roman legions commanded by Publius Cornelius Scipio captured Nova Cartago (Cartagena, founded by Hasdrubal) in 209 B.C. and Cádiz in 205 B.C., and destroyed Carthaginian rule in Spain.

The indigenous Hispanic population (perhaps 4 million) collaborated in the overthrow of the Carthaginians, but they were not prepared to submit to Roman tutelage. Over the next hundred years the Romans slowly extended their rule into the heart of the *meseta*, meeting fierce resistance. The fall of the Celtiberian city of Numancia near Soria in 133 B.C. terminated the most arduous period of the conquest, but it was not until the time of Augustus (27 B.C.–14 A.D.) that the Romans succeeded in subjugating the wild tribesmen of the far north and west. The names of towns such as Asturica Augusta (Astorga), Caesaraugusta (Zaragoza), and Pax Augusta (Badajoz) record the progress of the legions.

The Roman conquest brought the Hispanic peoples into the mainstream of European civilization, and for the first time the peninsula was unified under one government. The process of colonizing it and converting it into a province, endowed with Roman administration, citizenship, law, and language was a gradual one, extending over several centuries. The southern and eastern coastal regions obviously were most receptive to Roman influence, as the geographer Strabo noted in the first century A.D. The stationing of legionaries at strategic points, the settlement of veterans in colonies, and the development of provincial administration were among the chief instruments of the policy of Romanization. Vespasian granted Roman law in 73–74 A.D. to a number of towns in the peninsula, but when Caracalla granted Roman citizenship to all residents of the empire in 212 the Romanization of the Hispanic peoples in a legal sense was completed. The adoption of Roman manners, customs, and language was not so easily accomplished.

After the conclusion of the Second Punic War, in 197 B.C., Spain was divided into two provinces: *Hispania Citerior*, the east, center, and north, and *Hispania Ulterior*, the south and west. This division into Hither and Farther Spain explains the usage of the plural form to refer to the peninsula in the Middle Ages, as in *rex Hispaniarum, rey de las Españas*. After the whole peninsula had been subjugated, Augustus in 27 B.C. divided *Hispania Ulterior* into the provinces of Baetica and Lusitania. The former included most of modern Andalusia, and the provincial governor had his capital at Corduba. Lusitania, whose capital was Emerita Augusta (Mérida), consisted chiefly of modern Portugal and Extremadura. *Hispania Citerior*, or Tarraconensis as it was also known from the capital city Tarraco (Tarragona), extended from the east coast to Gallaetia in the northwest.

At the end of the third century A.D. Diocletian (284–305) effected a final reorganization of the provinces as part of his general attempt to reform imperial administration. The whole of *Hispania* formed a diocese within the Prefecture of Gaul and was divided into five provinces: Baetica, Lusitania, Tarraconensis, Cartaginensis, and Gallaetia. Nova Cartago (Cartagena), the capital of Cartaginensis, was located on the southeastern coast; from there the province reached well into the center of the peninsula. Gallaetia, the northwestern province, had

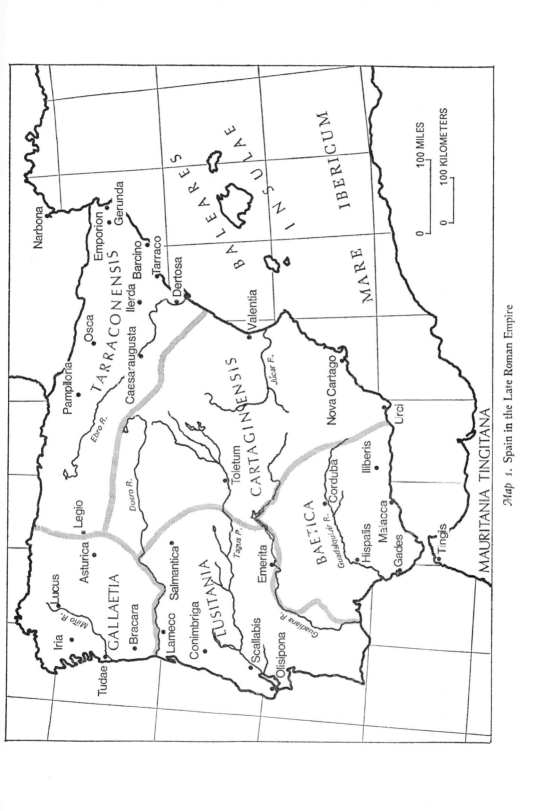

Map 1. Spain in the Late Roman Empire

Narbona

Emporion
Gerunda
Osca
Pamplona
TARRACONENSIS
Ilerda Barcino
Tarraco
Caesaraugusta
Dertosa

Ebro R.

Valentia

BALEARES INSULAE

Legio
Duero R.

Asturica
Lucus
Iria
GALLAETIA
Tudae
Bracara

Salmantica
Lameco
Conimbriga
LUSITANIA
Scallabis
Olisipona

Toletum
CARTAGINENSIS

Tagus R.
Júcar F.

Nova Cartago

Urci

Emerita
Guadiana R.

BAETICA
Corduba
Guadalquivir R.
Iliberis
Hispalis
Malacca
Gades
Tingis

MAURITANIA TINGITANA

MARE IBERICUM

100 MILES

100 KILOMETERS

0

0

its capital at Bracara Augusta (Braga). To these peninsular provinces were added the Balearic Islands and North Africa (Mauritania Tingitana), whose respective capitals were Pollentia (Pollensa) and Tingis (Tangier). The *vicarius Hispaniarum* had general responsibility for the peninsula, but each province was administered by a *praeses, rector,* or *iudex,* who had civil but not military power.

The essential unit of local administration was the municipality (*municipium, civitas*). Some of these were of native origin, while others were new Roman foundations. Aside from the provincial capitals already mentioned, the principal towns included: Hispalis (Seville), Toletum (Toledo), Barcino (Barcelona), Pampilona (Pamplona), Pallantia (Palencia), Legio (León), and Salmantica (Salamanca). Temples, arches, and other public works gave the towns a distinctly Roman appearance. The most outstanding symbols of Roman power still extant, and in some cases still used, include the aqueducts of Segovia and Tarragona, the amphitheatre of Tarragona, and the bridges of Alcántara, Mérida, and Salamanca. The urbanization of Spain hastened the process of Romanization. While the rural population long remained attached to ancient traditions, the townspeople more readily accepted Roman law, customs, language, dress, and religion, and consciously thought of themselves as Romans.

The municipality included both the urban nucleus (*urbs*) and an extensive rural district (*territorium*) including many villages and estates. The task of governing the municipality was entrusted to a *curia* of 100 *decuriones* or *curiales,* who elected the chief magistrates or *duumvires.* In the third century the burden of satisfying the insatiable tax demands of the imperial government fell heavily upon the *curiales* and ruined them as a class, and stifled initiative in municipal administration. In order to prevent the wholesale flight of the *curiales* from their responsibilities, the imperial government was compelled to bind them by law to their posts and to their station in life. The merchants and artisans who constituted the bulk of the plebeian class in the towns were similarly bound to their crafts and occupations.

In the country areas there were many small free holds (*fundus, predium*) sufficient to maintain a single family, but from the third century onward these lands were absorbed with increasing frequency by great estates (*villa, latifundium*). Small free proprietors found it more and more difficult to obtain a good yield and also felt the need to seek protection from more powerful men against the disturbances occasioned by civil wars and later by the barbarian invasions. As a consequence many proprietors gave up ownership of their land and became tenants on large estates and usually commended themselves to the protection of the landlord who eventually began to enjoy a real juridical power over them. As with other classes in society, the *coloni*, as the free men cultivating land on great estates were known, were bound to the soil in the fourth century. A large estate was usually administered by a steward (*villicus*) appointed by the landlord. The land was divided among the tenants who owed rents and labor services, but a certain portion was reserved for direct exploitation by the landlord. For this purpose he usually owned a large number of slaves, some of whom cultivated the land while others worked in his household. Under the influence of humanitarian impulses and Christianity, landlords often freed their slaves, but the freedman ordinarily remained a client under his lord's protection.

The economy of Roman Spain suffered the troubles which affected other regions of the empire in the third and fourth centuries. A flourishing commerce had developed along the southern and eastern coasts; from such ports as Cádiz, Cartagena, Tarragona, and Málaga, wheat, wine, olives, wax, honey, fish, and olive oil were exported to other parts of the Mediterranean world. In the interior the Romans constructed a network of roads covering about 13,000 miles which served to facilitate the transportation of troops and, at a later date, of goods. The Via Augusta running along the coast from Cádiz to Tarragona and thence into Gaul and Italy was the axis of the system. As trade began to decline in the third century, and gold and silver were steadily drained to the east, the government responded to the economic crisis by attempting to regulate wages and prices. Individuals were deprived of the fundamental freedom of movement and the right to change their occupations. This had deleterious effects upon life in town and country, as all sense of personal independence and initiative was stifled. A decadent economy and a stagnant, stratified society thus were part of the Roman legacy to the Visigoths. The territorial and personal tributes (*capitatio terrena, capitatio humana*), the system of tolls, and the obligation to perform certain public works (*munera*) were also part of that legacy.

One other element introduced during the Roman era contributed significantly to the civilization of the inhabitants and helped to unify them spiritually. Great obscurity surrounds the beginnings of Christianity in

Spain, but there is a tradition that Sts. Peter and Paul consecrated seven bishops to evangelize the people. It is also thought that St. Paul visited Spain, *circa* 63–67, as he promised to do in the Epistle to the Romans (15:23–28). The legend of St. James the Great's labors in Spain is of even more profound historical impact. No contemporary and none of the church Fathers mention his role in the peninsula, nor is he mentioned in any special way in the Mozarabic liturgy native to Spain; his martyrdom in Jerusalem makes it highly unlikely that he visited Spain or spent much time there. Early in the ninth century, however, his tomb supposedly was found in Galicia and became the center of the famous pilgrimage of Santiago de Compostela. As the patron of Spain, St. James was often seen fighting in battle by the side of the Christian rulers against the enemies of the faith, or so it was alleged. Yet there is no real historical evidence to demonstrate that he ever participated in the evangelization of the Hispanic people.

Whatever the details of evangelization may be, the work was accomplished quickly enough. Tertullian, writing about 202, speaks as if the whole peninsula were Christian. Pagan superstition persisted no doubt in many areas, and people in remote places, for instance, the Basques, remained untouched by Christianity for centuries. During the Decian persecution in the middle of the third century a number of Hispanic Christians were martyred, and there were also numerous victims of Diocletian's persecution at the close of the century. After the conversion of Constantine, as hostility between Rome and the church disappeared, Christianity flourished in Spain and became an effective means of Romanization. Ecclesiastical organization was based upon the civil territorial administration, so that metropolitan sees were established in the provincial capitals.

The growth of the Hispanic church in the fourth century was exemplified in various ways by the distinguished bishop, Hosius of Córdoba (d. 357), friend and counselor of Constantine, and chief papal representative at the Council of Nicaea in 325; by Paul Orosius, author of *Seven Books of History against the Pagans*, an attempt to demonstrate the failure of the pagan gods to protect their devotees from calamities over the course of history; and by the heresiarch, Priscillian (d. 385), whose execution by imperial officials foreshadowed the later collaboration of state and church in the suppression of heresy. One should also take notice of the Council held at Iliberis (Elvira) near modern Granada around 300–314; its most famous canon

required the clergy to observe a life of celibacy, a rule that eventually
became general in western Europe.

On the eve of the Germanic invasions of western Europe, *Hispania*,
after six hundred years of Roman presence, was highly Romanized and
Christianized. In spite of her subjugation by the barbarians, Roman
and Christian Spain survived and vanquished her conquerors.

PART I

The Visigothic Era

415–711

Gothorum antiquissimam esse gentem certum est. . . . Nulla enim gens in orbe fuit, quae Romanum imperium adeo fatigaverit.

Certainly the Gothic race is very ancient. . . . No people in the whole world so distressed the Roman Empire.

Isidore of Seville, *Historia Gothorum*, 1–2

CHAPTER 1

〜❧〜

The Visigothic Kingdom

The Visigoths

During the fifth century, Spain slipped gradually away from Roman rule into the hands of the barbarian tribes driven westward by the general tide of invasion. Vandals, Alans, and Suevi occupied the south, west, and north early in the century bringing war and destruction to the Hispano-Romans who seemed incapable of defending themselves. At the end of the century the Visigoths, the most powerful of the tribes to enter Spain, began to settle in Old Castile where their presence has been evident ever after in place names, racial structure, and customary law. They gradually extended their rule over the other tribes and conquered the last Roman outposts, but it was not until the seventh century that they established effective government over the entire peninsula. Their great misfortune was their inability to create a stable monarchy based on the principle of hereditary succession. Civil war was endemic during the centuries of their rule and ultimately contributed to the sudden collapse of their kingdom before the onslaughts of the Muslims early in the eighth century.

While the Visigoths, numbering perhaps 200,000 to 300,000, constituted the military ruling class, they did not radically alter the civilization of the peninsula. Due to differences in language, customs, and religion, their assimilation by the Hispano-Roman population of about six to nine million was difficult. The persistence of the name *Hispania*, rather than its replacement by some Germanic alternative, suggests the continuing strength of the Hispano-Roman tradition. The cultural ascendancy of the Hispano-Roman population is also manifest in the adoption by the Visigoths of the Latin language, the orthodox Christian religion, the imperial administrative system, Roman ideas of the state, of rulership, and of a written code of laws applicable to all men, regardless of racial origin. The substance of Hispano-Roman civilization, modified in various respects, survived throughout the Visigothic era, and it was this essentially Romance, rather than Germanic, legacy that was handed on to future generations. And yet, in spite of their cultural superiority, Hispano-Romans such as St. Isidore of Seville acknowledged the political and military achievements of the Visigoths and took patriotic pride in recording them. In this sense the Hispano-Romans accepted the Visigoths as their own.

The most significant element in the legacy of the Visigothic era was the concept of an indivisible kingdom embracing the whole of Spain. Inspired by this ideal and by the memory of the Visigoths, whose heirs they considered themselves to be, the rulers of the Christian kingdom of Asturias-León set as their goal the expulsion of the Muslim invaders and the reconstitution of the Visigothic state. Remembrance of the Visigothic kingdom thus gave an ideological justification to the reconquest.

The Kingdom of Toulouse

Settled along the Danube frontier in the late fourth century and already converted to Arian Christianity, the Visigoths were the first Germanic people to enter the Roman Empire in force. Fearing to suffer the fate of their neighbors, the Ostrogoths, who had been subjugated by the Huns, they requested permission in 376 to settle in the empire as *federati* or allies. Although Emperor Valens gave the necessary authorization, imperial officials dealt fraudulently and dishonestly with the Visigoths, causing them to rebel and to ravage Thrace. In haste, Valens prepared to crush them, but at Adrianpole in 378 his forces were routed and he was killed. The barbarians continued their rampage until they were brought under control by Emperor Theodosius (379–395) who settled them in Thrace and admitted their troops to the imperial army.

Toward the end of the century the rivalry between the regents governing the empire in the name of Theodosius's sons gave the ambitious Visigothic king Alaric the opportunity to seek his fortune. Leading his people through Thrace and Macedonia, he occupied Athens in 396; he then pressed westward attempting to enter Italy but was repulsed by the barbarian Stilicho, regent in the west. After Stilicho's murder in 408 Alaric was able to march unhindered through the peninsula, and in 410 sacked Rome, causing profound shock among the Romans, pagan and Christian alike. After three days the Visigoths left the city and continued southward, intending to cross into Africa, but Alaric's sudden death in southern Italy caused the abandonment of the project.

Athaulf (410–415), his successor, led the Visigoths through Italy into Gaul, where, under the assaults of the Suevi, Alans, Vandals, Burgundians, and Franks, imperial defenses had already broken down. The Suevi, Alans, and Vandals, who had had little previous contact with the empire, continued their marauding and entered Spain in 409. After laying waste the country for two years, the Suevi settled in the northwestern province of Gallaetia, as did the Asdings, one branch of the Vandal tribe. The Siling Vandals occupied Baetica in the south, while the Alans, an Iranian people, settled in the central provinces of Lusitania and Cartaginensis. Given the small number of barbarians, the occupation of the peninsula was far from complete, and for the moment Tarraconensis was left free of barbarians.

In the meantime, Athaulf, who as Orosius remarked, had dreamed of restoring the glory of the Roman empire, failed in his attempt to secure imperial permission to settle his people as *federati* in Gaul. Driven into Tarraconensis by the Romans, for a brief time he made Barcelona his headquarters, but he was assassinated in 415, as was his successor, Sigeric. Under their new king, Wallia (415–418), the Visigoths, threatened by starvation in Spain, tried unsuccessfully to pass into Africa. Thereupon they came to terms with the Romans and were recognized as allies and supplied with food (416). In the emperor's name the Visigoths now launched a series of campaigns against the other barbarians in the peninsula and nearly exterminated the Alans and the Siling Vandals. The remnants of these tribes joined the Asdings and the Suevi in Gallaetia. In 418, in return for these services, the Visigoths were allowed to settle in Gaul in *Aquitania secunda* and in part of Narbonensis. This was the beginning of the Visigothic kingdom of Toulouse.

For the next forty years the Visigoths had little to do with Spain, though they were very much involved in the defense of Gaul against other barbarians, including Attila's Huns. In Spain the Suevi and the Asdings continued their depredations and fought one another. About 421 the Asdings left Gallaetia and overran the province of Baetica, seizing Seville and Cartagena and even raiding the Balearic Islands. The

Vandal king, Gaiseric, led his people across the straits of Gibraltar to North Africa in 429; without great difficulty they conquered the province, and ruled it and the Balearic Islands until the Byzantine reconquest in 534.

The withdrawal of the Visigoths and then of the Vandals allowed the Suevi freedom to plunder the peninsula at will. Their destruction of Gallaetia induced Bishop Idatius to travel to Gaul in 431 to seek aid from the Roman general Aetius, but he could do nothing. Later Idatius tried to negotiate peace with the barbarians but to no avail. In 456 the Visigoths, led by King Theodoric II (453–466), who had recently helped to stop Attila at the Catalaunian Fields, returned to Spain with instructions from the emperor to destroy the Suevi. They easily defeated the Suevi and killed their king, but the Visigothic triumph, rather than benefiting the empire, prepared the way for the eventual Visigothic occupation of the peninsula.

In the next twenty years the chaos in the western empire continued unchecked and reached its culmination in the deposition of Emperor Romulus Augustulus in 476. His downfall also disrupted the fragile alliance between the empire and the Visigoths. Under the leadership of Euric (466–484), who gained the throne by murdering his brother, the Visigoths established an independent kingdom in Gaul and northern Spain. From his capital at Toulouse, Euric ruled the most powerful barbarian state in the late fifth century. The region in Gaul bounded by the Atlantic, the Loire, the Rhone, and the Pyrenees acknowledged his authority. In Spain his people occupied Tarraconensis and parts of Lusitania; the Suevi were forced back into Gallaetia, while Baetica and Cartaginensis were left to fend for themselves.

Despite the general collapse of the imperial government, Roman influence was still strong in the Visigothic kingdom. Not only did the Romans form the majority of the population, but they also filled many of the chief administrative positions, and continued to be governed by the Theodosian Code promulgated in 438. Euric, the ablest of the Visigothic kings, gained fame as the first great Germanic legislator, when the code of law bearing his name was published in Latin about 475. Some years later (506) his son Alaric II (484–507) issued a compilation based on the Theodosian Code known as the Breviary of Alaric. The difficulty of creating a common law for Visigoths and Romans and the persistence of the Visigoths in adhering to the Arian heresy created a broad gap between the rulers and the ruled.

During the reign of Alaric II a serious threat to Visigothic preponderance in Gaul emerged. Clovis (481–511), the greatest king of the Merovingian Franks, had subjected northern Gaul to his rule and by his acceptance of orthodox Christianity gained favor with the Gallo-Romans. As Gregory of Tours tells us, the wily Frank proposed to liberate southern Gaul from the hated and heretical Visigoths. Already Alaric II had revealed that he lacked the will to resist the Franks. When the Roman leader Syagrius, whom Clovis had expelled from northern Gaul, sought refuge at Toulouse, Alaric delivered him up to the mercy of the Franks, but this act of appeasement failed to save his kingdom. Crossing the Loire in 507, Clovis gave battle to the Visigoths at Vouillé (Vogladum) near Poitiers. "The Goths fled as was their custom," says Bishop Gregory; Alaric was defeated and killed, and the kingdom of Toulouse came to an end.

Following their victory, the Franks overran southern Gaul, occupying Toulouse, Bordeaux, and other cities, while their Burgundian allies entered Narbonne. Gesaleic (507–510), a bastard of Alaric II, could not check the invasion and was forced to flee to Barcelona. The intervention of the Ostrogothic king, Theodoric the Great (493–526), who had recently established his power in Italy, halted the progress of the Franks and Burgundians. No doubt he feared a possible threat to his own position, but he was concerned also to defend the rights of his grandson, Amalaric (510–531), the legitimate heir to the Visigothic throne. Theodoric drove the Franks and Burgundians out of Narbonensis and expelled Gesaleic from Barcelona. Although the Visigothic kingdom survived, it was now reduced to Septimania, a part of the province of Narbonensis, and the northern provinces of Spain. Until Theodoric's death the kingdom remained an Ostrogothic dependency, ruled by Ostrogothic governors. Much of the peninsula was still free of barbarians, but the inhabitants were abandoned to their own devices by the imperial authorities.

Not long after Theodoric's death, hostilities between the Franks and the Visigoths were resumed. At first Amalaric, by marrying Clovis's daughter Clotilde, established friendly relations with his northern neighbors, but his ill treatment of his wife and his attempts to force her to accept Arianism caused the Franks to renew their attack. Amalaric was expelled from Narbonne and fled to Barcelona, where he was murdered in 531. The Franks laid waste to Tarraconensis, seized Pamplona, and besieged Zaragoza, but their hope of extending their dominion south of the Pyrenees was not to be fulfilled. An Ostrogothic general, Theudis (531–548), the newly proclaimed king of the Visigoths, drove the Franks from Spain and regained control of Septimania, the southeastern corner of Gaul comprising the episcopal cities of Narbonne, Carcassonne, Nîmes, Maguelonne, Béziers, Agde, Lodéve, and Elne.

Although Frankish ambitions in Spain had been thwarted, the Visigoths had to face another challenge to their hegemony in the peninsula. The Byzantine Emperor Justinian (527–565) planned to reconquer the former Roman provinces abandoned to the barbarians by his predecessors. By 534 Byzantine forces had conquered the Vandal kingdom in North Africa and the Balearic Islands and were beginning the long struggle to destroy the Ostrogothic kingdom in Italy. Theudis recognized the threat to Spain and occupied Ceuta (Septum) on the North African coast, so as to close the straits of Gibraltar to a Byzantine invasion. In 542, however, the Byzantines were able to take possession of Ceuta. The murders of King Theudis in 548 and of his successor Theudigisil in the next year prepared the way for Byzantine intervention in the peninsula. Commenting on these murders in his *History of the Franks* (III, 30), Gregory of Tours said, "the Goths have taken up this detestable custom, that if any of their kings displeases them, they go after him with their swords, and then they make king whomever they wish." Heartened by the Byzantine conquest of North Africa, the Hispano-Romans of Baetica rose in revolt against King Agila (549–554) and routed him in a battle at Córdoba. A rival claimant to the throne, Athanagild, appealed to the Byzantines for help, and in reply Justinian dispatched a small fleet and an army from Sicily. Near Seville in 554 the rebels and their Byzantine allies defeated Agila, who fled to Mérida, where he was killed by his own men. Athanagild (554–567) was now the undisputed king of the Visigoths.

As one might expect, the Byzantines, whom Athanagild had summoned to Spain, did not withdraw, but seized possession of the province of Baetica and part of Cartaginensis, including the towns of Cartagena, Málaga, and Córdoba. Although he was able to wrest Seville from their grasp, Athanagild's efforts to expel them from the peninsula were futile. For about seventy years the Byzantines maintained a foothold in Spain, stretching along the southern and eastern coast from the mouth of the Guadalquivir to the mouth of the Júcar. Over the years the Visigoths whittled away at this territory, whose limits were never determined precisely, until the final conquest by King Swintila.

The Kingdom of Toledo

By the middle of the sixth century the power of the Visigoths, formerly centered in Toulouse, was located irrevocably in Spain. Since the time of Euric, the Visigoths had been penetrating deeper into the peninsula. In the course of the sixth century, especially after the battle of Vouillé, their settlement increased substantially. Although they were the preponderant power in the peninsula they were not the only one. The Suevi, though weak, still ruled Gallaetia; the Basques remained independent in their mountains, and the Byzantines controlled a large area in the south and east. The principal task facing the Visigoths in the late sixth century was that of unifying the peninsula under their rule. This was not only a political and military problem, involving conflict with the Suevi, Basques, and Byzantines, but there were also important legal, social, and religious differences dividing the Visigoths and Hispano-Romans. Until these were removed the Hispano-Roman majority would only tolerate the Visigoths as unwanted intruders.

During the reign of King Leovigild (568–586), who had been associated on the throne with his brother Liuva (568–573), the initial steps toward the solution of these problems were taken. A good general, Leovigild proved to be one of the most distinguished Visigothic rulers. According to Isidore of Seville, Leovigild established his residence at Toledo in the heart of Spain; henceforth Toledo would be the *urbs regia* par excellence. In imitation of the Byzantines, he began to wear royal vestments and to sit upon a throne; he was also the first of the Visigothic kings to coin money, in imitation of Byzantine coinage, with his own image and inscription. A legislator as well, he revised Euric's code and terminated the fourth-century imperial ban on intermarriage between Goths and Romans, an important step toward the ultimate assimilation of the races. The king clearly had a high conception of monarchy and hoped to transfer his power to his sons, to whom he entrusted the administration of certain provinces, as a means of ensuring their loyalty.

With great energy Leovigild set out to achieve the territorial unification of the peninsula. Between 570 and 572 he took Málaga, Medina Sidonia, and Córdoba, thus restricting Byzantine dominion to the eastern coastal region. He was equally successful in defeating the Basques in 581 and, in commemoration of his triumph, founded the city of Victoriacum (Vitoria). Although the Basques were never subdued entirely, they did have a new respect for his authority. Leovigild's most notable success was his conquest of the Suevi, who had been confined to the mountains in the northwest since the late fifth century and did not represent a major threat to the Visigoths. Through the missionary labors of St. Martin of Dumio, bishop of Braga, the Suevi were converted to orthodox Christianity in the middle of the sixth century. From about 574, Leovigild began to penetrate into the northwest and completed the conquest by 585. The last king of the Suevi was forced to enter a monastery.

The most serious obstacle to Visigothic rule in the peninsula was religion. As Arians, the Visigoths had a strong antipathy toward their Catholic subjects and frequently dealt harshly with them. Recognizing this difficulty, Leovigild in 580 convoked a synod of Arian bishops in hopes of converting the Catholic majority to Arianism. Although the Catholics were asked only to accept the Arian formula for the Trinity (*Gloria Patri per Filium in Spiritu Sancto*), they showed no disposition to do so, and this attempt to solve the religious problem failed.

The issue also clouded the king's relations with his first-born son, Hermenegild, who had been appointed duke of Baetica. Married to a Catholic Frankish princess, he came under the influence of St. Leander, bishop of Seville, and in 579 accepted orthodoxy. When summoned to Toledo, he declared himself in open rebellion and soon had the support of most of the towns in Baetica, as well as of the Byzantines and the still independent Suevi. Leander journeyed to Constantinople, seeking help for the rebels, but it was not forthcoming. Meanwhile Leovigild responded vigorously, defeating the Suevi and seizing Seville and Córdoba, the chief towns of Baetica. Hermenegild was captured and imprisoned but, after refusing to abjure Catholicism, he was murdered in 585 by his jailer. It seems unlikely that Leovigild had ordered his execution. Although Pope Gregory the Great, in his *Dialogues*, hailed Hermenegild as a martyr, contemporary peninsular Catholics, such as John of Biclaro, did not do so, but condemned him as a rebel and as a traitor for his alliance with the Byzantines. To some Hispano-Romans his actions appeared not as a defense of orthodoxy, but as a political uprising which the supporters of stable government could not condone.

Within a year Leovigild, the best of the Visigoths, whose organiza-

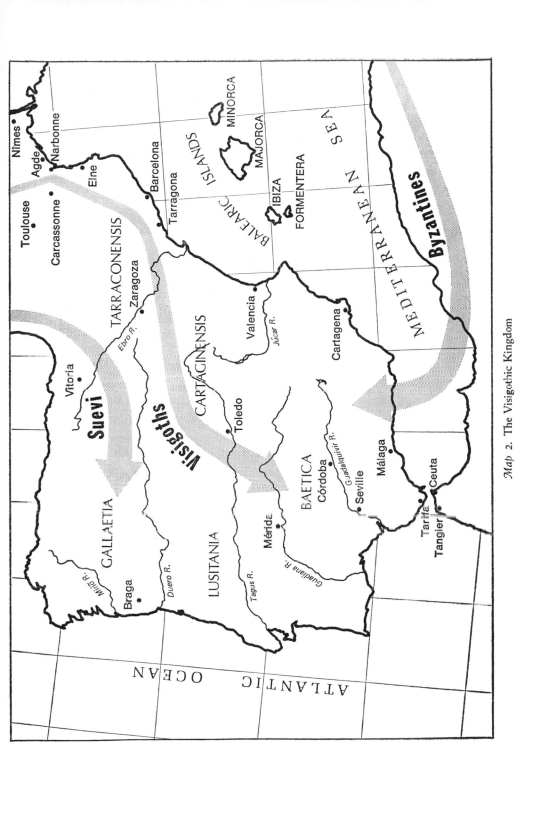

Map 2. The Visigothic Kingdom

tion of the state and extension of its frontiers did so much to strengthen the Visigothic realm, followed his son to the grave. Though he failed to resolve the religious issue, he probably realized the futility of attempting to force the orthodox majority to accept Arianism and may have recommended that his successor adopt the religion of the Hispano-Romans.

The Conversion of the Visigoths

Recared (586–601) peacefully succeeded his father and in 587, probably for reasons of public policy as well as personal conviction, announced his conversion to Catholicism. An assembly of Arian bishops followed his lead, but the Arians of Septimania revolted and appealed to the Burgundian king for help. The historian John of Biclaro regarded the defeat of the rebels and their allies in 589 as a divine reward for the king's conversion. In the same year at the Third Council of Toledo, at a gathering of sixty-two orthodox bishops, Recared read a profession of faith in the tenets of the Nicene Creed and promised his protection to the church. As the bishops shouted for joy, Leander of Seville extended their congratulations to the king. Recared's conversion and that of the Visigothic people eliminated one of the most serious causes of friction between the ruling caste and the subject population; religious unity now made possible a greater assimilation of the two races. To a much greater degree than before, the church was able to exercise its civilizing influence over the barbarians, whose Romanization proceeded rapidly in the seventh century.

As a consequence of Recared's abjuration of Arianism, relations between church and state became extremely close, so much so that historians such as Dahn have characterized the Visigothic state as a theocracy. No one would question the existence of a union of church and state in any medieval kingdom, but there is hardly any Spanish historian who today would speak of a theocracy in Visigothic Spain. Both church and state, as Isidore of Seville pointed out, had the same purposes, though they utilized different means; therefore they had the obligation to work in harmony with one another. By accepting orthodoxy, the kings did not surrender their authority to the bishops, but they made it possible for the bishops to exercise a much greater influence in public affairs. Just as the bishops recognized the monarchy as the only sure guarantee of law and order, the kings recognized the church as the most effective bulwark of their power. By appointing bishops, convoking councils, and sanctioning conciliar decrees, the kings were able to exercise a considerable measure of control over the church. At the same time the bishops exalted the institution of kingship and attempted to safeguard the person of the sovereign against a factious nobility. If the influence of the church appeared greater than that of the monarchy, this was the result of the essential weakness of the monarchy, its elective character.

The failure of the Visigothic kings to establish an hereditary monarchy laid the kingdom open to sedition and civil war. To avert these disorders the church councils tried to regulate the succession in accordance with the elective principle. Even though they might condemn arbitrary rule, in their anxiety to preserve stable government they were prepared to acknowledge anyone who gained the throne, even if by questionable means.

The problem of succession was especially acute during the seventh century. Although Recared's young son, Liuva II (601–603), succeeded to the throne, he was soon assassinated. His murderer, Witeric (603–610), apparently tried without success to revive Arianism, and in turn met a violent death at a banquet, a favorite scenario for regicide among the barbarians. Though eight of his predecessors had died naturally, Witeric was the tenth of the Visigothic kings to die by the hand of an assassin.

After the brief reign of Gundomar (610–612), Sisebut (612–621), the most Romanized of the Visigothic sovereigns and a close friend of St. Isidore, came to power. There are several extant Latin letters attributed to him in which he emphasized the ruler's accountability to God for waging war. His belligerence was directed chiefly against Byzantine positions in southeastern Spain, thus preparing the way for their final expulsion. At the same time he enacted rigorous legislation against the Jews, requiring them to accept baptism on penalty of death and confiscation of property. Several of his successors followed this unfortunate policy, thereby arousing the resentment of the Jewish community who at a later date could only welcome the Muslim invaders as liberators. Both Sisebut and his son Recared II, who reigned for only a few days, may have been murdered. Sisebut's most distinguished general, Swintila (621–631), finally expelled the Byzantines from the peninsula, thereby becoming the first king to rule the whole of Spain. St. Isidore had words of high praise for this monarch, but in his later years he apparently began to rule arbitrarily, and when he attempted to assure his son's succession by associating him on the throne, a rebellion broke out. With Frankish support, Sisenand, duke of Septimania, seized power and deposed Swintila, who, despite this misfortune, had the distinction of being the first king dethroned without also being murdered.

Acknowledging the insecurity of his own position, Sisenand (631–636) made an emotional appeal for support to the Fourth Council of Toledo in 633. Under the presidency of St. Isidore, the assembled bishops anathematized despotic kings and declared that Swintila by his evil ways had deprived himself of the throne. To protect Sisenand and future sovereigns, the Council proclaimed the inviolability of the king's person as the Lord's anointed, citing the Old Testament prohibition: "Nolite tangere christos meos." Hoping to avert the discord and rebellion so prevalent in the past, the Council decreed that upon the king's death, the magnates and bishops, by common counsel, should choose a successor. The Fifth and Sixth Councils of Toledo (636, 638), summoned by Sisenand's brother, King Khintila (636–640), attempted further to strengthen the sovereign's position by condemning sedition and by protecting the property rights of royal children and servants. Conciliar decrees were insufficient, however, to curb the morbid propensity of the Visigoths to revolt against their rulers. Thus Khintila's son, Tulga (640–642), was deposed, tonsured, and thrust into a monastery.

The octogenarian Khindasvinth (642–653), who dethroned Tulga, believed that the most effective means of retaining power was the use of terror. He executed hundreds of enemies and enacted a severe law subjecting conspirators and rebels to the penalties of mutilation, death, and confiscation of property. To these, the Seventh Council of Toledo (646) added ecclesiastical censures. No doubt such measures contributed to the tranquility of the next reign. Reccesvinth (653–672), who had been associated on the throne with his father, was a more conciliatory ruler and sought to mitigate the severity of this legislation. Although the Eighth Council of Toledo (653) declared that the law of treason was necessary for the well-being of the realm, and that the king was bound to uphold the laws, it acknowledged that he could dispense mercy.

Reccesvinth completed a project initiated by his father, namely, the compilation of a code of law applicable to all the inhabitants of the realm. Promulgated about 654, the *Liber Judiciorum,* one of the most significant legacies of the Visigothic era, terminated the duality of law and thus removed the last barrier to the assimilation of the Gothic and Roman populations. The code was a tangible manifestation of the survival of Roman civilization and of the fundamental role of the Hispano-Romans in the government of the Visigothic realm.

The Decline and Fall of the Visigothic Kingdom

When Reccesvinth died in 672 the Visigothic kingdom seemed at the height of its development. Territorial unity had been achieved; sources of religious and legal conflicts between the races had been eliminated, and a cultural level higher than in any other barbarian kingdom had been attained. Yet the state continued to suffer from fundamental weaknesses which neither royal legislation nor conciliar enactments were able to overcome. Despite the efforts of various kings to make the monarchy hereditary, it remained elective, thus encouraging ambitious magnates to conspire and rebel, even though these crimes were subject to harsh penalties. In essence, a sense of loyalty to the king seated on the throne was utterly wanting. In the last years of the kingdom's existence, rivalry among factions became especially intense and ultimately brought about the ruin of the Visigoths. An insufficiency of contemporary sources is a serious handicap to a clear understanding of the events preceding the Muslim invasion. Sources written a century or two after the fall of the kingdom must be used cautiously, since they are usually colored by a partisan effort to fix the blame on one faction or another.

The final unhappy chapter in Visigothic history began with the death of Reccesvinth and the election of his successor. In accordance with a decree of the Eighth Council of Toledo, the bishops and magnates who were assembled at Gerticos, where Reccesvinth died, proceeded immediately to an election. Their haste may have been due in part to a desire to affirm the elective nature of the monarchy and to prevent any member of Reccesvinth's family from seizing the throne; in any case they offered the crown to Wamba (672–680), a distinguished noble, who was reluctant to accept until threatened with a sword. So that his rights to the throne could not be impugned, he postponed his anointing until he arrived at Toledo. Scarcely had he assumed the kingship than a revolt broke out in Septimania. In order to suppress it, he dispatched Duke Paul, who promptly betrayed his trust, allied himself with the rebels and proclaimed himself king. Wamba, who had been occupied with a Basque uprising, hastened through Tarraconensis to Septimania. There he easily defeated the rebels and captured Paul (673), who was condemned to death, though the penalty was commuted to decalvation, lifelong infamy, and imprisonment. Wamba had crushed the rebellion with energy, but he had also encountered difficulties in raising troops. As a remedy he decreed that in the future all nobles and simple freemen, including the clergy, would be obligated to answer the summons to the royal host. This law, re-establishing an old custom, aroused ecclesiastical opposition, as did the king's erection of several new bishoprics, but there is no reason to believe that the bishops thereupon resolved to bring about his ruin.

In his brief career Wamba revealed exceptional competence and ability, but his reign ended rather abruptly in 680. On the night of 14 October he suddenly lost consciousness, and his courtiers assumed that he was dying. In accordance with custom, Julian, bishop of Toledo, tonsured the king and clothed him in penitential garb. When he awoke from his coma, Wamba found himself deprived of his right to rule, since the Sixth Council of Toledo had forbidden any tonsured person to wear the crown. Therefore he renounced the throne in favor of Erwig and retired to a monastery where he ended his days. According to the *Chronicle of Alfonso III*, written in the late ninth century, Erwig, a grandnephew of Khindasvinth, had indeed conspired to usurp the throne, and by administering a drug caused the king to lapse into unconsciousness. Nineteenth-century historians such as Dahn, Görres, and Gams, believed that Julian of Toledo collaborated in the conspiracy and was in fact the chief villain. Supposedly he wished to be rid of an energetic king who could not be dominated by the church, and to replace him with a weakling; on the other hand, F. X. Murphy has argued that evidence of Julian's involvement is so scanty as to be highly questionable.

The circumstances in which Erwig (680–687) attained the throne rendered his position precarious. Realizing this, he summoned the Twelfth Council of Toledo in 681 under the presidency of Bishop Julian; presenting documents in which Wamba designated him as his successor, Erwig appealed for recognition and support. Ziegler believes that these documents were forgeries, but the Council could not dispute their authenticity without provoking civil war. Thus the Council recognized Erwig, and released the people from their oath of allegiance to Wamba. Erwig's desire to conciliate his subjects was reflected in the

Council's pardon of those who had been punished under the terms of Wamba's law on military service. The Council also condemned Wamba's erection of new sees and declared that in future the metropolitan of Toledo, with royal consent, should have the right to name and to consecrate bishops of any diocese in the realm. This extension of Toledo's jurisdiction has been interpreted as Erwig's reward to Julian of Toledo for his assistance in the conspiracy against Wamba. Finally Erwig asked the Council to approve his stringent legislation against the Jews. Two years later the Thirteenth Council, on the king's urging, pardoned the Septimanians who had rebelled against Wamba.

If the *Chronicle of Alfonso III* is to be believed, Erwig made a final effort to reconcile the factions by marrying his daughter to Wamba's nephew, Egica, whom he designated, just before he died, as his successor. According to the same source, Egica (687–702) had no sooner ascended the throne than, on Wamba's insistence, he repudiated Erwig's daughter. Rather ominously he asked the bishops assembled in the Fifteenth Council of Toledo in 688 to release him from his oath to protect Erwig's family. When they did so, he set out to punish those whom he suspected of treachery, confiscating their goods, sending them into exile, or reducing them to servitude. Upon his complaint that the Jews were conspiring against him and were entering into treasonous contacts with their brethren in North Africa and with the Muslims, the bishops of the Seventeenth Council in 694 supported his proposal to deprive the Jews of their property and to reduce them to perpetual slavery.

Hoping to establish an hereditary monarchy in his own family, Egica associated his son Witiza (702–710) on the throne. He in turn elevated his young son, Akhila, to whom he entrusted the government of Septimania and Tarraconensis. Naturally these ambitious designs evoked hostility, and moreover, according to the *Chronicle of Moissac*, the king "was so given up to the love of women and by his example, taught the priests and the people to live in lust, that he aroused the anger of the Lord." The *Chronicle of Alfonso III* also denounced the king for corrupting the church by refusing to convoke councils, by violating the canons, and by compelling the clergy to take wives. For these reasons the "Goths perished under the sword of the Saracens."

The circumstances that led to the Muslim invasion of the peninsula a year after Witiza's death are involved in extraordinary confusion. In later accounts of the conquest it is not always possible to separate truth from legend. Although Witiza's son Akhila was proclaimed as king, his opponents controlled the royal city of Toledo and recognized Rodrigo, duke of Baetica, a grandson of Khindasvinth and a son of Theodofred who had been blinded by Egica. Rather than accept Rodrigo as king, Witiza's family reportedly sent envoys to Africa seeking Muslim assistance.

A mysterious personage known as Count Julian also figures in the events preceding the Muslim conquest. He is mentioned by all the Arabic chroniclers, but not by the early Christian ones. Modern authors have variously identified him as a Byzantine exarch who ruled Ceuta on the North African coast, as a Christian Berber who defended Tangier against the Muslims, or as a Gothic noble who was lord of Algeciras and Cádiz on the Spanish side of the straits of Gibraltar. Whatever his origin and official status, the Arabic chroniclers emphasize that he opposed Rodrigo's accession to power and collaborated in his downfall. They allege that his hostility to the king was born out of a desire for vengeance, as Rodrigo had ravished his daughter. For this reason Julian facilitated the Muslim entry into the peninsula.

Whatever the truth may be, and it will probably never be known entirely, the proximity of the Muslims to the peninsula eventually would have induced them to contemplate its conquest. Ever since Muhammad (d. 632) had proclaimed his message, his followers had been engaged in the continuing task of spreading Islam throughout the Mediterranean world. While Muslim armies overran Syria and pushed on toward the frontiers of India, others had advanced steadily across Egypt and Libya into North Africa. Carthage fell into their hands in 698, and Byzantine rule in North Africa came to an end. With the aid of the newly converted Berbers the Arabs were able to take Tangier in 708 and probably forced Count Julian to recognize their lordship over Ceuta in the next year. In October-November 709, Julian sent a reconnoitering expedition to Spain and reported the weakness of its defenses to the Muslims. But before undertaking any action on his own, Musa ibn Nusayr, governor of North Africa, consulted the caliph of Damascus who advised caution. A small expedition of about 400 men commanded by Tarif ibn Malluq landed in July 710 on the Spanish coast at Tarifa, which ever since has borne his name. After moving rapidly to Algeciras, he returned to Africa with booty and favorable reports.

After some months of further preparation Musa appointed the Berber freedman, Tariq ibn Ziyad, to command a force of about 7,000 men to carry out a more extensive investigation of conditions in the peninsula. Tariq landed on 27–28 April 711 on the rock of Gibraltar to which he gave his name. King Rodrigo, who had been engaged with the Basques, hastened to Córdoba where he assembled an army to oppose the intruders. Rather than move inland and deprive himself of the means of a rapid withdrawal from the peninsula, should that be necessary, Tariq chose to wait at Algeciras. The arrival of reinforcements brought his total strength to about 12,000 men. The fateful battle was joined at last on 19 July 711. The site traditionally has been placed on the Guadalete river between Jerez and Medina Sidonia, but Lévi-Provençal has located it on the river Barbate and the lagoon of La Janda not far from the coast.

In the midst of the battle, Witiza's sons, Sisbert and Oppa, who commanded the wings of the Visigothic army, abandoned their king, probably by prearrangement with the enemy. As a consequence, the Goths were routed, and King Rodrigo disappeared, perhaps a victim of the combat. The victors found only his white horse, a golden saddle encrusted with rubies and emeralds, and a gold mantle. In the words of the *Cronicon Albeldense* (78) : "And so the kingdom of the Goths perished and through fear and iron all the pride of the Gothic people perished." The defeat was complete, but if the family of Witiza hoped to regain the throne they were soon disillusioned. Tariq realized that the backbone of Gothic resistance had been broken and that the kingdom could be taken. His expedition, originally intended only to reconnoiter, had achieved one of the greatest victories in the annals of Islam.

In later days the Christians who survived the conquest tried to explain the destruction of the Visigothic kingdom by reference to the vices of Witiza or Rodrigo. Others saw the downfall of Spain as a divine punishment for the sins of the Visigoths. Without seeking to blame any individual, one can point to reasons of a more fundamental character which led to the collapse of the Visigothic state. The decrepitude of the state had been accentuated in the last thirty years of its existence by the conflict of factions. Lacking an hereditary monarchy, the state was left a prey to constant conspiracy and civil war. The most recent rivalries had not been healed at the moment of invasion, and the family of Witiza chose the decisive moment of battle to revive their partisan claims. The invasion was facilitated as well by Muslim control of the southern invasion route, namely, Ceuta and Tangier. The

Visigoths had never taken the precaution to secure firm control of those ports and the adjacent regions. In later centuries successive waves of invaders followed the path traced by Tariq in 711. In explaining the Muslim triumph one must also take into account the astounding combination of religious zeal and warlike enthusiasm which enabled Muhammad's disciples to overrun much of the Persian and Byzantine empires and to create an empire reaching from the borders of India to the Pillars of Hercules. Even if the Visigothic kingdom had not suffered from internal weaknesses, it seems unlikely that it would have been able to resist the impetus of the Muslim assault.

Whatever explanation one might offer, the lamentation of Alfonso X of Castile perhaps best expressed the traditional view of medieval Spaniards:

This kingdom, so noble, so rich, so powerful, so honored, was ravaged and destroyed by the discord among the people of the realm who turned their swords against one another, as if they were enemies . . . but they all lost because all the cities of Spain were taken . . . and destroyed . . . and the whole land was emptied of people and bathed in blood and tears; strangers occupied it; neighbors and householders were driven out; their wives were widowed and their children orphaned. . . . Spain weeps for her sons and cannot be comforted because they are no more. . . . What evil, what ruin has Spain not endured?   [*Primera Crónica General*, 558–559]

CHAPTER 2

Visigothic Government

The Formation of the Kingdom

In 418, after many years of wandering through the Roman Empire
without a fixed abode, the Visigoths achieved recognition as *federati*
with the right to settle in sections of southern Gaul and with the obligation to render military aid to the emperor. Retaining political autonomy under the rule of their own king and subject to their own law,
the Visigoths formed a kind of state within the state. This situation
changed as imperial power gradually disintegrated in the late fifth century. The authority of the emperor in the provinces of southern Gaul
and northern Spain was replaced by that of the Visigothic King Euric
who ruled both Goths and Romans, though each people probably continued to be governed according to its own law. The Visigothic kingdom, now established on a territorial basis, was centered at Toulouse
in southern Gaul, but due to the expansion of the Franks it was confined from the sixth century onwards to Spain and to the region of
Septimania just north of the Pyrenees. In the reign of Leovigild, Toledo replaced Toulouse as the seat of monarchy, but Visigothic rule did
not extend over the whole peninsula until Swintila's recovery of Byzantine coastal positions early in the seventh century.

The government of the realm was conducted in accordance with
ideas of Germanic, Roman, and ecclesiastical origin. Among the ancient
Germans the assembly of freemen directed the affairs of the community
and in time of war conferred supreme power upon a king. Government
was popular and military in character and lacked any territorial foundation until the settlement of the Visigoths in Spain. Through long
association with Rome the Visigoths had come to some understanding
of the state as a public institution based upon a defined territory and

55

held together by the allegiance of its citizens. Probably to a greater extent than elsewhere in the barbarian west, the Roman idea of the state (*res publica*) remained nearly intact, as suggested by the use of terminology such as *patria, utilitas publica, arca publica*, in the *Liber Judiciorum*, and by the distinction made between crimes against the fatherland or kingdom and those against the king. Roman influence also countered the Germanic inclination to regard the territory of the state as the king's private domain. The indivisibility of the kingdom was thus a fundamental characteristic of Visigothic rule.

The Visigothic kingdom, though influenced by the Roman concepts of public law and public welfare, was not a mere continuation of the late empire. Contrary to Dahn and Torres López, who insisted that the unity of the realm was based on the public bond between king and subject, Sánchez Albornoz argued that certain private relationships among men tended to undermine the public character of the kingdom and to encourage the development of a prefeudal society. In the late empire the seigneurial regime was fully developed. Roman magnates not only exercised a private jurisdiction over their tenants who commended themselves to their protection, but they also maintained bodies of armed retainers bound to them by a private oath of fidelity. These highly personal relationships were often interposed between the sovereign and his subjects.

Sánchez Albornoz has also presented ample proof of the survival of the Germanic *comitatus* in the Visigothic kingdom. The *comitatus*, according to Tacitus, was a company of warriors who freely pledged loyalty and service to a renowned chieftain in return for glory, booty, protection, and maintenance. Dahn and Torres López denied the existence of the *comitatus* in the Visigothic kingdom, but Sánchez Albornoz has shown that the *fideles regis* and *gardingi regis* mentioned in contemporary texts were especially bound to the king's service by a private oath of fidelity. The *fideles regis*, sworn to faithful and honest service (*fidele obsequium et sincerum servitium, vigilantia et custodia*), were magnates of the royal council, some of whom held offices in the royal household, while others did not. Provincial dukes and counts probably were included in their number. Of lower rank, but still enjoying high status among the aristocracy, were the *gardingi* or armed retainers, living in the palace, serving and protecting the king. Like the *antrustiones* of the Merovingian monarchy, they continued the tradition of the *comitatus*.

The Visigothic kings remunerated their *fideles* and *gardingi* with grants of royal lands, sometimes in full ownership or subject to certain conditions. Stipendiary grants (*in stipendio, causa stipendii*) were gratuitous, temporal, and revocable at will and can be properly described as benefices. While admitting the lack of documentary proof, Sánchez Albornoz believes that such concessions were made at times in return for military service on horseback. Grants of land, whether in full ownership or in usufruct, transformed the *fideles* and *gardingi* into rural landlords whose continued fidelity was a source of great strength to the monarchy. On the other hand, the armed retainers (*sagiones, bucellarii*) in the service of bishops and magnates and receiving similar recompense represented a threat to the crown.

By the seventh century the private bond between men was becoming the essential basis of political and social relations and tended to weaken the public character of the state. The Muslim conquest, however, interrupted the normal progression of Visigothic Spain toward a feudal society.

Kingship

The king, as the leader of his people and as the head of government, was responsible for defending the realm against external attack, preserving domestic tranquility, administering justice, and protecting the church. In addition to his private estates, he also enjoyed the revenues and income of the public patrimony.

Royal absolutism was curbed by the turbulence of the Visigothic nobility and the influence of the church. With their propensity to rebellion and assassination (the *morbus gothicus* or *detestabilis consuetudo* of Gregory of Tours), the magnates were always able to put an end to despotic government. After the Visigoths abandoned Arianism, the bishops, through the councils of Toledo, tried to guard the king against conspiracy and revolt, and also to limit his authority. Seeking to give a moral orientation to the state, they declared that the king received his power from God with the duty to rule justly in accord with the laws and the Christian moral code and to render a final accounting of his work at the divine tribunal. St. Isidore of Seville, who was chiefly responsible for formulating the political theory of the Visigothic era, argued that a king who ruled unjustly lost his character as king. Kings, he said, ought to uphold the law: "It is just for the prince to obey his laws. For when he himself shows respect for his laws, they

will be deemed worthy to be held by all" (*Liber Sententiarum*, III, 51).
The responsibility of the king and his people to obey the law was also
stated in the *Liber Judiciorum* (II, 1, 2): "Both the royal power and
the body of the people ought to be subject to reverence for the laws."

Although it has long been commonplace to describe the Visigothic
monarchy as an elective institution, it would be more accurate to say
that throughout Visgothic history the elective principle was in conflict
with the hereditary one. By associating their sons to the throne, successive kings labored to make the monarchy hereditary. In those instances where sons succeeded their fathers, it is not evident that any
formal election took place. Often enough, association to the throne or
designation by the preceding monarch was sufficient to secure the succession of a new king.

In the fifth century the establishment of an hereditary monarchy
seemed well under way, since the descendants of Theodoric I occupied
the throne from 418 to the death of Amalaric in 531. The crisis resulting from the expansion of the Frankish kingdom ushered in a transitional period, one in which the Visigothic kingship was conferred by
election. In the sixth century, once the crisis had passed and the center
of the kingdom was located in Spain, the family of Leovigild renewed
the attempt to promote hereditary succession. The effort failed, however, and following Swintila's overthrow, the Fourth Council of Toledo
(633) formally recognized the elective nature of the kingship. For the
first time the Council laid down the principle that the magnates and the
bishops should elect the king.

No one of us shall dare to seize the kingdom; no one shall arouse sedition
among the citizenry; no one shall think of killing the king; but when the prince
has died in peace, the chief men of all the people, together with the priests,
shall, by common consent, constitute a successor for the kingdom, so that while
we are united in peace, no division of the fatherland nor of the people may
arise through force or intrigue. [𝓜𝓗𝓓𝓔, II, 395]

Later councils added further details. The candidate should be of noble
Gothic origin and of good character; clerics, serfs, foreigners, and those
who had suffered the penalty of decalvation were excluded. As a
means of preventing the disorders attendant upon an interregnum, the
Eighth Council (653) decreed that the election should take place at
Toledo or in the place where the king died.

In view of this conciliar legislation it has been accepted generally that
churchmen were the staunchest advocates of elective kingship. Or-

landis, however, has insisted that the evidence does not reveal that the bishops displayed any special enthusiasm to uphold the elective principle, nor any decided preference for hereditary rule. On the contrary, Sánchez Albornoz has argued that the bishops were inclined to favor an hereditary monarchy in order to curb the conspiracies, rebellions, and assassinations which often attended the succession to the throne. In his opinion the decrees of the Fourth Council, regulating the elective system, represented a compromise between the wishes of the bishops and the magnates. The latter, rather than the bishops, had the most to gain from the preservation of the elective principle.

Despite the decrees of the councils, seventh-century kings such as Khintila and Khindasvinth, by associating their sons to the throne, attempted to transform the monarchy into an hereditary institution. In the last years of the century a clear case of election in conformity with the conciliar decrees was that of Wamba. No election seems to have taken place in the succession of the next three kings, two of whom were designated by their predecessors, and the third associated with his father on the throne. On the death of Witiza, the magnates, by electing Rodrigo, the last of the Visigothic kings, once more demonstrated their opposition to the hereditary principle. The sudden destruction of the kingdom immediately thereafter put an end to this controversy.

Upon his accession to the throne the king swore an oath to rule justly and received an oath of fidelity from his subjects, a public oath essentially different from the private pledge of his *fideles* and *gardingi*. Violation of the oath was condemned as sacrilege. Among the ancient Germans the elected king was raised upon a shield, but more refined ceremonial was adopted in the Visigothic kingdom. St. Isidore reported in his *Historia* (51) that Leovigild was "the first among them to sit upon a throne wearing royal vestments, for before him dress and seating were common to the people as well as the kings." The other symbols of royal power were the crown, sceptre, purple mantle, sword, and standard. Sometime after the conversion of the Visigoths, the custom of anointing the king was introduced. Although the anointing of Wamba is the first recorded instance, the custom may antedate his reign. Anointing conferred upon the king a quasi-sacerdotal character and protected his person against violence. This practice was adopted subsequently by the Franks and the Anglo-Saxons and thus became common throughout western Europe. Although the title *Rex Gothorum* expressed the tribal character of Visigothic kingship, the frequent use of the imperial title, *Princeps,* and the imperial surname, Flavius, emphasized the king's role as the head of state. From the time of Leovigild, the usual royal residence was Toledo, and, in the centuries to come, Christian tradition remembered it as the *urbs regia,* the symbol of the Visigothic monarchy.

The Royal Council and the Councils of Toledo

Once the Visigoths settled permanently in western Europe the traditional assembly of freemen by which they had regulated their affairs declined and disappeared. The dispersion of the Visigoths over a wide area in Gaul and Spain impeded, if it did not make impossible, their convocation to assemblies of this kind. In the sixth century the king relied for advice and support upon a much smaller council or *senatus* of prominent men (*seniores*), but this in turn, due to the extinction of old noble families and the progressive strengthening of royal power, disappeared in the following century.

The functions of the ancient assembly and the *senatus* passed, in the seventh century, to another organism called the *aula regia,* composed of officials serving in the royal court or bound to the king by special ties. The principal officers of the royal court (*officium palatinum*) included the treasurer (*comes thesaurorum*), the administrator of the royal patrimony (*comes patrimonii*), the head of the chancery (*comes notariorum*), the commander of the royal guard (*comes spatariorum*), the guardian of the stables and master of the household cavalry (*comes stabuli*), the chief chamberlain (*comes cubiculariorum*), the count of Toledo, and others. These officials and their subordinates, in continuous residence with the king, were responsible for the day-to-day activities of the central administration.

The *aula regia* also included magnates (*seniores, maiores palatii*) who resided at court without performing specific functions; bound to the king by the tie of commendation, they were known therefore as *fideles regis.* Also in residence, were the *gardingi* who formed the royal *comitatus.* As Sánchez Albornoz has shown, they were armed men, specifically sworn to the king's service, receiving maintenance from him, usually at court, or sometimes on lands granted to them as benefices or in full ownership. Finally the bishops of sees near Toledo in turn customarily resided each month at the royal court and were able to participate in the deliberations of the *aula regia.*

Thus the *aula regia* was composed of court officials (*officium pala-tinum*), the magnates (*seniores palatii*), the *gardingi*, and the bishops. The council had a consultative role, advising the king in matters of legislation, administration, war, foreign policy, and sitting with him as a judicial tribunal, but he was not obligated to follow its advice nor to submit his decisions for its approval.

After Recared's conversion, the bishops, through the councils of To-ledo, collaborated with the king in the affairs of government. The royal need for the moral support of the church largely explains the great in-fluence which the councils enjoyed in secular matters. Although the councils were primarily ecclesiastical assemblies, they were convoked by the king, who opened their deliberations. In his message (*tomus regius*) he set forth those questions of a spiritual or temporal character which he believed required the attention of the bishops. The councils, under the presidency of the oldest metropolitan, and later of the bishop of Toledo, treated first of ecclesiastical matters. During these sessions, usually lasting three days, only the prelates attended.

When the councils turned to secular matters the magnates of the *aula regia* attended to further the king's interests, but the councils re-mained essentially ecclesiastical bodies. They did not legislate for the state nor did they serve as secular tribunals. They did sanction the laws promulgated by the king, such as those concerning the Jews, the par-doning of rebels, the protection of the royal family; they regulated the forms of royal elections, and they acknowledged the legality of the king's accession to the throne. But the canons of the councils received the force of civil law only through confirmation by the king. It was to the interest of the church to secure civil support of conciliar decrees, just as it was to the interest of the king to obtain ecclesiastical sanction of his laws. In sum, the councils, as assemblies representing the church, tried to bolster the institution of monarchy and to set forth moral prin-ciples to guide the sovereign.

Provincial and Local Administration

In broad outlines the structure of Roman provincial and local ad-ministration survived in the Visigothic era. The old Roman provinces (Tarraconensis, Cartaginensis, Lusitania, Baetica, Gallaetia, together with Septimania, or Gallia Gothica, part of the province of Narbonen-sis) which now formed the Visigothic kingdom, had been governed by *rectores* or *iudices provinciae*, who were still appointed by the first

Visigothic kings. From the second half of the sixth century, however, the functions of these officials were assumed by a *dux*, the supreme civil and military governor of the province. At times the king appointed his sons as dukes in order to assure their eventual succession to the throne, but the office usually was given to prominent nobles, whose names, for example, Claudius, Paulus, often suggest that they were of Roman or perhaps Greek origin.

Much more important as administrative entities were the *territoria* or subdivisions of provinces. In the Roman era the *territorium* was the rural district surrounding a city and dependent upon the municipal *curia*. The importance of the *territoria* in the Visigothic kingdom was due to the decline of the municipalities (*municipia, civitates*), formerly the basic units of imperial administration.

Sánchez Albornoz has demonstrated that the municipalities suffered a steady economic decline from the third century and, as organs of administration, disappeared by the close of the sixth century. In earlier times the municipal *curia*, composed of the principal citizens, known as *curiales*, had been an honored institution, entrusted with the administration of the city and the rural area depending upon it. The *curiales*, subjected to heavy financial burdens by the imperial government, saw themselves threatened with ruin, but when they attempted to escape the responsibilities of the *curia*, the government made their office hereditary. The confusion accompanying the Germanic invasions and the collapse of imperial authority contributed further to the decline of the *curia*. Traditional offices such as *duumvir*, *aedilis*, and *quaestor* disappeared, while the *defensor civitatis* was reduced to the role of a local judge.

With the disintegration of municipal administration, the functions of the *curia* were conferred upon *iudices* or *comites* appointed by the king and removable at will. Usually residing in the city, the count and his lieutenant, the vicar, were responsible for the administration of justice, the collection of royal revenues, and the summoning of troops within the *territorium* which now replaced the municipality as the ordinary unit of local administration.

While villages and hamlets were subject directly to the count and his vicar, and did not form distinctive administrative units, village assemblies (*conventus publicus vicinorum*) regulated economic questions of interest to the community. On the other hand, lords of great estates (*villae, latifundia*) tended to enjoy a certain independence of territorial officials and often had extensive administrative responsibilities. Through their stewards and other agents, the lords maintained order and exercised civil and sometimes criminal jurisdiction over the villagers living on their estates who were often commended to their protection, and owed military service, rents, and personal services to them.

The Law and the Administration of Justice

When the Visigoths first settled in Gaul early in the fifth century the Roman empire acknowledged their right to be governed by their own customary laws. After the collapse of imperial power in the late fifth century the duality of law persisted, as the Visigoths continued to be subject to their own law, and the Gallo-Romans and Hispano-Romans to Roman law. In addition to a considerable body of vulgar Roman law, the Theodosian Code, promulgated in 438 by Emperor Theodosius II, remained in force. Thus, law in the early Visigothic kingdom was personal rather than territorial in its application.

The Visigoths originally regulated their affairs in accordance with custom, an unwritten law, developed over the centuries and deriving its binding force from long usage and the consensus of the people. In the late fifth century, under Roman influence, the Visigothic kings began to publish written laws for both their Gothic and Roman subjects. Even so, custom undoubtedly survived throughout the Visigothic era and, in the centuries following the Muslim conquest, reappeared in the full light of history.

The first written compilation of law in any of the Germanic states was the Code of Euric promulgated around 475. The work of Roman provincial jurists, who used elements of the Theodosian Code, the *Sententiae* of Paulus, as well as Germanic custom, the Latin text survives in 54 chapters in a palimpsest of Paris. Although largely Roman in tone, most historians believe it was intended to apply only to Euric's subjects, as Isidore of Seville suggested in his *Historia* (35): "Under this king the Goths began to have written enactments of laws; previously they were bound only by usages and customs." García Gallo, however, supported by Alvaro d'Ors and to some extent by Paulo Merêa, has insisted that from the beginning the Visigothic kings attempted to establish a territorial law. In this view, Euric's Code, by fusing vulgar Roman law and Gothic custom, was intended to put an end to the duality of law, but since it neither respected the integrity of Roman law nor codified Gothic custom, it was inadequate for the needs of both peoples.

Euric's son, Alaric II, in 506 promulgated a code known as the *Lex romana Visigothorum*, or simply as Alaric's Breviary. Prepared by a commission of jurists, the Breviary contained Roman law drawn from the Theodosian Code and other Roman sources. Its influence in western Europe, especially in southern Gaul, was considerable for centuries thereafter. Most historians believe it was intended to serve the needs of Alaric's Roman subjects, but García Gallo considers it a territorial law applicable to Goths and Romans. He argues that Alaric, faced by the impending threat of Frankish attack, sought to win the favor of the Gallo-Romans by accepting Roman law in full and giving it universal force in his kingdom. Thus Euric's Code ceased to have any effect. Again, most scholars dissent from this opinion.

Although a duality of law existed, Visigothic custom was not exclusively Germanic but was strongly influenced by the Roman, especially during the sixth century, thereby encouraging a tendency toward the unification of law. This may have prompted Leovigild's revision of Euric's Code between 572 and 586. In his *Historia* (51) St. Isidore noted that he "corrected those things in the laws which seemed to have been set down confusedly by Euric, adding many neglected laws and suppressing other superfluous ones." Although the text of this revision has not survived, individual laws are included in the later *Liber Judiciorum* under the rubric, *antiqua*. While Torres López and Galo Sánchez insist that Leovigild's revision was still a code for Visigoths only, García Gallo holds that it was a territorial law, replacing the Breviary and correcting and updating Euric's Code.

In the seventh century, Khindasvinth planned a new code of law of a territorial character that would embody the considerable amount of legislation enacted since the reign of Leovigild. Under the title *Liber Judiciorum*, the work was completed and promulgated by his son Reccesvinth *circa* 654. Erwig published a further revision in 681 including laws enacted since Reccesvinth. This was the final correction and reform of the text. Egica proposed a new revision in 693, but it does not seem to have been carried out. From time to time anonymous jurists corrected the text, and this corrected text is known as the *vulgata*.

A territorial law, binding on all the inhabitants of the realm without regard to their Germanic or Roman origin, the *Liber Judiciorum* terminated the duality of the law in the kingdom, thus removing one of the principal obstacles to the unification of the people. Lear has described the content of the *Liber* as Romance law, that is, an organic combination of both Roman and Germanic law. The text is divided into twelve books, and these into titles and laws dealing with civil, criminal, and procedural matters, as for example: the law, the legislator, judges, witnesses, procedures, marriage, inheritance, contracts, crimes, punishments, sanctuary, military obligations, foreign merchants, heresy, and so on. In addition to laws derived from the code of Leovigild, there are also laws of Khindasvinth and the later laws of Reccesvinth, Wamba, and Erwig, usually cited by the name of the king. The influence of conciliar decrees is notable, and the whole work has a distinctly Christian tone.

The most sophisticated and comprehensive codification promulgated in any of the barbarian kingdoms, the *Liber Judiciorum* continued to serve the Christian peoples of the peninsula until the revival in the twelfth century of Roman law embodied in Justinian's Code. In the thirteenth century, on the order of Fernando III of Castile, the *Liber Judiciorum* was translated into Castilian under the title *Fuero Juzgo*, and given to Córdoba and other cities as their municipal law. Thus as Galo Sánchez remarked, in one form or another it has been in use until our own times.

Although the *Liber Judiciorum* gave little attention to custom as a source of law, custom was ingrained in the minds of the people and persisted for centuries. In many areas it probably had greater binding force than the written law. After the collapse of the Visigothic kingdom, custom rose to the surface again and enjoyed a vigorous life throughout the early centuries of the reconquest. As Hinojosa pointed out, the numerous municipal *fueros* issued before the thirteenth century reflect the significance of custom in the daily lives of the people.

The administration of justice in the Visigothic kingdom had to be complicated, so long as the principle of the personality of law survived. The principle implied that Goths and Romans were subject to their own distinctive laws, but what law was followed in cases between Goths and Romans? Torres López, following Zeumer, believes that the law of the defendant was applied. Another complication arose from the ancient Germanic concept that litigation was primarily the private concern of the parties involved, rather than the public business. In their law codes, however, the Visigothic kings, influenced by Roman principles, assumed that the administration of justice was a function of the state under the direction of the king. The conflict between ideas of public and private justice undoubtedly continued throughout the Visigothic era, and García Gallo suggested that public justice triumphed only where royal functionaries were able to impose it.

Even before the duality of law was ended by the promulgation of the *Liber Judiciorum*, both Goths and Romans probably were being judged by the same functionaries. The judicial organization was not distinct from the civil administration, since administrative officers also enjoyed judicial powers. The king, assisted by the magnates of his court, was the supreme judge, with full jurisdiction and also with the power to dispense mercy. In special cases he could appoint judges (*pacis adsertores*) to act in his name. According to the *Liber Judiciorum* (II, 1, 27), "unjust judgments or sentences rendered by judges out of fear of the king or on his command, are invalid."

The ordinary judicial officers were the counts who were responsible for the general territorial administration, supplanting both the Roman provincial governors and the municipal magistrates. The *vicarius*, as the count's lieutenant, could also sit in judgment. Prominent men (*boni homines*) from the district served as assessors, offering advice on points of law or procedure, and *sagiones* acted as executive agents of the court, citing parties, seeing that judgments were carried out. Both the dukes and bishops had the general responsibility of supervising the administration of justice by the counts. The Portuguese scholar, Merêa, has argued that the *iudices territorii* who appear in the law codes were a distinct body of magistrates with jurisdiction in judicial subdivisions of the *territoria*.

The *thiufadus*, who is also recorded in the law codes, is the subject of much controversy. He has been regarded as the ordinary judge of the Visigoths, but this has been denied by Alvaro d'Ors, who does not believe that there were separate judges for Visigoths and Romans. In any case, by Leovigild's reign his jurisdiction was probably territorial; inasmuch as he has been identified with the *millenarius*, the military commander of 1,000 men, his jurisdiction was primarily over military crimes.

Of an entirely private character was the jurisdiction which landlords exercised on their estates. A landlord could adjudicate civil matters presented to him by those living on his estate, and he could also judge crimes committed in his household even by freemen. A landlord's slaves were especially subject to his jurisdiction, but he could not execute them until public judgment had been given. In general, landlords tended to close their estates, insofar as possible, to the jurisdiction of public functionaries. Finally, one should note the existence of church courts, dealing with ecclesiastical persons and property, and of courts for foreign merchants who were judged by their own magistrates according to their own law.

The civil procedure of the *Liber Judiciorum* was essentially Roman. A written or oral charge before the judge initiated the process. The court's bailiff (*sagio*), accompanied by witnesses, summoned the defendant, who had to appear in person or through his representative on the day and at the place assigned, or suffer penalties. A postponement could be granted on the grounds of illness, royal service, or some such reason. The presentation of documentary evidence and the use of witnesses was permitted in substantiation and in refutation of the charge. In important cases the judgment was rendered in written form under the signature and seal of the judge and witnesses.

In criminal cases the *Liber Judiciorum* did not admit the principle of collective responsibility, that is, the responsibility of the defendant's family or neighbors, nor did it recognize the blood feud. Ignorance of the law did not diminish responsibility, but the intent of the accused and not merely the damage done was given appropriate consideration. Thus accidental killing was not punishable to the same extent as murder. The social rank of criminals and of those against whom crimes were committed influenced the degree of punishment, but in general penalties were in proportion to the crime. Once an accusation was made it could not be withdrawn, but one who brought a false charge was subject to heavy fines (*calumniae*). The judge interrogated witnesses and scrutinized documents to determine credibility. Purgation was admitted, though not the accompanying band of *compurgatores* characteristic of Germanic law. There is little evidence of Germanic procedure, other than the ordeal of cold water, the principle of monetary compositions, and the penalty of decalvation. The use of torture and the penalties of reduction to slavery, confiscation, infamy, exile, imprisonment, mutilation, and execution, were typically Roman. The brutality of the times is suggested by a passage in the *Chronicle* of John of Biclaro describing the punishment meted out to Argimund, the rebellious duke of Baetica: "After being beaten and interrogated, his head was vilely shaved and his right arm was cut off. Then, paraded through the city of Toledo seated on an ass, he gave an example to all, and taught servants not to be arrogant to their lords."

Financial and Military Organization

In a simplified form the Roman financial administration continued to function in the Visigothic era. The Visigoths were probably slow to make a distinction between the patrimony of the state and that of the king, but Reccesvinth affirmed it at the Eighth Council of Toledo (653). Torres López does not believe that a new principle was enunciated, but that one previously recognized was restated. Property acquired by the king prior to his accession constituted his private patrimony, heritable by his descendants; property acquired after his accession was the public patrimony of which he had usufruct, but not ownership, and which passed to his successors rather than to his heirs.

The general supervision of the patrimony was entrusted to the *comes patrimonii*, while the *comes thesaurorum* was responsible for the moneys and precious objects kept in the royal residence. On the provincial level the dukes and especially the counts, assisted by many lesser officials, such as *villici* (administrators of royal estates), and *telonarii*, or toll collectors, had charge of the collection of royal revenues.

Royal revenues were determined by custom rather than by current need and thus tended to be fixed sums, and most were vestiges from the Roman era. Among them were rents payable by tenants on state domains, that is, lands formerly pertaining to the empire, lands without owners, lands confiscated from rebels, Jews, criminals, and such. Among direct imposts levied by the king was the land tax of the late empire, the *tributum soli* or *functio publica*, payable in coin or goods. It was collected originally only from lands held by Romans, but eventually it was applied to the lands of the Goths. In the course of time it tended to be confused with the private rent paid by tenants, and since no attempt was made to reassess land values, as had been done under the empire, the tax became a fixed charge.

Romans and Goths were obliged to pay a personal capitation (*capitatio humana*), though Sisenand authorized the Fourth Council of Toledo (633) to exempt clerics from this burden. The principal indirect tax was a toll on goods in transit (*teloneum, portorium*). Other indirect taxes disappeared. Royal income was augmented by fines, confiscation, booty, gifts from subjects or other kings seeking alliances, and personal services (*munera*), such as the provision of horses for royal messengers. No attempt was made to devise a budget. Royal expenses were limited to the maintenance of the king and his family, his household, officials, donations to the church, and to his *fideles*.

The Visigothic kings did not maintain a standing army, but their *fideles* and *gardingi* were pledged to render military service to them and formed an important element in the army. All freemen traditionally were obliged to perform military service when summoned to do so and to equip themselves suitably. Euric probably extended this obligation to Hispano-Romans and perhaps to slaves. The evident failure of many to answer the summons to war caused Wamba to re-enact the old law in 673, even extending it to the clergy, and to impose severe penalties on those who were delinquent in obeying it. Erwig modified the law somewhat by mitigating the harshness of its penalties.

Under the king as commander-in-chief and his lieutenant, the count of the army (*comes exercitus*), the troops were grouped in decimal units. The *thiufadus* or *millenarius*, the *quingentenarius*, *centenarius*, and *decanus* commanded groups of 1,000, 500, 100, and 10 respectively. Commanders were responsible for the punishment of infractions of discipline, desertion, failure to answer the summons, and so on. The chief remuneration of the soldiers consisted of booty. The army was constituted primarily by infantry forces, though Sánchez Albornoz pointed out that the cavalry had an important role, inasmuch as the *fideles* and *gardingi regis* and other chief men probably fought on horseback. Isidore of Seville, moreover, commented on the Visigothic predilection for horses: "They are remarkable enough in the use of arms and they fight on horseback not only with lances but also with darts. They enter battle both on horseback and on foot; nevertheless they prefer the swift course of cavalry, wherefore the poet says: 'There goes the Goth, flying on his horse' " (*Historia Gothorum*, 69).

CHAPTER 3

Visigothic Society
and Culture

The Population

For nearly three centuries the Visigoths dominated the political structure of the peninsula, but they were never more than a minority of the total population. Of the Germanic tribes who invaded the peninsula, the Alans and the Siling Vandals had been largely destroyed in wars with the Visigoths early in the fifth century. The survivors joined the Asding Vandals who crossed from Spain to North Africa in 429. The number of emigrants traditionally has been put at 80,000. Remaining behind were the Suevi, numbering about 100,000, who settled principally in Galicia where they preserved their independence until the end of the sixth century.

Not until the late fifth century did the Visigoths begin to occupy the peninsula in significant numbers. Due to Euric's expansionist policy, they took possession of the northeastern provinces, but only after the Franks expelled them from the kingdom of Toulouse did their colonization of Spain become more intensive. Archeology and the evidence of place names (Villa Gotorum, Godos, La Goda) indicate that they settled in relatively dense numbers in the upper regions of the central *meseta*, that is, in Old Castile, from Soria along the Duero river to the Campos Góticos around Palencia and Valladolid. Sánchez Albornoz believes that the evident Germanic influences in the later county of Castile are a reflection of Visigothic concentration in that region. Since statistical data for this period are unsatisfactory, estimates of the numbers of barbarians must be conjectural. Valdeavellano and others estimate that about 300,000 or 400,000 Visigoths settled among 9 million

Hispano-Romans; on the other hand, Vicens Vives gives figures of 200,000 Visigoths and 6 million Hispano-Romans.

Although the Visigoths were receptive to Roman ideas, their assimilation with the Hispano-Romans could not be achieved immediately. The process began soon after the Visigoths settled among the natives, but it did not result in the complete abandonment of barbarian customs. The law of Valentinian I and Valens (included in Alaric's Breviary) forbidding intermarriage between Romans and barbarians technically posed an obstacle to assimilation, but it does not seem to have been enforced rigorously. Late in the sixth century Leovigild, whose primary aim was the unification of the peninsula and its people, abrogated the law. Soon after, his son Recared accepted orthodox Christianity, thus eliminating the principal barrier separating the two peoples. The Suevi had been converted earlier in the century. The simultaneous existence of Visigothic and Roman law traditionally has been considered a major factor perpetuating the division of the races, but strong arguments have been adduced in favor of the territoriality of the law codes issued by the Visigothic kings. Although this controversy has not been settled, all agree that the tendency toward the unification of the law was apparent in Leovigild's reign and was completed about 654 with the promulgation of the *Liber Judiciorum*. The enactment of a single law for all the people of *Hispania* terminated the process of assimilation, if only in a juridical sense.

Standing apart from the Visigoths and Hispano-Romans and inferior to them in the eyes of the law were the Jews, whose religion and social isolation made them an object of suspicion and persecution. After Recared's conversion the Visigothic kings embarked on an anti-Jewish policy that reached its climax in the seventh century. The Third Council of Toledo (589), summoned by Recared, re-enacted Roman laws of the fourth century forbidding Jews to marry Christians, to own Christian slaves, or to hold public offices in which they would have power to punish Christians. In 613 King Sisebut went far beyond this by demanding that Jews accept baptism or leave the kingdom. In his *History of the Visigoths*, St. Isidore of Seville protested that forcible conversions were improper, since religion was a matter of persuasion and personal conviction. The Fourth Council (633), under his presidency, repeated this principle but insisted that Jews who had been baptized should be obliged to fulfill the precepts of the Christian faith. Children of apostates were to be taken from their parents and reared as Christians.

Under Khintila, the Sixth Council (638) returned to Sisebut's harsh policy requiring Jews to become Christians or to go into exile. The continuing hostility of the king and the church encouraged the Jews of Septimania to participate in the rebellion of Duke Paul against Wamba in 672, but the quick suppression of the uprising ended all hope of securing a mitigation of the laws. In the closing years of the century even more stringent legislation was enacted. At Erwig's urging, the Twelfth Council (681) ordered Jews to receive baptism within a year on pain of exile, confiscation, or decalvation. Jews were forbidden to practice circumcision, to celebrate their holy days, or to insult Christianity. The supervision and punishment of Jews was entrusted to the clergy rather than to civil officials. Some years later, Egica denounced the Jews for conspiring against him and summoned the Seventeenth Council (694) to deal with the crisis. In punishment of their perfidy, Jews who obstinately refused to accept the Christian religion were reduced to slavery, and their property was confiscated.

The Visigothic kings apparently were the initiators of the anti-Jewish policy, but the councils generally lent their support. No doubt the desire to achieve complete religious unity was a principal motivation for this policy, but royal greed must not be discounted. Confiscation of property was a frequent punishment inflicted on the Jews and must have increased royal income substantially. The persecution was essentially religious rather than racial, since Jews who converted were entitled to the same rights as other Christians. Some converts or descendants of converts (for example, St. Julian, bishop of Toledo, who is said to have been of Jewish origin) rose to high positions. Despite the abundance of legislation against them, the majority of Jews preserved their religious and racial homogeneity. It is not surprising that, in their own defense, they took political action against kings such as Wamba and Egica; nor is it surprising that they welcomed the Muslim invaders as liberators from a cruel oppression. Anti-Jewish legislation was a principal legacy of the Visigothic era to later generations of Spaniards.

The Social Structure

In spite of the settlement of the barbarians in Spain, the social structure of the former Roman provinces did not undergo any radical change. Society was divided broadly into two groups, the free and the unfree, of whom the former were the majority. Class distinctions arose from such conditions as ancestry, the possession of property, the exercise of public office, and a man's private relationship to the king or to other men.

Visigothic lords and survivors of the Roman senatorial class constituted the aristocracy. The fusion of both groups through intermarriage and other social and political relationships probably began with the first settlement of the Visigoths in the peninsula. The nobles (*seniores, maiores, primates, proceres*) were distinguished from the mass of ordinary freemen by birth, the possession of great estates cultivated by tenants, and service in the principal offices of the palace and the royal council and in local administration. According to the Fourth Council of Toledo (633), they acted as electors of the king. Many were *fideles* or *gardingi regis*, specially pledged to the king's service by a private oath of fidelity, and remunerated by grants of land in full ownership or in usufruct. Nobles also maintained their own companies of armed men (*buccellarii, sagiones*) commended to them by a private oath and similarly compensated. Private bands such as these greatly increased the power and prestige of the nobility, but they were also a disturbing element in society and a threat to royal authority.

As a class, the nobles enjoyed certain juridical privileges, for example, they could not be tortured or subjected to corporal punishment except in cases of extreme gravity. They were subject, however, to heavier fines than those imposed on simple freemen, and their properties frequently were confiscated in whole or in part. Wamba declared that nobles could be reduced to slavery for failure to answer the royal summons to war, while Egica enacted the same penalty for refusal to take the public oath of allegiance to the king. Sánchez Albornoz believes that Egica or Witiza emphasized the social distinction between nobles and simple freemen by establishing a higher *wergild* or monetary composition for the former. Men of talent but humble origin could be admitted to noble rank, but the aristocracy as a whole seems to have been developing as an hereditary class in the late seventh century.

Simple freemen (*ingenui, minores, inferiores*) of Gothic and Roman origin were the most numerous element in society. The law recognized that all freemen had certain rights and duties, but it also acknowledged that a great gap separated nobles from non-nobles. All freemen had juridical capacity and could sue in court, but simple freemen were subjected more often to torture and corporal punishment. Class distinctions among simple freemen arose from the possession of wealth and social independence. The urban population, composed chiefly of Hispano-Romans, tended to decrease both in importance and in numbers. The *curiales* of the late empire, who had been ruined by the excessive financial burdens imposed on them, no longer had any significant role in municipal administration and were fast disappearing as a class. The artisans and merchants who had been grouped into corporations or *collegia*, so the imperial authorities could more easily control and tax them, suffered a similar decline. Many townsmen realized that the urban economy had fallen on hard times and sought a new life in the countryside.

Among the rural population, free proprietors, both Roman *possessores* and Gothic *hospites*, who had acquired land by virtue of the division of the soil or perhaps through usurpation were the most prominent group. Difficult economic and political circumstances, however, caused many of them to surrender their property to great lords, agreeing to hold it henceforth as tenants in return for protection. Freemen without land could secure it on a rent-paying basis by commending themselves. In theory the man who commended himself to another remained a freeman, retaining his personal liberty, with the right to break the bond at any moment, but in that case he had to yield whatever he had received from his lord as well as one-half of whatever he had acquired in his lord's service. As few tenant farmers were willing to risk the loss of security by terminating the tie of commendation, the relationship tended to be for life and ultimately became hereditary. Commendation limited the tenant's freedom to some extent and also interfered with the public relationship between the king and his subjects.

Most rural freemen were probably *coloni* of Hispano-Roman origin. Although the *colonus* was theoretically free, capable of contracting marriage and suing in court, he did not have freedom of movement, bound as he was to the soil (*adscripti glebae*); that is, he could not leave the land, nor could he be expelled from it. The *coloni* were also commended to the protection of their landlords, to whom they paid rent and personal services, and the *capitatio* or poll tax. The law required *coloni* to marry persons of the same social condition. If a *colonus* married a woman from another estate the children were divided between the two lords. While the *colonus* enjoyed security in his tenure, his condition was hereditary and in many ways not much different from that of slaves.

Slaves (*servi, mancipii*) were totally lacking in liberty and possessed neither rights nor obligations. The slave juridically was a thing, an inanimate object, rather than a person, and his condition was hereditary. While slaves could not contract a legal marriage, their children as well as those of mixed unions between slaves and freemen were slaves. Children born to slaves of different lords belonged to the mother's owner. Capture in war, failure to pay debts, or the commission of crime were all punishable by slavery. Egica also attempted to enslave Jews who would not be baptized. While some slaves worked as domestics and perhaps enjoyed a life of some comfort, most lived in miserable conditions, cultivating the soil for the benefit of their owners. The church owned slaves, as did the king and the secular nobles, but it endeavored to mitigate the harshness of slavery and to encourage manumission.

An owner could free his slaves by an oral act in the presence of witnesses, or by a written charter, or by a will. The juridical condition of the freedman (libertus) was intermediate to that of freemen and slaves. The freedman was subject to more severe corporal punishment and higher monetary compositions than a man born free; nor could he testify against a freeman. He could not marry his former owner, and if he married a slave, his children would be slaves. Oftentimes he commended himself to the protection of his former owner. A typical formula for manumission read in part: "From this day forward, I establish and declare you to be a free man . . . and a Roman citizen, saving only this condition, that as long as I live you will remain in my protection as a free man" (CHDE, II, 123).

The Economy

Although data concerning the economy of the Visigothic realm are extremely sparse, there is no reason to believe that the advent of the barbarians precipitated a ruinous disruption of commerce and a sudden lapse into a closed agrarian economy. Ever since the third century the economy of western Europe had been declining steadily. The coming of the Visigoths did nothing to check this trend but instead gave impetus to the ruralization of society. While there is some evidence of commercial activity in the Visigothic era, agriculture remained the essential basis of the economy.

The division of the soil between Romans and Goths was the principal change effected by the invasions. By their alliance with Rome in 418 the Goths were entitled to receive lands in the provinces of Gaul.

García Gallo believes the division primarily affected the estates of the Roman senatorial class. The Roman landlord retained two-thirds of the land he cultivated directly (*terra dominicata*) and from which he derived the greater profit, but only one-third of the land cultivated by his *coloni* (*terra indominicata*). The Gothic settlers (*hospites*) received one-third of the landlord's reserve and two-thirds of his tenants' holdings. In effect Gothic and Roman *consortes* each received one-half of the land divided. Woods and pastures were not partitioned but were shared equally. Torres López argued that small holdings also were divided, but García Gallo considers that such a division would have made it impossible for either Romans or Goths to sustain themselves.

There is no evidence concerning the distribution of land once the Visigoths settled in the peninsula, but it was probably carried out in conformity with the principles outlined above. Menéndez Pidal has pointed out that the terms *sortes gothicae* and *tertiae romanorum*, referring to the share of each race in the land partitioned, are reflected in Castilian place names such as Suertes, Sort, Tertia, Tercias, Tierzo, and Tierz. Of course, there may have been instances in which the Goths simply dispossessed Roman landlords without the formality of a partition. In any case, given the small number of Visigoths and their preference for settlement in Old Castile, the distribution of the soil probably affected only a comparatively few Hispano-Romans.

Little substantial change took place in the exploitation of the soil, though the number of small freeholds probably declined as they were absorbed by the great estates. The latifundia of Roman times were the most characteristic forms of agricultural exploitation and continued to grow through confiscation, usurpation, and other means. The lord's residence (*curtis, atrium*), surrounded by the houses of his tenants, barns, and other buildings, was the center of the estate. While woods and pastures were utilized in common, the arable land was divided into the lord's reserve which he exploited directly, and the holdings of his tenants. The lord's bailiff (*villicus*) supervised the work of the tenants, and from time to time he summoned them to an assembly (*conventus publicus vicinorum*) to consider matters of common interest, such as planting and harvesting, use of pastures, and stray animals. Custom regulated these matters as well as the rents and services due from the tenants. Although this assembly was not an administrative organ of the state, it served as an instrument by which the lord could make known his will, and as a tribunal in which he could resolve conflicts among his tenants. Agricultural products were much the same as in the Roman era, that is, cereals, wines, vegetables, wheat, apples, olives, and such. The raising of sheep and other livestock was also important.

Trade within the peninsula and with other regions of the Mediterranean world did not suffer any abrupt interruption as a result of the barbarian invasions, though one may suspect that the volume of trade was less than what it had been in the last centuries of imperial rule. The *Liber Judiciorum* mentions foreign merchants (*negotiatores transmarini*) who were allowed to settle their disputes before their own judges. No doubt they included Syrians, Jews, and Greeks importing luxury items such as jewelry and exporting domestic products such as Cordoban leather. References in the legal texts to toll collectors (*telonarii*), and money changers and lenders (*argentarii*), and pecuniary compositions are indications of a continuing flow of goods and the circulation of money. Visits to Constantinople by Leander of Seville and John of Biclaro probably reflect the continuation of commercial contacts with Byzantium at least in the sixth century.

The monetary system of the Visigothic kingdom was essentially that of the late empire, that is, the gold *solidus*, the half *solidus*, and the *tremis* or third of a *solidus*. The *tremis*, weighing 1.5 grams was the usual coin in circulation. Both the Suevi and the Visigoths issued money bearing imperial inscriptions, but Leovigild issued coins with his own inscription, but of the same weight as the *tremis*. Vicens suggests that his coinage was an attempt to affirm his independence of the Byzantine empire which controlled a part of southern Spain.

While there is evidence of international trade and the circulation of money in Visigothic Spain, the decline of the cities and their population would seem to indicate a lessening of industrial production. The *collegia* of artisans still existed, but they do not seem to have had much economic importance. Industrial production was probably limited to essential items such as arms and tools. More than likely the imperial mines were still active, producing gold, silver, copper, iron, and lead for the benefit of the royal fisc. Miners were slaves, and work in the mines was often a punishment for crime. The increasing self-sufficiency of the latifundia contributed to the decline of industrial and commercial activity in the towns, but this was a gradual development, not a sudden consequence of the barbarian settlement in the peninsula.

The Organization of the Church

When the barbarians settled in Spain they introduced religious observances directly at variance with the orthodox Christianity of the Hispano-Romans. In the fifth century, Rekhiar, king of the Suevi (448–457), who were pagans, converted to orthodoxy, but his successor, Remismund (457–469), promptly adopted Arianism. Only in the middle of the sixth century, through the work of St. Martin of Dumio, bishop of Braga, were the Suevi finally won over to Catholic Christianity. In the late fourth century the Visigoths had been converted to Arianism by Bishop Wulfila (d. 383), who translated the Bible into their language. The Visigoths traditionally have been considered persecutors of the orthodox in Gaul and Spain, and there is ample evidence of the injuries which they inflicted on the bishops, their churches, and their goods. Abadal, Orlandis, Torres López, and others argue, however, that the reasons for the hostility of the Visigothic kings toward the orthodox clergy were chiefly political. Certainly there was no continuous religious persecution of the orthodox in either Visigothic Gaul or Spain. After Leovigild's failure to persuade the orthodox to enter the Arian camp, his son Recared in 587 adopted the religion of the majority. The union of Visigoths, Suevi, and Hispano-Romans in the profession of the orthodox faith prefaced the opening of a golden age in the history of the church in Spain.

The organization of the church, firmly established during the centuries of Roman rule, did not undergo any substantial transformation in the Visigothic era. The six civil provinces were also ecclesiastical provinces, namely, Tarraconensis (Tarragona, the metropolitan see), Cartaginensis (Toledo), Baetica (Seville), Lusitania (Mérida), Gallaetia (Braga), Narbonensis I, also called Septimania or Gallia Gothica (Narbonne). The metropolitan bishop exercised very real rights over his suffragans, by consenting to their elections, consecrating and installing them, hearing appeals from their decisions, summoning them to answer for their conduct, and presiding over provincial councils. Since Cartagena, the civil capital of the province of the same name, was in Byzantine hands from 554 to 622, Toledo was acknowledged as the metropolitan see in that province. The bishop of Toledo also presided over the Eighth Council (653) and all subsequent national councils, and the Twelfth Council (681) recognized his right to consecrate bishops for any see in Spain.

There were seventy-eight bishoprics in the Visigothic kingdom: 22 in the province of Cartaginensis, 10 in Baetica, 13 in Lusitania, 9 in Gallaetia, 15 in Tarraconensis, and 8 in Narbonensis, but none in the Basque country, whose people were still largely pagan. Generally, the diocese had the same limits as the Roman *civitas*. The bishop maintained his residence and his cathedral in the town, but his jurisdiction extended over the adjacent rural area.

The bishops originally were elected by the clergy and people of the diocese, but after Recared's conversion the king usually appointed them, and the Twelfth Council (681) expressly recognized his right to do so. In this connection one should note that Wamba's supposed reconstitution of dioceses in the peninsula rests upon forged documents dating from the twelfth century. The intellectual and moral level of the bishops, many of whom had been trained in monasteries, was generally high, though there were examples among them of simony, nepotism, and incontinence. Witiza is said to have compelled the bishops and the clergy to take wives, but this may be nothing more than a partisan attempt to blacken his memory. Each bishop had the obligation to visit all the churches of his diocese at least once each year. Of the income derived from tithes, the offerings of the faithful, and from landed estates cultivated by *coloni* and slaves, one-third was assigned to the upkeep of churches, one-third for the bishop's necessities, and one-third for the sustenance of the clergy. Conciliar decrees indicate that the third intended for the repair of churches was often diverted to other uses by the bishops, and many churches were falling into ruins. Priests were required to be freemen, pledged to continence in conformity with the canons of the Council of Elvira (c. 300–314), and were ordained for lifelong service in specific churches. The frequent repetition of the canons concerning priestly celibacy suggests that it was a constant problem. The Fourth Council provided that the education of young clerics should be entrusted to a master of doctrine.

The bishop's authority in his diocese was limited to a considerable extent by the existence of numerous private churches controlled by secular lords. García Villada believes that the origins of private churches can be traced to the late empire when prominent persons erected chapels and oratories in their homes or on their estates. According to Germanic custom the landlord considered these churches as his private property and insisted upon his right to appoint the priests to serve them and to dispose of whatever revenues accrued to them. Although the bishop ordained clergy to serve in private churches, he had little real jurisdiction over the churches themselves.

In accordance with the principles of the *privilegium fori* the Visigothic bishops exercised judicial powers over the clergy and over certain cases reputed to be primarily spiritual in substance, that is, involving the faith, ecclesiastical discipline, superstition, idolatry, infanticide, and so on. The bishops also had jurisdiction over the Jews. Penalties imposed by church courts included excommunication, public penance, seclusion in a monastery, fines, degradation, and exile. They could not inflict mutilation or capital punishment, but clerics could be degraded and then surrendered to the civil authorities for the imposition of a civil penalty. Decisions rendered in an episcopal court could be appealed to the metropolitan, to a provincial council, or a national council. Although appeals to Rome were probably few, two bishops who had been deposed did carry their plea to the pope. Finally, one should note that the bishops were also supposed to supervise the activities of local officers of the civil administration.

As already noted, the councils of Toledo played an especially prominent role in the history of the Visigothic church and state. Thompson suggests that national councils were banned until Recared's conversion. Thereafter, the king usually summoned the councils to treat of spiritual and temporal matters of national interest, and together with his magnates subscribed to the conciliar decrees, giving them the force of civil law. Although they considered such secular business as the regulation of royal elections, the councils always remained ecclesiastical assemblies and never became a national legislature or judicial tribunal. The weakness of the monarchy enabled the church, through the councils of Toledo, to exercise a profound moral influence over the state and its representatives.

The close relationship between church and state, reflected in the activity of the councils, has led some authors to conclude that the Visigothic bishops paid scant heed to papal authority. Cordial relations with Rome are attested, however, by the warm friendship between St. Leander of Seville and Pope Gregory the Great and by Recared's announcement of his conversion to the pope, whom he addressed as "a most reverend man, who is more powerful than the other bishops." The Councils of Braga (561), Seville (619), and the Fourth of Toledo (633) recognized papal primacy, as did St. Isidore in his *De officiis ecclesiasticis;* so too did the two deposed bishops who appealed to the

Roman see, "the head of all the churches." Much has been made of the fact that only eight papal letters sent to Spain in the seventh century have survived; at most this proves only that communication between Rome and Spain was difficult and that papal intervention in the affairs of local churches was less frequent than in later centuries. It is quite likely that many papal letters to Spain were lost.

In the course of the seventh century two incidents occurred which reflected what Ziegler called the self-contained and self-sufficient character of the church in Visigothic Spain. When Pope Honorius I exhorted the Spanish bishops not to be lacking in diligence against the Jews, the Sixth Council of Toledo (638) instructed St. Braulio of Zaragoza to reply. In very direct language Braulio informed the pope that he need not be distressed about the efforts of the Spanish bishops in this matter. Some years later Pope Leo II asked the Spanish prelates to express their adherence to the decrees of the Third Council of Constantinople (680–681) condemning Monothelitism. Their response, written by St. Julian of Toledo, as his *Apologeticum fidei*, elicited a request for clarification from Pope Benedict II. The bishops of the Fifteenth Council of Toledo (688), prompted perhaps by the feeling that their orthodoxy had been questioned unjustly, defended themselves in language that can only be described as blunt and bordering on the disrespectful.

Monasticism flourished in the Visigothic kingdom. St. Aemilianus (d. 573), later known as San Millán de la Cogolla, St. Toribio of Liébana, John of Biclaro, St. Martin of Dumio, St. Fructuosus, and others founded monasteries for both men and women throughout the peninsula. In addition to Martin of Dumio's translation of the *Sententiae Patrum Aegyptorum* and the lost rule of John of Biclaro, four monastic rules have come down to us. These are St. Leander's rule for the instruction of his sister and her companions, the rule of St. Isidore, and the two rules of St. Fructuosus.

Isidore and Fructuosus are the two chief legislators of Visigothic monasticism. The former was very much influenced by St. Benedict, and some have thought that he did little more than rewrite the Benedictine rule, but Pérez de Urbel believes that his principal master was St. Pachomius. In his *Regula monachorum*, Isidore discussed the essential aspects of monastic life with precision and clarity, particularly the physical structure of the monastery, the role of the abbot, vows, prayer and work, punishments, the care of the sick and the dead. Like St.

Benedict, his great virtue was his ability to fuse and to systematize the various elements at his disposal; he too lays emphasis upon moderation, so that even the ordinary man can lead the monastic life.

About thirty years later, St. Fructuosus (d. 665–667), a noble Goth, traversed much of the peninsula exhorting men to embrace the monastic life. Abbot of Dumio and bishop of Braga, he was, in Cocheril's opinion, "the most original and the most important Hispanic monastic legislator." His *Regula monachorum* and *Regula communis* are monuments of severity. Monks who were unable to observe the rule were subjected to harsh punishments such as fasts, imprisonment, lashes, and degradation. By means of an agreement or *pactum*, the monks promised a total obedience to the abbot in much the same way as the Goths pledged absolute fidelity to their lord or king. The following excerpt from the *pactum* found in the *Regula communis* illustrates the submission of the monks to their abbot:

We deliver our souls to God and to you, our lord and father, so that with Christ leading us and you teaching us, we may live in a monastery according to the edict of the apostles and the rule . . . and whatever you wish to proclaim, teach, do, declare, command, excommunicate or correct according to the rule, for the health of our souls, we, putting aside all arrogance, with humble hearts, intent mind and ardent desire, will fulfill entirely.   [*PL*, 87, 1127]

Among the distinctive characteristics of the Visigothic church was its liturgy, known traditionally as the Mozarabic rite. Although it has been attributed to St. Isidore, it was probably Roman in origin, introduced by the earliest missionaries in the peninsula. Oriental elements were perhaps due to the visits to Constantinople made by several Visigothic prelates, such as St. Martin of Dumio, John of Biclaro, and St. Leander. The Fourth Council of Toledo (633) insisted upon uniformity of rite, and St. Isidore, using older texts, probably redacted a complete breviary and missal for use in all churches. The Mozarabic breviary, missal, antiphonary, lectionary (*Liber Comicus*), ordinal, and sacramentary have all been preserved and published. In the eleventh century, under Cluniac influence and the pressure of Gregory VII seeking uniformity throughout the west, the Mozarabic liturgy was discarded in favor of the Roman.

The church of Visigothic Spain, by means of the *Collectio Hispana*, a collection of canons attributed to St. Isidore, deeply influenced the development of canon law in the west. The collection includes conciliar decrees, papal letters, and other materials organized systematically, and until the great revival of interest in canon-law studies in the eleventh and twelfth centuries, it ranked as the only well-organized, reasonably comprehensive, and most useful code of canon law in western Europe.

In sum, at a time when decay and corruption afflicted the church in many other areas of Europe, all the evidence seems to indicate that the church in Visigothic Spain was efficiently organized and served by highly trained and even scholarly bishops of good moral character who could take a justifiable pride in the orthodoxy of their doctrine, the spiritual condition of their people, and their moral influence over the civil authorities.

Literature and Learning

After achieving legal recognition early in the fourth century, the Christian church began to exercise an intensive influence over the civilization of the Roman world. In the field of scholarship, the most learned men of the day, educated in the classical tradition, were attracted to the study of Christian theology. Toward the end of the fourth century and the beginning of the fifth century the church Fathers, such as Augustine and Jerome, were at work incorporating the substance of ancient wisdom into Christian thought. While secular schools declined, monastic and episcopal schools, founded primarily to educate the clergy, continued the traditional curriculum based upon the seven liberal arts and also offered more advanced study of the scriptures and theology. Thus, at a time when the barbarians were overrunning western Europe, the clergy were beginning to dominate the world of literature and learning.

With the breakdown of imperial power, the church, as the custodian of the cultural heritage of Rome, had a major role to play in civilizing the barbarians. Despite their long contact with the empire, the Visigoths upon their settlement in the peninsula were still barbarians and had much to learn from the Hispano-Romans. The cultural superiority of the latter is proved by the continued use of Latin as the official language and as the proper vehicle of literary expression and by the disappearance, save for a few words (for example, *gardingus*, *thiufa*) of the Visigothic tongue.

During most of the fifth century the confusion attending the settlement of the Suevi, Alans, Vandals, and Visigoths was not conducive to the tranquil pursuit of wisdom. Idatius, bishop of Aquae Flaviae (Chaves) in Portugal (d. 470), lived through the terrors inflicted upon his native region by the Suevi and could not foresee the possibility of a more peaceful future. In his *Chronicle*, continuing that of St. Jerome (whom he visited in Bethlehem) from 379 to 468, he sadly recorded the disorder of the times; his method of dating events according to the era of Caesar, based on the date 38 B.C. when Augustus imposed a tribute on the empire, remained in general use in medieval Spain for centuries. Documents dated by the era are thirty-eight years in advance of the Christian era. The chronicle was continued to 567 by Victor, bishop of Tunis.

By the beginning of the sixth century the worst destruction was over and a greater calm pervaded the peninsula. The conversion of the Suevi and the Visigoths to orthodoxy made them more receptive to the civilizing influence of the church, and the steady assimilation of barbarians and Hispano-Romans contributed to the cultural revival of the seventh century. The very fine *Chronicle* of John of Biclaro, bishop of Gerona (d. 621), records the events of the critical years from 567 to 589, according to the reigns of the eastern emperors and the corresponding Visigothic kings. A former student in Constantinople (559–576), he had served as abbot of Biclaro (perhaps Bejar in Portugal) before becoming bishop. Although he suffered at the hands of the Arians, his Gothic origin probably explains his decided enthusiasm for the Visigothic monarchy. The *Chronicle* is the principal source for Leovigild's reign and concludes with the announcement of Recared's conversion at the Third Council of Toledo.

Among those who contributed substantially to the making of the new society was St. Martin of Dumio (d. 580). Born in Pannonia, he had visited the Holy Land, Rome, and Gaul before settling in Galicia, where he founded the monastery of Dumio and became bishop of Braga. As a monk and an abbot he provided guidance for his proteges by translating from the Greek the *Sententiae Patrum Aegyptorum,* a collection of sayings of the fathers of the monastic life. As bishop he compiled a small collection of canons, the *Capitula Martini,* but he devoted the greater part of his life to the instruction of the Suevi in the tenets of orthodox Christianity. In order to combat the persistent belief in idols and superstitions and to recall to the Christian faith those who had relapsed into paganism, he wrote the *De correctione rusticorum,* a catechetical work, which also contains interesting details concerning the customs of the Suevi. His *Formula vitae honestae,* dedicated to King Miro (570–584), is a treatise on the virtues: prudence, justice, continence, fortitude, and so on, and shows the clear influence of Seneca.

St. Leander, bishop of Seville (578–599), a contemporary of St. Martin, was one of the most influential figures of the century. He was born at Cartagena of Roman parents and after living as a monk was elected metropolitan of Seville. After instructing Hermenegild in the orthodox faith, he traveled to Constantinople probably to secure aid for the rebels; there he met the papal envoy, the future Pope Gregory the Great, who became his fast friend; later, Gregory dedicated his *Moralia* to him. Returning to Spain, Leander could not occupy his see because of the hostility of King Leovigild, but the times changed rapidly. Leander instructed Recared in the orthodox religion and presided at the Third Council of Toledo in 589 when the king announced his conversion. Leander's congratulatory discourse on that occasion has survived and has been described as an eloquent sermon worthy of the great Christian orator, St. John Chrysostom. These concluding lines are a specimen of his ability: "Now that we are all made one kingdom, it remains for us, with one heart, to ask God in our prayers for the stability of the earthly kingdom and for the felicity of the heavenly one, so that the kingdom and people who glorify Christ on earth, may be glorified by him not only on earth but also in heaven. Amen." Of Leander's other writings, mainly against the Arians, only his monastic rule, *Liber de institutione virginum et contemptu mundi*, an essay in praise of virginity, written for the benefit of his sister, Florentina, has come down to us. By organizing a school at Seville for the training of the clergy and by building up a library of the best pagan and Christian authors, Leander prepared the way for the fruitful labors of his brother, St. Isidore, who paid this tribute to him. Leander, he said, was "a man of eloquent speech, outstanding genius, illustrious life and learning, by whose faith and industry the people of the Gothic race were won away from the Arian madness to the orthodox faith" (*De viris illustribus*, 41).

Reared and educated by his brother, St. Isidore (599–636) succeeded Leander as bishop of Seville. In that capacity he served as adviser to kings and as the spiritual and intellectual guide of the Spanish hierarchy. Though not a creative genius, he was a man of great learning and broad intellectual interests with a great enthusiasm for the wisdom of the past. A prolific writer, his works include the *Regula monachorum* described above, the *Liber Sententiarum*, a clear and systematic summary of theology, and the *Liber de officiis ecclesiasticis,* a manual of instruction for the clergy. He also wrote two historical works, a *Chronicle* recording events from creation to the fourth year of Sisebut's reign, that is, to 616, and the *Historia de regibus Gothorum, Wandalorum et Suevorum,* extending to 624. Neither work has the color and vivid detail one finds in Gregory of Tours or Bede. Isidore's *Historia* begins with the famous *De laude Spaniae:*

Omnium terrarum quaequae sunt ab occiduo usque ad Indos, pulcherrima es, o sacra semperque felix principum gentiumque mater Spania.

Of all the lands there are from India to the West, thou, o Spain, sacred and always happy, mother of princes and of peoples, are most beautiful.

Isidore traced the origin of the Goths, using the chronicles already mentioned and following the chronological scheme of Idatius; the sections devoted to the Vandals and Suevi are quite short. Though an Hispano-Roman, Isidore had a frank admiration for the Visigoths and continually expressed a patriotic enthusiasm for *Hispania* and its barbarian rulers. His work was the first truly national, rather than universal, history to appear in the peninsula. His *Liber de viris illustribus* discusses the lives and writings of forty-six bishops, popes, and authors of the fifth and sixth centuries, most of whose works have been lost.

St. Isidore exercised his lasting influence on the Middle Ages through his *Etymologiae,* the first of the medieval encyclopedias. In twenty books he set out to summarize for the benefit of future generations the learning of the ancient world. The breadth of the work is indicated by the table of contents; after treating the seven liberal arts, medicine, and jurisprudence, he turned to God, the angels, man, the state; the remaining books discuss such a variety of subjects as human anatomy, animals, cosmology, geography, minerals, metals, coins, weights, measures, agriculture, war, architecture, clothing, food, drink, and tools. As an example of St. Isidore's method, the following may be cited:

Regnum a regibus dictum, nam sicut reges a regendo vocati, ita regnum a regibus. . . . Non autem regit, qui non corrigit. Recte igitur faciendo regis nomen tenetur, peccando amittitur. Unde et apud veteres tale erat proverbium: Rex eris si recte facias, si non facias non eris.

The kingdom is so called from kings, just as kings are so called from ruling. . . . Now he does not rule who does not correct. Thus a ruler acting rightly keeps the name of king, but by doing wrong he loses it. Hence among the ancients there was this proverb: You will be king if you do rightly; if you do not, you will not be. [*Etymologiae*, IX, 3]

Although he has often been ridiculed for giving fanciful or capricious etymologies for words, Isidore's achievement in synthesizing human knowledge both religious and secular, Christian and pagan, is nonetheless remarkable. He provided the European Middle Ages with an indispensable instrument which made it possible for untold thousands over many centuries to acquire the rudiments of learning.

Noting that none of his contemporaries wrote a biography of St. Isidore, Pérez de Urbel says they "were content to admire him, to read him and to plagiarize him." His friend St. Braulio called him "the glory of Spain, the pillar of the church," and the Eighth Council of Toledo (653) proclaimed him "the *doctor egregius* . . . the newest ornament of the Catholic Church." Later generations also honored his memory. Fernando I of León in 1063 asked his vassal, the Muslim king of Seville, to surrender the saint's body so that it could be given a new resting place in a recently erected church in León, dedicated henceforth to his memory. Two centuries later Alfonso X recognized the continuing value of Isidore's work by ordering the translation of the *Etymologiae* into Castilian, and Dante placed him in Paradise in the company of all the great theologians.

Throughout the later seventh century, several scholars continued the Isidorian tradition. St. Braulio, bishop of Zaragoza (631–651), a dear friend of St. Isidore, assumed the task of arranging the *Etymologiae* in their present form, though he had to ask insistently for a copy, saying "Render what you owe, for you are the servant of Christ and of Christians." In addition to a life of St. Aemilianus, founder of the abbey of Cogolla, and an account of the acts of the martyrs of Zaragoza, Braulio wrote many letters, chiefly on spiritual themes. Forty of them, including several to St. Isidore and the already-mentioned response to Pope Honorius concerning the repression of the Jews, have survived. Braulio's pupil, Taio, who succeeded him as bishop of Zaragoza (651–683), wrote a poorly organized *Liber Sententiarum* drawing heavily upon the writings of Pope Gregory the Great.

Several learned men graced the see of Toledo during the century. Among them were Eugene II, the Astronomer, Eugene III, the poet, St. Ildefonse, and St. Julian. Ildefonse (659–667), a Goth, served his apprenticeship as a monk and abbot before his election as bishop. Most of his works have been lost, but those extant include the treatise *De perpetua virginitate Sanctae Mariae*, a polemic against three Jews who had questioned Mary's virginity; the *De cognitione baptismi*, and the *Liber de viris illustribus*, a continuation of Isidore's book of the same name, including a notice of Isidore himself. St. Julian (680–690) was the last great writer of the Visigothic age. He is perhaps best known for his *Historia rebellionis Pauli*. His vigorous denunciation of the treacherous Duke Paul, coupled with a smoothly flowing narrative full of life, ranks his history as the best of its kind in the Visigothic period. An author whose knowledge of both pagan and Christian writers was profound and extensive, his other works include a biography of St. Ildefonse; the *De comprobatione sextae aetatis*, in which he demonstrated to the Jews (he was of Jewish origin) that the Messiah had come and that, in accordance with Augustinian theory, the world was in its sixth age; the eschatological treatise, *Prognosticum futuri saeculi*, setting forth the theology of predestination, original sin, heaven, hell, and purgatory; and the *Apologeticum fidei*, a treatise on the nature of Christ, mentioned above.

Within twenty years of Julian's death the Muslim conquest destroyed the Visigothic kingdom and interrupted the scholarly tradition to which St. Isidore had given such impetus. In the long, bleak centuries ahead, however, the Christian people still drew inspiration from that group of scholars whose work had enlightened the Visigothic age.

PART II

〜❦〜

The Ascendancy of Islam

711—1031

Troops of men will cross the sea to al-Andalus and will conquer it. By their splendor they will easily be recognized on the Day of Resurrection!

Al-Himyari, *Kitab al-Rawd al-Mitar,* 18

The Saracens occupied the Spains and seized the kingdom of the Goths. . . . The Christians are waging war with them day and night . . . until divine predestination commands that they be driven cruelly thence. Amen!

Cronicon Albeldense, 46

CHAPTER 4

〜 つ∽〜

The Emirate of Córdoba

Al-Andalus

The conquest of Spain early in the eighth century marked the culmination of nearly a century of Muslim expansion. The Visigothic kingdom collapsed, and the unity of the peninsula was shattered once more. The Muslims called the territory under their rule al-Andalus, a name possibly conserving the memory of the Vandals, or, as Vallve recently suggested, referring to the Atlantic region. Al-Andalus and *Hispania*, the name given to the peninsula by the Romans and Visigoths, symbolized the enmity between Muslims and Christians in the centuries that followed.

The foundations of a Muslim kingdom ruled by the Umayyad dynasty, independently of the eastern caliphate, were laid during the course of the eighth century, but several tiny Christian states also emerged in the northern reaches of the peninsula and began the centuries-long struggle for reconquest. The fortunes of war varied greatly over the next seven hundred years, but from 711 to 1031 Muslim ascendancy was seldom challenged successfully by the Christians. Christian triumphs were in direct proportion to Muslim strength or weakness, the greatest advances being made when al-Andalus was torn by internal crises. As the Christian hope of restoring the unity of the peninsula came closer to being realized, the name al-Andalus was restricted to a gradually decreasing territory. Today it survives as Andalusia, recording the last stage of Muslim occupation in the most southerly part of Spain.

The hostility manifested in Spain between Islam and Christianity, based upon mutual incomprehension and indeed upon an unwillingness to understand, raised formidable barriers to the assimilation of victors

91

and vanquished, and prolonged the military struggle for centuries. Despite religio-cultural differences, Muslims and Christians interacted upon one another, and the Muslims exercised considerable influence upon Hispanic civilization. Yet the links with the Roman and Visigothic past were not obliterated.

The Campaigns of Tariq and Musa

King Rodrigo's defeat near the Guadalete on 19 July 711 at the hands of Tariq, lieutenant of Musa, the governor of North Africa, sealed the fate of the kingdom of the Visigoths. The king was killed, and his army was dispersed; the defenses of the realm were breached and, as events proved, there were no serious obstacles to further Muslim penetration. Near Ecija the Berber chieftain routed the remnants of the Visigothic army and sent his lieutenants to seize Córdoba and to ravage the districts of Granada and Málaga. With guides provided by Count Julian he advanced along the old Roman road through Jaén to Toledo. At his approach, Sindered, the metropolitan, "not as a shepherd, but as a hireling," fled to Rome; many other citizens also abandoned the city, and it fell easily into Tariq's hands. At no time on this march did he encounter any significant opposition; it is quite possible, as Vicens Vives suggested, that the Hispano-Roman population, disgusted by the disorder perpetuated by their Visigothic rulers, rebelled and helped to bring down the kingdom. Certainly, the Jews and others who had suffered under Visigothic rule welcomed the invaders as liberators and collaborated with them. In return for their betrayal of King Rodrigo the sons of Witiza recovered their ancestral estates, and as the historian Ibn al-Qutiyya, a great-great grandson of Witiza, testifies, members of the family served as counts and judges of the Christians in Toledo, Seville, and Córdoba until the tenth century.

Meanwhile, Musa was outraged by the apparent insubordination of his lieutenant who had been sent to reconnoiter rather than to conduct an extensive campaign. Fearful that Tariq would reap all the glory and the profit of the conquest, Musa landed at Algeciras in June 712 with an army of about 18,000 Arabs. Instead of proceeding directly to Toledo, he elected to occupy the towns which Tariq in his haste to seize the capital had bypassed, namely, Medina Sidonia, Alcalá de Guadaira, Carmona, and Seville. Seville fell after a siege of a few months but revolted after his departure, only to be subdued again. Aided by Count Julian's guides, Musa advanced into Lusitania, meeting stiff resistance at Mérida, where the Visigothic nobility held out through the winter of 712 until forced to surrender on 30 June 713; according to the terms of the capitulation the Muslims seized the goods of the church and of those who had perished or fled.

At last Musa turned toward Toledo. Near Talavera he met Tariq whom he struck on the head with his riding crop, upbraiding him for insubordination and greed, but in spite of this outburst they settled down to pass the next several months in Toledo. After informing the caliph of his achievements, Musa set out in the spring of 714, marching in a northeasterly direction through Sigüenza and Calatayud to Zaragoza on the Ebro river. From there Tariq moved westward into Aragon and thence to León and Astorga, while Musa followed the course of the Duero river and then the Miño to Lugo in Galicia.

At Zaragoza, Musa had received a command from the caliph to return to Damascus, and upon arrival at Lugo he received another summons that he dared not disobey. The caliph apparently had heard complaints of Musa's avarice and abuse of power as governor of North Africa and probably wished to determine the real value of the conquest of Spain. Setting out in the summer of 714 on the journey across North Africa, with an immense booty and accompanied by 400 sons of Spanish lords, wearing golden crowns and belts (as Ibn al-Qutiyya testifies), Musa and Tariq arrived at Damascus in February 715, only to find that the caliph was dead and had been succeeded by his brother. Despite his great triumph, Musa was stripped of his honors and prosecuted on charges of embezzlement and died in ignominy. Tariq, whom the Muslim chroniclers exalted as the hero of this tale, apparently also died in obscurity.

In his absence Musa had appointed his son Abd al-Aziz to govern Spain. His forces seized Pamplona, Tarragona, Barcelona, and Gerona in the northeast and even crossed the Pyrenees into Septimania. He personally completed the subjugation of the western region of Spain, including Huelva, Beja, Evora, Santarém, Lisbon, and Coimbra; in the southeast Málaga and Granada (Elvira) were occupied. In April 713 he concluded an agreement with the Visigothic lord, Theodomir of Murcia, allowing him to retain a measure of autonomy within a specified district (which the Muslims thereafter called Tudmir), subject to the payment of tribute. The text of this, "the first diplomatic instrument in the annals of Muslim Spain," as Lévi-Provençal called it, follows:

In the name of Allah, the clement, the merciful! Letter addressed by Abd al-Aziz ibn Musa ibn Nusayr to Tudmir ibn Abdush. The latter receives peace and the promise, under the guarantee of Allah and of his Prophet, that there will not be any change in his situation nor in that of his people; that his right of sovereignty will not be contested; that his subjects will not be injured nor reduced to captivity, nor separated from their children nor their wives; that they will not be disturbed in the practice of their religion; that their churches will not be burned, nor despoiled of the objects of the cult found in them; all this, so long as he satisfies the charges that we impose upon him. Peace is granted to him on condition of the surrender of the following seven towns: Orihuela, Baltana, Alicante, Mula, Villena, Lorca and Ello. In addition, he will not give shelter to any person who may flee from us or who may be our enemy; nor will he do injury to anyone who may be protected by our friendship; nor will he keep secret information relative to the enemy which may come to his attention. He and his subjects will have to pay each year a personal tribute of one *dinar* in specie, four bushels of wheat and four of barley, four measures of malt, four of vinegar, two of honey and two of oil. These imposts will be reduced by one-half for slaves. Written in *rajab* of the year 94 of the hegira (April 713). [Al-Himyari, *Kitab al-Rawd al-Mitar*, 132–133]

The pact acknowledged the existence of a semi-independent Christian state along the southeastern coast centered at Orihuela in the modern province of Murcia. The *Chronicle of 754* described Theodomir as "a lover of letters, marvelous in eloquence, expert in battle" and noted that during the reigns of the Gothic kings Egica and Witiza he had defended the coast against Greek attacks. He was succeeded by Athanagild, probably his son, whom the chronicler calls an extremely wealthy lord.

Abd al-Aziz was murdered in 716 in the mosque of Seville (formerly the church of Santa Rufina) on the orders of the caliph of Damascus, who evidently distrusted all the members of Musa's family. By marrying Egilona, the widow of King Rodrigo, Abd al-Aziz roused the suspicion that he intended to embrace Christianity and to proclaim his independence; Muslim historians report that the former queen encouraged him to wear a crown and to demand the respect shown only to a king. His death closed the period of the invasion. In only a few years the Muslims had subjugated the greater part of the peninsula, and they now had to face the task of governing it.

The Organization of the Conquest and the Civil Wars

According to Muslim sources, the Caliph Umar, after inquiring about the geography of the peninsula and the security of its maritime communications with the rest of the Muslim world, planned to abandon it entirely, but he died before he could carry out his intention. By this chance, Muslim domination in Spain was perpetuated for centuries.

A succession of emirs or governors, usually appointed by the governor of North Africa, presided over the administration of al-Andalus in the caliph's name. Sometimes the caliph himself named the governor, and at times the troops in Spain revolted against a governor and proclaimed another in his place. Few of the emirs sent to Spain were endowed with great talent; most were proud, ambitious, greedy, and fanatical. Few remained in office for long; one served for five years, others for as little as six months. This rapid turnover contributed to the weakness of the administration, and the active participation of the governors in tribal rivalries was not conducive to stable and orderly government. About 716 Córdoba became the seat of government, replacing Seville, where Abd al-Aziz had his headquarters, and overshadowing Toledo, the royal city of the Visigoths, now considered too remote from the coast and from communication with Africa.

In the forty years following the conquest internal strife nearly precipitated the ruin of Muslim rule. Although united by the bond of religion, the conquerors were divided by deeply rooted hostilities. The Arabs who had accompanied Musa to Spain, numbering about 18,000, belonged to the two great ethnic groups, the Qaysites and Kalbites (Yemenites), whose rivalry antedated Muhammad, and did not diminish upon their settlement in Spain. A strong racial antipathy also existed between the Arabs, who formed the military aristocracy, and the Berbers, thought of as crude mountaineers, recently converted, with only a rudimentary knowledge of Islam. Tariq's force of about 12,000 consisted chiefly of Berbers, who were allotted the poorest lands in the northern and central regions of the peninsula. The Arabs, who occupied the more fertile areas in the south, held the Berbers in utter contempt.

The legal status of the vanquished depended on whether they accepted Islam. As people of the book (*ahl al-kitab*), that is, people who had received a divine revelation contained in their sacred writings, Christians and Jews were not compelled to give up their religion. They were protected (*dhimmi*) and paid a personal tribute or poll tax (*jizya*) to the Muslim authorities. Those who capitulated were permitted to retain their lands subject to the payment of a territorial tribute (*kharaj*), as exemplified in the case of Witiza's family and that of Theodomir of Murcia. Those who were subjugated by force could be deprived of their property and reduced to slavery. The lands so confiscated, together with ecclesiastical and state properties, were apportioned among the Muslims, though one-fifth (*khums*) was reserved for the caliph.

Christians subject to Muslim rule eventually adopted Arabic customs and language and came to be known as Mozarabs (*mustarib, mustaribun*), that is, like the Arabs. Important Mozarabic communities existed in Toledo, Córdoba, Seville, Mérida, and other towns. Subject to their own officials and their own law, the *Liber Judiciorum*, they continued to worship in their churches and to elect their bishops. In the chaotic years of the early eighth century the *Chronicle of 754* did not neglect to record the names of distinguished clerics who served the churches of al-Andalus. From time to time the Muslims despoiled the Christians, as for example, when Musa seized the church of Mérida, and when they took possession of one-half of the church of San Vicente in Córdoba for use as a mosque.

Many Christians, perhaps the majority, embraced Islam with the hope of enjoying greater security for themselves and their property. Converts to Islam (*musalim*) and their children who were born into the faith (*muwalladun*) were not subject to tribute, but the Muslims did not encourage conversions lest the number of tributaries be diminished. Slaves usually gained their freedom by conversion. For many years the Arabs held the *muwalladun* in disdain and denied them the opportunity to participate in the higher levels of government. The great rebellions of the ninth century were the fruits of this policy.

The unsettled condition of al-Andalus in the first years of Muslim rule was strikingly illustrated by the Berber revolt that began in Morocco with the seizure of Tangier in 740. Resentful of their inferior status and their mistreatment at the hands of their Arab governors, they accepted the Kharijite doctrine of the equality of all Muslims. As news of the uprising spread, the Berbers who had settled in the mountainous regions of Galicia and Cantabria abandoned their positions and marched southward, attacking the Arabs.

In the meantime the Moroccan Berbers defeated an army of about 30,000 Syrians sent against them by the caliph. Some 7,000 Syrians took refuge in Ceuta, where the Berbers promptly laid them under siege. As their supplies began to fail, the Syrians appealed to the governor of al-Andalus to allow them to cross the straits. Though reluctant to do so for fear that they would strip him of his power, he saw the possibility of using them against the Berber rebels in Spain. The Syrians were admitted to Spain in 741 and quickly disposed of the three major bands of Berbers threatening Toledo, Córdoba, and Medina Sidonia, but they refused to withdraw from the peninsula and deposed and crucified the emir. Order was not fully restored until 742, when a new governor sent by the caliph allotted the Syrians lands on which to settle, subject to the obligation of rendering military service; these military circumscriptions, already known in Syria, were called *junds*. Even after the suppression of the Berber rebellion, tribal hatreds among the Arabs continued unabated and facilitated the seizure of power by the Umayyad family in 756.

Muslim Penetration into Gaul: The Battle of Tours

While the Arabs were engaged in tribal warfare, the emirs of al-Andalus, prompted by a spirit of adventure and a desire to gain the merits of participating in the holy war, led several expeditions into Gaul. At that time the decadent Merovingian dynasty was about to be replaced by the Carolingian house, whose principal representative, Charles Martel, the mayor of the palace, was the uncrowned king of the Franks. In southern Gaul, Odo, duke of Aquitaine, who enjoyed a high degree of autonomy, had to bear the brunt of the first Muslim assaults.

Perhaps as early as 714, Tariq sent a detachment to occupy Barcelona and to cross the Pyrenees into Septimania or Gallia Gothica, once part of the Visigothic kingdom. The definitive occupation of Barcelona occurred in 717 or 718, and Narbonne, the capital of Septimania, fell to the Muslims in 720. From that base they raided as far west as Toulouse but in 721 were defeated by Odo of Aquitaine. Four years later the Muslims, after reaffirming their hold on Septimania, captured Carcassonne, plundered Nîmes, and mounted the Rhone as far north as Autun in Burgundy. On returning to Spain, however, they were attacked by the Basques, and the emir was killed. In the next several years the Muslim position in Septimania remained stable, but the rapid turnover of governors in al-Andalus did not permit extensive campaigns in Gaul.

The Emir Abd al-Rahman al-Ghafiqi, however, gathered a large army at Pamplona in 732 and crossed into Gaul through the pass of Roncesvalles. After defeating Duke Odo and sacking Bordeaux he advanced northward into Poitou and in October 732 encountered Charles Martel in the vicinity of Tours. In the ensuing battle Charles gained a resounding victory, and the emir perished on the field. The battle traditionally has been regarded as one of the decisive contests in history, on the supposition that, had the Muslims won, the whole of Gaul would have been theirs, but it does not appear that they had the capability to extend their rule over Gaul. The significance of the battle lies in the fact that it marked the most northerly advance of the Muslims and that it prompted the Franks to take more strenuous measures to defend their territory and to drive the infidels back into Spain.

Two years after the battle the Muslims again ravaged the Rhone valley, seizing Arles and Avignon, but Charles Martel forced them back to Narbonne and defeated a relieving force sent from Spain. In succeeding years, as the Berber revolt of 740 and tribal warfare in al-Andalus weakened the Muslim hold on Septimania, Pepin the Short, Charles Martel's son, increased the pressures on the enemy and probably in 751 (or 759) seized Narbonne. With that, Muslim rule in Septimania came to an end, and the Franks were in a position to penetrate into northeastern Spain.

The Origins of the Kingdom of Asturias

The emirs of al-Andalus devoted much less attention to the suppression of isolated nuclei of Christian resistance in the mountainous districts of northern Spain. From the time of Musa and Tariq, Muslim garrisons had been placed in the most strategic fortresses in the upper reaches of the peninsula, but in the remote regions of the middle Pyrenees their power was scarcely felt. In the northwest the mountaineers of Cantabria, Asturias, and Galicia laid the foundations of the kingdom of Asturias and initiated the reconquest of seven hundred years. Vicens Vives has noted the paradox that those who had most strenuously resisted absorption by Romans and Goths now became the champions of the Hispanic tradition.

The first leader of the Christian resistance was the almost legendary Pelayo, about whom the earliest testimony is given by the Chronicle of

Albelda, written in the ninth century. Supposedly a grand-nephew of King Rodrigo, he was expelled from Toledo by King Witiza, and came to Asturias where, after the Muslim invasion, he raised the standard of revolt. The later *Chronicle of Alfonso III*, seeking to link the Visigothic and Asturian monarchies and to make Pelayo the legitimate successor of Rodrigo, the last Visigothic king, asserted that he was of royal blood, and that the members of the royal family, most of whom had taken refuge in Asturias, elected him king. It seems more likely that he was simply the leader of an uprising by the Asturian mountaineers and that he had no conscious intent to resurrect the defunct kingdom of the Visigoths.

The sources cited above record that a Muslim expedition was sent to castigate Pelayo and his followers, who fled to the cave of Covadonga on mount Aseuva where Pelayo prepared to make his last stand. Bishop Oppa of Seville, one of the sons of Witiza, who accompanied the Muslim army, urged him to submit, saying:

"I know, brother, that it is no secret to you that not long ago all Spain was under the sole rule of the Goths and the army of all Spain was gathered together but could not resist the impetus of the Ismaelites; how much less able are you to defend yourself on the top of this mountain. But hear my advice and turn your mind from this purpose so you may enjoy many good things . . . in peace with the Arabs. . . ." To this Pelayo replied: "I will not associate with the Arabs in friendship nor will I submit to their rule. . . . For we trust in the Lord's mercy that on this little hill that you see the well-being of Spain and of the army of the Gothic people will be restored." [*Crónica de Alfonso III*, 9]

In the battle that followed, probably on 28 May 722, Pelayo routed his enemies; the enemy commander was killed, and Oppa was captured. "And thus liberty was restored to the Christian people . . . and by divine providence the kingdom of the Asturians was brought forth." Although later writers magnified the victory out of all proportion, the immediate military consequences for Islam were minimal. The *Chronicle of 754* has nothing to say about Pelayo or Covadonga, and this silence probably reflects the impact of the affair in al-Andalus where it must have been regarded as a minor skirmish. The Muslim attitude toward the northern rebels probably was expressed in words such as these reported by Ibn Hayyan: "What are thirty barbarians perched on a rock? They must inevitably die." Among the Asturians, however, Covadonga became the symbol of Christian resistance to Islam and a source of inspiration to those who, in words attributed to Pelayo, would achieve the *salus Spanie*.

Under the leadership of Pelayo's son-in-law, Alfonso I (739–757), the tiny base was broadened, and the kingdom of Asturias became a reality. Perhaps descended from the Visigothic King Leovigild, he came to power after the brief reign of Pelayo's son, Fáfila (737–739). The revolt of the Berbers in 740 and their withdrawal from the northern-most reaches of the peninsula enabled Alfonso I to establish the king-dom on a firm foundation and to extend his rule over Galicia, northern Portugal, Cantabria, Alava, and La Rioja. The Muslims maintained ad-vanced positions at Coimbra, Coria, Talavera, Toledo, Guadalajara, Tudela, and Pamplona. Thus the line of demarcation between Chris-tian and Muslim territories followed the course of the Duero river from Porto to Osma and then ran northward into the Basque country. Lack-ing sufficient forces to occupy the whole region abandoned by the Mus-lims, Alfonso I systematically laid waste the Duero valley, which for many years remained a great desert or no-man's land separating Astu-rias and al-Andalus.

The Foundation of the Umayyad Emirate of Córdoba

In the middle of the eighth century a dynastic revolution in Syria prepared the way for the eventual disintegration of the Muslim empire and the establishment of an independent Muslim state in al-Andalus. The Umayyad dynasty which had ruled the Muslim world since 661 was overthrown in 750 by the Abbasids, who attempted to slaughter all their rivals. One Umayyad, Abd al-Rahman, a grandson of the Caliph Hisham, survived the destruction to restore the fortunes of his family in Spain. Fleeing across North Africa he found a welcome among the Berbers of Morocco and established contact with his family's clients in Spain. The continued turbulence provoked by the rivalry of the Kalbites and the Qaysites offered him an opportunity to intervene in the peninsula. The Kalbites, seeing him as a champion of their cause, pledged their support; with that he landed at Almuñécar on 14 August 755 and began to gather an army.

Yusuf al-Fihri, the governor of al-Andalus, who was virtually inde-pendent, probably thought of making himself king and viewed the newcomer as an enemy. When negotiations failed, Abd al-Rahman ad-vanced to Córdoba; in a battle fought on 15 May 756 outside the city,

Yusuf was defeated and fled, but he later submitted. Abd al-Rahman made a triumphal entry into Córdoba where he was proclaimed emir, transforming al-Andalus into an independent kingdom and the new home of the exiled Umayyad dynasty.

During the next thirty years Abd al-Rahman worked tirelessly to secure the position he had won. He summoned to Spain other members of his family and their clients, showered them with favors, and organized an army of loyal mercenaries to defend his throne. Although he was inclined to be conciliatory toward his enemies and offered an amnesty to them, he was plagued continually by conspiracies and rebellions; after the failure of a revolt by the former governor in 759, he gave no quarter to his opponents. The Berbers, who had supported him initially, proved to be his most persistent antagonists, carrying on guerrilla warfare against him for many years until 776.

Preoccupation with the internal problems of al-Andalus did not allow him to devote much attention to the kingdom of Asturias, even if it seemed important to do so, which it probably did not. Fruela I (757–768), the son of Alfonso I, gained a minor victory over the Muslims at Pontuvium in Galicia, but his three successors, Aurelius (768–774), Silo (774–783), and Mauregatus (783–788), all related to him by blood or marriage, were shadowy figures of whom little or nothing is known, except that they seem to have been at peace with al-Andalus.

The northeastern frontier potentially presented a more serious danger. The governors of advanced posts such as Zaragoza, Barcelona, and Gerona, always tended to maintain a highly independent attitude toward the government at Córdoba. Now they had some justification for doing so, since they could regard Abd al-Rahman I as a rebel against the Abbasid caliph. Agents of the caliph, hoping to stir up rebellion, approached Sulayman ibn Yaqzan, governor of Zaragoza, who promised to collaborate with them. When a Cordoban army was sent against him, he realized the need for more effective support than the distant Abbasids could offer and decided to appeal to Charlemagne, king of the Franks (768–814).

Involved as he was in the affairs of Germany and Italy, Charlemagne probably did not think of expansion south of the Pyrenees as a major priority, but the possibility of quick success at little cost did attract him. Sulayman journeyed to Paderborn in Saxony where he pledged allegiance to Charlemagne and promised to surrender Zaragoza to him. He probably expected to continue as governor of the city and to enjoy a real independence of the emir of Córdoba under Carolingian protection. Charlemagne crossed the Pyrenees into Spain through the pass of Roncesvalles in the spring of 778. As he passed through Pamplona, the people offered their homage as did those of Huesca in Aragon. When he arrived at Zaragoza, however, he found the gates of the city closed against him, as Sulayman's lieutenant refused to admit the Franks. Much to his annoyance, Charlemagne was forced to establish a siege, but while it was in progress he learned that the Saxons had revolted against him once more. As their suppression was of far greater concern to him, he lifted the siege and set out on his return journey, taking Sulayman with him.

Traversing the pass of Roncesvalles on 15 August 778, Charlemagne's rear guard was attacked and wiped out by the Basques. Einhard, the royal biographer, reported that among the fallen were Eggihard, the seneschal, Anselm, count of the palace, and Roland, count of the march of Brittany. Centuries later the massacre became the subject of the first great epic of French literature, the *Chanson de Roland*, but the poem attributes the attack to the Muslims and portrays Charlemagne as the champion of Christendom against Islam. Some Muslims possibly did take part in the attack in order to liberate Sulayman. Upon his return to Zaragoza he was killed by his treacherous lieutenant, who in turn was forced to surrender the city to Abd al-Rahman I. Einhard's statement, therefore, that Charlemagne dominated "the entire chain of the Pyrenees mountains as far as the Ebro River" is not true.

Following his ill-starred expedition into Spain, Charlemagne realized that progress along the southern frontier would have to be more painstaking and gradual. He entrusted the defense of that frontier and the task of expansion into Spain to his son, Louis the Pious, whom he appointed king of Aquitaine. The surrender of Gerona in 785 was the first step in the Frankish advance to Barcelona.

Three years later on 30 September 788, Abd al-Rahman I died. A man of great energy and ability, he created an independent kingdom in al-Andalus and for thirty-two years, in spite of formidable opposition, succeeded in establishing orderly government. He also laid the foundations of the future greatness of Córdoba by beginning construction of the great mosque which still stands today as a marvel of architecture. Half of the church of San Vicente had been taken in 747, for use as a mosque, but as the increase in the Muslim population necessitated larger facilities, Abd al-Rahman purchased the other half and set his architects and builders to work. In spite of his success, he did not dare to take the title "prince of believers" or "commander of the faithful" (*amir al-muminin*) traditionally used by the caliphs, the successors of Muhammad. For almost two hundred years his descendants hesitated to assume the title and by commemorating the Abbasid caliphs in public prayers preserved the fiction that there could only be one legitimate successor to Muhammad.

In the century following the death of Abd al-Rahman I the Umayyad dynasty retained its grasp of sovereign power. As the throne passed from father to son, and several of the emirs enjoyed long reigns, the populace became accustomed to hereditary rule. On the other hand, the ninth century was a period of considerable disorder, and as it drew to a close the kingdom seemed to be on the verge of disintegration.

Hisham I (788–796), who succeeded his father, enjoyed a comparatively tranquil reign and gained renown for his piety and charity. A learned prince, he extended a cordial welcome to the jurists of the Malikite school, who adopted a rigorist interpretation of the Koran and the law, hostile to innovation and rationalist speculation. In the course of time, they came to dominate the juridical and theological thought of the kingdom and wielded great influence in public affairs. The general peace prevailing in al-Andalus enabled the emir to send expeditions every year to ravage the kingdom of Asturias. Overwhelmed by Muslim arms, King Vermudo I (788–791) abdicated in favor of his cousin, Alfonso II, known to history as the Chaste (791–842). His victory over the Muslims at Lutos in 795 restored Christian confidence, and the emir's death in the following year gave the Christians a respite from annual raids.

The long reign of al-Hakam I (796–822) was full of turbulence and discord. Provoked by conspiracies and rebellions, he displayed a terrible ferocity and gained a reputation for tyranny. At his accession his uncles tried to seize the throne, and one of them even visited Charlemagne at Aachen, seeking his help. The frontier towns of Mérida and Zaragoza were also hostile, and in 792 the citizens of Toledo—Mozarabs, Jews, and *muwalladun*—rebelled against the heavy financial burdens imposed upon them. The revolt was crushed, and as a lesson for the future the principal citizens, numbering about 700 or perhaps as many as 5,000, were executed, and their bodies were dumped into a ditch already prepared to receive them. Although these numbers are exaggerated, the massacre certainly terrified the Toledans, as it did the Muslim historians who recorded it.

The most serious challenge to al-Hakam's authority appeared in Córdoba itself. The Malikite jurists who had enjoyed such favor during his father's reign found their influence severely restricted and began to murmur against the emir, accusing him of evil ways, irreligion, drunkenness, and tyranny. A conspiracy was set afoot in 805 to depose him, but he discovered it in time and crucified seventy-two leaders. The citizens of Córdoba were stricken with terror, but their hostility continued unabated. For his security al-Hakam recruited a large bodyguard of Negroes, Franks, and Galicians who were placed under the command of the Christian Count Rabi who was also responsible for collecting the heavy taxes needed for the maintenance of this force. The citizenry, especially the *muwalladun*, crushed by the burden of taxes and bullied by the royal bodyguard, rose in revolt in the southern sector of the city in 818. Al-Hakam put down the uprising with great barbarity; three hundred notables were crucified, and the inhabitants were expelled from the district, which was then razed to the ground. Most of the refugees fled to Morocco, but one enterprising group traveled to Alexandria in Egypt, where they dominated the city until their expulsion in 827. They sailed then to Crete where they founded a kingdom that lasted until the Byzantine reconquest in 961.

The Development of the Christian States

While al-Hakam I was occupied with domestic strife, Alfonso II made a conscious effort to restore in Asturias the civil and ecclesiastical order of the Visigothic monarchy. In the words of the *Cronicon Albeldense* (58): "In Oviedo he established all things and the entire order of the Goths, both in the church and the palace, as it had been in Toledo." Although there was no legal connection between the Visigothic and Asturian kingdoms, the Visigothic tradition was not forgotten and perhaps received new life from the Mozarabs who took refuge in Asturias. Alfonso II used the characteristic titles of the Visigothic kings and surrounded himself with palatine officials whose offices were reminiscent of the Visigothic court. Oviedo, the royal city, became the seat of a bishopric and was embellished by the erection of palaces, churches, baths, and other public buildings. Alfonso II may also have initiated the historiographical tradition linking the Visigothic and Asturian monarchies.

An event with extraordinary consequences for the future was the discovery, sometime during the reign, of a tomb purported to be that of the Apostle St. James the Great, said to have evangelized Spain centuries before. The details of the discovery are recorded only in a late eleventh-century document, but the existence of the tomb was admitted at least from the end of the ninth century. The story has it that a hermit heard angels singing and saw bright lights illuminating the place where the Apostle was buried. He informed Bishop Theodomir of Iria Flavia in Galicia who discovered the tomb and notified the king. A church was erected on the site, which came to be known as *Campus stellarum*, the field of stars, or Santiago de Compostela. The shrine of the Apostle became one of the great European centers of pilgrimage and eventually contributed to the broadening of cultural and commercial relations between Spain and northern Europe. Belief in the existence of the Apostle's tomb undoubtedly gave a great psychological uplift to the people of Asturias and strengthened their will to resist the infidels. Indeed, Américo Castro argues that the cult of St. James had its origins in a conscious attempt to create an anti-Muhammad, a Christian patron and protector who could counter and overcome the power of the prophet and his followers. St. James became the patron of Spain, the hope and the mainstay of the Christian people in times of stress and threatening ruin.

The eleventh-century Muslim historian, Ibn Hayyan, offers this appreciation of the legend of St. James:

Santiago is . . . one of the sanctuaries most frequented, not only by the Christians of Andalus, but by the inhabitants of the neighboring continent, who regard its church with veneration equal to that which the Muslims entertain for the Kaba at Mecca . . . pretending that the tomb . . . is that of Yakob (James), one of the twelve apostles. . . . They say that he was bishop of Jerusalem and that he wandered about the earth preaching . . . until he came to that remote corner of Andalus; that he then returned to Syria where he died. . . . They pretend likewise that after the death of Yakob his disciples carried his body and buried it in that church. [Al-Maqqari, *History of the Mohammedan Dynasties in Spain*, tr. Pascual de Gayangos, II, 193]

Because of dissension in al-Andalus, for most of his reign Alfonso II was spared the ravages of Muslim attacks. Occasionally he took the offensive with some success and in 798 occupied Lisbon, though the Muslims later recovered possession. In the course of these wars Frankish sources relate that he sent envoys bearing trophies of war and Muslim captives to Charlemagne and his son, Louis the Pious. Einhard, for example, relates that Charlemagne "so closely bound Alfonso, king of Galicia and Asturias, to himself that whenever the latter sent letters or messengers to him, he ordered that he be styled simply as his own man," a phrase implying that he was Charlemagne's vassal, but this seems to be an exaggeration of their relationship.

Although Alfonso II probably received little direct assistance from Charlemagne, Carolingian influence and authority south of the Pyrenees increased perceptibly. After the occupation of Gerona in 785 the Franks concentrated on extending their rule into the mountainous regions of the Segre river, that is, to Vich, Caserras, and Cardona. The Muslims made their last incursion into Gaul in 793. After sacking Gerona, and ravaging the suburbs of Narbonne, they defeated Duke William of Toulouse on the banks of the Orbieu near Carcassonne; although they gathered much booty, the frontier remained unchanged. Not long after, the Muslim governors of Barcelona, Zaragoza, and Huesca, whose allegiance to the regime at Córdoba was always tenuous, sought alliance with the Franks. Charlemagne in 797 sent an embassy to Harun al-Rashid, the Abbasid caliph of Baghdad, perhaps with the hope of gaining his alliance against the Umayyads. Be that as it may, Louis the Pious, king of Aquitaine, encouraged no doubt by overtures from Spain, laid siege to Barcelona and captured it in 801, but efforts to extend the frontier as far south as Tortosa at the mouth of the Ebro river were unavailing. Tortosa remained in Muslim hands for the next three hundred years. Louis the Pious's accession to the imperial throne in 814 and the ensuing dissension within his own family halted the Frankish drive into Spain and eventually encouraged the independence of the conquered territory.

In the next fifty years the Franks organized their conquests along the Pyrenees. The *limes hispanicus* or Spanish March, a prefiguration of Catalonia, eventually included the counties of Sobrarbe, Ribagorza, Pallars, Cerdagne, Urgel, Besalú, Ampurias, Vich, and Barcelona. Settlers came chiefly from Septimania to repopulate the counties, occupying the land in accordance with the principle of squatters' rights (*aprisio*). Many of them were descendants of the Visigoths and Hispano-Romans who had fled from Spain at the time of the Muslim invasion. Imperial capitularies of 812, 815–816 regulated the process of colonization and the administration of justice. As a result of Frankish rule the social and political structure of the counties was based on feudal customs; in this respect Catalonia was uniquely different from the other Christian states in Spain. Frankish influence on the liturgy, the law, the art and architecture of the counties was also strong. Even though the counties secured *de facto* independence as a result of the disintegration of the Carolingian empire later in the ninth century, they always retained significant social and cultural ties to the region north of the Pyrenees.

To the west of Catalonia, in the region around Jaca, the future county of Aragon was beginning to take form under the rule of Aznar Galindo. Farther west in the mountains around Pamplona, the Basques, some of whom apparently were still pagans, jealously guarded their independence, despite the efforts of Asturians, Franks, and Muslims to subdue them. After successively throwing off the yoke of the Umayyads and the Carolingians, they regained their independence under their chieftain, Iñigo Arista, whose descendants ruled until the beginning of the tenth century. Until then, evidence concerning these tiny Pyrenean states is quite scanty.

The Mozarabic Martyrs of Córdoba

Al-Hakam I, who had checked rebellion and disorder in al-Andalus by a policy of calculated ferocity, died in 822, leaving the kingdom to his son Abd al-Rahman II (822–852). Learned and pious, he quickly gained renown as a patron of scholars, poets, and musicians, and his court became the cultural center of western Islam. He also proved to be an able ruler and organized the central and local administration; with only a few changes, his work survived until the end of the caliphate. During the greater part of his reign al-Andalus enjoyed relative internal peace, enabling him to send expeditions nearly every year to harry Asturias, Barcelona, and the Spanish March.

Both Asturias and al-Andalus experienced the first raids by the Norsemen who launched their attacks upon the British Isles and the Carolingian empire at the close of the eighth century. A Norse fleet, after sacking Bordeaux, attempted a landing at Gijón in Asturias in 844, but Ramiro I (842–850) repelled them; undaunted, they continued westward to La Coruña and, after plundering the neighborhood, sailed southward to Lisbon, which they also sacked. Their next objective was Cádiz, but when they sailed up the Guadalquivir and assaulted Seville, the emir sent an army to drive them away. A number of them were captured and accepted Islam in order to save their lives; others

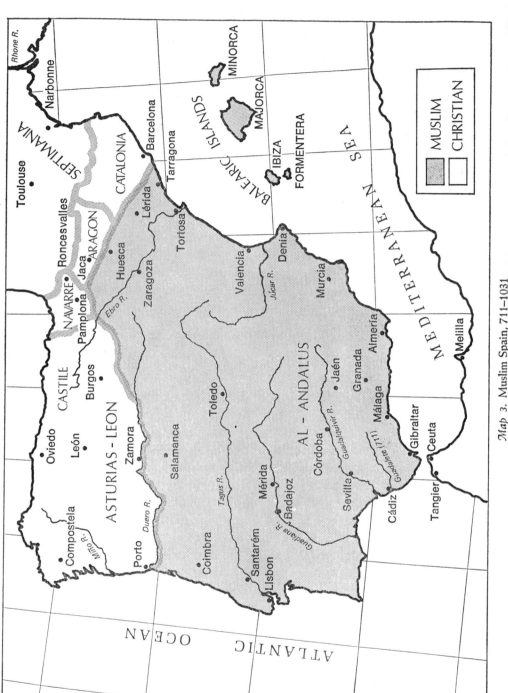

Map 3. Muslim Spain, 711–1031

made their escape to the north and again sacked Lisbon. As events were to show, neither western Europe nor Spain had seen the last of the Norsemen. In order to deal with any future attacks, the emir ordered the construction of shipyards and a fleet to guard the river approaches to Seville.

A few years later, in 848–849, the fleet was used to reestablish Umayyad rule over the Balearic Islands, whose population was largely Christian. Failing to receive any assistance from the Franks, the islanders submitted to the emir and agreed to pay the usual tribute in return for protection. Abd al-Rahman II's ambitions, however, did not extend beyond the western Mediterranean. The Byzantine Emperor Theophilus sought his alliance in 839 against the Abbasids of Baghdad, and also suggested that he should attempt to curb the activities of the Cordoban exiles who had overrun Crete. The emir, courteously but firmly, disclaimed any responsibility for the exiles and refused to enter an alliance, preferring, he said, to place his trust in Allah, who, he hoped, would eventually restore the Umayyads to their rightful position as rulers of the Muslim world.

Toward the close of his reign the hitherto docile Mozarabs of Córdoba, in an unprecedented manifestation of patriotic and religious feeling, openly defied their rulers by denouncing Muhammad and the Islamic religion. The response of the authorities was swift and sure, as blasphemy of the prophet was an intolerable and unpardonable crime, punishable by death. Even so, the Christians continued to challenge the regime for several years, deliberately courting death in the hope of gaining the crown of martyrdom.

Although they enjoyed freedom of worship and the privilege of self-government under Islamic protection, the Mozarabs were clearly an inferior group who often experienced the contempt of their Muslim neighbors. In the century since the first Muslim invasion the Christians had developed an active hatred for the Arabs, whom they regarded as foreign intruders. Early in the reign of Abd al-Rahman II the Mozarabs of the frontier towns of Mérida and Toledo rebelled against him. The Mozarabs of Mérida even addressed an appeal for help to Emperor Louis the Pious, who responded in 826, expressing sympathy for their plight and denouncing the injustice of the emir who constantly increased the tributes they owed and used force to collect them. He urged them to stand fast until he could send military assistance and assured a warm welcome to those who wished to settle in his dominions. But the great distance between Mérida and the kingdom of the Franks precluded any effective assistance from him. Thus the emir was able to reduce Mérida and Toledo to submission.

The resistance of the Mozarabs of Córdoba was documented by two outstanding representatives of the Christian community, namely, Eulogius, a priest, who justified their deeds in several books, and his friend, the learned layman, Paulus Alvarus. Contrary to those who wished to preserve the existing accommodations with Islam, both men argued that the Christians were constantly harassed by the Muslims; that they were subject to burdensome tributes; that their churches were destroyed; and their priests subjected to public vilification and even stoning when they passed through the streets of the city. They were especially dismayed by the loss of so many of the faithful to Islam. Mixed marriages seem to have been frequent, particularly between Christian women and Muslim men; the children of these unions were raised as Muslims. They also decried the impact of Islamic culture upon young Christians who neglected their own heritage in order to study Arabic literature and to imitate Arabic customs. Rather than keep silent, Eulogius urged the necessity of speaking the truth and of giving public testimony to one's belief in Christ and one's repudiation of "the damned and filthy prophet," Muhammad.

When the priest Perfectus publicly denounced Muhammad as an agent of the devil, an adulterer, and a liar in 850 and suffered the supreme penalty for his blasphemy, the quest for martyrdom among the Mozarabs of Córdoba began. At intervals over the next nine years more than fifty persons appeared before the Muslim authorities to condemn the prophet and to suffer the inevitable penalty of death. But there were many Christians who believed that it was sheer folly to pursue such a course and who refused to recognize as martyrs those who voluntarily sought execution. Hoping to put a stop to the martyrs' movement, the emir appealed to the moderates among the Christian leaders. On his command a council of bishops was convened at Córdoba in 852, under the presidency of Recafred, metropolitan of Seville, who demanded the condemnation of the martyrs. The council redacted an ambiguous decree forbidding the faithful to court martyrdom, but it did not censure those who had already been executed. This satisfied no one and did not bring the end of the martyrs' movement; nor did the imprisonment of Eulogius. Indeed, Abd al-Rahman's death later in the year was looked upon by many as divine retribution for his persecution of the Christians.

His son and successor, Muhammad I (852–886), had no hesitancy in adopting stringent measures to suppress the opposition. "An enemy of the church of God and a malevolent persecutor of the Christians," as Eulogius called him, on the day of his accession he dismissed all the Christians from his service unless they accepted Islam. The Mozarabic *exceptor* or tax collector, Gómez, "a Christian in name only, who was distinguished for his vices and his wealth," chose not to give up his lucrative position and became a Muslim. The emir also ordered the destruction of recently erected churches and issued a general decree condemning all Christian men to death and their wives and daughters to a life of prostitution, unless they converted to Islam. His ministers pointed out, however, that this was an impolitic regulation which, if carried out, might arouse even stronger hostility to the regime. Therefore it was not enforced.

The Revolt of the Muwalladun

The reign of Muhammad I and those of his immediate successors constituted one of the most critical periods in the history of Muslim domination in Spain. The resistance of the Mozarabs, while the source of aggravation and annoyance, had more serious consequences when it encouraged other forms of opposition among other segments of society. The outbreak of armed rebellion among the *muwalladun* offered a formidable challenge to the Umayyad dynasty and nearly destroyed it. These descendants of Christian converts to Islam had discovered in a century of Muslim rule that they did not enjoy the full freedom and equality to which they were entitled. In spite of their profession of faith they were looked upon with suspicion and contempt by the Arabic aristocracy and had little chance to attain prominent positions in government or society. Resentful of their inferior standing, they turned against their overlords and for fifty years kept al-Andalus in a constant state of turmoil. Though it is anachronistic to speak of their revolt as a manifestation of Hispanic nationalism, as some Spanish historians have done, they were clearly motivated by an antipathy toward the Arabs, whom they viewed as foreign intruders. Opposition developed not only among the *muwalladun* along the frontiers, but also in the heart of al-Andalus, and for the first time the Asturian Christians tried to assist the rebels. When the *muwalladun* of Toledo, aided by the large Mozarabic population of the city, revolted, King Ordoño I of Asturias (850–866) promptly responded to their appeal for help, but the emir's forces routed the Toledans and Asturians on the Guadacelete in 854. Though momentarily cowed, Toledo did not finally abandon her defiance for nearly eighty years.

Given the questionable loyalty of the Toledans, it is not surprising that the emir should have blocked the election of Eulogius as bishop, for his presence in the city would only have served to incite the populace to revolt again. Though he had been released from prison, he was arrested again for having given shelter to a young girl of Muslim parentage who had fled from her family's home so that she could live as a Christian. For that crime he was executed in March 859. Without him to exhort and to lead them, the Mozarabs lost the fervor that had impelled them to sacrifice their lives in defiance of Islam. The martyrs' movement subsided, and this strange era in the history of the Mozarabs of Córdoba came to an end. The hostility of the *muwalladun*, however, continued unabated and became more widespread and more dangerous as the years passed.

Among the most famous families of *muwalladun* were the Banu Qasi, who were entrenched in Zaragoza, Huesca, and Tudela on the Upper Frontier where they successfully ignored and defied the government at Córdoba. Descended from Fortun, the son of Count Casius, who converted to Islam at the time of the conquest and became a client of the caliph of Damascus in order to retain his lands, privileges, and honors, their adherence to Islam was more a matter of convenience than conviction. Musa, the head of the family, had such regard for his own power that, according to the *Chronicle of Alfonso III*, he called himself "the third king in Spain." His ambition to extend his dominions to the west brought him into conflict with Ordoño I who defeated him in 859, but his sons, who succeeded him after his death three years later, were more inclined to collaborate with the Asturians in opposition to the Umayyad regime.

Ordoño I's support of the *muwalladun* and his repopulation of previously deserted zones in the Duero valley and the towns of León, Túy, Astorga, and Amaya prompted Muhammad I to send expeditions to ravage Asturias. Despite them, the Asturians were not cowed. Ordoño's young son, Alfonso III (866–910), later known as The Great (*el magno*), seized Porto at the mouth of the Duero and began to repopulate the region between the Miño and the Duero. He also erected many castles on his eastern frontier to block further Muslim incursions into that area; in this way, Castile, the land of castles, originated as the western bulwark of the kingdom of Asturias.

Like his father before him, Alfonso III maintained close ties with the Banu Qasi and incited rebellion elsewhere in al-Andalus. Along the Lower Frontier Alfonso threw his support to Ibn Marwan, a *muwallad* of Galician origin, who seized control of Badajoz on the Guadiana in 875 and skillfully turned back Umayyad forces sent against him; Ibn Marwan even captured the emir's chief minister and handed him over to Alfonso III who held him for ransom. Ibn Marwan was expelled from Badajoz in 877 and sought refuge at the Asturian court, but this proved to be only a temporary setback. With the intention of chastising the Christians, Muhammad I dispatched a large army to Asturias in 878; but Alfonso III won a great victory at Polvoraria and a few days later completed the rout of the enemy in the valley of Valdemora. Muhammad I asked for a truce, perhaps the first time that an emir of Córdoba submitted to the will of the king of Asturias. Alfonso III's success encouraged many Asturian Christians to believe that the days of Muslim rule in Spain were numbered; a contemporary expressed this conviction in the following words: "Christ is our hope that upon the completion in the near future of 170 years from the entrance of the enemy into Spain they will be annihilated and the peace of Christ will be restored to the holy church" (*Cronicon Albeldense*, 86).

Although this hope proved illusory, rebellions and secessionist movements in al-Andalus continued to favor Alfonso III. At the expiration of the truce and coincidentally of 170 years from the time of the first Muslim invasion, he carried out a raid deep into Muslim territory, attacking Coimbra and Mérida, crossing the Guadiana toward the Sierra Morena and defeating an enemy force at Mount Oxifer. No Christian king had penetrated so far into al-Andalus.

The renewal of the truce with Asturias was essential to allow Muhammad I a free hand to deal with rebels such as the Banu Qasi on the Upper Frontier and Ibn Marwan, who returned to Badajoz in 885. The most prolonged and dangerous threat to the Umayyad regime, however, came from the southernmost part of al-Andalus in the modern province of Málaga. From the security of Bobastro, a fortress in the mountains of Ronda, Umar ibn Hafsun, a *muwallad* descended from a Gothic count, carried on guerrilla warfare against the government and very nearly destroyed it. According to Ibn al-Qutiyya, he dominated the region between Algeciras and Tudmir (Murcia) and enjoyed the support or alliance of other rebel leaders and the masses of the *muwalladun* and Mozarabs.

After the death of Muhammad I, his son al-Mundhir (886–888), a valiant and energetic prince, devoted his brief reign to the suppression of Ibn Hafsun. While besieging Bobastro, al-Mundhir died suddenly, perhaps as some Muslim historians charged, poisoned by his brother Abd Allah (888–912), who succeeded him. The new emir was indeed a man of suspicious temper who executed several members of his family whom he found untrustworthy. Confronted by rebellions along the frontiers and in the very heart of the kingdom, he found his authority restricted to the region around the capital. His most dangerous opponent, Ibn Hafsun, occupied fortresses and towns along the Guadalquivir, directly threatening Córdoba, and initiated inconclusive negotiations with the Abbasid caliph of Baghdad. Abd Allah defeated Ibn Hafsun in 891 and captured Poley, the fortress which had served as the base for his attacks upon Córdoba, but in spite of this the rebel leader's influence and power was not changed substantially. Around 898 Ibn Hafsun took the bold and unprecedented step of becoming a Christian, thereby underlining his fundamental opposition to the Umayyads and all they stood for. Perhaps, as Cagigas suggests, many *muwalladun*, impelled by an intensified patriotism and a desire for independence, followed his lead and returned to the religion of their forefathers, but it is difficult to assess the extent of this movement and its impact upon the rebellion. As Ibn Hafsun's influence seems to have begun to wane thereafter, it would seem that his conversion was premature and the cause of confusion and disunity among the rebels. Abd Allah defeated Ibn Hafsun in 904, but the rebellion was not yet crushed.

The chaotic conditions in al-Andalus during the closing decades of the ninth century and at the opening of the tenth century enabled the Christian states to establish themselves on a firmer foundation. In the northeast, Wifred the Hairy, count of Barcelona (873–898), took advantage of the disintegration of the Carolingian empire to secure a *de facto* independence and through inheritance, conquest, and repopulation broadened his dominions to include the several Catalan counties, namely, Ausona (Vich), Gerona, Cerdagne, Besalú, and Urgel. All this he bequeathed to his heirs, but the custom of dividing the inheritance among all the sons hindered the unification of the Catalan counties for

many years. As the progenitor of the dynasty that ruled Catalonia for
centuries, Wifred holds a special place in Catalan history. Farther west
a new dynasty emerged in the kingdom of Navarre. Sancho I Garcés
(905–926), the founder of the Jimena dynastry that ruled in Pamplona
for centuries, apparently came to power with the assistance of Alfonso
III, who, by placing Sancho I in his debt, perhaps sought to secure an
acknowledgement of his supremacy.

Continuing the colonization of the Duero valley, Alfonso III repopulated Zamora, Toro, Simancas, and other places. Many Mozarabs,
fleeing from al-Andalus, settled in these new towns and elsewhere in
the kingdom of Asturias and by their presence helped to make known
and to reinvigorate the Visigothic tradition. Alfonso III also raided al-
Andalus at will. Nothing better illustrates the debility of the Umayyad
regime than the Asturian devastation of the neighborhood of Seville
in 901. Alfonso III led an expedition into the territory of Toledo in the
following year and collected tribute from the inhabitants, probably in
return for a promise of protection. His last years, however, were
clouded by familial discord. His sons, according to Sampiro, bishop of
Astorga, writing a century later, "conspired among themselves and
expelled their father from the kingdom." The deposed monarch made
a pilgrimage to Santiago de Compostela and then with the permission
of his sons made a last incursion into Muslim territory before he died.
Although Sampiro's account has been questioned, it has not been dis-
proven. The deposition probably occurred at the close of 909, and the
king died in December 910. In spite of this inglorious end he had enjoyed a long and highly successful career and ranks among the leading
sovereigns of Asturias.

Abd Allah succumbed in 912 without having resolved the crisis con-
fronting the Umayyad dynasty. The bankruptcy of his reign was
summed up in these words by the compiler of the *Akhbar Majmua*:
"Public revenues diminished considerably because all the provinces
were in the hands of rebels. . . . Disorder spread everywhere and the
power of Umar ibn Hafsun was increasing." Although Abd Allah
gained victories over his opponents, he failed to compel their submission. But their inability to act in concert for any prolonged period of
time enabled him to preserve the rights of his family and to transmit
them intact to his grandson, Abd al-Rahman III, the first of the Spanish
Umayyads to assume the title of caliph.

CHAPTER 5

The Caliphate of Córdoba

The Century of the Caliphate

At the commencement of the tenth century al-Andalus appeared on the verge of disaster, but the remarkable talents of Abd al-Rahman III averted the destruction of the kingdom and reaffirmed and strengthened its unity. Indeed, the tenth century proved to be an epoch of unrivaled splendor in the history of Muslim domination in Spain. Recovering from the blows they had received from both external and internal foes, the Umayyads restored order to the peninsula and established hegemony over the Christian states. As a symbol of the new order Abd al-Rahman III reclaimed the title of caliph lost by the dynasty nearly two hundred years before. Córdoba, the seat of his power, attained unprecedented heights both as a center of commerce and of civilization, with a population of approximately a quarter of a million, a figure unmatched by any other western city and equaled only by Baghdad and Constantinople. The fame of the city reached far beyond the confines of the peninsula and was celebrated in verse by the German nun, Hrotswitha of Gandersheim, who hailed it as "the new imperial city, the glittering ornament of the world, shining in the western regions."

The new-found unity and direction of Spanish Islam considerably limited the expansion of the Christian states and threw grave doubt upon their ability to drive the Muslims from the peninsula. It was now a far more hazardous thing to challenge the power of the caliphate; though the Christians occasionally triumphed over Muslim arms, in the second half of the century they were compelled to bow their necks under the Umayyad yoke. And yet the Umayyads did not employ their overwhelming military superiority to destroy the Christian states or even to annex substantial segments of their territory. Thus, the Chris-

116

tians survived the trials of the tenth century with the hope that a brighter day would soon come.

The effective usurpation of the caliph's power by his chief minister at the close of the tenth century ushered in an era of decadence which gave way to widespread civil war in al-Andalus. The agonies of the early eleventh century finally reached their dénouement; the caliphate was abolished, and the unity of al-Andalus was replaced by many petty kingdoms.

Abd al-Rahman III

Abd al-Rahman III (912–961), the first caliph of Córdoba, mounted the throne at the age of twenty, already respected for his courage and intelligence. Designated successor by his grandfather, Abd Allah, he was of mixed blood, the son of a Frankish mother and grandson of a Basque princess. Contemporaries described him as handsome, blue-eyed, and light-haired, equally at home in Arabic and in the emerging Romance tongue. His origin and temperament enabled him to bring together the conflicting racial elements that had for so long thrown al-Andalus into turmoil. He approached the task of pacifying the kingdom realistically and methodically, by pledging a pardon to all those rebels who submitted to his authority and sure punishment for those who continued in opposition. The Arabic tribal factions that had so long disturbed the peace in Seville, Carmona, and other cities renewed their allegiance and supported his campaigns against his chief antagonist, Ibn Hafsun, who has been described by one chronicler as "the refuge of dissidents and heretics." The old rebel, after terrorizing al-Andalus for nearly thirty years, breathed his last in 917, though his four sons continued the resistance until their final capitulation in 928. At that time Abd al-Rahman III visited Bobastro and ordered the disinterment of Ibn Hafsun's body, which was then crucified at the gates of Córdoba as a warning to future rebels. Following the suppression of the Banu Hafsun, the Banu Marwan of Badajoz and the Banu Qasi of the Upper Frontier acknowledged Umayyad sovereignty. By 932 al-Andalus again enjoyed internal tranquility under the firm hand of Abd al-Rahman III. In part his success was due to the death of rebel leaders, but he also tried to eliminate some of the causes which had provoked discontent among the Mozarabs and the *muwalladun*. He guaranteed the former full freedom to practice their religion without harassment and offered to all his subjects equal opportunity to participate in public affairs and to rise in his service. His conciliatory attitude is suggested by certain remarks attributed to his chief minister who pointed out that the Christians were not to be treated with disdain but with justice and equity. This too was his policy with regard to the *muwalladun*, whose allegiance grew firmer year by year. Given new impetus, the assimilation of all the disparate elements in the population proceeded more rapidly than before.

The event of greatest import for the future of al-Andalus was the assumption by Abd al-Rahman III of the title of caliph (*khalifa*) and prince of all believers (*amir al-muminin*) on 16 January 929. Until then the Umayyads of Córdoba, while maintaining their political independence in Spain, had recognized at least in theory the supremacy of the Abbasid caliphs of Baghdad as the rightful successors of Muhammad and rulers of the Muslim community. Abd al-Rahman III elected to end this fiction, by reasserting the ancient rights of his family. In his instructions to his governors ordering them to address him by this title he explained that his continued failure to assume it might be construed as a renunciation of it:

Because the most high God . . . has shown his preference for us . . . and has extended our fame throughout the world and exalted our authority . . . we have decided that we should be addressed by the title Prince of Believers, and that in the letters we send as well as in those we receive this title should be accorded us. Anyone, other than ourselves, who uses it, does so improperly and is an intruder and arrogates to himself a title that he does not merit. We recognize, moreover, that by neglecting to use this title that is due to us, we are abandoning a right that belongs to us. [*Crónica anónima de Abd al-Rahman III*, 59]

Henceforth his name and that of his successors would be commemorated in public prayer in all the mosques of Spain. As caliph, he claimed absolute and infallible authority in both the spiritual and temporal realms. As the true successor of Muhammad he was the sole leader and guide of the Muslim community, the faithful interpreter of the will of God as expressed in the Koran. The title of caliph emphasized his royal majesty and sovereign power and exalted him far above the ranks of ordinary mortals. Only the very bold and irreligious would attempt to challenge his authority in the future. He also assumed, as a symbol of his sovereignty, the honorific surname, al-Nasir li-din-Allah, meaning, the defender of the religion of God. An elaborate court ceremonial served to render him inaccessible to the masses and to endow him with a certain air of mystery. In order to emphasize his inaccessibility still further he constructed a great palace at Madinat al-Zahra, a few miles outside Córdoba and transferred all the departments of state to that site.

His desire to imbue his subjects with a stronger sense of loyalty and obedience prompted his assumption of the caliphal title, but the emergence of the Fatimid caliphate in North Africa in 909 probably also contributed to his decision. The Fatimids, Shiite sectaries who claimed descent from Muhammad's daughter Fatima, had overthrown the dynasties that ruled Algeria and Morocco and, as they moved westward, became a very real threat to the Umayyad regime. Even Ibn Hafsun had established communication with them and, if they had tried to enter the peninsula, they probably would have found substantial support. To counteract possible Fatimid designs on Spain, Abd al-Rahman took the precaution of occupying Melilla in 927, Ceuta in 931, and Tangier in 951. Thus he controlled the ports most convenient for an invasion of the peninsula and was also able to establish a protectorate over northern and central Morocco. After several indecisive naval encounters, the Fatimids overran much of Morocco in 959 and confined the caliph's influence and authority to his coastal positions. The Fatimids were more concerned, fortunately, with the extension of their dominion into Egypt and established their capital at Cairo in 972. Their withdrawal freed the Umayyads from any anxiety and enabled them to resume their efforts to control the destinies of Morocco.

The rivalry of the Fatimids, Abbasids, and Umayyads probably induced Abd al-Rahman III to initate diplomatic exchanges with the Byzantine Emperor Constantine VII Porphyrogenitus, the natural enemy of both eastern caliphates. A century before, Emperor Theophilus had vainly proposed an alliance with the Umayyads against the Abbasids. According to Ibn Hayyan, the caliph solemnly received Byzantine envoys at Córdoba in September 949, and a month later his representatives were received at Constantinople, where they encountered Liutprand of Cremona, ambassador of the king of Italy. Little substantive action was agreed upon, though it is probable that exchanges of envoys continued until the end of the tenth century.

Ambassadors from prominent western personages such as Hugh of Arles, king of Italy, and Otto the Great, king of Germany, also came to Córdoba, apparently to protest raids by Muslim pirates along the coasts of Italy and France. The Germans found the caliph's response offensive, and in 953 Otto sent Abbot John of Gorze to Córdoba, with a letter equally insolent in tone. For almost three years John of Gorze was refused admission to the caliph's presence because of his intransigent attitude. In the meantime the caliph sent Recemund, the newly appointed bishop of Elvira, to consult with Otto the Great at Frankfort. After establishing cordial relations with the German king, Recemund returned to Córdoba in June 956 with instructions for John of Gorze to conclude a treaty of friendship with the caliph. Thus at last John was received by the caliph, but at this point his biography, which describes in detail the circumstances of his mission and his astonishment at Mozarabic acceptance of Umayyad rule, breaks off before recording the final outcome of the affair.

The Kingdom of León

The tenth century was, on the whole, a bleak period in the history of Christian Spain. The reintegration of sovereign authority in al-Andalus enabled the caliph to dominate Asturias and her neighbors. Internal strife and the emergence of a semi-independent county of Castile weakened Asturias, but precisely in this century of near despair Asturian pretensions to lordship over the whole of Spain were put forward in grandiloquent language, perhaps with the deliberate intent of giving hope to those who had little reason for hope.

After the death of Alfonso III, who had raised the kingdom of Asturias to new heights of glory, his three sons, García I (910–914), Ordoño II (910–925), and Fruela II (910–925), partitioned the realm as though it were a family patrimony. García took León and Castile, Ordoño retained Galicia, which he had probably ruled in his father's lifetime, and Fruela held Oviedo and Asturias. García, the oldest son, established his court at León, which lay more nearly in the center of the kingdom and at the juncture of the all important lines of communication. The growth of the population and the strengthening of the frontiers during the late ninth century made such a move feasible, since León was no longer exposed to direct enemy assault. Upon García's death, Ordoño II took possession of his kingdom and erected in León a palace and a cathedral truly worthy of a royal city. He and his successors were known thereafter as kings of León, but this did not imply any essential change in the structure of the state. The kingdom of León was simply a continuation of the kingdom of Asturias.

In the course of the tenth century the Leonese developed a concept of peninsular hegemony expressed principally in the title *imperator* applied to the kings of León by their subjects or by other Christian princes. No tenth-century king of León personally used the title. Although the meaning of the title has been much debated, Menéndez Pidal has suggested that it was a new manifestation of the neo-Gothic ideal. From the time of Alfonso II the Asturian kings had made a conscious effort to restore the ceremonial of the Visigothic monarchy and to preserve Visigothic law, while the official historiography of Alfonso III's court deliberately attempted to demonstrate that the Asturians were the heirs of the Visigoths. The title *imperator*, meaning "king of kings," expressed a claim to political supremacy over the whole of Spain, whether Christian or Muslim, and proclaimed the responsibility of the kings of León to recover their heritage, to reconquer the ancient territory of *Hispania*, and to expel the Muslims from the peninsula. The earliest authentic references to the title are found in three charters of Ordoño II dated 916 and 917, in which he called himself *filius Adefonsi magni imperatoris*. In Menéndez Pidal's opinion the imperial idea originated at this time, perhaps as a device for asserting Leonese supremacy over Sancho I, the new king of Navarre, or for preserving a semblance of unity in the kingdom which the sons of Alfonso III had divided among themselves. Sánchez Albornoz finds these arguments wholly unconvincing, and suggests that Ordoño II may only have wished to express filial devotion by calling himself "son of Alfonso, the great ruler." He admits that the idea of empire was inspired by the neo-Gothic ideal, but believes that the idea developed gradually and began to assume a true significance only in the second quarter of the tenth century, partly as a reaction to Abd al-Rahman III's assumption of the title of caliph, and in any case as an expression of Leonese aspirations to predominance throughout Spain. Vicens Vives, on the other hand, believes that imperial terminology is used so ambiguously at this time as to be almost meaningless and impossible to interpret precisely.

In the early years of the tenth century Ordoño II, the most vigorous of Alfonso III's sons, with the active cooperation of Sancho I Garcés, king of Navarre, attempted to conquer La Rioja, the region lying between Castile and Navarre. Ordoño II won a substantial victory over the Muslims in 917 at San Esteban de Gormaz, which together with Osma, Simancas, and Zamora, was a major link in the defenses of the Duero valley. Elated by this success, the Christians made repeated in-

cursions into La Rioja, attacking Nájera, Tudela, Arnedo, and Calahorra. Though still preoccupied with the restoration of order in al-
Andalus, Abd al-Rahman III determined to punish the aggression of
the kings of León and Navarre. Advancing to the north in the summer
of 920, he seized Osma, Gormaz, and Calahorra, and routed the Christian kings on 26 July at Valdejunquera, southwest of Pamplona. After
ravaging lower Navarre he returned to Córdoba with every reason to
believe that his enemies would hesitate to attack again. Surprised and
infuriated when they renewed their raids, he marched directly to
Pamplona in July 924 and thoroughly sacked it. Sancho I could do
nothing to halt the destruction of his chief stronghold and was reduced
to impotence for the remainder of his career. His son, García I Sánchez
(926–970), by marrying the heiress to the county of Aragon, linked
the county to the kingdom of Navarre in a union that was to last for
a century.

After the death of Ordoño II and the very brief reign of his brother,
Fruela II, a dynastic crisis developed in León. With the help of the king
of Navarre, Alfonso IV (925–930), Ordoño's son, gained the throne,
but in 930 he abdicated in favor of his brother, Ramiro II (930–951),
and retired to the monastery of Sahagún. Within the year, however,
Alfonso IV abandoned the cloister and attempted to recover the throne.
Hastily returning from the frontier, Ramiro II captured and blinded
him, together with the three sons of Fruela II, thereby eliminating all
potential rivals.

A bold and aggressive monarch, Ramiro II was an implacable foe of
the caliph of Córdoba and had the unique honor of humiliating him
on the field of battle. At the beginning of his reign he attempted unsuccessfully to aid the rebels of Toledo, but in 933 he defeated a Muslim army near Osma, and compelled the governor of Zaragoza to pay
tribute. Intent on crushing the king of León, the caliph assembled a
powerful army and advanced toward Zamora, one of the key fortresses
in the Duero valley; near Simancas he encountered Ramiro II who
soundly defeated him on 1 August 939, and completed the rout a few
days later at Alhandega, south of Salamanca. On returning to Córdoba
in disorder, Abd al-Rahman vented his rage by crucifying 300 of his
officers as traitors to the faith. In the future he did not dare risk his
person in combat with the Christians. The ensuing respite enabled
Ramiro II to repopulate the lands between the Duero and the Tormes.

Ramiro II's aggressive policy toward al-Andalus was hampered severely by the rebellious attitude of Fernán González, count of Castile (923–970), hero of legend and epic, and the true founder of an independent Castile. The formation of Castile, the ancient Bardulia, had its beginning in the ninth century, when the numerous castles that gave the province its name were erected as a buffer against Muslim expeditions sent to ravage Asturias and León. Castile formed a county of the kingdom of Asturias by the middle of the ninth century, and in 882 the district around a small fort or *burgus*, the nucleus of the future town of Burgos, the *caput Castellae* of later centuries, was repopulated. In the meantime the Castilian frontier steadily advanced to the Arlanzón, the Arlanza, and the Duero rivers.

Though a dependency of the kingdom of Asturias-León, Castile at an early date developed a distinctive character and identity. The hardy men of the Cantabrian and Basque mountains who settled Castile were pioneers filled with a spirit of adventure and self-confidence. Freemen and free proprietors, they firmly resisted the constant assaults of the Muslims and refused to yield their liberty to any man. Their law was custom, rather than the written law of the Visigoths that prevailed in the more conservative regions of León. Their language too was different, and they developed a literature of an epic and popular character in the Germanic rather than the Isidorian tradition.

Under Fernán González the ties binding Castile to León were weakened, and the county was transformed into the hereditary domain of his family. In the early years of the reign he collaborated with Ramiro II against the Muslims, but in 943 he raised the standard of revolt. Moving swiftly, Ramiro II seized González and threw him into prison, only to release him and to restore the county to him two years later. Although Ramiro II affirmed his supremacy, his peaceful relations with González rested on precarious foundations thereafter.

The Decadence of León

With the passing of Ramiro II in January 951, the kingdom of León entered upon a period of civil discord that weakened its defenses and left it a prey to Umayyad intervention. This dismal era opened with a series of disputes over the throne. Ordoño III (951–956), son of the deceased king, ascended the throne, only to be challenged by his half-brother, Sancho, supported by Fernán González and the Navarrese King García I. But Ordoño overcame his opponents and successfully countered Muslim attacks on the frontiers. González, who had renewed his allegiance, also won a signal victory over the Muslims at San Esteban de Gormaz in 955.

Shortly after concluding a truce with the caliph, Ordoño III died, and a new controversy over the succession erupted. The magnates recognized his half-brother, Sancho I (956–966), whose obesity (*cum esset crasus nimis*) made it difficult for him to walk and impossible for him to mount a horse. In spite of his physical handicaps, he repudiated the truce with the caliph who promptly attacked him. Thereupon the nobles, led by Fernán González, deposed him and elected Ordoño IV (958–960), son of Alfonso IV, and known to history as "the bad." In order to regain his throne, Sancho I decided to reduce and to seek military assistance from Córdoba. The caliph gladly sent his Jewish physician, Hasday ibn Shaprut, to Pamplona, where Sancho had taken refuge, to cure him of his disability; but to conclude the alliance Sancho and his grandmother, the queen of Navarre, had to make a humiliating journey to Córdoba. Accompanied by a large Muslim army, the now slender Sancho I (*ad pristinam leuitatis astuciam reductus*) returned to León in 960 and recovered his kingdom, beginning the second stage of his reign.

Not long after, the Caliph Abd al-Rahman III, who had made this triumph possible, died at his great palace at Madinat al-Zahra outside Córdoba. His long reign of nearly fifty years witnessed the pacification of al-Andalus and the attainment of an unprecedented prosperity and a new level of civilization. Though he curbed the audacity of the Christian states, he failed to destroy them or to annex any of their territory, and he could not obliterate the memory of Ramiro II's victory over him at Simancas in 939. His personality overshadowed that of his son, al-Hakam II (961–976), a cultivated prince and a lover of good literature, who was in every way a worthy heir, capable of guarding well the brilliant legacy entrusted to him.

During the fifteen years of al-Hakam II's reign the tranquility of al-Andalus was scarcely disturbed, allowing him greater freedom to intervene in the destinies of the Christian states. When Sancho I refused to fulfill the conditions of his alliance with Córdoba, namely, the cession of ten fortresses along the Duero river, the caliph proffered his assistance to Ordoño IV, who had taken refuge at his court. Lest Ordoño do anything foolish, the caliph required him, before taking any major decision, to seek counsel with two Mozarabic judges of Córdoba and the metropolitan of Seville, but these arrangements came to naught when Ordoño died at Córdoba in 962. Meanwhile Sancho I prepared to defend his realm and concluded alliances with García I of Navarre, Fernán González, and the counts of Barcelona, Borrell II (940–992), and his brother Miro (940–966). The caliph responded to this challenge by sending his armies to lay waste León, Castile, and Navarre, humiliating the Christians on all sides and compelling them to make peace.

After the death of Sancho I in 966, a victim of poisoning, the kingdom of León for the first time had to endure a minority, a fact which in itself testifies to the acceptance of the concept of hereditary monarchy. Ramiro III (966–984), the five-year-old son of the dead king, was acknowledged as his successor. Equally without precedent was the fact that his aunt Elvira assumed the direction of the government.

During the minority, al-Hakam's supremacy in Spain was unquestioned. The Christian princes vied with one another in seeking to acknowledge his lordship. Not only did León send envoys with pledges of lasting friendship, but so too did Sancho II Garcés (970–994), king of Navarre, García Fernández, who succeeded his father Fernán González as count of Castile in 970, and Borrell II, count of Barcelona. The Byzantine Emperor John Tzimisces sent ambassadors to Córdoba in 972 as did Otto II, the western emperor, in 974. The following description of the reception of the Catalan ambassador conveys some idea of the protocol observed on these occasions:

The Caliph al-Hakam was seated on a throne in the alcove of the Eastern Salon. . . . First the counselors were received and seated according to their rank. . . . Earlier Jahwar ibn Al-Shaykh had been sent to the ambassadors of Count Borrell, with a squadron of cavalry and a small group of Christians of Córdoba to act as interpreters. He returned with them and with Borrell's gift to the Caliph al-Hakam, consisting of thirty Muslim captives, including men, women, and children, and not counting loads of brocade and arms. . . . Permission was given for them to enter the caliph's chamber. . . . At the door of the throne room they prostrated themselves . . . until they reached the caliph, whose hand they kissed. They then stepped back and still standing, presented their credentials. After looking them over, the caliph questioned them about their lord Borrell . . . and the condition of their country. . . . They responded as seemed appropriate. . . . At the end of the session, they returned to their lodgings. . . . The caliph ordered that help be given to the captives who had been turned over to him, so they could return to their lands. [Isa al-Razi, *Anales palatinos*, 4]

The caliph also made his influence felt in Morocco where, after the withdrawal of the Fatimids to Cairo in 972, the Idrisids tried to establish their supremacy. By 974, however, this threat was overcome, and Morocco was again safely within the Umayyad sphere of influence. Peaceful relations with the Christian states were abruptly terminated by the aggressive attitude of the count of Castile, but in July 975 the Umayyads inflicted a thorough defeat upon the combined forces of León, Castile, and Navarre at Gormaz, and their humiliation was complete.

The Dictatorship of Almanzor

Al-Hakam II's death in October 976 closed the epoch of greatest splendor in the history of the caliphate of Córdoba. In the next quarter century al-Andalus was held in the grip of a dictator, known as Almanzor, who exercised an absolute military superiority over the entire peninsula. León, Galicia, Castile, Navarre, and Catalonia were devastated as never before. But by excluding the true sovereign absolutely from any share in the government, Almanzor hastened the destruction of the caliphate and the end of the Umayyad dynasty.

Upon the death of al-Hakam II, a court conspiracy was set on foot to prevent the accession of his ten-year-old son, Hisham II (976–1009), whom he had designated as his heir. The boy's mother, Subh, determined that her son should rule, enlisted the support of the wazir, al-Mushafi, and of Ibn Abi Amir, the future Almanzor, who quickly thwarted the conspiracy. Hisham II was duly recognized as caliph; al-Mushafi was appointed hajib or first minister, and Ibn Abi Amir was named counselor of state. Together they suppressed all opposition in the court and in the administration.

Ibn Abi Amir, who now came to prominence, was a young man about thirty-six years of age, descended from the original Arab conquerors of Spain. After completing his education, he entered the civil service and rose rapidly. Placed in charge of the patrimony reserved for al-Hakam's son, he apparently gained the affection of Subh, who, according to rumor, became his mistress. Under her protection he steadily accumulated power and offices, being appointed inspector of the mint, judge of Seville and Niebla, chief of the central police, and inspector of troops sent to Africa. In this last capacity he distinguished himself by suppressing the Moroccan rebels. He was a man of great skill and intelligence, shrewd, tactful, and insinuating, ambitious, ruthless, and unscrupulous.

Unwilling to remain for long subordinate to al-Mushafi, he sought to gain popularity among the Cordobans and to establish a reputation as a military commander. Although his career had been concentrated chiefly in the civil service, he did not hesitate to assume command of an expedition that ravaged Salamanca in February 977; on this occasion great booty was accumulated and distributed liberally among his troops. He also assiduously cultivated the most distinguished Cordoban general, Ghalib, who helped him to depose and imprison al-Mushafi in March 978. With the complaisance of the caliph's mother, Ibn Abi Amir was appointed *hajib* and now had at his disposal the full resources of the state.

Ibn Abi Amir continued the policy of tolerance and assimilation carried out by the first two caliphs. He gave the *muwalladun* every opportunity to participate in government, and there is no evidence that he persecuted the Mozarabs. His armies included numerous Christians who were well treated and permitted to celebrate their festivals even on campaign. To win favor with the rigorist theologians of Córdoba he despoiled the great library formed by al-Hakam II and burned many books of philosophy and science. The administrative organization was continued as before, although its offices were removed to Madinat al-Zahira, another palace, this one constructed by Almanzor to the east of Córdoba. The extent of his usurpation of power was described by al-Himyari in these words:

He denied the caliph any participation in the affairs of government. . . . Once the seat of power was transferred to the palace of al-Zahira, the caliph was left alone and ignored. People no longer spoke about him; his door remained closed and he no longer appeared in public. No one feared the slightest evil from him nor expected the slightest benefit. Of sovereign attributes he retained only the right to inscribe his name on the coinage, to be commemorated in the Friday prayers, and to use the title of caliph. [*Kitab al-Rawd al-Mitar*, 169–170]

Though not trained as a military man, he maintained a highly efficient military machine and took the important step of abolishing the tribal organization of the army; he preferred to rely on Berber mercenaries imported from North Africa, who were grouped in units without regard to their tribal origins. The Berber and Christian mercenaries who served him proved extremely loyal, in part because they profited immensely from the booty taken in his wars. Muslim authors reported that he led fifty-two expeditions against the Christian states. Al-Marrakushi commented: "He made many conquests and seized fortresses which had resisted all those who had preceded him. He filled al-Andalus with booty and captives, with the sons and daughters of the Christians and their wives." Though he wrought great destruction, his campaigns did not extend the frontiers of al-Andalus nor did they destroy any of the Christian states. In fact his expeditions may have cost more than the booty gained, but they served other purposes. By conducting a nearly continuous holy war he was able to make the Christians appear as a threat to Islam, thus consolidating popular support behind himself while diverting attention from his own usurpation of the caliph's power.

Jealous of the extraordinary power and influence of Ibn Abi Amir, whose popularity and military prowess now overshadowed his own, General Ghalib turned against him in 981 and sought alliance with the Christian rulers, Ramiro III of León, Sancho II of Navarre, and García Fernández, count of Castile. But Ibn Abi Amir attacked swiftly and won a succession of victories over his enemies, and with the defeat and death of Ghalib eliminated the last serious opposition to his rule. Returning from this campaign he assumed the honorific title, al-Mansur billah, that is, victorious through Allah. This in itself was an encroachment upon the prerogatives of the caliph, as the title was a symbol of sovereignty. By the name Almanzor, the dictator became known and feared as the scourge of Christian Spain.

The outbreak of civil war in 982 enabled him to intervene directly in the affairs of the kingdom of León. The Galician nobility rose in revolt against Ramiro III and proclaimed as king Vermudo II (984–999), son of Ordoño III. As Vermudo advanced to León, Ramiro fled to Astorga where he died in 984. In order to overcome all opposition and to secure his throne, Vermudo II concluded a treaty with Almanzor who agreed to lend him troops in exchange for an annual tribute. Vermudo II's abject submission was matched by that of Sancho II of Navarre, who offered his daughter as a wife to the dictator. She became a Muslim and the mother of his son, Abd al-Rahman, known familiarly as Sanjul, in memory of his Christian grandfather.

The only Christian state which had not yet experienced Almanzor's military might was the county of Barcelona; but in the summer of 985 he marched through the Levant and, after defeating Count Borrell II, sacked and burned the city of Barcelona. This was the worst punishment the city had yet suffered. Count Borrell appealed for help to the

1. The Crown of Reccesvinth. Courtesy of the Museo Arqueológico Nacional, Madrid.

2. The Ivory Box of al-Hakam II. Courtesy of the Museo Arqueológico Nacional, Madrid.

3. The Castle of Calahorra, Córdoba. Photograph by J. F. O'Callaghan.

4. The Palace of Ramiro I on Monte Naranco, Oviedo. Photograph by courtesy of James Powers.

5. The Crucifix of Fernando I of León. Courtesy of the Museo Arqueológico Nacional, Madrid.

6. "The Adoration of the Magi." Courtesy of The Metropolitan Museum of Art, The Cloisters Collection, New York, 1930.

7. The Tomb of Armengol X, Count of Urgel, and Dulcia, Wife of Armengol VII. Courtesy of The Metropolitan Museum of Art, The Cloisters Collection, New York, 1948.

8. Fresco from the Chapter House of
San Pedro de Arlanza. Courtesy of
The Metropolitan Museum of Art,
The Cloisters Collection, New York;
gift of John D. Rockefeller, Jr., 1931.

9. "Pedro the Cruel at Prayer." Courtesy
of the Museo Arqueológico Nacional,
Madrid.

10. Torre de Comares, the Alhambra, Granada. Photograph by J. F. O'Callaghan.

11. Portal of the Collegiate Church, Toro. Photograph by courtesy of James Powers.

12. João I of Portugal. Courtesy of the Museu Nacional de Arte Antiga, Lisbon. Published with the permission of the Ministério da Educação Nacional, Direcção-Geral dos Assuntos Culturais.

13. The Castle of Belmonte. Photograph by courtesy of James Powers.

French court, but the rivalry between the Carolingian and Capetian families stood in the way of a favorable response. Hugh Capet, after winning the throne in 987, offered to help if Borrell would first come to France to pledge homage and fealty. The count declined to do so and in effect severed the feudal bond with the French monarchy, although Catalan public documents continued to record the regnal years of the Capetian kings until the mid-twelfth century.

In spite of the demonstrated superiority of Almanzor's forces, the Christians did not abandon all hope of resistance. But when Vermudo II foolishly expelled the Cordoban mercenaries from León in 987, Almanzor responded swiftly by plundering Coimbra, León, Zamora, and the abbeys of Sahagún and San Pedro de Eslonza. Two years later he ravaged Castile and seized Osma, but his triumph was embittered by the defection of one of his sons, Abd Allah, who sought refuge with the count of Castile. Bowing to Almanzor's insistent demand, Count García surrendered the rebellious youth who was promptly decapitated. Still vengeful, Almanzor soon incited the count's son, Sancho, to rebel and then took advantage of the revolt to invade Castile; he defeated Count García near Medinaceli and took him prisoner to Córdoba where he died. Sancho García (995–1017) succeeded his father as count of Castile and agreed to pay tribute to Almanzor as the price of peace.

Although he had attained the pinnacle of power, Almanzor's ambitions were not entirely satisfied. By conferring the title of *hajib* on another son, Abd al-Malik, in 991 he revealed his desire to make the post an hereditary one. Five years later he assumed the title *malik karim*, that is, noble king, and may even have considered proclaiming himself caliph, but he was wise enough to avoid that fatal mistake. Though Subh, who had favored him for so long, now turned against him, the youthful Hisham II, lacking any will of his own, did not hesitate to confirm Almanzor's title. From then on, Almanzor sealed official documents with his own seal and maintained a court that was in every way a royal one. Poets surrounded him and accompanied him into battle to chant his glories. Truly he was the sovereign of al-Andalus in everything but name.

Almanzor undertook his most spectacular campaign in the spring of 997. His objective was the great Christian shrine and center of pilgrimage, Santiago de Compostela. Advancing through Portugal he reached Compostela on 11 August, sacked the town, and razed the church over the Apostle's tomb. The doors of the church were carried off to be used for shipbuilding, and the bells were hung in the great mosque of Córdoba. It is an irony of history that Fernando III, after conquering Córdoba in 1236, compelled Muslim captives to carry the bells of Santiago back to the shrine. The destruction of Compostela did more than the devastation of the countryside to undermine Christian morale. Perhaps precisely for this reason, in the darkest days of Leonese history, the royal courtiers consciously set out to strengthen and exalt the monarchy by the more frequent use of the title *imperator* with its implied claims to supremacy throughout the peninsula.

Almanzor continued his harassment of the Christian states. Vermudo II of León obtained a truce and then died leaving the kingdom to his five-year-old son, Alfonso V (999–1028). Sancho II of Navarre was succeeded by his son, García II (994–1000), who died after suffering a new invasion by Cordoban troops. In the same year Almanzor laid waste Castile and plundered Burgos. As he was returning from an expedition to La Rioja in 1002, however, he fell ill and died at Medinaceli. These verses attributed to Almanzor are his judgment of his career:

> Thus I surpassed in power all men of power,
> Excelled them in glory until I found none to excel!*

The Christian attitude toward him was expressed by an anonymous author in these words:

At that time in Spain divine worship perished; all the glory of the Christian people was destroyed; the treasures stored up in the churches were plundered; but at last after enduring such great ruin, the divine mercy deigned to lift this yoke from the necks of the Christians. . . . After many horrible massacres of Christians, Almanzor was seized in the great city of Medinaceli by the demon which had possessed him while he was alive, and he was buried in hell. [*Historia Silense*, 71]

The Destruction of the Caliphate

Although there was every reason to believe that the jealousies, ambitions, and intrigues which had been repressed for so long would now provoke a violent reaction against the dictator's family, nothing of the sort occurred. Hisham II, trained to submission, was quite content to

---

* In A. R. Nykl, *Hispano-Arabic Poetry and its Relations with the Old Provençal Troubadours* (first published, Baltimore, 1946; reprinted 1970, by The Hispanic Society), 55; used with permission of The Hispanic Society.

advance the fortunes of the Amirid family and confirmed Almanzor's son, Abd al-Malik, in the post of *hajib*. Abd al-Malik intended to continue his father's policy without modification. The Christian states remained as docile as before; the counts of Castile and Barcelona asked for a truce, and the Leonese allowed Abd al-Malik to arbitrate a dispute concerning the regency for Alfonso V. The Mozarabic judge of Córdoba was sent to León to decide the issue. The abject condition of León and Castile was further revealed when they were required to send troops to assist Abd al-Malik in laying waste the county of Barcelona in 1003. Muslim sources report that he led at least seven expeditions against the Christian states, plundering Galicia, Navarre, Castile, and Catalonia, but his campaigns were evidently not as profitable as those of his father. The Cordobans compared him unfavorably with Almanzor, who had kept the slave market well supplied with Christian captives. Setting out on campaign in October 1008, Abd al-Malik fell ill and died at the early age of thirty-three, perhaps, as some Muslim chroniclers suggested, the victim of poison administered by his younger brother, Abd al-Rahman, known popularly as Sanjul, who took control of the government.

He was a libertine lacking in political wisdom, and immediately committed a blunder which his predecessors had avoided. He persuaded Hisham II, who had no children, to appoint him heir presumptive to the caliphal throne; instead of bridling with resentment at such arrogance, the caliph graciously acquiesced. In his proclamation of November 1008 he declared that he had long searched for one to whom he could entrust the great burdens of the caliphate. Now through divine inspiration he had discovered that there was no one more worthy than Sanjul, a man distinguished by his ancestry, his fear of God, his enlightenment, energy, and intelligence. Thus Hisham prepared the way for the replacement of the Umayyad dynasty by the Amirids.

Deceived by the calm with which this proclamation was received, Sanjul set out from Córdoba in February 1009 to attack the Christians. His departure was the signal for an uprising led by members of the Umayyad family and the Arab aristocracy, who hated the presumption of the Amirids and their Berber mercenaries. The rebels sacked Madinat al-Zahira, the palace built by Almanzor, and also seized the caliph's palace, Madinat al-Zahra. Neither structure ever recovered from the destruction wrought at this time. The ruination of both palaces symbolized the approaching end of the caliphate. Complaisant as ever, Hisham II abdicated in favor of Muhammad II (1009–1010), a great-grandson of the first caliph. Sanjul learned of the revolt at Toledo but, as he began to return, his troops deserted him, and he was taken prisoner and killed by his guards; his body was trampled under horse's hooves and crucified at the gate of the *alcazar* and his head was mounted on a spear. Thus the Amirid regime came to an end.

The new caliph, Muhammad II, was not the man to restore order or to give good government. Fearing a reaction in favor of Hisham II, he gave out the news that his predecessor was dead, and a body purporting to be Hisham II's was given solemn burial; but no one was deceived by this farce. The Berber troops who had served the Amirids for so long now revolted and proclaimed Sulayman, another grandson of Abd al-Rahman III as caliph. The Berbers appealed to Count Sancho García of Castile, who thus found himself the unexpected arbiter of the destiny of al-Andalus. With Sancho García's assistance, the Berbers defeated Muhammad II in November 1009; Muhammad tried to save the situation by restoring Hisham II to power and presented him to the people of Córdoba, but it was too late. The Berbers and Castilians entered the capital and plundered it; once again Hisham II was deposed, and Sulayman was enthroned as caliph. Muhammad fled and contracted an alliance with Count Ramon Borrell I of Barcelona (992–1018) and his brother, Count Armengol of Urgel. With their support he advanced on Córdoba, defeated his Berber opponents, and entered the city in triumph in June 1010. It was now the Catalans' turn to sack Córdoba, but within two weeks of their departure from the smoldering city Muhammad II was assassinated. Hisham II recovered his throne, but was forced to abdicate for the third time in May 1013. He died shortly afterwards in prison, though some sources reported that he escaped to the east.

The disintegration of al-Andalus, now thrown into wild disorder, proceeded without letup. The succession of caliphs was bewildering, as few of them reigned for more than a year or two, and none of them could claim universal authority. Sulayman (1013–1016), whom the Berbers had installed in Córdoba, was overthrown and executed by Ali ibn Hammud (1016–1018), the governor of Ceuta, who became the first caliph who was not a member of the Umayyad family. In the next decade the Umayyads and Hammudids struggled for control; from 1018 to 1031 there were no less than six caliphs, namely, the Hammudids, al-Qasim (1018–1021), Yahya ibn Ali (1021–1023, 1025–

1027); and the Umayyads, Abd al-Rahman IV (1018), Abd al-Rahman V (1023–1024), Muhammad III (1024–1025), and Hisham III (1027–1031). Fittingly, Hisham III, the last of the caliphs, belonged to the Umayyad house, but his indolence and lack of resolution prompted the Cordoban aristocracy to depose him and to abolish the office of caliph. With the end of the caliphate of Córdoba, not the slightest semblance of unity remained in al-Andalus.

For the next fifty years until the advent of the Almoravids from North Africa, Muslim Spain consisted of numerous small states or *taifas* ruled by petty kings (*reyes de taifas, muluk al-tawaif*). Each of them ordinarily assumed the title of *hajib* to preserve the fiction that he was exercising authority simply as the chief minister of a nonexistent caliph. Each of them probably hoped to restore the caliphate in his own person, but that proved impossible. The *taifas* basically fell into three broad groups representing different ethnic strains. The Berbers of the Sinhaja and Zanata tribes, who had been brought to Spain to serve in Almanzor's army, established themselves in the southernmost section of the peninsula. The slaves (*saqaliba*) of northern European origin who had gained prominence in the court and in the administration dominated the eastern coast, while elsewhere indigenous elements of Arab, Berber, or *muwallad* stock assumed power.

There were about twenty-three *taifas* early in the eleventh century. Córdoba, after abolishing the caliphate, was governed by an aristocratic council, and then by the Banu Jahwar until annexed by Seville in 1070. At first Seville was also governed by a council, but it soon became a kingdom ruled by the Banu Abbad, the most famous dynasty of the period; they gradually subjugated a number of smaller *taifas* in the adjacent regions, including Carmona (1067), Ronda (1059), Morón (1066), Arcos (1068), Huelva, Saltes, Niebla, Silves, Santa Maria del Algarve, and Mértola. On the Lower Frontier the Banu-l-Aftas ruled Badajoz and the adjacent regions of Portugal, while the Banu Dhi-l-Nun governed Toledo. Zaragoza, Tudela, Lérida, and Tortosa on the Upper Frontier fell to the Banu Hud; the Banu Razin seized Albarracín and the Banu Qasim, Alpuente. A grandson of Almanzor founded a kingdom in Valencia, while farther south the enterprising Mujahid, a slave of Christian origin, seized Denia and the Balearic Islands and overran Sardinia in 1015; in the following year, however, the Pisans and Genoese drove him out. Almería and Murcia also constituted tiny kingdoms. In southern Spain, the Banu Hammud ruled

Algeciras until its annexation by Seville in 1058 and Málaga until its annexation by Granada in 1057. Granada became the seat of a kingdom ruled by the Banu Ziri. As one might expect, the *taifas* were constantly at war with one another, but gradually the larger states conquered or absorbed the smaller ones, so that by the late eleventh century the numbers had been considerably reduced. Those still remaining included Badajoz, Toledo, Seville, Granada, Almería, Denia and the Balearic Islands, Valencia, Alpuente, Albarracín, and Zaragoza.

The Christian States in the Early Eleventh Century

While the caliphate of Córdoba was suffering the agonies of dissolution, the Christian states enjoyed a respite in which to repair the damage inflicted by Almanzor. For the second time in its history the kingdom of León was ruled by a minor, Alfonso V, whose succession points up the strength of the hereditary principle. His uncle Sancho García, count of Castile, who had aspired to control the regency, took advantage of the minority to seize lands between the Cea and the Pisuerga rivers, thus laying the basis for a long controversy between León and Castile. When Alfonso V came of age in 1008 the reconstruction of the kingdom was his major task, as León and other towns were in ruins and many rural areas were deserted. In a general *curia* or council of bishops, abbots, and nobles (*omnes pontifices, abbates et optimates regni Hispaniae*), meeting at León in 1017, he completed his labors by promulgating the first territorial law dating from the period of the reconquest, a *decretum generale* treating the affairs of church and state; a charter or *fuero* was also given to the city of León. Menéndez Pidal conjectured that the council met following the solemn coronation of Alfonso V as emperor and that the convocation of the bishops and magnates of the kingdom of Spain was intended to reaffirm Leonese hegemony throughout the peninsula. Although it is evident that the imperial concept was strengthened during this period, an imperial coronation is not mentioned by any source and seems quite unlikely. Only at the close of his career was Alfonso V able to take advantage of the civil wars in al-Andalus, but he died while engaged in the siege of Viseu. The accession of his nine-year-old son, Vermudo III (1028–1037), opened the third minority in the history of León, and prepared the way for Navarrese interference in the affairs of the kingdom.

The kingdom of Navarre reached its apogee in the Middle Ages during the reign of Sancho III Garcés (1000–1035), better known as

Sancho el mayor. For much of the tenth century Navarre had played a secondary role among the Christian states, and at critical moments her rulers had tended to be overly submissive to the Muslims. With Sancho el mayor, Navarre moved to the forefront and enjoyed a *de facto* hegemony in Christian Spain. Through marriage, his family had acquired the adjacent counties of Aragon, Sobrarbe, and Ribagorza. Berenguer Ramon I (1018–1035), count of Barcelona, expecting help against the Muslim rulers of Zaragoza, Lérida, and Huesca, became his vassal, but in the long run the relationship brought no real profit to either party. Sancho also maintained friendly relations with the count of Gascony in southwestern France, but his hopes of inheriting that county were never fulfilled.

Sancho el mayor also exercised a preponderant influence over Castile and León. While posing as friend and protector of his youthful brother-in-law, García Sánchez, count of Castile (1017–1029), he strengthened his hold over the county and attracted many adherents among the Castilian nobility. His interests in the kingdom of León were represented and guarded by his sister, Urraca, widow of Alfonso V, and regent for her stepson, Vermudo III. Influenced by the French feudal tradition, Sancho el mayor, unlike the kings of León, championed the concept of the patrimonial state, heritable and divisible among heirs. Perhaps as Menéndez Pidal suggested, the nobles of Castile and León were inclined to look favorably upon him in the hope that under his aegis a greater feudalization of public offices and lands would be possible.

As Count García Sánchez grew to manhood, he realized that he had to free himself from Navarrese tutelage. For this reason he sought a rapprochement with León, to be effected by his marriage to Vermudo III's sister; as her dowry, she would receive the lands between the Cea and the Pisuerga that Alfonso V had recovered from Castile in 1017. This, it was hoped, would remove a major cause of conflict and would bolster Castile against Navarre, her aggressive neighbor to the east; but while preparing for the wedding the young count was murdered in 1029.

There is no proof that Sancho el mayor, who had accompanied García to León, was implicated in the crime, but he reaped the profit. In his wife's name he took possession of Castile, but, probably as a pledge against its absorption into the kingdom of Navarre, he designated his second son, Fernando, as heir to the county. In this way the Navarrese dynasty was established in Castile.

Encouraged by this success, Sancho el mayor then began to intrude upon the affairs of the kingdom of León. He arranged the marriage of his son Fernando to Vermudo III's sister, and the disputed lands between the Cea and the Pisuerga were transferred to Castile as her dowry. But this only whetted Sancho's appetite. Attempting to restrict the scope of Vermudo III's authority by referring to him only as emperor in Galicia, he called himself by contrast *rex Dei gratia Hispaniarum*, thereby laying claim to that peninsular supremacy previously attributed to the king of León. As he obviously was the most powerful of the Christian rulers, he probably concluded that he, rather than Vermudo III, should rightly be called *imperator*. Thus in 1034 he occupied the city of León, the "imperiale culmen" as he called it, and coined money in affirmation of his new dignity as *imperator*.

His triumph, however, was brief. In the following year he died rather suddenly, and Vermudo III, who had taken refuge in Galicia, regained possession of the kingdom of León. Sancho el mayor helped to draw Christian Spain out of its isolation and to incorporate it fully into the life of western Christendom. Through his kingdom of Navarre, feudal concepts penetrated into the peninsula. He encouraged the pilgrimage to Compostela, a principal vehicle for the transmission of French ideas, and for the convenience of pilgrims modified the difficult route through Alava and the Cantabrian mountains. Under his auspices the Cluniac reform was introduced into the monasteries of Oña, Leire, and San Juan de la Peña, whence it spread to other centers and reached a climax in the second half of the century. In the political sphere his work was incomplete and inconclusive. Although he unified all the Christian states except Catalonia, his adherence to the patrimonial concept made any permanent union of these states impossible. His death shortly after occupying León and assuming the imperial title allowed him no opportunity to give new vigor to an imperial tradition already grown old and decrepit. In Menéndez Pidal's view, he was an antiemperor who did not understand the origin and foundation of that tradition. Contrary to the neo-Gothic concept of a unitary kingdom, he divided his dominions among his sons and also failed to assume any responsibility for the continuation of the reconquest, and at no time did he attempt to profit from the discord in al-Andalus. His principal contribution to peninsular development was to open Spain to northern European influences. For this reason Menéndez Pidal has called him the first of the "Europeanizers" of Spain.

CHAPTER 6

Government, Society, and Culture in al-Andalus, 711–1031

The Emirs and Caliphs of Córdoba

From the beginning of the period of Muslim conquest al-Andalus was but a province in an empire ruled by the caliph of Damascus, an empire extending from the borders of India to the straits of Gibraltar. Although the Muslims penetrated into the deepest sectors of the peninsula and even crossed into southern Gaul, they did not long remain in occupation of the far north. By 740 their forces were withdrawn from the northwest, and by 751 they were driven from Narbonne by Pepin the Short. In the years that followed, the Christians slowly advanced to the south, but in the period under review they progressed no farther than the Duero river. Thus about three-quarters of the peninsula was in Muslim hands during the first three centuries of the reconquest. At the opening of the tenth century the Balearic Islands were definitively conquered, and a few years later various north African ports including Ceuta, Melilla, and Tangier were occupied by Umayyad troops.

The seat of government, after a very brief stay at Seville, was removed in 716 to Córdoba where it remained throughout the Umayyad era. The governors (*wali, amir*) of al-Andalus, appointed by the governor of North Africa or occasionally by the caliph of Damascus, were seldom in office for more than a year or two and had to contend with the ferocious strife between Berbers and Arabs and among the Arab tribes. It is indeed cause for wonder that in spite of recurring political crises and military upheavals, the governors were able to retain control of the peninsula and even to lead raiding expeditions into Gaul. This would seem to be a measure of the total collapse affecting the native population who were evidently too disorganized to attempt to overthrow the Muslims. If the disorder and confusion that characterized the dependent emirate had continued into the later eighth century, it seems likely that it would have resulted in the eventual destruction of Muslim rule.

Al-Andalus became an independent kingdom in 756 when the Umayyad prince, Abd al-Rahman I, whose family had been deprived of the caliphate in the east, seized power. His position, however, was anomalous. In the Muslim world, government rested upon an essentially religious foundation. Islam was a community of believers governed by the laws of Allah, administered by the prophet, Muhammad, and his successors, the caliphs. The caliph wielded both spiritual and temporal authority, for indeed the one could not properly be separated from the other. In the eyes of Abd al-Rahman I, the Abbasid caliph ruling in Baghdad was a usurper, but instead of claiming the caliphate he allowed the caliph's name to be commemorated in public prayer (*khutba*) and thus implicitly acknowledged him as the legitimate successor of Muhammad. At the same time he did not permit the eastern caliph to exercise any real power, whether political or spiritual, in al-Andalus.

Abd al-Rahman III took the logical step of assuming the titles of caliph and *amir al-muminin*, that is, prince of all believers or commander of the faithful, in 929. In so doing he broke the last tenuous tie with the caliphs of Baghdad. No radical change in the structure of the state took place, though the authority of the sovereign was greatly strengthened. As the representative of the prophet, the caliph was the supreme head of the community and wielded an absolute power in spiritual and temporal affairs. He appointed and removed at will all state functionaries, acted as judge of last resort, served as commander-in-chief of the army, and, as *imam*, led his people in public prayer. The responsibility for maintaining the integrity of the law of Islam and for guarding the spiritual and temporal well-being of his subjects was his alone.

From the time of Abd al-Rahman I, the Cordoban monarchy was hereditary, though the principle of primogeniture was not operative. The ruler exercised the right to designate any one of his male relatives as his heir. The throne usually passed from father to son, but in one instance Abd Allah succeeded his brother, al-Mundhir. An anonymous chronicler described the advent of Abd al-Rahman III in these terms:

His grandfather, the *imam* Abd Allah, preferred him to his own sons and designated and prepared him to be his successor. . . . The chief functionaries of state put all their expectation in him, certain that power was going to be his. When his grandfather died, they caused him to take his place in the caliphate, to the exclusion of the dead man's sons. . . . His enthronement . . . took place easily and without opposition. It is also said that when the *imam* Abd Allah fell ill, he took off his ring and gave it to him, letting it be known that he named him as his successor. He was seated on the throne to receive the oath of fidelity of his subjects. . . . The first to swear were his paternal uncles . . . then his grandfather's brothers. . . . After the members of the caliphal family, notable persons and clients . . . then the most important people among the inhabitants of Córdoba, jurists, magnates, members of noble houses also swore. . . . Letters were sent to the governors of all the provinces asking them to give the oath of fidelity. [*Crónica anónima de Abd al-Rahman III, 2*]

There was only one minority in the history of the Umayyad regime, that of Hisham II, in whose name Almanzor wielded dictatorial power. The prestige of the family was such, however, that even at the height of his career, Almanzor did not dare to depose that inept young man. When Sanjul, Almanzor's son, persuaded Hisham II to designate him as heir to the throne, the Arab aristocracy rebelled. In the next quarter-century of civil war, caliphs were proclaimed and deposed by rival military forces, but with the exception of three members of the Hammudid family, who ruled between 1016 and 1027, all of the caliphs, including the last, belonged to the Umayyad dynasty.

After the establishment of the caliphate, the sovereign was surrounded by the pomp and ceremony proper to his exalted position. The insignia of sovereignty included the throne, crown, scepter, seal, and ring with his device on it, and also the right to use an honorific name. Almanzor's assumption of such a name was a usurpation of a sovereign attribute. Access to the caliph's presence was extremely difficult. During Almanzor's dictatorship, Hisham II was continually secluded and when traveling was garbed as a woman so no one could recognize him. The excavations at Madinat al-Zahra, site of the caliphal palace outside Córdoba, reveal an extraordinary beauty and sumptuousness; taken together with numerous contemporary descriptions of the strict protocol regulating the court, they suggest the profound impression that the caliph's power and dignity must have made upon his subjects and upon foreign visitors. The historian Ibn Said attributed the success of the Umayyads to their impartial administration of justice and to the splendor and magnificence they displayed in public, thus arousing a reverential awe among their subjects. "When this salutary awe and impartial justice had vanished, the decay of their empire began" (Al-Maqqari, *History of the Mohammedan Dynasties in Spain*, tr. by Pascual de Gayangos, I, 98).

Royal Administration

The central administration, organized chiefly under the direction of Abd al-Rahman II, was patterned upon that of the eastern caliphate, which in turn was modeled upon Byzantine and Persian practices. Administrative offices were located initially in the *alcazar* of Córdoba, but were later moved to Madinat al-Zahra and then to Madinat al-Zahira. The Arabs enjoyed a monopoly of administrative posts until the first caliph opened the road to advancement to all of his subjects, regardless of racial origin.

Supervising the entire civil administration and serving as a kind of prime minister was the *hajib* or "doorkeeper." He outranked all other officials and was the only one to deal directly with the caliph. As the indispensable intermediary between the caliph and subordinate officials and subjects, he was the heart and center of the government. Ibn Khaldun summarized the functions of the *hajib* in these words: "In the Umayyad dynasty in Spain, the office of doorkeeper was that of the person who guarded the ruler from his entourage and from the common people. He was the liaison officer between the ruler and the *wazirs* and lower officials. In the Umayyad dynasty the office of doorkeeper was an extremely high position." (*The Muqaddimah*, tr. by Franz Rosenthal, II, 14). Almanzor used the post to make himself dictator and then bequeathed it and all of his accumulated powers to his sons. The petty kings later used the title to justify their exercise of public authority.

The other important officers of the central administration had the title of *wazir* or vizier. Ibn Khaldun described their functions as follows:

The Umayyads in Spain at first continued to use the name *wazir* in its original meaning. Later they subdivided the functions of the *wazir* into several parts. For each function they appointed a special *wazir*. They appointed a *wazir* to furnish an accounting of government finances; another for official correspondence; another to take care of the needs of those who had suffered wrongs; and another to supervise the situation of people in the border regions. A special house was prepared for all these *wazirs*. There they sat upon carpets spread out for them and executed the orders of the ruler, each in the field entrusted to him. [*The Muqaddimah*, II, 12]

The title, without reference to specific functions, but purely as a mark of dignity, eventually was given to many public officials, and carried with it a state pension which the caliph sometimes doubled; in such instances the *wazir* was said to be the holder of two wazirates (*dhu-l-wizaratayn*).

The chief department of state was the chancery or secretariat (*kitaba*), headed by a *wazir* with the title *katib* or secretary. In the tenth century Abd al-Rahman III established four principal offices within the chancery, each under the direction of a *wazir*; one was concerned with correspondence from provincial officials, another with correspondence from the frontiers, marches, and coasts; a third supervised the execution of administrative decrees approved by the caliph, and the fourth received petitions and forwarded them to the proper officials for processing. The caliph also had a personal secretary at his service. Chancery documents were stylized pieces of literature, written in rhythmic prose and full of citations from the Koran, indicating that the secretaries were men of high culture. A regular postal service, making extensive use of carrier pigeons, assured prompt communication between the central government and the provinces.

An equally important pillar of the state, as Ibn Khaldun called it, was the treasury (*khizanat al-mal*). Although the treasurers (*khazin al-mal, sahib al-makhzan*) were usually drawn from the Arab aristocracy of Córdoba, many of the lesser functionaries were Mozarabs and Jews. The public revenues derived from imposts, direct and indirect, legal and extralegal, were administered separately from the private revenues of the caliph, and will be discussed below.

In addition to the officers of public administration there were numerous persons attached to the royal household who enjoyed varying degrees of influence with the caliph. Many were slaves of northern European origin who constituted the royal bodyguard or served in other domestic capacities. They were often given their freedom and endowed with great estates; because of their wealth and influence they were held in contempt by the Arab aristocracy. The more important household officers were the constable responsible for the royal stables, the chief of the kitchens, the custodian of the palace and other buildings, and the falconer.

Following the conquest, al-Andalus was divided into five administrative areas roughly corresponding to Andalusia, Galicia and Lusitania, Castile and León, Aragon and Catalonia, and Septimania. By the middle of the tenth century, however, provincial administration had been reorganized more efficiently. At least twenty-one provinces, probably identical with those of the Visigothic kingdom, existed; many of them later formed the petty kingdoms of the eleventh century. The caliph appointed and removed provincial governors (wali) at his pleasure. Appointing a governor, al-Hakam II instructed him in these words recorded by Isa al-Razi: "Ask God's help; temper your authority with mercy; don't be ambitious; don't favor certain persons to the prejudice of others. . . . The caliph has decided to entrust you with command of half the province of Rayyu, in his eyes, one of the most important in all al-Andalus, on account of its seacoast, its territory, its tributes and estates. Watch what sort of servant you prove to be" (Anales palatinos, 62). The governor usually had his residence in the chief provincial town and maintained a court with secretarial and financial departments in imitation of the royal court.

Given the chronic state of war with the Christian states, the northern frontiers (thaghr) were subject to military governors (qaid) endowed with broad powers. At first there were three frontier districts or marches, namely, the Upper Frontier, including Catalonia and Aragon, with its capital at Zaragoza, the Middle Frontier extending along the borders of León and Castile with its headquarters at Medinaceli, and the Lower Frontier centered at Toledo and bordering Galicia and Portugal. In the tenth century the Lower and Middle Frontiers were merged as one. The great distances separating the marches from Córdoba enabled the governors to rule as autonomous lords and at times to break entirely with the central government. The governors of Zaragoza especially enjoyed a high degree of independence and were able to transform their dominions in the Ebro valley into a principality transmissible to their heirs.

The municipalities of al-Andalus lacked any true self-government, since the central administration controlled the appointment and removal of municipal officials. From time to time frontier towns such as Toledo were able to shake off, if only temporarily, the domination of the central government. The duties of the principal municipal functionaries will be described below, in connection with the administration of justice.

The Law and the Administration of Justice

In the Muslim community, law was the will of God, immutable and permanently binding on the faithful. Failure to obey the law was tantamount to defiance of God himself and was punishable both in this life and in the life to come. God revealed the law explicitly in the Koran, implicitly in the customs or *sunna* and in the consensus of the community (*ijma*). The Koran was the primary and infallible source of law, containing the word of God as revealed directly to Muhammad. As juridical precepts were scattered throughout the text, scholars were faced with the task of trying to present the law in a more systematic fashion. Muslims believed that Muhammad's conduct, inspired by God, could serve as a model for others, and for this reason his companions had preserved and transmitted by word of mouth traditions (*hadith*) concerning his habits and behavior (*sunna*). The consensus of the community (*ijma*) concerning specific observances was regarded as a diffused revelation from God and as a legitimate source of law. Given the divine promise revealed in the Koran that the community would never fall into error, the possibility of an heretical consensus was ruled out, and consensus itself became an assurance of infallibility.

The task of the jurists (*al-faqih*) was to determine the juridical principles contained in the Koran, the *sunna*, and the consensus. Jurisprudence (*fiqh*), as Ibn Khaldun put it, consisted in "the knowledge of the classification of the laws of God which concern the actions of all responsible Muslims, as obligatory, forbidden, recommendable, disliked or permissible" (*The Muqaddimah*, III, 3). The jurists had to set forth the meaning of texts, establish the authenticity of traditions, resolve contradictions, and determine the applicability of specific rules of law. They ordinarily held that legal texts should be interpreted literally; but when the texts failed to cover specific points of law, the jurists attempted to resolve difficulties by means of analogy.

By the middle of the ninth century four schools of law had come to be acknowledged as orthodox. It was during the reign of Hisham I that the doctrine of the Malikite school, founded by Malik ibn Anas (d. 795), was introduced into Spain and gained official recognition. Thenceforward Malikite jurists dominated the religio-legal thought of al-Andalus, upholding a strict orthodoxy and dogmatic unity. So successful were they in suppressing dissident views and hounding dissenters out of the kingdom that al-Andalus never had to endure the religious quarrels so prevalent in other parts of the Muslim world.

The caliph, as supreme judge, was primarily responsible for the administration of justice. The Umayyad emirs were accustomed to hold weekly audiences at which anyone could seek justice, but Abd al-Rahman III dispensed with this practice. In matters concerning the revealed law of God, the most important judge was the *qadi* of Córdoba. Al-Khushani's tenth-century *History of the Judges of Córdoba* contains anecdotal biographies, descriptions of cases presented to them and their judgments. He summarized the importance of the office in these words:

Inasmuch as the post of judge of Córdoba became the highest dignity in the empire, after that of the caliph, . . . the responsibilities of this authority before God have made it a very serious post, a terrible, imposing task. . . . Some men were fearful that something unfortunate would happen to them in the afterlife and they feared God, because they had to answer not only for their personal conduct in their own affairs, but also in other matters entrusted to their direction. There were in al-Andalus, especially in the capital, men distinguished for their wisdom and piety, to whom the office of judge was offered, but they did not wish to be appointed; though urged, they were unwilling to accept, solely for fear of God, considering the consequences that their souls might suffer in the future life. [*Historia de los jueces de Córdoba*, 6]

The *qadi* usually was a learned jurist of the Malikite school, a man of high moral standing and simple habits, who insisted on retaining his freedom to give judgment in accordance with the law and without interference from the sovereign. The terms of a commission given to one of the earliest judges illustrate the qualities expected in a *qadi*:

He should take God's Book and the *sunna* of the Prophet Muhammad . . . as guides whose light will direct him on the right road. . . . In mediating between litigants he should examine, question and inquire by the most skillful and well-intentioned methods and listen attentively to the testimony of witnesses and carefully attend to the arguments and proofs presented by each party. . . . His ministers, counselors and aides should be . . . men wise in religious law. . . . The bailiffs and attendants who help him in fulfilling his judicial functions should be honest and continent men . . . totally divorced from corruption, because whatever they do will be imputed to the judge they serve and the people will cast blame on the judge. . . . When the judge has reached thorough certainty and is sure of the truth, he ought not to delay his judgment. [*Historia de los jueces de Córdoba*, 7–8]

The *qadi* was a judge of last resort in questions relating to wills, inheritances, divorces, the rights and property of orphans, and so on. Attended by assessors, doorkeepers, and scribes, he held court daily in a corner of the mosque, where litigants appeared in person or through their representatives to plead their cases and to present documents or witnesses whose testimony was recorded by scribes. Before passing judgment he might consult with legal scholars who issued written opinions (*fatwa*) based upon precedent, declaring what was licit according to divine law. In effect, they attempted to reconcile legal principles and the public good. Ibn Sahl (d. 1093) compiled a collection of *fatwa* which served as models for future judicial decisions. Just as the *qadi* could not compel anyone to appear before him, he did not always have an effective means of enforcing his decisions. His moral prestige was so high, however, that litigants seldom refused to abide by the judgment rendered.

In the chief provincial towns justice was dispensed in the same manner. Each provincial *qadi* originally received a delegation of authority from the *qadi* of Córdoba, but by the tenth century he was appointed directly by the caliph. The decisions of the provincial judges were final and could not be appealed to another court, but the *qadi* of Córdoba occasionally reviewed cases already decided by other judges.

Since the *qadi*'s jurisdiction was limited to those types of litigation of which the revealed law took cognizance, other judges administered justice of a more secular character. Among them was the *sahib al-mazalim* or lord of injustices, who was authorized to correct abuses of power and spoliation of the people by public officials. Julián Ribera suggested that the *justicia mayor* of Aragon who figures so prominently in the thirteenth and fourteenth centuries was a Christian imitation of the lord of injustices. The *sahib al-shurta* or prefect of police was responsible for the punishment of crime. With the coercive power of the government at his disposal he could use methods not available to the *qadi* and could compel people to appear before him and could use whatever measures might be necessary to repress violence and disorder. The functions of the *sahib al-madina* or lord of the city appear to have been similar to those of the prefect of police, though the scanty evidence at hand indicates that these were two distinct offices. The responsibility of preventing and punishing fraudulent practices in commercial transactions fell to the *sahib al-suq* (also called *muhtasib*) or inspector of markets. It should be noted, finally, that Mozarabs and Jews had their own magistrates and their own law, though in cases between Muslims and non-Muslims, Muslim courts had jurisdiction.

The Financial Administration

The Umayyad financial administration resembled that of the eastern caliphs. The public treasury, derived chiefly from tolls, tributes, imposts on Christians and Jews, and such, was kept in the *alcazar* of Córdoba and was administered separately from the private treasury of the sovereign (*khassiyat bayt al-mal*). In the mosque, the *qadi* guarded the revenues of foundations (*waqf*) established by devout Muslims for the upkeep of mosques and other public buildings and for charitable purposes. Only in exceptional circumstances could he allow portions of this money, the treasury of the Muslim community (*bayt al-mal al-muslimin*), to be used by the sovereign.

Provincial governors were responsible for the collection of tributes and imposts, and after paying their own expenses they forwarded the surplus to Córdoba. The *khazin al-mal* or secretary of the treasury disbursed these sums to cover expenses connected with the maintenance of the court, the army, the civil administration, public works, and so forth. Various estimates indicate that public revenues rose from about 600,000 gold *dinars* under al-Hakam I, to 1,000,000 under Abd al-Rahman II, to 6,245,000 under Abd al-Rahman III. Of the last total, 5,480,000 *dinars* were received as land tax and the rest as indirect taxes. The money was divided into three parts, for the payment of salaries and maintenance of the army, the upkeep of public buildings, and the needs of the caliph. The caliph is also reported to have had 20,000,000 *dinars* in his treasury, a sum doubled by his son.

The sources of royal income may be classified as legal or extralegal, depending on whether they were authorized by divine law. From time to time popular protests against illegal taxes reached the point of riot and rebellion, and any ruler seeking to curry favor with the populace had only to abolish or reduce illegal taxes. For example, in remitting a portion of the tax due, al-Hakam II ordered that this should be widely publicized, "so that the people might know the favor he bestowed on them, and that the ignorant, as well as the wise, the stupid, as well as the clever, should be equally well-informed."

Imposts authorized by divine law included the alms contributed by all Muslims to the community. Though originally a voluntary act, alms-giving became a fixed obligation and a major source of public revenue, consisting of *zakat*, a tax of about 10 percent levied on capital goods such as animals, merchandise, gold and silver, and so on. In addition,

Muslims paid a land tax (*ushr*) varying between 10 percent and 20 percent. Christians and Jews living under Muslim rule were required to pay a personal tribute (*jizya*) as a sign of protection; this sum was levied monthly on all adult, able-bodied freemen, and varied according to their social condition. Women, children, the crippled, the blind, and the aged were exempt, as were monks, beggars, and slaves. Christians and Jews who had capitulated to Islam were obligated to pay a land tax (*kharaj*) usually of about 20 percent of the value of the harvest. If the proprietor became a Muslim, the land tax was still owed to the government. The lands of those subjugated by force were treated as the booty of war, and the sovereign's share of the booty both in land and goods amounted to one-fifth (*khums*). Export and import duties and market tolls were also levied at variable rates. Unclaimed property, estates without heirs, the confiscated property of rebels or apostates, flotsam and jetsam, and the profits of coinage were additional sources of income.

Illegal imposts (*magharim*), such as poll taxes collected monthly from Muslims, sales taxes (*qabala*), and such, were levied frequently. The obligation to give hospitality to the sovereign was also transformed into an annual tax. From time to time tributes (*jibaya*) were received from the Christian rulers, the semi-independent Muslim princes of the frontier provinces, or from the Berbers of North Africa. The caliph also received a goodly income from his private estates (*mustakhlas*), which were cultivated by rent-paying peasants. The royal domain was often augmented by the confiscation of property belonging to the nobility or others who incurred the monarch's wrath. The income from crown lands was administered separately from the public revenues by the *sahib al-diya*.

The Military Organization

The nearly constant state of war existing between al-Andalus and the Christian states necessitated the development of an efficient military establishment, but this was not easy to accomplish. The Umayyad army was formed essentially by contingents from districts owing military service, by mercenaries, and by religious volunteers, but the usefulness of each of these groups varied according to time and circumstances.

Early in the eighth century the Syrian *junds* were authorized to settle in certain districts of al-Andalus where they had the usufruct of agricultural properties on condition that they perform military service when summoned. These rights and obligations passed by hereditary right to their descendants. By the tenth century the term *jund* was applied to others who owed military service, no matter what their origin. The names of able-bodied freemen, Arabs, Berbers, *muwalladun* were inscribed on provincial registers so that they could be summoned when needed. All Muslims had the religious duty of fighting in defense of the faith, though in practice no attempt was made to compel all of them to serve. Christians and Jews were ordinarily forbidden to bear arms, but in practice many Christians were hired as mercenaries. Although statistics given by the historian Ibn Hayyan indicate that in 863 Muhammad I could summon about 22,000 horsemen, the effectiveness of conscripted troops was always uneven.

A corps of professional soldiers paid regular wages proved to be a more valuable instrument of war. Al-Hakam I was the first to recruit large numbers of mercenaries, including Berbers and Sudanese Negroes as well as Christians from northern Spain and even from beyond the Pyrenees. His palatine guard of 3,000 horse and 2,000 foot became a permanent institution in Muslim Spain. Although many of the guardsmen were slaves or freedmen, they came to enjoy an exceptional political and military importance, and were bitterly hated by the populace.

Participation in the holy war was considered an act of great religious merit, and the opportunities in Spain were almost limitless. Al-Himyari described al-Andalus as "a territory where one fights for the faith and a permanent place of the *ribat*." The Umayyad armies always included religious volunteers, men who hoped to share in the booty of war but also to gain entrance into paradise through service in defense of Islam. For example, Isa al-Razi mentioned that in 975, "bands of volunteer soldiers from the citizenry of Córdoba set out for the Upper Frontier. . . . Day after day, desiring to participate in the holy war, they set out. . . . The government was astonished by the bravery of the volunteers, who were not obliged to do this, and praised their holy courage." When not engaged in battle the volunteers (*al-murabitun*) were stationed in frontier garrisons (*ribat*) where they adhered to an ascetic regimen. Place names such as La Rábida are derived from these garrisons. Although Asín and Castro have stated that the Christian military religious orders, which came into existence in the twelfth century, were simply an imitation of the military ascetic organizations of the *ribat*, the Christian tradition of monasticism and chivalry was the primary source from which the orders sprang.

In the late tenth century, Almanzor, distrusting both the palatine guards and the Arab aristocracy, reorganized the army by abolishing the tribal units on which it was based. In the new army, men were grouped together without regard for ties of family or patron. Many Muslims were exempted from military service in return for a monetary payment. With these sums Almanzor began an intensive recruitment of Berbers from North Africa and, to a much lesser degree, of Christians. The Berberization of the army transformed it almost exclusively into a cavalry force. Although these barbarians were staunchly loyal to Almanzor, they had much to do with the destruction of the caliphate and the plundering of palaces and towns after his death.

There is little precise information concerning the internal division of the army during the Umayyad era. Descriptions of military reviews held during the reign of al-Hakam II mention Cordoban infantry armed with shields and lances, a force numbering about 16,000, together with mounted light cavalry, mounted Negro archers wearing white capes, heavy cavalry, and other regiments, all distinguished by their banners decorated with lions, dragons, leopards, and eagles. The technical military vocabulary of the Spanish Muslims was very largely adopted by the Christians. Among the numerous examples that may be cited are words such as *alcaide* from *al-qaid*, a commander of troops, *aceifa* from *al-saifa*, the annual expeditions usually undertaken in the summer; *atalaya* from *al-talia*, a watchtower; *almirante* from *amir al-bahr*, lord of the sea or admiral. Arabic terminology for fortifications also passed into Castilian, and there are many place names such as Alcalá de Henares, Alcalá de Guadaira, Calatayud, Calahorra, Calatrava, and so forth, which derive from Muslim strongholds.

The naval raids of the Norsemen and of the Fatimids in the ninth and tenth centuries compelled the Umayyads to organize their coastal defenses and to construct fleets of warships. Abd al-Rahman III is reported to have had a fleet of about 200 ships at his disposal. The principal naval base during the Umayyad era was located at Pechina near Almería, but there were important shipyards for the construction and repair of vessels at Seville, Alicante, Algeciras, and other ports.

The Social Structure

Early in the eighth century, when the fusion of Visigoths and Hispano-Romans seemed to be reaching maturity, the Muslim invasion injected new racial strains as well as new religious beliefs into the life of the peninsula. To the indigenous elements were added indeterminate numbers of Arabs, Berbers, Syrians, and other orientals, united solely by their common adherence to Islam. Once again racial, linguistic, legal, and religious barriers were raised between the conquerors and the conquered.

Lévi-Provençal has remarked that any attempt to calculate the size of the population of Muslim Spain is in vain, due to a lack of sufficient statistical data. On the other hand, Vicens Vives estimated the total population of the peninsula at the time of the conquest at 6,000,000 and argued that the general prosperity during the Umayyad era encouraged a steady increase in numbers. During the tenth century al-Andalus was probably one of the most densely populated regions in Europe; settlements tended to be concentrated in the most fertile zones, that is, in the valleys of the Ebro and the Guadalquivir and in the Levant.

All Muslims theoretically were equal before God and the law, but numerous differences, among them racial origin, wealth, and learning, served to establish social classes. The Arabs, though few in number, constituted the military and landed aristocracy (khassa), owning the best lands and filling the chief positions in the administration. Probably no more than 18,000 Arabs entered the peninsula in the first wave of invasion; thereafter relatives and dependents of the Umayyads settled in al-Andalus, but the number of Arabs did not increase appreciably. In the first century of Muslim rule their ancient tribal rivalries contributed greatly to the disorder of the realm. Several Arab families established semi-independent lordships until Abd al-Rahman III succeeded in suppressing them and reaffirming the sovereign power. From then on, the political and military influence of the Arab aristocracy was held in check, especially as the caliph encouraged the development of a new nobility of service.

The mass of ordinary freemen (amma) were Berbers, muwalladun, and Mozarabs, settled as merchants and artisans in the towns or as farmers and shepherds in rural areas. The Berbers were the most numerous of all the newcomers to the peninsula. About 12,000 crossed the straits with Tariq, but there was a steady influx from Morocco during the centuries of Muslim predominance. Most were settled along the frontiers of Castile and Extremadura where they formed a kind of rural proletariat, devoted chiefly to sheep-raising. In the tenth century many others were recruited in Morocco for service in the army.

The descendants of the Visigoths and Hispano-Romans constituted the largest element in the population. Of those who submitted willingly or unwillingly to Muslim rule, the majority eventually abandoned the Christian religion in favor of Islam. Their motives were probably more material than spiritual, for, as Muslims, they were not subject to the payment of the poll tax. Yet conversion did not automatically guarantee them full equality with other Muslims. In general the *muwalladun* formed the humbler classes in society, the small merchants, artisans, and farmers. Their assimilation into Muslim society was rather superficial, and while they learned Arabic, they continued to speak a Romance derivative of Latin. Many retained their Christian family names, though others provided themselves with Arabic genealogies and eventually intermarried with the Arabs. On the whole, the *muwalladun*, occupying a lower social rank, tended to be excluded from participation in government on the higher levels. In protest, many of them revolted in the ninth century, and some even returned to the religion of their forefathers, though reconversions were not typical. Abd al-Rahman III had the political wisdom to see the necessity of integrating them fully into Muslim society and of encouraging their efforts to achieve wealth and position. By reconciling them to the regime, he hastened the process of cultural assimilation and facilitated their many contributions to the civilization of al-Andalus in the eleventh century.

An indeterminate number of Mozarabs, forming important communities in Toledo, Seville, Córdoba, and Mérida and probably also in certain rural areas, remained faithful to Christianity, continuing to worship in their churches and to be governed according to the *Liber Judiciorum* by their own magistrates: the *comes* or *defensor*, who served as their representative before the caliph; the *censor* who adjudicated their lawsuits; and the *exceptor* who collected their tributes. They paid tribute monthly, though women, children, monks, beggars, and the blind, and infirm were exempt. Gradually they were forced to live in special quarters of the cities, usually outside the walls. At the time of the conquest the general level of culture among them was probably higher than that of the Arabs and certainly of the Berbers, but in the course of time they succumbed to the attractions of a more refined Arabic society, adopting Arabic names and customs as well as the language of the conquerors. In the century of the caliphate, after the martyrs' movement subsided, they led a rather tranquil existence, and many found employment at court. Even so, throughout the Umayyad era there was a steady emigration of Mozarabs to the Christian states.

The status of the Jewish community was similar to that of the Mozarabs, though there is little information concerning the Jews until the eleventh century. Most, probably, were descended from Jews settled in the peninsula before the conquest, though their numbers were undoubtedly increased through immigration. Few of them converted to Islam. They enjoyed freedom of worship and the right to live according to their own law and customs; their chief rabbi was responsible to the ruler for the community. In addition to Hebrew, they also spoke Arabic and the popular Romance. Some, such as Hasday ibn Shaprut, attained prominence in the caliph's service. While living in their own quarters in the towns, they enjoyed considerable freedom and prospered economically and were particularly active in the slave trade. Later under Almoravid rule, they were persecuted, along with the Mozarabs, and fled to Christian Spain or to other parts of the Muslim world.

The population of al-Andalus included an indefinite, though substantial, number of slaves. Among them were some of Hispanic origin, tillers of the soil who had not embraced Islam, though once they did so they obtained their freedom. The constant state of war with Christian Spain and the flourishing slave trade in the Mediterranean kept al-Andalus well supplied with slaves. These included Negroes from the Sudan and others of European origin (saqaliba) : Slavs, Franks, Germans, Norsemen, and so on. Spain was not only a major market for slaves but also a base from which they were shipped elsewhere in the Muslim world. Owners did not possess the power of life and death over them, nor could they inflict excessive punishments; it was considered good practice to treat one's slaves well and even to liberate them after faithful service. On one occasion al-Hakam II freed more than 100 slaves, both male and female; some received their freedom immediately, while for others it was postponed, in some instances until after his death; but all received appropriate documents declaring their free status. In the tenth century freedmen (mawla, mawali) formed a very large class in Muslim society; they continued to be bound by moral ties to their former masters and could claim their protection. Slaves in the service of the caliph were both numerous (it is estimated that there were about 14,000 in Córdoba in the tenth century) and influential. Some, as eunuchs, guarded the harem; others served in administrative offices or in the royal guard. They usually became Muslims and were freed by the caliph, to whom they were fiercely loyal. Under Abd al-Rahman III they formed a new military and bureaucratic nobility, controlling the direction of governmental policy for a century. As Ibn Idhari noted they "served in the palace, but they ruled in it like lords." Their arrogance and wealth aroused the hostility of all, but especially of the Arab aristocracy who had lost their former influence and authority. The slaves also played an important role in the collapse of the caliphate and in the organization of the *taifas*.

With the exception of the Mozarabs and Jews, the diverse ethnic groups in al-Andalus were gradually assimilated to one another by their acceptance of Islam with its laws and customs touching almost every aspect of public and private behavior. While conscious of belonging to a world-wide Muslim community, the Spanish Muslims were also inspired by sentiments of a more particular character, and were bound together by common aspirations and attitudes, an attachment to their ancestral traditions, and an affectionate regard for their homeland, al-Andalus, the *Hispania* of their forebears.

The Economy

The prosperity of al-Andalus contrasted sharply with the economic conditions prevalent in Christian Europe. During the last centuries of the Roman Empire, commerce and industry in western Europe declined, and the Germanic invasions tended to accelerate this development. The Belgian historian Henri Pirenne argued that the expansion of Islam was the fundamental cause of the decline of the western European economy, disrupting trade and industry, ruining the cities, eliminating the mercantile classes, causing the disappearance of money as the ordinary medium of exchange. Few historians today would accept Pirenne's thesis in its totality, but in any case the greater part of Spain fell under Muslim rule and participated actively in the economic life of the Muslim world. In the century of the caliphate, due to the pacification of the countryside, al-Andalus attained the height of its prosperity. Its cities gained renown as centers of commerce and industry, populated by merchants who carried on an extensive trade with Africa, the Near East, and Byzantium, and by artisans who produced goods of fine workmanship for the domestic market and for export. Gold and silver coins circulated throughout the country, and the agricultural regions shared in the general prosperity.

Agriculture was the backbone of the economy. When the Muslims invaded the peninsula, they seized the lands belonging to the Visigothic state, to the church, and to individuals who had fled or were killed. Those who were subjugated by force were either dispossessed or allowed to remain in precarious occupation of their lands, subject to the payment of tribute. Other proprietors capitulated in order to retain their property on condition of paying tribute. Of the lands taken, one-fifth (khums) was reserved for the state and cultivated by tenants, some of whom were perhaps captives taken in war. The remaining four-fifths of the landed booty was distributed among the victorious soldiers. Some, especially the Arabs, obtained possession of latifundia in the regions of Andalusia, the Levant, Toledo, and the Ebro valley. Some latifundia were probably broken up and parceled out among the Berbers and the natives, but small holdings of this sort were found chiefly in the northern and central areas.

Sharecropping, a system which the Muslims inherited from the Byzantine empire and introduced into Spain, appears to have been the normal means of exploiting the latifundia. Contracts between the owner and the sharecroppers, who usually lived in small villages (al-daya, aldea) near the lands to be cultivated, often ran for many years. Each supplied an equal amount of seed, for instance, of wheat or barley, but the sharecropper (munasif, shariq) in return for one-half of the harvest assumed the task of plowing, sowing, and harvesting, using his own work animals and tools; he might also be required to give the owner a lamb or a sheep during the year. Sometimes he was entitled to only a quarter of the harvest; on other occasions he was supplied with work animals and three-quarters of the seed to be sown and so received a smaller proportion of the harvest.

Among the most important agricultural products were wheat and barley, usually cultivated in the dry zones of Andalusia and the Levant. The wheat supply seems to have been just sufficient for domestic needs, but even then wheat was imported from North Africa, and from time to time famine occurred. Commenting on the famine of 915, one Muslim chronicler wrote: "The misery of the people reached unheard-of extremes and disease and plague took such hold upon the needy that it became impossible to bury all the dead." Olive and fruit trees (figs, oranges, lemons) grew in abundance, especially in the districts of Seville, Córdoba, Jaén, and Málaga. Olive oil (*al-zayt, aceite, al-zaytuna, aceituna*) was exported to Morocco and the east. Vineyards were also extensive, and even though the Koran prohibited the use of wine, indulgence was so widespread that al-Hakam II proposed uprooting the vines, but this order was not carried out. In the eastern coastal regions melons, beans, lettuce, sugar cane (*al-sukkar, azúcar*) and rice (*al-ruz, arroz*) were grown; linen was cultivated in the valley of the Genil, cotton in the region south of Seville, and silk in the districts of Granada and Murcia. Madder and woad were raised for purposes of dyeing cloth.

In addition to the introduction of exotic plants, such as rice and sugar cane and different vegetable species, the Muslims also improved the irrigation systems, rendering fertile the *vegas* of Andalusia and the *huertas* of Murcia and Valencia. The system of control and inspection established by the Muslims has influenced irrigation in Valencia and Murcia to the present day, and numerous technical terms have passed into modern Spanish, such as *noria* from *naura*, a water wheel, *acequia* from *al-saqiya*, a canal, *aljibe* from *al jub*, a well. In these areas the cultivators of the soil usually lived on small farms (*al-qarya, alquería*).

The breeding of livestock and the exploitation of mineral resources also contributed to the prosperity of al-Andalus. The Berbers were particularly active in raising sheep, though it is not known whether they introduced into Spain the system of *transhumancia*, that is, the annual migrations of sheep from north to south. Work animals such as asses and oxen were raised, and horses were especially valued because they gave a man prestige and served to distinguish him from the simple foot soldier. Spain was famed for its mineral wealth in ancient times. Gold was found in the beds of rivers, iron in the vicinity of Huelva and Constantina, lead near Cabra and mercury at Almadén, the mine par excellence (*al-madin*), the richest source of mercury in western Europe. In the Roman and Visigothic eras, mines were considered the property of the state, but under Umayyad rule they appear to have been exploited by private persons.

In contrast to northern Europe, where urban centers declined in economic importance following the Germanic invasions and the expansion of Islam, the cities of al-Andalus increased in population and wealth. Torres Balbás has estimated the population of the major cities of al-Andalus as follows: Córdoba, about 250,000; Toledo, 37,000; Zaragoza, 17,000; Valencia, 15,500; and Málaga, 15,000. These old Roman towns had been declining in the Visigothic era, but now, because of the development of industry and commerce, they took on new life and surpassed in size most of the cities of Christian Europe. An important textile industry supplied wool, linen, and silk to both the domestic and foreign markets. Abd al-Rahman II established a silk factory at Córdoba; leather production was also centered in the capital. Toledo was famed for its arms and armor, and Játiva was the center for the manufacture of paper which was exported throughout the Muslim world. In the middle of the ninth century Abbas ibn Firnas discovered the secret of making glass. Al-Andalus also was noted for fine metalwork, especially in gold and silver.

Men engaged in the same craft usually lived together in the small narrow streets near the mosque and the town market (al-suq, zoco). Their associations were scrutinized by the government, and one of the more distinguished artisans ordinarily was held responsible for the activities of his fellows. The sahib al-suq (zabazoque, al-muhtasib, al-motacén) or inspector of the market, saw to it that fair prices were charged, that honest weights and measures were used, and that disputes were settled peaceably. On one occasion a local cheat was paraded through the principal market of Córdoba while a herald cried out before him: "This is Ibn Umar, a thief and a criminal, who, by his cheating, consumes the wealth of Muslims. Recognize him so you may avoid him."

Near the main gate of the town merchants established their warehouses (al-funduq, alfondiga, alhondiga), filled with foreign and domestic products. A flourishing commerce was carried on within al-Andalus over the old Roman roads linking the principal towns. Following the ravages of the Norsemen, the Umayyads built a fleet for coastal defense and overseas trade. Pechina near Almería, the chief port on the south-eastern coast, was visited frequently by ships from Syria, Egypt, and Byzantium, while Seville maintained contacts chiefly with Moroccan ports. Customs duties collected at these ports constituted a major source of revenue in the tenth century. Al-Andalus exported textiles, olive oil, arms, and slaves, and imported spices and other luxuries as well as slaves. In a letter purportedly written by Hasday ibn Shaprut, a Jew in the caliph's service, one finds this description of the trade relations of Umayyad Spain:

Merchants come from the ends of the earth, and traders from all the countries and far away islands stream into it. . . . They bring spice and precious stone and royal merchandise and noble trade and all the precious goods of Egypt. . . . From year to year our purchases from the merchants of Mesopotamia and the traders of Khorasan, and the merchants of Egypt, and the merchants of India reach 100,000 *dinars*. This is the amount of our purchases year after year and it is only so because of the great number of merchants who come from all the lands and their islands. [Howard Adelson, *Medieval Commerce* (Princeton, 1962), 139–140]

Money was the ordinary medium of exchange in al-Andalus. Besides Roman and Visigothic coins, the first Muslim governors put into circulation newly minted gold and silver coins. Shortly after his entrance into Toledo in 713, Musa coined money with a Latin inscription testifying to the oneness of the Deity: *In nomine Dei non Deus nisi Deus solus non Deus alius*. The minting of the gold *dinar*, a coin based on the Byzantine *solidus*, was a right reserved to the caliph; therefore the independent Umayyad emirs ceased to issue the *dinar*. When Abd al-Rahman III assumed the title of caliph, he also reorganized the mint (*dar al-siqqa*, ceca) at Córdoba under the direction of the *sahib al-siqqa*. There were at least fourteen mints throughout the kingdom. In addition to silver coins, such as the *dirham* valued at one-tenth of a *dinar*, the caliph also minted gold *dinars* bearing an inscription in praise of Allah, the ruler's name, and the place and date of minting. In accordance with the prohibitions of the Koran no images appeared on the coins. Ibn Hawqal reported that the caliph minted 200,000 *dinars* each year. Many of these coins found their way across the frontiers, where they were imitated by the Christians in the eleventh century.

The imitation of Muslim coinage is only one example of the impact of al-Andalus upon the economy of the Christian states. Although commercial contacts between the Muslim and Christian worlds were limited, the more advanced agricultural and industrial techniques of al-Andalus were brought to Christian Spain especially by Mozarab *emigrés*. The numerous loan words which have passed into Castilian, such as those referring to agricultural products, weights, and measures (*qafiz, cahiz*), markets, tariffs (*tarifa*), and customs duties (*al-diwan, aduana*), are suggestive of the extent of Muslim influence.

Literature and Learning

As the Muslims extended their rule over the provinces of the Byzantine and Persian empires in the seventh and eighth centuries, they came into contact with the philosophical and scientific thought of the ancient civilizations. Gradually assimilating the wisdom of the past, they developed a distinctive culture which, under the patronage of the caliphs, flourished at Baghdad and eventually spread throughout the Muslim world. The first Muslims to enter Spain, however, were rude barbarians from the deserts of Arabia and the mountains of Morocco whose contact with Greco-Roman civilization was still minimal. During the first century and a half of their domination in al-Andalus, civil wars and rebellions, the illiteracy of the masses, and the stringent thought-control of the Malikite jurists did not provide a suitable environment for the flowering of literature and learning.

By the middle of the ninth century, however, Córdoba became the center of a potentially significant civilization. In large measure this was due to the patronage extended by the Emir Abd al-Rahman II to scholars and poets. A highly cultured man in his own right, he established a brilliant court and embellished the capital by erecting fine mosques, palaces, bridges, and gardens; he also developed a library that served many scholars in the following century. The most influential courtier was the musician Ziryab, a Persian, who had held high position in the court at Baghdad, but who, on falling out of favor, had emigrated to the west. Skillfully avoiding the usual palace intrigues, he became the arbiter of good taste and fashion, introducing eastern refinements in dress, hair styles, table manners, and social intercourse. The emir doted on him and loved to hear him sing and discourse on history, poetry, art, and science.

During the century of the caliphate, Córdoba became a very real rival to Baghdad as the cultural center of the Muslim world. The Caliphs Abd al-Rahman III and al-Hakam II were learned men who extended a cordial reception to scholars from Europe, Africa, and Asia. Al-Hakam was probably the best-educated of the caliphs and even in the midst of his public duties displayed an inclination for study and meditation. His court was filled with philosophers, poets, grammarians, and artists, and his library is said to have included as many as 400,000 volumes. Nowhere in western Europe was a similar collection to be found. His concern for learning is also revealed by his decree ordering that royal rents from shops in the Cordoban market be assigned to a pious foundation to support teachers of poor children. "This foundation was of great utility and enormous merit, for, thanks to it, God made heirs of the Koran persons whose parents were not in a position to do so." The Cordoban aristocracy imitated the caliph and vied with one another in acquiring books and extending their patronage to learned men. Almanzor, after securing supreme power in the state, unhappily purged the royal library of books considered unorthodox and immoral, hoping in this way to win favor with the Malikite jurists. Even so, he was a well-educated man who was said to go into battle accompanied by forty poets charged with the responsibility of recording his triumphs in verse. In spite of the breakdown of government after 1031, the Umayyad tradition was continued by the *taifas*, and their age became the golden age of Islamic culture in Spain.

Probably the majority of people in al-Andalus, especially in the cities, were bilingual. The Latin tongue and its Romance derivative survived among the Mozarabs, but it was also known and used by the Arabs, Jews, and *muwalladun*. Arabic, of course, was the official language of government and of literature, and the preferred instrument of expression of the poets, the philosophers, and the historians.

The people of al-Andalus had great admiration for poetic skill. Emirs and caliphs are reported to have written verses and to have cultivated and patronized poets whose praise they coveted. Poets, then as now, could make a man appear more virtuous and honorable than he was or destroy him with a few biting lines. Al-Hakam II, according to Isa al-Razi, ordered the arrest of a "group of insolent Cordobans who . . . were given to mocking talk . . . to speaking evil of the caliph, to ruining the reputation of people and to spreading their maledictions abroad by means of the poems they composed." García Gómez has noted that much of the poetry of the Spanish Muslims is delightful and charming and full of imagery, but it generally suffers from an extreme intellectual poverty. Poets celebrated royal victories and public assemblies and sang of love and beauty and nature, but they failed to develop narrative or epic poetry. From the east the Arabs brought to Spain the classical lyric in the verse form known as *qasida*, which in its original state celebrated a memorable event in the life of the Bedouin in the desert. Hispano-Arabic poetry of the caliphal age tended, however, to reflect a more refined and aristocratic way of life. Its themes were treated with sensuous feeling, and there is an ethereal and somewhat unreal quality to it. Among many examples the following lines from the pen of Ibn Abd

Rabbihi (d. 940), one of the greatest poets of the caliphal era, can be cited:

> Oh gazelle's eyes, beguiling,
> Oh sister of the moon, in shining,
> Whenever your eyes look toward me
> From behind veils and curtains
> I lay my hand on my heart
> For fear that it might start to fly.*

Nykl, who translated the above lines, notes that the poetry of this period was still largely imitative, and only after the fall of the caliphate were the poets able to give free rein to their imaginations.

Muslim scholars, like their Christian contemporaries, were very much concerned with the concept of God and man's relationship to Him. The study of philosophy was inextricably linked to theology, but the rude culture of the first invaders of al-Andalus, coupled with the strict orthodoxy of the Malikites, impeded the early development of philosophical speculation. Nor was there a strong philosophical tradition in pre-Muslim Spain, as Miguel Cruz Hernández has pointed out. Philosophy began to flourish after Spanish Muslims, who had visited the east for study or pilgrimage, brought back the newest doctrines. The earliest philosopher to appear in al-Andalus was Ibn Masarra of Córdoba (d. 931), whose father had been very deeply influenced by the Mutazilite doctrines which he encountered in the east. Adopting the ascetic ideas of Sufism, Ibn Masarra retired to a hermitage in the mountains near Córdoba and soon attracted many followers. Although his books are no longer extant, Asín Palacios has succeeded in reconstructing his essential thought, characterized by mysticism and moral austerity, from long citations found in the writings of the thirteenth-century philosopher, Ibn al-Arabi. The principal source of Ibn Masarra's ideas was the neo-Platonism of pseudo-Empedocles; for this reason he was accused of pantheism, of denying the physical reality of the punishments of hell, and of holding the doctrine of free will. These opinions so aroused the ire of the Malikites that Ibn Masarra elected to go into exile to Mecca; he returned to Spain only during the more liberal regime of Abd al-Rahman III. In spite of alternating periods of

---

* From a poem by Ibn Abd Rabbihi, in A. R. Nykl, *Hispano-Arabic Poetry and its Relations with the Old Provençal Troubadours* (first published, Baltimore, 1946; reprinted 1970, by The Hispanic Society), 39–40; used with permission of The Hispanic Society.

tolerance and persecution the followers of Ibn Masarra continued to propagate his doctrines for more than a century after his death.

The influence of the Malikite jurists also restricted the development of scientific studies, but mathematics and astronomy were considered necessary for dealing with such practical matters as determining the calendar. During the caliphate, Maslama of Madrid (d. 1008) gained fame as a mathematician, astronomer, and alchemist; his writings included a treatise on the astrolabe, a commentary on Ptolemy's *Planisphaerium*, and an edition of al-Khwarizmi's *Astronomical Tables*. Important advances in medical science were also achieved during the caliphate. With the help of a Byzantine monk, Hasday ibn Shaprut (d. 970), a Jewish physician and diplomat in the service of Abd al-Rahman III, translated the *Materia Medica* of Dioscorides, a copy of which the Emperor Constantine Porphyrogenitus had sent to the caliph. Abu-l-Qasim, better known as Abulcasis (d. 1013), one of the physicians of al-Hakam II, wrote a voluminous medico-surgical encyclopedia, a classic work in use for centuries; not only was it later translated into Latin by Gerard of Cremona, but also into Provençal and Hebrew.

The earliest historians of Muslim Spain are known to us through fragments of their writings preserved by later authors. One of the first historians whose work has survived was Abd al-Malik ibn Habid (d. c. 853/4), but his history of al-Andalus from 711 to 839 has not yet been edited. Not until the time of the caliphate did a group of historians of the first rank emerge, reflecting the higher level of civilization in that century. Among them is the author known to the Christians of a later time as el moro Rasis. Ahmad ibn Muhammad al-Razi (d. 955) wrote the first general history of Spain from the Roman era until his own time, but the Arabic text has survived only in fragments cited by later authors. Centuries later, King Dinis of Portugal ordered a translation of the Arabic text to be made, and a Castilian version of the Portuguese translation is extant in the so-called *Crónica de 1344*. Fragments of the *Annals of the Caliph al-Hakam II* written by Isa al-Razi, son of el moro Rasis, have also survived. Contemporary with Rasis was the judge al-Khushani (d. 971), the author of one of the most entertaining of Muslim historical works, a series of notable pen portraits and anecdotes entitled a *History of the Judges of Córdoba;* using official documents as well as tradition and legend, he provides us with the most vivid picture of daily life and activity in the tenth century.

Another historian, Ibn al-Qutiyya (d. 977), is especially interesting because he was a descendent of King Witiza, as his name "Son of the Goth" indicates. A great-great-grandson of Sara, daughter of Witiza's son Olmundo, he was born in Seville and wrote a *History of the Conquest of Spain* extending to the death of Abd Allah. His sources included oral tradition as well as earlier written works. Though he took great pride in his Gothic ancestry, he was wholly devoted to the Umayyad dynasty and displayed great disdain for the Christians. Paying scant attention to chronology, he recounts numerous anecdotes and court intrigues and says very little about frontier warfare with the Christians.

An anonymous compilation probably put together early in the eleventh century is the *Akhbar Majmua* or *Collection of Traditions*, from the invasion to the reign of Abd al-Rahman III. Full of anecdote, legend, and snatches of poetry, its value is uneven, but it remains one of the most important sources for the first century of Islamic rule in Spain. One of the finest historians was Abu Marwan ibn Hayyan (d. 1076) who lived during the age of the *taifas*, but the portions of his *al-Muqtabis* or *History of Spain* which have survived relate to the reigns of Abd Allah and al-Hakam II. His information, veracity, critical sense, and literary skill rank him as the finest historian of the age; regrettably most of the fifty works attributed to him are lost. Mention also should be made of an anonymous *Chronicle of Abd al-Rahman III* which relates the first eighteen years of his reign. Largely dry and annalistic, it is especially interesting in its treatment of the rebel Ibn Hafsun.

CHAPTER 7

Government, Society, and Culture in Christian Spain, 711–1035

The Formation of the Christian States

In contrast to al-Andalus, Christian Spain during the era of the Umayyads existed only as fragments—states varying in size and importance. From west to east they were the kingdom of Asturias-León, the kingdom of Navarre, the counties of Aragon, Sobrarbe, and Ribagorza, and the Catalan counties of Pallars, Urgel, Cerdagne, Rousillon, Besalú, Ampurias, Ausona (Vich), Gerona, and Barcelona. The Christian states expanded slowly, principally in times of disorder in al-Andalus. The greatest advance was made in the west where the rulers of Asturias-León occupied and colonized vast areas abandoned by the Muslims, extending as far south as Porto at the mouth of the Duero river and eastward along the valley of the Duero into Castile. Early in the tenth century the seat of government was moved from Oviedo, far to the north, to León which enjoyed more immediate communication with the repopulated areas. The Navarrese also moved southward from Pamplona, touching the borders of Castile, but the Aragonese still clung to Jaca and the foothills of the Pyrenees and had not reached the Ebro river. Catalonia was repopulated in the ninth century as the Muslims were driven south of Barcelona, but the Catalans still maintained close ties with the lands of southern France and had not reached the Ebro. At the close of this period, Sancho el mayor, king of Navarre, united the counties of Aragon, Sobrarbe, and Ribagorza, as well as Castile and León, and upon his death in 1035 bequeathed these dominions to his sons. As a result, Castile and Aragon attained the status of kingdoms.

The Leonese Imperium

Until the advent of Sancho el mayor and his dynasty, the most important of the Christian states, by reason of its size and the activities and aspirations of its rulers, was the kingdom of Asturias-León. In recent years scholars have debated whether the kings of León, to whom the title *imperator* was sometimes applied by their subjects in the tenth century, had developed a concept of empire and whether a Leonese *imperium* existed in fact. None of the tenth-century kings of León called himself emperor, but they did use titles such as *rex magnus, princeps magnus,* and even *basileus,* which suggest more than ordinary royal status. The term *regnum imperium* was also used to designate the king's reign and kingdom.

Interpretations of these data have varied greatly. Ernest Mayer suggested that the use of the imperial title was intended to enunciate Leonese independence of the Carolingian empire, but the empire of the tenth century was no threat to León. García Gallo argued that the title had no meaning other than the power of command, once enjoyed by generals (*imperatores*) of the Roman republic. His suggestion that the title was applied to a ruler who had won a great victory is unconvincing, because the kings of León in the late tenth century suffered repeatedly at the hands of the Muslims.

Menéndez Pidal's explanation, summarized in chapter 5, may be recapitulated here. He held that the title *imperator* should be understood, not in the primitive sense proposed by García Gallo, but in the medieval sense of emperor, that is, king of kings, a ruler claiming supremacy over other rulers. The use of the title was a refinement of the neo-Gothic ideal of the Asturian monarchy, and was intended to express Leonese aspirations to supremacy over all other rulers in the peninsula, whether Christian or Muslim. In no way was the title a challenge to the Holy Roman Empire whose sovereigns had pretensions to universal hegemony.

While admitting that the imperial idea derived from the neo-Gothic ideal, Sánchez Albornoz has suggested that it began to take form during the reign of Ramiro II. A vigorous ruler who triumphed over the caliph himself at Simancas in 939, he probably inspired in his courtiers a desire to exalt his majesty by giving him a title equally as expressive of supreme power as the title of caliph used by the Umayyads of Córdoba. Lévi-Provençal, without entering a detailed discussion of the matter, had already proposed that the imperial title was an imitation of Umayyad practice. In the late tenth and early eleventh century, when the throne of León was occupied by a succession of minors, who were humiliated more than once by Almanzor, the imperial title was applied to the sovereign more often than before. In Sánchez Albornoz's view, a conscious effort was being made to strengthen a weak monarchy and to safeguard its claims to supremacy against challenges from both Muslim and Christian rulers.

In his several studies Menéndez Pidal attempted to demonstrate that the Leonese *imperium* existed as a juridical institution and was acknowledged as such by the rulers of the other Christian states. Sánchez Candeira, while at first concurring, later concluded that one could not maintain that the Leonese empire had an actual, juridical existence, and Sánchez Albornoz has sustained the same opinion. All would agree that the Leonese sovereigns and their courtiers had a conception of imperial power and an aspiration to predominance throughout the peninsula. Insofar as their supremacy was acknowledged by the other Christian rulers, the idea of empire held out the possibility of the restoration of Hispanic unity in the future.

The Impact of Feudalism

From the ninth century onward, feudalism was a principal factor in the life of northern Europe, and its influence was also felt in Spain. The foundations of government and society rested upon private contracts between the sovereigns and the great men of the realm who were his vassals and who were in turn lords of vassals. Pledging homage and fealty to his lord, the vassal assumed the obligation of performing military and court service in return for protection and maintenance; maintenance took the form of a benefice or fief, that is, an estate or public office held in usufruct by the vassal, and heritable by his heirs. Thus the feudal relationship tended to be rooted in the land over which the vassal exercised dominion, i.e., the right to administer justice and to exercise public functions. As the landlord of an estate he was also entitled to receive rents and services from his tenants and to exercise juridical powers over them. The general consequence of the growth of feudalism and its union with the seigneurial system was the weakening of royal authority; public offices were held by hereditary right, not by royal appointment, and private bonds of loyalty supplanted the public oath of fidelity to the crown. The efficacy of royal government, therefore, depended upon the strength of the feudal ties linking the king and his vassals.

Under Carolingian influence, feudalism developed early in the Catalan counties, as Charles the Bald's capitulary of 844 addressed to the inhabitants of the county of Barcelona reveals:

Let the Spaniards (*Spani*) know that we have granted them permission to commend themselves in vassalage to our count, just as other free men do; and if anyone receives a benefice from the one to whom he is commended, let him know that he should render to his lord for it such service as our men customarily render to their lords for similar benefices. [*MHDE*, II, 466]

The Catalan counts were vassals of the Frankish king, holding their offices as benefices, but the heritability of benefices, recognized in a capitulary of 877, encouraged the foundation of dynasties and a tendency toward independence in the Spanish March. The counts of Barcelona, in the late tenth century, while acknowledging the titular sovereignty of the Capetian kings of France, refused to become their vassals. Subinfeudation was also characteristic of Catalan feudalism. Viscounts pledged homage and fealty (*hominaticum et fidelitatem*) to the Catalan counts, receiving investiture (*potestas*) of their offices as benefices held by hereditary right. Other nobles entered into similar relationships, accepting the typical feudal obligations of military and court service. In sum, the characteristic customs and institutions of French feudalism were also found in Catalonia and reached their fullest development in the eleventh and twelfth centuries.

In the other Christian states feudalism never reached maturity, though its constitutive elements existed in embryonic and uncoordinated form. Visigothic Spain had reached a prefeudal stage of development characterized by private oaths of fidelity, the existence of dependent tenures, the granting of immunities, and the seigneurial regime. But the Muslim invasion and the peculiar circumstances of the Asturian-Leonese reconquest impeded the natural evolution toward the linking of vassalage with the granting of benefices, as in northern Europe. The kings of Asturias-León were surrounded by *fideles*, vassals bound by private oath to give faithful service; prelates and magnates enjoyed similar relationships with the lower nobility (*infanzones, milites*). Until the eleventh century when *vassalus* came into common usage, the term *miles* ordinarily meant vassal. In return for military service, the vassal received money (*solidata*) or a benefice (*prestamum*), recoverable by the lord upon the termination of the vassal's service. On the other hand, persons who were not vassals sometimes received monetary compensation or benefices in exchange for military service. The relationship between lord and vassal was not hereditary and could be terminated by either party at any moment. As the relationship was not necessarily bound up with the concession of benefices, it retained a highly personal character seldom found elsewhere in Europe.

The failure of feudalism to develop fully and to transform the character of the state must be attributed to the historical conditions surrounding the origin and growth of the kingdom of Asturias-León. A strong monarchy and a large class of freemen were the principal obstacles to the growth of feudalism. The continuing state of war with the Muslims bolstered the power of the king as the military leader primarily responsible for defense and for the preservation of Asturian-Leonese independence. Military success not only enhanced the king's prestige, but also added to his resources. Claiming ownership of all reconquered territory, the king was able to reserve large estates for himself and to reward his followers for their loyalty to him. Those who repopulated the newly conquered lands were for the most part small, free proprietors, hardy frontiersmen, who gave allegiance to no lord save the king. The nobility, on the other hand, lacking the military and financial power which only the possession of large estates could give, were unable to offer serious challenge to the king's authority.

Kingship

To what extent the Christians in the first centuries of the reconquest were consciously aware of the abstract idea of "the state" is difficult to ascertain. In the concrete, the king was the acknowledged head of a political community, whose members pledged public allegiance to him. He had the traditional responsibility to administer justice, to guard the Catholic faith, to defend the frontiers, and to appoint subordinates to carry out various public functions. The Isidorian tradition of the just ruler accountable to God was well known and acted as a limitation upon any tendency toward the abuse of authority. The responsibility of preserving the territorial integrity of the realm seems to have been recognized, at least until the early tenth century, when the sons of Alfonso III, regarding it as a private patrimony, partitioned it among themselves, but this custom did not become rooted in the kingdom until the advent of Sancho el mayor and his descendants.

The king's primary role as a military leader required that an adult male be chosen to assume the royal responsibilities. The kings who ruled Asturias-León in the eighth and ninth centuries were descended from Pelayo and his son-in-law Alfonso I, but Sánchez Albornoz believes that the monarchy was fundamentally elective. The hereditary principle gained strength, however, because of the succession from father to son, and in spite of the upheavals of the tenth century, it continued to gain acceptance, as the accession of three minors in 966, 999, and 1028 testifies. With the triumph of hereditary right, the idea that the kingdom was the patrimony of the royal family and divisible among heirs was more widely accepted.

In the kingdom of Navarre, though we are much less informed about its internal development, a similar tension between election and hereditary right seems to have been operative. The descendants of Iñigo Arista held the kingship until they were supplanted by the Jimena family early in the tenth century. Hereditary succession also came to prevail in the counties of the Spanish March, although titular sovereignty pertained to the Carolingian and Capetian kings of France. The descendants of Wifred (873–898), as counts of Barcelona, enjoyed an exceptionally long tenure extending to the early fifteenth century.

Alfonso II, who is said to have revived the ceremonial of the Visigothic court is also the first Asturian king known to have been anointed (*unctus est in regno*, 791). The making of the king (*ordinatio*) became a more solemn rite as the years passed. By the tenth century it consisted of the coronation, anointing, and enthronement of the king, who also received the scepter and mantle, the symbols of his rank and authority. The elevation of Ordoño II in 914 is described by the *Historia Silense* (44) in these words: "All the magnates, bishops, abbots, counts and chief men of Spain, gathered together in a solemn general assembly, acclaimed him and made him king, and the diadem was placed upon him and he was anointed in the throne of the kingdom at León by twelve bishops." The ceremony, which usually took place in the cathedral of León, was also enhanced by the celebration of a solemn mass and the chanting of the *Te Deum*. At this time the king swore to govern in accordance with the law, and his subjects pledged their allegiance to him. The *Antiphonary of León*, based upon a Visigothic ritual of Wamba's time, contains the orations and other ceremonies for the ordi-

natio of the king and probably reflects the actual practices of the tenth century.

The king was not, as the early Visigothic kings were, the head of a tribal community (*rex Gothorum*), but the ruler of a territory and its inhabitants, as expressed in his title: king of Oviedo or king of León (*rex Ovetensis, rex Legionensis*). The king of Navarre was usually called king of Pamplona.

The Royal Council

The principal agency aiding the king in the conduct of public affairs was his council, called *palatium* or *aula regia*; the term *curia regis* did not come into use until the eleventh century under French influence. Alfonso II made an early attempt to give some formal organization to this body, by reviving at Oviedo, his chief seat, the palatine order which had existed at Toledo under the Visigothic kings, but the business of government was simplified and did not require a complicated central administration. Sánchez Albornoz has demonstrated that the royal council, in both its ordinary and extraordinary sessions, performed the secular functions of the Visigothic *aula regia* and also the ecclesiastical tasks of the councils of Toledo.

The ordinary sessions of the council were attended by all those persons who customarily accompanied the king on his travels, such as members of the royal family, magnates who were friends and counselors of the king (*consiliarii regis*), royal vassals (*fideles* or *milites regis*), and officials. The palatine officials who formed the backbone of the council were the *armiger* or *alferez*, the royal standard-bearer and commander of troops, who received the king's coronation oath and held the sword before him as the symbol of royal authority; the *maiordomus* who supervised the household and the administration of the royal domain and the collection of royal rents; the notary (*notarius*) who drafted royal documents and kept the archives; the *strator*, in charge of the king's stables; the treasurer (*thesaurarius*) who had custody of objects of value belonging to the king; the chamberlains (*cubicularii*) who cared for his bedchamber and clothing; and the chaplains who tended to his spiritual needs.

Whenever circumstances warranted, the king convened his council in extraordinary session, summoning the bishops, abbots, nobles, and provincial governors of the whole kingdom. Together with those who ordinarily attended the council, they advised the king on those matters which he chose to set before them. After dealing with ecclesiastical affairs, that is to say, the creation of new bishoprics, the appointment or removal of bishops, the foundation of monasteries, and the regulation of clerical morals, the council turned to secular business such as the granting of charters or the promulgation of laws such as the *decreta* enacted by Alfonso V at León in 1017. The council's most important function was to serve as a judicial tribunal with general jurisdiction to hear suits of prelates and nobles and even of simple freemen. Though the extraordinary council was only a consultative body, whose proposals had only that force which the king chose to give them, it did in fact act as a curb on royal absolutism.

Territorial Administration

As the Muslim invasion broke down the administrative structure of the Visigothic era, the emerging Christian states had to create for themselves territorial subdivisions on an entirely new basis. The series of counties established in the Pyrenees originated for the most part as territorial districts of the Carolingian empire but gradually became independent in the tenth century. The counts affirmed their hereditary right to rule the counties and to exercise on their own behalf the administrative, judicial, financial, and military powers once entrusted to them as agents of the emperors. Though lacking the royal title, the counts were virtually independent. Subdivisions of the counties were administered by vicars or viscounts (*vicarii, vicecomites*), who held their offices as benefices.

Even after the colonization of the Duero valley in the tenth century, the administrative districts (*mandationes, commissa*) of the kingdom of Asturias-León were limited in extent. Castile was one of the largest counties and, because of its condition as a frontier province, acquired a certain autonomy and in the late tenth century became the hereditary domain of Fernán González and his descendants. Elsewhere, officials, sometimes with the personal title of count (*comites, potestates*), were appointed by the king to serve solely at his pleasure, and not by hereditary right; each was responsible for the maintenance of public peace, the administration of justice, the collection of taxes, and the levying of troops. In return for his services, he retained a portion of the taxes and fines collected. His subordinates included *maiorini* who supervised the exploitation of royal estates, collecting tributes and rents; and *sagiones*, who summoned troops, cited litigants to court, inflicted corporal punishments, and so on.

From time to time the king granted the privilege of immunity, usually to properties of bishops and monasteries. Although the privilege was given infrequently, it was given in perpetuity. A charter of immunity given by Alfonso III to the monks of Sahagún in 904 reads in part: "We designate you to rule, on behalf of the church, whatever men may be inhabitants of the village of Zacarías . . . so that they shall all attend to your command concerning the fulfillment of whatever may be useful to the church. . . . You, Sancho, shall not dare to disturb them for any cause" (*MHDE*, II, 490). By prohibiting royal officers to enter the immune land (*cautum*) to perform their duties, the administration of the district, the dispensing of justice, the collection of taxes and fines, the levying of troops were effectively entrusted to the immunist, subject only to the general supervision of the king, who could correct any abuse of authority.

Municipal government scarcely existed in the ninth and tenth centuries when so many old towns in the Christian states were ruined or scantily populated; even important administrative and military centers, Oviedo, León, Pamplona, Jaca, and Barcelona, lacked a specifically municipal government. Although Herculano argued that the Mozarabs restored the Roman municipality in the Christian towns, Sánchez Albornoz demonstrated that it had already disappeared in the late Visigothic era and that, for the most part, life remained centered in rural settlements subject to the jurisdiction of territorial officials. Only as urban life began to revive in the eleventh century did rulers begin to issue charters establishing municipal governmental autonomy.

The Law and the Administration of Justice

In the Christian states of the ninth and tenth centuries the *Liber Judiciorum*, the territorial law of the Visigoths, had limited application, probably because few copies were available, and only the most enlightened judges were acquainted with it. The influx of Mozarabs into the kingdom of León helped to prolong its influence there, but in Castile it was rejected as a source of law, and in Catalonia the capitularies of the Carolingian kings (812, 815, 816, 844) had greater impact.

In all the Christian states the chief source of law was custom, unwritten law sanctioned by usage from time immemorial. Local custom was sometimes embodied in charters of settlement (*cartae populationis*) issued by a ruler in order to colonize a certain place; some of the rights and responsibilities of the settlers, for instance, the payment of tribute, were set down in the document. Charters (*fueros*) given by the ruler to the people of a specific locality usually regulated in greater detail such matters as administration, tributes, services, legal procedures and penalties, but the charters did not purport to be comprehensive codes of local law. The earliest *fueros*, appearing in the middle of the tenth century, are indeed quite brief. Among the most important was the *fuero* given to the city of León by Alfonso V in 1017; on the same occasion he promulgated fourteen *decreta*, the first genuinely territorial laws for the kingdom of León.

The administration of justice was very much influenced by Germanic ideas. Litigation was regarded essentially as the private concern of the parties. On the other hand, the king did have a responsibility to see that justice was done, especially when a violation of the king's peace was alleged. The king's peace protected his family, his residence, public assemblies, courts, markets, highways, pilgrims, merchants, and so on. Anyone committing a breach of the peace in any of these places or against any of these persons was guilty of an offense against the king, and the matter would be dealt with by the king's agents. Both the king and the local authorities, the *potestates* or counts, and the lords of immunities, presided over courts. In the *Fuero* of León, Alfonso V declared that "in León and in all the cities and in all the districts (*alfozes*) there shall be judges chosen by the king who shall judge the suits of all the people." Each court had civil and criminal jurisdiction, and each was a court of first instance; there was no hierarchy of courts and no system of appeals. The king's court usually heard litigation involving the great men of the realm, though it was always possible for an ordinary freeman to bring his case to the king's attention. The courts of the *potestates*, counts, and immunists resolved disputes among the inhabitants of the districts involved.

The procedure employed in the courts was basically Germanic and was essentially the same in both civil and criminal cases. Litigation was initiated by the will of the parties who directed the process through its various stages, while the judges sat as spectators and intervened decisively only to determine the form of proof. The suit (*intentio*) began when the litigants agreed to appear in court, or when the *sagio* or public officer summoned the defendant to appear on a specified day. In order to compel his appearance and to oblige him to abide by the outcome of the trial, the plaintiff was allowed to take a pledge (*pignus*) from the defendant's goods or to require him to name someone who would act as security (*fideiussor, fidiator*) for him. If the defendant could not give a pledge or name a surety, he could be imprisoned. The litigants appeared in person, though in accordance with Roman and Visigothic tradition they could be represented by *assertores*, who spoke for them. Each party presented oral allegations and denials. When their respective positions were clearly determined, the decisive phase of the process began, that is, the proof. The fundamental responsibility of the presiding officer was to appoint *iudices* to determine the proof to be used; in the king's court the *iudices* were selected from the magnates or prelates in attendance; in the local courts they were chosen from the *boni homines* of the district. The defendant ordinarily was obliged to undergo the proof, though there were instances in which the plaintiff was allowed to do so.

The proof usually took the form of an oath of purgation, supported by a specific number of compurgators; unless impugned by the other party the oath proved the case. The oath of a noble was worth more than that of a freeman. Witnesses might also be summoned, but their role was secondary. The ordeal or appeal to the judgment of God was also a common form of proof. The ordeal was a physical test undertaken on the assumption that God would intervene to save an innocent party from harm. A late-tenth-century description of the ordeal of hot water, the ordeal usually employed, relates: "I, Salamirus, an innocent man, underwent the ordeal of hot water (*ad pena caldaria*) and with my hands I threw hot stones out of the hot water and on the third or fourth day I appeared in the council unharmed and clean. . . . I Abbot Alfonso . . . by my hand put this innocent man to the ordeal of hot water and he threw hot stones out of it and on the third or fourth day . . . unharmed and not burned by the heat he stood in the council of the faithful in the presence of all and he appeared restored and uninjured" (*ES*, 19, 375–379). The judicial duel or trial by battle was also an appeal to the judgment of God. Once the proof was executed, the judges of proof reported the results to the president of the court who gave sentence recognizing or confirming the right of one of the litigants as determined by the proof. An account of the proceedings (*agnitio*) was then drawn up. The execution of the sentence was sometimes left to the parties themselves, who might have come to agreement either before or after the proof, or to the *sagiones* in the service of the court.

In criminal cases, the king or his representative collected a fine (*calumnia*) from the guilty party and often inflicted additional punishments, including confiscation, exile, mutilation, and hanging. The *Cronicon Albeldense* (59) praised Ramiro I as "the staff of justice. He tore out the eyes of thieves and by fire put an end to magicians and with marvelous speed undercut and destroyed tyrants." The right of private vengeance was always recognized, and once the family of a murdered man defied the murderer in a public gathering, they could seek to kill him. Monetary compositions for murder and for lesser bodily injuries were intended, however, to alleviate recourse to blood feuds. The extent of the injury or the rank of the person killed determined the amount of the composition. Thus the murder of a noble could be compensated for by payment of 500 *solidi*, while 300 sufficed for a simple freeman.

A special tribunal which appeared in the city of León in the tenth century, probably due to the influence of Mozarabic immigrants, was the tribunal of the book. The book was the *Liber Judiciorum*, the law code of the Visigothic kingdom, still in use among the Mozarabs in al-Andalus. The tribunal of the book was a court of first instance, but it also heard appeals in accordance with Visigothic tradition. The Castilians, however, took exception to appeals from the judgments of their courts and rejected the *Liber Judiciorum*.

Financial Administration

The financial administration of the Christian states was rudimentary in character. Royal expenditures were limited, and no clear distinction between the public treasury and the king's private patrimony was maintained. Not only were clergy and nobles exempted from the payment of public imposts, but so too were ordinary freemen as an inducement to the colonization of reconquered regions. The bulk of the royal income was derived from rents and services owed by tenants living on royal estates.

The estates of the crown (*realengo*) were frequently expanded by reconquest. Enunciating the principle that all conquered and deserted lands pertained to the crown, the king exploited these himself or allowed others to do so. Tenants on royal estates paid in kind a tribute (*functio, censum, tributum*), varying in quantity from place to place, which represented a fusion of the rent paid by tenants to their lords and the public tribute of the Visigothic era. The king also collected fees in kind for the use of his woodland (*montaticum*) and his pastures (*herbaticum*). The use of woods, rivers, and salt pits pertained exclusively to the king as a regalian right (*ius regale*). The king was also entitled to the rents and labor services due to other landlords.

Among the public revenues of the crown, surviving from Roman and Visigothic times under a variety of names, imposts on persons and goods in transit were still of some importance (*teloneum, quadragesima, lezda, portaticum, pedaticum*). The king also received fines levied on persons convicted of crime, or upon those who failed to perform military service (*fonsadera*) or guard duty (*anubda*); these last eventually became regular payments for exemption from these services. All the king's subjects owed him hospitality (*hospicium*), and certain duties, for example, the repair of roads and bridges (*facendera*), transportation (*conductum*), and service as soldiers, guards, guides, or messengers.

The Army

Given the necessity of constantly defending the frontiers against Muslim attack, the rulers of the Christian states required all able-bodied men to perform military service. This included participation in major expeditions (*fonsado*), raids (*cabalgata*), garrison duty (*anubda, vigilia*), and the defense of beleaguered fortresses (*apellido*). The assembled host was commanded by the royal *armiger* or *alferez* and included the *fideles* or *milites regis*, the king's vassals, the forces of the magnates and counts and immunists. The nobility, who usually fought on horseback, were oftentimes vassals of the king or of great lords who remunerated their services by monetary payments (*solidata*) or by the grant of benefices. The host also included mounted soldiers of non-noble rank, simple freemen, later called *caballeros villanos*, who were sufficiently well-to-do to own horses and the accouterments for fighting on horseback. The peasants who served as infantry forces were ordinarily allowed during the tenth century to send one out of every three men to the host; the two who remained behind had to provide the soldier with an animal for transport. The booty taken in war was divided into five parts, one of which was reserved solely for the king (*quinto*), probably in imitation of Muslim practices.

The Social Structure

The possibilities of determining with any degree of accuracy the size of the population in the Christian states are even more limited than they are for al-Andalus. The remote mountainous zones of the northern periphery where the Christians preserved their independence had never been thickly populated and certainly were not during the first centuries of the reconquest. Alfonso I devastated the Duero valley because the scarcity of population made it impossible to establish permanent settlements there. The constant ravages of the Muslims must also have prevented any rapid increase in population. Only in the late ninth and tenth centuries were there sufficient Christians to carry out the colonization of the Duero valley, but even then the total population was probably quite small.

Remnants of the Hispano-Gothic aristocracy constituted an important element in the population. At the end of the Visigothic era, as old differences were disappearing, the assimilation of Hispano-Romans and Visigoths was proceeding quickly. The leaders of society had begun to think of themselves as forming one race, the *gens Gothorum* or the *Hispani.* An indeterminate number of the Hispano-Gothic nobility fled before the Muslim invaders and took refuge in Asturias or Septimania. In Asturias they supported Pelayo's rebellion and, with the native leaders of the region, came to form the aristocracy in the new kingdom. They were also responsible for the reconquest and resettlement of the Catalan counties. The mass of the population in the northern mountains consisted of indigenous Galicians, Asturians, Cantabrians, Basques, and others who had not been entirely assimilated into Roman or Visigothic society. As the reconquest opened up new lands for settlement, these mountaineers began to move southward and in so doing lost some of their regional characteristics.

Mozarabs fleeing from al-Andalus formed an especially significant element in the Christian states. From the ninth century onward they came to settle in the north, and established important colonies in León, Zamora, Toro, Galicia, and to a lesser extent in Castile, where they devoted themselves to agriculture, the crafts, governmental administration, the monastic life, and many other activities. In general, they brought with them a higher level of culture, new artistic styles, improved techniques of farming and craftsmanship, as well as an idealized concept of the Visigothic state which influenced the neo-Gothic revival and the later development of the imperial idea. In the formation of the Christian states the Mozarabs represented a conservative tradition which looked with nostalgia to a happier past. In the changing circumstances of the tenth and eleventh centuries the predominant role in shaping the course of the Christian states passed into the hands of the Castilians, a young and vigorous people unhampered by the venerable traditions of the past.

In the early centuries of the reconquest there were Franks, who settled chiefly in the Pyrenees in the territories which formed the Spanish March, but the great influx of Franks and other northern Europeans as pilgrims and crusaders did not occur until the eleventh century. There were few Muslims or Jews in the Christian states until the rapid progress of the reconquest in the eleventh and twelfth centuries. Muslims in Christian territory were for the most part prisoners of war reduced to slavery. The Jews probably preferred to live in al-Andalus, where the economic opportunities were substantially greater and where they were ordinarily assured of toleration.

The Muslim invasion totally disrupted the society of the Visigothic era, so that in each of the Christian states social classes emerged in response to the new circumstances of life. A rigid separation of classes was not easily established, because the twin tasks of reconquest and repopulation favored the development of a society of freemen. A brave man who distinguished himself by feats of arms in the struggle against Islam could acquire noble status, while a poor man of servile origin, by taking part in the colonization of new lands, could acquire land of his own as well as the condition of a free man. In Asturias-León the simple freeman typified the rural population. In Catalonia, on the other hand, a society developed based upon the feudal bonds of vassalage and benefice and the commendation of the peasantry to the great lords.

The nobility who appeared in the several Christian states were in part descended from the aristocrats of the Visigothic era and in part were a new nobility brought into being by their services to the sovereign in government or in war. As a privileged class, the nobles participated directly with the ruler in the government of the state and the defense of the frontiers, and were exempt from the payment of tribute. The higher nobility (*magnates, optimates, proceres, seniores, barones*) held the principal offices in the royal palace, served as governors of provinces, and were usually bound to the king by the personal tie of vassalage (*fideles regis*). Usually they held in full ownership or in benefice landed property of considerable extent, though there were few latifundia save in Galicia. In Catalonia, the several counts, theoretically governing in the name of the Frankish kings, but independent in fact, constituted the higher nobility together with their vassals, the viscounts.

Nobles of secondary rank, whose political, economic, and military importance was not as great, were known as *milites* or knights, a term which describes their primary function as mounted warriors. They also came of distinguished ancestry, as the Romance term *infanzones* indicates. As vassals of the magnates, they were recompensed for their services in coin or in lands granted as benefices. In Catalonia the vassal had an hereditary right to his benefice, but this was not so in Asturias-León.

The majority of people were settled on the land as freemen, proprietors or tenants, sometimes commended to a lord's protection, oftentimes not. The process of repopulation enabled many simple freemen (*ingenui*) to acquire property in full ownership, especially in Castile and in the lands of the Duero valley. These were hardy adventurers, full of confidence in themselves and determined to preserve their independence both of the Muslims who attacked them and the magnates who sometimes tried to dominate them. Some freemen were prosperous enough to own horses and the equipment necessary for fighting on horseback. Given the exposure of Castile to constant Muslim raids, the services of these mounted troops (*caballeros villanos*) were highly prized. Thus in 974 Count García Fernández granted the mounted freemen of Castrojeriz the same privileges as the *infanzones* of Castile, namely, exemption from tribute. In Catalonia there were some free proprietors holding allodial land, that is, in full ownership, but they were the exception. The number of freemen working as hired hands or inhabiting the towns was limited, as the towns had not yet achieved any economic importance.

In addition to free proprietors there were many freemen who were tenants cultivating the lands of others. Insecurity and violence due to Muslim attacks, civil wars, and other calamities induced many rural freemen to commend themselves to the protection of their landlords, but by so doing they sometimes lost their freedom of movement. Freemen without lands of their own, or the means of subsistence, commended themselves to a lord who provided them with food, clothing, shelter, and work in his household. They could not leave without his consent and, if they did, could be reduced to slavery. Most commonly a man commended himself to a lord, surrendering all or part of his lands to the lord, but retaining the right of usufruct subject to the payment of rent. In Galicia and Portugal this was called a pact of *incommuniatio* and was usually for an indefinite term, though sometimes it was perpetual. In León and Castile free proprietors who commended themselves to the protection of a lord were known as *homines de benefactoria* (later *hombres de behetría*), that is, men who had entered a contract that was highly beneficial to themselves. Given the scarcity of lords holding large estates, these small proprietors could freely choose a lord and just as freely break the bond to seek another lord; they retained their lands and paid only a rent to the lord, losing neither their goods nor their personal liberty. In Catalonia free proprietors commended themselves to lords, pledging homage and promising an annual rent for the lands they cultivated. The relationship between the Catalan lord and his non-noble vassals (*homines proprii et solidi*) at first could be broken freely by either party, but it quickly tended to become hereditary.

Many other tenants, similarly commended, perhaps the majority, had much less freedom of movement. Some, tenants on the great estates of Galicia, León and Catalonia, were descended from the *coloni* of Roman and Visigothic times and were bound to the soil; others, not having lands of their own, obtained them from lords, but as a condition of the grant had to give up their freedom to leave the land whenever they wished. Inasmuch as they owed tribute to their lords, they were known by the generic name of *tributarii* or in Catalonia as *villani de parata*. In Galicia and León, tenants bound to the soil were also called *iuniores*, a term found in the Theodosian Code, referring to their inferior status as well as to their obligation to pay tribute. From the tenth century onward they were also known as *collatii*, a term that spread into Castile, Navarre, and Aragon. In Aragon and Navarre the term *mesquini* was used and, in Catalonia, *pagenses, commanentes, stantes*.

Peasants bound to the soil enjoyed the juridical condition of freemen, though in fact they were deprived of freedom of movement, an essential element in human liberty. This condition was heritable. As new lands were opened for colonization, many peasants sought to improve their lot by fleeing from their lords to the areas being repopulated, where they had the possibility of obtaining land of their own without any dependence upon a lord. Lords, of course, endeavored to check the flight of their peasants by various measures. Alfonso V touched on this problem in 1017 and sanctioned practices that no doubt had become customary during the tenth century. Anyone proven to be a *iunior* had to live on the estate to which he was bound and to satisfy all the obligations arising from his condition; but he was also permitted to leave and to settle elsewhere, if he wished, taking his personal belongings with him, with the reservation that he had to surrender one-half of his movable goods to his lord. He could also alienate his rights to the land to another *iunior* who would assume all the obligations attached to it.

Slavery continued to exist in Christian Spain, though it is likely that at the time of the Muslim conquest many slaves were able to regain their liberty. Captured Muslims and persons convicted of crime or incapable of paying their debts could be enslaved. Slaves (*servi, mancipii, pueri*), in a juridical sense, were considered as objects rather than persons; they could be bought or sold; they could not appear in court, and their owners were responsible for their crimes. On the other hand, their condition was ameliorated somewhat, since they were allowed to contract marriages with the consent of their owners and even to have personal possessions. Some slaves, especially Muslim captives employed in the household, were entirely subject to the will of their owners. Others were more fortunate in that they were settled on the owner's land with the responsibility to cultivate it and to pay a rent and services. The condition of these rural slaves differed little from that of free peasants who were bound to the soil. Like the *iuniores*, slaves sometimes attempted to flee to zones being repopulated in the hope of gaining the status of freemen owning land. Slave uprisings took place occasionally, as in the later eighth century when "the slaves, opposing their lords, by the king's efforts were captured and reduced to their earlier servitude." From time to time slave owners emancipated their slaves, sometimes in a last will and testament, usually by a charter of liberty (*carta ingenuitatis*) in which the owner declared the slave free and a Roman citizen (*civis romanus*), a formula which evidently had survived over the centuries. The freedman occasionally was entirely free to go his own way, but often he was bound by commendation to the protection of his former owner. In many instances the manumission of a slave probably did little to change his social or economic status since he probably continued to work in his lord's household or to cultivate the land he had occupied as a slave.

The Economy

In the first centuries of the reconquest the economy of Christian Spain was decidedly less advanced and less prosperous than that of al-Andalus. The remote mountainous areas of the peninsula occupied by the Christians had not enjoyed a vigorous economic life even in Roman and Visigothic times. There were no great cities such as Córdoba and Seville in the Christian north; León and Barcelona were renowned as seats of government, not as centers of trade and industry. The Christian states did participate in a minimal commercial relationship with al-Andalus and the lands north of the Pyrenees, as the circulation of Umayyad and Carolingian coinage testifies, but there were undoubtedly few native merchants, and there was little native industry of importance.

The predominantly agrarian economy of the Christian north was deeply influenced by the reconquest and its economic and social corollary, repopulation. In the late ninth and tenth centuries the repopulation of the Duero valley, deserted since the devastation by Alfonso I in the eighth century, was begun in earnest. The process was initiated with the occupation of a series of advanced positions constituting a defensive line; fortifications were erected around these positions, and communications with the heart of the kingdom were assured by the erection of a line of castles; finally the settlers took possession of the land (pressura), plowed it, and cultivated it (scalio). The kings of Asturias-León claimed reconquered and deserted land as their own, and thus controlled its settlement. The king could direct repopulation himself, or he could authorize a count, a magnate, a bishop, or an abbot to do so. In such cases a colonizing expedition advanced to the place of settlement; after building the necessary fortifications, they took possession of the land, unfurling the royal standard and sounding a trumpet. Attractive conditions offered to prospective colonists were often stated in written charters of settlement (cartae populationis). Among the important places colonized in these early centuries were Astorga (854), León (856), Amaya (860), Coimbra (876), Zamora (893), Burgos (896), Simancas (899), Osma (912), Salamanca, Avila, and Sepúlveda (940). In many instances, simple folk, lacking any authorization whatsoever, squatted on the land and began to cultivate it and only later obtained royal recognition of their rights. Settlers came from the mountains of Galicia, Cantabria, and the Basque country, and there were also many Mozarabs who fled from al-Andalus. The pioneers who settled the frontier lands of León and Castile were for the most part freemen, owning the land on which they were settled and independent of every lord save the king.

In the valleys of the Pyrenees which had been little affected by the Muslim invasion, the number of freemen in possession of their own land was also large. In Catalonia, from which the Muslims withdrew only gradually, there were many deserted areas requiring repopulation. This was effected by *aprisio* (from *prehendere*, to seize, to take hold of). Early in the ninth century, Charlemagne and Louis the Pious issued capitularies *pro hispanis* in which they admitted the right of refugees from Spain to the lands they had occupied in Septimania. The same principle was applied by the Catalan counts. At times they directed colonization themselves or authorized abbots and magnates to do so, but most often the land was simply occupied by ordinary folk who, after thirty years' occupancy, acquired a real right of ownership.

One of the major consequences of repopulation was the predominance both in Catalonia and in the Duero valley of small freeholds (*mansus, hereditas*) owned by freemen and transmissible by hereditary right to their children. In the mountainous regions of Asturias, Galicia, Cantabria, the Basque country, and the Pyrenees, where the chief activity was the raising of livestock, the typical settlement was the isolated *villa*, that is, the farmhouse and its appurtenances, barns, stables, cultivated lands, pastures, and so forth. In the plains of the Duero valley, where farming predominated, proprietors usually grouped their houses in villages (*vicus*) near a castle or monastery which could serve as a refuge in time of war. Each house had an adjacent garden, but the fields to be cultivated lay beyond the village. Woodland and pastureland were exploited in common, though they belonged to the king, to whom tribute was due. The village community regulated its common affairs, such as the use of pastures, the determination of boundaries, in an assembly (*concilium, conventus*) of freeholders. In the course of time some *villae* became centers of larger settlements, and thus the word came to mean a village rather than a simple farmhouse.

The abundance of land for settlement and the consequent growth of small freeholds impeded the development in Christian Spain of the great estates so characteristic of northern Europe. In Galicia, however, bishoprics and monasteries possessed extensive domains, and some magnates were able to acquire substantial holdings in Asturias and

León. In Catalonia the influence of feudalism encouraged the growth of large estates at the expense of small farms. In the early centuries of the reconquest these estates generally were not compact, self-sufficient units, but there was a natural tendency toward expansion and consolidation which became more pronounced with the progress of the reconquest in the eleventh century. The exploitation of the great estates scarcely differed from the Visigothic era. The monastery, castle, or seigneurial *villa* constituted the center of the estate; of the arable land a portion was set aside as the lord's reserve to be cultivated by his slaves or tenants, and the rest was apportioned among the tenants who owed rents and services. Tenants were obligated to work for a fixed number of days on the seigneurial reserve, usually at the seasons for plowing, sowing, and harvesting (*opera, sernas*). They also paid fees for the use of the lord's mill, bakery, and winepress. The lord collected fees for consenting to the marriage of female tenants, for permitting a tenant to alienate his holding, and he was also entitled to the best chattel of a deceased tenant (*nuntio, luctuosa*). The administration of the estate was entrusted to a bailiff (*maiordomus, maiorinus, bajulus, prepositus*), often a peasant himself.

In marked contrast with al-Andalus there was little improvement in agricultural techniques, nor was there any appreciable increase in the variety of products. The most important were wheat, barley, oats, vegetables, apples, figs, linen, flax, hemp, and olives (cultivated to some extent in the Duero valley). Vineyards in many areas (for example, La Rioja) supplied the Christians with a variety of wines. In addition to horses and cattle, sheep were raised and their production came to be one of the foundations of the Castilian economy. While in the Pyrenees sheep grazed on the mountainside and in the valleys, in the central *meseta* they began to travel along the *cañadas* or sheep walks from the northern mountains to the banks of the Duero. The reconquest opened new pastures for them, and perhaps the need for pastures gave a stronger impulse to the reconquest. In each community, sheep were pastured in a *mesta*, a term which eventually came to be applied to a vast organization of sheep owners throughout the kingdom of Castile.

Prior to the eleventh century there was little industrial activity in Christian Spain, save that which met the needs of local communities. On the great estates, carpenters, cartwrights, blacksmiths, tailors, and other craftsmen (*ministeriales*) produced clothing, furniture, weapons, household utensils, tools, and so on. Sánchez Albornoz has pointed to the existence of villages in Asturias-León whose names, Ferrarios, Rotarios, Ollarios, indicate that the inhabitants devoted themselves to the manufacture of iron goods, wheels, pots, or tiles. There were also itinerant artisans (*artifices*) who went from village to village with their tools to earn a living. Others maintained small shops in the villages or towns where they plied their trade.

As industrial production served local needs, so too trade was limited to local markets usually held weekly. There, agricultural products as well as craft goods and some exotic merchandise were exchanged. The market was held under the protection of the public authority of the king or count who guaranteed the security of persons and their goods. Violation of the peace of the market (*bannus, cautum*) was punishable by fine. Public imposts were levied at the entrance to the market, and a public official, the *zabazoque* or *almotaçaf* (*sahib al-suq, al-muhtasib*), inspected the market to protect purchasers against false weights and measures, to maintain order, and to settle disputes. In addition to products of local origin, silks, tapestries, and other textiles from the Muslim world, and weapons and fabrics from the lands north of the Pyrenees were sometimes offered for sale to wealthy lords and churchmen. By the eleventh century some enterprising merchants established permanent shops and warehouses (*alfondegas*) in the principal northern towns.

In spite of the Muslim conquest and the backward state of the economy, money did not cease to circulate in Christian Spain, though in the more remote areas barter was the ordinary means of exchange. Among the coins in circulation were the Visigothic gold *tremis* or third of a *solidus*, the old Roman and Byzantine coin, and gold *solidi* coined in Galicia by the kings of the Suevi. There were also silver *dirhams* from the mints of al-Andalus and silver *solidi* from Carolingian and Capetian France. The Carolingians coined the silver *denarius* in Barcelona, but in the tenth century the name of the Frankish sovereign was no longer inscribed on newly minted coins. The kings of Asturias-León did not coin money of their own, nor did they authorize anyone to do so. By the late ninth century the gradual disappearance of the gold *tremis* and the more frequent circulation of Carolingian and Umayyad coins resulted in the effective establishment of a silver standard in Christian Spain. In the tenth century a silver *solidus* had the equivalent value of one sheep or one *modius* (about eight kilograms) of wheat.

The number of coins in circulation was probably insufficient to meet all the requirements of trade, so barter was often necessary.

The Church, Literature, and Learning

The church survived the Muslim conquest with less change in its organizational structure in al-Andalus than in the independent Christian states. On the other hand, defection among the faithful in al-Andalus was extensive. The ecclesiastical provinces of Toledo, Mérida, and Seville fell largely within Muslim Spain, while most of the provinces of Tarragona and Braga remained in Christian hands. As Tarragona itself was in Muslim territory and in ruins, the metropolitan see was not restored there until the early twelfth century; in the interim, the counties of the Spanish March continued under the jurisdiction of the metropolitan of Narbonne. Braga, lying in no-man's land, was uninhabited, and the bishopric was apparently moved to Lugo, just as Dumio was transferred to Mondoñedo, and Iria Flavia to Compostela, following the discovery of the tomb of the Apostle St. James in the early ninth century. Many bishoprics in the frontier zones disappeared entirely as the bishops and their people sought refuge farther north. All told, there were about eighteen bishoprics in al-Andalus and not quite a dozen in Christian Spain in the ninth century. The latter number increased eventually with the expansion of the Christian states and the restoration of sees or the establishment of new ones, such as Oviedo, founded by Alfonso II. The Christian rulers in general exercised the right to establish sees, to determine boundaries, to appoint bishops, and eventually, to summon councils. In al-Andalus, the bishops continued to be elected according to the Visigothic tradition, though it is possible that the caliph was consulted beforehand. Eulogius was elected bishop of Toledo by the provincial bishops, but Muhammad I refused to allow him to take possession, but this was an exceptional case. There does seem to be evidence of irregularities, including simony, in the election of the bishops, but they were not appointed by the caliph, as Dozy held. The exception to this might be Recemund, who obtained the see of Elvira through the caliph's intervention.

Communications between Rome and the church in Spain were infrequent, though there are extant several papal letters to the Mozarabic bishops. In letters of 782 and 785, for example, Pope Hadrian I noted that the Christians of Baetica, the southernmost province, were in conflict concerning the date of Easter and the problem of predestination, and that their contact with Muslims and Jews led to mixed marriages, divorce, concubinage among the clergy, and ordinations contrary to the canons.

Notices of church councils are scanty. In al-Andalus a council met at Córdoba in 839 to deal with the acephalous heretics, and in 852 the emir assembled the bishops at Córdoba to take a stand against the Mozarabic martyrs. A number of diocesan or provincial councils seem to have been convoked in Christian Spain. Alfonso V, in the *curia* held at León in 1017 to deal with both ecclesiastical and secular business, stated the principle that in all future councils the affairs of the church would be discussed first.

The monastic life continued to flourish in al-Andalus, where monasteries for men and women were found in the principal cities or in the suburbs. From the late eighth century onward, as monks emigrated from al-Andalus, there was a revival of monasticism in the Christian states. The emigrés repopulated many newly conquered regions and founded famous monasteries such as Sahagún, San Pedro de Cardeña, San Miguel de Escalada, and so forth. The monastic rules of Sts. Isidore and Fructuosus continued to be used, and the Benedictine rule was also widely known.

The cultural level of the Mozarabs of al-Andalus, as the direct heirs of the tradition of St. Isidore of Seville, was considerably higher than that of the northern Christians, but, with the passage of time, they succumbed to the influence of the brilliant Arabic civilization beginning to develop. To a certain extent the juxtaposition of Christian and Muslim belief encouraged theological controversy among the Mozarabs. Aside from some rather bizarre theological novelties of passing interest, the Mozarabs of the late eighth century were most agitated by the heresy of adoptionism. This doctrine was propagated chiefly by Elipandus, metropolitan of Toledo, and Felix, bishop of Urgel in the Spanish March, who held that Christ, insofar as he was man, was the adopted son of God. They hoped apparently to refute the Muslim charge that Christians believed in three Gods; the idea that Christ was only the adopted son of God was not too far removed from the Muslim view of Christ as one of the prophets. Opposition to this teaching came from various quarters. In Asturias, the monk Beatus of Liébana and Eterius, bishop of Osma, wrote a lengthy refutation and were promptly attacked by Elipandus in the most violent language. Charlemagne summoned Felix of Urgel to appear before a council at Regensburg in 792 to recant, while Pope Hadrian I condemned the heresy. Even so, Felix and Elipandus persisted in their belief until death early in the ninth century.

One of the consequences of this controversy was to cast doubt upon the orthodoxy of the Mozarabic liturgy that had been in use in Spain since the earliest days of Christianity. In justification of adoptionism Elipandus had cited passages from the liturgy, and in responding to him Carolingian writers such as Alcuin argued that the liturgy was shot through with heresy. Neither Elipandus nor Alcuin was correct, but the suspicion thrown upon the liturgy at this time was revived in the eleventh century and was one reason for its abandonment and the introduction of the Roman liturgy in its stead.

The most distinguished representative of Mozarabic culture was Eulogius of Córdoba (d. 859) who gained fame as the spiritual adviser of the Cordoban martyrs and who suffered martyrdom himself. His writings include the *Memoriale Sanctorum, Documentum martyriale,* and *Liber apologeticus martyrum,* all written in defense of the martyrs. In these works he displayed a good knowledge of the church Fathers, the Visigothic doctors, various pagan authors, and especially of the Scriptures. These words spoken to the *qadi* of Córdoba, in defense of his having sheltered a young convert from Islam, suggest something of his character and purpose:

Judge, the office of preaching is enjoined upon us and it is fitting to our faith that we hold out the light of faith to those who inquire of us and that we should not deny those things that are holy to anyone hastening along the journey of life. . . . Wherefore . . . I explained that faith in Christ was the road to the kingdom of heaven. Willingly would I do the same for you, if you should think to ask me.   [Alvarus, *Vita Eulogii,* 5]

The judge, firm in his own convictions, did not accept this tentative offer and ordered the execution of Eulogius.

Equally learned was his very dear friend and schoolmate, Paulus Alvarus, a layman who died about 861. Besides a *Life* of Eulogius, he also wrote the *Indiculus luminosus,* a treatise in justification of the martyrs. In a very famous passage he decried the impact of Islamic culture upon young Christians:

Who, I ask, is there today among our faithful laymen who studies the sacred scriptures and inquires into the Latin writings of the doctors? . . . Rather, our Christian young men, . . . distinguished by their pagan learning, proud of their Arabic eloquence, avidly study the books of the Chaldeans. . . . They know not the beauty of the church and they despise the streams that water the paradise of the church. Alas, Christians do not know their own language, nor do the Latins study their own language, so that in the whole assembly of Christ one would scarcely find one among a thousand who is capable of addressing a letter of salutation to his brother in correct form. And yet there are a great many, without number, who learnedly expound the pomposities of Chaldean letters, adorning the final clauses of their letters with poetic verses of greater erudition and beauty than those of the pagans themselves. [*Indiculus luminosus*, 35]

Not many years later Abbot Samson of Córdoba (d. 890) wrote an *Apologeticum* in refutation of the heresy of anthropomorphism (the notion that God has a human body) espoused by Hostigesis, bishop of Málaga. Written with clarity and precision, the book is the principal work of dogmatic theology and also the last original production of the Mozarabs of Córdoba to come down to us. It is also a chief source concerning the scandals afflicting the Mozarabic church in the later ninth century.

Eulogius, Alvarus, and Samson typify the Isidorian tradition and its resistance to the blandishments of Islam. By the tenth century the Mozarabs had accepted the new order and proved to be as adept in the use of Arabic as of Latin or Romance. The most influential Mozarab of that time was Recemund, bishop of Elvira, also known as Rabi ibn Zayd, who represented the caliph at the German and Byzantine courts. There he became acquainted with Liutprand of Cremona, who dedicated his *Antapodosis*, a history of contemporary Europe, to him, as a man "worthy of reverence and filled with all holiness." Recemund himself was the author of the *Calendar of Córdoba* in Latin and Arabic, containing notices of Christian feast days, as well as miscellaneous information about monasteries, basilicas, agriculture, medicine, and astronomy.

Although the Mozarabs of the tenth century failed to produce original theological or literary compositions, their schools continued to prepare men for the service of the church, and there too the Bible, the liturgical books, collections of conciliar decrees and writings of the church Fathers were copied faithfully, in some of the finest examples of Visigothic script. Without intellectual brilliance, but without sacrificing essential beliefs, the Mozarabs preserved their Christian heritage, in circumstances of exceptional difficulty.

As one might surmise, the cultural attainments of the northern Christians during these early centuries were quite limited. In general, there is an extreme paucity of literary works of every kind, and those extant betray little originality. The uncertainty of the times, the constant threat of Muslim attack, no doubt discouraged scholarly activity in a region that had never been a cultural center in Roman or Visigothic times. In Asturias, Beatus of Liébana, mentioned above as an opponent of adoptionism, is also noted for his commentary on the Apocalypse; his work is not particularly profound, but the extant *codices* contain remarkable examples of miniature illumination. The flight of scholars, men like Theodulf of Orleans, Claudius of Turin, and Prudentius Galindus, to the court of Charlemagne, contributed to the cultural deficiency in northern Spain. These men came from the Spanish March, but the attraction and opportunities of the imperial court obviously were too great to be resisted. Even so, there remained important intellectual centers in Catalonia. The library of the Benedictine monastery of Santa Maria de Ripoll was one of the best in Europe and served as an inducement to Gerbert of Aurillac, the future Pope Sylvester II, to visit Catalonia in the late tenth century. Whether he also visited Córdoba is much debated.

The principal historical works of this period are anonymous chronicles. The earliest Christian source after the Muslim conquest is the so-called *Mozarabic Chronicle of 754* (or *Continuatio Hispana*, as Mommsen called it), once attributed to Isidore, bishop of Beja. The work of a Spanish cleric living under Muslim rule, perhaps in Toledo, it extends from 611 to 754. The author is strangely vague in his comments upon the circumstances leading to the Muslim invasion, King Rodrigo's defeat, and the treachery of Witiza's sons. He is much fuller when recording the activities of the early Muslim governors of Spain, their invasions of Gaul, and the civil wars of the early eighth century, but he knows nothing of the beginning of Christian resistance in Asturias.

The success of the kings of Asturias in dealing with the infidels probably encouraged their desire to record the origin and progress of the kingdom and its hopes for the future. If the conjectures of Sánchez Albornoz are correct, Alfonso II compiled a chronicle of Asturian history, now lost, that served as the basis for the later ninth-century chronicles emphasizing the continuity of the Visigothic and Asturian monarchies. The *Chronicle of Albelda* (*Cronicon Albeldense*), written about 881-883, and later continued to 976, stresses the history of the Goths and the Asturian kings and is especially detailed on the reign of

Alfonso III. About the same time, an anonymous author, probably a Mozarabic cleric from Toledo, composed the so-called *Prophetic Chronicle*, the text of which was included in part in the *Chronicle of Albelda*. The special interest of the *Prophetic Chronicle* lies in its interpretation of the prophecy of Ezekiel; identifying the Visigoths with Gog, the son of Japhet, and the Muslims with Ismael, the author declared that the Muslims would dominate Spain for 170 years, and, according to his calculations, the imminent end of their rule was at hand. Events seemed favorable enough to the Christians at the time to justify this expectation.

General opinion holds that the *Chronicle of Alfonso III* in its primitive form was composed by the king himself, but that an ecclesiastic, probably Sebastian, bishop of Orense, turned it into better Latin. An official chronicle written after 883, it extends from 672 to 866. The author regards the Asturian kings as heirs of the Visigoths, and when he discusses recent events he reflects the optimism which the successful prosecution of the reconquest had engendered. For much of the history of the tenth century we are dependent upon the *Chronicle* of Sampiro, bishop of Astorga (1035–1041), covering the years from 866 to 982. Though accurate and impartial, the work suffers from excessive brevity.

Aside from these works and some fragments of verse and the like, the literary remains of Christian Spain in the first centuries of the reconquest are sparse indeed. Yet in the courts, the cathedrals, and monasteries, despite the vicissitudes of war, the cultural tradition was kept alive, and libraries containing the great books of the past were being formed. On this necessary foundation greater intellectual labor was accomplished in the eleventh and twelfth centuries, when success in the reconquest, greater domestic tranquility, and increased communication with the rest of Christian Europe provided a milieu conducive to prolonged study and thought.

PART III

∽ᘓᘔ∼

A Balance of Power, from the Fall of the Caliphate to Las Navas de Tolosa

1031-1212

Los moros llaman Mafómat e los cristianos Santi Yague.

The Moors call on Muhammad, and the Christians on Santiago.

Cantar de mio Cid, 731

CHAPTER 8

Alfonso VI, the *Taifas*, and the Almoravids

The Eleventh Century

The eleventh century was a period of transition characterized by the integration of Christian Spain into western Christendom and by the political restructuring of al-Andalus. The Christian states intensified their relations with northern Europe, especially with France and the papacy, in every way and entered the mainstream of European civilization. Knights, monks, pilgrims, merchants, artisans, and scholars came from the lands north of the Pyrenees, sometimes in search of novelty and adventure, but more often to settle and to make a new life for themselves. Many of them were fortunate to attain high rank in the civil and ecclesiastical hierarchies; all of them contributed to the process of Europeanizing Christian Spain. The process was not without its cost, however, for it required the abandonment or modification of some hallowed traditions.

The new age was signaled also by the appearance of two new kingdoms, Castile and Aragon, which ultimately overshadowed the older realms of León and Navarre. Navarre, which, under Sancho el mayor's leadership, had seemed destined to unify Christian Spain, was quickly eclipsed and isolated by her neighbors. León continued to aspire to supremacy throughout the peninsula, but the future lay with the adventurous people of the frontier kingdom of Castile. Although the two kingdoms were reunited during most of the eleventh century, Castile retained her distinctive identity, and the Castilians provided the driving force in the reconquest. The fragmentation of al-Andalus following the abolition of the caliphate left the many petty kingdoms at the mercy of the Christian states whose rulers exacted tribute from them and threatened them with ultimate extinction. The balance of power, so long weighted against the Christians, seemed to shift decisively in their favor after the fall of Toledo in 1085. Any expectation of the imminent downfall of Muslim power was, however, premature, for the sect known as the Almoravids crossed from Morocco to restore Muslim unity and to throw the Christians back upon their heels. Thus, as the century drew to a close, the future of the reconquest was still clouded with uncertainty.

The Ascendancy of Fernando I

In conformity with the patrimonial principle, Sancho el mayor distributed his several realms among his sons and erased the unity of the Christian states as easily as he had created it. His oldest son, García III (1035-1054), received the kingdom of Navarre, expanded to include Castilian lands from Santander to Burgos, La Rioja, and the Basque provinces of Alava, Guipúzcoa, and Vizcaya. Fernando I (1035-1065) held the county of Castile which, though its eastern frontier was limited by the cessions to Navarre, was augmented on the west at the expense of León; his wife Sancha brought him as her dowry lands extending from the Cea to the Pisuerga river. An illegitimate son, Ramiro I (1035-1063), inherited the county of Aragon, and the youngest son, Gonzalo (1035-1043/5), the counties of Sobrarbe and Ribagorza; after his assassination these counties were annexed to Aragon. All the sons of Sancho el mayor eventually bore the title of king, and in this way Castile and Aragon attained the status of kingdoms.

Of all the brothers, Fernando I, whom an admiring chronicler hailed as *rex magnus*, achieved the greatest success. Not only did he reunite León and Castile and counter the ambitions of his brothers, but he also lorded it over the *taifas*. His first challenge came from Vermudo III, who repossessed the kingdom of León immediately after the death of Sancho el mayor. His hopes of restoring Leonese dominance and curbing Castilian independence were thwarted, however, by his defeat and death in the battle of Tamarón in 1037. Fernando I triumphantly claimed the kingdom of León in his wife's name and was solemnly crowned in the cathedral in 1039. The reunion of León and Castile, accomplished by Castilian arms, revealed the maturity of that erstwhile frontier county and marked the first step toward Castilian ascendancy in the peninsula.

The Castilian lands annexed to Navarre gave substantial cause for hostility between Fernando I and his older brother, García III, who was jealous of his success in gaining the kingdom of León. Their enmity was resolved when Fernando I emerged triumphant in the battle of Atapuerca in 1054, leaving García III dead upon the field. García's son, Sancho IV (1054–1076), inherited the kingdom of Navarre, but he had to cede part of La Bureba to Fernando I, whose eastern frontier was thereby extended as far as the Ebro river.

Victorious over his enemies and secure in possession of his realms, Fernando I convened a council of bishops and magnates to meet at Coyanza around 1055 "for the restoration of Christendom." Besides promulgating decrees regulating ecclesiastical discipline and renewing the enactments of the council held at León in 1017, the king and the assembly pledged to uphold the traditional laws of the kingdom of León and to assure the equitable administration of justice.

Ramon Berenguer I, count of Barcelona (1035–1076), a contemporary of Fernando I, effected a similar work of reorganization and reconstruction in Catalonia. Though at first he shared the government with his younger brothers, by 1054 through their renunciations he obtained sole authority in Barcelona, Gerona, and Ausona (Vich). Possession of these counties, the essential nucleus of Catalonia, enabled him to dominate the whole of Catalonia and to persuade the counts of Ampurias, Urgel, Besalú, Cerdagne, and Pallars to recognize his suzerainty. Furthermore, by inheriting the dominions of his nephew, Roger III, count of Carcassonne and Razès, viscount of Béziers and Agde, in 1066, he acquired a special interest in Languedoc, which influenced the policy of his successors for several generations. The linguistic, cultural, feudal, and family ties linking Catalonia and Languedoc were especially strong, and until the opening of the thirteenth century the formation of a state uniting these territories under the rule of the count of Barcelona seemed to be a very real possibility. Unification was continually hindered, however, by the common practice of dividing the comital patrimony among the heirs.

In another respect, too, Ramon Berenguer I holds a unique place in the history of Catalonia because it was he who promulgated the earliest texts of the *Usages of Barcelona* containing the fundamental law of Catalonia and the essential principles upon which the structure of Catalan society was established.

Both Ramon Berenguer I and Fernando I tried to profit from the disorganized conditions prevailing in Muslim Spain. The numerous petty kingdoms that had emerged there in the early years of the eleventh century gradually were reduced in number as the larger ones absorbed the smaller ones. From west to east the principal *taifas* were Badajoz, ruled by the Aftasids, Seville by the Abbadids, Granada by the Zirids, Toledo by the Banu Dhi-l-Nun, Málaga by the Hammudids, Denia and the Balearic Islands by the descendants of Mujahid, Zaragoza and Lérida by the Banu Hud, and Valencia by the Amirids. Through their inability to cooperate with one another, the *taifas* succumbed individually to the pressure exerted by the Christian rulers.

Fernando I seized Lamego and Viseu in 1055, advancing his western frontier south of the Duero into what was to become Portugal, but he was not yet prepared to attempt the conquest and annexation of large segments of Muslim territory. By compelling the *reyes de taifas* to pay tribute, he and the other Christian rulers filled their treasuries in preparation for the day when conquest and colonization would be feasible. Of the several *taifas*, only Zaragoza bordered on all the Christian realms; each of them eyed it as a natural zone for expansion. Thus while Ramon Berenguer I levied tribute on Lérida, the eastern sector of the kingdom, Ramiro I of Aragon threatened Zaragoza itself. To counter this aggression, al-Muqtadir, king of Zaragoza (1046–1081), offered tribute to Fernando I, whose troops routed the Aragonese at Graus in 1063 and affirmed Leonese supremacy in that region. Ramiro died soon after and was succeeded by his son, Sancho I Ramírez (1063–1094). Meanwhile, al-Mamun of Toledo (1043–1075), al-Mutadid of Seville (1042–1069), and al-Mutawakkil of Badajoz (1067–1094) also promised to pay tribute to León. The king of Seville, in addition to the tribute money, even yielded the body of St. Isidore to be reinterred in a church recently erected by Fernando I in León, as a future pantheon of kings. The *Historia Silense* (100) reported that al-Mutadid threw a brocaded cover over the coffin and sighed: "Now you are leaving here, revered Isidore; well you know how much your fame was mine!" Fernando I capped his successful manipulation of the Muslim rulers by taking Coimbra in July 1064 after a siege of six months. As his western frontier now reached the Mondego river, the future county of Portugal began to take shape under the administration of the Mozarabic leader, Sisnando Davídiz, whom Fernando appointed as count in that district.

In the same year, an army of French knights assaulted the fortress of

Barbastro in the kingdom of Zaragoza, blocking access to the plains of the Ebro river. This first occasion on which Frenchmen participated in significant numbers in the reconquest is indicative of increasing French interest in peninsular affairs. The expedition might be thought of as the first of the crusades, as Pope Alexander II granted to the participants the plenary indulgence characteristic of the later crusades to the Holy Land, saying: "By the authority of the holy apostles, Peter and Paul, we relieve them of penance and grant them remission of sins." While Boissonade greatly exaggerated by saying the Cluniac monks preached the crusade throughout the Christian world, other French scholars, such as Villey and Rousset, wishing to reserve the honor of proclaiming the first crusading indulgence to Urban II, have challenged the authenticity of Alexander II's bull. Dufourneaux has remarked, on the other hand, that if the expedition lacked the juridical character of a crusade, the crusading spirit pervaded its organization.

A sizeable French army, together with Catalan and Aragonese contingents, under the leadership of Guillaume de Montreuil (whom Ibn Hayyan called the papal standard-bearer), Robert Crespin of Normandy, Duke William VIII of Aquitaine, and Count Armengol III of Urgel, captured Barbastro in August 1064, after a siege of forty days. Although the defenders were guaranteed safe conduct, the Christians fell upon them as they left the city and slaughtered them; Muslim women were violated, and young boys and girls were seized as slaves. The booty was immense. Placing the city under the sovereignty of Sancho I of Aragon, the victors succumbed to the luxury of Muslim life and surrounded themselves with harems and dancing girls, but their enjoyment of the spoils of war was abruptly terminated in the following year when al-Muqtadir of Zaragoza recovered possession. The crusade of Barbastro contributed nothing of permanence to the reconquest, though it did point up the possibilities of spiritual and material gain awaiting those Frenchmen who chose to take part in future peninsular wars. The massacre of the defenders of Barbastro also exemplified the difference in the attitudes of those Christians who had continual contact with Muslims and those who did not. The zeal and fanaticism displayed by the latter contrasted sharply with the comparative tolerance of the former.

It is something of a paradox that those who seemed destined to further the reunification of the peninsula often retarded the process. Convening an assembly of magnates and bishops at León in 1063 for the dedication of the church of San Isidoro, Fernando I announced his intention to distribute his dominions among his sons. The oldest, Sancho II (1065–1072), received the kingdom of Castile as far west as the river Pisuerga and also the tributes owed by the king of Zaragoza. The second son, Alfonso VI (1065–1109), his father's favorite, received the kingdom of León and the tributes of Toledo, and the third son, García (1065–1072), was awarded the kingdom of Galicia and the district of Portugal with the tributes of Badajoz and Seville. The king's daughters, who were forbidden to marry, received lordship over all the monasteries of the three kingdoms. By dividing the kingdom into three parts, Fernando I not only violated an age-old Leonese tradition but also undid his own work. According to the thirteenth-century *Primera Crónica General* (813), his son Sancho protested the partition declaring: "In ancient times the Goths agreed among themselves that the empire of Spain should never be divided, but that all of it should always be under one lord." Though his protest was to no avail at the moment, he later took steps to rectify what he considered to be a grave injustice.

When the king of Zaragoza refused to pay tribute, Fernando I set out on his last campaign, ravaging as far south as Valencia, until illness forced him to return to León. On Christmas Day 1065, he placed his crown and mantle on the altar of San Isidoro of León and, asking God's mercy, assumed the garb of a penitent. Two days later he died and was buried in the church near his father and his predecessors. An excellent king in many respects, the conqueror of Coimbra, the overlord of Zaragoza, Toledo, Badajoz, and Seville, called *Yspanus rex* by the *Chronicle of Nájera*, by dividing the realm among his heirs he sowed the seeds of future discord.

Determined to subordinate the whole of Spain to the rule of one lord, Sancho II of Castile, a bold and energetic prince, set out to assert his pre-eminence over his neighbors and to deprive his brothers of their share in the partition. He compelled al-Muqtadir to renew the payment of tribute, but his claims to suzerainty over Zaragoza were disputed by his cousins, Sancho IV of Navarre and Sancho I of Aragon. He also quarreled with Alfonso VI, whom he defeated at Llantada in 1068, though he gained no territory. He was more successful in dealing with his youngest brother, García, whom he deposed as king of Galicia in 1071 and forced to flee to Seville.

Early in the following year Sancho II defeated Alfonso VI again and expelled him from his kingdom. While Alfonso sought refuge at To-

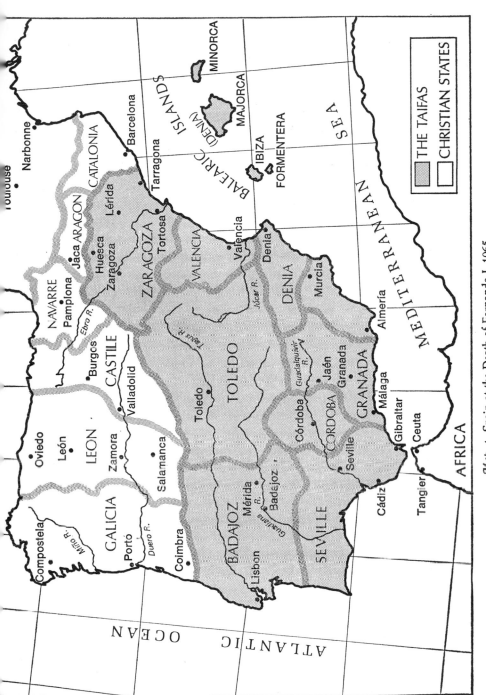

Map 4. Spain at the Death of Fernando I, 1065

ledo, Sancho was anointed and crowned as king of León. Thus for the third time in less than a century León and Castile were reunited through the military action of the ruler of Castile. Though he might well now be called *dominator Hispaniae*, Sancho's triumph was brief; he was struck down by the hand of an assassin thought to be in the employ of his sister Urraca, who conspired to help Alfonso VI (toward whom she displayed a more than sisterly love) to regain his throne. Alfonso promptly returned to take possession of the kingdom of León and, since his brother had died without children, to claim Castile as well. The Castilian nobility, led by Rodrigo Díaz de Vivar, Sancho's chief military commander, suspected Alfonso of complicity in the assassination, and before accepting him as sovereign, required him to exculpate himself by swearing an oath of purgation. Rodrigo Díaz, whom history knows as the Cid (*sidi*, or lord) or as the Campeador (*Campidoctor*, master of the battlefield) was admitted into the king's favor and became his vassal, but their relationship was never cordial, and eventually the king, perhaps jealous of the Cid's prowess, dismissed him from his service.

Later in the year García, the third brother, returned to Galicia, but Alfonso arrested him and kept him in prison until his death eighteen years later. Thus Alfonso VI reunified the kingdom divided by his father seven years before. By adopting the title *rex Hispaniae* thereafter, he indicated his pretensions to supremacy throughout the peninsula.

The assassination of Sancho IV of Navarre in 1076 enabled Alfonso VI to resolve the conflict over frontiers which had agitated Castile and Navarre since the days of Sancho el mayor. Taking advantage of the situation Sancho I of Aragon invaded Navarre, occupied Pamplona, and obtained recognition as king, thereby reuniting Aragon and Navarre until 1134; at the same time Alfonso VI annexed the provinces of La Rioja, Alava, Vizcaya, and a part of Guipúzcoa, considerably augmenting the Castilian territory.

Pope Gregory VII and the Hispanic Kingdoms

During Alfonso VI's long reign, Christian Spain experienced a constantly expanding influence from beyond the Pyrenees. The influx of pilgrims journeying to Compostela increased rapidly, while French monks introduced the Cluniac observance into many monasteries, and French knights, seeking fame and fortune, came in large numbers. At the same time there was a more frequent and a more effective exercise of papal authority. Under the leadership of Gregory VII (1073–1085), the papacy was freeing itself from the domination of the Roman factions and of the Roman emperor and attempting to carry out a general reform of the church. Papal action in the Hispanic kingdoms touched chiefly on two major themes, namely, papal sovereignty over the peninsula and the Mozarabic liturgy.

Both Gregory VII and his predecessor, Alexander II, seem to have believed that the papacy had a definite responsibility for the prosecution of the reconquest. Alexander II had supported the expedition of the French knights against Barbastro in 1064 and, in spite of its fleeting success, sanctioned a similar enterprise being planned by Count Ebles de Roucy with the backing of the Abbot of Cluny. Soon after his election, in April 1073, Gregory VII instructed his legates in southern France to lend every encouragement to de Roucy's expedition. In a letter to "all the princes wishing to go to Spain," he stated: "We believe that it is not unknown to you that the kingdom of Spain belonged from ancient times to St. Peter in full sovereignty (*proprii iuris*) and, though occupied for a long time by the pagans, since the law of justice has not been set aside it belongs even now to no mortal, but solely to the apostolic see" (*DP*, 12). In accordance with the terms of his agreement with the Holy See, de Roucy was to hold any future conquests in the name of St. Peter. Suger, abbot of St. Denis, in his life of King Louis VI of France, reported that de Roucy (whom he describes as rapacious and tumultuous) led a large army, such as kings command, into Spain, but none of the peninsular sources mention it, and it seems not to have achieved any important success.

A papal policy of reconquest which ignored the Hispanic rulers and relied upon expeditions such as that of de Roucy can only be described as foolish. Gregory VII may well have come to realize this, but he did not abandon papal claims to the peninsula. He wrote to the "kings, counts and other princes of Spain," in June 1077, exhorting them to rule justly, but also reminding them that "the kingdom of Spain was given by ancient constitutions to Blessed Peter and the Holy Roman Church in right and ownership" (*DP*, 24). It has usually been assumed that by "ancient constitutions" he meant the Donation of Constantine, a forgery, whereby the first Christian emperor purportedly gave the papacy great power and authority in western Europe. Other interpretations have been offered but with less plausibility. Luciano de la Calzada's suggestion that the pope wished to assert only a spiritual sovereignty seems quite unrealistic. Gregory VII's desire to secure an acknowledgment of papal sovereignty does not mean that he sought to exercise direct temporal power in the peninsula, but he probably hoped that the Hispanic rulers would establish feudal relationships with Rome, similar to those already binding the rulers of Naples and Sicily, Hungary, and Denmark. Sancho I of Aragon, brother-in-law of Count Ebles de Roucy, on the occasion of a visit to Rome in 1068, gave an example by offering himself as a *miles Sancti Petri*, or vassal of St. Peter, promising to pay an annual tribute. Count Bernat of Besalú did likewise in 1077. Pledges of this sort could only encourage papal pretensions.

Alfonso VI, the most powerful of the Christian princes, apparently refused to recognize papal claims and, by using the title *imperator totius Hispaniae*, affirmed as explicitly as possible traditional Leonese aspirations to hegemony throughout the peninsula. Menéndez Pidal considered this a declaration of Hispanic independence. Whether this interpretation be true or not (and de la Calzada believes that it is not), Gregory VII did not press the issue. Rather, by addressing Alfonso as the "glorious king of Spain" to whom Christ had given greater honor and glory than the other kings of Spain, he seemed to accept Alfonso's supremacy in the peninsula.

In the strictly ecclesiastical order, Gregory VII attempted to substitute the Roman for the Mozarabic liturgy. Dating from the early Christian centuries, the Mozarabic liturgy was still in use in both the Christian and Muslim parts of Spain. In the mind of Gregory VII, whose whole policy tended toward centralization and uniformity, native liturgies were suspect and were seen as obstacles to ecclesiastical unity. Writing to the kings of León and Navarre in March 1074 he implied that because of the growth of Priscillianism and Arianism in Spain during the early centuries of the Christian era and the prolonged rule of the Visigoths and Muslims, the Mozarabic liturgy was tainted and not quite orthodox. Even though the liturgical books of the Mozarabic rite had been approved in Rome in 1065, Gregory VII obviously had reservations on this count and expressed the hope that the Hispanic Christians would accept the Roman liturgy, that of the see of St. Peter, in place of that of Toledo.

Under Frankish influence the Catalan counties had long ago aban-/ doned the Mozarabic liturgy. The Cluniac monks who flocked to Spain in the eleventh century became active proponents of the Roman liturgy and, with the approbation of Sancho I, helped to introduce it into the kingdom of Aragon in 1071. Alfonso VI, who was open to extrapeninsular influences, was not averse to the adoption of the Roman liturgy, but he recognized that the Mozarabic liturgy had strong support. As a means of overcoming popular resistance, he submitted the question to trial by combat, pitting champions representing the two liturgies against one another. The defeat of the Roman champion seemed a clear sign of divine approbation of the Mozarabic liturgy, but the king was unwilling to accept this judgment as final and caused

a great fire to be set in the middle of the square, and two books, the one containing the Roman liturgy, the other the Toledan liturgy, were thrown into it, on condition that the liturgy found in the book that escaped unscathed would be accepted. But when the Toledan liturgy took a great leap out of the flames, the angry king kicked it back into the fire, saying: "Let the horns of the laws bend to the will of kings." [*Crónica Najerense*, III, 49]

In the context of contemporary notions of law, these appeals to the judgment of God clearly favored the retention of the Mozarabic liturgy and contradicted the wishes of the king and the pope.

A frustrated Alfonso VI appealed to the pope in 1078 to send a legate to convince his people of the need for change, and he also asked his good friend, Abbot Hugh of Cluny, to send a monk to become abbot of Sahagún, one of the most prestigious monasteries of his kingdom, to advance acceptance of the Roman liturgy. The monk Robert, chosen for this task, became a champion of the Mozarabic cause, however, and evidently encouraged the king in his liaison with one of the queen's ladies-in-waiting. Menéndez Pidal views Robert as an adventurer who hoped to gain high position in the church, while de la Calzada suggests that he was attempting to oppose the increasing papal intervention in Spain as a threat to Cluny's ecclesiastical hegemony there. The latter argument seems particularly weak, and it is likely that Menéndez Pidal's assessment of the situation is the correct one.

Resolved to bring the matter to an end, Gregory VII sent a legate to convene a council at Burgos in 1080 to effect the adoption of the Roman liturgy throughout León and Castile. On the pope's insistence Robert was removed as abbot of Sahagún and replaced by another

Cluniac, Bernard de Sauvetot. The pope also threatened Alfonso VI with excommunication if he failed to put aside his mistress. The abandonment of the Mozarabic liturgy symbolized the full integration of Christian Spain into western Christendom; no longer was the peninsula isolated from the main currents of European civilization. From this time forward, papal authority touched the lives and actions of the Hispanic rulers and their people to a greater extent than ever before. Menéndez Pidal has pointed out that a council held at León in 1090 completed the papal trimuph by ordering the elimination of the Visigothic script from all ecclesiastical books and the use of the Carolingian or French hand. A major effect of this was that books written in the traditional peninsular script were unintelligible to later generations trained to read a more modern hand. Thus "an abyss was opened between the archaic and the modern culture."

The Fall of Toledo

Alfonso VI had the great honor of fulfilling a long-held ambition of the Leonese kings, namely, the conquest of Toledo, the ancient seat of the Visigothic monarchy. He initially continued his father's policy of imposing tributes upon the taifas, but gradually turned toward active conquest. While he derived considerable profit from the economic exploitation of the taifas of Seville, Granada, Badajoz, Toledo, and Zaragoza, he was tempted constantly to increase his demands. Thus Abd Allah, king of Granada (1074/5–1090), wrote in his memoirs that it was Alfonso's intention to set the Muslim princes against one another and by exacting ever-increasing tributes to exhaust their resources and their power to resist. Count Sisnando Davídiz, Alfonso VI's envoy to Granada, said as much:

Al-Andalus belonged to the Christians from the beginning until they were conquered by the Arabs. . . . Now . . . they want to recover what was taken from them by force, and so that the result may be final, it is necessary to weaken you and waste you away with time. When you no longer have money or soldiers, we will seize the country without the least effort. [Lévi-Provençal, "Les Mémoires de Abd Allah," Al-Andalus, 4 (1936) 35–36]

This oppression of the petty kings provoked a reaction among their subjects, who accused them of a humiliating subservience to the infidels and of betraying the Muslim faith. Popular hostility ultimately brought about the downfall of the taifas, but Alfonso VI gained no advantage from it.

In the past he had enjoyed excellent relations with al-Mamun of Toledo, who had sheltered him during his exile from León. Al-Mamun
was a patron of poets and scholars who raised his kingdom to the
heights of prosperity and broadened its frontiers by annexing Valencia
and Córdoba. After his death his ineffectual grandson, al-Qadir (1075–
1085) was unable to defend the kingdom against the attacks of his
neighbors. Valencia proclaimed its independence, and al-Mutamid of
Seville (1069–1091) seized Córdoba, while the citizens of Toledo became increasingly hostile to their ruler. Al-Qadir fled the city in 1080
and appealed to Alfonso VI to aid him; the Toledans, meanwhile, invited al-Mutawakkil of Badajoz to rule over them. Alfonso VI seized
Coria, his first important conquest beyond the Tagus, and promised to
restore al-Qadir to power, on condition that he eventually surrender
Toledo and move to Valencia, where if necessary Alfonso's armies
would install him. Thus with Leonese support, al-Qadir was able to
return to Toledo in April 1081, and al-Mutawakkil fled. As the price
of his restoration al-Qadir had to pay tribute to Alfonso VI and yield
control of the principal castles guarding the approaches to the city. The
king's determination to have Toledo is revealed in a letter he wrote to
Pope Gregory VII concerning the future appointment of an archbishop
in that city.

At this time Alfonso VI, influenced by jealous courtiers, forced his
most distinguished vassal, Rodrigo Díaz, into exile; he perhaps viewed
the Cid as a dangerous man, too independent in judgment and action.
Whatever the reason, the tie of vassalage was broken, and the Cid began the long peregrinations that led him first to Zaragoza and ultimately to Valencia. Together with a small band of followers he left the
kingdom of León in 1081 "para ganar su pan," to seek his livelihood
elsewhere. At first he went to Barcelona where the brothers, Ramon
Berenguer II (1076–1082) and Berenguer Ramon II (1076–1097), refused his offer of service. Then he journeyed to Zaragoza where he
received a warmer welcome. That kingdom was divided between al-
Mutamin (1081–1085) who ruled Zaragoza proper, and his brother
al-Mundhir, who ruled Lérida and Tortosa. The Cid entered al-Mu-
tamin's service and successfully defended Zaragoza against the assaults
of al-Mundhir, Sancho I of Aragon, and Ramon Berenguer II, whom he
held captive briefly in 1082. Shortly thereafter Berenguer Ramon, by
assassinating his brother, gained sole control of the county of Barcelona.

In acting as the protector of Zaragoza, the Cid probably believed that he was serving the best interests of his erstwhile lord, Alfonso VI, who for many years collected tribute from Zaragoza and considered it his dependency. But the rulers of Aragon-Navarre and Barcelona also hoped to make inroads into the area. By repelling them, the Cid was preserving Leonese claims to overlordship and eventual conquest in Zaragoza. Thus when Alfonso VI sent troops to besiege the city in 1085, the Cid made no attempt to oppose them, as he had the forces of the other Christian princes; but as he was still out of favor with the king, he could offer no active assistance during the siege.

Meanwhile al-Qadir's position in Toledo was becoming more untenable every day. His enemies within the city continued to conspire against him and hoped to induce one of the other Muslim rulers to depose him. The more moderate element preferred submission to Alfonso VI and appealed to him to besiege the city, so that after a decent interval and an honorable resistance they could surrender without fear of being charged with treason to Islam. In the meantime Alfonso VI ravaged the kingdom of Seville for failure to pay tribute and reached the southern extremity of the peninsula at Tarifa. As he rode out to the surf, he exclaimed in exultation: "This is the very end of Spain and I have set foot upon it." Complying gladly with al-Qadir's request, he established a formal siege of Toledo at the end of the summer 1084.

Failing to secure relief from the other Muslim states, Toledo surrendered on 6 May 1085. Alfonso VI guaranteed to the inhabitants the security of their persons and properties, subject to the payment of a poll tax. The Muslims who remained in the city were granted the right to worship freely and to retain possession of the chief mosque; those who wished to leave could do so freely, taking their goods with them. Upon entering Toledo, the king appointed the Mozarab, Sisnando Davídiz, count of Coimbra, as governor, in a deliberate move to placate the different religious elements, but his tolerant attitude toward the Muslims scandalized many, especially the French queen, Constanza, and the French clergy, such as Bernard de Sauvetot, abbot of Sahagún, who was now installed as archbishop of Toledo. As there was no church suitable for use as a cathedral, Archbishop Bernard, during the king's absence from the city, seized the chief mosque. Outraged by this breach of the terms of capitulation, Alfonso VI threatened to punish the archbishop severely, but the Muslims persuaded him not to, lest they suffer later. Three years after the fall of Toledo, Pope Urban II acknowledged the primacy of that see in the Iberian peninsula, thereby provoking opposition from other metropolitan sees in the next 150 years. In fulfillment of promises given, Alfonso VI sent his troops to install al-Qadir, the hapless king of Toledo, as ruler of Valencia, and to remain there to protect and sustain him.

The surrender of Toledo was an event of great transcendence in the history of medieval Spain. Alfonso VI was able to occupy both the city and a broad region in the Tagus valley reaching from Talavera on the west to Guadalajara on the east. Although Toledo was threatened frequently in the next century, it remained in Christian hands, and the frontier was never pushed back from the Tagus. Toledo formed the nucleus of the region later known as New Castile and quickly eclipsed León, the old seat of royalty, as the political center of the peninsula. In recognition of the importance of his conquest, Alfonso VI began to use the title *imperator toletanus*.

With the surrender of Toledo and its dependencies a substantial number of Muslims were incorporated into his dominions. Hitherto the Muslims usually elected to abandon their settlements rather than submit to Christian rule, but from 1085 onward they tended to remain in their ancestral homes. The Christian rulers, for the most part, were inclined to be tolerant of the *mudéjares*, as the Muslims living in their kingdoms were called. Several Muslim chronicles report that Alfonso VI described himself as emperor of the two religions, perhaps to emphasize his sovereignty over both Christian and Muslim communities, or, as seems more likely, to assert his claim to rule over the whole peninsula and all its people, both Christian and Muslim. This notion is clearly expressed in another of his titles: *imperator constitutus super omnes Hispaniae nationes*.

The king's entrance into Toledo marked the fulfillment of one of the most cherished dreams of his predecessors, the kings of Asturias and León, who almost from the earliest times, as the self-proclaimed heirs of the Visigoths, hoped to reconstitute the Visigothic kingdom. The capture of Toledo, "once the ornament of the Christians of all Spain," and the seat of the Visigothic kings, seemed to augur the rapid dissolution of al-Andalus.

The Advent of the Almoravids

Alfonso VI in 1085 stood at the pinnacle of glory. In possession of Toledo, protector of Valencia, he had reason for elation and could plan

the conquest of Zaragoza and eventually of the other *taifas*. The poet
Ibn al-Gassal warned his fellow Muslims of the threat facing them:

> O people of al-Andalus, hasten your horses;
> To remain here is folly . . .
> We live with an enemy who does not go away.
> How can we live with a serpent in the basket?
>
> [Huici, *Las grandes batallas de la reconquista*, 19]

The kings of Seville, Granada, and Badajoz now fully realized that they
lacked the resources and energy to deal effectively with Alfonso VI. If
they failed to act in concert and to secure external assistance, he would
surely destroy them all. Their only salvation seemed to lie in an appeal
to the Almoravids of North Africa, though that entailed a potential
threat of conquest from that quarter.

The sect of the Almoravids had its origin in the preaching of Abd
Allah ibn Yasin, who, about fifty years before, attempted to enkindle
a new zeal for the faith among the Berber tribes of the Sahara. With a
band of disciples he established a fortress-monastery or *ribat* on an
island in the Niger river. The men of the *ribat* (*al-murabitun*, almoravids) devoted themselves to ascetic practices while waging war against
those who refused to accept their interpretation of Islam. The Almoravids, who covered their faces with a veil, were fanatical puritans who
insisted upon a rigorous observance of Muslim law, condemning the
use of wine, the imposition of taxes not sanctioned by the Koran, and
the custom of having more than the four wives permitted by law.
Under the leadership of Yusuf ibn Tashufin (1061–1106), a rude Berber endowed with great military talent, who called himself emir of the
Muslims (*amir al-muslimin*) and acknowledged the supremacy of the
Abbasid caliphs of Baghdad, the Almoravids conquered Morocco and
western Algeria. After taking Tangier in 1077 and Ceuta in 1084,
Yusuf was easily able to cross the straits into Spain, but he waited until
he received an appeal from the *reyes de taifas*.

The contrast between the Almoravids and the petty kings of al-
Andalus could not have been greater. The former were barbarian no-
mads who viewed the latter as effete lovers of luxury who bore their
religious obligations lightly. In summoning the Almoravids to their aid
the *reyes de taifas* were running the risk of self-destruction, but they
had no other choice. Al-Mutamid of Seville summed up the feelings of
his colleagues when he remarked that he preferred to herd camels for
the Almoravids than to guard the pigsty of Alfonso VI. Thus, with the

concurrence of Abd Allah of Granada and al-Mutawakkil of Badajoz, he addressed an appeal to Yusuf ibn Tashufin, who responded favorably.

The Almoravids landed at Algeciras in June 1086 and advanced to Seville; from there, accompanied by the kings of Seville, Granada, and Málaga, they continued to Badajoz. Alfonso VI, on learning of the invasion, abandoned the siege of Zaragoza, recalled his troops from Valencia, and appealed to Sancho I of Aragon for help. Early in the fall Alfonso VI set out to meet the enemy and engaged them in a major battle at Zallaqa (Sacralias, Sagrajas), northeast of Badajoz on 23 October 1086. At first the Christians drove the forces of the *reyes de taifas* back to Badajoz, but Yusuf seemed unconcerned for their fate, as he remarked: "What is it to me that those people are massacred? They are all enemies!" But then, ordering the Almoravids to move forward in a compact mass to the sound of war drums, he stemmed the tide, and by nightfall routed the Christians. In the *Rawd al-Qirtas*, Ibn Abi Zar records grimly that piles of heads severed from bodies of defeated Christians were loaded on carts and sent to the cities of al-Andalus to give visual testimony to the completeness of the victory.

The disaster was probably not so great as it seemed. Instead of pursuing the enemy, Yusuf returned immediately to Africa, ostensibly because of the death of his son, but it is possible that his losses were such that he could not engage in a prolonged campaign in Spain. His cupidity had been aroused by the gifts showered upon him by the *reyes de taifas*, but he was not yet ready to dispossess them. Alfonso VI had been beaten badly, and his pride had surely suffered a grievous blow, but he had not lost any territory and remained firmly in possession of Toledo. Soon after the battle a number of French nobles, including Duke Odo of Burgundy and Count Raymond of Toulouse (who later gained fame as a leader of the First Crusade), arrived in answer to his appeal for help, but in view of the departure of the Almoravids, their services did not seem to be needed, and they returned home.

Emboldened by the victory at Zallaqa, the *reyes de taifas* refused to continue paying tribute to Alfonso VI, but they were incapable of checking a renewed Christian offensive. The Cid, readmitted to the king's service, and authorized to hold by hereditary right whatever lands he could occupy in the eastern part of the peninsula, established himself as the protector of al-Qadir in Valencia and made his power felt throughout the adjoining regions. Other Christian forces, using the castle of Aledo near Murcia as a base, carried out marauding expeditions deep into the heart of al-Andalus. So exasperated were the *reyes de taifas* that they felt constrained to summon the Almoravids again.

Yusuf ibn Tashufin returned to Spain in June 1089, but only al-Mutamid of Seville and some lesser lords joined with him in an attempt to expel the Christians from Aledo. When he learned that Alfonso VI was preparing to relieve the castle, Yusuf abandoned the siege and returned to Morocco. Now he began to think seriously of deposing the *reyes de taifas* for the good of Islam. Throughout al-Andalus the jurists incited hostility toward the petty kings, charging them with immorality and subservience to the Christians. The devout might well ask whether such impious libertines and corrupters of public morals should be allowed to rule over the Muslim community. The poet al-Sumaisir expressed the feelings of many when he reproached the kings, saying: "To revolt against you is a duty, for you make common cause with the Christians. To withdraw from your allegiance is not a crime, for you yourselves have withdrawn your allegiance to the prophet." (Dozy, *Histoire de l'Espagne Musulmane*, III, 136). For his part, Yusuf sought the opinion of the jurisconsults of Spain and Morocco and even of the distinguished eastern preceptors al-Ghazzali and al-Turtushi, all of whom concurred in justifying whatever action he might take against the Muslim princes of Spain.

Returning to the peninsula, Yusuf deposed Abd Allah, the last of the Zirid kings of Granada, and his brother Tamim, king of Málaga, in September 1090, and sent them as prisoners to Morocco, where Abd Allah composed his memoirs, a significant historical record for the period. While Yusuf seized Córdoba in March 1091 and prepared to besiege Seville, al-Mutamid appealed to Alfonso VI to rescue him. Realizing that if he failed to intervene, the Almoravids would soon control the whole of al-Andalus, Alfonso VI called upon his subjects to grant him an extraordinary tribute so that he could take the necessary measures to check the enemy advance. His troops threatened Granada and attempted to relieve Seville, but the Almoravids took the city by assault in November 1091. Al-Mutamid ended his days as a prisoner in Morocco. Meantime the Almoravids overran the southeastern coast taking Almería, Murcia, Denia, and Játiva.

With the conquest of Granada, Córdoba, Seville, Málaga, and Murcia, Yusuf became master of a substantial segment of al-Andalus. Badajoz, Valencia, and Zaragoza were the only major kingdoms still independent. The Almoravids seized Badajoz in 1094 and executed al-Mutawakkil, who attempted to gain Christian support by ceding Lisbon and other places to Alfonso VI, though eventually the Almoravids recovered them. With the overthrow of al-Mutawakkil, Yusuf controlled an empire straddling the straits of Gibraltar, including the whole southern section of the peninsula from the Atlantic to the Mediterranean. Through a series of uninterrupted triumphs the Almoravids had restored the unity of al-Andalus and confronted Christian Spain with the most serious threat since the days of Almanzor.

The Cid and the Defense of Valencia

The Almoravids met their first reverses at the hands of the Castilian exile, Rodrigo Díaz de Vivar, the Cid Campeador. Though reconciled with Alfonso VI, he remained in the east where he dominated al-Qadir, king of Valencia. The Valencian Muslims, contemptuous of their ruler, looked for deliverance to the Almoravids, who were advancing from the south. In high expectancy the Valencians revolted in October 1092 and killed al Qadir, but the Cid intervened and by establishing a tight siege of the city, prevented its surrender to the Almoravids; they sent reinforcements but decided not to offer battle to him. Left to their own devices the citizens, after a siege of twenty months, were reduced to starvation and surrendered on 17 June 1094. The Cid was generous enough, allowing Muslims to worship freely and to retain their property, subject only to the payment of tributes authorized by the Koran. At first he resided outside the city but eventually established himself in the *alcazar* and from that vantage point was more easily able to govern his realm and to suppress any signs of disloyalty or intrigue. Though content to call himself lord of Valencia, he was sovereign in all but name.

The Almoravids advanced against Valencia in great strength in October 1094, but the Cid met them at Cuarte just outside the walls and routed them; this was their first reverse since their initial invasion. For the next five years the Cid remained in unchallenged control of Valencia. His death, at the age of fifty-six on 10 July 1099, was a cause of great sorrow to Christians on both sides of the Pyrenees. The Poitevin *Chronicle of Maillezais* recorded his death, saying: "Count Rodrigo died in Spain in Valencia; his death caused the most profound sorrow in Christendom and great joy among the pagan enemies." Through his life and actions he won the affection and admiration of many of his contemporaries and of future generations. In his lifetime an anonymous author was inspired to celebrate his exploits in the poem, *Carmen Campidoctoris*. Within fifteen years of his death a cleric who had followed him in his wanderings composed the *Historia Roderici*, a detailed and informative biography, the first historical work in Christian Spain whose central figure was someone other than the king. Some fifty years after his death the *Cantar de mio Cid*, the great epic of medieval Castile, was put in written form. These texts reflect the impact of the Cid's personality upon his age and reveal that he was not a bandit or *condottiere*, fighting only for material profit, as he has sometimes been pictured, but rather a true champion, the defender of Christian Spain and a faithful vassal to his king.

For nearly three years after his death, his widow, Jimena, aided by her son-in-law, Count Ramon Berenguer III of Barcelona (1097–1131), maintained the lordship of Valencia. The Almoravids besieged the city for seven months in 1101 but withdrew when they learned that Alfonso VI was bringing relief. Concluding that Valencia could no longer be defended, he ordered Jimena to abandon the city; thus she returned to Castile, bringing her husband's body to be buried in the monastery of San Pedro de Cardeña. The Almoravids occupied the burning ruins of Valencia in May 1102. Not until a hundred and thirty years later were the Christians able to return.

After the occupation of Valencia, the Almoravids controlled the whole of Muslim Spain, with the exception of the kingdom of Zaragoza. Pedro I (1094–1104), the new king of Aragon and Navarre, continued his father's aggression against that kingdom and in 1096 gained a major victory over al-Mustain (1084–1110) at Alcoraz. As a consequence, Huesca, one of the key points guarding the approaches to Zaragoza, surrendered. Pedro I in 1101 also recovered Barbastro, which the French knights had occupied temporarily thirty years before. In spite of the work of reconquest still to be accomplished, Pedro I announced his intention to go on a crusade to the Holy Land, until he was dissuaded by Pope Paschal II who offered crusading indulgences to those who fought against the infidels in Spain. From this time on, the military expeditions of the reconquest ordinarily received the canonical status of crusades. Pedro I died in 1104, leaving to his brother, Alfonso I (1104–1134), the task of conquering Zaragoza. Two years later Yusuf ibn Tashufin, the emir of the Muslims, died, bequeathing to his son, Ali (1106–1143), an immense empire extending from the borders of the Sudan through North Africa to Spain.

The reign of Alfonso VI was also drawing to a close. Despite several marriages, he had no legitimate son and was confronted by the difficult problem of providing for the succession. His daughter, Urraca, could legitimately aspire to the throne, along with her husband, Raymond of Burgundy, a cousin of Duke Odo, who had come to Spain in response to Alfonso VI's call for help before the battle of Zallaqa. While the others returned home, Raymond remained to seek his fortune and married Urraca around 1091. A few years later the king ceded Galicia to them, as a sort of subkingdom. Raymond's authority there was similar to that of a viceroy.

The succession of Raymond and Urraca to the Leonese throne seemed to be assured, but rivals unexpectedly appeared. Raymond's power in the west was undermined when the king, around 1094, granted the *terra portucalense*, the land of Portugal, to his illegitimate daughter Teresa and her husband, Henry of Burgundy, a grandson of Duke Robert and a nephew of Queen Constanza. There has been much discussion concerning the powers they received, but Merêa appears to be correct when he states that they held Portugal by hereditary right as vassals of the king and exercised regalian rights there. The concession of the region from the Miño river to Coimbra and beyond to Henry and Teresa was the first step toward the foundation of an independent kingdom of Portugal.

Raymond and Urraca doubtless regarded Henry and Teresa with unfriendly eyes, but an even more serious challenge to their future hopes appeared when a son, Sancho, was born to Alfonso VI around 1100. As the boy's mother was the Moorish princess, Zaida, a widowed daughter-in-law of al-Mutamid of Seville, there were many, especially among the French clergy in Spain, who opposed Sancho's rights to the throne. In order to prevent his eventual succession, Raymond of Burgundy realized that he would need Henry's support; but Henry, not content to strengthen his hold on Portugal, was also attempting to secure territory in León at Raymond's expense. Raymond persuaded Abbot Hugh of Cluny to intercede with Henry on his behalf. The upshot of this was a pact concluded by the two Burgundian lords probably in 1105, as Bishko has suggested, providing for the future partition of the kingdom as follows:

I Count Raymond . . . swear that after the death of King Alfonso I will give you (Henry) Toledo and all the land subject to it, and you shall hold all the land which you now receive by my grant, on such condition that you shall be my vassal, and shall hold it from me as lord; and after I give this to you, you shall leave to me all the lands of León and Castile. . . . I also swear that if I first obtain the treasure of Toledo, I will give you a third, keeping two-thirds for myself. [*PL*, 159, 944–945]

By these concessions and by making Henry his vassal, Raymond hoped to secure his loyalty and support in any future struggle with Sancho for the crown.

The deaths of Raymond in 1107 and of Sancho in 1108, fighting the Almoravids at Uclés, changed the picture entirely. An assembly of notables acknowledged Urraca as heir to the throne, but the claims of her son by Raymond of Burgundy, Alfonso Raimúndez, the future Alfonso VII, were passed over in silence. Realizing that political and military circumstances required that his daughter be married again, Alfonso VI tried to find a suitable husband for her; at last, in spite of some objections, he settled on Alfonso I, king of Aragon and Navarre. This match would have the advantage of uniting all the Christian states except Catalonia and would present a solid front against the Almoravids.

Before the marriage ceremony took place Alfonso VI died on 20 June 1109 at the age of seventy-nine. A man of great talent and great pride, by virtue of his conquest of Toledo he gained a distinguished place among the many kings of Spain. Though his reign began auspiciously, the advent of the Almoravids checked the reconquest and forced the Christians to stand on the defensive for at least a century. The title "emperor of the two religions" was rendered meaningless after his defeat at Zallaqa, but he clung tenaciously to Toledo, and refused to abandon the Tagus frontier. Despite his personal faults, his arrogance, and his unhappy relations with the Cid, he was indeed a great king.

CHAPTER 9

Alfonso VII and the
Leonese Empire

The Twelfth Century

During the reign of Alfonso VII, in the first half of the twelfth century, the concept of a Leonese empire, developed centuries before, reached its culmination and briefly acquired a juridical existence. In fact, however, Alfonso VII's claims to dominion over the whole of the peninsula were never fully admitted by his contemporaries. Several developments directly challenged Leonese hegemony. The prospective union of Aragon-Navarre and León-Castile, foreshadowed by the marriage of Alfonso I and Urraca, never became a reality. Instead the union of Aragon-Navarre was dissolved and replaced by the union of Aragon and Catalonia, thereby creating a major counterweight to León-Castile in the east. In the west, the count of Portugal shook off the fiction of his dependence upon León-Castile and proclaimed himself king. As a consequence, Alfonso VII's attempts to assert Leonese leadership in peninsular affairs were made especially difficult. His partition of his own realm at the close of his reign was in fact, whether he realized it or not, an admission that the idea of a Leonese empire was bankrupt.

Conditions prevailing in Muslim Spain at this time enabled the Christian states to make important progress in the reconquest. The opportunities for territorial expansion helped the rulers of Aragon, Catalonia, and Portugal to affirm their independence of León. The Aragonese conquest of Zaragoza, the northernmost Muslim outpost in the peninsula, marked a significant advance in the development of that kingdom, while the temporary occupation of Majorca by the count of Barcelona revealed the eventual direction of Catalan expansion. The

215

unity imposed upon Muslim Spain by the Almoravids proved to be ephemeral. These zealots had achieved their heights of glory under the leadership of Yusuf ibn Tashufin. His sons and heirs simply lacked his capabilities and could not preserve the unity of his empire. The Spanish Muslims eventually threw off their rule, while the Almohads, a new sect, appeared in North Africa to challenge Almoravid domination. As the Almoravid empire collapsed on both sides of the straits, the Christian rulers were able to profit by the ensuing disorder to capture Lisbon, Tortosa, and Almería. By mid-century, however, the Almohads entered the peninsula and reduced al-Andalus to obedience and for many years thereafter constituted the most serious threat to Christian Spain since the days of the caliphs.

Urraca and Alfonso I

The future of Christian Spain seemed immeasurably enhanced by the marriage in September 1109 of Alfonso VI's daughter Urraca (1109–1126) and Alfonso I, king of Aragon and Navarre. By the terms of the contract their children would inherit their several kingdoms. If there were no children, each spouse was declared the heir of the other. The union of all the Christian states, with the exception of the Catalan counties, seemed assured. As an expression of that unity, Alfonso I began to use the title *imperator totius Hispaniae*.

In reality there were several formidable obstacles to any permanent union. The king and queen were temperamentally unsuited to one another; Urraca was vain and capricious, while Alfonso was brusque and impetuous and more inclined to think of himself as a knight in God's service than as a husband. The French clergy, under the leadership of Archbishop Bernard of Toledo, objected to the match not only on canonical grounds, pointing out that as great-grandchildren of Sancho el mayor the royal couple were related within the prohibited degrees; but they also protested because Alfonso Raimúndez, Urraca's son by Raymond of Burgundy, was excluded from the Leonese succession, save in case of a default of other heirs. Moreover, Henry of Burgundy, now that both Raymond and Sancho were dead, conceived the hope of winning the crown for himself. Thus from the start the marriage was a sad one, the cause of family discord and civil war.

Within a year Pope Paschal II nullified the marriage on the grounds of consanguinity. Acting on papal authority, Archbishop Bernard threatened the king and queen with excommunication if they failed to separate, but for four bewildering years Alfonso I refused to do so. From time to time he had to wage war against his wife, her sister and brother-in-law, and her son's partisans. Urraca vacillated, at times attempting to expel her husband from León, at other times accepting a reconciliation with him. Henry of Burgundy took advantage of the confusion to further his own ambitions until his death in 1114, but his widow, Teresa, proved no less aggressive. In Galicia attempts were made to establish an independent sovereignty for Alfonso Raimúndez, who was crowned by Diego Gelmírez, bishop of Compostela; but an attempt to seize León in his name was thwarted. Meanwhile the Almoravids occupied Zaragoza, ravaged the Tagus valley, and captured Santarém. Wearied of a struggle that grew more senseless as each day passed, Alfonso I finally announced in 1114 that he no longer intended to live with Urraca in a union condemned by the church. With that, he withdrew to his own realms, leaving her to manage hers as best she could.

At first she tried to reach a settlement with her son and his supporters. Gelmírez, the bishop of Compostela, appeared to be in an especially vulnerable position. Alfonso VI had entrusted him with the civil administration of Compostela in 1100, even granting him the right to coin money, though not without some hesitation. Now the increasing number of burghers of Compostela formed a commune in opposition to the bishop and appealed to Urraca to support their demands for self-government. With her approval they assumed control of the town government in 1116, but within the year she changed her mind again and agreed to restore Gelmírez to full authority.

When she entered Compostela in 1117, accompanied by the bishop, the citizenry revolted. After plundering the episcopal palace they set fire to the bell tower of the cathedral where the queen and the bishop had taken refuge. Urraca was informed that she could come out safely:

As the fire was already spreading within, the queen, urged by the bishop, accepted their guarantees and came out of the tower; but when the rest of the mob saw her coming out, they made a rush upon her and seized her and knocked her to the ground in a muddy wallow; like wolves they attacked her and ripped off her clothes, leaving her body naked from her breasts on down; for a long time she lay shamefully on the ground in the presence of all. Many wanted to bury her under stones and one old lady of Compostela struck her harshly on the cheek with a stone. [Historia Compostelana, I, 114]

In the midst of this confusion Gelmírez was able to escape in disguise.

After the more responsible citizens rescued Urraca, she summoned her son Alfonso, whose troops cowed the townsmen into submission. The commune was dissolved, and Gelmírez was reinstated with full spiritual and temporal powers.

In the years following, until his death in 1139, he worked steadily to exalt the prestige and authority of his see. Pope Calixtus II, brother of Raymond of Burgundy and uncle of Alfonso Raimúndez, raised Compostela to archiepiscopal rank in 1120 and assigned to it all the metropolitan rights of the see of Mérida, until it should be liberated from the Muslims. Besides Compostela, Urraca granted Gelmírez lordship over the whole of Galicia, exempting him from military service and attendance at the royal court. The continuous influx of pilgrims visiting the shrine of the apostle also contributed to the wealth and distinction of his see. To celebrate his glories and those of Compostela he authorized his clerics to compile the *Historia Compostelana*, an important record for the period.

The Reconquest: Ramon Berenguer III and Alfonso I

During the years of civil strife in León, Ramon Berenguer III, count of Barcelona, worked to give a major impetus to Catalan expansion. By inheritance he acquired the counties of Besalú (1111) and Cerdagne (1117), and by his marriage with Douce, the heiress to Provence (1112), strengthened Catalan interests north of the Pyrenees. Provence and Catalonia, long united by language and the poetry of the troubadours, now professed allegiance at least temporarily to a common ruler. During the following century the counts of Barcelona were very much concerned with the preservation of their power north of the Pyrenees, though it is doubtful that they would ever have succeeded in forming a trans-Pyrenean state. In the course of time their claims were challenged by the counts of Toulouse, by the German emperors (who considered Provence part of the empire), and by the kings of France.

Ramon Berenguer III led the first tentative overseas adventure of the Catalans, who had not hitherto embarked on any significant maritime enterprise, though their coastal trade was growing. On the other hand, the republic of Pisa had taken an active role since the early eleventh century in combating the Muslims in the western Mediterranean. Pisa and Genoa collaborated in expelling the Muslims from Sardinia in 1016, and now the Pisans proposed to conquer the Balearic Islands, ruled by Mubashir Nasir al-Dawla. Giving his approval to the project,

Pope Paschal II conceded crusading indulgences to the participants, and appointed a cardinal as legate. The Pisans sailed to Catalonia in 1113 and appealed to Ramon Berenguer III to join them and to become their leader. The anonymous *Liber Maiolichinus de gestis Pisanorum*, an eyewitness account of the progress of the crusade, hailed him as the *dux pyrenus*, the *rector Pyrenee*, and the *Catalanicus heros*. The name Catalonia also appears for the first time in this text. William VI of Montpellier, the viscount of Narbonne, and other lords from Languedoc and Provence also pledged their collaboration.

The fleet sailed from Catalonia in June 1114 and quickly overran Majorca and Ibiza. In an attempt to divert Ramon Berenguer, the Almoravids of Zaragoza attacked Barcelona, but the Catalans drove them off and defeated them at Congost de Martorell. Early in the following year Ramon Berenguer returned to Barcelona, and the Christians soon evacuated the islands. As the king of Majorca died at this time, the Almoravids sent a fleet to take possession, and the islands remained in Muslim hands for another century. Although the venture had only temporary success, it greatly stimulated Catalan interest in overseas trade and prepared the way for the eventual conquest of the islands.

In the meantime Alfonso I, after severing his relations with Urraca, concentrated his energy upon the conquest of Zaragoza. His brother, Pedro I, by capturing Huesca in 1096, had opened the road to the capital. Al-Mustain, the king of Zaragoza, was killed in battle with the Christians at Valtierra in 1110. His son, Abd al-Malik, succeeded him, but the citizens of Zaragoza were unwilling to accept any accommodation with the Christians and invited the Almoravids to send a garrison to occupy the city. Abd al-Malik fled, and the last independent *taifa* passed under Almoravid rule.

In order to achieve the conquest of Zaragoza, Alfonso I appealed to the nobility of southern France, many of whom had taken part in the First Crusade. Among those who brought troops and siege machinery to his aid were Gaston de Béarn, Centule of Bigorre, and Bernard Ató of Carcassonne. At a council held at Toulouse, French knights were urged to join the crusade against Zaragoza, and Pope Gelasius II, who was traveling through southern France, granted crusade indulgences to the participants; a new element was introduced when he offered partial indulgences to those who contributed to the reconstruction of the church of Zaragoza. The host, including Aragonese, Catalans, Castilians, and Frenchmen, seized the fortresses leading to Zaragoza and established a formal siege of the city in May 1118. Attempts by the Almoravids to send reinforcements were thwarted, and the populace gradually was reduced to starvation. Entering the city in triumph on 18 December, Alfonso I treated the Muslims generously enough; those who wished to leave could do so, though most preferred to remain behind, retaining their possessions but subject to the payment of an annual tribute. Later, most of the Muslims were removed to the suburbs of the city. The king in January 1119 granted the first of many privileges (the so-called *privilegio de los veinte*) to the Christians who chose to settle in Zaragoza. Three years later he organized the Confraternity of Belchite, similar to the military Orders of the Temple and the Hospital, to defend Zaragoza; eventually the Confraternity was absorbed by the Temple.

The conquest of Zaragoza was an accomplishment almost as significant as the fall of Toledo in 1085. For several centuries Zaragoza stood as the northernmost bastion of Islam in the peninsula and effectively blocked any Christian advances south of the Ebro. Now the Christians stood astride the river and soon began to move southward in preparation for the eventual conquest of the kingdom of Valencia. The immediate fruit of Alfonso I's conquest was the surrender of Tudela, Tarazona, Borja, and other towns; in the spring of 1120 he besieged Calatayud and defeated a relieving force of Almoravids at Cutanda; this was the worst defeat they had suffered thus far. As a result, Calatayud and Daroca fell to the Aragonese, and the frontier was pushed well south of the Ebro.

The declining strength of the Almoravids made apparent by Alfonso I's successes in the Ebro valley was even more clearly revealed by his celebrated march through Andalusia. The Mozarabs of Granada, finding the rule of the Almoravids intolerable, appealed to him for deliverance, promising to join him with 12,000 warriors; though undoubtedly exaggerated, this figure suggests that the number of Mozarabs in Granada and the vicinity was still substantial. Elsewhere their numbers probably had declined, as many elected to remove to Christian territory. Attracted by the prospects of great booty and glory, Alfonso I, with a large force, set out from Zaragoza in September 1125. As he proceeded along the coast, bypassing Valencia, Alcira, Denia, Játiva, and Murcia, he was joined by bands of Mozarabs. Turning westward to Guadix he reached the outskirts of Granada early in January 1126. Although many Mozarabs left the city to join his army, there was no general uprising within. According to Ibn Idhari, he reproached the Mozarab leader Ibn al-Qalas, for failure to fulfill his promises. The latter replied that Alfonso's late arrival rendered a surprise attack impossible, as the Almoravids had had time to gather their troops and to bring reinforcements from Africa.

Lacking the machinery necessary to conduct a prolonged siege, Alfonso I set out through the mountains toward Archidona and Antequera, probably to establish contact with the Mozarabs there. After returning to Granada, he proceeded westward, attacking Ecija, Baena, and Cabra and defeated the Almoravids in a pitched battle near Lucena. Turning eastward once more, he retraced his route to Zaragoza. The Anglo-Norman historian Ordericus Vitalis reported that he settled 10,000 Andalusian Mozarabs in the Ebro valley. As for those who remained behind, the qadi Ibn Rushd (grandfather of the philosopher Averroës) declared that they had broken their pact with Islam and ought to be sent into exile. The emir of the Muslims, Ali ibn Yusuf, ordered them to be transported to Morocco, where many of them later served the Almoravids in their wars against the Almohads; eventually some of these displaced Mozarabs were able to return to the peninsula. The number of those remaining in al-Andalus cannot be ascertained, but it is likely that very many sought refuge in the Christian states.

The march to Granada, a spectacle without concrete results, was Alfonso I's last triumph. A new generation of Christian leaders began to emerge to challenge his supremacy and to rival his accomplishments. While he was still in Andalusia, his former wife, Urraca, died in March 1126, and her son by Raymond of Burgundy, Alfonso VII (1126–1157), nicknamed "the little king" (al-sulaytin) by the Arabic sources, assumed sole power in the kingdom of León. His accession inaugurated the Burgundian dynasty that ruled León and Castile until the coming of the Trastámaras in 1369. The new king moved quickly to recover Burgos, Carrión, Soria, and other Castilian strongholds still in the hands of Alfonso I, who was unwilling to yield at first, but eventually agreed to the reconstitution of the frontier between Castile and Navarre as it had existed in the days of Sancho el mayor. Alfonso I also ceased to use the imperial title, thereby acknowledging that it pertained by right to the ruler of León. In the westernmost part of the peninsula, Afonso Henriques, son of Henry of Burgundy and Teresa, asserted himself and forced his mother to withdraw from Portugal in 1128; she died two years later. Afonso Henriques, count of Portugal

(1128-1185), showed no inclination to acknowledge the sovereignty of Alfonso VII and steadily laid the foundations of Portuguese independence. As the contemporary *Chronica Gothorum* put it, with a bit of exaggeration:

He received the kingdom and the Lord, through him, extended the frontiers of the Christians and expanded the bounds of the faithful people from the river Mondego, that flows by the walls of Coimbra, to the river Guadalquivir that flows by the city of Seville, and from the great sea to the Mediterranean sea. [Blöcker-Walter, *Alfons J*, 151]

Meanwhile, Alfonso I, after a brief incursion into Gascony where, on behalf of his vassal Gaston de Béarn, he besieged Bayonne, resumed the task of reconquest and repopulation in the Ebro valley. Advancing in the direction of Lérida, he captured Mequinenza in 1133; but at Fraga, between Lérida and Mequinenza, he met with disaster at the hands of the Almoravids on 17 July 1134. Thoroughly defeated, he fell ill later in the summer and died on 7 September. An accomplished soldier and a true crusader, known by the nickname, the battler (*el batallador*), he will always be remembered as the conqueror of Zaragoza. Yet the unique problems raised by his last will and testament show that he was not endowed with a fine political sense.

The Leonese Empire and the Union of Aragon and Catalonia

Alfonso I died without heirs of his body. His will, drawn up in 1131 and ratified just three days before his death, made the usual bequests to religious houses, but then named as his heirs and successors in the kingdoms of Aragon and Navarre the military Orders of the Holy Sepulchre, the Hospital, and the Temple. "To these three," he declared, "I grant my whole kingdom and also all that I have conquered in the whole territory of my kingdom . . . so that they may hold and possess it in three equal parts" (*ES*, 50, 393). The terms of this remarkable document reflect the king's crusading zeal and his high regard for the recently organized military Orders. He confidently believed that they could be entrusted with the task of continuing the reconquest; he seems not to have considered that their principal interests were always likely to be centered in the Holy Land, or that the Aragonese and Navarrese were likely to oppose the cession of the kingdoms to them.

No one in Aragon or Navarre took the will seriously. The day after his death the Aragonese nobles assembled at Jaca and elected his brother, Ramiro II (1134-1137), as king. Ramiro was a Benedictine monk, and for this reason Alfonso I had not designated him as his successor. His religious status weakened his title to the throne, but his election seemed to be the only means of preventing the kingdom from falling into the hands of the military Orders. Ramiro II himself explained that he accepted the crown "not out of any desire for honor or ambition or arrogance but only because of the needs of the people and the tranquility of the church." About the same time the Navarrese magnates met at Pamplona and elected as their king García IV Ramírez (1134–1150), a descendant of Sancho el mayor. As a result, the union of Aragon and Navarre effected by Sancho I Ramírez in 1076 was dissolved.

The death of Alfonso I offered Alfonso VII the opportunity to revive traditional Leonese Castilian claims to the kingdom of Zaragoza. According to the *Chronica Adefonsi Imperatoris,* Alfonso VII immediately proceeded to Nájera, where García Ramírez became his vassal, just as earlier kings of Navarre had become the vassals of Fernando I and Alfonso VI. Then Alfonso VII continued to Aragon where he was received cordially by Ramiro II, who delivered the city of Zaragoza to him. It would seem that neither García Ramírez nor Ramiro the Monk was prepared to assume the responsibility for defending Zaragoza and its territory. In effect the future of Zaragoza rested with Alfonso VII, who placed a garrison there; later in the year he granted it as an *honor* or tenancy to his brother-in-law, Ramon Berenguer IV, count of Barcelona (1131–1162), who became his vassal.

Alfonso VII's prestige was never higher than at this time. Besides the new king of Navarre and the count of Barcelona, he included among his vassals, William, lord of Montpellier, Alphonse Jourdain, count of Toulouse, a grandson of Alfonso VI, and Zafadola (Sayf al-Dawla), son of the last Muslim king of Zaragoza, who accompanied Alfonso VII on his first expedition into Muslim territory, reaching Jerez and Cádiz, in 1133. The royal chronicle, noting the list of his vassals, boastfully proclaimed that "the bounds of the kingdom of Alfonso, king of León, extended from the great ocean sea beyond Santiago as far as the Rhone river."

In order to solemnize his pre-eminence in Spain, Alfonso VII was crowned as emperor in the cathedral of León on Pentecost Sunday, 26 May 1135. The assembled bishops and magnates, following divine counsel, decided to proclaim him as emperor "because King García and Zafadola, King of the Saracens and Count Ramon of Barcelona and

Count Alphonse of Toulouse and many counts and dukes of Gascony and France were obedient to him in all things." He received a golden crown, encrusted with precious jewels and a scepter and mantle. By virtue of his coronation he gave juridical reality to the old Leonese idea of empire, but, as will be seen, the reality died with him, though the idea lived on for another generation.

Meanwhile Pope Innocent II, mindful of the fact that the kings of Aragon were vassals of the Holy See, watched developments with particular interest. Not only did he demand that Alfonso I's will be carried out; he also refused to recognize either of the kings who claimed the inheritance. Ramiro the Monk was not inclined to step aside, however, and for the avowed purpose of perpetuating the dynasty, married Agnes of Poitiers, a sister of Duke William IX of Aquitaine in 1136. When she gave birth to a daughter, Petronila, later in the year, the survival of the dynasty was assured. In the hope of eventually uniting Aragon to the kingdom of León, Alfonso VII proposed that the new-born princess be married to his oldest son. A union of this sort would have isolated Navarre permanently and prevented its expansion in the future, just as an extension of Leonese-Aragonese power along the Ebro to the sea would have thwarted the further growth of the Catalan counties. In the long run both Navarre and Catalonia, whether they liked it or not, probably would have been incorporated into the union.

García Ramírez of Navarre revealed his opposition by forming an alliance with Afonso Henriques of Portugal; together they waged desultory warfare along the frontiers of León-Castile. As the Aragonese nobility also refused to accept the proposed Leonese marriage, Ramiro II offered his daughter's hand to Ramon Berenguer IV, count of Barcelona. Just a few years before, his father, Ramon Berenguer III, entering the military Order of the Temple, divided his dominions between his sons; Ramon Berenguer IV inherited the counties of Barcelona, Gerona, Vich, Besalú, and Cerdagne; his brother Berenguer Ramon received the county of Provence. By reason of this division, the potentially powerful union of Catalonia and Provence was dissolved.

The betrothal of Petronila and the count of Barcelona took place at Barbastro on 11 August 1137. Ramiro delivered the kingdom of Aragon to Ramon Berenguer IV, who promised to respect the laws and privileges of the people. In deference to his father-in-law and in acknowledgment of his own status as a prince-consort, he did not assume the royal title, but called himself simply Prince of Aragon. With these arrangements concluded, Ramiro retired to the Benedictine abbey of San Pedro de Huesca, where he died in 1157. When his daughter attained the appropriate age in 1150, her marriage was solemnized.

The union of the kingdom of Aragon and the Catalan counties of Barcelona, Gerona, Vich, Besalú, and Cerdagne was one of the most significant developments in the history of medieval Spain. Rivalries that had arisen of late were now set aside, and the joint resources of the federated states could be devoted to their common advantage. Although it is usual, after the union of 1137, to refer to the whole eastern section of the peninsula as the kingdom of Aragon, it is well to remember that this territory constituted a confederation of states, ruled by a common sovereign, in Aragon called a king, but in Barcelona a count. The federative character of the union is best expressed by the term, Crown of Aragon. Each state retained its identity, its forms of government, its capital (Zaragoza, Barcelona), its language and institutions. By temperament, tradition, and culture the peoples of Aragon and Catalonia differed from one another. The Aragonese, essentially a landlocked people, were linked by language and customs to Castile. The Catalans, on the other hand, had closer linguistic ties to Languedoc, and by virtue of their geographic position eventually developed a great Mediterranean empire. There is much to be said for Soldevila's view (albeit a Catalan view), that in the Crown of Aragon Catalonia was "the directing and dynamic element." In spite of the obvious differences between Catalans and Aragonese the union achieved in 1137 was not disrupted in the medieval era.

Immediately after the betrothal Ramon Berenguer IV sought to come to an agreement with Alfonso VII, to whom he renewed his pledge of homage and fealty, acknowledging Alfonso's suzerainty over Zaragoza and its territory. They also agreed to partition Navarre and in the next few years waged inconclusive warfare against García Ramírez. By making peace in 1140 he preserved the independence of his kingdom; but since the idea of partitioning Navarre always held a certain attraction for its neighbors, the future of the kingdom remained in doubt.

Ramon Berenguer also had to dispose of the claims of the military Orders. In the period from 1140 to 1141 the Hospital, the Temple, and the Holy Sepulchre renounced their rights to the inheritance of Alfonso I. In future years they were amply compensated by grants of land and fortresses in Aragon and Catalonia. Pope Hadrian IV in 1158 formally confirmed Ramon Berenguer's rights to all the lands willed to the

Orders by Alfonso I. Thus the crisis provoked by his testament was satisfactorily resolved.

The union of Aragon and Catalonia was one aspect of a major political restructuring taking place in the peninsula during the twelfth century. In the far west an independent Portugal began to take shape under the aggressive leadership of Afonso Henriques, who was determined to free the county of Portugal from subjection to León. At the time of his assumption of power, the Portuguese territory extended from the Miño river eastward to Bragança and southward to Coimbra. Two possible avenues of expansion lay open to him, namely, northward across the Miño into Galicia or southward from Coimbra into Muslim territory. In the first years of his reign, while Alfonso VII was preoccupied with the problems of the Aragonese succession, Afonso Henriques persistently tried to extend his rule into Galicia. But while he was able to take Túy and other fortresses, the Muslims assaulted the castle of Leiria which he had recently erected on the road from Coimbra to Santarém. Unable to maintain a war on two fronts, he had to make peace with Alfonso VII in 1137, promising to restore the captured fortresses and to aid him against his enemies, Christian or Muslim. The tenor of the agreement seems to imply that he acknowledged the emperor's suzerainty, but this was a political necessity. Afonso was now free to strengthen the fortifications of Leiria and to chastize the Muslims, over whom he gained his first major triumph at Ourique in July 1139. Though the *Chronica Gothorum* commented simply, "thus Afonso by the favor of divine protection gained a great triumph over the enemy," later legend related that Christ appeared to him before the battle to assure him of victory. Muslim power in the western peninsula was hardly cast down, but subsequent generations magnified the victory out of all proportion and hailed it as a tribute to the Portuguese national character.

His success at Ourique may have decided him to declare the fullness of his dominion in Portugal. Extant documents reveal that after 1139, instead of entitling himself simply *infans* or *princeps*, as he had in the past, he adopted the title of king (*rex Portugalensium*), which was tantamount to a declaration of independence. By placing his kingdom under papal protection and pledging homage and fealty to the Holy See, he took another significant step to strengthen and secure his independence. Professing himself a *miles beati Petri et Romani pontificis,* "a knight of Blessed Peter and of the Roman Pontiff," he promised to pay an annual tribute of four ounces of gold in return for papal protection. A formal document setting forth these terms was published on 13 December 1143. Earlier in October, Alfonso VII met Afonso Henriques at Zamora and, evidently accepting the fait accompli, recognized him as king of Portugal. Herculano believed that Afonso became a papal vassal after this meeting, but Erdmann has shown that the reverse is true. In the spring of 1144 Pope Lucius II wrote to Afonso Henriques, graciously accepting the proferred tribute and extending protection; but the letter was addressed simply to the *Portugalensium dux.* Not until 1179, when the independence of Portugal was firmly established, did Pope Alexander III address Afonso Henriques as king.

The Coming of the Almohads

In the meantime the Almohads, who were to prove one of the most dangerous enemies of Christian Spain, were spreading their teachings throughout Morocco and undermining the Almoravid regime. The founder of this new sect was Abu Abd Allah ibn Tumart (d. 1130) of the Berber tribe of the Masmuda. After making a pilgrimage to Mecca, he studied for some time at Baghdad, where he became acquainted with the doctrines of the famed philosopher al-Ghazzali (Algazel, d. 1111). Disillusioned by the sterility of orthodox theological teaching, al-Ghazzali discovered new inspiration in Sufism, a manifestation of popular piety, expressed through asceticism and mysticism. His book, *The Revival of Religious Sciences,* was burned at Córdoba on the insistence of the Malikite jurists. Fortified by the wisdom of his teachers, Ibn Tumart returned to North Africa where he zealously denounced the corruption and impiety he saw. The Malikites condemned him, however, for arguing that the allegorical interpretation of the Koran was necessary at times to achieve a fuller understanding of the text, and that excessive reliance upon the literal interpretation had given rise to an anthropomorphic conception of God. For this he accused the Almoravids and their supporters of infidelity and materialism. It was indeed ironical that those who not long before had been regarded as the most devout followers of Muhammad were now condemned as pernicious enemies of the faith.

Ibn Tumart in 1121 proclaimed himself the *mahdi* or rightly guided one, descended from the family of the prophet, who would come at the end of time to render justice and to secure the final triumph of Islam. He gave his followers the name *al-muwahhidun* or Almohads, that is, those professing belief in the absolute unity (*tawhid*) of God. From their chief seat at Tinmallal in the Atlas mountains they launched a holy war against the Almoravids. After Ibn Tumart's death, under the capable direction of his designated successor or caliph, Abd al-Mumin (1130–1163), the Almohads destroyed the Almoravid empire. Ali ibn Yusuf, who was the emir of the Muslims, died just before the final collapse; his son Tashufin (1143–1145), fleeing from Oran with the intention of taking ship to Spain, was killed by a fall off a cliff. The Almohads occupied Tlemcen and Oran, and in 1147 Fez and Marrakech surrendered to them. At that time Ishaq ibn Ali, the last of the Almoravid dynasty, was killed, and the Almoravid empire came to an unfortunate end.

The revolt in Africa encouraged the enemies of the Almoravids in Spain to try to overthrow the regime. The Almoravids there had lost that fervor and strict observance of the law that had once gained them the backing of many who despised the laxity of the *reyes de taifas*. The thirteenth-century historian al-Marrakushi accused them of apathy, concern for their own comfort, and an inordinate attention to women. The Almoravids also levied extra-legal taxes and dealt harshly with Jews and Mozarabs and generally held the inhabitants of the peninsula in contempt. Thus anti-Almoravid sentiment was deep and strong; it needed only to be stirred up.

For about three years prior to the coming of the Almohads in 1147, Muslim Spain was torn by confusion and anarchy. The authority of the Almoravids was challenged and cast down and was supplanted by that of many petty rulers, a new generation of *reyes de taifas*. The Christian princes were able to ravage al-Andalus with comparative impunity and even to achieve some conquests of major significance. Only after ten years had elapsed were the Almohads securely in control of al-Andalus and only then were the lines hardened again along the frontier.

The first uprisings against Almoravid rule began in the western sector of the peninsula. One of the earliest rebels was Ibn Qasi, a mystic very much influenced by the teachings of Ibn Masarra and al-Ghazzali and by Sufi asceticism. Proclaiming himself the *mahdi*, he seized Mértola in the Algarve in 1144, but his attempts to establish relations with the Almohads in Morocco failed because of his pretension to the title claimed by Ibn Tumart. Other leaders, in conjunction with Ibn Qasi or independently of him, expelled the Almoravids from Evora, Beja, Silves,

Badajoz, Huelva, and Niebla. Almoravid government in the Algarve practically ceased.

The Almoravids were overthrown in Córdoba in January 1145 by the *qadi* Ibn Hamdin, who invited Alfonso VII's vassal, Zafadola, to assume government of the city, but he was quickly expelled, and Ibn Hamdin declared himself emir of the Muslims. Zafadola then tried to establish himself in Jaén and Granada. In the east, the Almoravids were driven from Murcia and Valencia, where Ibn Mardanish (1147–1172) emerged as king. Thus within a year's time the unity of al-Andalus was destroyed, but none of the new chieftains was strong enough to impose his authority upon the others.

Taking advantage of discord among the rebels, Ibn Ganiya, the Almoravid governor of Seville, ousted Zafadola from Granada and Ibn Hamdin from Córdoba. With Seville, Córdoba, and Granada under his control Ibn Ganiya seemed well on the way to re-establishing Almoravid rule once again, but at this point Alfonso VII intervened. Responding to an appeal from Ibn Hamdin, he marched into the heart of Andalusia and occupied the suburbs of Córdoba (May 1146), leaving the Almoravids in control of the inner city. Reports of the landing of the Almohads impelled Ibn Ganiya to negotiate with Alfonso VII and to become his vassal, promising him an annual tribute and surrendering Ubeda and Baeza. Retiring from Córdoba, Alfonso VII took possession of those towns and then seized Calatrava, a key fortress linking Toledo with Andalusia, and the future seat of one of the principal Spanish military Orders (January 1147).

The first contingents of Almohads arrived in Spain in May 1146 in answer to an appeal from Ibn Qasi of Mértola, who had abandoned his pretensions as *mahdi* and recognized Abd al-Mumin as caliph. After occupying Tarifa and Algeciras, the Almohads advanced westward into the Algarve, receiving the submission of Jerez, Niebla, Mértola, Silves, and Badajoz. They expelled the Almoravids from Seville in January 1147 and forced Ibn Ganiya to surrender Córdoba and Jaén and to retire to Granada, where he died in 1148.

The Reconquest: Lisbon, Almería, Tortosa, and Lérida

The unstable situation in al-Andalus, as the Almohads tried to subdue both the Almoravids and the new *reyes de taifas*, offered the Christian rulers an excellent opportunity to make substantial territorial gains at Muslim expense. Afonso Henriques, Alfonso VII, and Ramon Berenguer IV all joined in the assault against the enemy. With the exception of Almería, the Almohads were never able to retake the towns conquered by the Christians in 1147–1148.

For Afonso Henriques of Portugal the coincidental arrival of a fleet of crusaders from northern Europe made it possible for him to achieve the conquest of Lisbon. There is some evidence to indicate that around 1140–1142 he planned to attack Lisbon with the help of an Anglo-Norman fleet commanded by William Viel and his brother Ralph. Nothing is known of the campaign, save that the Anglo-Normans developed a strong antipathy to the king of Portugal.

As a preliminary step toward the conquest of Lisbon, Afonso seized Santarém on 15 March 1147. Situated on the Tagus, about forty-six miles north of Lisbon, Santarém had been the center of activity for frequent Muslim raids on Portuguese territory and especially for attacks against Afonso's most advanced position, the castle of Leiria, defending the approaches to Coimbra. The capture of Santarém opened the road to Lisbon, a populous and prosperous seaport, at the mouth of the Tagus. Reports of the coming of a new crusading fleet prompted Afonso to prepare for the attack on Lisbon.

Many northern Europeans, stimulated by the preaching of St. Bernard of Clairvaux, set out to participate in the Second Crusade. Among them were contingents from Germany, Flanders, Normandy, and England, numbering about 13,000, who set sail in 164 ships from Dartmouth, England, in May 1147, intending to cross the Mediterranean to the Holy Land. Their leaders included Hervey de Glanvill, Saher of Archelle, Christian of Ghistelles, and Count Arnold of Aerschot.

On arrival at Porto they were greeted by Pedro Pitões, the bishop, who invited them to aid the king in an attack on Lisbon. The bishop declared that this was a just war, worthy of their talents: "Act like good soldiers, for the sin is not in fighting war, but in fighting for the sake of booty." When the fleet reached Lisbon on 28 June, Afonso Henriques outlined his proposals, and an alliance was concluded. He guaranteed to the crusaders the plunder of Lisbon and the ransom of captives; those who wished to settle there would be given lands and would be assured the protection of their native customs and liberties. The king also exempted them and their descendants from the payment of tolls in any part of his realm. He promised to continue the siege until surrender unless forced to desist by mortal illness or by an attack on his kingdom from some other quarter.

The archbishop of Braga, sent to persuade the Muslims to surrender, charged that they had "held our cities and lands already for 358 years," and urged them to "return to the homeland of the Moors, whence you came, leaving to us what is ours." When this drew a negative response, the siege commenced in earnest. Catapults and towers were constructed, and the city was blockaded on all sides. The defenders appealed in vain to their fellow Muslims to relieve them; realizing that their chances of victory were steadily lessening, they eventually asked for a truce to negotiate the terms of surrender. After a siege of seventeen weeks the Christians made their triumphal entrance into Lisbon on 24 October 1147. Although the Muslims were permitted to leave freely, the city was sacked, and many were killed, including the Mozarabic bishop, whose name has not been recorded. The crusaders also occupied the nearby fortresses of Sintra to the west and Palmela south of the Tagus. Many of the crusaders elected to settle in Lisbon, and one of them, Gilbert of Hastings, was installed as bishop. The conquest of Lisbon, which has been described by an Anglo-Norman priest, a participant, rivaled in importance the capture of Toledo in 1085 and Zaragoza in 1118.

While Afonso Henriques was achieving the greatest triumph of his career, Alfonso VII and Ramon Berenguer IV were engaged in the siege of Almería, a port on the southeastern coast; long a major center of Muslim trade with Africa and the East, it had also gained fame as a pirate's nest (*marinorum latronum sedem*). The people of Genoa and Pisa were especially anxious to eliminate this threat to their own developing trade in the western Mediterranean and proposed its conquest to Alfonso VII, who invited his vassals, Ramon Berenguer IV, García Ramírez of Navarre, and William of Montpellier to collaborate. The campaign began on 1 August 1147; blockaded by land and sea, the city capitulated on 17 October and was promptly garrisoned by the emperor. The siege is described in the Latin *Poem of Almería*, included in the royal chronicle.

Returning from Almería, Ramon Berenguer IV made an agreement with the Genoese to assist him in the conquest of Tortosa, near the mouth of the Ebro. Since the days of Louis the Pious, the city had steadfastly repelled Christian assaults, but its independence was shortly to be terminated. Pope Eugene III granted a crusade indulgence to those who took part in the attack; after a siege of six months the city surrendered on 31 December 1148. Fresh from this victory Ramon Berenguer moved against the fortresses of Lérida, Fraga, and Mequinenza farther up the river. All three surrendered on 24 October 1149. With that, he had completed the reconquest of the Ebro river valley. From its source to the sea the river was in Christian hands, and the task begun by Alfonso I had been brought to a happy conclusion.

This succession of Christian victories excited the hope of the imminent destruction of Muslim rule in Spain. So confident were Alfonso VII and Ramon Berenguer IV that they signed the treaty of Tudellén (27 January 1151) defining their respective shares of Muslim territory and renewing their earlier agreement to partition Navarre. The regions of Valencia and Murcia were allotted to Ramon Berenguer for future conquest, but he promised to hold these lands as the emperor's vassal. Thus, while acknowledging Aragonese and Catalan interests in the reconquest, the treaty upheld traditional Leonese pretensions to hegemony throughout the peninsula. Needless to say, the proposed partition of Navarre, now ruled by Sancho VI (1150–1194), the son of García Ramírez, was never carried out. As for Valencia and Murcia they were in the hands of Ibn Mardanish, known to the Christians as *el rey Lobo*. Probably descended from a family of Hispanic Christian origin, he dominated the eastern sector until his death in 1172 and proved to be the most tenacious opponent of Almohad expansion. As such, he maintained close relationships with the Christians, concluding treaties with Pisa and Genoa, offering tribute to Ramon Berenguer IV, and becoming the vassal of Alfonso VII.

The Almohads, meantime, had consolidated their rule in North Africa and were beginning to extend their control over Muslim Spain, occupying Málaga in 1153 and Granada in 1154. As they proceeded eastward they began to threaten Alfonso VII's prize, Almería, and besieged it by land and sea in 1157. The defenders were able to hold out in the citadel, but Alfonso VII and Ibn Mardanish were unable to relieve them. Thus Almería fell to the Almohads and remained in Muslim possession for the next three centuries.

As he was returning home, Alfonso VII, "emperor of Castile and of all Spain," fell ill and died on 21 August 1157. A worthy rival of Charlemagne, according to the *Poem of Almería*, he was his equal in lineage, bravery, and deeds of war:

Facta sequens Caroli, cui competit aequipari.
Gente fuere pares, armorum vi coequales.
Gloria bellorum gestorum par fuit horum.

[*Chronica Adefonsi Imperatoris,* p. 166.]

A fortunate monarch, who ruled at a time when the Almoravid empire was beginning to disintegrate, he was able to ravage al-Andalus almost at will, and to affirm the old Leonese claim to drive the Muslims from the peninsula. His pre-eminence among Christian princes was contested only by Afonso Henriques of Portugal. Alfonso VII, however, was the last emperor, the last sovereign to assert a real right to hegemony throughout the peninsula. Just before his death he divided the realm between his sons, Sancho and Fernando, and in so doing separated Castile from León, and dealt a mortal blow to the idea of an Hispanic empire seated in León.

CHAPTER 10

The Duel with the Almohads

The Almohads and the Five Kingdoms

The second half of the twelfth century was one of the most critical times in the history of the reconquest. The Almohads, after destroying the Almoravid empire, consolidated their hold in Morocco and restored the balance of power in Spain. Though unable to reconquer Toledo, Zaragoza, or Lisbon, they inflicted great damage upon the Christian states and kept them almost continually on the defensive. Two great battles, the one an extraordinary victory for the Muslims at Alarcos, the other an equally important triumph for the Christians, highlighted the struggle for dominion. The rout at Las Navas marked the beginning of the end of Almohad power and assured the ultimate triumph of Christian Spain which, as an entity, now began to assume the political form it was to retain for centuries.

The idea of a Leonese empire dominating the peninsula and directing the reconquest no longer conformed to the political realities. Castile began to emerge as the dominant kingdom, whose continued growth and future pre-eminence seemed to be guaranteed by the vast expanse of Muslim territory still to be conquered. The independence of Portugal, once, like Castile, a frontier province of the kingdom of León, was established on solid foundations. Nor was Navarre, wedged between Castile and Aragon and so denied the possibility of further territorial expansion, dependent upon León in any way. Lastly, the united states of Aragon and Catalonia constituted a formidable challenge to both León and Castile. In some respects, the kings of Aragon were hampered by an ambivalent policy that prompted them to pursue political ambitions in Languedoc, while also trying to profit from the reconquest. The issue was resolved at the beginning of the thirteenth

234

century when their interests in Languedoc suffered an irreparable blow on the battlefield of Muret.

In sum, the kingdom of León was now only one of several Christian states, each following its own independent course. Whatever theoretical unity the idea of a Leonese empire had given to Spain in the past was shattered, and within a generation the idea itself ceased to have any meaning.

The Heirs of Alfonso VII

When Alfonso VII died returning from his futile journey to relieve Almería, his sons Sancho III (1157–1158) and Fernando II (1157–1188) succeeded him, the former as king of Castile, the latter as king of León. That the oldest son received the kingdom of Castile rather than León, the traditional seat of empire, was indicative of the changing concepts of the time. Young and vigorous, with a bright future before him, Sancho III clearly expected to enjoy his father's pre-eminence and in February 1158 renewed the treaty of Tudellén with Ramon Berenguer IV, delimiting their respective zones of reconquest and pledging cooperation against Navarre. The prince of Aragon also agreed to hold the kingdom of Zaragoza as a vassal of Sancho III, as it had been held of Alfonso VII.

Some months later Sancho III and Fernando II met at Sahagún to map plans for the future. Pledging to maintain peace and friendship and to aid one another against all princes, except Ramon Berenguer IV, they also proposed to partition Portugal; Fernando was given the privilege of dividing the Portuguese territory as he wished, but Sancho was to choose whichever part suited him. Turning to al-Andalus, the brothers marked out areas for future conquests; the western region from Lisbon to Niebla, including Mérida, Badajoz, Evora, and Mértola, was reserved for Fernando II, who would also receive half of Seville and its revenues. The treaty did not envision the expansion of Portugal to its present-day limits, but the brothers were reckoning without the indomitable character of Afonso Henriques, nor did they realize the obstacles which the Almohads were to put in the way of the reconquest.

Historians will never know what noble deeds Sancho III might have achieved; he died on 31 August 1158, leaving the throne to an infant of two years, whose mother had died in childbirth. The minority of Alfonso VIII (1158–1214) was a period of great disorder in the kingdom of Castile, as the noble families of Lara and Castro struggled for power and control of the child-king. Had he attempted it, Fernando II might have succeeded in depriving him of his kingdom; he did enter Castile, in response to a plea from the Castros, and for several years kept a garrison at Toledo. He was even recognized as his nephew's tutor, but he was never able to gain custody of his person. Fernando II eventually withdrew from Castilian affairs, leaving the Laras in the ascendancy. In the meantime, Sancho VI of Navarre took advantage of the minority to settle old scores by seizing Logroño and other towns on the Castilian frontier. When Alfonso VIII attained his majority in 1169, he married Leonor, the daughter of King Henry II of England and Eleanor of Aquitaine. Though the duchy of Gascony was supposed to be her dowry, it was never surrendered to Alfonso VIII and so became the object of future controversy.

A child also ascended the throne of Aragon in 1162 upon the death of Ramon Berenguer IV. By his capture of Tortosa and Lérida, he completed the reconquest of Catalonia and by his marriage with Petronila effected the union of Catalonia and Aragon. On the other side of the Pyrenees he defended the interests of his nephew, Ramon Berenguer, marquess of Provence (1144–1166), against the encroachments of the count of Toulouse; they had to recognize, however, the suzerainty of Frederick Barbarossa, the Roman emperor, over Provence.

Aragon and Catalonia were the inheritance of Alfonso II (1162–1196), Ramon Berenguer IV's son by Petronila. She yielded all her rights to Aragon in 1164, and two years later the young king also inherited Provence from his cousin. As marquess of Provence, his vassals included the viscount of Béziers and Carcassonne, the lords of Narbonne and Montpellier, but he also had to contend with the continuing challenge of the count of Toulouse and the imperial claims to overlordship. At the outset of his reign he established close and friendly relations with Alfonso VIII, whom he promised to assist in warfare against Navarre.

The Almohads in al-Andalus

While the new Christian rulers were establishing themselves, the Almohads were extending their control over al-Andalus. They held Seville, Córdoba, and other important cities, but resistance among the Hispanic Muslims, led by Ibn Mardanish of Murcia, was strong. The Caliph, Abd al-Mumin, was preoccupied with the conquest of Algeria and Tunisia and only came to Spain in 1160; but after ordering the construction of a town and fortifications at Gibraltar, he returned immediately to Morocco, leaving his sons to deal with the rebels in Spain. Ibn Mardanish, aided by his father-in-law, Ibn Hamusk, had already seized Jaén, Ubeda, Baeza, Carmona, and Ecija, but their joint forces were routed by the Almohads near Granada in 1162. The new Caliph, Abu Yaqub Yusuf (1163–1184), increased the pressure against Ibn Mardanish, who was defeated in the plain of Murcia in 1165. Thereafter his power and influence began to decline, as his supporters, including Ibn Hamusk, began to turn away and make peace with the Almohads. One by one the towns of the kingdom of Murcia opened their gates to the enemy, and when he died in 1172 Ibn Mardanish counseled his son to offer allegiance to the caliph. With that, the Almohad subjugation of al-Andalus was complete. But Ibn Mardanish's resistance for so many years deflected the Almohads from making any major assault upon the city of Toledo and the kingdom of Castile during the critical years of Alfonso VIII's minority.

While the Almohads were still contending with Ibn Mardanish, Fernando II and Afonso Henriques were trying to push their frontiers southward, though rivalry and jealousy prevented them from undertaking any joint enterprise. Knowing that his neighbors in León and Castile intended to partition his kingdom, Afonso made repeated incursions into Galicia, but he came to recognize that greater profit was to be had from the reconquest. In 1158, for example, he captured Alcácer do Sal, a position of great military importance in the Alentejo, the region south of the Tagus river. Additional conquests were made on his behalf by a valorous knight, known as Giraldo Sempavor, the Fearless (*Giraldus qui dicebatur sine pavore*), who has been called the Portuguese Cid. His tactic was surprise; with a band of adventurers and thieves he struck the enemy when they least expected it, in the darkness of night or in inclement weather. During 1165–1168 he seized Evora, Trujillo, Cáceres, Montánchez, Serpa, and Juromenha in the area between the Tagus and the Guadiana. But his most audacious attack was carried out against Badajoz in May 1169; after gaining control of the town he summoned Afonso Henriques to assist him in taking the citadel.

News of the Portuguese entrance into the city alarmed Fernando II, who decided to intervene because, according to the treaty of Sahagún, Badajoz and the other places taken by Giraldo were reserved for Leonese conquest. As he advanced upon the city his opponents took to flight but were soon captured; Afonso Henriques broke his leg on this occasion and ever after found it difficult to mount and ride a horse. Fernando II "who was never conquered in battle, but who was always overcome by the entreaties of the downtrodden," liberated his illustrious prisoners but required the surrender of Montánchez, Trujillo, and other places. He left Badajoz in the hands of the Muslims, who agreed to hold it as his vassals until such time as he was able to occupy it himself; but as soon as he departed, they repudiated him and opened the gates to the Almohads. Giraldo vainly renewed his harassment of Badajoz, but soon defected to the Almohads, who beheaded him in 1174 when they suspected him of conspiring with Afonso Henriques. His death closed an heroic chapter in the history of Portugal, and the initiative now passed to the Almohads.

During the next quarter-century, when the Almohads launched a series of devastating assaults upon the Christian states, Fernando II, Alfonso VIII, and Afonso Henriques entrusted the defense of the frontiers in large part to several military religious Orders. Although the Templars and Hospitallers were established in the peninsula, their participation in the reconquest, save in Portugal and Aragon, was rather limited. The Christian princes relied more heavily upon native military Orders, which constituted a permanent military force, garrisoning the fortresses along the frontier and ready to take the offensive at any moment. The first of the Hispanic Orders was established at Calatrava, a fortress guarding the main road from Toledo to Andalusia. Alfonso VII captured Calatrava in 1146, and appointed the Templars to defend it; but fearing that they would not be able to hold it against the Almohads, they asked Sancho III to relieve them. He vainly sought among his nobles for someone to assume this responsibility, until Abbot Ramón of the Cistercian monastery of Fitero in Navarre offered to do so. Sancho III ceded Calatrava to him and his successors in 1158. With the support of the archbishop of Toledo, Ramón garrisoned the fortress, and many of the defenders assumed the monastic habit while continuing to serve as soldiers. Thus the Order of Calatrava came into being. Pope Alexander III approved it in 1164, and the Order was formally affiliated with the Order of Cîteaux in 1187.

Evora, in the Alentejo, conquered in 1166, became the seat of a military Order for which there is documentary evidence from 1176; from the beginning and after the transfer of its headquarters to Avis in 1211, it was affiliated with Calatrava and followed its customs. The Order of

San Julián del Pereiro probably originated in Extremadura in 1167, though the first certain evidence of its existence is Alexander III's bull of confirmation in 1176. Also affiliated with Calatrava, it came to be known as the Order of Alcántara, after its chief seat was established there on the Tagus in 1218.

The Order of Santiago, destined to become the richest and most powerful of all, was founded by Pedro Fernández in the city of Cáceres in 1170. Fernando II gave his wholehearted encouragement and richly endowed the knights in his kingdom; Alfonso VIII granted them the fortress of Uclés, east of Toledo in the Tagus valley, and from that base they eventually pushed southward into the *campo de Montiel*. Pope Alexander III approved the Order in 1175.

Seeking to combine the ideals of monasticism and chivalry, the military Orders pledged to defend Christendom against the infidels and for more than a century were largely faithful to that trust.

The Almohad Offensive against Christian Spain

With the annexation of Ibn Mardanish's kingdom of Murcia in 1172, the Almohads were free to commence hostilities against all the Christian states. Almohad armies advanced toward Toledo, besieging Huete in 1172, and ravaging the vicinity of Talavera in 1173. Turning against León in 1174, they seized Alcántara, which Fernando II had taken eight years before, but they were unable to capture Ciudad Rodrigo, which he had recently repopulated. Pope Alexander III offered indulgences to those who fought the Almohads and excommunicated anyone who collaborated with them. In response to enemy attacks, Fernando II led a plundering expedition deep into Muslim territory in 1177, going beyond the Guadalquivir as far south as Jerez. The Portuguese also raided the neighborhood of Seville, destroying some ships in the river.

Alfonso VIII began an important campaign against the Almohads at this time. His first concern, however, was to settle quarrels with Sancho VI of Navarre, who had occupied Castilian lands. The two kings agreed to submit their dispute to the judgment of Henry II of England, who found in favor of Castile in 1176. Although the litigants accepted his decision, conflict over the frontiers continued for many years to come. With this matter resolved, at least temporarily, Alfonso VIII, aided by Alfonso II of Aragon, laid siege to Cuenca, east of Toledo, and forced it to surrender on 14 September 1177. A bishopric was established there, and the new settlers received a detailed *fuero* which became the model for *fueros* granted to many other towns. The acquisition of Cuenca assured the defense of Castile's eastern frontier and also encouraged Aragon's southward expansion.

In return for his assistance at Cuenca, Alfonso VIII released Alfonso II from his obligation of vassalage for Zaragoza and its dependent territory, the lands which Ramon Berenguer IV had agreed to hold as a vassal of Alfonso VII. The two kings concluded a treaty of even greater importance for the future at Cazola on 20 March 1179. Pledging mutual aid against all other rulers, but especially against the king of Navarre, they also agreed to partition the *terra Hyspanie*. The Muslim territories of Valencia, Játiva, Biar, Denia, and Calpe were reserved for Alfonso II and his heirs, while the regions beyond fell to the lot of Alfonso VIII. The treaty differed from the pact of Tudellén (1151) in two significant respects. In the first place, the kings of Aragon thereafter would hold any conquests freely and independently, without any kind of feudal subordination to Castile; secondly, while the whole of the kingdom of Valencia as far as Alicante was allotted to Aragon, Murcia was assigned to Castile.

Soldevila believes that Alfonso II committed a grave blunder by yielding those rights to Murcia which the treaty of Tudellén had guaranteed to Aragon. The pact of Cazola, however, while perhaps limiting Aragon's future territorial expansion, did acknowledge the equality of Aragon and Castile and ended once and for all any pretense that the reconquest was primarily the business of the western kingdoms. It should also be pointed out that Alfonso II was determined to be quit of any feudal bonds to Castile or to any other power; for this reason he avoided doing homage to Frederick Barbarossa for Provence, and he also abandoned the custom of dating his charters according to the regnal years of the French kings, an implicit recognition of French sovereignty.

While the treaty of Cazola provided Aragon with a potential opening to the south, much of Alfonso II's attention was given to the defense of his interests north of the Pyrenees. Count Raymond V of Toulouse consistently attempted to undermine the Catalan position in Provence; his partisans went so far as to assassinate Alfonso II's younger brother, Ramon Berenguer, who served as his procurator in Provence. The count of Toulouse also sought aid from Genoa, which aspired to control the Provençal coast, but Alfonso II countered this by forming an alliance with Pisa, Genoa's longtime rival. Alfonso also strengthened his ties with the counts of Foix and Bigorre, the viscounts of Béarn and Nîmes, and the lord of Montpellier. By 1185 a peace treaty with Toulouse was concluded, giving Alfonso II a reasonably secure position in Provence.

The other Christian rulers, in the meantime, while distracted by personal and territorial rivalries, were mainly engaged in a continuing struggle against the Almohads. Portuguese, Leonese, and Castilian troops ranged widely through al-Andalus, threatening Seville, Córdoba, Málaga, and other towns, while the Almohads responded by attacks all along the Tagus river, especially in the vicinity of Toledo, Santarém, and Lisbon. Provoked at last, the Caliph Abu Yaqub Yusuf assembled a formidable army and crossed the straits into Spain in the spring of 1184. From Seville he marched to Badajoz and then turned westward into Portugal where he besieged Santarém. Afonso Henriques valiantly defended the town, and Fernando II hastened to help him, though it must be said that Afonso was not immediately certain that he came with friendly intent. As the caliph raised the siege and began to withdraw, the Christians attacked, throwing his army into a panic; he was mortally wounded and died upon his arrival in Seville. His son Yaqub, known as al-Mansur (1184–1199), returned promptly to Morocco, to deal with uprisings there, and left the Christians free to resume their raids.

The defense of Santarém was the last great achievement of Afonso Henriques, the first king of Portugal, of whom the *Chronica Gothorum* remarked, "he protected the whole of Portugal with his sword." Pope Alexander III, on 23 May 1179, formally acknowledged "the intrepid destroyer of the enemies of the Christian name and the energetic defender of the Christian faith," as *rex Portugalensium*, thereby confirming Portuguese independence. The conqueror of Lisbon died on 6 December 1185, leaving the kingdom to his son, Sancho I (1185–1211).

Fernando II outlived his longtime rival by three years. A genial prince, the soul of liberality, he repopulated important areas of his kingdom and thwarted Portuguese efforts to occupy parts of Galicia, but he achieved only limited success in the reconquest. At his death on 22 January 1188 his son Alfonso IX (1188–1230), then only seventeen years of age, succeeded him.

The Ascendancy of Alfonso VIII

The death of these two kings left Alfonso VIII of Castile as the most influential and powerful of the Christian rulers; but his efforts to dominate his neighbors eventually drove them to join forces against him, at a time when the Almohads still constituted a grave menace to the whole of Christian Spain.

As events were to show, the bitterest opponent of the king of Castile was his cousin, Alfonso IX of León. Inexperienced and scarcely of adult age, Alfonso IX came to power in trying circumstances. His father's excessive generosity had weakened the royal power, and his stepmother tried to stir up opposition to his rule. Both Portugal and Castile were hopeful of taking advantage of these disorders to extend their frontiers at his expense.

With the intention of establishing himself firmly on the throne and of securing broad support among his subjects, Alfonso IX held an extraordinary meeting of his *curia* at León in April 1188. This assembly has an exceptional significance because for the first time in the history of Christian Spain and indeed in the history of western Christendom, representatives of the towns were summoned to attend the king's court together with the bishops and magnates. With the assembling of these three elements of society, it can be said that the medieval *cortes* or parliament had come into being at an earlier time than elsewhere in Europe. Alfonso IX declared his intention to uphold the good laws of his predecessors and to restore order to the land; he also began a review of his father's concessions and recovered royal rights and properties that had been alienated. Later in the year he attended the *curia* held at Carrión by Alfonso VIII, to whom he pledged homage and fealty. No doubt he did so to avert any further conflict with Castile, but ever after he considered the act of homage a supreme humiliation forced upon him in a time of weakness by his more powerful neighbor.

While Alfonso IX was securing his throne, thousands of Europeans were preparing to hasten to the Holy Land to liberate Jerusalem, which had been taken by Saladin in 1187. As at the time of the Second Crusade, fleets from northern Europe carrying Danes, Germans, Frisians, Flemings, Englishmen, and Frenchmen, passed along the Portuguese coast, and aided in the reconquest. One fleet stopped to capture and plunder the port of Alvor, but after killing the inhabitants, the crusaders continued their journey. A second fleet arrived at Lisbon in July

1189 and accepted Sancho I's proposals for a joint attack on Silves in the Algarve, the southernmost sector of the future Portuguese territory. While he marched overland, the fleet sailed southward, landing the crusaders who seized the suburbs and established a siege. Silves was gradually starved into submission and surrendered on 1 September; after sacking the city the crusaders resumed their pilgrimage to the Holy Land. In the following year the caliph attempted to recover Silves; failing that, he marched northward to besiege Santarém, defended by Sancho I and a band of English crusaders. The caliph withdrew but returned in 1191 and succeeded in capturing not only Silves, but also Alcácer do Sal, Palmela, and Almada. Thus Portuguese advances in the Alentejo were wiped out, with the exception of Evora.

At this crucial time the Christian rulers, instead of collaborating against the Almohads, were preparing to open hostilities against Alfonso VIII of Castile, a ruler whom they charged with an overweening ambition to dominate them all. Alfonso II, whose relations with Castile had cooled perceptibly since the treaty of Cazola, joined Sancho VI of Navarre in an anti-Castilian pact in 1190; in the next year the isolation of Castile was completed when the kings of Aragon, León, and Portugal promised to join together against Alfonso VIII and never to make a separate peace. The ensuing warfare was a source of scandal, especially to Pope Celestine III who sent his legates to restore concord and unity in Christian Spain. The kings of Castile and León were persuaded to make peace in 1194, but resentments ran too deeply to be suppressed permanently.

The Battle of Alarcos

The renewal of peaceful relations between Castile and León came none too soon, because the Caliph, al-Mansur, had decided to respond on a massive scale to the recent Christian incursions into al-Andalus. Landing with a large army at Tarifa in June 1195, he proclaimed the holy war and advanced to Córdoba; he then proceeded northward through the Puerto del Muradal (Despeñaperros) into the *campo de Calatrava* and encamped between Salvatierra and Alarcos. At the first word of the invasion, Alfonso VIII hastened to Alarcos, a new fortress he was erecting on the Guadiana near the modern town of Ciudad Real. Instead of waiting for expected reinforcements from Alfonso IX, he chose to give battle to the enemy on 19 July 1195, but he suffered a defeat of disastrous proportions and fled in disorder to Toledo. The victors, who compared their triumph with that of Zallaqa in 1086, occupied Alarcos, Calatrava, and other fortresses guarding the road to Toledo. Al-Mansur fortunately chose not to invest Toledo at this time but retired with the spoils of war to Seville. Little did he realize that this was the last great victory of the Muslims in Spain.

In this moment of tribulation Alfonso VIII found himself confronted once more by the hostile kings of León and Navarre. Alfonso IX, demanding the cession of certain disputed border fortresses, began to lay waste the Tierra de Campos, while Sancho VII of Navarre (1194–1234) resumed his father's efforts to annex La Rioja. The Almohads, who concluded an alliance with Alfonso IX and sent him troops, simultaneously ravaged the Tagus valley, seizing Trujillo, Plasencia, and other places; but in order to be free to subjugate the Muslims of Majorca, the caliph granted Alfonso VIII a truce in 1197. Upon the caliph's death soon afterwards, he was succeeded by his son, al-Nasir (1199–1213), known to Christian writers as Miramamolín, that is, *amir al-muminin*, prince of believers.

Alfonso II of Aragon, realizing the evil of continuing warfare among the Christian princes, had assumed the role of peacemaker and tried to persuade them to lay down their arms, but he died on 25 April 1196. Although he had considerably augmented his power and prestige in Provence and Languedoc, in his last will he destroyed his labors and those of his predecessors to form what Soldevila called "un gran estat occitánic," a great Occitanian state. He bequeathed the kingdom of Aragon and the counties of Pallars and Rousillon to his oldest son, Pedro II (1196–1213), but he left Provence, Millau, Gavaldá, and Razès to his second son, Alfons II. This was not the first time that Provence was separated from the crown of Aragon, but it was in fact the last time, and the possibility of a permanent union of the two regions was eliminated. Pedro II, the new king of Aragon, a young man in his twenties, followed a policy of cooperation with Alfonso VIII and agreed to a joint partition of Navarre.

Meanwhile, Pope Celestine III took several radical steps to compel Alfonso IX to cease his attacks on Castile. He excommunicated the king of León on 31 October 1196, releasing his subjects from their oath of allegiance, and offering indulgences to those who took up arms against him, just as if he were a Muslim. Both Alfonso VIII and Alfonso IX soon realized the futility of their struggle and accepted a solution proposed by Queen Leonor of Castile. She suggested that Alfonso IX marry her daughter Berenguela, who would receive as a dowry the disputed fortresses held by Alfonso VIII. The wedding accordingly took place at Valladolid in October 1197.

Although the prospect of friendlier relations between Castile and León and possibly their eventual reunion was now in sight, Alfonso IX and Berenguela were related within the prohibited degrees so their marriage could not be sanctioned by the papacy. Thus in 1198 Pope Innocent III excommunicated them and imposed an interdict on León until they separated. Only in the spring of 1204, after four children had been born, including the future Fernando III, did they dissolve their marriage, and only then were they freed of ecclesiastical censures. The immediate result of the separation was the revival of animosity between the kings of León and Castile, but in 1206 they reached a new agreement, endowing Berenguela's son with the lands and fortresses she had received from her father and her husband. Thus the peace was preserved.

Celestine III had also attempted to bring about peace between Castile and Navarre. As an inducement to peace, he recognized Sancho VII as king of Navarre in 1196, although the popes, ever since the separation of Aragon and Navarre in 1134, had refused to address the Navarrese rulers by the royal title. Sancho VII did not succumb to papal blandishments, however, and even went so far as to appeal to the Almohads for help. After Alfonso VIII settled his quarrel with León, he devoted his full energy to the expulsion of the Navarrese from Castilian territory and the conquest of the Basque provinces of Guipúzcoa and Alava. A few years later he also made a brief incursion into Gascony, claiming it as his wife's dowry, but he was unable to take Bayonne or Bordeaux and withdrew. A truce with Navarre in 1207 left him in possession of the recently conquered provinces. Aragon and Navarre signed a similar pact in the following year, and León and Castile renewed their treaty of peace and friendship in 1209. Thus all the Christian princes were in concord at last.

The Crusade of Las Navas de Tolosa

For several years Christians and Almohads had been at peace, while the former resolved their disputes and the caliph conquered Majorca. But the military Orders and the bishops, led by Rodrigo Jiménez de Rada, archbishop of Toledo, had become increasingly anxious to resume hostilities against the Muslims. Pope Innocent III wrote to the archbishop in 1209 urging him to persuade his king to take up arms in a crusade against the infidels. When Infante Fernando, the king's son, dedicated his sword to the crusade, the pope lauded him and asked other princes to follow his example, threatening with excommunication any prince who attacked his Christian neighbors. Meanwhile, not requiring these promptings, Pedro II seized Adamuz, Castellfabit, and Sertella, the first important Aragonese conquests in the Muslim kingdom of Valencia.

The renewal of Christian raids prompted Miramamolín to cross the straits again in May 1211. From Córdoba he marched northward along the road which had led his father to Alarcos in 1195. He stopped in July to besiege the castle of Salvatierra, the chief seat of the knights of Calatrava since the loss of Calatrava itself in 1195. Set in the heart of a region held by the Muslims, Salvatierra was a symbol of Castilian determination to undo the effects of Alarcos. An ever-present challenge to the Muslims, it was, according to the caliph, the "right hand of the lord of Castile," and he hoped to cut it off. For two months the knights valiantly defended the castle until Alfonso VIII, unable to relieve them, authorized them to surrender. Since the summer was at an end, Miramamolín decided to return to Córdoba, preferring to resume the campaign in the spring. Though he boasted loudly of his triumph, the resistance of Salvatierra made it impossible for him to launch any serious attack against Toledo at this time. "God doubly saved the whole land through that castle," the *castrum salutis*, the castle of salvation, as Archbishop Rodrigo called it. The loss of Salvatierra, however, was a grave blow for Castile and for the knights of Calatrava who were homeless once more; the death of Infante Fernando, of whom so much had been expected, added to the king's grief.

During the winter months all Castile was busy preparing for the assault that was sure to come in the spring. Alfonso VIII sent Archbishop Rodrigo to Rome to ask the pope to proclaim a crusade; before returning, the archbishop sought recruits in Italy, France, and Germany. Innocent III wrote to the French bishops urging them to exhort the faithful to hasten to aid the king of Castile; he also granted crusading indulgences to Alfonso VIII and his people, and admonished the Christian rulers to preserve the peace among themselves.

The kings of Aragon and Navarre pledged their assistance to Castile, but Alfonso IX made his cooperation dependent upon the restoration of border fortresses held by Alfonso VIII. While the others were preparing for the coming crusade, he attacked Portugal, whose king, Sancho I, had died in March 1211. Known as the Settler, Sancho's principal work had been the repopulation of the central and eastern regions of the kingdom. His last years were troubled by conflicts with the bishops, and he also quarreled with the papacy because of his delay in paying the tribute promised by his father. In his will, he bequeathed certain royal domains to his daughters, thereby arousing the anger of his son and successor, Afonso II (1211–1223), who insisted that the royal patrimony was indivisible. While Portugal was thrown into a turmoil, Alfonso IX launched an assault and routed the Portuguese at Valdevez. Despite the preoccupations of the kings of León and Portugal, many of their subjects did take part in the crusade against the Almohads.

During the octave of Pentecost a cosmopolitan army began to assemble at Toledo. Among the French crusaders were the papal legate, Archbishop Arnald Amaury of Narbonne, Archbishop William of Bordeaux, Count Centule of Astarac, Viscount Raymond of Touraine, Theobald of Blazon, and others. As the Christian army set out from Toledo on 20 June 1212, it was divided into three sections. Diego López de Haro, lord of Vizcaya, led the vanguard composed of the troops from beyond the Pyrenees; then followed Pedro II of Aragon and the count of Ampurias, and finally the rearguard under the command of Alfonso VIII, accompanied by Archbishop Rodrigo, the other bishops, and the masters of the military Orders.

Proceeding southward, the French and other ultramontane crusaders seized the castle of Malagón on 24 June and slaughtered the garrison. Next they reached Calatrava, whose *alcaide* surrendered on 1 July after a brief siege; later he was executed by the caliph for cowardice. Alfonso VIII allowed the defenders to leave and restored the fortress to the Order of Calatrava, but at this point the ultramontanes, complaining of the heat, the lack of booty, and the king's refusal to allow them to sack Calatrava, abandoned the crusade. Only the archbishop of Narbonne and Theobald of Blazon remained with the Hispanic forces. As they resumed their march, they were joined by Sancho VII of Navarre. Without difficulty, the army seized Alarcos, Piedrabuena, Benavente, and Caracuel, but bypassed Salvatierra rather than engage in a protracted siege. Hastening on through the Puerto del Muradal, the crusaders reached Las Navas de Tolosa on 13 July.

Meanwhile, Miramamolín had set out from Córdoba and blocked the Christian advance. For two days, as they prepared for the final struggle, the armies faced each other. Archbishop Rodrigo exhorted the crusaders and absolved them of their sins. When the battle began on 16 July, Diego López de Haro commanded the center of the Christian army, with Sancho VII on his right and Pedro II on his left, while Alfonso VIII and the military Orders held the rear. In the ensuing combat the kings of Aragon and Navarre carried out a pincers movement, and Alfonso VIII rushed forward, breaking the enemy lines. Sancho VII drove forward through a circle of Negro slaves chained to one another to guard Miramamolín's tent. The caliph took to flight and did not rest until he had reached Jaén; there he wrote to his subordinates trying to disguise with rhetoric the extent of his defeat. The Christian triumph was complete. Thousands of Muslims were left dead on the field, and the booty was immense. The tapestry covering the entrance to the caliph's tent was sent as a trophy of war to the monastery of Las Huelgas near Burgos, where it still hangs in testimony of the victory. An exultant Alfonso VIII sent Miramamolín's standard and tent, with a detailed account of the crusade, to Innocent III:

On their side 100,000 armed men or more fell in the battle, according to the estimate of the Saracens whom we captured. But of the army of the Lord . . . incredible though it may be, unless it be a miracle, hardly 25 or 30 Christians of our whole army fell. O what happiness! O what thanksgiving! though one might lament that so few martyrs from such a great army went to Christ in martyrdom. [DP, 514]

The king's daughter Berenguela communicated news of the victory to her sister, Blanche, wife of Prince Louis of France: "Our father, the king and lord, conquered Miramamolín in a pitched battle; we believe this to be a signal honor, because until now it was unheard of that the king of Morocco should be overcome on the battlefield" (González, El reino de Castilla en la época de Alfonso VIII, III, 572). During the next few days the crusaders occupied several castles and the towns of Baeza and Ubeda, though the latter were soon recovered by the Muslims. The shortage of supplies and the outbreak of pestilence then compelled the king to terminate the campaign and to return to Toledo.

The Christian victory at Las Navas de Tolosa ended once and for all the Almohad threat to Christian Spain and hastened the decline of the Almohad empire. The equilibrium hitherto existing between Christians and Muslims was upset, and the balance of power was tipped decisively in favor of the Christians. The victory was the greatest ever

achieved in the course of the reconquest, and it made possible the subjugation of the greater part of al-Andalus in the next forty years.

Returning from the field of battle, Alfonso VIII's immediate concern
was to make peace with Alfonso IX who had taken advantage of the
crusade to seize several Castilian fortresses. The kings of Castile, León,
and Portugal concluded a truce at Coimbra in November and agreed
to collaborate against the Muslims in the future. The immediate result
of this new-found harmony was Alfonso IX's capture of Alcántara, a
fortress situated on the Tagus and soon to become the headquarters of
the Order of Alcántara.

Pedro II and the Albigensian Crusade

Before the end of the year 1213, Pedro II of Aragon, who had fought
valiantly at Las Navas de Tolosa, met his death on the field of Muret,
a victim of the Albigensian Crusade. A form of Manicheism, the Albigensian heresy, also know as Catharism, had gained a strong base in
Languedoc where the rulers of Barcelona always had had important
feudal interests. St. Dominic (Domingo de Guzmán), a canon of Osma,
devoted his life to preaching to the heretics and founded the Order of
Preachers in 1209 to carry on the work. Ecclesiastical efforts to repress
the heresy were unavailing, however, and the secular authorities,
namely, Count Raymond VI of Toulouse and Raymond Roger Trencavel, viscount of Béziers and Carcassonne, failed to collaborate with
the church.

Had he wished to do so, Pedro II could not have ignored these developments. That he was no friend of heresy is indicated by the law
he published in 1197 banishing heretics from his dominions under
threat of confiscation of property and death at the stake. On the other
side of the Pyrenees he numbered among his vassals the counts of Foix
and Comminges, and the viscounts of Béarn, Béziers, and Carcassonne;
besides, his brother Alfons ruled the march of Provence. Although the
counts of Toulouse traditionally had opposed Catalan intervention in
Languedoc, Raymond VI, perhaps to protect himself against the threat
of papal condemnation, was disposed to seek a rapprochement, and in
1200 married Pedro II's sister, Leonor. Four years later, in order to
strengthen his position in southern France, Pedro II married Marie of
Montpellier, a marriage that made him the lord of Montpellier. He was,
however, a faithless and dissolute husband who spent little time with

his wife, so that it was almost by chance that the future Jaime I was born to the royal pair in 1208.

Pedro II in 1204 journeyed to Rome where he renewed the feudal bond established by King Sancho Ramírez (1063–1094) between Aragon and the Holy See. Offering his kingdom to the pope, Pedro swore fidelity to him and his successors, promising to defend the Catholic faith, and in acknowledgment of his status as a papal vassal pledged payment of an annual tribute. For his part, Innocent III extended his protection to him and solemnly crowned him. Both king and pope expected to draw tangible profit from this new relationship. By his actions Pedro II demonstrated to the whole world his unshakable allegiance to the papacy and to the Catholic faith; at the same time he obtained a guarantee of papal protection against any intrusion into his dominions by enemy forces, including any which the pope might employ to extirpate heresy. Perhaps Innocent III thought to use his faithful vassal against the heretics; at the very least he could expect Pedro not to interfere with any military action taken against them under papal auspices.

For some time the pope had been contemplating the possibility of a crusade against the Albigensians and had attempted in vain to interest Philip Augustus, king of France. The assassination of the papal legate, Peter of Castelnau, in January 1208 convinced the pope of the urgent need to launch the crusade. Accusing Count Raymond VI of instigating the murder, the pope excommunicated Raymond and invited good Christians to take up arms against him and the heretics. The prospect of enriching themselves at the expense of the count of Toulouse and the other lords of Languedoc attracted many warriors from northern France. Amidst a horrible slaughter they seized Béziers and Carcassonne in July–August 1209 and deposed Raymond Roger Trencavel, who died soon after. Simon de Montfort, invested as viscount and elected as leader of the crusade, now began preparations to attack the lands of the count of Toulouse.

Thus far, Pedro II, while protesting the action of the crusaders against his vassal, Raymond Roger Trencavel, had not intervened directly. As a papal vassal he could not thwart the purposes of the crusade, yet he could not stand aloof while his vassals and his brother-in-law were ruined and his own interests were undermined. At first he refused the homage proferred by de Montfort for the viscounties of Béziers and Carcassonne, but in 1211, hoping to bring about an accommodation of conflicting interests and to safeguard the lands of the count of Toulouse from conquest, he agreed to do so. At the same time the future marriage of Pedro II's son and heir, Jaime, with de Montfort's daughter was arranged; as surety that the pact would be fulfilled Jaime, then aged three years, was delivered into de Montfort's custody. As a counterweight to these ties with de Montfort, the king of Aragon married his sister Sancha to the count of Toulouse's son, Raymond.

In spite of these agreements, the pacification of Languedoc was not achieved. Abetted by the papal legates, who refused to accept Raymond VII's protestations of repentance and adherence to the orthodox faith, de Montfort resumed his plans to conquer Toulouse. Pedro II, after participating in the campaign of Las Navas de Tolosa, appealed to Innocent III, charging de Montfort and the legates with attacking his vassals and his brother-in-law, all of whom were good Christians. While the pope announced his intention to investigate and ordered a suspension of military operations, Pedro II decided to give active support to the count of Toulouse and to crush de Montfort. The climax came on 12 September 1213 when the king of Aragon and his allies, the counts of Toulouse, Foix, and Comminges and the viscount of Béarn, besieged the castle of Muret, near Toulouse. De Montfort hastened to relieve the fortress. Knowing the numerical superiority of his own forces and holding his adversary in utter contempt, Pedro II chose to fight a pitched battle. Rashness, lack of coordination, and poor generalship on the one side, and skill and determination on the other, enabled de Montfort to rout his enemies. Pedro II, who, according to the *Chronicle* of his son Jaime I, had spent the preceding evening in amorous pursuits and was too tired to stand for the reading of the gospel in the morning's mass, fell on the field of battle. In order to safeguard his reputation from any taint of heresy, the *Crònica general de Pere III* (34) explained that he was called Pedro the Catholic "because he loved the Church," and that he "went into that region only to help his sisters . . . and the count of Toulouse, not to give aid to any infidel or enemy of the Christian faith." But as a Castilian chronicler commented: "Happy would that king have been had he concluded his life immediately after the noble triumph in the battle of Las Navas de Tolosa."

The victory at Muret greatly enhanced the prestige of Simon de Montfort who continued his conquest of the county of Toulouse with renewed zeal. Muret also hastened the end of an independent Langue-

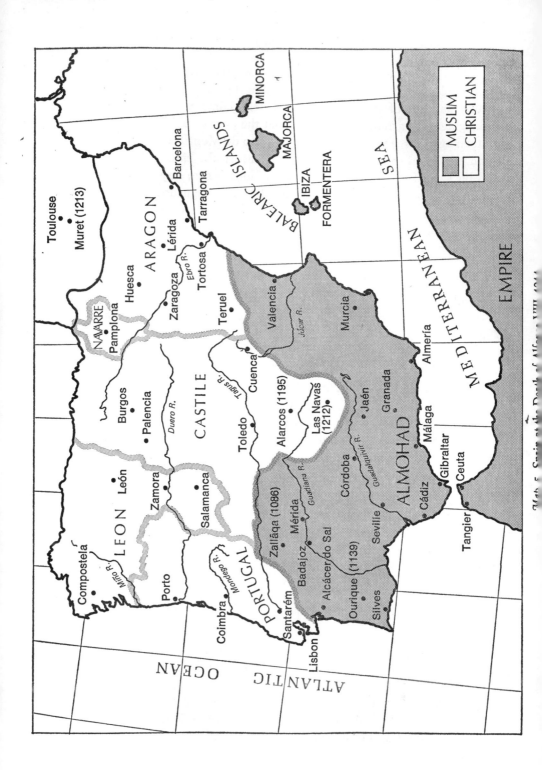

Map 5. Spain at the Death of Alfonso VIII, 1214

Muret (1213)
Toulouse

ARAGON
Huesca
Pamplona
NAVARRE
Zaragoza
Lérida
Barcelona
Ebro R.
Tortosa
Tarragona
Teruel

BALEARIC ISLANDS
MINORCA
MAJORCA
IBIZA
FORMENTERA

Burgos
Palencia
CASTILE
Duero R.
León
LEON
Zamora
Salamanca
Compostela
Miño R.
Porto

Toledo
Cuenca
Tagus R.
Valencia
Júcar R.
Alarcos (1195)
Las Navas (1212)
Murcia

PORTUGAL
Mondego R.
Coimbra
Santarém
Lisbon

Zallāqa (1086)
Badajoz
Mérida
Guadiana R.
Alcácer do Sal
Ourique (1139)
Silves

Córdoba
Guadalquivir R.
Jaén
Granada
Seville

ALMOHAD

Almería
Málaga
Cádiz
Gibraltar
Ceuta
Tangier

MEDITERRANEAN SEA

EMPIRE

ATLANTIC OCEAN

MUSLIM
CHRISTIAN

doc, which, within not too many years, would pass into the hands of the Capetian dynasty. Catalan dreams of political domination and expansion north of the Pyrenees and the possibility of uniting the peoples of Catalonia, Provence, and Languedoc were destroyed once and for all. For this reason, Soldevila summarized Pedro II's reign in two words: bankruptcy and ruin.

Miramamolín, the vanquished of Las Navas de Tolosa and the last great Almohad caliph, followed Pedro II to the grave at the end of the year 1213, perhaps poisoned by his subordinates. In view of the tender age of his son Abu Yaqub Yusuf, al-Mustansir (1213–1224), truces were arranged with Castile and Aragon.

Alfonso VIII met his death on 6 October 1214, and his queen and faithful companion, Leonor, died twenty-six days later. One of the great kings of medieval Spain, during his reign of fifty-six years he suffered the worst humiliation of any Christian king on the battlefield of Alarcos, but he was fortunate in being able to redeem his honor at Las Navas de Tolosa. When he ascended the throne the Almohads were a serious menace to the whole Tagus valley, but at the end of his career the Christians were secure in their holdings as far south as the Guadiana, and the gates of Andalusia were open to them. In the more tranquil areas of civil society, he recognized the value of learning and education and founded the first university in the peninsula at Palencia early in the thirteenth century. His many children included Berenguela, mother of the future St. Fernando III, and Blanca or Blanche, wife of Louis VIII of France and mother of St. Louis IX. Since his oldest son, Fernando, predeceased him, the throne passed to the youngest child, Enrique I (1214–1217), a boy of only eleven years.

CHAPTER 11

Government, 1031–1212

Territorial Realignments

In the nearly two hundred years from the fall of the caliphate of Cór-doba to the defeat of the Almohads at Las Navas de Tolosa, the po-litical structure of the peninsula developed with a greater complexity than previously had seemed likely. The disintegration of al-Andalus into numerous petty kingdoms coincided with the ascendancy of San-cho el mayor, king of Navarre, who extended his rule over Aragon and Castile and even occupied León for a brief time. But the prospect of union among the Christian states was premature, for he divided his dominions among his sons, each of whom assumed the title of king. Thus Castile, once a semi-independent county in the kingdom of León, and Aragon, once briefly under Carolingian rule, attained the status of kingdoms. Although Fernando I of Castile annexed León in 1037, the two kingdoms were separated again at his death in 1065; seven years later his son Alfonso VI reunited them until the partition between the sons of Alfonso VII in 1157. The final reunion did not take place until 1230. The emergence of Portugal as a distinct entity and then as an in-dependent kingdom ruled by its first self-proclaimed king, Afonso Henriques, contributed further to the dismemberment of the old king-dom of León. To the east of León the kingdom of Navarre was united to Aragon by Sancho I in 1076, but the union was dissolved upon the death of Alfonso I in 1134. Throughout the remaining medieval cen-turies Navarre preserved its independence of the other peninsular states, despite their manifest intention to destroy it. Aragon, on the other hand, was linked with Catalonia in 1137 by the marriage of Petronila and Ramon Berenguer IV. This union of peoples with disparate interests, languages, and customs was the most significant and durable of the epoch.

Early in the eleventh century al-Andalus was fragmented into many small kingdoms continually at war with one another, but by the middle of the century their numbers were reduced as the larger states absorbed or conquered the smaller ones. Disunity among the *taifas* left them a prey to the Christians, who exacted tribute and then seized their territory. The capture of Toledo in 1085, the first major triumph of the Christian reconquest, moved the frontier from the Duero to the Tagus where, despite many vicissitudes, it was to remain for more than a century. The Almoravids, summoned to halt the Christian advance, dispossessed the petty kings and incorporated al-Andalus into their empire. Yet the reconquest continued, and Alfonso I's seizure of Zaragoza in 1118 revealed the weakness of the Almoravid regime, which collapsed by the middle of the twelfth century. Taking advantage of these circumstances, the Christians seized Lisbon, Tortosa, and Lérida in the short space of two years. The Almohads, after overrunning North Africa, restored the vigor of Spanish Islam and seriously threatened the Christian states, pushing them back to the Tagus, but they failed to recover any of the major towns that had fallen into Christian hands. Alfonso VIII's victory at Las Navas de Tolosa closed this period, moving the Castilian frontier beyond the Guadiana and raising the very real possibility of conquering Andalusia. Thus within two hundred years each of the Christian states substantially enlarged its territory, but the unification of Christian Spain was made more difficult than ever before.

Empire and Kingdom

In the early centuries of the reconquest the idea of empire evolved as an expression of Leonese aspirations to rule the whole of Spain as the heirs of the Visigoths. The recognition of the king of León as *imperator* by the other Christian princes seemed to suggest that the eventual establishment of a truly Hispanic unity under his aegis was not impossible. Alfonso VI used the imperial title with a significant qualification; by calling himself emperor of Spain (*imperator Hispaniae, imperator constitutus super omnes Hispaniae nationes*), he emphasized as explicitly as possible the traditional Leonese ambitions, challenging the tendencies toward independence among the other Christian states and repudiating Pope Gregory VII's assertion that *Hispania* pertained to the patrimony of St. Peter. Alfonso VI's claims to universal dominion in the peninsula were also reflected in one of his charters referring to his rule over "all the kingdoms of Spain of both the Christians and the pagans" and in the title "emperor of the two religions" attributed to him by Muslim sources. While the other Christian princes acknowledged him as emperor, they did not admit that his power extended over their kingdoms. Thus his empire, like that of the tenth-century kings, was never a reality.

Sánchez Albornoz, pointing to the influence of feudalism in the eleventh and twelfth centuries, suggested that the idea of empire might have been translated into actuality by the feudal subordination of the other Christian rulers to the king of León. Alfonso VII seemed to have had this in mind when he tried to bind the other princes to himself by means of vassalage. Recognized as suzerain by the count of Barcelona, the king of Navarre, the count of Toulouse, and others, he was solemnly crowned as emperor at León in 1135:

The king was vested in a rich cape of marvelous workmanship and they placed on his head a crown of fine gold and precious stones and placed the scepter in his hands. And then with King García holding him by the right arm and Ariano, bishop of León on his left, together with the bishops and abbots they led him before the altar of St. Mary, chanting "*Te Deum laudamus*" to the end, and shouting "*Vivat Adefonsus Imperator*." After the blessing had been given to him, they celebrated mass according to the custom of the feast . . . and he ordered a great banquet to be prepared in the royal palace, and counts and princes and dukes served at the royal table. Then the emperor ordered that great gifts be given to the bishops and abbots and the rest and that alms of clothing and food be given to the poor. [*Chronica Adefonsi Imperatoris*, 70]

Although Menéndez Pidal believed that this ceremony was only a repetition of earlier imperial coronations, Sánchez Albornoz emphasized its unique character. For the first time the king of León was solemnly crowned and acclaimed as emperor, and for the first time the Leonese empire existed in a juridical sense. The possibility of unifying Spain in the empire of León was never closer to reality, but before his death in 1157 Alfonso VII committed the grave blunder of giving his sons the rank of kings and dividing León and Castile between them. Although Fernando II of León and Alfonso VIII of Castile occasionally used the title of *rex Hispaniae*, the Leonese empire was effectively dissolved; the *regnum Hispaniae* gave way to the five kingdoms of León, Castile, Portugal, Navarre, and Aragon-Catalonia by the end of the twelfth century.

Private relationships between the ruler and his subjects had a greater importance during this period, and certain rulers, regarding the kingdom as a private patrimony, partitioned it among their heirs. Yet the concept of the state as a public institution survived and was indeed affirmed and strengthened by the reception of Roman law in the twelfth century, as references to the status, utility, or necessity of the kingdom (*status regni, utilitas regni, necessitas regni*) suggest.

Ramon d'Abadal has pointed out that the opportunity to proclaim Catalonia as a kingdom arose when Ramon Berenguer IV, count of Barcelona, married Petronila of Aragon. The jurists in his court hesitated, however, because of the traditional, though largely theoretical, sovereignty of the king of France over the Catalan counties. Influenced by Roman law, they advanced as a compromise the theory of a principedom, a Catalan state ruled by a *princeps*, a ruler possessed of the sovereign powers, though not the title of king. This greatly strengthened the position of the count of Barcelona, transforming him from a mere feudal lord into a veritable sovereign in Catalonia; it also gave Catalonia greater cohesion and unity, but Catalonia's status as a principality was always inferior to that of the kingdom of Aragon.

Kingship

The king or prince incarnated the authority of the state, promoting the public welfare, guarding the rights of the church, giving true justice, protecting the innocent, enacting salutary laws, and defending the frontiers. Fernando II of León described the king's functions as follows: "The office of kings is to cultivate justice, to extirpate evil, to do good to good men, to conserve the rights of the church." The compilers of the *Usages of Barcelona*, noting that "the faith and justice and truth of the prince, by which every kingdom is governed, are worth a kingdom and more than a kingdom," and that "the land and its people will perish under a wicked ruler, without truth and justice," attributed to Ramon Berenguer I this declaration (article 64): "We declare and command that all the princes who succeed us in this principality shall always hold to a sincere and perfect faith and true speech, so that all men, noble and non-noble . . . may trust in them and believe in them. . . . And all men . . . shall help the princes to keep, to hold, and to guard their faith and their word."

By the beginning of the eleventh century the principle of hereditary succession was well-rooted in each of the Christian states. The custom of election fell into desuetude, save in exceptional circumstances: for example, the Castilians elected Alfonso VI after the assassination of his brother in 1072, and following the death of Alfonso I in 1134 both the Aragonese and the Navarrese elected separate monarchs. Otherwise the succession ordinarily passed from father to son, or from brother to brother as in the case of Pedro I and Alfonso I of Aragon. The principle of primogeniture usually determined the heir to the throne, as Sancho I and Afonso II of Portugal indicated in their wills. The kingdom was partitioned occasionally, however, to provide for more than one son; thus Fernando I divided his realm among three sons, and Alfonso VII between two. Ramon Berenguer I of Barcelona left his dominions to be ruled jointly by his two sons, but within a few years one assassinated the other and gained sole control of the principality. The right of minors, admitted in the late tenth century, allowed Alfonso VIII of Castile and Alfonso II of Aragon to occupy the throne. Although the *Liber Judiciorum* prohibited clerics from accepting the crown, the difficult situation created by the last will of Alfonso I caused the Aragonese to summon his younger brother Ramiro II from his monastic refuge to become king. Once married and the father of a daughter, Petronila, he withdrew again to his monastery. Although Fernando I claimed León and Castile by virtue of his marriage, the first female to rule in her own right was Urraca, the daughter of Alfonso VI. Even during her marriage to Alfonso I she retained full rights of sovereignty in her kingdom. Petronila similarly had title to the kingdom of Aragon during her marriage to Ramon Berenguer IV, and she specifically yielded the kingship in 1164 to her son Alfonso II. The turbulence of Urraca's reign and the rivalries and jealousies created by the partitioning of the realm served to strengthen the principle of primogeniture and the belief that the oldest son had an exclusive right to the whole kingdom, and to discourage the claims of female heirs, while not entirely denying them.

Occasionally contemporary sources mention the traditional ceremonies of anointing and coronation. The *ordinatio* contained in the tenth-century *Antiphonary of León* may have been replaced by the *Ceremonial of Cardeña*, a twelfth-century text containing a ritual similar to that used in France. The *Historia Silense* (80) reported that Fernando I "was consecrated in the church of Blessed Mary of León and anointed as king by Servando, of venerable memory, Catholic bishop of the same church." Alfonso VII was crowned on three occasons: in 1111 at Compostela by Bishop Diego Gelmírez who gave him the royal sword and scepter and a golden crown; in 1126 at León after the death of his mother; and again in 1135, this last being his imperial coronation. A contemporary text describes the coronation of Pedro II of Aragon in Rome in 1204 in the monastery of St. Pancratius as follows:

He (Innocent III) caused the king to be anointed by the hand of Peter, bishop of Porto, and then he crowned him by his own hand, giving him all the royal insignia, viz., the mantle, scepter, orb, crown and miter, and he personally received from him the oath whose tenor follows: "I, Pedro, king of Aragon, profess and avow that I will always be faithful and obedient to my lord the pope, Innocent, and his Catholic successors and the Roman Church and I will keep my kingdom faithfully in that obedience, defending the Catholic faith and persecuting the heretical depravity. . . ." Then the king . . . returned . . . to the basilica of St. Peter, placing the scepter and diadem on the altar and receiving from the hand of the lord pope, the sword of battle; he offered his kingdom to Peter, the prince of the apostles, and pledged a tribute for it. [MHDE, II, 583–584]

In this way, he became a vassal of the papacy and was entitled to papal protection.

The king's subjects usually swore an oath of allegiance to him, either in his presence on his accession or before his representatives. The men of Tortosa swore to Alfonso II of Aragon in 1162 "that we will always be faithful to you in all things, both concerning your body and its members and all your honor and concerning all your justices and laws, and that we will aid you always with good faith to have and to hold and to defend the honor you have and hold or which anyone has or holds for you, against all men and women who may wish to take it from you. Through God and these four holy Gospels" (MHDE, II, 566).

Calling himself king by the grace of God, the sovereign listed all the lands over which he ruled; for example, Fernando II called himself king of León and Galicia, while Alfonso VIII customarily used the title king of Castile and Toledo. Alfonso I was entitled king of the Aragonese and the Pamplonians, but after the separation of the two realms and the union of Aragon and Catalonia, his successors devised new titles. Thus, Ramon Berenguer IV, count of Barcelona, used the title prince of Aragon, but his son Alfonso II was king of Aragon, count of Barcelona, and marquess of Provence. Afonso Henriques, after initially describing himself as the prince of the Portuguese, assumed the royal title and became a papal vassal, but not until 1179 did the pope address him as king of the Portuguese.

After the disintegration of the caliphate of Córdoba, the so-called *reyes de taifas* (*muluk al-tawaif*) did not dare to assume the title of caliph. Each of them preferred to call himself *hajib*, suggesting thereby that he was only the caliph's chief minister. On the other hand, these petty princes did not hesitate to use the honorific titles associated with the caliphs as symbols of sovereignty. The usage of titles such as al-Mutamid, al-Muqtadir, al-Mustain, and so forth, prompted a poet to write these mocking verses, cited by al-Marrakushi:

> What disgusts me in al-Andalus
> Is to hear Muqtadir and Mutadid there
> Royal titles out of place
> Like the cat which, by puffing itself up,
> Imitates the strength of the lion.   [*Kitab al-Muyib*, 65]

Within the limited extent of his dominions each of the *reyes de taifas* enjoyed the fullness of power and strove to make it hereditary, though few families survived more than two or three generations. Far greater was the authority of the Almoravid and Almohad rulers whose empires straddled the straits of Gibraltar. Recognizing the Abbasid caliph of Baghdad as the true successor of Muhammad, the Almoravid rulers contented themselves with the use of the title *amir al-muslimin*, that is, prince of the Muslims. On the other hand, the Almohads were not slow to claim the caliphal title and the honorific titles associated with it. From the title *amir al-muminin*, commander of the faithful or prince of believers, the Christians derived the name *Miramamolin* which they used to refer to any one of the Almohad rulers. Among the Almoravids and Almohads, royal power passed by hereditary succession, though the principle of primogeniture was not operative. Upon the sovereign's death, one of his sons previously designated as heir, was proclaimed, as in these words cited by al-Marrakushi on the accession of Abu Yaqub: "Recognize the prince of believers . . . as the companions of God's Messenger promised submission and obedience in what is pleasing and in what is not, in what is easy and in what is difficult" (*Kitab al-Muyib*, 270). Those present pledged allegiance, and deputations were sent from the provinces with written professions of loyalty. The seat of government during the rule of the Almoravids and the Almohads was Marrakech in southwestern Morocco.

The Development of Feudalism

Feudalism reached maturity in Catalonia in the eleventh and twelfth centuries and exercised a stronger influence than ever before in the other Christian states. To some extent, the authority of the ruler was modified by feudal customs. In the feudal hierarchy of Catalonia, illustrated by the code of feudal laws promulgated by Ramon Berenguer I around 1058, the count of Barcelona, who also ruled the counties of Gerona and Ausona, ranked as *princeps*, the suzerain of the counts of Ampurias, Urgel, Besalú, Cerdagne, and Pallars; the king of France in theory was sovereign over all. Within each of the counties the viscounts or vicars held their offices as fiefs, transmissible by hereditary right; below them were *comitores*, who may have formed part of the count's retinue or may have assisted him in administration; the *vasvassores*, or *milites* in the lowest rank, were vassals of the viscounts and *comitores*. Each baron or knight held his fief as a lordship in which he exercised public functions of jurisdiction in minor civil and criminal cases (low justice) and seigneurial rights over the peasants who cultivated his estates.

As in France, the feudal contract was established by the ceremony of homage (*homenatge*), fealty (*sagrament*), and investiture (*potestad*, *postad*). There were, however, distinctive features to Catalan feudalism. It was customary for the vassal to give his lord a sum of money, in proportion to the value of the fief, as a guarantee that he would fulfill his obligations (*firma de directo*). At any time the lord could demand that the vassal surrender the fief to him; if the vassal refused, he could be denounced as a traitor. The vassal could alienate his fief with the consent of his lord, who was entitled to a third of the sale price (*laudamio*) and, if he wished, could recover the fief by offering the same price as a prospective buyer (*fatica*). Fiefs were transmissible by hereditary right to male heirs and, in their default, to females. A vassal could designate one of his sons as heir, but if the vassal died intestate, the lord could give the fief to any one of the surviving sons. Catalan feudalism also recognized the right of a vassal to hold from more than one lord and distinguished between homage given absolutely to one lord (*homenatge soliu*) and limited homage given to several (*homenatge no soliu*). If the vassal defied his lord or refused him homage or abandoned him in battle, his fief could be confiscated.

In the western kingdoms, feudal customs were widely diffused, but they did not attain maturity, nor did they transform the essential character of the state. The pilgrimages to Santiago, the advent of the Cluniac monks, and the establishment of the Burgundian dynasty in León, Castile, and Portugal, all served to increase feudal influences and to introduce the terminology of French feudalism. The increasing numbers of royal vassals and vassals of magnates, the frequent grants of immunities, the cession of certain public offices as benefices, the submission of Ramon Berenguer IV as a vassal to Alfonso VII, of Afonso Henriques and Pedro II as vassals of the Holy See, all testify to the importance of feudalism.

In the west the term vassal came into use, though it did not supplant the older *miles* or *caballero*, and it could also be used in a broader sense to mean all the king's subjects or natural vassals. The pact between lord and vassal was called *pleyto e homenage*, whereas in France and Catalonia the central act of the ceremony was the joining of hands (*immixtio manuum*), in León and Castile the vassal ordinarily kissed his lord's hand, saying, "Sir, I kiss your hand and I am your vassal." The bond could be terminated at any moment by either party; though there was a tendency to prolong it for life, it never became hereditary. If the vassal wished to break it, he was obliged to send one of his men to his lord to announce the end of the relationship, saying, "Sir, I kiss your hand for him and from now on he is no longer your vassal." Obliged to surrender horse and arms and whatever benefices he might have received from his lord, the vassal pledged never to injure him thereafter, even though no longer in his service. A royal vassal might go into exile to seek a new lord; if the king declared him *in ira regia*, as Alfonso VI did in the case of the Cid, the vassal was forced into exile, but he could take with him his men-at-arms (*mesnaderos*) or *vasallos de criazón*, whom he had educated and maintained in his household and who, because of their very personal relationship with him, could never abandon him. Those vassals to whom he paid money could leave him after assisting him in finding a new lord. Contrary to Catalan practice, no vassal was permitted to contract simultaneously with more than one lord.

As in the past, vassals were compensated for their military and other services by payments of money (*soldadas*) or by grants of land in benefice (*prestimonia, atondos,* or *honores*). The *prestimonium* of León, Castile, and Portugal was a grant limited to a definite term, sometimes for life, but never transmissible by hereditary right; moreover, it was sometimes given to one who was not a vassal of the donor. Thus it lacked the technical character of the fief. In Aragon and Navarre the king often granted public authority over certain districts to his vassals to hold as a benefice or *honor*, by the early twelfth century the *honor* was ordinarily held by hereditary right. Similarly, in León, Castile, and Portugal, especially in the twelfth century, the king ceded territorial administration or the tenancy of castles to his vassals to hold as a benefice. The tenancy was limited in time, though often held for life; the tenant never acquired an hereditary right, and the king was always free to demand surrender of the tenancy.

In spite of obvious feudal influences the western kingdoms never experienced the development of a true feudalism. Vassalage and benefice were not indissolubly linked, as they were in Catalonia and northern Europe. Vassals did not always receive benefices, and benefices were not always given to vassals; nor did the benefice ever become an hereditary possession. Above all, feudalism failed to undermine the public structure of the state. The monarchy remained strong precisely because it continued to fulfill the fundamental role of leadership in the war against the Muslims. From that conflict the king reaped substantial profits in the form of booty, tribute, and reconquered lands, enabling him to preserve his financial independence and to recompense his vassals with even greater frequency in coin, rather than in the cession of land or public offices. Although territorial administration was indeed given in benefice, the king, at least in León, Castile, and Portugal, could always recover it. Nor when granting immunities did the king divest himself of sovereign powers; only rarely did he yield the right of coining money or excuse an immunist from the obligations of military and court service. At all times he reserved the right of intervention in an immunity to deal with cases of especial gravity. Finally, to counter an ambitious nobility, the king could always depend upon the full support of the freemen of the great *concejos* or municipalities dominating the lands between the Duero and the Tagus.

The Royal Council

In exercising his functions as administrator, legislator, judge, and commander-in-chief, the sovereign relied upon the collaboration of his council. In Catalonia the council or *curia* was fundamentally a feudal assembly composed of the count's vassals fulfilling one of their principal obligations: suit to court. The council or *curia regis* (a term borrowed from French usage) in the western kingdoms evolved from the Astur-Leonese *palatium*, which had performed the tasks of the Visigothic *aula regia* and councils of Toledo. The *curia* continued to function in both ordinary and extraordinary sessions, and its constitutive elements were essentially the same as in the past, but in the course of the twelfth century it ceased to deal any longer with ecclesiastical as well as secular affairs. One of the results of the Gregorian Reform was the frequent convocation of church councils, sometimes under the presidency of a papal legate, to deal with questions of specific interest to the clergy. This had the effect of generally excluding ecclesiastical business from the discussions of the *curia regis*.

The king's ordinary or small council consisted of administrative officials who usually accompanied him on his travels, members of the royal family, and various prelates, and magnates who occasionally joined his entourage. The principal palatine officials, whose attendance at meetings of the ordinary council was obligatory, in Guglielmi's opinion, were the *mayordomo* and *alferez* (*armiger, signifer*), usually prominent nobles and vassals of the king, and the chancellor (*cancellarius*), ordinarily a cleric. The *mayordomo* directed the administration of the royal household, guarded the king's treasure, and supervised the collection of his revenues. The *alferez* was the royal standard-bearer and, under the supreme authority of the king, the commander of the royal host. The office of chancellor, the chief innovation of this period, another reflection of French influence, first appears in the reign of Alfonso VII who entrusted it to Diego Gelmírez; thereafter it was annexed in perpetuity to the archbishopric of Compostela. After the partition of the realm in 1157 the Castilian chancellorship was held by several ecclesiastics until it was finally conceded to the archbishop of Toledo. In the hands of prelates such as these the chancellorship was more of an honor than a responsibility. The task of preparing royal documents continued to be the primary responsibility of the notary, assisted by a number of scribes. From the time of Alfonso VI, it was customary to affix a seal to royal charters as a guarantee of their validity. Alfonso II in 1180 eliminated the last symbolic vestige of Aragonese dependence upon France, surviving from the Carolingian era, by ordering that royal documents should no longer record the regnal years of the French kings.

Lesser persons who probably participated in the sessions of the ordinary council included: porters (*portarii*), who issued citations in the king's name and executed his commands; chaplains; the members of the royal guard (*militia palatii, schola regis*); and legal experts who assumed especial importance as Roman law began to have a stronger influence in the Hispanic kingdoms. The ordinary council advised the king in matters of legislation, justice, finance, diplomacy, war, and so on. In numerous texts the king declared that he acted "with the counsel of the chief men of my *curia*," or "with the counsel and approbation of the nobles of my *curia*," whose names were listed in confirmation of his charters.

In general outline, the royal council of the Muslim rulers preserved the organization and ceremonial of the Umayyad era. Inasmuch as the *reyes de taifas* themselves used the title *hajib*, once the designation of the caliph's chief minister, the title *wazir* regained the meaning it had elsewhere in the Muslim world. The *wazir* became a powerful figure as the head of the central administration and the sole intermediary between the sovereign and lesser officials of the court. In the Almohad era, the office of *hajib* reappeared but apparently in subordination to the wazirate. Other officials included the secretaries entrusted with royal correspondence, military affairs, and finance. Ibn Khaldun noted that the financial minister (*sahib al-ashgal*), with responsibility for the collection and disbursement of royal revenue, had a goodly share of royal authority. Members of the royal family and the *shaykhs* of the Almoravid and Almohad tribes exercised considerable influence upon the ruler through their participation in deliberations on matters of great import.

In the Christian states, the king summoned an extraordinary session of his *curia* when he wished to resolve affairs of paramount importance. The great council (*curia plena, curia generalis, curia solemnis*) differed from the ordinary council mainly in composition. Among those present, besides members of the royal family and palatine officials, were archbishops, bishops, abbots, and magnates, specially summoned to meet at a certain time and place. For example, around 1055 Fernando I summoned "the bishops, abbots and chief men of the whole realm" to Coyanza, and a few years later Ramon Berenguer I, "with the assent and acclamation of the magnates of the land," published the first of the *Usages of Barcelona*. On several later occasions the kings of Aragon convoked their great council to promulgate the Peace and Truce of God. The assembly of archbishops, bishops, abbots, counts, princes, dukes, and judges convened by Alfonso VII in León in 1135, on the occasion of his imperial coronation, met in the cathedral on the first day to discuss "those things that . . . are convenient for the salvation of the souls of all men." Following the coronation, the assembly gathered on the third day in the royal palace to treat "those things that pertain to the welfare of the kingdom of the whole of Spain." The council concerned itself with the restoration of church property, the punishment of criminals, the repopulation and cultivation of lands destroyed by warfare, and the prosecution of the war against the Muslims. This assembly had a mixed character, in that it dealt with ecclesiastical as well as civil affairs, but later in the twelfth century the royal council generally limited itself to secular concerns.

Alfonso IX convoked one of the most significant public assemblies in the history of medieval Spain in July 1188. In order to affirm his leadership in troubled circumstances, he summoned his council to meet in the cloister of the church of San Isidoro in León. In attendance were the archbishop of Compostela, the bishops and magnates and "the elected citizens from each city" (cum electis civibus ex singulis civitatibus). Nothing is known of the manner of their election, nor can it be determined whether they were procurators endowed with full powers (plena potestas) to act in the name of their towns; but for the first time in European history we have unequivocal evidence of the presence of representatives of towns in a meeting of the royal council. Town representatives may have attended the councils held by Alfonso VIII of Castile in 1187 and 1188, but this cannot be affirmed with certainty. In virtue of the presence of townsmen in the Leonese curia of 1188, that assembly can be regarded as the first meeting of the medieval parliament or cortes. Nor was the attendance of townsmen at the time an isolated event. The king at Benavente in 1202 called together the bishops and royal vassals "and many men from each town of my kingdom" (et multis de qualibet villa regni mei) ; he summoned the bishops and magnates and "a multitude of citizens sent by each city" (civium multitudine destinatorum a singulis civitatibus) to his council at León in 1208. The presence of townsmen in these meetings is indicative of the importance that the towns had attained in the political, military, and economic life of the kingdom. Populated by freemen, they dominated vast areas south of the Duero extending to the Muslim frontier and were responsible for the administration and defense of those regions. The urban militia forces supplied to the royal host, and often sent on incursions into Muslim territory, were by no means negligible. Their loyalty to the crown was nearly always secure. In the twelfth and thirteenth centuries the towns began to gain in prosperity through the development of trade and industry, and the king found in their wealth a useful source of revenue to meet the ever-increasing costs of government.

Sánchez Albornoz has argued that the towns were summoned to send representatives to the royal council precisely in order to give their consent to taxation. This custom had its recorded beginnings at the *curia* of Benavente in 1202, when Alfonso IX sold his right to coin money for seven years to his subjects for one *maravedí* payable by each person. In effect, during seven years the king promised not to devalue the coinage, a measure that could increase his revenue while causing great harm to the economy through inflation and a rise in prices. The towns preferred to pay the king a subsidy for a specified term in order to avert possible economic ruin. At the end of that time, presumably, though the evidence is not certain, the king had to summon the *cortes* again to obtain the subsidy (*moneda forera*) which became, then, a regular form of taxation. It is also likely that representatives of the towns were summoned to the royal council to pledge their allegiance to the heir to the throne; this may also have occurred at the council of 1202. For whatever reason, the addition of townsmen transformed the character of the royal council and held out to the towns the opportunity to exert a direct influence upon royal policy.

Territorial Administration

In the eleventh and twelfth centuries increasing concessions of immunities, and the development of municipalities, tended to dissolve the counties as major territorial divisions in the western kingdoms. The responsibility for the defense of a district, town, or fortress was usually given as a benefice (*honor*) or tenancy to a royal vassal (called *tenens* in León, Castile, and Portugal, *senior* in Aragon and Navarre, or *alcaide*, from *al-qaid*, if he held a castle); in Aragon and Navarre, but not elsewhere, he held the benefice by hereditary right. In Old Castile many civil responsibilities, especially in the administration of justice, were assumed by *maiorini* (*merinos*) whose original duty was to collect royal revenues; a *merino mayor*, noted first in 1180, apparently appointed subordinate *merinos* for smaller Castilian districts. In the

Catalan counties, vicars (*vicarii*) had military and civil functions below the count, while in more limited areas bailiffs (*bajuli*) continued to serve as fiscal agents.

Grants of immunities to prelates, monasteries, military Orders, and nobles became more numerous than before. Pledging homage to the king, the immunist received a charter conferring upon him a specified district "with every royal right, to hold in perpetuity by hereditary right." The immunist had authority to grant charters to the villages or towns within his lordship, or to enact more general decrees, as did Diego Gelmírez, archbishop of Compostela, in 1113, and to appoint judges, administer justice, levy fines, exercise police powers, demand military service, and collect various tributes and services ordinarily due to the crown. While the immunist had considerable independence, he was limited by his feudal obligation to serve the king in war and peace and to attend the royal court when summoned; Diego Gelmírez's exemption from these duties was an exception. The king, moreover, reserved the right to intervene when the immunist was negligent in the exercise of his jurisdiction, and in four specific instances, namely, treason, rape, robbery, and the destruction of highways, and sometimes homicide; infrequently he reserved the right to hear appeals from the immunist's tribunal. He also required the payment of *fonsadera* and *yantar*, sums paid in lieu of military service and hospitality. The king only exceptionally granted the right to coin money to an immunist; the only known instances are Alfonso VI's concession to Diego Gelmírez and Urraca's donations to the abbey of Sahagún and to the cathedral of San Antolín in Palencia.

In al-Andalus the provincial administration developed during the Umayyad era apparently continued after the downfall of the caliphate. Under the Almoravids and Almohads, al-Andalus was a sort of viceroyalty administered by various members of the royal family. Granada seems to have been the chief seat of government under the Almoravids, but the Almohads preferred Seville, which attained the apogee of its prosperity and affluence in the twelfth century. The sovereign appointed and removed governors at will, oftentimes after only a year or two in office; among the principal provinces were Seville, Córdoba, Jaén, Granada, Málaga, Murcia, Baza, Almería, Beja, Silves, Badajoz, Valencia, and Majorca. In his treatise on laws and customs, Ibn Abdun, writing during the Almoravid domination of Seville, noted that a governor ought to take counsel with the *qadi*, the jurists, and men of religion; "he should repress tyranny and brutality" and should remember that "whoever, whether prince or jurist, does not respect the law will perish by the law."

The Municipalities

The development of municipalities was the most basic transformation of the territorial administration in the Christian states. As the Roman municipal organization had long since disappeared, the forms of town government that eventually emerged were creatures of the reconquest rather than survivals or revivals from the Roman era. In the early centuries of the reconquest, the essentially agricultural and pastoral settlements of the Duero valley were centered around a fortress or burg (as in Burgos, Burgo de Osma), which served as a refuge in time of attack and also encouraged the development of a sense of identity and common interest among the neighbors of the district.

In the eleventh and twelfth centuries some of these communities, especially between the Duero and the Tagus, increasing in population and in political, economic, and military importance, began to lose their rural character, though never entirely, and to become urban centers or towns. With the reconquest, towns like Toledo, Zaragoza, Lisbon, and Tortosa, already enjoying a flourishing mercantile and industrial activity, passed from Muslim to Christian hands. By the twelfth century many towns had obtained royal recognition as organs of territorial administration, embracing an urban nucleus and a dependent, but quite extensive, countryside (*terminus, alfoz*), including many villages. Directly dependent upon the king, these municipalities or *concejos*, as they were called, enjoyed administrative autonomy, with their own laws, institutions, and officials. The *concejo* possessed a juridical personality, which found external expression, as Valdeavellano has remarked, in the walls enclosing it. Towns sought at all costs to preserve their dependence upon the king and to avoid falling under the domination of a lord; thus in 1118 Alfonso VII promised the citizens of Toledo that he would never give the city "in benefice, nor would there ever be there any lord but himself." Ecclesiastical and secular lords (for example, the bishops of Lugo, Túy, Oviedo, Porto, Palencia, and so on) were particularly loath to yield autonomy to the urban communities beginning to develop within their lordships. Some communities such as Compostela and Sahagún revolted against their lords, but towns under ecclesiastical domination seldom obtained more than elementary liberties, while the essential powers of government remained in the lord's hands.

The basic rights, privileges, and obligations of the *concejos* were often embodied in charters (*fueros*) granted, sometimes voluntarily, sometimes under pressure, by the king or lord. Often the text was drafted by the townsmen themselves on the basis of their past customs and privileges; sometimes they adopted and copied the charter of another town. The *fuero* guaranteed the inhabitants in the possession of their properties and the right to "live under one equal law," and regulated the election of officials, the payment of tributes and services or exemption therefrom, military obligations, the administration of justice, the collection of fines, and so on. *Fueros* varied in length and in the degree of self-government conceded.

In most towns the king was represented by a noble (*senior civitatis, dominus ville, alcaide*) who was primarily responsible for the defense of the citadel (*alcazar*), the maintenance of public order, and the general safeguarding of the rights of the crown. In Aragon and Navarre the *senior* usually had considerable control over the municipal administration, including the right to appoint certain magistrates. In towns and villages located within immunities, the lord generally controlled the administration and the appointment of officials.

The principal organ of municipal government was the *concejo* (*concilium*) or assembly of neighbors (*vicini, boni homines, cives*), that is, the adult male property owners, living in the municipal district, who were admitted to citizenship. In these early centuries the *concejo* was a democratic body in which each person had a right to speak and to cast his vote, though nobles, clergy, and foreigners ordinarily were not permitted to take part in its deliberations. The *concejo* assembled at the sound of a bell or a horn on Sunday following Mass; questions of justice, taxes, military service, the policing of the market, the establishment of weights and measures, the election of magistrates and other administrative officers were discussed and treated. As the town grew in wealth and population, the townsmen came to dominate the *concejo* and the municipal government, reducing the rural inhabitants of the district to a secondary participation.

In León, Castile, and Portugal the political and judicial head of the town, called a *iudex* or *juez*, was elected by the *concejo*, ordinarily for a one-year term. In the administration of justice he was assisted by several *alcaldes* (*al-qadi*), two, four, six, or so, chosen annually from the parishes (colaciones) into which the municipality was divided. In Aragon and Navarre the king or lord appointed the local magistrate (justicia, alcalde, zalmadina, from sahib al-madina), from among the boni homines of the city. Among the other officials were iurati or fideles chosen by the concejo to control its finances; merinos who collected fines and other taxes; the almotacén (al-muhtasib) or zabazoque (sahib al-suq), the inspector of the public market, especially of weights and measures and prices; notaries, scribes, and messengers (andadores); police officials (sayones, alguaciles, porteros) who excuted judicial sentences, arrested criminals, seized pledges, and so on; toll collectors; the alferez who carried the concejo's standard when the militia was summoned to war; and a host of others who guarded pastures, vineyards, woods, and the like.

In Catalonia the towns attained administrative autonomy only in the thirteenth century. Many towns lay within the fiefs of great lords, but the more important ones belonged to the royal domain, and their development was closely controlled by the crown. The king's representatives, namely, the vicar and bailiff, directed municipal administration, with the assistance of a small council of good men (probi homines). Under the influence of the Italian and Provençal communes this primitive organization gave way in the thirteenth century to a more sophisticated regime, in which executive authority in the municipality (universitas) was entrusted to consuls or keepers of the peace (paciarii, pahers), in numbers of two, four, or six, aided by a council of twenty or thirty; the vicar continued to preside over the communal organization, but took a somewhat less active role in the direction of its affairs.

Self-government was entirely lacking in the towns of al-Andalus, where officials were appointed by the sovereign. The prefect of the city (sahib al-madina) was responsible for the maintenance of public order and, according to Ibn Abdun, "ought to be a person of maturity, good morals, with a knowledge of the law," and strength of character to shun corruption, extortion, and drink. The qadi continued to serve as the principal judicial officer, and the al-muhtasib had the task of inspecting the market and guarding against fraud and deceit in commercial transactions.

The Law and the Administration of Justice

A great diversity of law prevailed in the Christian kingdoms. The Visigothic Liber Judiciorum had only restricted acceptance, chiefly in

León and among the Mozarabs, because of the resurgence of customary law and the development of municipal privileges. Custom was the predominant source of law for several centuries, though much of it was never written down. In Castile, judges claimed the right to give judgments in conformity with the principles of equity, if custom was unclear or unjust. Recognized as sources of law, collections of these judicial decisions (*fazañas*) were compiled in the twelfth century, preserving the essential details of the suit and the judgment given, and thereby serving as precedents for the settlement of similar cases.

During these centuries the customs of many rural and urban settlements concerning the liberty of persons and property, tributes, fines, military service, judicial citations, pledges, proofs, and penalties were written down in charters (*fueros*). The oldest of these tend to brevity, while some of those issued in the later twelfth century are veritable codes of municipal law. As some *fueros* were superior to others in content and completeness, the better ones were widely diffused and copied, thereby tending to bring about a certain uniformity of law, at least within regions. Among the charters whose influence extended well beyond their immediate environs were the *Fuero* of Jaca (1063), the *Fuero* of Sepúlveda (1076), and the *Fuero* of Sahagún (1085). The most comprehensive Castilian *Fuero* was that given to Cuenca in 1177 by Alfonso VIII and subsequently adopted in many other places in New Castile and Lower Aragon. Gibert described it as the product of a "juridical syncretism," as it was based on Castilian, Visigothic, and Roman law.

While written local law multiplied throughout the peninsula, the enactment of territorial laws also became more common as rulers, under the influence of Roman law, assumed the power of legislating and also recognized the importance of having a uniform law applicable to all the inhabitants of their kingdoms. Among the most famous of these compilations was the *Usages of Barcelona*. Recognizing the deficiency of the *Liber Judiciorum* and the Carolingian capitularies in feudal matters, Count Ramon Berenguer I promulgated various laws that formed the primitive nucleus of the collection later known as the *Usages*. Included were the *Usualia de curialibus usibus* issued around 1058, in which the count recorded the basic feudal customs of Catalonia. About two years later he enacted what Valls Taberner called the "constitutional charter of the county of Barcelona . . . the oldest monument and the fundamental basis of the old Catalan public law." As reconstructed by Valls, this compilation established and regulated executive, legislative, and judicial functions. Additional texts relating to the Peace and Truce of God were also included, and the whole work was given a new cast, according to Abadal, by the jurists in the service of Ramon Berenguer IV; they attempted to impose a concept of monarchical sovereignty upon the characteristic feudal customs included in the compilation. The *Usages* became the fundamental law of Catalonia thereafter.

Alfonso IX of León enacted territorial laws in his *curia* of 1188. Swearing to uphold the good customs of his predecessors, he guaranteed his subjects security in their persons and property and promised to make justice available to everyone. Of special significance was his pledge of a full and fair hearing in his court to anyone accused by another; not until the accused had been cited in writing to appear in court to be judged according to law would any action be taken against him. False accusations would be punished severely. These laws have been compared to the *Magna Charta*, aptly enough in that Alfonso IX, like King John, declared that he would abide by the laws of the realm and guarantee due process of law to his subjects; but, unlike John, Alfonso IX was not a tyrannical king confronted by a rebellious baronage, nor did his decrees acquire the unique prestige and influence of *Magna Charta* in later centuries. Alfonso IX's constitutions concerning the administration of justice, the repression of public disorders (1194), and the regulation of ecclesiastical property (1202, 1208) also had territorial application.

As other examples of territorial laws, one might mention the constitutions promulgated by Alfonso II of Aragon in a *solemnis curia* held at Huesca in 1188, and those of Pedro II, also issued at Huesca, in 1208. A law of Alfonso VIII of Castile (1191), giving security to all the clergy and to religious houses in all the kingdoms of Spain and guaranteeing the right of sanctuary, may also be cited. The earliest extant territorial laws of Portugal are those enacted by Afonso II in the *curia* of Coimbra in 1211, safeguarding the rights of the church and providing for the protection of the weak against the strong.

Belief in the public responsibility for upholding the law and administering justice grew ever stronger in this period. Although the notion that justice was a private affair did not entirely disappear, the revival of Roman law emphasized that the administration of justice was one of the essential reasons for the existence of the state, a function which the sovereign could not surrender to others. Thus the *Usages of Barcelona* (94–95) asserted that "it is given only to the sovereign to do justice to evildoers, namely, murderers, adulterers, poisoners, thieves, rapists, traitors . . . and since the land cannot live without justice, so it is given to the sovereign to do justice; and as it is given to him to do justice, so it is licit for him to release or to pardon whomever he wills." The development of this idea was influenced by the Peace and Truce of God, proclaimed by the church in order to secure protection and safety for widows, orphans, pilgrims, merchants, clergy, and other poor and defenseless persons, and to prohibit warfare during the festal seasons of the Christian year. The Peace and Truce of God originated in France and then spread to Catalonia, where Alfonso II proclaimed it in 1173, adding to the usual spiritual penalty of excommunication, secular punishments for violators. Pedro II promulgated constitutions relative to the Peace and Truce of God in 1198 and 1202. Throughout the peninsula the king extended his peace or protection (*cautum*) to public assemblies, courts, markets, churches, monasteries, highways, and private houses, and violators were subject to the payment of fines (also called *cautum*). Efforts were made to limit the right of private vengeance and to bring all serious crimes to the judgment of the royal courts.

The judicial organization was still linked intimately with public administration. Thus the royal court, in addition to functioning as an administrative organ or as a consultative assembly, also sat as a tribunal of justice. Judicial business was one of its most important activities. Lords responsible for territorial administration and lords of immunities exercised jurisdiction in varying degrees, but most litigation was probably handled in the municipal courts. The obligation to render impartial justice according to the law of the land was enunciated by the Aragonese barons in 1134: "He (the king) shall keep them in good justice and his *alcalde* shall judge them in good justice, by the *fuero* of the land" (*MHDE*, II, 469). Alfonso VII "ordered his judges to act justly, strictly uprooting the evils of those men found to act contrary to justice and the decrees of kings . . . not sparing the rich and powerful instead of the poor, but determining all things according to the nature of the fault" (*Chronica Adefonsi Imperatoris*, 71).

All courts had civil and criminal jurisdiction, and their judgments were usually final, though, under the influence of Roman law, appeals were allowed with greater frequency. For example, in the lordships of the military Orders, appeals might be carried from the judgment of a *comendador* to the master of the Order or perhaps to the king. Appeals could also be directed to the tribunal of the book in León, that is, an appeal to the *Liber Judiciorum.*

The concept of justice as a public function was reflected in the fact that with increasing frequency litigation was initiated by royal agents, especially in criminal cases or in cases involving a violation of the king's peace. With the gradual introduction of Roman law in the twelfth and thirteenth centuries the distinctive Germanic character of judicial procedure was modified. The defendant could still be compelled to appear in court by means of pledges (*pignus, prenda*) taken by the plaintiff; the *fueros,* however, usually declared that no one was to take a pledge from another's goods without being accompanied by a public official; Alfonso IX of León in 1188 prohibited anyone to take as pledges animals used for plowing or agricultural implements. The defendant might also name another person to act as surety (*fideiussor, fiador*) for him. Anyone who refused to attend the summons to court was subject to the loss of his goods and imprisonment and even the supreme penalty. The inhabitants of privileged *concejos* were required to demand justice and to give justice only in the courts of the *concejos;* but if a man wished to press a case against someone from another *concejo,* the suit would be heard at a designated place midway (*medianedo*) between the two towns.

During the eleventh century and the early twelfth century the process was conducted much as it had been in the past. The parties presented their respective charges and countercharges until the issue at law was clear, and then a form of proof, such as compurgation or the ordeal, was determined by judges of proof chosen from those present. In the twelfth century there were often permanent *iudices* or *iustitiae* in the royal court who performed this function; in the *concejos,* the *alcaldes* usually did so. In the *Poem of the Cid,* the functioning of the royal court in the Cid's suit against the *infantes* of Carrión is clearly portrayed. The Cid presented oral charges, and judges specially appointed for the purpose rendered judgment; the use of the judicial duel as a form of proof is also depicted. As late as 1184 and 1207 Alfonso VIII of Castile confirmed the results of judicial duels fought to settle property disputes, but the *fueros* frequently excluded these barbaric forms of proof from the municipal courts. Under Roman influence, witnesses and documents assumed a much greater role in the proof than before. In the late twelfth century the most common means of resolving issues, especially those involving property, was the inquisition (*inquisa*, *pesquisa*), an inquiry conducted by royal inquisitors (*exquisitores*, *pesquisitores*) or by those agreed upon by the parties. Their task was to summon a jury of knowledgeable persons (*boni homines*) from the locality and to obtain information from them under oath. The inquisitors then presented a written report to the presiding judge who opened it and confirmed the findings. To some extent the inquisition was also used to identify criminals, for example, thieves.

Penalties for crimes were still rather barbarous. According to the *Usages* (94–95), the sovereign possessed the right of cutting off hands and feet, putting out eyes, imprisonment, hanging, and in the case of women, of cutting off their noses, lips, ears, and breasts. Alfonso VII instructed his judges to punish criminals by cutting off their hands and feet and by hanging, while Alfonso IX ordered that thieves should be hanged, drowned, or boiled alive. Crimes such as homicide, rape, and the like could still be compensated for by the payment of a sum of money. The *calumnia* (*caloña, coima*) payable to the king for such violations of the peace constituted an important source of royal income.

In al-Andalus, the Koran remained the fundamental law of Islam, while Christians and Jews continued to live according to their own laws. The notorious laxity of the *reyes de taifas* in the observance of the law encouraged the Almoravids to overthrow them and to impose a rigid orthodoxy. As interpreters of the law the Malikite jurists enjoyed a prominance they had seldom known in the past. In their turn, however, the Almohads cast aspersions on the orthodoxy of the Almoravids and presented themselves as the only faithful adherents of the law; but the regime they established was no less strict than that of the Almoravids. In every town the *qadi*, a judge appointed by the sovereign, pronounced judgments according to the revealed law of God. Writing early in the twelfth century, Ibn Abdun of Seville, emphasized that the *qadi* should be a man of prudence, compassion, impartiality, and learning, who would always remember that he was God's servant and would have to render an account to God for his actions. His principal task was to settle litigation on the basis of divine law, but he also had special care of orphans and the administration of the funds of pious foundations. In giving judgment he was always expected to reflect and to consult with men learned in the law. Ibn Abdun also discusses judges of lesser importance (*hakim*), as well as the *sahib al-madina*, who was especially concerned with criminal cases, and the *al-muhtasib* or inspector of markets. All were expected to be men of incontestable honesty, and natives of the country "because they know better than others the affairs of the people."

The Financial Administration

Royal revenues increased in the eleventh and twelfth centuries, but so did expenditures. A host of officers (merinos, bajuli) collected royal revenues on the local level. In the western kingdoms the general administration of these sums seems to have been entrusted to a chief almojarife, often a Jew. The nobles and clergy continued to be exempt from taxation, and many other exemptions were granted to favor the dependents of churches, monasteries, and military Orders.

The traditional sources of royal revenue included rents from the estates of the royal domain (pectum, pecho), payable for the use of the land and in recognition of the king's dominion over it. Tenants paid fees for the use of woods, pasturage, ovens, mills, and wine presses; they also owed personal service on royal lands and were subject to various inheritance taxes. Revenues of a public character included tolls levied on goods and persons in transit (portazgo, portagem, peaje, peagem), judicial fines payable by those convicted of crime, and fines levied on those who violated royal commands or broke the king's peace. In addition the king collected fonsadera, a sum payable in lieu of personal military service, and he was entitled to receive lodging and hospitality on his travels; this was also converted into a money payment (cena, yantar, colheita), payable even if he did not visit the locality. Freemen could be required to perform public works such as the repair of roads, bridges, castles, fortifications (facendera), or to provide transportation for the king and his representatives (conducho).

The financial necessities of the Christian kings greatly increased during the eleventh and twelfth centuries, partly because of the expansion of the royal bureaucracy, but especially because of the nearly continual warfare with the Almoravids and the Almohads. In the early eleventh century Fernando I and his contemporaries levied tribute (parias) on the reyes de taifas, but that extraordinary source of income was terminated abruptly when the Almoravids overthrew the taifas. In order to defend his kingdom against the Almoravids, Alfonso VI, in return for concessions, raised an exceptional tribute from his subjects: "I do this, with the consent of your will, so that you, infanzones and peasants in each populated settlement, shall pay me two *solidi* this year, this one time, and they will not be demanded of you again" (*ES*, 35, 411). This was the origin of the tax known as *petitum* or *pedido*, which, as its name indicates, was requested by the king, though we do not know how consent was given thereafter. The extraordinary needs of the crown caused Alfonso IX and Pedro II to resort to the manipulation of the coinage, but in view of the ensuing popular outcry, the former promised in 1202 not to debase the coinage for a term of seven years in return for a tribute (*moneta*); Pedro II seems to have obtained a similar tribute (*monedatge*) three years later. Just before the crusade of Las Navas "all the clergy of the kingdom of Castile, on the petition of the kingdom, granted half of all their revenues in that year to the lord king." As the expenses of the reconquest mounted, the need to obtain consent to frequent levies of this sort encouraged the summoning of bishops, nobles, and townsmen to the *cortes*, whose origins are closely linked to the fiscal necessities of the crown.

Under the *reyes de taifas*, taxation tended to be capricious and excessive, especially in view of the tributes demanded of them by the Christian rulers. The levying of illegal taxes was one of the chief complaints which the jurists leveled against the *taifas* to justify their overthrow by the Almoravids. The Almoravids pledged only to levy those taxes sanctioned by law, but eventually they too succumbed to the temptation to raise money by illegal means and were condemned for it by the Almohads. Under the Almohads the financial administration was more efficiently organized. A *wazir* administered the *diwan* or treasury of both realms, that is, of Morocco and al-Andalus. As in the past the revenues of the sovereign were distinct from those of the state. Governors of provinces were required to come to the capital with their registers recording income and expenditures. These were inspected by *almojarifes* appointed for the purpose. Taxes included the *kharaj* or land tax and *zakat*, a tax on movable goods, as well as sales taxes and customs duties.

The Military Organization

The principle of universal military service, long observed in Spain, was stated in the *Usages of Barcelona* (68) in this way:

If for any reason the prince should be besieged or if he himself should besiege his enemies, or should hear that any king or prince is coming to war against him, and if he should warn his people . . . all men, both knights and foot soldiers, who are of age and capable of fighting, immediately as they hear or see [the warning], shall aid him as quickly as they can.

While, in theory, all able-bodied men were subject to military service, numerous exemptions were often granted. The *fueros* sometimes required that only a limited number of inhabitants of a *concejo* perform military service, or else the obligation was restricted to once a year. Even so, the militia forces of the towns and especially their cavalry (*caballeros villanos*) constituted a major element in the royal army and made significant contributions to the reconquest.

The military services of the nobility were increasingly feudalized, that is, the noble did not have to serve unless he received wages (*soldadas*) or benefices (*prestimonia*). The lower nobility (*infanzones, caballeros*) owed service to their lords under the same conditions. The tributes collected from the *taifas*, and extraordinary revenues such as the *petitum*, enabled the king to pay his vassals rather than to cede land to them. This limited the development of feudalism in the western states. In Catalonia, of course, where feudalism was fully developed, military service was a fundamental obligation of each vassal and was rendered in return for his fief. The military obligations of the Aragonese nobility as set forth in 1134 stipulated that "when the king has need of them for a pitched battle or for the siege of a castle, they should aid him with bread [i.e., at their own expenses] for three days and no longer. . . . And the lords who hold royal honors should serve the king for them, wherever he may be in his body, three months in the entire year, from the time of setting out, through their time in the host and their return" (*MHDE*, II, 469–470). In effect, there were definite limitations upon the duty of rendering military service.

The principal innovation in military organization was the establishment in Spain of the military Orders of the Temple and the Hospital, which had originated in the Holy Land after the First Crusade. Their example subsequently encouraged the foundation and development of the native Orders of Calatrava, Alcántara, Santiago, and Avis, which thereafter had a primary role in the reconquest. The Orders assumed responsibility for the defense of the most important frontier castles, and they provided a basic nucleus for the armies engaged in major encounters with the enemy. Despite a natural tendency to rivalry, they recognized the necessity of collaboration and common action in dealing with the Muslims. This, coupled with a military and monastic discipline, was the chief reason for their success. Each of the Orders was headed by a master, a title emphasizing his military role; the castles were entrusted to *comendadores*, usually with a sufficient complement of knights under their command. The development of the military religious Orders was one manifestation of the influence of the crusades in Spain. The character of the reconquest as a holy war was given firmer emphasis, and the promise of remission of sins was held out to the participants, who were also assured that, if they died fighting the infidels, they would gain immediate entrance into heaven.

The Christian rulers had only a limited need for naval forces in this period, but it should be noted that Diego Gelmírez, the enterprising archbishop of Compostela, built a number of ships to defend the coasts of Galicia against pirates from northern Europe and from Muslim lands. The Portuguese kings employed the fleets of northern crusaders enroute to the Holy Land in their campaigns against Lisbon and Silves; similarly Pisan and Genoese fleets participated in the conquest of Majorca and the capture of Almería and Tortosa. It was not until the thirteenth century that the Christian rulers employed their own naval forces in the reconquest.

In al-Andalus the *reyes de taifas* who, on the whole, displayed a notable lack of enthusiasm for the holy war, depended heavily upon mercenary forces, many of whom were recruited among the Berbers of North Africa. The military posture of Muslim Spain improved remarkably after the Almoravid invasion, for the Almoravids or men of the *ribat*, highly disciplined practitioners of asceticism and the military art, were wholly dedicated to the expansion of Islam by the sword. The fear struck in the hearts of Christians on hearing Almoravid war drums is mentioned in the *Cantar de mio Cid* (2345–2347) :

> En la ueste de los moros los atamores sonando.
> A maravilla lo avien muchos dessos cristianos,
> Ca nunca lo vieran, ca nuevos son llegados.

> In the host of the Moors the drums are sounding.
> Many of the Christians wondered at it
> For they were newly come and had not heard it.

In warlike zeal the Almohads probably surpassed the Almoravids. The armies of both sects were organized on a tribal basis, but it is interesting that both employed Christian mercenaries, especially in North Africa. The Almohads developed one of the most powerful fleets in the western Mediterranean; its fame was such that Saladin asked for its help in taking the Syrian ports held by the crusaders.

CHAPTER 12

Society and the Economy, 1031–1212

The Social Structure

In the two centuries following the collapse of the caliphate of Córdoba the population of the Iberian peninsula increased, as did the
numbers of the distinct racial groups. There were several reasons for
this. A natural rise in the birth rate appears to have occurred, as is suggested by the more intensive settlement of lands between the Duero
and the Tagus rivers, the organization of towns there, and the continuing attempt to push the frontier beyond the Tagus to the borders
of Andalusia. The general expansion of the European economy north of
the Pyrenees was accompanied by a remarkable population growth
that impelled people to move from their ancestral homes in search of
better places to live. Many of them came to settle permanently in Spain.
The population also rose in al-Andalus as the successive invasions of
the Almoravids and Almohads injected new elements; the great cities of
Seville, Córdoba, Granada, Málaga, Valencia, and Murcia grew in
physical size to accommodate a much larger population. At the same
time, the fall of Toledo, Lisbon, Tortosa, Lérida, and other towns,
while augmenting the population of the Christian states, produced an
equivalent loss in Muslim Spain.

The ethnic composition of Christian Spain included Galicians, Leonese, Castilians, Portuguese, Aragonese, Catalans, Basques, and others
descended from the ancient Iberian, Roman, and Visigothic stock. By
this time differences in language and customs were defined sufficiently
to set off these groups one from another. In addition there was an ever-
increasing number of Franks, the generic name for all those northern
Europeans who settled in the peninsula. They came from Germany,
England, Italy, and from Gascony, Toulouse, Provence, and other re-

gions of France. Some followed the pilgrim road to Santiago de Compostela; others came as exponents of Cluniac or Cistercian monasticism, others as crusaders anxious to participate in the war against the
Muslims, and still others as merchants in search of trade. The clerics
among them soon filled abbacies and bishoprics; nobles such as Henry
and Raymond of Burgundy married into the royal family and founded
dynasties in Portugal and León-Castile. Most achieved less spectacular
fortunes and were content to settle in the burgeoning towns along the
pilgrim route and in some of the newer settlements to the south. The
charters or *fueros* given to many localities reveal the presence of substantial numbers of Franks, who usually were authorized to have their
own laws; in 1118, for example, Alfonso VII granted a charter to all
the citizens of Toledo, namely, to the Castilians, Mozarabs, and Franks.

The progress of the reconquest resulted in the incorporation of much
larger numbers of Mozarabs, Jews, and Muslims into Christian territory than ever before. When Toledo, Zaragoza, Lisbon, Tortosa,
Lérida, and the surrounding rural areas were conquered by the Christians, the natives were allowed to remain, and most, whether Christian
or not, probably did so. The *fueros* acknowledged their existence and
their right to continue being governed according to their own laws. The
Mozarabs, as Christians familiar with Latin, Arabic, and Romance,
played an especially important role in bridging the cultural gap between
the Christians of the north and the Muslims of the south.

Information concerning the Jews in Christian Spain during this
period is quite ample. Important Jewish colonies were located in the
major cities, but also in many small towns. Popular attitudes toward
the Jews are reflected in the *Poem of the Cid* which describes with
equanimity and no adverse comment the Cid's deception of the Jewish
moneylenders of Burgos. Later, the Cid, praying to Christ, records the
common charge that the Jews were responsible for His death:

> A los judios te dexeste prender; do dizen monte Calvarie
> Pusiéronte en cruz por nombre de Golgotá.

> You allowed the Jews to seize you. On Mount Calvary
> Known as Golgotha, they put You on the cross.
>
> [*Cantar de mio Cid*, 347–348]

In the *fueros* of the eleventh and twelfth centuries the rights granted to
Jews varied a good deal. In some instances, as in the *Fuero* of Zorita,
Jewish settlers were guaranteed the same rights and the same wergild

as Christians. In litigation between Christians and Jews, four judges, two from each faith, would hear the case. On the other hand many *fueros* indicate the inferior status of Jews. The *Fuero* of Cuenca stipulated that the wergild of a murdered Jew should be paid to the king "for the Jews belong to the king and are assigned to his treasury." Since Jews were always considered as an important source of revenue, for this reason, though not only for this reason, they were under the guardianship by the crown. The influx of northern Europeans into Christian Spain tended to exacerbate Christian-Jewish relations, as a few examples will demonstrate. The Council of Coyanza as early as 1055 forbade Christians to live with or eat with Jews; the Council of Gerona in 1068 ordered Jews to pay tithes on lands acquired from Christians, and in 1081 Pope Gregory VII warned King Alfonso VI not to allow Jews to exercise public authority over Christians. "For to subordinate Christians to Jews," he said, "and subject them to their power, what is this, if it is not to oppress the Church of God and to exalt the synagogue of Satan?" (*DP*, 38). The hostility to Jews reflected in this statement also found expression in the decrees of the Third and Fourth Lateran Councils of 1179 and 1215 forbidding intermarriage between Christians and Jews and requiring Jews to wear a distinctive dress. In spite of these strictures the Christian rulers in the peninsula employed Jews as physicians, counselors, envoys, tax collectors, and entrusted them with a major responsibility for organizing supplies for the armies sent against Muslim Spain.

The Muslims who elected to remain in Christian territory were known as *mudéjares*, a word of disputed origin, derived from *al-mutaakhkhirun*, meaning those who had submitted to Christian rule. In the early centuries of the reconquest the Muslims withdrew before the Christian advance, but in this period, as Coimbra, Viseu, Toledo, Lisbon, Zaragoza, Calatayud, and other cities were captured, many Muslims elected to remain, preserving their property, their law, and their religion, subject to the payment of a poll tax. For example, the *sahib al-madina, qadi,* and good men (*probi homines*) of Tortosa, on behalf of their community (*aljama*) promised to pay Alfonso II an annual tribute of 400 gold *mazmudis*. The guarantees given in the capitulation for a city were not always observed; Archbishop Bernard of Toledo, for example, seized the mosque of that city for use as a cathedral. In the cities the Muslims usually were obliged to live in separate quarters. Their treatment in the *fueros* varies considerably; at times the murder of a Muslim was punished the same as the murder of a Christian, but in other cases harsh dispositions reveal a belief in their inferiority to Christians. Like the Jews, they were forbidden to marry Christians and were supposed to wear distinctive garb, and to pay tithes on lands acquired from Christians. Unlike the Jews, they seldom found employment in the service of the ruler, probably because they were not always trusted, and because so many of them belonged to the lower classes in society and lacked the qualifications for service.

In al-Andalus the fusion of various ethnic elements—the Arabs, Berbers, Syrians, and descendants of the preconquest population—had made significant progress by the beginning of the eleventh century. Lévi-Provençal has pointed out that a distinctive Hispano-Muslim type recognizable throughout the Muslim world had developed. The people of al-Andalus no longer thought of themselves as orientals but were fully aware of their Hispanic roots and identity. The highly civilized character of the *Andalusiyyun*, as they called themselves, contrasted sharply with the barbarity of the Almoravids and Almohads who entered the peninsula in the eleventh and twelfth centuries. These newcomers were Berber mountaineers and herdsmen who were suddenly impelled by their new-found faith to embark on the road to conquest. Those who settled permanently in al-Andalus were chiefly garrison forces, members of the military caste, aggressive and intolerant, on difficult terms with the indigenous Muslim population who regarded them as intruders.

Christians and Jews generally benefited from the easygoing attitude of the *reyes de taifas*, an inheritance from the caliphate. The Almoravids and Almohads, on the contrary, were no more tolerant of religious minorities than they were of Muslims who dissented from their interpretation of Islamic teaching. This attitude had deleterious effects upon the Mozarabic and Jewish communities. Churches and synagogues were attacked, and Christians and Jews were subjected to insults, reflecting the utter contempt in which they were held by their Muslim overlords. For these reasons there was a steady emigration of Mozarabs to Christian territory. Alfonso I of Aragon in 1126 granted a charter of liberties "to all you Mozarabic Christians whom I brought, with the help of God, out of the power of the Saracens and led into the lands of the Christians. . . . Because you left your homes and your estates for the name of Christ and out of love for me and came with me to populate my lands, I grant you good customs throughout my realm" (Simonet,

Historia de los Mozarabes, 824). Condemned for having broken their pact with Islam, those who remained behind were deported to Morocco, thereby greatly reducing, if not extinguishing altogether, the Mozarabic population in al-Andalus. In the second quarter of the twelfth century, when the Almohads were destroying the Almoravid empire in North Africa, many of these transplanted Mozarabs returned to the peninsula and were allowed to settle in the Tagus valley in the vicinity of Toledo. Others who remained in Morocco were employed by the Almoravids as tax collectors, entrusted especially with the task of collecting taxes not authorized by the Koran.

The Jews always had a prominent place in Muslim Spain, but especially during the period of the *taifas*. Al-Idrisi reported that the most prosperous Jewish community was found at Lucena; the city was largely populated by Jews and only a small number of Muslims inhabited the suburbs. Jews were employed in a variety of offices by the *reyes de taifas*. Samuel ibn Naghrila (d. c. 1056) and his son Joseph, for example, acted as chief ministers for the king of Granada; after Joseph's assassination, however, a general massacre of Jews followed. Under the Almoravids and Almohads the Jews suffered intermittent persecution; the people of Córdoba in 1135, for example, sacked and burned the Jewish quarter. In his treatise on public administration in Seville, Ibn Abdun linked Jews and Christians with lepers, and insisted that they be obliged to wear a distinctive sign "that will make it possible for them to be recognized and will constitute for them a mark of ignominy." Under the active persecution of the Almohads the synagogues were destroyed, and many Jews were forced to embrace Islam or to go into exile. Many sought refuge in Christian Spain, while others, such as the great scholar Maimonides, traveled as far away as Egypt. According to Ibn Idhari, one of the greatest merits of the Almohad Caliph, al-Mansur, was his insistence that the Jews wear distinctive clothing: "This was because they had become so bold as to wear Muslim clothing and in their dress looked like the noblest among them, mingling with the Muslims in external affairs, without being distinguished from the servants of God. . . . He imposed a fashion upon them . . . the sleeves of their tunics were a cubit in length and another in width, and black, with black burnooses and black caps" (*Al-Bayan al-Mugrib*, I, 204). The color later was changed to yellow. In recording this decree, al-Marrakushi noted that there was neither synagogue nor church in Morocco and that, although the Jews adhered to the Muslim religion, only God knew what was in their hearts.

Class distinctions in the Christian states were becoming more pronounced, but society was still open enough for a simple freeman to attain noble rank and for a man of servile origin to become a freeman. Feudal concepts colored many social relationships, especially in Catalonia, but also in other areas where feudalism was not as fully developed.

Those who were most directly concerned with feudal relationships were the nobility, who formed two broad categories, the magnates and the knights, both actively engaged in the political and military life of the realm. The magnates, known in the western kingdoms from the twelfth century as *ricos hombres* or rich men (the term first appears in a charter of Sancho VI of Navarre dated 1162) and in Catalonia as *barones*, usually held large estates, either in their own right or as benefices from the ruler. They attended his court and considered themselves his natural counselors; hundreds of charters of this period indicate that the ruler seldom acted without first taking "the counsel of my barons." They also were entrusted with major offices of territorial administration, and their forces constituted a significant part of any royal army. Their influence extended to the church too, because their relatives often filled important bishoprics or abbeys. Among the most influential baronial families were the Lara, Haro, and Castro families in Castile, the Cardona and Moncada in Catalonia, and the Alagón in Aragon; generally, the number of such families was small.

Just as the magnates usually were vassals of the king, so the secondary nobility, known as *milites* or *caballeros*, and distinguished by their lineage and profession of arms, were vassals of the magnates. In the western realms the term *infanzones*, signifying their descent from great men, often was applied to them, as in this charter of 1093, speaking of the "knights who are not born of inferior parents but who are of noble origin and are called in the vulgar tongue *infanzones*." In the course of the twelfth century they were also called *fijosdalgo*, from whence comes the modern word, *hidalgos*. Various etymologies for this word have been proposed, but it probably derives from the Latin *filius de aliquod*, meaning a man of worth or substance; eventually *infanzón* and *fijodalgo* were used interchangeably. In León-Castile the expression *caballeros fijosdalgo*, emphasizing their role as knights and their noble rank, distinguished them from the *caballeros villanos* or non-noble knights of the towns. Because the king could confer noble status upon anyone, a distinction was made in Aragon among nobles by birth (*infanzones ermunios*), those ennobled by royal charter (*infanzones de carta*), and the inhabitants of a particular locality who were ennobled (*infanzones de población*).

The nobility were a privileged class, justiciable only in the royal court and exempt from the payment of tributes of any kind. As their lands were exempt, non-nobles were forbidden to acquire them, and nobles could not acquire lands belonging to taxpayers, lest those lands become exempt. Nobles were obliged to serve in war only when they received recompense from their lords in the form of money or benefices. Above all, they were tenacious in defense of their privileged condition; in 1134, for example, the barons and *infanzones* of Aragon asked Alfonso VII to confirm the *fueros* and usages they had enjoyed since the days of Pedro I. Among other things, they claimed the right to be judged according to law, to be exempt from various tributes, and to be subject to the loss of their *honores* only in case of one of the following transgressions: the murder of one's lord, adultery with the lord's wife, using the *honor* received from one lord to serve another. After the battle of Las Navas de Tolosa, Alfonso VIII asked the Castilian *ricos hombres* and *fijosdalgo* to present a written statement of their customs, so that he could confirm what was good and make any necessary emendations. This purportedly was the origin of the so-called *Fuero Viejo*.

In theory the clergy did not constitute a social class, but the prelates, that is, the bishops and abbots, enjoyed the same privileges, and at least in the temporal sphere often shared the same interests as the nobles. Not only did they attend the royal court and supply military forces for the royal army, but they were also exempt from tribute and were lords of large estates or even of towns, for example, Compostela and Palencia.

Though no systematic study of society in al-Andalus during this period has been undertaken, the general outlines are clear. In the eleventh century the aristocracy of the caliphate became the new ruling class in the several *taifas*. Around each of the petty kings groups of people distinguished by birth or talent constituted the new royal courts. The advent of the Almoravids and the Almohads superimposed a new nobility upon the native aristocracy. The brothers and uncles (called by the honorific titles *sayyid* and *shaykh*) of the sovereign formed the first rank in the new hierarchy; immediately below them were the leaders (*shaykhs*) of the different tribal groups. Al-Mutamid of Seville, in a letter to Yusuf ibn Tashufin in 1086, noted an essential difference between the Berbers and the aristocracy of al-Andalus when he said: "Among us, the Arabs of al-Andalus, the tribes have been dissolved; their unity has been destroyed and their genealogies have been lost. . . . We are not here as tribes but as dispersed bands without parentage or friendship" (*Al-Hulal al-Mawshiyya*, 60–61). Unlike the Almoravids and Almohads, who were still organized in tribes and still very much concerned with their genealogy, the nobility of the peninsula were a blend of many different ethnic elements and were neither pureblooded Arabs or Berbers and are perhaps best described as *Andalusiyyun*.

The families of the *reyes de taifas*, that is, the Banu-l-Abbad, the Banu Hud, the Banu Dhi-l-Nun, and later the Banu Mardanish, were the natural leaders of the native aristocracy. Other patrician families, for example, the Banu Hajjaj and Banu Khaldun of Seville, and the Banu Sahib al-Sala of Beja, possessed large estates in the vicinity of the principal cities and ordinarily had a monopoly of the principal public offices. Ibn Abdun urged the Almoravids to entrust these offices to native men of honor and distinction. Insisting that nobles should be treated with greater consideration than ordinary men, he argued that they should not be subjected to corporal punishment for offenses against religious law. In the turbulent conditions of this time many nobles not only suffered bodily punishment but even loss of life on the grounds of treason.

Both the number of simple freemen and the number of those living in towns in Christian Spain increased significantly, due to an influx of immigrants from other lands, the conquest of cities already populated by persons engaged in mercantile and industrial activity, and a steadily expanding economy that encouraged the revival of old towns and the development of new ones. Whereas the inhabitants of Lisbon, Toledo, Barcelona, and other towns gained their daily bread as merchants and artisans, many of the people settled in the towns of the central *meseta*, such as Segovia, Avila, and Salamanca, were warriors, owners of flocks, and farmers. No matter what their occupation, persons settled in towns, having houses there and having resided there for a year and a day, had full rights of citizenship (*vicinitas*). This meant that they could participate in the government of the town through its council; they could serve as magistrates or represent the town in its relationships with other towns or with the crown. Townsmen in every case were recognized as freemen, with all that that implied, namely, the right to enter into contracts, to buy and sell property, to go and come as one pleased.

Social distinctions within the urban population became manifest as soon as some persons accumulated more wealth than others. The documents at times speak of *maiores* and *minores*, that is, the great men and the lesser men. In the western states, townsmen who owned horses (*caballeros villanos*), and were able to take part in military expeditions as mounted troops, were recognized as more important than simple foot soldiers (*peones*); these non-noble knights were usually exempt from personal services such as road repair and many forms of tribute. By the end of the twelfth century they seem to have gained control of the principal offices of town government and probably were the representatives ordinarily sent by the towns to the king's council or *cortes*. The social distinctions in the towns of the central *meseta* are clearly illustrated in a contemporary chronicle. Recounting the settlement of Avila at the close of the eleventh century, the text points out the distinction existing even then between the *serranos*, who dedicated themselves exclusively to warfare and the defense of the town as cavalry forces, and the artisans and tradesmen (*menestrales, ruanos*). "The *serranos* held that they were true Castilians and as such they had never known artisans among them, but only knights and squires and they had always lived as knights and not otherwise; and they had never entered into marriage with artisans nor with merchants nor with anyone other than noble knights, nor would they do so for anything in the whole world" (*Crónica de la población de Avila*, 23). This passage sharply delineates the class consciousness of the knightly element in Avila and their disdain for men who worked with their hands. In later centuries this contempt for labor became even more pronounced and contributed to the weakness of the middle class in the kingdom of Castile.

In al-Andalus a similar increase in the urban population took place in the eleventh and twelfth centuries. The geographer al-Idrisi reported that cities such as Seville, Córdoba, Málaga, Granada, Almería, Murcia, Alicante, and so forth were well populated, and there were many other towns with sizeable populations. The aristocracy often resided in the towns and maintained sumptuous palaces there; but in addition scholars, theologians, professional men, merchants, and artisans, Jews, and

Christians constituted the urban population. Ibn Abdun found occasion to censure the behavior of several of these groups; he complained of the lawyers who abused their clients, and he insisted that lawyers ought not to be allowed to represent women because their only concern was to seduce the women. In similar vein he found fault with the mercenaries and Negro soldiers in Seville who wore the Almoravid veil and therefore were treated with the honor due only to men of high rank. Though documentation is scanty, it would appear that a highly complex urban society existed in al-Andalus and that conflicts between social classes in the towns occurred frequently during this time of political upheaval.

Despite the increase in the urban population the majority of people in both Christian and Muslim Spain were still settled in country areas. In the Christian states some free proprietors (*villanos* in the west, *payeses* in Catalonia), owning their own land, as a protection against disorder commended themselves to the more powerful. In the earlier centuries freeholders in the Duero valley had been able to do so on advantageous terms because of the scarcity of lords with great estates in that region. These *homines de benefactoria* were able to choose a lord, and to sever ties with him at any moment without losing their holdings. In the eleventh and twelfth centuries, however, the relationship between the lord and the men commended to him tended to become hereditary. A distinction thus arose between those who could freely choose a lord wherever he might be found and those who were bound to a particular lord and his descendants. A charter of *circa* 1074, for example, provided that the recipient of lands would serve the donor for life and thereafter could serve "whomever will show favor to you (*qui tibi benefecerit*) from the rising to the setting of the sun." The last phrase indicates the individual's freedom to seek a lord anywhere in the realm, or, as the later expression put it, *de mar a mar*, from sea to sea. By contrast, in 1162 a freeman, in his own name and that of his descendants, pledged to serve his lord and his descendants, thus constituting what came to be known as a *behetria de linaje*. Although the bond between lord and man was a highly personal one, it was based upon the possession of land by the one commending himself. The term *benfetria* or *behetria* thus came to be applied to the land itself, and whoever was in possession of it had the rights and obligations of a *homo de benefactoria*. *Behetrías* were found principally in Castile in the

Duero valley and did not extend southward because of the development of the great *concejos* in the region between the Duero and the Tagus.

Most rural freemen were tenants commended to the protection of their lords. As large estates developed in Galicia, León, and Catalonia, more and more men fell into this status, but the ties binding them to the soil were never unbreakable. The notion that a man was subject to his lord because of the lands he occupied rather than because of his person was evidently gaining ground and seems to be the basis for the distinction between *iuniores per hereditatem* and *iuniores de cabeza*. The former held lands in tenancy and owed tributes for them but could leave under certain conditions; the latter were bound to the lord by a personal tie and owed him personal services and were not as free to leave. With the repopulation of many lands under the direction of great lords, many peasants, known as *solariegos* (from *solar*, a place of settlement), accepted lands on a tenant basis and submitted to the lordship of another. Their status apparently differed from that of *iuniores* only in the types of tribute owed to their lords. Some Leonese and Castilian *fueros* required the *solariego* who wished to leave the land to give all his goods to the lord, but other *fueros* permitted him to take all his movables (not merely half as prescribed for *iuniores* in the Leonese *decreta* of 1017) and to sell his rights in his holding to another *solariego*.

Catalan lords, concerned lest their tenants abandon the land and move to newly developed regions, insisted that they accept commendation and agree to pay a redemption for permission to leave. In effect, these tenants were bound to the soil unless the lord was willing to allow them to leave and unless they were able to pay the redemption. In the most recently acquired parts of Catalonia, peasants had much greater freedom of movement. In Aragon and Navarre the condition of the *mezquinos* who were bound to the soil did not change appreciably, but the conquest of the Ebro valley brought large numbers of Muslim sharecroppers (*shariq, exarico*) under Christian rule. Details concerning the structure of rural society in al-Andalus during this period are woefully lacking, but the majority of freemen probably cultivated the lands of great estates on a sharecropping basis.

The number of slaves in both Christian and Muslim Spain probably increased, not only because of a natural rise in the birth rate among the already existing slave population, but also because of the capture of many more persons who were reduced to slavery. The condition of slaves used to cultivate the soil differed little from that of tenants on the lord's estates. The slave, of course, was always a chattel and did not have any of the juridical rights of a freeman. In Christian Spain many Muslim slaves were utilized in the households of lords as personal servants and workmen. Manumission continued to be practiced, usually by the concession of a letter of freedom (*carta ingenuitatis*). A letter of 1143, for example, specifies the rights of two former slaves: "Wherefore, from this hour forth, you shall have permission to testify, to sue, to litigate, to respond, to buy and sell, and to carry on other affairs among free and noble men. But we retain your persons in our service and our fealty, so that from today onward you may serve us faithfully and with great humility all the days that my daughter and I shall live" (*CHDE*, II, 287). Thereafter they were at full liberty to go wherever they wished. The retention of former slaves in some type of personal dependence upon their lords, at least during the lifetime of the lord, seems to have been the most usual practice. The many military expeditions dispatched against Christian territory during this period filled the slave markets of al-Andalus, so that people of ordinary circumstances often were able to own slaves. Women slaves often graced the harems of Muslim rulers, more than one of whom was the child of a Christian mother. Negro slaves were also imported from Africa. As in the past, freedmen (*mawla, mawali*) sometimes attained wealth and power in al-Andalus. Mujahid, king of Denia and the Balearic Islands, for example, was a freedman, formerly a slave of Almanzor's family.

The Economy

During the eleventh and twelfth centuries western Europe experienced a remarkable economic expansion. An urban, industrial, commercial economy based upon the widespread use of money as a medium of exchange came into being. International trade throughout the Mediterranean flourished as never before, as Venice, Genoa, and Pisa broadened their contacts with the Byzantine empire and, partly as a result of the crusades, established commercial relations with Syria, Palestine, Egypt, and North Africa. In the north, trade between England, Flanders, and the Scandinavian countries stepped up and gradually spread across the face of Europe, following the principal rivers, the natural arteries of communication. The expansion of trade between north and south, east and west, between the Christian and Muslim worlds, was accompanied by a greater circulation of money, the development of credit instruments, and an increased production of goods not merely for local consumption but for national and international distribution. The increased volume of trade was made possible by the activities of an ever-growing class of merchants and artisans, who at first tended to be itinerant but gradually settled in towns; old towns took on new life, and new towns were built from nothing. As the towns constituted an expanding market for agricultural products, the colonization and cultivation of more and more land was undertaken. At the same time, the peasants discovered the opportunity to seek a new life as workmen or merchants in the towns; by emigrating from the countryside to the urban areas, they were often able to achieve a greater degree of freedom and prosperity.

The developments described above also took place in Spain, though in accordance with the peculiar conditions and circumstances of peninsular life. While the Christians pushed their frontiers beyond the Ebro and Tagus rivers, opening up vast areas to colonization, commercial contacts between the Christian states and al-Andalus were broadened, and merchants from France and Italy and other countries began to enter the peninsula. Consequently a number of towns began to delevop and flourish along the pilgrimage route to Santiago de Compostela. Pilgrims, and merchants seeking to serve their needs, came across the Pyrenees to Jaca in Aragon or Pamplona in Navarre and then proceeded westward through Estella, Logroño, Nájera, Burgos, Sahagún, León, Astorga, and Ponferrada. In the eleventh century Sancho el mayor of Navarre, Sancho Ramírez of Aragon, and Alfonso VI of León endeavored to facilitate the journey by erecting hospices, repairing and building roads and bridges. Noting that Alfonso VI "built all the bridges from Logroño to Sahagún," the *Crónica Najerense* (III, 57) also mentioned that "merchants and pilgrims traveling through his entire realm feared nothing for themselves or for their goods." Many of these visitors settled in villages and towns along the way and opened trade relations between their new homeland and northern Europe. The increasing influence of the Franks, the most important mercantile element in the western kingdoms, is illustrated by the challenge they offered to the lordship of the abbots of Sahagún and the archbishops of Compostela. As in northern Europe, the burghers tried to throw off the political power of prelates and to secure rights of self-government. In fewer numbers, merchants and craftsmen settled in the municipalities of the zone from the Duero to the Tagus; those towns therefore were slow to develop significant mercantile or industrial activity.

Along the coast of the Bay of Biscay, Santander, Laredo, Castro Urdiales, and other towns were beginning to develop trade relations with the French towns of Bayonne and Bordeaux. Alfonso VIII in 1192 assigned to the bishop of Burgos a tenth of the tolls on cloth, arms, and other merchandise imported to Santander or Castro Urdiales or any other port in the diocese. Some years later, in 1210, he settled San Vicente de la Barquera, giving the inhabitants the *Fuero* of San Sebastián, with the additional provision that the rules applying to the arrival of ships at Santander would also apply to San Vicente. In the thirteenth century these towns on the Bay of Biscay organized an association to defend their interests, both against the bishop of Burgos and against their French neighbors. It should also be pointed out that the growth of Castilian shipping in this area made it possible to provide a fleet to assist in the conquest of Seville in 1248.

The Muslim geographer al-Idrisi referred to the Bay of Biscay as the sea of the English; in so doing he implied the existence of fairly regular contact between the Iberian peninsula and the lands to the north, that is, France and the British Isles. In the ninth and tenth centuries the Norsemen frequently raided the coasts of the peninsula and even passed through the straits of Gibraltar. During the period of the crusades various groups going to the Holy Land sailed around Spain and through the straits, often stopping enroute to take on supplies and to trade or plunder. King Sigurd I of Norway, for example, in 1108 attacked Sintra, Lisbon, and Alcácer do Sal on his way to the Holy Land; another group identified only as Normans attacked Ceuta on the North African coast in 1143–1144. Some of those in the Anglo-Flemish fleet that helped to capture Lisbon in 1147 had apparently visited the area before for trade, plunder, or piracy. In the later twelfth century Porto and Lisbon began to develop as important ports, and the Portuguese rivers, the Miño, Duero, Mondego, and the Tagus, facilitated commercial development. By the thirteenth century the Castilian towns on the Bay of Biscay found competition from Portugal too much to be endured.

Until the eleventh century the Mediterranean was a Muslim lake, and the possibilities for Christian maritime commerce were limited. But Venice, Genoa, and Pisa broke the Muslim monopoly and opened up trade with Sardinia, Corsica, Sicily, Tunis, Tripoli, the Balearic Islands, and Christian Spain. The participation of Count Ramon Berenguer III in an assault on Majorca in 1115 was a sign of growing Catalan interest in overseas expansion and commerce, but it should be noted that the Pisans provided the fleet which made the assault possible. Thirty years later the Genoese supplied the ships which enabled the Christians to take Almería and Tortosa. As an inducement for their collaboration in the attack on Tortosa, Ramon Berenguer IV promised the Genoese a third of the city and exemption from all tolls. Tortosa, according to al-Idrisi, was a city with an important shipbuilding industry; its possession no doubt helped in the development of a native Catalan merchant fleet. It would seem that until the early thirteenth century the Catalans did not have a merchant fleet of any consequence, but a stipulation in the *Usages of Barcelona* (60) that "all ships coming to or departing from Barcelona shall be under the Peace and Truce of God" indicates an increasing maritime trade. Benjamin of Tudela in 1150 reported that ships from Alexandria, the Holy Land, Greece, Africa, Pisa, Genoa, Sicily, and Marseille visited Barcelona. The natural advantages of the chief city of Catalonia thus enabled it to become an important point of contact between east and west, between the Christian and Muslim worlds.

Along the coast to the south of Barcelona and Tortosa and extending all the way to the straits of Gibraltar were a number of ports with a substantial share in Mediterranean trade. These included Valencia, Denia, Alicante, Cartagena, Murcia, Almería, Málaga, Algeciras, Tarifa, Niebla, Huelva, and Silves. Almería was, without question, the principal seaport in all of Spain; it totally eclipsed nearby Pechina, the chief port of the Umayyad era. Ships from Egypt, Syria, and the entire Mediterranean world made their way to Almería, whose people were noted for their industry and application. Al-Idrisi remarked that, at the time of his writing, the city was in Christian hands, having been taken by Alfonso VII and the Genoese, and its people had been enslaved and its buildings destroyed. Though recaptured by the Almohads in 1157, the city subsequently never quite regained its former prosperity.

A number of the great cities in the heart of the peninsula were conquered by the Christians during this period and therefore contributed substantially to the economic growth of the Christian states. A flourishing urban economy already existed in towns such as Toledo, Zaragoza, Calatayud, Cuenca, and Talavera, where Jews, Mozarabs, and Muslims continued to practice their crafts and to maintain an active commerce.

In al-Andalus, towns and trade had prospered in earlier centuries, so that the contrast with the commercial and industrial development of the Christian north was sharp. The most populous and prosperous city was no longer Córdoba but Seville, the former seat of the Abbadid family and then the headquarters of the Almohads in the peninsula. The latter did much to embellish the city and to foster the development of its commerce and industry. Granada, a small settlement long over-shadowed by nearby Elvira, came to prominence as the capital of the Zirid kings, but even after their overthrow by the Almoravids, the city continued to grow in size and prosperity. Jaén, Carmona, and Badajoz were some of the other towns noted for their active economy.

The carrying trade was largely in the hands of the Muslims, the Genoese, and Pisans, and to a lesser extent, the Hispanic Christians. Shipbuilding was a major industry in Alicante, Alcácer do Sal, Alge-ciras, and Tortosa. From these and other ports a variety of goods were shipped to different areas of the Mediterranean. Almería exported pot-tery, glass, silken robes of different colors and patterns; Denia shipped grain and paper, while Málaga and Silves exported figs (al-Idrisi de-scribed the figs of Silves as delicate, appetizing, and exquisite). Seville exported olives and olive oil. The ports of the Bay of Biscay probably shipped iron, wood, and fish to the north. Weapons of various kinds evidently figured in trade, as this prohibition in the *Usages of Barcelona* (123) suggests: "Christians may not sell arms to the Saracens without the consent of the prince." Imports included cloth of varied material, foods, especially spices, slaves, and luxury items.

Overland trade followed the old Roman roads and newer routes such as the pilgrimage road to Compostela. According to the *Usages* (62), "highways and roads . . . ought to be under the Peace and Truce . . . so that all men, both knights and pedestrians, merchants and busi-nessmen, going and coming along them, may go and come securely and quietly, with all their goods, and without any fear." Professional mer-chants from different countries, Jews, Christians and Muslims, met at fairs to engage in wholesale exchange. Important fairs were held at Granada, Córdoba, and Carmona; Alfonso VII authorized the holding of fairs at Valladolid for a week following the Nativity of the Virgin, and at Sahagún for three weeks after Pentecost; others were held at San Zoil de Carrión, Brihuega, and Alcalá de Henares. In every case the fair was protected by the ruler, who guaranteed the security of those persons who attended.

In most cities economic activity was centered in one or more public markets (al-suq, azogue, zoco). The principal market usually was located in the central plaza; in Toledo, for example, the plaza was known, as it is today, as the zocodover (suq al-dawabb), because it was given over to the trading of pack animals. Around the square, small shops were grouped where merchants and artisans offered their goods for sale. The streets running off from the square usually were devoted to separate crafts. In both Muslim and Christian Spain town markets were carefully regulated and supervised by the al-muhtasib or almotacén appointed by the government. Ibn Abdun insisted that the supervisor should be intelligent and incorruptible and should assign a place to each craft so that all those engaged in it could be found more easily. In any important town, such as Toledo, Zaragoza, or Seville, there were men engaged in several major occupations, for example, supplying food for the citizenry, that is, meats, fruits, vegetables, fish, olives, spices, wines, and the like; then there were the builders, bricklayers, carpenters, and toolmakers; the clothing merchants, tailors, dyers, tanners, and shoemakers. The moneychangers also played a prominent part in the commerce of the city, but care should be taken, said Ibn Abdun, that they not be allowed to demand usury. Physicians, barbers, apothecaries, masseurs, musicians, gamblers, storytellers, dancers, and prostitutes also plied their respective professions and trades.

Since Ibn Abdun does not discuss the subject, Lévi-Provençal believes that there was little corporate organization of the crafts and professions in Muslim Spain in the twelfth century. In commenting upon the different groups involved in the public market, Ibn Abdun showed special concern to prevent fraud and emphasized that this was one of the principal responsibilities of the al-muhtasib. But he also insisted that no one should be allowed to practice a profession or craft of which he was not a master. He especially condemned the pharmacist who prepared medicine or drugs which harmed rather than helped the patient, and he noted that a mistake made by one practicing medicine under false pretenses could lead to the loss of life: "the error that a physician may commit is hidden by the earth covering the grave of the dead man." For these reasons he proposed that each of the crafts and professions should be supervised by a prudent and responsible man (amin) who would resolve disputes and guard against deceit. To what extent these recommendations were implemented is difficult to ascertain.

Artisans and tradesmen in Christian towns were beginning to organize confraternities (cofradías, confratrias) in the twelfth century, for both spiritual and economic purposes, that is, to provide spiritual comfort to the members in time of distress, but more importantly to defend their economic interests. The ordinances to be observed by the muleteers and merchants (los recueros e los mercadantes) of Atienza at the close of the twelfth century illustrate this point. The members (confrades) declared that they were forming a brotherhood (ermandat) for the honor of God and of his saints and "for the defense of our goods." A provost, or presiding officer, assisted by six others (los seys), resolved disputes involving the members. A chapter meeting (cabildo), probably a gathering of officials, was held each year a week before a meeting of the confradría, apparently a plenary assembly of all the members. Other regulations concern the participation of the members in spiritual functions.

The principal industries were textiles, metals, and mining. Silk, cotton, linen, and woolen cloth was manufactured, especially in al-Andalus, but weaving was becoming an important industry in the Christian north. The weavers of Soria, for example, formed a confraternity in the twelfth century. Tools and weapons of all sorts were made throughout the peninsula for domestic use but also for export. Toledan steel was still renowned as ideal for swords and other weapons; Toledan shields, for example, are mentioned in the Song of Roland. Paper was manufactured at Játiva and shipped throughout the Mediterranean. Gold, silver, copper, iron, and lead were mined in the region around Granada and Constantina, and iron was mined in the Asturian mountains and eventually became a major export. The most famous mines were the mercury mines at Almadén to the north of Córdoba. One thousand workers were said to be employed there in different phases of the operation. The Christians seized the mines in the mid-twelfth century, and for a time they were exploited for the benefit of the Order of Calatrava, but they were soon recovered by the Almohads and remained in their possession until the thirteenth century. Salt pits were exploited extensively, especially in the vicinity of Atienza; portions of the revenues obtained were often assigned by the king to bishops or abbots.

The expansion of trade necessitated a substantial increase in the quantity of money in circulation. Most of the reyes de taifas coined money in imitation of the coinage of the caliphate; much of that money found its way to the Christian states in the form of tribute. Count

Ramon Berenguer I was the first Christian ruler to coin gold money: *mancusos* imitating the gold *dinars* of the king of Málaga. The *Usages of Barcelona* (66) attributed the principle of the immutability of the coinage to him, stating, "the coinage, both of gold and silver, should be so diligently guarded that it may not be increased in copper in any way, nor diminished in gold or silver, nor in weight." In practice, however, all rulers tended to manipulate the coinage to their own advantage. For example, Pedro II asked Pope Innocent III to release him from the oath he had taken to maintain his father's coinage; he argued that it was so thoroughly debased as to be the cause of "grave scandal among the people."

Sancho Ramírez of Aragon coined money at Jaca, the so-called *jaqueses*. Although the monarch ordinarily reserved the right to coin money to himself, Alfonso VI authorized Diego Gelmírez, the bishop of Compostela, to coin money in 1108. A century later Afonso II of Portugal ordered counterfeiters to lose their goods, their hands, and their feet. Pointing out that a diversity of coinage would lead to depreciation and rising prices, Ibn Abdun emphasized the importance of allowing only one coinage to circulate within the kingdom. The coins most in use in al-Andalus were gold *dinars* minted by the Almoravids; in 1172 Alfonso VIII of Castile issued coins of this type, known as *morabetinos* or *maravedís*, a name recalling their origin as Almoravid money. These quickly became the basic coinage in the Christian states.

In spite of the growth of trade and industry and the increasing number of people settled in towns, agriculture remained the essential foundation of economic life in both Christian and Muslim Spain. As Ibn Abdun remarked: "Since agriculture is at the basis of civilization the whole of life and its principal advantages depend upon it." For this reason he urged the ruler to encourage the cultivation of the soil and to protect farmers working in the fields. Farmers on both sides of the border had reason to want protection, inasmuch as they were harassed by constant raids and threatened by conquest. Significant changes in the frontier and the possession of land occurred during this period, on the whole favoring the economic development of Christian Spain.

From the Duero valley the Christians steadily moved southward, reaching the Tagus river at Toledo in 1085, at Lisbon in 1147, and the Ebro river at Zaragoza in 1118 and at Tortosa in 1148. The colonization of the region from the Duero to the Tagus was effected under the aegis of the king who authorized the creation of broad municipal districts including a fortified urban center and a substantial rural area dotted with villages. These settlements initially were highly rural in character, since their inhabitants gained their livelihood principally from pasturage and the exploitation of the soil as well as from warfare against the Muslims. The booty obtained in frequent raids into Muslim territory made up for the inadequacy of the local economy, but it also encouraged raiding as a way of life and retarded the growth of the more prosaic activities of craftsmen and merchants.

The rich lands of lower Aragon below Zaragoza were exploited very much as in the past by the large Muslim population remaining there after the Christian conquest. Christians settled there, too, but in small numbers, taking possession of vacated lands; but for the most part the land remained in the hands of Muslim proprietors or sharecroppers subject to Christian landlords. The colonization of the region from Barcelona to Tortosa was carried out generally under the direction of the count of Barcelona who offered privileges to those who would settle there. Large numbers of Catalans thus discovered an opportunity to improve their economic and juridical condition.

In the late twelfth century the region between the Tagus and the Guadiana was in dispute, but by the early thirteenth century it was definitively in Christian hands. The king entrusted the settlement of this zone principally to the recently established military Orders. The knights of Alcántara held a large zone in Extremadura along the Portuguese frontier, while the knights of Calatrava occupied the *campo de Calatrava*, directly south from Toledo, and the knights of Santiago held the *campo de Montiel* to the east of that. The knights of Avis played a major role in the colonization of the Alentejo, the Portuguese territory beyond the Tagus river south of Lisbon. The native military Orders and the Knights Templar and Hospitaller performed a similar function in the lands acquired by the king of Aragon from Zaragoza to Teruel. In view of the threat of daily raids and armed conflicts of varying importance, settlements in these frontier zones tended to be rather sparse until the thirteenth century. In al-Andalus the latifundia of earlier centuries evidently survived the vicissitudes of the several upheavals caused by the collapse of the caliphate, the overthrow of the *reyes de taifas*, and the invasions of the Almoravids and the Almohads; though landlords might come and go, the peasantry remained in occupation of their ancestral lands.

During the eleventh and twelfth centuries great estates became more numerous and more substantial in all the Christian kingdoms. The foundation for their development was the cession of extensive tracts to bishops, abbots, magnates, and military Orders. Other lands might be acquired subsequently by purchase, exchange, marriage, gift, bequest, or outright usurpation. In many instances freeholders bequeathed their property to the church after death; in other cases they ceded it immediately but retained usufruct for life. At other times a freeholder might be despoiled of his rights and reduced to tenant status.

On any great estate the landlord usually reserved a portion for his immediate use. The center of his reserve or demesne (*terra indominicata*) was a court (*curtis*) surrounded by various buildings, including his house, granaries, wine cellar, stable, workshops, mill, bakery, smithy, and church. The reserve was cultivated by serfs or day laborers, or by tenants required to perform a few days' service on his land. A bailiff (*villicus, maiorinus, bajulus*) supervised the administration of the estate, directed the work, and collected the rents. Tenants holdings, common lands used for pasturage, and woodland constituted the most extensive part of the estate. Depending upon the terrain, the use to which the land was put, and the need for defense, tenants' houses might be grouped together in a village or scattered over a wide area. In the arid zones of al-Andalus, for example, the peasants usually lived in a fortified center from which they went out each day to tend the olive trees or vineyards. In the irrigated areas, the isolated farmhouse (*cortijo, alquería, al-qarya*), with its livestock and dependencies, was most common. In the mountainous regions of the north the peasants' houses usually were widely scattered, but in the central *meseta* they were grouped together in villages or towns.

Tenants held land under a variety of conditions. In earlier centuries many had received precarious grants of land to be held indefinitely in return for rent; gradually the term was extended for life and then became hereditary. In the western kingdoms the *prestimonium* was a similar concession, but it could be revoked at any time by the grantor. At times a proprietor granted land on condition that the tenant plant a vineyard; after seven years of sharing the yield with the owner, the tenant received ownership of half the land. Sharecropping was most common in al-Andalus and in lower Aragon where there was a large Muslim peasantry. The proprietor provided the land, a portion of seed, tools, and animals, and received a share of the produce ranging from one-sixth to one-half.

In the Christian states, cultivators owed the landlord a rent usually in kind, though later in money (*censum, forum, infurción, parata*). In the west this tribute was often called *martiniega* or *marzadga*, because it was paid on St. Martin's day or in March. Tenants also had to perform services on the lord's reserve several times each year, especially at planting and harvesting (*opera, sernas*). Services on the repair and construction of roads and bridges (*facendera*), guard duty (*anubda*), hospitality (*alberga, pausataria*), and so forth could also be demanded. Peasants also had to pay the lord for the use of his mill, ovens, or smithy (*maquilas, llosol*), and for the right to cut wood in the forest (*montazgo, forestatge*). When a tenant died, his son inherited his holding but had to give the best chattel to the lord (*nuntium, mortuarium, luctuosa, lexia*). If there were no heirs, the holding reverted to the lord, but the deceased could leave his land to a friend or neighbor who would have to pay the lord a fee for the privilege of inheritance (*mañería*). The lord also received payment from women of servile or semiservile condition who wished to marry (*ossas, huesas*).

Catalan peasants were subject to a series of burdens that came to be known as the "evil usages." Tenants bound to the soil could leave it only after paying the price of their redemption (*redimentia, remensa*), a sum fixed arbitrarily by the lord. If a man died intestate, leaving a wife and children, the lord took one-third of his movable goods; if only the wife survived, the lord took one-half (*intestia*); if a man died without heirs, his lands reverted to the lord, but could be taken up by a friend or neighbor upon payment of a fee (*exorchia*). If a tenant's wife committed adultery, the lord claimed half of her goods; if she acted with the consent of her husband, the lord took all (*cugucia*). A tenant who caused a fire had to pay the lord a fine (*arsina*). The last of the "evil usages," called *firma de spolii*, was a payment made by the tenant for the right to mortgage lands held by the lord to guarantee the dowry of the tenant's wife. The lords of great estates in Catalonia and Aragon also claimed the *ius maletractandi*, the right to coerce the peasants, to imprison them and confiscate their goods or even to kill them. Pedro II in the *curia* of Cervera in 1202 acknowledged the practice in Catalonia, though restricting it to the estates of secular lords. The burdens imposed upon the Catalan peasantry eventually provoked them to the point of rebellion in the later Middle Ages and resulted in substantial change in their condition.

Agricultural products varied from one region to another. Staples such as wheat, barley, oats, fruits, and vegetables were cultivated throughout the peninsula, depending upon conditions of soil and climate. In the Duero valley, for example, the land was given over to the growing of wheat and other cereals, while in Valencia oranges were the principal crop. Cotton, linen, and silk were grown in the vicinity of Granada and Almería; rice, sugar cane, figs, and bananas were also major crops of al-Andalus. Olive groves were found in many parts of the peninsula, some near Zamora, but the most luxurious were those in the *ajarafe* of Seville, a zone forty miles long by twelve miles wide reaching to Niebla. Vineyards were planted in many areas, for example, in La Rioja, eventually one of the most important wine-producing regions of Spain. Although much of the soil was dry and barren, irrigation systems were utilized in most parts of Spain, but especially in Valencia, Murcia, and Andalusia. In Christian Spain the land usually was left fallow every other year so that it could regain its fertility; fields to be cultivated ordinarily were not enclosed but left open.

Dairy cattle were raised in the humid, mountainous regions of north-central Portugal, Galicia, Asturias, the Basque provinces, and Catalonia, and also in al-Andalus. Bishko has pointed out that, as the reconquest extended into the subhumid or arid plains of the central *meseta*, cattle-ranching was developed or, as he put it, invented. Cattle were allowed to roam widely over open range lands of New Castile, Extremadura, and the Alentejo, and their owners developed the techniques of herding, grazing, round-ups, branding, and the like that characterized cattle-ranching centuries later in the New World. In this respect Spain was unique in medieval Europe. As important as cattle-ranching became in the thirteenth century, sheep-raising was the dominant element in the economy of the central *meseta*. Flocks of sheep were moved annually along sheepwalks (*cañadas*) extending from the base of the Pyrenees to the Ebro river in the east, to the Duero, and thence to the Tagus in the west. Royal charters of the twelfth century reveal an increasing concern for sheepherding and often guaranteed free pasturage throughout the realm to sheep belonging to bishops, nobles, monasteries, and others. Disputes inevitably arose between the sheepherders and the farmers and others through whose lands the sheep passed. Both cattle and sheep were eagerly sought by raiding parties on both sides of the frontier. Ibn Idhari noted that on one occasion the cavalry of Avila seized 50,000 sheep and 2,000 cows. The figures may be exaggerated, but they are an indication of the importance of livestock as booty in the never-ending border warfare.

CHAPTER 13

Religion and Culture, 1031–1212

An Age of Revival

The nearly two hundred years from the fall of the caliphate of Córdoba to the death of Alfonso VIII of Castile witnessed the tentative beginnings of a truly significant Christian culture in Spain and the full flowering of Islamic culture. Christian Spain was open to all the influences of northern Europe and received a steady influx of pilgrims, monks, knights, merchants, and others who contributed to the reform of the church, the growth of schools and universities, and the introduction of Roman and canon law. The church was organized more solidly than before and maintained continual contacts with Rome, accepting the Roman liturgy in place of the Mozarabic, receiving the monastic reforms of Cluny and Cîteaux, and creating indigenous military Orders to oppose the Muslims. Formal studies of the scriptures, the writings of the Fathers, and the law, were undertaken with greater success, while at the same time a native literature in the vernacular tongue began to take shape.

The cultural development of al-Andalus, based upon the assimilation by the Muslims of the wisdom of the ancient world, reached its apogee during the era of the *taifas*. For all their inadequacies in the political realm, these petty sovereigns were notable patrons of scholars and were oftentimes scholars themselves. Poets, philosophers, scientists, historians created a Golden Age in the eleventh century. Even though the atmosphere tended to be more repressive during the domination of the Almoravids and Almohads, there was no substantial decline in intellectual and artistic activity. Christian and Muslim cultures came into closer contact as the great Muslim cities, Toledo, Zaragoza, Tortosa, and Lisbon, were captured by the Christians. Toledo attained fame for its school of translators who turned into Latin the writings of Arabic scholars as well as those of the ancient Greeks. In this way the wisdom of the Greeks and Arabs, especially in the fields of philosophy, science, and medicine, was made known to western Europe and profoundly influenced the development of western civilization.

The Church

For the church the eleventh and twelfth centuries were a period of transition, characterized by destruction in al-Andalus, restoration and reorganization in the Christian north. Emigration to the Christian kingdoms, persecution by the Almoravids and Almohads, deportation to North Africa, attempts at forced conversion to Islam, all contributed to a substantial decline in the Mozarabic communities of al-Andalus. On the other hand, as the frontiers of the northern states expanded, old bishoprics, some of them abandoned centuries before, were restored, and new bishoprics were created. Ecclesiastical organization, thrown into chaos by the Muslim invasion, was refined and defined, largely through the intervention of the papacy.

Greatly increased papal interest and involvement in the affairs of the peninsular church is apparent from the rapid multiplication of the number of papal letters addressed to peninsular personages. The submission of the kings of Aragon and Portugal as vassals of the Holy See, papal claims to peninsular territory as part of the patrimony of St. Peter, encouragement of French military expeditions against the Muslims, and the extension of crusading privileges to all who fought against Spanish Islam, are all signs of growing papal influence. Papal legates frequented the peninsula, both to reform the church and to persuade the Christian rulers to put aside their quarrels and to join forces against Islam.

The progress of the reconquest facilitated and made necessary the reorganization of dioceses and ecclesiastical provinces. The five provinces of earlier centuries had long since been upset by the Muslim invasions, but attempts now were made to reconstitute them. No one of the newly organized provinces had precisely the same limits as in the Visigothic era, and not all the bishoprics of that time were restored. The metropolitan status of Toledo, conquered in 1085, was never in doubt, but its claims to primacy over all the churches in Spain were hotly contested. Urban II confirmed the primacy in 1088, but the other metropolitans continued to challenge it until the thirteenth century. The suffragan sees belonging to the province of Toledo included Segovia, Sigüenza, Osma, Palencia, Cuenca, and Albarracín (Segorbe). Paschal II explicitly confirmed the status of Braga, restored around 1070, as the metropolitan see in the ancient province of Galicia, and in so doing helped to strengthen Portuguese independence. The suffragan sees were Astorga, Lugo, Túy, Mondoñedo, Orense, Porto, Coimbra, and Viseu. Mérida, the metropolitan see of the province of Lusitania, remained in Muslim hands, thereby giving the bishop of Santiago de Compostela the opportunity to lay claim to Mérida's rights. The bishops of Compostela evinced far-reaching ambitions early in the eleventh century when they began to speak of their see as "an apostolic see." This title, based upon the supposition that the Apostle St. James had been buried there, provoked papal objections, and Pope Leo IX expressly forbade its use. Pope Calixtus II conceded the metropolitan rights of Mérida in 1120 to Diego Gelmírez, the bishop of Compostela, until the recovery of Mérida; but four years later the pope suppressed the archiepiscopal status of Mérida for good, transferring it in perpetuity to Compostela. Given the ancient rights of Braga in the province of Galicia, the suffragan sees of Compostela were located for the most part in León and Portugal, though one or two were in the kingdom of Castile; they included Zamora, Salamanca, Avila, Coria, Ciudad Rodrigo, Plasencia, Badajoz, Lamego, Idaña, Evora, and Lisbon. The distribution of sees between Braga and Compostela occasioned an intense rivalry, encouraged by the kings of Portugal and León, who strongly objected to the intervention of foreign prelates in the ecclesiastical affairs of their kingdoms. Disputes over boundaries were frequent among the twelfth-century metropolitans, and as a consequence the bishoprics of León, Oviedo, and Burgos were declared exempt from the jurisdiction of any archbishop.

After the Muslim conquest the bishoprics of the ancient province of Tarragona were subordinated to the jurisdiction of the metropolitans of Narbonne or Auch in southern France. In the tenth century, efforts were made to reorganize an ecclesiastical province in Catalonia, but they were not successful until 1089. Then the rights of Tarragona were assigned to the bishopric of Vich; after the reconquest of Tarragona in 1117 the archiepiscopal see was re-established there. The suffragan sees were Gerona, Barcelona, Vich, Lérida, Urgel, Tortosa, Huesca, Zaragoza, Pamplona, Tarazona, and Calahorra. In al-Andalus the metropolitan see of Seville was served without interruption by a succession of bishops until the middle of the twelfth century when the last of them, Clement, fled to Toledo. Notices of other bishoprics are scanty and incomplete, but there were bishops in Medina Sidonia, Córdoba, Elvira-Granada, Málaga, and Niebla. Bishops also served Christian communities in Toledo, Lisbon, and Zaragoza while those cities were under Muslim rule; the Cid established a bishopric temporarily in Valencia when he seized that city. The persecution of the Almoravids and Almohads seems to have caused the disappearance or dispersal of most of the bishops of al-Andalus, some of whom found refuge in Christian Spain. Around 1140, Archbishop Juan of Seville apparently abjured his faith at least temporarily under the threat of torture and drew a reprimand from Hugh of St. Victor. As Hugh presented it, Juan's defense was something like this: "Not the tongue, but conscience, makes one a Christian. . . . The Lord himself knows that I denied him unwillingly. The tongue did so, but not conscience. Indeed, I denied him with my mouth, but I confess him in my heart." Urging him to confess his fault, Hugh responded: "O miserable man. . . . Look at yourself. . . . What a shepherd of Christians! How can you feed the sheep of Christ whom you yourself have lost?" (𝒫ℒ, 176, 1014). The subsequent collapse of the province of Seville is reflected in the papal privilege given to the archbishops of Toledo allowing them to restore bishoprics in reconquered territory lacking a metropolitan.

A sign of the increasing vitality and stability of the church during this period is the number of councils convened by papal legates or by archbishops. In the eleventh century mixed secular and ecclesiastical assemblies were convened by monarchs, for example, the Council of Coyanza, about 1055, and the Council of Jaca, about 1063. Cardinal Hugh Candidus held an important Council at Gerona around 1068, and in the twelfth century councils that were essentially ecclesiastical in composition and function were held at Compostela in 1114 and 1124, Palencia in 1129, and so on. Provincial councils were convened with increasing frequency in this period. These assemblies promulgated the Peace and Truce of God in Aragon and Catalonia, and enacted canons regulating tithes, clerical discipline, the monastic life, and similar matters.

The problem of lay investiture which caused so much controversy elsewhere in Europe was of no great consequence in the peninsula. The Council of Coyanza did stipulate that laymen should have no control over churches or the clergy, and the Council of Palencia forbade the clergy to receive churches from the hand of a layman. In the early centuries episcopal elections usually were carried out by the provincial bishops and confirmed by the king, but the king's role in the election, even if he nominated the candidate, was not considered an abuse or a violation of the canons. In the later twelfth century the king authorized the election and often proposed a candidate, but the cathedral canons were theoretically free to choose whomever they wished, and to present him to the archbishop for consecration. At times elections were the cause of rivalry and led to papal intervention. Early in the twelfth century, for example, Bishop Julián of Málaga was expelled from his see and languished in an Almoravid prison for seven years. In his absence the bishops of the province chose the archdeacon of Málaga as his successor. Upon his release from prison Julián appealed to Pope Paschal II who restored him and admonished the clergy and laity, "inasmuch as you live among the Saracens as among wolves and lions, so much the more carefully should you strive to please God" (DP, 70–71).

The bishop's most intimate counselors constituted the cathedral chapter. The canons, who in some instances followed a common life, were generally an educated class of men, as their responsibility for assisting the bishop in the administration of his see required. The principal capitular officers were the dean, chanter, treasurer, sacristan, archdeacon, and master of scholars. The last named had the important function of educating young boys and men for the priesthood. In the cathedral schools the substance of priestly education was provided, though some fortunate persons were able to study at the emerging universities beyond the Pyrenees or at Palencia and Salamanca within the peninsula. The parish clergy, especially in rural areas, were probably acquainted with the rudiments of Latin necessary for the celebration of mass, but otherwise deficient in education and discipline.

Clerical discipline was a major concern of the many councils held during this time. The clergy were required to wear dress appropriate to their calling, to avoid the use of arms, the practice of usury, hunting, hawking, simony, and concubinage. The problem of enforcing clerical celibacy appears to have been a continuing one. Ibn Abdun painted a very black picture of the clergy of Seville accusing them as follows:

The clergy indeed are debauched, fornicators and sodomites. Christian women should be forbidden to enter the church except on days of liturgical services and religious feasts, since they customarily go there to eat, drink and fornicate with the clergy. There is not one of the latter who does not have two or more mistresses. . . . The clergy should be ordered to marry, as is done in the east. [*Seville musulmane,* 154]

His charges probably reflect the bias of a censor of public morals and of an intolerant enemy of Christianity, but contemporary Muslim poets also allude to the abuse of wine and sexual indulgence by Christian clergy and laity.

The clergy were supported by tithes, first fruits, stole fees, and gifts. Numerous battles over tithes took place, especially between bishops and monastic or military Orders claiming exemption. Jews and Muslims who acquired lands formerly held by Christians were obliged to pay the tithes customarily due from those lands. The clergy were justiciable in ecclesiastical courts presided over by the archdeacon; appeals could be carried to the bishop and archbishop and ultimately to the papal court, which began to intervene much more frequently in litigation. The expansion of ecclesiastical jurisdiction often caused conflict with the secular courts and prompted rulers to attempt to set limits; for example, Afonso II of Portugal in 1211 declared that suits against the clergy and crimes committed by them could be adjudicated in church courts, but all other suits belonged to the crown.

The suppression of the Mozarabic liturgy, one of the most far-reaching changes of the era, exemplified the growing northern European influence in the peninsula and especially the impact of the papacy, which, under the leadership of Gregory VII, followed a policy of centralization and uniformity. King Sancho I of Aragon, with the collaboration of the papal legate, adopted the Roman liturgy in 1071; Alfonso VI of León vacillated for several years but eventually yielded. The Council of Burgos in 1080 formally confirmed the acceptance of the Roman liturgy in Spain. Thereafter, the Mozarabic rite remained little more than an historical curiosity.

The adoption of the Roman liturgy was partly the result of the introduction of Cluniac monasticism into Spain. Founded in 910 by the duke of Burgundy, Cluny effected a reform of Benedictine monasticism in many parts of Europe and eventually in Spain. Monastic life suffered severely from Muslim ravages in the tenth century, thus necessitating extensive reconstruction and restoration in the following century. Sancho el mayor, king of Navarre, by inviting Cluniac monks to reform the monasteries of Leyre, Oña, and San Juan de la Peña, gave the initial impetus to this task. His son, Fernando I, pledged to pay an annual tribute to Cluny as a sign of his affection, and the Council of Coyanza, held under his auspices, required all monasteries in the kingdom of León-Castile to follow the Benedictine Rule. Alfonso VI doubled the tribute promised to Cluny and established Sahagún as a center of Cluniac reform and influence in his kingdom. Many monasteries accepted the Cluniac interpretation of the Benedictine Rule, and many others submitted directly to the jurisdiction of the abbot of Cluny. As a consequence, the peninsula was inundated by French monks, many of whom subsequently benefited from royal favor and were elevated to the sees of Braga, Toledo, and Compostela.

By the end of the eleventh century Cluniac influence in Spain had reached its apogee, and shortly a new monastic reform supplanted it. The monastery of Cîteaux, founded in 1098 in Burgundy, became the center of a new attempt to recapture the primitive spirit of St. Benedict. Under the leadership of St. Bernard of Clairvaux, the most distinguished churchman of the early twelfth century, Cistercian monasteries were established all over Europe. The white monks came to Spain, probably first to Fitero in Navarre, and then to many other abbeys, such as Moreruela in León. Many older monasteries accepted the Cistercian reform, and many new ones were created, such as Poblet in Catalonia and Alcobaça in Portugal. Perhaps the most famous of all was Las Huelgas de Burgos, a Cistercian nunnery established by Alfonso VIII of Castile and endowed with extraordinary civil and ecclesiastical privileges. As part of an international congregation, Cistercian monasteries were subject to annual visitation by abbots of the monasteries whence they took their origin, and their abbots were required to attend an annual general chapter at Cîteaux.

Other religious Orders, the Premonstratensians, Carthusians, Canons regular of St. Augustine, and so forth, also established houses in the peninsula. Several military religious Orders, attempting to unite the highest ideals of asceticism and chivalry, played an especially important role in the reconquest. The Knights Templar and the Knights Hospitaller, founded in the Holy Land early in the twelfth century, also acquired property in the peninsula. Largely in imitation of them, the native military Orders of Calatrava, Santiago, Alcántara (San Julián del Pereiro), and Avis (Evora) were founded in the third quarter of the twelfth century. Calatrava, Alcántara, and Avis followed an adaptation of the Benedictine Rule and were affiliated to the Order of Cîteaux, with the right to participate in its general chapters and subject to the visitation of its abbots. The knights of Santiago followed a modified version of the Rule of St. Augustine. While the Orders tried to preserve the essential customs of the monastic life, such as community prayer, ascetic exercises, poverty, chastity, obedience, and the like, all these had to be adjusted to their principal responsibilities of a military character.

While northern European religious and ecclesiastical currents deeply influenced peninsular developments, the impact in Spain of the Waldensian and Albigensian heresies then ravaging Languedoc was scant indeed. Pedro II of Aragon, however, in 1197 promulgated a decree strictly commanding all heretics "to leave . . . our kingdom . . . as enemies of the cross of Christ and violators of the Christian faith and as public enemies of ourselves and of our kingdom. . . . If after the appointed time anyone should discover them in all our land, two-thirds of their goods shall be seized for the fisc, the other third by the discoverer, and their bodies shall be burned by fire" (CMCH, III, 401–402). This was the first enactment of the death penalty by fire for heretics in western Europe. One native of his realm, Durando of Huesca, and several companions, calling themselves *Poor Catholics*, renounced the Waldensian heresy and obtained permission from Innocent III to form a small group to preach the orthodox faith to their former coreligionists. There is some evidence of their activity in the archdiocese of Tarragona, but their principal sphere of operation seems to have been in Languedoc. There too, Pedro II became involved in the Albigensian Crusade, but his interest was chiefly political and feudal.

The incorporation of thousands of Muslims into Christian territory occasioned only tentative efforts to convert them. Abbot Hugh of Cluny around 1074 sent the monk Anastasius to Spain to preach to the infidels, but as his biographer noted, his efforts were in vain:

To prove the certitude of the Christian faith and to uproot the hardness of Saracen cruelty, after celebrating the solemnities of the mass, he offered to undergo the ordeal by fire. But the Saracens would not acquiesce in his conditions, namely, that if he emerged unscathed, they would hasten to the grace of baptism. But when, through blindness and hardness of heart, they refused to be moved in any way, he shook the dust from his feet in testimony against them and returned to his monastery. [PL, 149, 429]

Many years later Peter the Venerable, abbot of Cluny, visited Spain and decided to secure a translation of the Koran so that he could refute Muslim doctrine more effectively. The Englishman, Robert of Ketton, completed the translation into Latin in 1143, providing western Europeans for the first time with a precise knowledge of the contents of this fundamental Muslim text. It is noteworthy that interest in converting the Muslims was most evident among northern Europeans rather than peninsular Christians. The latter probably had long since accepted the notion of coexistence with Muslims and did not yet make any significant attempt to convert them. At the close of the twelfth century, Pope Celestine III asked the archbishop of Toledo to send a bilingual priest to serve the needs of the Christian people in al-Andalus and Morocco. Although this mission was directed to the Christians, it marks the beginning of an attempt to revivify and to expand the Christian faith in Morocco. Early in the thirteenth century, Franciscan missionaries undertook the task of establishing a formal mission to serve the needs of the Christians there and also to proselytize among the Muslims. The impetus for this came, however, from St. Francis himself, rather than from the Christians of Spain.

Christian Literature and Learning

The cultural achievements of Hispanic Christians of this era were slight in comparison to the accomplishments recorded in al-Andalus and northern Europe, but several significant developments did take place. In the city of Toledo, where Christians, Muslims, and Jews came into daily contact, the important task of translating and assimilating the wisdom of the Muslim world was carried out. Under the patronage of Archbishop Raimundo (1125–1152), an international community of scholars made Toledo the intellectual capital of Christian Spain and the principal link between Latin and Arabic civilizations. To some extent Seville served as the source for books that were translated, as Ibn Abdun complained: "Books of science ought not to be sold to Jews or Christians, except those that treat of their own religion. Indeed, they translate books of science and attribute authorship to their coreligionists or to their bishops, when they are the work of Muslims" (*Seville Musulmane*, 206). Among the personages assembled at Toledo were Gerard of Cremona, who translated several of Aristotle's works from Arabic into Latin; Domingo González, archdeacon of Segovia, and Joannes Hispanus, a converted Jew also known as Ibn Dawd or Avendaut, who collaborated on several translations. Jointly or separately they were responsible for translations of Avicenna's *Logic* and *Metaphysics*, al-Ghazzali's *Metaphysics*, and Avicebron's *Fons Vitae*. González also wrote a number of philosophical works intending to reconcile Christianity with Aristotelian, Neoplatonic, and Muslim philosophy.

Another Jewish convert, Pedro Alfonso of Huesca (d. 1110), using Arabic sources, compiled astronomical tables that facilitated the study of astronomy in northern Europe. He also published a collection of moral fables and tales, entitled *Disciplina Clericalis*, destined to circulate widely and to contribute to the common fund of stories later utilized by writers such as Boccaccio. In his *Dialogues*, an apologetic treatise intended to refute the beliefs of Jews and Muslims, Pedro Alfonso revealed a precise and accurate knowledge of the Koran and of Islamic doctrine; on this account his book proved to be eminently useful to missionaries and preachers in the thirteenth century.

Historical writing occupies a substantial place in the literature of this period. A succession of chronicles recapitulated the history of Spain from the Gothic era until mid-twelfth century. The anonymous *Chronicle of Silos (Historia Silense)* written about 1115 by a Mozarabic monk from Toledo, includes the text of Sampiro's *Chronicle*, but extends the history through the reign of Fernando I. Pelayo, bishop of Oviedo (d. 1129), utilized the earlier chronicles of Isidore, Alfonso III, and Sampiro, in his *Liber Chronicorum*, which is useful mainly for the period 894 to 1109; unfortunately, in order to exalt his diocese, he interpolated the texts that fell into his hands and is responsible for such inventions as Wamba's alleged division of the sees of Spain. The *Chronicle of Nájera (Crónica Najerense)* written about 1160, makes intelligent use of the earlier sources and is valuable for the reigns of Fernando I and Alfonso VI. Distinctively Castilian in tone, as its account of the Cid reveals, its use of poetic material marks a new departure in historiography.

Much more detailed than any of these works is the *Chronica Adefonsi Imperatoris*, an account of the reign of Alfonso VII to 1147. Divided into two parts, the first treating internal affairs and the second the wars with the Muslims, it is a eulogy of the king and tends to give a providential interpretation of history. The author was a man of solid biblical culture whose book reveals a literary skill not found in the earlier chronicles. A poem in hexameters, describing the preparations for the conquest of Almería, concludes the work.

The sources mentioned thus far are centered upon the activities of the kings of León-Castile. The *Historia Compostelana*, on the other hand, is largely a biography of Diego Gelmírez, the first archbishop of

Compostela, who evidently wished to leave a record of his achievements and the privileges obtained for his see. The work recounts the discovery of the Apostle's tomb and briefly sketches the previous history of the diocese, but the bulk of it concerns Gelmírez and his dealings with Alfonso VI, Urraca, and Alfonso VII. A number of royal and papal letters as well as the decrees of councils are included in the text.

In addition to these narratives, there are many compilations of annals which simply record events year by year. Among them the *Chronica Gothorum* is important as an account of the activities of Afonso I Henriques. Others include the *Chronicon Complutensis*, *Chronicon Conimbricensis*, *Chronicon Lamecensis*, *Chronicon Burgense*, *Annales Castellanos I, II*, *Annales Compostellani*, *Chronicon Rivipullense*, *Chronicon Dertusense*, *Chronicon Rotense*, *Chronicon Villarense*, and so on. Most of them extend into the late twelfth century and are useful primarily for establishing the chronology of events described more fully in the narratives cited above.

The greatest literary achievement of this period, without doubt, is the *Cantar de mio Cid*, written in the Castilian vernacular about 1140. The origins of the vernacular are lost in earlier centuries, though fragments of words and passages appeared in Mozarabic texts. By the twelfth century the languages of the people were being used to express the finest sentiments of the human soul. The great French epic, the *Song of Roland*, heralded the deeds of Roland and Charlemagne against the Moors in Spain and undoubtedly aroused crusading zeal among the many French knights who came to Spain during this century. At the same time, the troubadours, some of whom enjoyed the patronage of Alfonso II of Aragon, were writing beautiful lyrics in praise of noble ladies and elaborating the ideas of courtly love, while the *juglares* or traveling minstrels of Castile were beginning to sing songs in honor of ancient heroes.

The *Cantar de mio Cid*, extending to nearly 4,000 lines, is an extraordinary piece of literature portraying the career of Rodrigo Díaz de Vivar, the Cid. The poem is historically accurate in its description of persons, events, and places. The language is simple and direct, the tone objective and realistic, with none of the exaggerations that characterize so much of the action in the *Song of Roland*. The Cid was an authentic hero, a man of flesh and blood, whose memory was still vivid to those who heard the poem fifty years after his death. Exiled from his native land, *Castiella la gentil*, a victim of the anger (*ira regis*) of Alfonso VI of León, the Cid invaded Muslim Spain to earn a living (*ganar su pan*) for himself and his vassals. The booty won was immense, but could not compare with the richest prize of all, the city of Valencia, where the Cid became lord. The loyalty of a vassal to his lord is emphasized not only by the Cid's unshakeable fidelity to the king who dismissed him, but also in the equally firm allegiance of the Cid's vassals to him. As the poet said: "Dios, que buen vassallo, si oviesse buen señor!"—"God, what a good vassal, if only he had a good lord!"

The Cid's actions reveal contemporary attitudes toward Jews and Muslims. He practiced deceit upon Jewish moneylenders, and he was generally tolerant of and friendly to Muslims who were not his enemies. But in battle with the Moors, "en el nombra del Criador e d'apostol santi Yague," he fought bravely and victoriously. Though invincible, he was nevertheless human, and occasionally his sword blows missed their target. The crusading spirit is evident in these lines, in which Bishop Jerome, after absolving the knights from their sins and promising them a reward in heaven, asks the Cid's permission to strike the first blows:

> El obispo don Jerome la missa les cantava;
> la missa dicha, gran sultura les dava:
> "El que aquí muriere lidiando de cara,
> préndol yo los pecados, e Dios le abrá el alma.
> A vos, Cid don Rodrigo, en buena çinxiestes espada,
> yo vos canté la missa por aquesta mañana;
> pídovos una dona e seam presentada:
> las feridas primeras que las aya yo otorgadas."
> Dixo el Campeador: "desaquí vos sean mandadas."
>
> Bishop Jerome sang mass for them
> And gave them absolution:
> "Whoever dies fighting here,
> I take away his sins and God will have his soul.
> For you Cid Don Rodrigo, who girded sword in good hour
> I sang the mass this morning.
> I ask a favor of you; let it be granted to me.
> Let me strike the first blows."
> "From this moment," said the Campeador, "they are yours."
> [*Cantar de mio Cid*, 1702–1710]

The poet also shows us the Cid as husband and father, but there is nothing here that smacks of courtly love. The Cid has no mistress, but bears a deep affection for his wife: "Ya doña Ximena, la mi mugier tan cumplida, commo a mie alma yo tanto vos quería"—"O, doña Jimena, my perfect wife, I love you as my own soul" (278–279). Alfonso VI, overwhelmed by reports of the Cid's deeds and by the munificent gifts he sent to him, received him again into favor and arranged the marriage of his daughters to the *infantes* de Carrión, who represented the highest ranks of the nobility. But they proved to be cowards in battle and dishonored their wives. The Cid's challenge to them in the king's court and the subsequent judicial duel resulting in their defeat are vivid portrayals of contemporary legal procedures. Afterwards the Cid married his daughters to the princes of Navarre and Aragon, and the poet concluded his work triumphantly:

> Veed qual ondra creçe al que en buen ora naçió
> quando señoras son sues fijas de Navarra e de Aragón.
> Oy los reyes d'España sos parientes son,
> a todos alcança ondra por el que en buena naçió.

> See how he grows in honor, he who was born in good hour.
> Now his daughters are queens of Navarre and Aragon.
> Today the kings of Spain are his relations.
> All increase in honor, through him born in good hour.
> [*Cantar de mio Cid*, 3722–3725]

A good man, a loyal vassal, and a brave warrior, the Cid overcame adversity and gained honor and fame for himself and his family and indeed for the kings of Spain who are now his kinsmen. His impact upon society is also suggested by the Latin *Carmen Campidoctoris*, evidently written in his lifetime, when his name was already celebrated among the kings of Spain:

> Unde per cunctas Ispanie partes
> celebre nomen eius inter omnes
> reges habetur, pariter timentes
> munus solventes. [Menéndez Pidal, *La España del Cid*, II, 883]

The *Historia Roderici*, on the other hand, is a prose account written in unembellished style before 1118 to record the victories of the warrior "who was never conquered by anyone." As these writers make plain, the Cid symbolized the fundamental virtues of the people of Castile.

Literature and Learning in al-Andalus

While the cultural horizon of Christian Spain was just beginning to be broadened, the cultivated society of the caliphate of Córdoba survived the political collapse of the early eleventh century and continued to flourish under the *reyes de taifas*. In his book *In Praise of Spanish*

Islam, al-Shaqundi (d. 1231) noted that "after the breaking of the necklace and the scattering of its pearls," the petty kings, as partakers of the caliphal heritage, vied with one another in their patronage of poets and scholars and their encouragement of literature and learning. This was a Golden Age in no way inferior to that which preceded it. Literary figures from the entire Muslim world were welcomed at the courts of Toledo, Badajoz, Valencia, and Zaragoza, though the Abbadid court of Seville outshone them all, chiefly because of the brilliance of al-Mutadid (1042–1069) and his son al-Mutamid (1069–1091), both distinguished poets.

Though much of the poetry of the age was artificial and false, as García Gómez has remarked, from time to time the poets succeeded in giving voice to the noblest sentiments of mankind. The poems of Ibn Zaydun (d. 1070), for example, describing his love for the Princess Wallada, a noted poet in her own right, who eventually rejected him, reveal emotions common to all men in all times:

> We passed the night alone, with no other companion
> But friendship and union; and while happiness and
> Slumber fled from the eyelids of our detractors,
> The shadows of night retained us in secret bonds
> Of pleasure, until the tongue of morning began to
> Herald our names.   [Al-Maqqari, *History of the Mohammedan*
> *Dynasties of Spain*, tr. by Pascual de Gayangos, I, 39]

The sensuous beauty of these lines is characteristic of the classical lyric poetry of the Spanish Muslims.

In the eleventh and twelfth centuries Muslim Spain made a unique contribution to Arabic poetry by means of the verse forms known as *muwashshah* and *zajal*. Said to have been invented by a tenth-century poet, the *muwashshah* was written in classical Arabic and usually consisted of five or six stanzas. Its essence, however, was the final couplet or *kharja*, which unlike the rest of the poem, was written in the colloquial tongue or in Romance, or sometimes in a combination of the two. These lines usually were spoken by a woman, reflecting upon her lover. A number of examples have been discovered in recent years by Stern and have attracted the attention of Spanish scholars especially, because they give evidence of the Romance language spoken in al-Andalus. The following is an example of a *kharja*:

> Que farayo o que serad de mibi?
> **Habibi,**
> **non te tolgas de mibi.**

What will I do, what will become of me?
Beloved,
Do not go away from me.   [Stern, *Les chansons mozarabes*, 16–17]

The principal difference between the *muwashshah* and the *zajal* is that the latter was entirely in colloquial rather than classical Arabic, and it reflected an increasing attraction of the aristocracy to the passions and violence of the crowd. In origin the *zajal* was probably a type of vulgar street song, made popular among the aristocracy by Ibn Quzman (d. 1160–1169), whose poetry is usually humorous, satirical, and obscene in character. Many years ago Julián Ribera called attention to the influence of the *zajal* on the development of Provençal lyric poetry, noting that William IX of Aquitaine, the first of the troubadours, utilized verse forms similar to the *zajal*. Menéndez Pidal has also emphasized this influence. Among other critics, Gerald Brenan thinks it unlikely that the French peasantry would borrow the *zajal* for their folk songs; rather he suggests that it may have been a primitive type of folk song common to all the peoples of the western Mediterranean.

Equally debated is the influence of Spanish Islam upon the idea of courtly love, one of the most significant and far-reaching developments of northern European society in the twelfth century. A highly idealized and romantic conception of love in which the lover is depicted as the submissive and obedient servant of his beloved is characteristic not only of Hispano-Arabic poetry, but also of the troubadour lyrics. Menéndez Pidal has stressed this relationship, and there are many who are inclined to agree. There is strong opposition to this thesis, of course, especially from those who point to ancient writers such as Ovid as sources for some of the ideas of love current in twelfth-century Europe.

The argument in favor of Hispano-Arabic influence is given added weight when one takes into account the work of Ibn Hazm of Córdoba (994–1064), one of the greatest writers of al-Andalus. Standing in the transitional period between the fall of the caliphate and the emergence of the *taifas*, he was a poet, theologian, philosopher, historian of religion, and statesman. He participated in the Umayyad struggle to retain the caliphate, but after the downfall of Abd al-Rahman V in 1023 he retired to devote himself to study. His most famous book, which Lévi-Provençal says is most representative of the culture of al-Andalus and which García Gómez has called the *Vita nuova* of Hispanic Islam, is *The Dove's Neck Ring* (*Tawq al-Hamama*), a treatise on love. Written at the request of a friend, the book discusses and illustrates by means of stories, verses, and personal reminiscences, the theory and practice of love in all its manifestations. He considers why and how people fall in love, including love at first sight, communication between the lovers by glances, signs, letters, and intermediaries, the pangs of separation from one's love, jealousy, the necessity of secrecy, and the destruction of the love relationship. His concept of love is essentially platonic. Although physical beauty is the immediate cause of love, and physical union is a part of love, he believes that love is basically the union or reunion of souls separated at creation. A few passages will reveal something of his style:

> I am jealous, because of you, of the glance of my eye;
> And I fear lest the touch of my hand make you melt . . .

> When I was prevented from being near to my lady
> And she insisted on avoiding me, and did not treat me justly;
> I began to content my eyes with her dress
> Or was contented with something she had touched.*

The similarity of his work to the theme of courtly love in Provençal lyric poetry and in Andreas Capellanus's *Art of Courtly Love* has been noted by many authors, including Nykl, his translator. Contrary to Jeanroy, who denies any influence of Ibn Hazm's work on courtly love, Parry has emphasized that the Spanish writer expresses two themes characteristic of courtly love, namely, the superiority of the beloved to her lover, and the ennobling influence of love. On the first point, for example, Ibn Hazm remarks, "The surprising thing which happens in love is the submissiveness of the lover to his beloved." Though he does not say in so many words that the lover's character is ennobled by his love, he does say that the lover tries to improve himself and to develop his good qualities so as to make himself more attractive to his lady: "And how many a stingy one became generous, and a gloomy one became bright faced, and a coward became brave, and a grouchy-dispositioned one became gay and an ignoramus became clever and a slovenly one in his personal appearance 'dolled up,' and an ill-shaped one became handsome" (*The Dove's Neck Ring*, tr. by A. R. Nykl, 16). The issue is still unresolved, but it seems likely that further ex-

---

* From a poem by Ibn Hazm, in A. R. Nykl, *Hispano-Arabic Poetry and its Relations with the Old Provençal Troubadours* (first published, Baltimore, 1946; reprinted 1970, by The Hispanic Society), 97; used with permission of The Hispanic Society.

ploration of the origins of courtly love will extend rather than lessen Ibn Hazm's role and that of other Spanish Muslim poets.

Ibn Hazm was also the author of a *Critical History of Religious Ideas*, a book hailed by many as the first comparative history of religion. In it he offered a sharp critique of Islamic belief, as well as of Judaism and Christianity, but his tendency toward rationalism and his opposition to the orthodox theologians caused his book to be burned at Seville. On hearing that, he is said to have remarked: "Do not speak to me of burnt vellum and paper; do not lament the information contained in them and destined for mankind. For if the books are burnt, their contents are not so; since they are still alive in my head" (Al-Maqqari, tr. by Pascual de Gayangos, I, 37). Watt has suggested that the connecting link between his theology and *The Dove's Neck Ring* is his concern for language as the instrument used by God to communicate with man. In the treatise on love Ibn Hazm tried to use both prose and poetry as skillfully as he could, and in his theological writings he emphasized the need to understand God's word in the Koran as clearly as possible. Although he had no followers, his approach to theological speculation heralded the dominant trend of the twelfth century.

If controversy rages concerning Hispano-Arabic influence upon the idea of courtly love, there is, on the contrary, general agreement as to the impact of the Spanish Muslims on the development of philosophical inquiry in western Christendom. Through translations made in Syria in the eighth and ninth centuries the Arabs had become acquainted with the Greek philosophers, especially Aristotle, and in the tenth century Alfarabi of Baghdad became the first important Muslim exponent of Aristotelian ideas. Of even greater influence was Ibn Sina or Avicenna (d. 1037), a universal genius, who endeavored to explicate Muslim belief in accordance with Aristotle's doctrine. Such efforts eventually provoked the hostility of al-Ghazzali or Algazel (d. 1111), a philosopher who came to the conclusion that rational speculation was idle and worthless, and so turned to mysticism. In his *Rebuttal of the Philosophers*, he pointed out the errors and contradictions, as he saw them, in the works of Alfarabi and Avicenna.

Algazel's writings had considerable influence upon Ibn Tumart, the founder of the Almohad movement, and this in turn had a direct bearing upon the development of philosophy in al-Andalus. Aside from Ibn Masarra in the tenth century there was little true philosophical study there before the twelfth century. The Malikite jurists took a dim view of philosophy, but they were also opposed to Algazel and caused his *Revival of Religious Sciences*, in which he expounded Muslim teaching, to be burned. When the Almohads came to power, the climate gradually changed, and debate concerning the views of the Aristotelians and of Algazel was permitted and even encouraged. Just before the Almohads gained control of Spain, Ibn Bajja or Avempace (d. 1138), the earliest of the Spanish Aristotelians, in his *Rule of the Solitary*, challenged some of Algazel's ideas and also emphasized the wise man's responsibility to remain detached from the corruption of the world.

The first to attempt an effective answer to Algazel was Ibn Tufayl (d. 1185), physician to the Almohad caliph and author of a philosophical novel or romance, called *Hayy ibn Yaqzan*, that is, *Alive, son of Awake*. This is the tale of a young man who from infancy is reared by a gazelle on a deserted island. Without family or friends or any human contact, but solely through the perception of his senses and the power of his intellect, he acquires knowledge of nature and the universe and a conception of God. He is a philosopher self-taught. His isolation ends with the coming of Asal, another young man, who in society had worked out a rational critique of religious orthodoxy and now sought to devote himself to contemplation. They discover through conversation that they have come to essentially the same conclusions and to the same idea of God and his relationship to man. But their attempt to propagate their views among the people of another island ends in failure. This leads Ibn Tufayl to the conclusion that while a few intellectuals may profit from the study of philosophy and philosophical religion, the masses are incapable of grasping these nuances and will always remain bound to the simple and ordinary teachings of religious orthodoxy.

The greatest of the Spanish philosophers, a pupil of Ibn Tufayl, was Ibn Rushd, known to the western world as Averroës (1126–1198). A distinguished jurist, *qadi* of Córdoba and physician attending the caliph, he had a profound influence upon western European philosophy. Immersing himself in the study of Aristotle, whom he regarded as exemplifying the highest development of the human intellect, he sought to purify his doctrine of Neoplatonic elements intruded into it and reflected in the writings of Avicenna, and he also set out to refute Algazel in a book called *The Rebuttal of the Rebuttal*. His major works consisted of commentaries on Aristotle: (1) the middle commentaries, in which he gave the content of Aristotle but in such a way that it was not easy to distinguish it from Averroës' explanations; (2) the great commentaries, in which he presented portions of Aristotle's writing followed by his commentary, and (3) the little commentaries which summarized Aristotle's conclusions.

Averroës tried to harmonize religion and philosophy without synthesizing them or obliterating differences between them. He was aware that there were apparent contradictions between what one believed through religious faith and what one grasped by the use of reason, and he held that both philosophy and revealed religion were true. But he did not teach the so-called double truth, namely, that a proposition may be true in theology while its opposite is true in philosophy. Rather he argued that the truth is comprehended on different levels depending upon one's learning and education. The ordinary uneducated man accepts revelation in the Koran without further ado, whereas a man of reasonable education seeks rational explanation for the truths of revelation, and the philosopher in the fullest sense of the term tries to achieve a complete and absolute demonstration of religious truth. There is then no contradiction between religious and philosophical truth, though there may be differences in the comprehension of that truth.

Muslim scholars had little enthusiasm for Averroës, whose approach they found too rationalistic. Through the intervention of the Malikites he was exiled to Morocco in 1196, where he died two years later. The measure of his rejection by the Muslim world is suggested by the fact that scarely any of his Arabic writings survive. His teaching is known principally through Latin or Hebrew translations made in the thirteenth century. His commentaries caused great perplexity in northern Europe, partly because of the difficulty of determining what was Aristotelian doctrine and what was commentary, and partly because he held views unacceptable to orthodox Christians, such as his denial of the immortality of the individual soul. In general, Christians held both Aristotle and Averroës in suspicion for most of the thirteenth century, until direct translations of Aristotle's works from the Greek were made available. On the other hand, a group of scholars known as Latin Averroists, whose leading exponent was Siger of Brabant, openly proclaimed themselves followers of Averroës, thereby incurring the opposition of the hierarchy and of theologians such as Thomas Aquinas.

While Christian Europe was attempting to meet the challenge of Averroës's thought, another Spaniard, Ibn al-Arabi (d. 1240), was spreading a new mystical gospel throughout the Islamic world. After studying at Seville he went on pilgrimage to Mecca about the beginning of the thirteenth century and spent the rest of his life in the east, until his death at Damascus. His doctrines, which are confused and contradictory, drew heavily upon Neoplatonic theories and also seem to reflect Christian influences. But his pantheism and monism of being ran counter to orthodox belief; moreover by describing himself as the "seal of the saints" who would fulfill the "seal of the prophets," Muhammad himself, he seemed to be downgrading the prophet. Asín Palacios has noted the resemblance between Dante's *Divine Comedy* and Ibn al-Arabi's description of a journey from hell to paradise, based upon the story of Muhammad's ascent to heaven. In spite of his unorthodox views, his influence, especially in the eastern world, was immense.

Religious and philosophical speculation obviously had an important place in the intellectual history of al-Andalus in the eleventh and twelfth centuries, but scientific study also attracted many scholars, some of whom had considerable influence beyond their own country. Among them were al-Zarqali (d. 1087), or Azarquiel, compiler of the astronomical tables that served as the basis for tables prepared under the direction of Alfonso X; Ibn Zuhr, or Avenzoar (d. 1162), whose medical treatises were translated into Latin; and al-Bitruji, or Alpetragius (d. 1202), whose *Book of Astronomy*, based on Aristotle's *Physics*, was translated into Latin and gave rise to controversy with the defenders of the Ptolemaic system of the universe.

Of the writers of history during this period, reference has been made to Ibn Hayyan (d. 1076) whose extant historical work is concerned with the caliphal era. A unique source consists of the memoirs of Abd Allah, one of the *reyes de taifas*, the last Zirid king of Granada (1073–1090), who had the misfortune to be deposed by the Almoravids and sent into exile in North Africa. Only three fragments of his work, covering the years 1064–1077 and 1080–1089, are extant, but they are full of information relating to the petty kingdoms, to Yusuf ibn Tashufin, and to Alfonso VI. The work of another writer, Ibn al-Qama (d. 1116), describing the siege and capture of Valencia by the Cid, survives only in passages translated in Christian chronicles of the thirteenth and fourteenth centuries. The principal contemporary source for the history of the Almohads is the chronicle of Ibn Sahib al-Sala (d. c. 1200–1210), secretary to the Caliph Yusuf I. Only the second of his three volumes survives. This work, relating the history of the Almohad caliphs, and covering the years 1159–1173, has exceptional importance, as Huici has pointed out, because it is the only record by a contemporary with access to first-hand information. Dedicated exclusively to the Almohad empire, it is accurate and detailed, and includes a number of documents, its only fault being the author's adulation of the caliphs. Somewhat later Abd al-Wahid al-Marrakushi (d. 1224), a native of al-Andalus, who settled in the east in 1217, wrote a history of the Muslim west in response to the request of a friend. A pleasant and entertaining author, he reviewed the history of Muslim Spain from the conquest to the Almoravids and treated the Almohad era somewhat more fully, but his account of contemporary events is based largely upon a faulty memory.

Finally, mention should be made of Ibn Bassam (d. 1147) and Ibn Bashkuwal (d. 1182), both of whom compiled biographical dictionaries, giving information about literary figures; Abu Bakr of Tortosa (d. 1130), whose *Light of Princes*, a book of moral instruction for rulers, is full of historical anecdotes, and al-Shaqundi (d. 1231), the author of *In Praise of Spanish Islam*, in which he records the literary and cultural achievements of his people, in response to the deprecating challenge of a Moroccan author.

Jewish Literature and Learning

The attention traditionally given to study in the Jewish communities bore wonderful fruit in the eleventh and twelfth centuries, a truly Golden Age in the history of medieval Judaism. In the Umayyad era, Hasday ibn Shaprut is said to have welcomed to Córdoba several distinguished Jewish scholars from the east who gave impetus to the development of Talmudic studies in Spain. During the period of the *taifas*, Samuel ibn Naghrila (d. c. 1056), *wazir* of the king of Granada, acted as patron and protector of scholars, and achieved fame as the author of a commentary on the Talmud and of some other treatises now lost. He also wrote poetry, though it is not considered of high quality.

Among those who enjoyed his protection was Solomon ibn Gabirol (d. 1070), a native of Málaga, who spent most of his life at Zaragoza where he died. He has been hailed as one of the great poets of medieval Jewry. His Arabic poems celebrate secular themes, but his Hebrew religious poetry has long been used in the synagogues. His most famous hymn, *The Kingly Crown*, included in the Sephardic ritual for the Day of Atonement, extols God's goodness and power and calls upon Him to be merciful and forgiving of men. The following passages in Husik's translation reveal something of the style of this beautiful prayer:

Thou art light, and the eyes of every pure soul shall see thee; for the clouds of iniquity alone hide thee from her sight. . . . Thou art most high, and the eye of the intellect desireth and longeth for thee; but it can only see a part, it cannot see the whole of thy greatness . . . Thou art wise, and wisdom which is the fountain of life, floweth from thee; and compared with thy wisdom, the knowledge of mankind is folly.*

Ibn Gabirol was known to the Latin west, however, as Avicebron, the author of a major philosophical work called *Fons Vitae*, the *Fountain of Life*. The Arabic original of this work is no longer extant; the Latin translation was done by Domingo González and Joannes Hispanus. Nowhere does Ibn Gabirol give any indication of his Jewish origin, either by citing the Bible or the Talmud, nor does he attempt to reconcile his religious belief with philosophy. It is not surprising, therefore, that the Latin scholastics thought he was an Arab, or that his influence upon Jewish philosophy was negligible. The *Fountain of Life* is a speculative treatise inspired by Neoplatonism, although, according to Husik, it lacks literary grace and tends to be rather confused and tedious. Ibn Gabirol's development of the hylomorphic theory, attributing matter and form to spiritual as well as corporeal beings, had the greatest impact upon the Latins. His notion of a universal being composed of matter and form became the source of controversy later between Thomists and Scotists. He tended to personify the Will of God and to treat it as an emanation from the divine nature. All inferior beings emanated from the Divine Will, which he saw as bringing the universe into being and conserving it. Although generally neglected by his fellow Jews, Ibn Gabirol had a considerable influence upon the Augustinian school among the Latin scholastics of the thirteenth and fourteenth centuries.

The study of philosophy among the Spanish Jews eventually evoked an outspoken attack by Judah Halevi (d. c. 1150), one of the greatest Jewish poets and a prophet in his own time. A native of Toledo and a physician, he traveled widely among the Jewish communities in Spain and gradually developed an intense awareness of the unique place of

* From *The Kingly Crown*, by Solomon ibn Gabirol, in Isaac Husik, *A History of Mediaeval Jewish Philosophy* (New York: Harper, Torchbook ed., 1966), 76; used with permission of The Jewish Publication Society of America.

the Jews in history. This eventually led him to protest against the efforts of some Jewish leaders to seek favors and places at the courts of Christian and Muslim rulers as a means of securing the safety of the Jewish people. For these reasons, toward the close of his life he decided to return to Palestine, the home of his ancestors. He reached Damascus, but it is not known certainly whether he got to Jerusalem. Halevi was a poet of extraordinary beauty, whose works include poems of love and worldly pleasures as well as beautiful hymns such as the following:

> Spirit and flesh are Thine,
> O Heavenly Shepherd mine;
> My hopes, my thoughts, my fears, Thou seest all;
> Thou measurest my path, my steps dost know.
> When Thou upholdest, who can make me fall?
> When Thou restrainest, who can bid me go?
> O would that I might be
> A servant unto Thee,
> Thou God by all adored.
> Then though by friends outcast,
> Thy hand would hold me fast
> And draw me near to Thee, my King and Lord.*

The unique relationship between God and the people of Israel is the theme of Halevi's principal work, the *Kusari*. As a defense of Judaism against contemporary threats from rationalism and from Christian and Muslim supremacy, it has a similarity to St. Augustine's *City of God*, and Baer thinks that Halevi may even have read that work of apologetics. The *Kusari* is based upon the story of the tenth-century king of the Khazars, a Turkish people settled in the Caucasus, who were converted to Judaism, after the king had consulted with a Muslim, a Christian, and a Jew. In the form of a dialogue between the king and a rabbi, Halevi sets forth the superiority of Judaism to other religions and points out the defects of philosophy. He is familiar with the terminology of the Neoplatonists and to some extent of the Aristotelians, but he rejects the attempt by the philosophers to develop a natural theology. Rational speculation, in his view, can never fathom the mystery of God nor offer a certain guide for man's conduct. We know God through revelation, and this is the only sure foundation for religion.

Although certain Jewish aristocrats were attracted to and influenced

* From a poem by Judah Halevi, in *The Standard Book of Jewish Verse*, compiled by Joseph Friedlander, ed., G. A. Kohut (New York: Dodd, Mead, 1917), 436–437; used with permission of Dodd, Mead & Co.

by the current ascendancy of Muslims and Christians, Halevi emphasized that God and Israel were joined by a very special bond not shared
by other peoples. The Jews are God's Chosen People, to whom He
gave the original language, a sacred language, Hebrew, a special homeland, Palestine, and a law, the Torah, all as distinctive marks of His
favor. Through all the travail of history, God has maintained and preserved the Jewish people, and for Judah Halevi this is the best evidence
of God's existence. In his book Halevi appealed to his fellow Jews to
become more fully conscious of the authenticity and continued viability
of their tradition and history and not to be beguiled by rationalism nor
by the deceptions of Christians and Muslims.

His contemporary, the poet Moses ibn Ezra (d. 1135), who fled
from the terror of the Almoravids to the kingdom of Castile, shared
Halevi's fears and expressed his sorrow that some of his coreligionists
were beginning to adopt the ways of their Christian neighbors:

> Fortune has hurled me to a land where the lights of my understanding
> dimmed
> And the stars of my reason were beclouded with the murk of falter-
> ing knowledge and stammering speech.
> I have come to the iniquitous domain of a people scorned by God and
> accursed by man
> Amongst savages who love corruption and set an ambush for the
> blood of the righteous and innocent.
> They have adopted their neighbors' ways, anxious to enter their midst
> And mingling with them they share their deeds and are now reckoned
> among their number.
> Those nurtured, in their youth, in the gardens of truth, hew, in old
> age, the wood of forests of folly.*

In spite of Halevi's strictures against philosophy, twelfth-century
Jews were much attracted to the new ideas of Aristotle being disseminated throughout Spain. The first of the Spanish Jews to be fully
acquainted with Aristotle, albeit through the writings of Arabic philosophers, was Abraham ibn Daud (d. c. 1180). In his book, *Exalted Faith*,
he set out to achieve a harmony between the tenets of Judaism and
Aristotelian philosophy. His work was thorough and systematic, but
he has generally been overshadowed, and nearly ignored, because of
the attainments of Moses Maimonides, a younger contemporary. Ibn

* From a poem by Moses ibn Ezra, in Yitzhak Baer, *A History of the Jews in
Christian Spain* (Philadelphia: The Jewish Publication Society, 1966), I, 63–64; used
with permission of The Jewish Publication Society of America.

Daud also wrote an historical treatise, *A Book of Tradition*, which is valuable for the history of the Jewish communities in Spain.

The greatest of the Jewish Aristotelians was Moses Maimonides (d. 1204). Born at Córdoba, he was forced by the intolerance of the Almohads to abandon his homeland, going first to Morocco and finally to Egypt where, until his death, he served as physician to Saladin. His principal writings were the *Mishneh Torah*, a Hebrew code of law; a commentary in Arabic on the *Mishnah*; and the Arabic *Guide for the Perplexed*. Written in Egypt around 1190, the last-named work was translated into both Hebrew and Latin. Maimonides says he wrote it for philosophers who found difficulty in reconciling their religious beliefs with the truths discovered by human reason.

His purpose was to harmonize religion and reason, to establish the rational and philosophical supports for revealed truth. Whenever possible, he tried to provide rational explanations or arguments for basic religious tenets, such as the existence of God, the creation of the world, the freedom of the will, and so on. He drew these arguments from Aristotle whom he regarded as exemplifying the fullest development of human reason. He employed no less than twenty-six rational proofs for the existence of the one God, some of them akin to those used later by Thomas Aquinas. But he was aware of the limitations of philosophy and realized that in some instances it was impossible to demonstrate the truths of religion by means of reason. Thus one accepts the creation of the world as described in the Book of Genesis as a tenet of one's faith, though it cannot be demonstrated by philosophy. In this respect his attitude was similar to that of Aquinas, and in general his approach to all these questions was very much like that of the scholastics.

Though Aquinas and other Christians spoke of Maimonides with respect, his work aroused a storm of controversy among the Jews throughout the world, who already recognized him as a master of the Talmud. Whereas the intellectuals found his exposition of religion in accordance with reason attractive and helpful, the traditionalists were scandalized by what they believed to be the rationalization of religion. The attack on Maimonides began in Spain and quickly spread into France. Attempts there to ban his writings evoked countercondemnations from those who adhered to Maimonides's teaching. The controversy reached such intensity that the enemies of Maimonides allegedly called upon the papal inquisition in southern France early in the thirteenth century to cause the destruction of his work. Thus, as Baer has noted, one significant effect of the dispute was the intrusion of the inquisition into Jewish concerns.

From the foregoing it is clear that the cultural level of the Muslims and Jews of the eleventh and twelfth centuries was considerably higher than that of the Christians of northern Spain. The Christians were still preoccupied with military affairs and the colonization of reconquered territory. Only gradually did they begin to devote themselves to formal study and to take advantage of the opportunity to study abroad in the emerging Universities of Paris and Bologna. One can find evidence of an increasing number of educated clergymen, men trained in theology, civil and canon law, in the latter part of the twelfth century, and one can find evidence of foreign masters who accepted teaching positions in Christian Spain, but the fruition of their work came only in the thirteenth century.

PART IV

❧❧

The Great Reconquest and the Beginnings of Overseas Expansion

1212—1369

Christus, Deus et homo, ex parte nostra. Ex parte vero maurorum, infidelis et dampnatus apostata Machumetus.

Quid ergo restat?

On our side, Christ, God and Man. On the Moors', the faithless and damned apostate, Muhammad.

What more is there to say?

Chronique latine des rois de Castille, 43

CHAPTER 14

The Great Reconquest

The Thirteenth Century

The thirteenth century saw the rapid reconquest of the greater part of al-Andalus, the definitive formation of the Christian states, and the beginnings of Catalan expansion into the Mediterranean area. The Almohads never fully recovered from the staggering blow suffered at Las Navas de Tolosa in 1212, and as a result, in the years following, conspiracies, rebellions, and civil wars were chronic among the Muslims of al-Andalus and Morocco. The Hafsids eventually broke with the Almohads and established an independent state in Tunisia, while in the western regions of Morocco, the Banu Marin (Benimerines or Marinids) steadily consolidated their power and, after occupying Marrakech, brought about the downfall of the last Almohad caliph in 1269. Long before that date al-Andalus had ceased to be ruled by the Almohads, but the petty kings who replaced them were incapable of preventing the advance of Christian armies to the south.

In the reconquest the Christian states completed their expansion and defined the frontiers that they were to retain with only minor changes until the close of the medieval era. Navarre, the smallest of all, cut off from further territorial expansion in the twelfth century, passed under the rule of a French dynasty, and for some time thereafter her fortunes were linked with those of France. In the west, Portugal penetrated into the Algarve, thus achieving her ultimate limits; Aragon in the east overran Valencia and also conquered Majorca. In so doing she embarked upon the first stage of a significant Mediterranean expansion, laying the foundations of the future Spanish overseas empire. In the center of the peninsula, Castile occupied the valley of the Guadalquivir, so that by the middle of the century all that remained to the Muslims was the kingdom of Granada whose rulers were compelled to pay tribute to

333

Castile. Insofar as Castile was the only Christian state whose borders touched upon Granada, she alone had any evident role to play in the reconquest in the future; she alone could expect to profit from the conquest of the last Muslim stronghold in Spain.

The Minorities of Jaime I and Enrique I

The early medieval period came to a close with the demise of the two sovereigns, Pedro II of Aragon, vanquished at Muret, and Alfonso VIII of Castile, the conqueror of Las Navas de Tolosa. Their successors, Jaime I and Enrique I, as well as the new Almohad Caliph, Yusuf al-Mustansir, were minors. As usual, the nobility of the three realms attempted to usurp royal authority, revenues, and estates.

At the time of his father's death Jaime I of Aragon (1213–1276) was five years of age and a virtual prisoner of Simon de Montfort, whose daughter he was intended to marry. The death of his mother, Marie of Montpellier, left him entirely an orphan. The Aragonese nobility appealed to Pope Innocent III, who, as suzerain of Aragon, persuaded de Montfort to release the king to the papal legate, Cardinal Peter of Benevento, in May 1214. The legate summoned a meeting in August at Lérida of Catalan and Aragonese bishops, magnates, and "other prudent men" to arrange for the government of the realm. Jaime I was duly acknowledged as sovereign, and his great-uncle, Sanç, count of Rousillon, was appointed procurator with authority to govern the realm. As a guarantee of tranquility during the critical years ahead, the Peace and Truce of God was proclaimed, and a truce was arranged with the Almohads. The king and his young cousin, Ramon Berenguer V, count of Provence, were delivered into the custody of the master of the Temple who lodged them in a fortress at Monzón. Although the royal chronicle implies that the king was imprisoned there so that his great-uncle could usurp the throne, there is no evidence to substantiate this allegation.

The procurator's first concern was to avenge his nephew Pedro II. For this reason he supplied military forces to Raymond VI who hoped to recover the county of Toulouse from Simon de Montfort. De Montfort had been recognized by the Fourth Lateran Council as count of Toulouse, viscount of Béziers and Carcassonne and duke of Narbonne. Although Raymond was able to re-enter the city of Toulouse in September 1217, Pope Honorius III immediately demanded that the Aragonese withdraw their assistance under threat of ecclesiastical censure and even of a crusade; therefore, Sanç desisted from further intervention in Languedoc. Even so, after de Montfort's death in 1218, Raymond VI and his son were able to recover much of the county. In the meantime the Aragonese bishops and magnates had undermined the procurator's authority and had secured the release of Jaime I from the castle of Monzón. Sanç had no choice but to resign. In effect, Jaime I, aged a mere ten years, was thought fit to administer his affairs himself.

During the next several years while he was growing up the nobles threw the kingdom into great disorder. Those principally responsible for this unhappy state of affairs were the very counselors nominated by the pope. In this atmosphere of intrigue, conspiracy, and rebellion, the king's character was formed. He learned gradually to adapt himself to the habits of his adversaries and by 1227, through guile and force, succeeded in overcoming them and in restoring a semblance of order to the realm.

Meanwhile the kingdom of Castile was also undergoing the travail of a royal minority. After the death of Alfonso VIII in 1214 (and that of Queen Leonor a few weeks later) the throne was occupied by his eleven-year-old son, Enrique I (1214–1217), under the guardianship of his older sister Berenguela, a woman of great prudence, wisdom, and energy. Challenged by a faction among the magnates who demanded custody of the king, she agreed to entrust him to Count Alvaro Núñez de Lara, as procurator, under the following conditions: that he not make war against any neighboring state, nor deprive anyone of his estates, nor grant property to anyone, nor impose any tribute, without her consent. The count subsequently paid little heed to these restrictions and by his offensive conduct brought the kingdom to the verge of civil war. Suddenly, however, his ambitions were wrecked when Enrique I, while playing with some companions, was struck on the head by a stone and died a few days later in June 1217.

Although Count Alvaro tried to keep the king's death a secret, Berenguela discovered the truth and promptly summoned her son Fernando from León where he was living with his father, Alfonso IX. As the oldest surviving child of Alfonso VIII, Berenguela could claim the kingdom for herself, but on the petition of the people in an assembly at Valladolid on 2 July, she yielded her rights to her son, Fernando III (1217–1252), who was proclaimed king of Castile. Berenguela deliberately concealed from Alfonso IX, her former husband, news of her brother's death and her intention to surrender the kingdom to Fernando III. When he discovered what had happened, Alfonso IX considered the possibility of attempting to unite León and Castile under his own rule and, encouraged by appeals from Count Alvaro, who hoped to regain his lost influence, invaded Castile. As the summer wore on, however, he realized that there was little support for his cause, and withdrew to his own kingdom. Father and son made peace in August 1218, promising to live in harmony with one another and to undertake joint action against the Muslims. With her son's accession assured, Berenguela now arranged his marriage to Beatrice, daughter of Philip of Swabia and granddaughter of Frederick Barbarossa. The wedding was solemnized in 1219 at Burgos in "a most memorable council . . . to which a multitude of magnates, knights and chief men of the cities had been summoned." This union established the first important link between Castile and Germany and gave the future Alfonso X, the child of the royal couple, his claims to the Holy Roman Empire.

In the Almohad dominions, Abu Yaqub Yusuf, al-Mustansir (1213–1224) succeeded his father, al-Nasir, as caliph. Still in adolescence, he was easily dominated by the Almohad tribal lords, but the Muslim chroniclers are unanimous in speaking of the tranquility of his reign and note that he undertook no military expeditions. Truces concluded with Castile and Aragon minimized warfare with the Christians.

On the other hand, the Portuguese, assisted by a fleet of crusaders on their way to the Holy Land to take part in the Fifth Crusade, conquered Alcácer do Sal. A combined German-Frisian fleet under the leadership of Count William of Holland and Count George of Wied left the English channel in June 1217. When they arrived at Lisbon in late July, Bishop Sueiro persuaded them to join in an attack on Alcácer do Sal, a strongly fortified position at the mouth of the Sado river that had served as a base for Muslim raids in the vicinity of Lisbon. While the Germans with about 180 ships agreed to collaborate, the Frisians continued their journey to the east, plundering the Muslim ports of Santa Maria de Faro and Rota and occupying Cádiz, whose inhabitants fled before them. The German fleet reached Alcácer on 30 July, while the Portuguese forces, led by the bishops of Lisbon and Evora, and the military Orders, arrived three days later. The caliph ordered troops from Seville, Córdoba, and Jaén to relieve the beleaguered fortress, but they were repulsed on 11 September. A month later, on 18 October, the hapless defenders surrendered Alcácer, and the road to the Algarve was opened to the Portuguese.

The conquest of Alcácer was planned and executed without the intervention of Afonso II of Portugal. From the beginning of his reign, his principal concern was not to seek fame in battle with the Muslims, but to bolster and consolidate royal power. His quarrel with his sisters over their inheritance was settled in 1216 by a compromise which safeguarded the ultimate rights of the crown to the properties in dispute, while guaranteeing the princesses a life revenue. His efforts to curb the dissipation of the resources of the royal patrimony also brought him into violent conflict with the bishops and secular lords. From 1216 onward he began to review charters granted by his predecessors, reserving the right to confirm them or not. Four years later he dispatched commissioners into the provinces to conduct inquisitions into the condition of great estates. Local people were summoned to testify under oath concerning land tenure, seigneurial rights, rights of patronage of churches and monasteries and the like. In this way it was expected that usurpations of royal rights and properties would be discovered. Of course, the landlords, both lay and ecclesiastical, were antagonized by these proceedings.

The prelates were also angered by the king's violation of ecclesiastical immunities, for example, by his insistence upon receiving hospitality for himself and his entourage, by his trial of clerics in civil courts, and the like. Estevão Soares da Silva, the aggressive archbishop of Braga, after his remonstrances went unheeded, excommunicated the king and placed the kingdom under interdict and then fled to Rome to appeal to Pope Honorius III who agreed to release the king's subjects from their oath of fealty; but the issue was still unresolved when the king died, a victim of leprosy, on 25 March 1223.

The reign of his son, Sancho II (1223–1248), a boy about twelve years of age, began in difficult circumstances. His counselors reached a settlement with the archbishop, pledging to indemnify the church for damages done by royal officials and to punish those responsible for such outrages. Once this had been done the archbishop promised to lift the interdict, to absolve the dead king from the sentence of excommunication, and to allow his burial in consecrated ground. For the moment, peace reigned in Portugal, but the old quarrels flared again with even greater bitterness and eventually led to the new king's deposition.

The Collapse of the Almohad Empire

When the uneventful reign of Caliph al-Mustansir came to an end in January 1224, a struggle for power commenced among the Almohads, and their empire began to suffer the long process of disintegration. While Abd al-Wahid succeeded to the caliphate in Morocco, the Almohad princes in al-Andalus seemed intent on returning to the old regime of the *taifas*. Al-Adil, governor of Murcia, proclaimed himself as caliph (1224–1227) and was recognized by Seville, Córdoba, and Granada. On the other hand, Abu Zayd, governor of Valencia, remained steadfast in his allegiance to the caliph in Morocco, at least for the time being; but his brother, Abu Muhammad, declared his independence in Baeza, whence the name by which he was commonly known, al-Bayasi. The Moroccan Almohads deposed and executed Abd al-Wahid in September, thereby making it possible for al-Adil to cross the straits and to take possession of Marrakech. At his departure, however, the loyalty of al-Andalus to his cause was very much in doubt.

The sudden breakdown of government in al-Andalus offered excellent opportunities to the Christian princes. For some time Alfonso IX had been raiding the neighborhood of Cáceres, a fortress blocking his advance to Badajoz and Mérida on the Guadiana river; bad harvests and consequent famine, however, prevented Fernando III from undertaking any military campaigns until 1224. After taking Quesada in September he received a pledge of homage and fealty from al-Bayasi and his brother Abu Zayd of Valencia, who evidently hoped to establish themselves more securely with Castilian support. Al-Bayasi accompanied Fernando III on his devastation of the countryside about Jaén and Granada in the summer of 1225 and as a warranty of his good faith surrendered Martos and Andújar to him. After the king returned to Toledo, al-Bayasi, aided by Castilian troops, defeated his opponents outside Seville and won the support of Córdoba and of many other towns and fortresses. This was the high point of his career, but his dependence upon Castile was revealed to everyone when he humbly acquiesced to Fernando III's demand that he surrender several fortresses and admit a Castilian garrison into the citadel of Baeza. Al-Bayasi and the Castilians made a second, though less fortunate attack on Seville in March 1226; the defeat cost al-Bayasi the allegiance of most of the places that had acknowledged him in the previous year. The Córdobans, fearing that he would admit the Christians into their city, rose in rebellion and drove him out to Almodóvar, where he was assassinated. At news of his death the Castilian garrison in Baeza occupied the town, and the inhabitants fled.

Since al-Adil's withdrawal to Morocco the responsibility for the defense of Almohad interests in al-Andalus rested with his brother, Abu-l-Ala, governor of Seville. Lack of support from Morocco, as well as a supreme confidence in his own ability, induced him to proclaim himself caliph and to assume the honorific name al-Mamun (1227–1232). Though he expected to be recognized by the Almohads in Marrakech, they betrayed him by executing his brother and placing his nephew Yahya (1227–1236) on the throne. A long war between uncle and nephew followed, giving encouragement to rebels on both sides of the straits.

A major uprising against al-Mamun in al-Andalus was not long in coming. Ibn Hud (1228–1238), said to belong to the lineage of the kings of Zaragoza, raised the standard of revolt in Murcia in August 1228, charging the Almohads with oppression and declaring himself the liberator of the people. Unlike other rebels who pretended to the caliphal title, he put himself forward as a representative of the Abbasid caliph of Baghdad and began to massacre the Almohads as heretics. Al-Mamun was unable to crush the rebellion, and since the need to establish himself in Marrakech was pressing, he left Spain for Morocco in the summer of 1229. Ibn Abi Zar avers that he obtained 12,000 men from Fernando III on condition that he cede ten border fortresses and erect a church in Marrakech, but this is untrue; he did conclude a truce of one year with Castile and took 500 Christian soldiers with him, but these, like others who had served the Almoravids and Almohads in the past, were chiefly adventurers and exiles willing to fight anywhere for pay. With his departure, Almohad rule in al-Andalus ceased. Ibn Hud was acknowledged by Almería, Granada, Jaén, Córdoba, and Málaga; and even Seville, long the chief seat of the Almohads in Spain, opened its gates to him (October 1229). Within a year he became master of the greater part of al-Andalus, with the exception of Valencia, Niebla, and the Algarve.

But he was no more able than the other Muslim leaders to stop the Christian reconquest. After taking Cáceres in the summer of 1227, Alfonso IX pressed his advance to the Guadiana and laid seige to Mérida. As the acknowledged champion of Spanish Islam, Ibn Hud was duty bound to attempt to relieve the city, but he suffered a rout near Alange, southeast of Mérida; according to Lucas of Túy, "the blessed St. James visibly appeared in this battle with a host of white knights, who valiantly overthrew the Moors." Whatever the truth of this story of saintly intervention may be, Mérida capitulated in March 1230. The

Muslim defenders also abandoned Elvas which was occupied by Portuguese knights in the name of Sancho II, who also seized Juromenha on the Guadiana. In the meantime Alfonso IX moved westward along the river to Badajoz which surrendered after a brief siege. A bishopric was established there, but the old metropolitan see of Mérida was not restored because of the opposition of the archbishop of Compostela.

The road to Seville now lay open before Alfonso IX, but the honor of conquering that metropolis was not to be his. He died on 24 September and was buried at Compostela. A sovereign of great capability, he has often been charged with a greater concern for his own pride and self-interest than for the good of Christian Spain. His desire to uphold his rights and the integrity of his kingdom against the threat of domination by Alfonso VIII is understandable, but his alliance with the Almohads in Castile's gravest hour was not to his credit. In the last fifteen years of his reign he devoted his energy principally to the reconquest and helped make possible his son's eventual conquest of the chief cities in Andalusia.

Fernando III had just returned from a fruitless attempt to besiege Jaén when he learned of his father's death. He immediately set out for León to claim the throne, though he was not without competitors. Alfonso IX had never publicly settled the question of the succession, and besides Fernando III, his son by Berenguela of Castile, he had two surviving daughters by Teresa of Portugal, his first wife. Both marriages had been dissolved on the grounds of consanguinity. The possibility of civil war was averted by the two former queens, Berenguela and Teresa, who negotiated a settlement at Benavente on 11 December 1230. The *infantas* renounced their claims in favor of Fernando III who promised each of them an annual pension. Thus at last and for all time to come, the kingdoms of León and Castile, so often separated in the past, were reunited, and their total resources were made available to Fernando III for the task of destroying the remnants of Muslim power in Spain.

Jaime I and the Conquest of Majorca

While the other Christian rulers were waging war against the Almohads, Jaime I of Aragon, known to later history as the Conqueror, carried out his first major enterprise. As he grew to manhood he suppressed revolt and strengthened his grasp on his kingdom and developed his interest in the reconquest. The curtailment of Catalan interests in

Languedoc as a result of his father's defeat and death at Muret perhaps inclined him to consider more seriously the possibilities of expansion within the peninsula. Upon the expiration of the truce arranged at the beginning of his reign, he vainly attempted to capture the impregnable fortress of Peñíscola in 1225, and ravaged the district of Teruel in the next year. These campaigns did not enhance his reputation for prowess, but they did induce Abu Zayd, lord of Valencia, to offer tribute to him.

While expansion southward into the territory of Valencia was a logical undertaking, one in which the nobles of Aragon were specially interested, Jaime I's initial success was the conquest of Majorca. Centuries earlier the Muslims had wrested the Balearic Islands from the Byzantine empire, but after the collapse of the caliphate of Córdoba, the islands, together with Denia on the mainland, formed one of the *taifas*. The Almoravids later occupied the islands, but after their downfall the Banu Ganiya established their independence there and defied Almohad efforts to conquer them. For several years the Banu Ganiya used Majorca as a base from which to attempt the conquest of parts of North Africa. The Almohads succeeded in gaining control of the islands in 1203, but after the caliph's death in 1224, they became independent again.

For more than a century the Catalans had been interested in the conquest of Majorca. Count Ramon Berenguer III joined a Pisan expedition which overran the island in 1114, but the occupation was only temporary. Since then, numerous projects for conquest had been suggested, and by the early thirteenth century the Catalans themselves possessed the naval power necessary to complete the task. The coming of age of Catalan maritime enterprise is indicated by Jaime I's privilege to the merchants of Barcelona in 1227, just before the expedition to Majorca, stipulating that Catalan exports to Ceuta, Alexandria, and other places should be carried in ships of Barcelona, rather than those of Genoa or Marseille. As the Catalans participated more actively in Mediterranean commerce, they also encountered the characteristic risks of the sea, including piracy. Majorca was a notorious base for pirates, whose attacks on Catalan ships prompted Jaime I to demand restitution; on receiving a hostile response from Abu Yahya, king of Majorca, he declared war, and as Desclot relates, "swore to God that he didn't wish to be called king if he failed to seize (his enemy) by the beard." Possession of Majorca and the other islands would guarantee the Catalans against piracy in the future, actively stimulate Catalan commercial development, and perhaps lead to closer ties with the Levant.

Thus the king, who was then about twenty years of age, summoned the Catalan *corts* to Barcelona in December 1228 and announced his intention to undertake the conquest of Majorca. The assembly lauded his proposal and granted him an extraordinary *bovatge*, or aid, to help finance the expedition, even though this tax had been granted to him at the beginning of his reign and was not usually granted again. On instructions from Pope Gregory IX, the legate Cardinal Jean d'Abbeville offered crusade indulgences to all who accompanied the king. A large military force and a fleet of about 150 ships was assembled in the ports of Tarragona, Salou, and Cambrils.

Setting sail on 5 September 1229, the fleet immediately encountered a storm; although some advised the king to return to port, he insisted on continuing the journey. In sight of the Balearic Islands another storm came up, but a landing was made in the bay of Palma on the night of 8–9 September. After overcoming the first resistance of the Muslims the crusaders established the siege of the city of Palma and occupied part of the island. When negotiations for the surrender of Palma broke down, the crusaders assaulted the city on 31 December 1229 and with much butchery took possession of it. The king himself reported that, "as the Saracens told us, the first to enter on horseback was a white knight with white arms, and we believe that he was St. George, since we find in histories that Christians and Saracens have often seen him in other battles" (*Crònica de Jaume I*, 84). The king of Majorca was captured and died soon after.

The subjugation of the rest of the island was completed by Palm Sunday 1230. Most of the Muslim inhabitants chose to withdraw to the other islands or to North Africa, thereby making possible an intensive Catalan colonization. The *repartiment*, or book recording Jaime I's distribution of land and estates to those who aided in the conquest, has come down to us. The Catalan language and law, the *Usages of Barcelona*, were established throughout the island. Barcelona was granted freedom of trade with Majorca, and Genoa, Pisa, and Marseille were rewarded for their collaboration with the cession of houses and trading privileges.

The Muslims of Minorca recognized Jaime I as their sovereign in

July 1232 and surrendered several strategic castles to him, but the occupation of the island was not carried out until 1286. The king ceded the islands of Ibiza and Formentera as fiefs to the archbishop of Tarragona, who occupied them in 1235. The conquest of Majorca and the smaller islands was the first significant triumph for the king and the first step in the extension of Catalan power into the Mediterranean.

The Conquest of Córdoba, Valencia, and Murcia

As the situation of the Muslims in al-Andalus steadily worsened, the Christian rulers were encouraged to continue their offensive without letup. The Spanish Muslims had little reason to expect any useful assistance from their coreligionists in Morocco; there, al-Mamun, without having overcome his opponents, died in 1232, leaving the throne to his young son al-Rashid (1232–1242). While the civil war continued, the Hafsid family, under the leadership of Abu Zakariyya, established an independent emirate at Tunis. In the peninsula Ibn Hud controlled Seville, Córdoba, and Granada, and after occupying Algeciras and Gibraltar, made an unsuccessful attempt to dominate both sides of the straits by seizing Ceuta. His prestige was further enhanced by the arrival of an embassy from the Abbasid caliph who recognized him as his faithful servant. Ibn Hud failed, however, to compel Abu Zayd of Valencia to submit to him, and his authority apparently did not extend into the western region known as the Algarve. A serious rival now appeared to threaten him and to help bring about his downfall.

Ibn al-Ahmar (1232–1273), founder of the Nasrid dynasty and the kingdom of Granada—which survived until 1492—rose in revolt against Ibn Hud at Arjona in 1232. In Cagigas's view, his uprising was a reaction of the Hispano-Arab aristocracy against the popular movement headed by Ibn Hud. Once Ibn al-Ahmar declared himself, he was acclaimed by the people of Jaén, Carmona, and Córdoba. Seville also threw off its allegiance to Ibn Hud, but for the moment its citizens preferred to be governed by their qadi, who joined Ibn al-Ahmar in defeating their common enemy in 1234. Thereupon Ibn al-Ahmar murdered his ally and seized control of Seville, but the populace, angered by this treachery, drove him out, and Córdoba and Carmona also rejected his rule. Despite these upheavals, Ibn Hud was not able to gain any advantage and finally acknowledged his rival's rule in Arjona and Jaén. The agreement was intended to serve only until such time as either party felt strong enough to resume hostilities with a chance of ultimate victory.

Taking advantage of the discord in al-Andalus, Fernando III, assisted by the bishops, magnates, military Orders, and militia of the towns, carried out an offensive along a broad front. While he captured Ubeda (1233) and ravaged the territory around Arjona and Jaén, his vassals seized Trujillo, Medellín, Alange, Santa Cruz, and Magacela in Extremadura (1233–1235), thus advancing closer to Córdoba and Seville. At the same time, Sancho II of Portugal moved southward along the course of the Guadiana river, taking Moura and Serpa in 1232 and Aljustrel southwest of Beja in 1234.

The climax of this advance came quite unexpectedly at the close of 1235 when a small band of Castilians, helped by the Muslims within, gained entrance into one of the suburbs of Córdoba. Fernando III received their urgent summons for help at Benavente in León in mid-January 1236. Although he had recently concluded a truce with Ibn Hud, who promised to pay tribute, he felt that he could not fail to aid his vassals, who "for his service and the honor of the Christian faith had exposed themselves to such great danger." Setting out at once with only a few companions, he braved rainstorms and floods and rode rapidly by the most direct route to Córdoba, arriving on 7 February, to the great joy of his vassals. It was still some time, however, before an army could be assembled to besiege the city.

As expected, Ibn Hud came to relieve the city but advanced no farther than Ecija and then returned to Seville, leaving part of his army to watch in idleness while Córdoba suffered her final agony. As the spring came on, the besiegers destroyed the fields and tightened the siege. Realizing that no help was to be expected from Ibn Hud, the defenders offered to surrender. Once the "ornament of the world," the seat of the Umayyad caliphs, Córdoba capitulated on 29 June 1236. Fernando III allowed the inhabitants to leave, taking with them whatever they could carry, but if they wished to remain, they were free to continue the practice of their religion. The king of Castile was, as al-Himyari remarked, "a mild man, one with political sense." On the other hand, the great mosque with its labyrinth of columns and arches dating from the first Umayyads in Spain was consecrated as a cathedral. To repair an ancient wrong, as Archbishop Rodrigo tells us, "King Fernando caused to be carried back to the church of Santiago and restored to it, the bells of Santiago which . . . Almanzor had carried away to the mosque of Córdoba where, to the distress of the Christian people, they were hung as lamps" (*De rebus Hispaniae*, IX, 17). The king also required Ibn Hud to pay an annual tribute, part of which was due to Ibn al-Ahmar with whom Fernando III made an alliance just before the surrender of the city. The historian al-Maqqari summed up centuries of Muslim feeling when he noted that Córdoba had "passed into the hands of the accursed Christians (may God destroy them all!)."

The conquest of Córdoba opened the whole valley of the Guadalquivir to Fernando III, and in the next few years many towns and fortresses traditionally dependent on the city submitted to him. The loss of the city and the burden of paying an increased tribute was a grave blow to Ibn Hud's popularity. Sedition spread through al-Andalus, and in January 1238 he was murdered at Almería by one of his lieutenants. Ibn al-Ahmar derived the immediate profit from his rival's death; proclaimed as king at Málaga and Almería, he established his chief seat at Granada, where he began the fortifications which eventually became the palace of the Alhambra.

While Fernando III was engaged in the campaigns culminating in the conquest of Córdoba, Jaime I, the conqueror of Majorca, embarked upon the arduous task of subjugating the Muslim kingdom of Valencia. At his accession the Catalan frontier lay not too far south of Tortosa at the mouth of the Ebro river, and the Aragonese frontier lay beyond Teruel, but Jaime I as yet had made no gains in the area. For several years Abu Zayd, a descendant of the first Almohad caliph, served as governor of Valencia and enjoyed a *de facto* independence; but his hold weakened steadily, and in 1229 he was overthrown by Zayyan ibn Mardanish, a grandson of that Ibn Mardanish who had opposed the Almohads for so long in the late twelfth century. Abu Zayd took refuge with the Christians and even embraced their religion, taking the name of Vincent.

In view of the circumstances, Christian intervention in Valencian affairs was inevitable. The conquest of this rich and prosperous region held a particular attraction for the nobles of Aragon who looked forward to the prospect of booty and large estates for themselves. Jaime I, a born warrior imbued with the crusading spirit of the age, needed no urging to begin the campaign. Together with the bishops, nobles, and chiefs of the military Orders of the Temple, the Hospital, Santiago, and Calatrava, he took the crusader's vow at Monzón in 1232. Other crusaders came from Languedoc, where Pope Gregory IX authorized the preaching of the crusade. The conquest began with the taking of Mor-rella and Ares. The king penetrated deep into Valencian territory in July of the following year to besiege and capture Burriana on the coast; among the many other fortresses taken, were Villafamés, Pulpis, Chivert, Cervera, Cuevas de Vinromá, and Peñíscola in the northern region known as the Maestrazgo. These acquisitions opened the road to Valencia.

For about two years other concerns distracted the king from the con-tinuance of the campaign. The future of the kingdom of Navarre be-came a matter of some importance to him as the reign of Sancho VII, one of the heroes of Las Navas de Tolosa, drew to a close. Since he had no children, his proper heir was his sister Blanca, the wife of the count of Champagne. Jaime I, however, hoping to reunite Navarre and Aragon, persuaded Sancho VII (who had no liking for his brother-in-law) to adopt him as his heir in 1231. They also agreed to aid one another against Fernando III who, mindful of his predecessors' ambi-tion to partition or absorb Navarre, was watching the situation care-fully. When Sancho VII died in 1234, his nephew Thibault of Cham-pagne came to take possession of a kingdom rightfully his, and the Navarrese made it clear that they preferred him to Jaime I or Fernando III. Although both rulers were inclined to intervene, they accepted a situation they could not change. With the accession of Thibault I (1234–1253), the kingdom of Navarre passed into the hands of the Champagne dynasty, and thereafter its fortunes were closely tied to France. The new sovereign spent little time in his kingdom and, having no prospect of expanding it by reconquest of Muslim-held territory, went off on crusade to the Holy Land in 1238–1242, where he gained scant distinction.

Thwarted in his ambition to annex Navarre, Jaime I turned to the more congenial business of taking a second wife. His marriage to Leonor of Castile was nullified in 1229 on the usual grounds of con-sanguinity, though their son Alfonso was acknowledged as the legiti-mate heir to the throne. The king married Violante, daughter of King Andrew II of Hungary, in 1235. A strong-minded woman, she con-vinced her husband that he should award Majorca and his future con-quests in Valencia to the children yet to be born of their union, reserving only Catalonia and Aragon proper for Alfonso. The desire to provide an inheritance for his children by Violante was the source of much discord in later years, but at the moment it probably incited Jaime I to complete the conquest of Valencia.

After he renewed his crusader's vow at the *cortes* of Monzón in 1236 and received a new subsidy to finance the enterprise, he announced his intention to capture the city of Valencia. As he put it in his chronicle, "once we have the chicken, then we will also have the eggs." The assault on Valencia commenced when the Christian forces established themselves on the Puig de Cebolla (Puig de Santa Maria), a hill overlooking the city. Ibn Mardanish tried to drive them off but was severely beaten in 1237. Seeing the need for external support, he appealed to Abu Zakariyya, the Hafsid emir of Tunis, and recognized his sovereignty. A fleet bearing food, arms, and money sailed from Tunis in August 1238, but finding Valencia blockaded by the Christians, it landed the supplies at Denia, a considerable distance to the south, and returned home. Unable to obtain the supplies, Ibn Mardanish found himself on the verge of starvation and offered to surrender. According to the terms of the capitulation dated 29 September 1238, "all the Moors, both men and women, who wish to leave Valencia, may leave and go safely and securely with their arms and all their movable belongings. . . . We also wish and grant that all those Moors who wish to remain in the district of Valencia shall remain in our trust safely and securely. . . . We also give you a firm truce" (*MHDE*, II, 616). Jaime I entered the city on 9 October, where he caused the mosque to be consecrated as a cathedral and began the task of distributing houses and fields among his victorious companions-in-arms. Two years later, for the governance of his new realm, he promulgated the *Fori regni Valentie* or *Furs de Valencia* (the Catalan version was issued in 1261), a code of law very much influenced by Roman law. While the Christians rejoiced over their good fortune, the Muslim world was filled with wailing. Al-Himyari recorded the lament of a poet, recalling the fall of his native city: "Like a bird of prey, the enemy seized the city by the throat. . . . The call to prayer in the mosque was quickly silenced. . . . The infidel has destroyed the Muslim faith there, and the sound of the bell has replaced the call of the muezzin" (*Kitab al-Rawd al-Mitar*, 103–105).

As Jaime I marched south from Valencia, he approached the limits of Aragonese expansion as agreed upon in 1179 by Alfonso II of Aragon and Alfonso VIII of Castile. Simultaneously, his future son-in-law, Alfonso of Castile, was establishing Castilian authority throughout the district of Murcia. Perhaps inevitably Castilians and Aragonese came into conflict at this point.

The Murcian towns had been thrown into a state of confusion by the assassination of Ibn Hud in 1238. In Murcia itself, Ibn Mardanish, after his expulsion from Valencia, was able to restore a semblance of order, but he was soon driven out, and the family of Ibn Hud seized control of the city and dependent towns. But to avert the threat of subjugation by Ibn al-Ahmar or perhaps by the emir of Tunis, they decided to accept Fernando III as their overlord and protector. Since he was ill when their envoys arrived, he dispatched his oldest son Alfonso to receive the submission of the Murcian towns. The *infante* entered Murcia on 2 April 1243 and received the homage of the Banu Hud, but Lorca, Cartagena, and Mula were at first unwilling to bow to Castilian rule. In return for Castilian protection, the Murcian lords became Fernando III's vassals and surrendered half the public revenue to him; at the same time, they continued to govern their towns as in the past, coining money, maintaining military forces, and so on. Cagigas comments that Murcia was a true *mudéjar* state, a Muslim state under Christian sovereignty.

After securing recognition in Murcia, Alfonso set out to take possession of Alcira and Játiva, towns reserved for Aragonese reconquest, according to the treaty of Cazola (1179). Seeing his protests fall on deaf ears, Jaime I allowed his troops to occupy Villena, Sax, Bogarra, and Salinas, in the zone reserved for Castilian expansion. A war between the Christians was averted, and negotiations toward a settlement were opened, though at first they were carried on in a hostile atmosphere, and harsh words were exchanged. In the end, a treaty was signed at Almizra on 26 March 1244, confirming the essential points of the treaty of Cazola. Thus Villena and other towns were given up to Castile, while Jaime I was now free to take Alcira, Játiva (1244), and Biar (1245). With that, the Aragonese reconquest essentially was completed. The reduction of the remaining Muslim strongholds in al-Andalus was reserved for the Castilians, though the Aragonese frequently lent assistance, and from time to time Jaime I's successors tried to modify the settlement at Almizra in order to acquire part of Murcia.

One of the significant features of the conquest of Valencia and the submission of Murcia to Castilian sovereignty was the continued existence in both regions of great numbers of Muslims. They had withdrawn from the northern parts of the Valencian kingdom, chiefly in the modern province of Castellón de la Plana, leaving vast areas to be settled by the Christians. The Catalans settled along the coasts and the Aragonese in the mountainous inland districts. Farther south, while the cities such as Valencia were largely populated by Christian settlers, and the Muslims were confined to certain quarters, the rural population still remained Muslim for the most part. The presence of such a vast number of infidels posed many problems for Jaime I and later for Alfonso X of Castile. The Muslims of Valencia, under the leadership of al-Azraq, revolted in 1248 against Jaime I, who suppressed them easily enough and then ordered their expulsion from the kingdom. As the command was not fully carried out, a substantial Muslim population remained there. Not until the expulsion of the Moriscos in the seventeenth century was the problem finally resolved.

The Deposition of Sancho II of Portugal

While the kings of Aragon and Castile could derive increasing satisfaction from their triumphs over the Muslims, Sancho II of Portugal was continuing his march down the Guadiana to the sea. He captured Mértola in 1238 and probably Ayamonte at the mouth of the river on the Gulf of Cádiz; Tavira and Cacela just west of Ayamonte fell in 1239. Thus the Muslims in the southwestern corner of Portugal were isolated from their coreligionists in Niebla and Seville.

Sancho II did not have the distinction of completing the Portuguese reconquest. Though he possessed undoubted talents as a soldier, he was not capable of dealing firmly and effectively with the turbulent clergy and nobility who had been quarreling with the monarchy since the time of his father and grandfather. On the one hand the prelates maintained a continuing charge that royal agents violated ecclesiastical immunities and did violence to the clergy; the nobles, angered by Afonso II's attempt to recover royal rights and revenues, took advantage of Sancho II's youth and inexperience to defy his representatives, and to refuse service and tribute owed to him. The bishops and magnates also vied with one another in the usurpation of rights pertaining to monasteries. The bishops were accused of infringing monastic exemptions by demanding the payment of tithes when they were not owed and by imposing interdicts and excommunications on monasteries that refused to submit.

In order to justify themselves and to secure support in their struggle with the crown, the bishops frequently appealed to Rome. The papal legate, Cardinal Jean d'Abbeville, vainly tried to restore peace and harmony between church and state in 1229, but before a decade had passed other papal commissioners imposed sentences of interdict and excommunication upon the king. These were confirmed by Pope Gregory IX, who, despite his admiration for the king's work in the reconquest, could not permit canon law and the rights of the church to be impugned, as alleged by the clergy.

Pope Innocent IV was much less inclined than his predecessor to tolerate the failings of the Portuguese king and took steps to bring about his downfall. The pope drew up an extraordinary indictment of Sancho II at the General Council of Lyons in March 1245. He accused him of destroying the prosperity of the realm; of allowing men, women, and children, clergy and laity, to be killed with impunity; of tolerating incest, rape, extortion, incendiarism, profanation of churches; in a word, of encouraging the spread of anarchy throughout the realm. Although these accusations are undoubtedly exaggerated, they do give evidence of a lack of firmness on the king's part and of the determination of the clergy and their allies among the nobility to destroy him.

A few months later, on 25 July, after the archbishop of Braga and the bishops of Porto and Coimbra reported that the condition of the kingdom had not improved, the pope undertook to remedy its ills. Addressing himself to the people of Portugal, he declared that for the good of civil and ecclesiastical society it was necessary to repair the good order of the realm; he proposed to entrust this responsibility to the king's brother Afonso. The pope did not depose Sancho II, but explicitly reserved his rights to the throne, while taking those measures which he thought necessary to save the kingdom from immediate ruin. There seems little doubt that Afonso, who had left Portugal some years before and married Matilda, countess of Boulogne, had participated in intrigues directed against his brother. He signed a pact at Paris on 6 September with the Portuguese bishops, pledging his intention to administer the affairs of the realm in a spirit of justice and honor, to uphold the rights of the church, to eradicate evil customs and abuses, and to take counsel with the prelates on all those matters touching the good estate of the realm.

Early in the following year, using the titles *curator et visitator*, he arrived at Lisbon and confirmed the rights and privileges of the citizenry. Civil war broke out almost immediately, inasmuch as Sancho II was not prepared to abandon his kingdom; yet his popularity had declined to such a point that he could count on only a few supporters. Alfonso of Castile, to whom he apparently ceded Portuguese rights to the lands east of the Guadiana, from Moura to the sea, lent some assistance. Castilian help was minimal, however, since Alfonso was soon summoned by his father to take part in the siege of Seville. Sancho II was forced to retire to Toledo, where he died on 4 January 1248, a victim of his own weakness and of the concerted opposition of the prelates and magnates of Portugal. Martim de Freitas, the *alcaide* of Coimbra, who staunchly resisted Afonso's efforts to seize the city, surrendered only after he traveled to Toledo to view with his own eyes the dead body of his sovereign.

As Sancho II left no children, his brother claimed the throne under the name Afonso III (1248–1279) and renewed his pledge of good government. On the whole he encountered no significant opposition and could count upon the support of most of the towns. By turning his attention to the reconquest of the Algarve, the last Muslim outpost in the Portuguese zone of expansion, he did much to enhance his position. With the help of the military Orders of Avis and Santiago and of the towns, he occupied Faro in March 1249 and then reduced Albufeira, Porches, Silves, and other positions. The frontier was pushed to the sea and, once the Algarve was conquered, Portugal was complete.

The Conquest of Jaén and Seville

The revolution in Portugal occurred at a time when Fernando III was beginning the climactic campaign that ended with the fall of Seville, the jewel of al-Andalus. After the murder of Ibn Hud in 1238 the city pledged its allegiance to the Almohad caliph, al-Rashid. Within a year or so Ibn al-Ahmar, now the undisputed master of Granada, Jaén, Arjona, Málaga, and Almería, on the pretext of restoring the prestige and authority of the Almohad dynasty, but in fact to strengthen his own position, also pledged allegiance to al-Rashid. After the caliph's death in 1242, Ibn al-Ahmar recognized as his sovereign, Abu Zakariyya, the emir of Tunis, who sent him considerable sums of money which he used for the expansion of the mosque of Granada, in a city whose population was increasing steadily.

Growing bolder each day, Ibn al-Ahmar took advantage of Fernando III's illness and the absence of his son in Murcia to attempt the recovery of Andújar and Martos. Once he regained his health, the king of Castile assembled his troops to lay waste the countryside about Jaén and Granada and in 1244 captured Arjona and several adjacent towns. Now he determined to take Jaén itself, one of the keys to al-Andalus, though he knew from his failures in 1225 and 1230 that this was an arduous task. Jaén was an almost impregnable fortress with powerful walls dominated by a castle perched high on a hill overlooking the city. In preparation for the siege, Castilian troops systematically destroyed the crops and cut off all avenues of supply and then sat down before the city in August 1245 to await the capitulation. The defenders gradually were reduced to starvation and realized that Ibn al-Ahmar was powerless to assist them; they made peace with Fernando III in March 1246, and Ibn al-Ahmar agreed to the surrender of Jaén. As the Muslims evacuated the city, the king was free to distribute lands and houses to his followers; the mosque became a cathedral, and a bishopric was established there. Ibn al-Ahmar also became a vassal of Fernando III, promising to serve him in peace and war, to attend his *cortes*, and to pay a tribute of 150,000 *maravedís* over a term of twenty years.

After the fall of Jaén, logic directed Fernando III's attention to Seville. As he already held Córdoba, there was every reason for him to continue his advance southward along the Guadalquivir to Seville, the most opulent city in al-Andalus and also a seaport with access to the Mediterranean and the Atlantic. At the time, Castile's only contact with the sea was along the coast of the Bay of Biscay. Seville, though, in the past twenty years, had lived an extremely agitated existence. At various times she had acknowledged Ibn Hud, Ibn al-Ahmar, al-Rashid, and in 1246 Abu Zakariyya of Tunis. After the fall of Jaén, Seville made a separate peace with Fernando III and pledged the payment of tribute, but hostilities quickly developed. In the course of a conflict between the Sevillans and the governor sent by the emir of Tunis, one of Seville's most influential citizens, reportedly also a friend of Fernando III, was assassinated. This, according to the Muslim chroniclers, gave the king of Castile a pretext for assaulting the city. The prospects for success seemed good. There was little likelihood that the Hafsids of Tunis or the Almohads would be able to send any substantial reinforcements. Ibn al-Ahmar, the chief Muslim prince in al-Andalus, was Fernando III's vassal, pledged to assist him, as indeed he did, in war, even against his fellow Muslims. Thus Seville stood in isolation from the rest of the Muslim world.

The conquest of Seville was the most complex military operation undertaken by Fernando III. His armies included contingents led by his son Alfonso, his ally Ibn al-Ahmar, the bishops, nobles, towns, and military Orders. His first task was to break the ring of fortresses guarding access to the city and to cut off all sources of supply. As his troops devastated the countryside, the towns on the various routes from Córdoba to Seville capitulated: Alcalá de Guadaira (1246), Carmona, Constantina, Reina, Lora, Cantillana, Guillena, Gerena, and Alcalá del Rio (1247). The Muslims of these towns were allowed to remain in possession of their houses and other properties under the sovereignty of the king of Castile. By July 1247 the Castilians had advanced to the outskirts of the city and established a siege.

Although Seville was cut off by land, she still retained communication with Triana on the western side of the Guadalquivir by means of a bridge of boats, and she also had access to the sea. Realizing this, Fernando III instructed Ramón Bonifaz of Burgos to assemble a fleet to complete the blockade of the city. With the exception of Alfonso VII's capture of Almería in 1147 with the aid of Genoese and Pisan ships, this was the first time that the Castilians found themselves in need of a fleet. Bonifaz gathered the necessary ships, thirteen galleys and a number of smaller vessels, from ports on the Bay of Biscay. When he reached the mouth of the Guadalquivir he encountered enemy ships from Seville, Ceuta, and Tangier but drove them off and sailed up the river, breaking the bridge of boats linking Seville and Triana. As their supplies dwindled, the defenders appealed to the Almohad Caliph, al-Said (1242–1248); but he was intent upon the destruction of the Hafsids, and died before he could send any help to Seville, even had he wished to do so.

Without hope of relief and faced with the certainty of starvation the defenders capitulated on 23 November 1248. The terms of surrender allowed them to depart with their movable goods; they were given safe conduct to Jerez or, if they chose, to Ceuta, on ships provided by the victors. The *alcazar* was surrendered immediately to a Castilian garrison, and a month was allotted in which the Muslims could settle their affairs preparatory to exodus. Ibn Khaldun, himself a descendant of an old family of Seville, reported that the chief families eventually resettled in Tunis, the Hafsid capital. Others retreated to other towns in al-Andalus, while still others remained in Seville. Fernando III, "the tyrant, the cursed one," as one Muslim writer called him, made his triumphal entrance into the city on 22 December 1248. Then he began the process of establishing a bishopric there and of distributing houses and lands among the victors. Numerous towns in the surrounding regions recognized him as their sovereign.

The reign of Fernando III was the most fruitful of the Castilian reconquest, though his success was dependent in large measure upon his grandfather's triumph over the Almohads at Las Navas and the subsequent collapse of the Almohad unitary state. Like the other Christian rulers, he profited from the dissension and disunion among the Muslims of al-Andalus, extending his frontier into the valley of the Guadalquivir and affirming his suzerainty over the kingdom of Granada, the last Muslim bastion in Spain. In the *Setenario* (9–10), his son Alfonso noted that God favored Fernando III "through the union of the kingdoms of Spain, so that what other kings had lost for lack of wisdom or evil counsel . . . God joined together so that he might inherit it in peace." Fernando III wanted his realm to be called an empire, "not a kingdom and he wanted to be crowned as emperor as were others of his lineage," but he decided that "it was not the time to do it." The language used by Archbishop Rodrigo in dedicating his *De rebus Hispaniae* to Fernando III, "serenissimo invicto et semper Augusto domino suo," also reveals the king's ambition. The opportunity to restore the empire in Spain was allowed to slip by, but remembrance of his father's intentions probably encouraged Alfonso X in his own efforts to obtain the title of Holy Roman Emperor.

While so much of Fernando III's energy was expended in the reconquest, he did not neglect the development of institutions and culture. A patron of scholars, he fostered the Universities of Salamanca and Palencia and encouraged the use of Castilian, rather than Latin, as the official language of government and administration. He also initiated the preparation of a uniform code of law for the kingdom, a task continued by his son. The *cortes*, as an assembly of prelates, magnates, and townsmen representing the estates of the realm, emerged from obscurity, and the meeting held at Seville in 1250 marked the culmination of a half-century of growth and development.

Berenguela, for many years her son's principal counselor, died in 1246. Death came to Fernando III on 30 May 1252 while he was planning an invasion of North Africa, hoping to take advantage of the downfall of the Almohad empire to safeguard his kingdom against the possibility of a new Muslim intrusion from that quarter. He was buried in the cathedral of Seville and raised to the honors of the altar in 1671 by Pope Clement X.

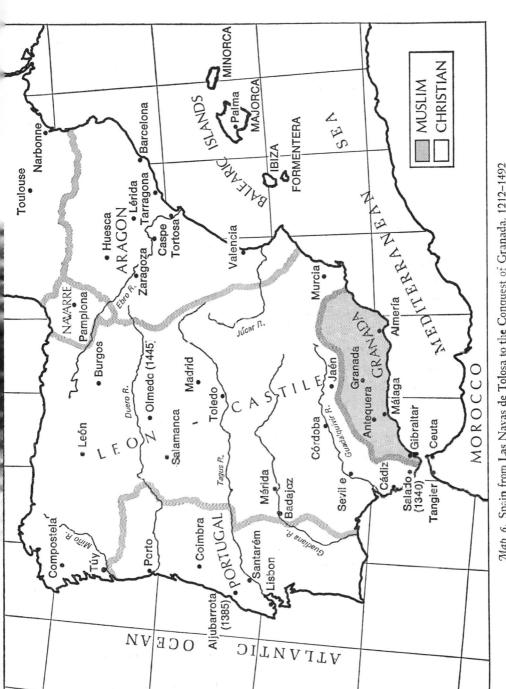

Map 6. Spain from Las Navas de Tolosa to the Conquest of Granada, 1212–1492

MUSLIM
CHRISTIAN

ATLANTIC OCEAN

MEDITERRANEAN SEA

BALEARIC ISLANDS

MINORCA
MAJORCA
•Palma
IBIZA
FORMENTERA

Toulouse
Narbonne

NAVARRE
Pamplona

ARAGON
•Huesca
Lérida
Tarragona
Zaragoza
Caspe
Tortosa
Barcelona

Ebro R.

Valencia

Júcar R.

LEON
•León
Burgos
Olmedo (1445)
Salamanca
Madrid
Toledo

Duero R.

Tagus R.

CASTILE

Murcia

GRANADA
Almería
Granada
Jaén
Málaga
Antequera
Córdoba
Guadalquivir R.
Sevil e
Cádiz
Gibraltar
Ceuta
Salado (1340)
Tangier

MOROCCO

Compostela
Túy
Porto
Coimbra
Santarém
Lisbon
PORTUGAL
Aljubarrota (1385)
Mérida
Badajoz
Guadiana R.
Miño R.

The words supposedly spoken by Fernando III on his deathbed to his son reflect a contemporary estimate of his achievement:

You are richer in lands and good vassals than any other king in Christendom. . . . I leave you the whole realm from the sea hither, which the Moors won from Rodrigo, king of Spain. All of it is in your dominion, part of it conquered, the other part tributary. If you know how to preserve in this state what I leave you, you will be as good a king as I was, and if you win more for yourself, you will be better than I was, but if you diminish it, you will not be as good as I was.   [*Primera Crónica General*, 1132]

The exultation felt by all Spaniards when they contemplated the extraordinary accomplishments not only of Fernando III, but also of Jaime I, Sancho II, and Alfonso IX, was expressed by the canonist, Vincentius Hispanus (d. 1248). Rejecting the idea that all kingdoms were subordinate to the Holy Roman Empire, he declared with pride: "The Spaniards alone gained an empire by their valor. . . . The Spaniards rule Blessed Lady Spain; ruling by virtue of their audacity and probity, they are winning dominion over her and expanding it. . . . O Spain, who can count your praises?" (For the Latin text see Gaines Post, *Studies in Medieval Legal Thought: Public Law and the State, 1100–1322* [Princeton, 1964], 490, n. 190).

On the contrary, despair, dejection, and resignation to the will of God were the feelings most commonly voiced by Muslim poets and writers forced to emigrate from their native country, a land for which they all retained a deep affection. Their sense of loss and ruin is perhaps summed up best in these lines of the poet al-Rundi:

> Ask Valencia what became of Murcia,
> And where is Játiva, or where is Jaén?
> Where is Córdoba, the seat of great learning,
> And how many scholars of high repute remain there?
> And where is Seville, the home of mirthful gatherings
> On its great river, cooling and brimful with water?
> These centers were the pillars of the country:
> Can a building remain when the pillars are missing?
> The white wells of ablution are weeping with sorrow,
> As a lover does when torn from his beloved;
> They weep over the remains of dwellings devoid of Muslims,
> Despoiled of Islam, now peopled by Infidels!
> Those mosques have now been changed into churches,
> Where the bells are ringing and crosses are standing;

. . .

This misfortune has surpassed all that has preceded,
And as long as Time lasts, it can never be forgotten!

. . .

What an opprobrium, when once powerful people
Have been humbled to dust by tyrants and injustice!
Yesterday they were kings in their own palaces,
Today they are slaves in the land of the Infidels!*

* From a poem by al-Rundi, in A. R. Nykl, *Hispano-Arabic Poetry and its Relations with the Old Provençal Troubadours* (first published, Baltimore, 1946; reprinted 1970, by The Hispanic Society), 338–339; used with permission of The Hispanic Society.

CHAPTER 15

Alfonso X and the Lure of Empire

The Aftermath of the Great Reconquest

The untimely death of Fernando III in 1252 closed the age of the great reconquest. Muslim territory in the peninsula was reduced to the kingdom of Granada in tributary vassalage to Castile, a relationship that no one ever considered permanent. The conquest of Granada, however, like Fernando III's projected invasion of Morocco, was postponed indefinitely and the threat of a new Muslim assault into Spain, which he hoped to avert, soon became a reality. In the meantime the Christian rulers were reminded of the constant domestic peril caused by the presence of vast numbers of Muslims within their dominions. The rapidity of the reconquest in the thirteenth century was such that there were not enough Christians to colonize the newly conquered regions, whose defense and retention, therefore, was doubly difficult. As for the Muslims, no serious attempt was made to convert them, to assimilate them, or to expel them; but as their loyalty was never guaranteed, they eventually joined their coreligionists in Granada and Morocco in hostilities against the Christians. The problem of the *mudéjares*, as Muslims living in Christian territory were called, was one of the chief legacies of the reconquest.

In order to hold the conquered territory, immense estates were ceded in full ownership to the nobility and to the military Orders who had collaborated in the reconquest. Enormously enriched in this way, and possessing for the first time a strong base in the land, the nobility were able to present a formidable challenge to the monarchy. As the sovereign, imbued with the principles of Roman law, inclined to the concept

358

of royal absolutism, the traditional role of the nobility as his indispensable counselors and collaborators was brought into question. Constitutional struggles between the crown and the nobility inevitably ensued and to some extent contributed to the further growth of parliamentary institutions.

Spain's gradual incorporation into the mainstream of western European life reached fruition in the late thirteenth century. No longer did the peninsula exist in political, economic, or cultural isolation, but the increasing participation of the Hispanic rulers in the public affairs of western Europe was often extraneous and detrimental to the fundamental interests of Spain herself.

Alfonso X of Castile

Alfonso X (1252–1284), known to history as *el Sabio*, the Wise or the Learned, succeeded his father as king of León and Castile. Well educated, and experienced in war, he was apparently destined to continue brilliantly the tasks so far advanced by Fernando III. From a cultural standpoint the reign has exceptional significance because of the work that he and the scholars associated with him accomplished in the fields of literature, history, and law. In the political sphere, however, his achievements were less than distinguished. His quest for the crown of the Holy Roman Empire distracted him from Castilian affairs, and from the business left unfinished at the time of his father's death. His ambition, his vast expenditure of money, his tendency toward absolutism, and his indecision in resolving the question of the succession to the throne brought his career to an unhappy conclusion.

Immediately after his accession he busied himself with the colonization of Seville and the surrounding territory, distributing houses, lands, vineyards, olive groves, and the like to the settlers who came from Castile, Galicia, Navarre, Portugal, the Basque provinces, and even from Catalonia. Alfonso X had greater riches at his disposal than any other Spanish king, but while he retained a substantial share of the spoils for himself, he was indeed generous to those who had participated in the recent conquests. The *Libro del Repartimiento* drawn up on his orders contains the list of grantees and the estates given them.

Alfonso X also had to compel obedience from the Muslims of several towns who took advantage of his father's death to repudiate Castilian sovereignty. He besieged Jerez, whose inhabitants offered to recognize him as their lord, provided that they be allowed to retain their houses and lands. Not having sufficient Christians to populate the city, he accepted but placed a garrison in the citadel as a guarantee of future loyalty. Arcos, Lebrija, Medina Sidonia, and other towns surrendered on the same terms. Then, in preparation for the African invasion proposed by his father, he ordered the construction of docks and arsenals at Seville and sought crusading indulgences from the pope, but other concerns required its postponement.

Among them was a dispute with Afonso III of Portugal concerning Portuguese conquests east of the Guadiana river and in the Algarve, the southernmost sector of modern Portugal. Portuguese historians believe that Alfonso X, before he became king, obtained rights to the Algarve from the Muslim king of Niebla, but Ballesteros argues that Sancho II of Portugal, in return for assistance against his brother, ceded the Algarve to the Castilian prince. It is also possible, as Herculano suggested, that Afonso Henriques and Fernando II may have agreed to set their future boundaries along the line of the Guadiana. In any case, Sancho II had annexed Moura, Serpa, and Ayamonte, east of the river, and Afonso III seized Aroche and Aracena, also east of the river. Once Alfonso X became king, he decided to press his claims to the disputed territories. Desultory warfare followed until 1253 when a preliminary settlement was arranged. Although his wife, Matilda of Boulogne, was still alive, Afonso III agreed to marry Beatriz, Alfonso X's illegitimate daughter; until a son was born to the couple and attained the age of seven, Alfonso X would have usufruct of the Algarve, but thereafter Portugal would have it in full sovereignty and would also retain the fortresses east of the Guadiana. The pact of 1253 laid the groundwork for the eventual resolution of the controversy and allowed both monarchs to turn their attention to other matters.

Under the rule of Afonso III Lisbon supplanted Coimbra as the favorite royal residence and as the principal seat of administration. Like his contemporaries elsewhere, he was strongly influenced by Roman conceptions of royal authority, but at the same time he had to contend with an emerging tradition of parliamentary government. Afonso III summoned the first Portuguese *cortes*, an assembly of prelates, magnates, and "good men of the towns" to Leiria in February 1254. The presence of the townsmen reflected the king's need to deal with them in order to increase his revenues. Royal debasement of the coinage was a common device for doing so, but it caused economic upset and proved the necessity to develop alternative means of raising money.

Thus the *cortes* of 1254 offered the king a tribute called *monetágio* in return for his promise to guarantee the coinage for seven years. At the end of that period he devalued the coinage, but the outcry was so vociferous that he had to accept stringent restrictions imposed by the *cortes* of Coimbra in March 1261. The original value of the old money was restored, and a relative equivalency was given to the new money. Only at the end of four years and then only for two years was he allowed to resume the minting of new money in limited quantities. Thereafter for the rest of his reign he was forbidden to coin money. His successors were to be permitted to issue new coinage only once in the course of their reigns, but they did not abide by this rule. In order to help the king meet his financial needs the *cortes* enacted a general property levy, but there were so many exemptions that the tax burden fell inevitably on the humbler classes. While admitting the king's right to coin money, the *cortes* of 1261 established the principle that authorization by the *cortes* was required before he could do so; in this respect a real limitation was imposed on royal power.

Though he acquiesced in these determinations, Afonso III labored constantly to bolster royal authority. He resumed his father's inquisitions in order to recover royal lands wrongfully seized by prelates, nobles, and others; although he was able to put an end to abuses and extortions practiced by many nobles and bishops, it is not surprising that he eventually ran afoul of them as had his predecessors.

Meanwhile, Alfonso X, an extraordinarily ambitious monarch, tried to impose his suzerainty over Navarre, while raising nearly forgotten pretensions to Gascony and urging his rights to the throne of the Holy Roman Empire. Upon the death of Thibault I, king of Navarre and count of Champagne, Alfonso X, no doubt recalling the precedent set in 1134 when García Ramírez pledged homage and fealty to Alfonso VII, demanded that the new king, Thibault II (1253–1270), become his vassal. When Castilian troops began to gather along the frontier, the Navarrese appealed to Jaime I of Aragon who gladly pledged his support to prevent Castile from occupying the country. A stalemate ensued, and by 1256 Alfonso X gave up, for the time being, his attempt to reduce Navarre to the status of a feudal dependency.

With respect to Gascony, he revived claims deriving from his great-grandparents, Alfonso VIII and Leonor, the daughter of Henry II of England. The possibility of Castilian intervention was raised when the unruly Gascon nobility, disgusted with the government of Henry III of

England, appealed to Alfonso X. Henry III, however, offered to negotiate; according to the treaty concluded at Toledo in April 1254, Alfonso
X yielded his rights to Gascony to his sister Leonor, who was to marry
Edward, the son and heir of the English king. Thereafter Gascony
ceased to be an issue in Anglo-Castilian relations.

During much of his reign Alfonso X's greatest preoccupation was his
desire to win the crown of the Holy Roman Empire. Ever since the
papal deposition of Emperor Frederick II in 1245, civil war between
papalists and imperialists raged in both Germany and Italy. When the
antiemperor elected by the papalist faction died in 1256, Alfonso X
determined to press his rights to the throne vigorously. As the son of
Beatrice of Swabia, a granddaughter of Frederick Barbarossa, he belonged to the Hohenstaufen family and could expect to find substantial
support for his candidacy. Richard of Cornwall, a brother of the English king, appeared, however, as a rival. Both men expended great
sums of money to gain adherents, so it was not surprising that a double
election took place in 1257. Richard came to Germany to receive the
crown and the homage of his followers, but Alfonso X urged his claims
from afar, naming an imperial vicar and sending money to his partisans.
Jofre de Loaysa, one of his counselors, remarked that his expenditures
were "almost unbelievable, so that it was necessary for him to ask the
men of his realm for services and to impose unaccustomed tributes on
them." This proved to be a powerful cause of domestic discontent
thereafter. If the Castilians were lukewarm in their support of Alfonso
X's imperial ambitions, Jaime I was clearly hostile; recalling traditional
Leonese imperialist pretensions in Spain, he rejected the notion that Alfonso X might be regarded as "an Hispanic emperor or that our realms
and dominions are in any subjection to him, by reason of empire." The
pope, too, was disinclined to recognize Alfonso X, for he represented
the Ghibelline party, a group traditionally hostile to the papacy. In
actuality neither Richard nor Alfonso X was able to secure a firm grasp
of the imperial crown, but in spite of the obstacles the king continued
to believe that all would eventually admit the justice of his cause.

Jaime I and the Withdrawal from Languedoc

While Alfonso X remained steadfast in his pursuit of empire, Jaime
I was liquidating the last vestiges of Catalan hegemony in Languedoc.
There, Catalan interests were dealt a mortal blow by the Albigensian
Crusade. Simon de Montfort's victory over Pedro II destroyed the pos-

sibility of creating a Catalan state embracing Catalonia, Languedoc, and Provence. The way was now opened for the French monarchy to extend its power into the county of Toulouse and the march of Provence. Raymond VII was recognized as count of Toulouse but was obliged to give his daughter in marriage to Alphonse of Poitiers, a brother of King Louis IX. On the count's death in 1249, Toulouse passed, by right of inheritance, to Alphonse and his wife. A few years before, Charles of Anjou, another brother of the French king, married the heiress of Ramon Berenguer V, marquess of Provence and cousin of Jaime I. Thus younger members of the Capetian dynasty were entrenched in both Toulouse and Provence, regions in which the counts of Barcelona had long had both family and feudal connections.

Jaime I realized that he could revive feudal claims in Languedoc only at the risk of a quarrel with the powerful French monarchy. Choosing rather to abandon whatever rights he might have, in May 1258 he signed the treaty of Corbeil with Louis IX who was anxious to guarantee his brothers' dominions against any Catalan threat. Thereby Jaime I renounced claims to Carcassonne, Béziers, Foix, Agde, Nîmes, Albi, Narbonne, Toulouse, and other places, and two months later yielded his claims to Provence to Queen Margaret of France, a daughter of Ramon Berenguer V. For his part, Louis IX, as the successor of Charlemagne, renounced rights to Rousillon, Conflent, Cerdagne, Barcelona, Urgel, Ampurias, Besalú, Gerona, and Vich, that is, the frontier territories that had once constituted the Spanish March. The Catalans had enjoyed a *de facto* independence from the tenth century, but only now in 1258 were all legal ties between Catalonia and the kingdom of France severed. The pact was sealed by an agreement that Philip, heir to the French throne, should marry Jaime I's daughter, Isabel; before the century was over this union encouraged an attempt to place a Capetian prince on the throne of Aragon.

Following the treaty of Corbeil, Jaime I's only possessions north of the Pyrenees were the county of Rousillon and the lordship of Montpellier. Catalan historians have lamented his withdrawal from Languedoc, but there was little likelihood that he could have overcome the greatly superior power of France. Any attempt to advance ephemeral claims north of the Pyrenees would have involved Aragon in a long and self-destructive conflict with France. In the circumstances Jaime I's policy seems to have been the only realistic one.

Alfonso X and the Revolt of the Mudéjares

The legacy which Alfonso X received from his father included a proposed invasion of Morocco, for so many centuries a principal sustenance and support for the Muslims of al-Andalus. The challenge offered to the Almohads by the Banu Marin or Marinid dynasty made Castilian intervention an ever more attractive possibility. Alfonso X began to prepare a fleet and appointed an admiral or *adelantado de la mar* in 1260 "because we greatly desire to carry forward the work of the crusade overseas for the service of God and the exaltation of Christianity." News from Morocco encouraged him to speed his preparations: the governor of Salé, a town on the Atlantic coast adjacent to Rabat, was preparing to revolt against the Marinid Emir, Abu Yusuf Yaqub b. Abd al-Haqq (1258–1286) and called on Alfonso X for help.

He sent a fleet from Cádiz to Salé in early September 1260. Assuming that the fleet had come for purposes of trade, the Muslims, who were just breaking the fast of Ramadan, were totally surprised and unable to oppose the landing. The Castilians easily gained entrance into the city and gave themselves over to killing, rape, and pillage. When the Emir, Abu Yusuf, hastened to the rescue the Castilians decided to withdraw; entering their ships on the night of 21 September, after setting fire to the city, they made their escape. The *Chronicle of Alfonso X* reported that the king was highly pleased by the expedition to Salé, but it seems that it failed to achieve his objectives. He may have intended to establish a permanent base there to facilitate further expansion. The capture and temporary occupation of Salé, however, constituted the sum and substance of his crusade to Africa. While it brought no permanent advantage to Castile, it did provoke the enmity of the Marinids.

The need to broaden Castilian access to the sea apparently led Alfonso X to recover possession of Cádiz and to conquer Niebla. Cádiz had submitted to Fernando III but evidently regained its independence after his death. Alfonso X probably occupied the port in the summer of 1260 before the expedition set sail for Salé. Niebla capitulated in February 1262 after a siege of nearly ten months. With it, Alfonso X also won control of the port of Huelva on the Atlantic coast. Alfonso X also hoped to acquire the ports of Gibraltar and Tarifa, but when he demanded that Ibn al-Ahmar, king of Granada, yield them to him, he was refused. Though he came to Seville each year to renew his homage and to pay tribute to Alfonso X, the king of Granada realized that if Castile gained control of the straits of Gibraltar the Spanish Muslims would no longer be able to summon aid from Morocco, and Granada would inevitably be absorbed by Castile.

Rather than submit meekly to that fate, Ibn al-Ahmar decided to challenge Alfonso X. In conjunction with Ibn Hud, king of Murcia and a vassal of Castile, he organized a conspiracy among the Muslims subject to Castilian rule. Plans for simultaneous risings in all the towns of Andalusia were readied by the beginning of 1264. The Muslims of Seville were expected to capture Alfonso X, but as it turned out he was absent from the city when the revolt broke out. Although the Marinids were still preoccupied with the struggle against the Almohads in Morocco, they sent a contingent of 3,000 volunteers to take part in the holy war. These hardy warriors distinguished themselves by their bravery and also by their arrogance, but their presence incited the Muslims of al-Andalus to greater resistance to the Christians. In order to balance his dependence upon the Marinids, who at some future date might become a threat to his sovereignty, Ibn al-Ahmar renewed his homage to the Hafsid emir of Tunis. The revolt probably began at the end of May 1264, and Alfonso X seems to have been taken entirely by surprise. In his letters he declared that Ibn-Ahmar sent messengers to break the bond of vassalage and to inform him that Granadan troops were already invading Castile. Proclaiming Ibn al-Ahmar as their king, the rebels quickly seized Lebrija, Arcos, Vejer, Rota, Medina Sidonia, Sanlúcar, Jerez, Murcia, Moratalla, and Lorca, but Seville, Córdoba, Jaén, Cartagena, and Orihuela remained safely in Christian hands. Several of the towns in Andalusia formed a *hermandad* in April 1265 to defend their interests against the Muslims.

Once aware of the seriousness of the situation, Alfonso X took steps to suppress the revolt. Medina Sidonia, and other towns, were recovered by September, and Jerez, after a siege of five months, surrendered on 9 October; Sanlúcar and Cádiz were recaptured in the following year. The Muslims of these towns were allowed to depart and to settle in Granada or Morocco; Christians were brought in to settle in the towns, but there remained many deserted areas. To Alfonso X's great good fortune, the Muslim governors (*arraez*, or *al-rais*) of Málaga, Guadix, and Comares, belonging to the family of the Banu Ashqilula, revolted against Ibn al-Ahmar because of the favor he showed to the volunteers from Morocco. In response to their appeal,

Alfonso X invaded the *vega* of Granada in the spring of 1265. Realizing that little could now be gained from a continuation of the conflict, Ibn al-Ahmar asked for a truce in August; he pledged payment of a yearly tribute of 250,000 *maravedis* and agreed to assist Alfonso X in the reconquest of Murcia. For his part, Alfonso X promised not to give further support to the Banu Ashqilula, but neither he nor Ibn al-Ahmar abided fully by the terms of the pact.

While the greater part of Andalusia was now pacified, the rebels still held out in Murcia. As soon as he learned of the revolt, Alfonso X appealed for help to his father-in-law, Jaime I, who convened an assembly of Catalan prelates and nobles at Barcelona in July 1264 and another with the Aragonese bishops and nobles at Zaragoza in November. In order to help the king of Castile, he asked for a special subsidy and offered three reasons in justification:

First, because I do not wish to betray my daughter (the queen of Castile) nor my grandchildren, nor do I wish to disinherit them; secondly . . . although I need not aid him out of valor or duty, yet I should help him because he is one of the most powerful men in the world, and if I do not aid him now and he emerges safely from the conflict in which he now finds himself, he will always hold me as his mortal enemy . . . and if he can pressure me, he will do so as often as he can and he will have good reason. Thirdly . . . if the king of Castile loses his kingdom, we will be badly off in our own kingdom. Therefore it is better to hasten to defend his kingdom now, than to have to defend ours later. [*Crònica de Jaume J*, 382]

After much grumbling the Catalans voted to give him the tax called *bovatge*, though they reminded him that he "had no right to it" because he had collected it twice before, at his accession, and when he began the conquest of Majorca.

The Aragonese nobles refused his request for the *bovatge* saying, "My lord, we in Aragon don't know what the *bovatge* is." All his efforts to secure their support were unavailing, even when he reminded them that Catalonia "the best kingdom in Spain, the most-honored and most noble," had generously contributed to his need. The nobles turned against him, charging him with violating the traditional customs of Aragon, of adjudicating lawsuits according to civil and canon law, and of taking the counsel of legists, men trained professionally in Roman law. The nobles objected to the reception of Roman law and the tendency of the lawyers in the king's service to use it to bolster and expand royal power, at the expense of what the nobles considered to be their traditional rights. Given the strength of the opposition, Jaime I found it necessary to accede to some of their demands. He swore to uphold the laws and customs of the realm in an assembly at Exea in April 1265 and promised to appoint the *justicia* of Aragon, the chief judge of his court, from the ranks of the knightly class and to give him authority to adjudicate suits between the crown and the nobility, "with the counsel of the *ricos hombres* and knights in the *curia*." This was intended to guarantee the nobles judgment by peers; it foreshadowed later attempts to render the *justicia* independent of the king and to further curtail the powers of the monarchy.

After settling this dispute, at least for the time being, Jaime I advanced to the frontiers of the kingdom of Murcia in the fall of 1265. The Muslims of Elche and other towns quickly submitted and were guaranteed possession of their houses and fields, their right to worship freely and to be judged according to their own law by their own judges. The city of Murcia surrendered on similar terms after a short siege at the end of January 1266. The king's only demand was that the Muslims give up the great mosque adjacent to the *alcazar* so that he could make it a Christian church. When they objected, he queried: "Do you think it proper that you should have the mosque at the gate of the *alcazar* and that I, when I am asleep, should have to hear in my head the cry, Allah lo Sabba o Allah?" (*Crònica*, 445). As one might expect, the king had his way. Loyally abiding by his promises and by the treaty of Almizra (1244) which designated Murcia as Castilian territory, he restored the city and other reconquered towns to Alfonso X. Large numbers of Catalans were settled there, however, and the Catalan tongue came to be spoken widely in this part of the kingdom of Castile. As Ramon Muntaner put it: "They are true Catalans and speak the finest Catalan (*bell catalanesc*) in the world." The text of the *Repartiment de Murcia*, describing the distribution of houses and properties to Jaime I's followers, is extant. As the number of Christians increased, many Muslims emigrated to the neighboring kingdom of Granada.

While the rebellion of the *mudéjares* was crushed, Alfonso X and Ibn al-Ahmar apparently continued at odds; the former refused to abandon the Banu Ashqilula, realizing that by protecting them he would always have the upper hand of the king of Granada. For the time being Ibn al-Ahmar bowed to the inevitable and renewed his pledge of vassalage and the payment of tribute, probably in late 1266 or 1267. On the other hand he could hope to derive some advantage from a conflict beginning to develop between Alfonso X and the Castilian nobility, but until it reached a climax he bided his time.

The Settlement of the Algarve

The threat posed by the revolt of the *mudéjares* was of such gravity that Alfonso X had turned for help not only to Jaime I, but also to Afonso III of Portugal. As an inducement he showed a disposition to come to terms concerning their respective boundaries. There had been friction along the border despite the marriage alliance of 1253; the marriage itself was threatened when Afonso III's first wife, Countess Matilda of Boulogne, charged him with bigamy and appealed to the pope. The king, however, refused to separate from Beatriz of Castile, thereby prompting the pope to impose an interdict on those places where the royal couple resided. After Matilda's death in 1263 the interdict was lifted, the king's marriage to Beatriz was approved, and their children, including Dinis, heir to the throne, then aged two, were legitimated.

Alfonso X and Afonso III concluded an important pact on 20 September 1264, not long after the outbreak of the Muslim revolt. In the circumstances both men undoubtedly realized the necessity of harmony. Thus Alfonso X yielded all effective authority in the Algarve, including the right to make laws, to administer justice, to hear appeals, and to dispose of lands and estates. The Portuguese, on the other hand, were obligated to aid him in his lifetime with fifty knights, and Castilian officers were to hold certain castles in the Algarve as a guarantee that this service would be performed. Portuguese historians maintain that Alfonso X gave up the Algarve fully, the service of fifty knights being only a condition of alliance and not a recognition of Castilian sovereignty or feudal lordship. On the contrary, Ballesteros believes that Alfonso X did retain these rights, as his continued use of the title "king of the Algarve" suggests. The text of the document referring to "the aid and service for the Algarve of fifty knights which ought to be given to me during my lifetime" seems to imply a feudal obligation, though perhaps of more symbolic than actual value. In any case, Afonso III was determined to be free of it and in 1266 sent Dinis, then about five years old, to visit his grandfather at Seville, ostensibly to receive the honor of knighthood from him, but in fact to ask that the service of fifty knights be canceled. Alfonso X joyously received his grandson, but when he consulted the nobles they advised him, much to his annoyance, never to give up the service owed by the king of Portugal. Alfonso X, however, had already decided to accede to the request.

The kings of Castile and Portugal met at Badajoz on 16 February 1267 to conclude a treaty of peace, promising mutual friendship and assistance. Out of love for his grandson, and in gratitude for the aid given by the king of Portugal during the revolt of the *mudéjares*, Alfonso X yielded all rights to the Algarve, including the service of fifty knights, and instructed his lieutenants to surrender to Portugal the castles they held for him in the Algarve. This was an absolute cession of Castilian rights to the Algarve, though Ballesteros suggested that by continuing to use the title "king of the Algarve," Alfonso X sought to keep alive some vestigial claim to suzerainty; he might have used the title, however, with reference only to the territory of Niebla. The two kings also agreed upon a delimitation of their borders, with the river Guadiana from Elvas and Badajoz to Ayamonte on the Atlantic Ocean as the dividing line. In effect, Portugal surrendered Aroche, Aracena, Moura, and Serpa east of that line; to the north of Elvas, Arronches and Alegrete remained to Portugal, while Marvão and Valencia de Alcántara were adjudged to Castile. As a result of this agreement, Portugal attained substantially the frontiers she has today, with the exception of the districts of Moura and Serpa and of Riba-Coa, including the towns of Almeida, Vilar Maior, and Alfaiates; these were incorporated subsequently into the kingdom during Dinis's reign.

Christian Spain and the Latin East

The restoration of peace in the peninsula raised the possibility of greater Hispanic involvement in the affairs of the Latin kingdom of Jerusalem and the Latin empire of Constantinople. In the past, because of the reconquest, the papacy usually discouraged the rulers of Christian Spain from participating in the crusades; for this reason the same indulgences that could be obtained in the Holy Land were granted to those who took part in the reconquest.

Once the greater part of al-Andalus had been conquered and the Muslims suppressed or reduced to tributary status, there seemed no reason why Hispanic Christians should not take a more active role in the crusades in the eastern Mediterranean. The situation of the Latin kingdom was exceedingly precarious after the Muslim recapture of Jerusalem in 1244. The Christians entertained the fleeting hope of converting the pagan Mongols who advanced into Syria and of forming an alliance with them for the destruction of Islam, but it was not to be, as the Mongols were defeated in 1260 and were forced to withdraw to central Asia. Jaime I, according to his own account, made preparations for a crusade at that time, but a prolonged tempest delayed his departure, and he finally abandoned the enterprise.

The foundations of the Latin empire of Constantinople were equally shaky. Emperor Baldwin II's financial needs were such that he contracted enormous debts with the Venetians and had to deliver his son and heir into their hands as a pledge of repayment. To obtain the prince's release, Empress Marie de Brienne, a niece of Fernando III and a cousin of Alfonso X, visited Rome, Paris, and Burgos. While the pope and the king of France offered her two-thirds of the needed funds, Alfonso X, no doubt hoping to enhance his international reputation and to further his imperial ambitions, insisted on paying the entire sum. His generosity in redeeming the heir to the throne, however, could not save the Latin empire from destruction. Michael VIII Paleologus, emperor of Nicaea, recaptured Constantinople in 1261 and doomed Baldwin II and his family to a life of exile.

Meanwhile, the Egyptian Mamelukes seized many towns and fortresses in what remained of the kingdom of Jerusalem and conquered the great city and principality of Antioch in 1268. The response to the papal appeal for a crusade was lukewarm, but Louis IX of France and Jaime I of Aragon did promise to take part. The pope urged the latter to terminate his adulterous relations with a Castilian lady before setting out on the pilgrimage to the Holy Land. Once again the possibility of an alliance with the Mongols was discussed, and Jaime I sent an envoy to the court of the Mongol khan. Alfonso X, with whom he spent Christmas 1268, advised Jaime I not to trust the Mongols or to put his faith in their promises. Alfonso X refused to take any direct part in the expedition, but he did offer to assist with money and some knights. Jaime I's envoy returned in the spring, accompanied by two Mongols and a representative of the Byzantine emperor, who pledged the support of their sovereigns in the effort to recover the Holy Sepulchre.

In seven months' time all was ready, and the fleet set sail from Barcelona on 4 September 1269, but once more fierce storms scattered the ships. Believing that it was God's will that he not continue, Jaime I returned home, landing on the French coast. What he had hoped would be the crowning achievement of his life and a great service to Christianity that would avail him divine pardon for a life of uninhibited sensuality, ended as a fiasco. Some of his ships and his two bastard sons did reach the Holy Land, but aside from delivering supplies they made no significant contribution to the crusade and returned to Aragon by February 1270.

Thibault II, king of Navarre and count of Champagne, also took part in the crusade, accompanying Louis IX of France to Tunis. After the death of the French king in August 1270, his brother Charles of Anjou, king of Sicily, forced Tunis to accept a commercial treaty and then terminated the crusade. Thibault II died shortly after returning to Sicily and was succeeded by his brother Henry (1270–1274).

Still believing that it was possible to revive the crusading ardor of times past, Pope Gregory X (1271–1276) summoned a General Council to meet at Lyons in 1274 and invited the crowned heads of Europe to attend. Jaime I, now an old man, was the only monarch to do so. He pledged his collaboration and offered much advice as to the strategy to be employed, but, his views were rejected by the master of the Temple and others who were more knowledgeable in the affairs of the east than he was. At this, the king, confident that he had upheld "the honor of all Spain," asked the pope's permission to withdraw. As he gave spurs to his horse, admiring bystanders remarked: "The king is not as old as they said! He could still break a lance against the Turks!" At this time the king asked the pope to crown him, but when the pope asked him to pay the arrears of tribute owed to the Holy See since Pedro II's coronation in Rome in 1204, he replied: "We did not come to his court to bind ourselves with tribute." Before leaving the Council Jaime I confessed to the pope "all our good and bad works, insofar as our memory was faithful to us, and he gave us his absolution, imposing on us as a penance only that we should persevere in the good and keep ourselves from evil" (*Crònica de Jaume I*, 537–542). Hardly had he returned home than he fell again into adulterous ways with the wife of one of his vassals and so merited a sharp reprimand from the pontiff. Plans for the crusade, as will be seen, came to naught.

The Revolt of the Castilian Nobility

Like most European sovereigns of the late thirteenth century, Alfonso X of Castile showed little interest in the fate of the Holy Land. Rather than pursue transitory fame by leading a crusade to the Orient, he preferred to seek the apparently more tangible goal of recognition as

Holy Roman Emperor. Besides the opposition of Richard of Cornwall and the papacy, pressing domestic problems prevented him from undertaking the "ida al imperio," the journey to the empire. Until he resolved them and assured himself of the tranquility of the frontiers, he could not leave the peninsula.

His innovations in matters of law and taxation were the fundamental reasons for the steady growth of opposition within the kingdom of Castile. In common with other rulers, he was greatly influenced by the principles of Roman law and utilized them in the preparation of the *Fuero Real*, a code of municipal law, which he granted to many towns, and the *Espéculo de las leyes*, the earliest redaction of the *Siete Partidas*, evidently intended to become a uniform law throughout the realm. The concept of royal power exemplified in these texts was often at variance with the older medieval notion of a delicately balanced relationship between the sovereign and his subjects, each having certain rights and obligations. A crisis arose when the nobles charged the king with upsetting the balance by denying them their rights. Greatly enriched as they were by the spoils of war in Andalusia, their challenge to royal authority was indeed a formidable one. The townsmen too were fearful of losing their traditional rights and privileges and were especially distressed by the king's frequent requests for extraordinary taxation. The royal chronicle echoed their oft-voiced complaint that his quest for the empire "brought great poverty to the kingdoms of León and Castile."

The nobles, out of sympathy with Alfonso X's idea of kingship, brought many specific complaints against him. Keenly aware of his predilection for Roman law, they accused him of contravening the old laws; of failing to maintain in his court *alcaldes de Castilla* or *alcaldes de fijosdalgo*, who would judge their fellow nobles—an implied objection to the presence of Roman legists in the court and a defense of the principle of judgment by peers; of tolerating abuses of authority by subordinate royal officials; of levying the *alcabala*, a new tax on merchandise collected in Burgos for the repair of the city walls; of diminishing their rights and resources by establishing new towns and villages; of yielding Castilian claims to the Algarve; of expending vast sums of money to secure the imperial throne and to celebrate the marriage of his son Fernando de la Cerda and Blanche, daughter of Louis IX of France, in November 1269.

Led by the king's brother, Felipe, for whom Alfonso X had displayed great affection, the discontented magnates began to weave their plots and to enter into communication with his potential enemies. No doubt Alfonso X now perceived the wisdom of his father-in-law who advised him always to keep the support of the clergy and townsmen, "because they are people whom God loves more than the knights, since the knights are more prompt to rebel against authority" (*Crònica de Jaume I*, 498).

King Henry of Navarre saw the possibility of utilizing the rebels to recover frontier lands in dispute with Castile, but Alfonso X neutralized him by arranging a marital alliance between their families. Ibn al-Ahmar, king of Granada, was only too pleased to encourage the conspirators, but as a safeguard against future developments, he appealed to the Marinids in Morocco to succor their coreligionists in Spain. The *Crónica de Alfonso X* (22) notes that the rebels also contacted Abu Yusuf, the Marinid emir, who expressed his willingness to help them against "Alfonso de los Tuertos," "Alfonso of the wrongs," who had injured them by issuing "false coinage and by violating the good *fuero* that you have used since antiquity." For the time being, however, he still had to crush opposition to his rule in Morocco and could not intervene in al-Andalus.

The nobles confronted the king at Burgos in 1272 reiterating their demands; though he refuted their arguments one by one, he did offer to make some concessions and to confirm his promises in the presence of the *cortes*. When that assembly convened at Burgos in September, the nobles expressed fear for their safety and now objected to the levying of extraordinary taxes upon their dependents, although they had previously given their consent. Despite the king's efforts to reason with them, a number of them, intent upon a breach with him, withdrew from the *cortes*. The king, however, continued to seek some accommodation and also attended to the petitions and complaints of the bishops and townsmen. He confirmed the traditional customs of the nobility and also the *fueros* of the towns, thereby significantly modifying his plan to develop and apply a single royal law for the entire realm. In return for this, the towns granted him a tax levy every year "until the affair of the empire was concluded."

The death of Richard of Cornwall in April 1272 indeed seemed to enhance Alfonso X's chances of gaining unanimous recognition as Holy Roman Emperor. At this time all his thoughts and actions were dominated by the desire to go abroad for that purpose. In order to obtain the necessary money and to pacify the realm, he was willing to abandon, or at least to postpone, his efforts to impose a uniform law upon the kingdom.

Repudiating the bond of vassalage, Felipe and other nobles rebuffed the king's conciliatory efforts and announced that they would go into exile to the kingdom of Granada. Unable to restrain his bitterness, Alfonso X reproached his brother for aiding the king of Granada, "the enemy of God, of the faith, of the king and of his kingdoms." "You," he said, "as the son of King Fernando and Queen Beatriz, and as the brother of King Alfonso, ought better to safeguard the lineage from whence you come and the duty that you owe to it" (*Crónica de Alfonso X, 29*).

Ibn al-Ahmar gave the exiles a welcome worthy of their rank and condition and concluded an alliance with them, but he died shortly after their arrival. As the first of the Nasrid dynasty that ruled longer than the Umayyads, Almoravids, or Almohads, he performed a remarkable feat in establishing his kingdom when Christian power appeared most invincible; by skillful diplomacy he preserved his independence of Castile while also avoiding dangerous entanglements with the Muslims of North Africa. Although there was some opposition to the succession of his son, Muhammad II (1273–1302), the Castilian exiles helped him to secure the throne.

Alfonso X's negotiations with the rebels, even after they left the kingdom, eventually bore fruit, and he received them into his favor once more in 1274, after confirming their *fueros* and acceding to other demands. He also renewed his pact with Granada; Muhammad II pledged homage and promised to pay an annual tribute of 300,000 *maravedís*, as well as any arrears due, and also to make a special contribution to Alfonso X's "journey to the empire." Alfonso X's refusal to abandon the *arraeces* of Málaga, Guadix, and Comares remained a sore spot and was to be the cause of future discord.

The reconciliation with the rebels and the renewal of peace with Granada allowed Alfonso X to step up his preparations for the journey that he hoped would see the fulfillment of his fondest dreams. Setting out at the end of 1274, he traveled to Beaucaire in southern France where he was received by Pope Gregory X in May 1275. The pope, however, had already recognized Rudolf of Hapsburg as emperor and insisted that Alfonso X renounce his imperial pretensions once and for all. The pope wished to restore peace and unity to the Holy Roman

Empire and to persuade the emperor to succor the Holy Land; from the papal standpoint Alfonso X's candidacy was divisive. Although the king's disappointment was immense, the papal decision against him was fundamentally sound, as events in Spain soon made clear.

The Invasion of the Banu Marin

As soon as Alfonso X departed for France, the king of Granada, irritated by his continued support of the *arraeces*, decided to break the recently concluded peace treaty. He appealed to the Banu Marin of Morocco for help and threatened the *arraeces*, who submitted to him, considering how precarious their situation was in the absence of the king of Castile.

Abu Yusuf, the Marinid emir, received the summons from Granada with great enthusiasm, for he had long desired to engage in the holy war in Spain. The time was now propitious for, after many years of warfare, he had conquered the Almohad empire. The last Almohad caliph died in 1269, and, shortly after, Abu Yusuf entered their capital at Marrakech. Except for the region of Tlemcen, the greater part of western Morocco was now in his hands. As a condition for his help he demanded that Muhammad II cede the ports of Algeciras and Tarifa to him. This would enable him to cross the straits at will, but it also represented a possible danger to Granada's independence. Alfonso X understood very well the importance of these ports and had vainly attempted to obtain them from Muhammad II. The first contingent of Marinid forces crossed from Alcácer Seguir to Tarifa in May 1275; after making peace with the ruler of Tlemcen, Abu Yusuf landed at Tarifa in August, and confirmed his agreements with Muhammad II. While the Granadan forces set out to ravage Christian territory around Jaén, the Marinids advanced along the Guadalquivir to the vicinity of Córdoba, spreading destruction far and wide.

At the first news of the Moroccan invasion, Infante Fernando de la Cerda, heir to the throne and governor of the realm in his father's absence, summoned the host and hastened to the frontier; but at Villarreal he fell ill and died suddenly on 25 July 1275. His death was a grievous blow, but the Christians had yet to suffer other disasters. Near Ecija on 7 September, Abu Yusuf gave battle to Castilian troops commanded by Nuño González de Lara, *adelantado de la frontera*. The Muslims gained a victory such as they had not enjoyed since Alarcos. Nuño was killed, and his head was severed from his body and sent to the king of Granada as a trophy of war. Remembering the services he had received from the dead knight and perhaps doubting the wisdom of his summons to the Banu Marin, Muhammad II sent the head to the Castilians for honorable interment. With grotesque exaggeration Ibn Abi Zar reported that the Muslims cut off the heads of 18,000 dead Christians and piled them high; the muezzin then mounted upon the pile to recite the evening prayer after battle. A month later, Sancho, archbishop of Toledo, one of the sons of Jaime I, was defeated and killed while attempting to check Muslim raids in the neighborhood of Jaén.

In the meantime, Sancho, younger brother of the deceased Infante Fernando, assumed supreme command and hastened to Córdoba where he reorganized the defense of the frontiers and ordered a fleet from Seville to blockade Algeciras, cutting Abu Yusuf's communications with Morocco. When Alfonso X returned from France at the close of the year, he offered a truce to the enemy who gladly accepted it. In the spring of 1277 Abu Yusuf returned to Spain for the second time and ravaged the districts of Seville, Córdoba, and Jerez, but Alfonso X remained on the defensive, avoiding any direct confrontation on the battlefield. Meanwhile the Banu Ashqilula ceded Málaga to Abu Yusuf, so frightening the king of Granada that he proposed an alliance with Castile to expel the Marinids from the peninsula. Accepting the alliance, Alfonso X sent a fleet in the summer of 1278 to blockade Algeciras; his army joined the siege in February 1279. A Marinid fleet succeeded in breaking the blockade in the summer, and the besiegers, who were suffering from disease and a lack of food, were easily driven off. After the deliverance of Algeciras, Abu Yusuf, preoccupied with problems in Morocco, made peace. Scarred and wounded, but without loss of territory, Castile emerged from the crisis. Abu Yusuf was unable to return to the peninsula for two years, and then he appeared in an entirely new role, as the ally of Alfonso X.

While his kingdom had thus far survived the Muslim peril, the death of his oldest son in 1275 caused Alfonso X intense grief. Now he was faced with the difficult juridical problem of determining the succession. In accordance with the principle of primogeniture and representation, Fernando de la Cerda's oldest son, Alfonso, was entitled to recognition as heir to the throne, but this had never been promulgated as the law of the land. On the contrary, Infante Sancho appealed to custom which dictated that a king's surviving sons should take precedence over his grandsons; therefore he asked his father to acknowledge him as the rightful heir. Many of the prelates and nobles and the majority of the townsmen assembled in the *cortes* in 1278 supported Sancho, and the king finally admitted his right. The decision, however, was the source of considerable discontent and greatly complicated Castilian relations with both France and Aragon.

Philip III of France (1270–1285) was already at odds with Castile concerning the succession to Navarre. There King Henry died, leaving the kingdom to his daughter Jeanne I (1274–1305), but both Castile and Aragon indicated a desire to dispossess her. Threatened by a Castilian invasion, the widowed queen of Navarre took her daughter to France and called upon Philip III for protection. Responding with enthusiasm, he betrothed the child-queen to his son, the future Philip IV; in this way Navarre became for many years an appendage of France. Castilian partisans stirred up civil war in Navarre, however, and the outbreak of a full-scale war between France and Castile seemed imminent. French hostility was intensified by Alfonso X's decision to disinherit the *infantes* de la Cerda, his grandsons, who were also nephews of Philip III.

Pedro III of Aragon

In the closing years of his life Jaime I of Aragon was confronted with similar problems relating to the succession. His determination to partition his dominions among his sons was the cause of great bitterness. Over the course of his reign, in spite of numerous protests, he divided the realm six times. The definitive partition made in 1262 between his two surviving legitimate sons, Pedro and Jaume, conceded to the former Aragon, Catalonia, and Valencia, while Majorca, the counties of Rousillon and Cerdagne, and the lordship of Montpellier were assigned to the latter. As might have been expected, there was little love between the brothers. Pedro also developed a strong hatred for his father's bastard Ferran, whom he charged with conspiracy and drowned in the river Cinca.

Family discord caused Jaime I great tribulation, but the revolt of the Muslims in Valencia, encouraged by the Marinid invasion of Castile, was too much to bear. As he set out to crush the rebels, he fell ill and died on 27 June 1276 and was buried in the Cistercian monastery of Poblet. His reign, lasting sixty-three years, was of transcendent importance. Although he yielded Catalan interests in Languedoc, he completed the peninsular expansion of the realm and by his conquest of the Balearic Islands pointed the way to future development in the Mediterranean. At the same time he encouraged the growth of Catalan commerce, fostered the introduction of Roman law, protected the University of Montpellier, and purportedly wrote an autobiography, the *Llibre dels Fets*, or *Chronicle of Jaime I*. Generous, bold, and licentious, he typified the good and bad characteristics of thirteenth-century chivalry; yet in spite of his failures and defects, his fame as the conqueror has not been diminished over the centuries.

Though comparatively brief, the reign of his son Pedro III (1276–1285), a man of energy, initiative, and audacity, had a decisive effect upon the history of the Mediterranean. The conquest of Sicily was to be the great work of his career, but before embarking upon that enterprise he had to ensure domestic peace and to gain the friendship or neutrality of his neighbors. He was crowned in the cathedral of Zaragoza in November 1276 by the archbishop of Tarragona, in conformity with the papal privilege granted to his grandfather in 1204. Unlike him, however, he declared that he was not a vassal of the Holy See and that he received his crown neither for nor against the Roman church. His repudiation of the feudal tie with the papacy was later charged against him as proof that he was an enemy of the church.

His first task was to quell disorder and rebellion. The lands of the Muslim rebels in Valencia were systematically laid waste, and after a siege of six months they were forced to surrender their principal refuge, the castle of Montesa. With that, the revolt collapsed, and they gave him no further trouble. On the other hand, the barons of Catalonia, who had shown signs of restlessness during the last years of his father's reign, now conspired against him, protesting his failure to come to Barcelona to take the customary oath to uphold the liberties of Catalonia; they also refused to pay the *bovatge*, arguing that they were not obligated to pay this tax until it was voted by the *corts*. Jaume II, king of Majorca (1276–1311), tended to favor the rebels, and only in 1279 was he compelled to pledge homage and fealty to Pedro III; but he always remained a vassal of questionable loyalty, always ready to encourage his brother's enemies. The rebels yielded to Pedro III in the following year and asked his pardon. Thereafter they rendered valuable service in the Sicilian venture.

The establishment of amicable relations with his neighbors was a somewhat more difficult task. Pedro III's relations with France and

Castile, both potential enemies, were complicated by the arrival at his court in January 1278 of his sister Violante, queen of Castile, and Blanche, widow of Fernando de la Cerda, and her two sons. While Blanche traveled to France to enlist the support of her brother, Philip III, she left her sons in the custody of the king of Aragon. Taken by surprise and greatly upset by the sudden departure of his grandchildren, his daughter-in-law, and his wife, Alfonso X tried to conciliate Philip III who demanded that the rights of his nephew, Alfonso de la Cerda, to the Castilian throne be upheld. Alfonso X's proposal in 1280 to establish a vassal kingdom at Jaén for the benefit of his grandson was rejected by Philip III and also by Infante Sancho who opposed any diminution of his inheritance by a partition of the realm. Early in the following year Alfonso X and Pedro III signed a treaty of alliance, agreeing to a partition of Navarre; but Sancho, looking to the future when he would be king, promised the Castilian share to Aragon. In return he expected that his chief rivals, the *infantes* de la Cerda, would continue to be kept in close confinement. Thus they became hostages to be used by Pedro III, as circumstances required, to gain advantages from Castile or from France.

Considering the possibility of future Castilian hostility, he arranged a marital alliance with Portugal in 1281. There, Afonso III, who had gained the throne with ecclesiastical support, found himself involved during the last years of his reign in a violent struggle with the bishops. His efforts to recover royal properties seized by the clergy and nobility provoked such opposition that in 1266 the archbishop of Braga and most of his colleagues journeyed to Rome to accuse him of extortion, the destruction of church property, and the violation of ecclesiastical immunities. For several years the controversy dragged on until Pope Gregory X demanded that the king respect the rights of the church on pain of excommunication. Afonso III, at the *cortes* in 1273, indicated his readiness to remedy any abuses, but in fact nothing was done. Thus a papal legate in 1277 formally pronounced the sentence of excommunication against him, releasing his subjects from their oath of allegiance, and also imposing an interdict on the kingdom. Although he promised to give satisfaction to the papacy and the bishops, Afonso III died in February 1279 before the matter was resolved. He had been a capable ruler who, besides completing the reconquest, had encouraged the development of institutions and the growth of trade. His son Dinis (1279–1325), then eighteen years of age, but already a man of independent spirit, showed no haste to come to terms with the papacy and for a number of years continued to endure the censures pronounced against his father. His marriage in 1281 to Pedro III's daughter, Isabel, was intended to contain potential Castilian ambitions to peninsular domination.

The Fall of Alfonso X

The reign of Alfonso X, which had begun so auspiciously thirty years before, was now coming to a disappointing and unhappy conclusion. In the past few years the struggle with the Moors greatly strained his resources, and his incessant demands for tax levies sorely tried the patience of his people, who complained that they were being reduced to penury. When he proposed coining two new moneys, rather than impose another direct tax, the *cortes* of Seville in 1281 responded, "more out of fear than love," that he should do what he thought best. But when he revealed his intention to resume negotiations with France and the papacy concerning the future of the *infantes* de la Cerda, his son, Sancho, angered by the possibility of losing any portion of the kingdom, exchanged sharp words with him. At that Alfonso X threatened to disinherit him, and Sancho replied, "the time will come when you will wish you had not said that." Thereupon Sancho left Seville and began to gather supporters on all sides, including his mother, Queen Violante, his brothers, Dinis of Portugal, Pedro III of Aragon, the masters of the military Orders, the nobles and many of the towns. Summoning an assembly or *cortes* to Valladolid in April 1282, he exposed his grievances against his father and assumed direction of the government, "but he would not consent to be called king of his kingdoms during the lifetime of his father."

Abandoned by his family and many of his subjects, Alfonso X, holding out in Seville, turned for help to his former enemy, Abu Yusuf, the Marinid emir of Morocco. Realizing that dissension in the Castilian royal house might work to his great profit, the emir promptly crossed the straits to Algeciras in the summer of 1282. Near Seville he received his protégé, the king of Castile, and loaned him 100,000 gold *dinars,* accepting as security the crown worn by Alfonso X and his father. In Ibn Khaldun's time the crown still rested in the palace of the Banu Marin and was considered one of the glories of the dynasty. The Moroccans laid waste the countryside around Córdoba, defended by Sancho, and then moved into the heart of the peninsula as far as Toledo and Madrid, reaping much booty. In the spring of the following year, they renewed their raids in the Tagus valley, but at the end of the season the emir returned to Morocco.

Meanwhile Sancho began to discover that his brothers and many of the nobles who had pledged their allegiance were of fickle mind. Not satisfied with the riches he promised them, they began to return to the king's side, no doubt hoping to strike a better bargain with him. Both the king and his son quickly realized the foolishness of their quarrel and made tentative efforts at reconciliation. Nothing was settled, however, when Alfonso X died at Seville on 4 April 1284. In his last will he disinherited his son, giving the realm to Alfonso de la Cerda, and creating vassal kingdoms at Seville and Murcia for his younger sons Juan and Jaime, who had returned to their former loyalty. The will was not carried out, however, for as soon as he learned of his father's death, Sancho IV (1284–1295) claimed the entire interitance. One can only regret that Alfonso X, an admirable scholar, poet, legist, historian, scientist, a truly learned man, was not an equally gifted statesman and politician. The contemporary Catalan historian, Bernat Desclot summarized Alfonso X's character and his difficulties in these words:

He was the most generous man who ever lived, for there was no man, or knight, or minstrel who came to ask anything from him who went away empty-handed. On this account his realm was much less wealthy and the people could not endure the burdens he caused them or the many evil laws he imposed on the land, as well as the coinage which he changed and issued. . . . For this reason the barons of Castile and León and of the whole realm deprived him of his sovereignty. [Crònica, 5]

CHAPTER 16

The Overseas Expansion of
the Crown of Aragon

The Beginning of a New Era

As the thirteenth century gave way to the fourteenth and a new generation of leaders came to the fore, political interest and activity centered
upon two principal issues. In the first place, the crown of Aragon, cut
off from the possibility of making any further substantial territorial acquisitions in the peninsula was impelled to seek a future overseas. The
conquest of the Balearic Islands and the growth of Catalan maritime
trade inevitably encouraged other ventures in the Mediterranean. This
further stage in Aragonese expansion was inaugurated by Pedro III, "a
second Alexander, by virtue of chivalry and conquest." As will be seen,
the resolution of the problems created by his intervention in the so-
called Sicilian Vespers required the nearly constant attention of the
courts of Aragon, France, England, Naples, and the papacy for more
than twenty years. However brilliant his success in seizing Sicily, his
heirs were unable to unite it to the crown of Aragon, so it passed into
the hands of a cadet branch of the royal family. The repercussions
arising from the Aragonese thrust into the central Mediterranean were
to be felt for centuries thereafter.

The second issue, one that directly concerned Castile, but which
could affect the future of all the Christian states, had to do with control
of the straits of Gibraltar and the prevention of another invasion by the
Banu Marin of Morocco. As usual the Nasrids of Granada played a
double game in order to preserve their own independence with respect
to their equally dangerous Christian and Muslim neighbors. Castilian
efforts to deal with this matter were complicated by the continuing con-

troversy over the claims to the throne of the *infantes* de la Cerda, a problem that affected Castilian relations with France and with the other peninsular states and, in some measure, encouraged the turbulence of the nobility during two successive royal minorities. The possibility of French action against both Castile and Aragon was very real, once the crowns of France and Navarre were united by marriage. Portugal remained somewhat detached from these problems, but she did succeed in rectifying her frontier slightly at Castilian expense.

Pedro III and the Sicilian Vespers

Pedro III's outstanding achievement, for which he merited the appellation, the Great, was the conquest of Sicily, an event that touched off a long chain of consequences. Sicily's future became a matter of grave international concern in 1245 when the pope divested Emperor Frederick II of his authority over the kingdom of Naples and Sicily, a papal fief since 1059. Many years elapsed, however, before the papacy found a champion willing and able to expel Frederick II's heirs from southern Italy. Charles of Anjou, a brother of Louis IX of France, was eventually persuaded to do so. After defeating Manfred, Frederick II's illegitimate son, in 1266, Charles entered Naples in triumph; two years later he overcame the emperor's grandson, Conradino. Thus the male line of the Hohenstaufen family, "that race of vipers," as the pope called them, was extinguished. Charles of Anjou was now free, or so it seemed, to lord it over all of Italy and to prepare the conquest of Byzantium, a project that had beguiled more than one of his Norman and Hohenstaufen predecessors.

In the wake of his triumph, loyal servitors of the Hohenstaufen dynasty scattered to all quarters, and a number of them found refuge at the court of Aragon. Pedro III in 1262 had married Manfred's daughter, Constance; after the deaths of Manfred and Conradino, she could claim the Sicilian throne, and the fact that public documents from 1268 onward referred to her as queen was a clear indication of her pretensions. Aside from this, the Aragonese had other reasons to look with disfavor upon Charles of Anjou. By his marriage with the heiress of Provence he had acquired possession of a territory long held by the royal house of Barcelona in one or another of its branches; any possibility for the re-establishment of Catalan influence there seemed ended for good. Moreover, Charles controlled the port of Marseille, a growing rival to Barcelona in the maritime trade of the western Mediterranean. Finally, as master of Sicily, Charles had an interest in Tunis that ran counter to Aragonese aspirations there.

While Jaime I was king he was not inclined to champion, in any aggressive way, the cause of his son and daughter-in-law, for to do so would lead to entanglements with both France and the papacy. Once Pedro III ascended the throne, however, he was free to develop and pursue his own policy. After affirming his authority at home, Pedro III set out to win allies or to neutralize prospective opponents. His custody of the *infantes* de la Cerda and marital alliances contracted with Portugal and England served to counterbalance the possible enmity of either Castile or France. In order to protect his southernmost flank, recently the scene of a Muslim uprising, he concluded a five-year truce with Granada. He also established friendly relations with the maritime republics, Genoa and Pisa.

These diplomatic activities were accompanied by the preparation of a large fleet in the ports of Catalonia. Foreign powers viewed this with alarm, but Pedro III announced that his purpose was to lead a crusade against the infidels. There was considerable plausibility in this, for Aragonese relations with the Hafsid emirs of Tunis, though peaceful for many years, had recently turned more hostile. In the reign of Jaime I the Catalans, after initially profiting from piracy against Tunisian ships, developed more legitimate commercial relations with Tunis and established merchant colonies there. Jaime I encouraged this, as it was a source of wealth for the crown as well as for his subjects, and from time to time the emirs sent him gifts of money as a sign of their friendship. Tunis, however, was situated directly opposite Sicily, and Charles of Anjou had taken advantage of his brother's crusade of 1270 to exact tribute and trading rights from the emir. Thus competition for economic ascendancy in Tunis was another point of conflict and contention between the crown of Aragon and the house of Anjou.

When he came to power, Pedro III, interpreting in a legalistic way the spontaneous gifts made by the emirs of Tunis to his father, demanded the payment of tribute on a regular basis. Upon the refusal of al-Watiq (1277–1279), he decided to support the latter's uncle Abu Ishaq in his effort to seize the throne. A Catalan fleet helped Abu Ishaq to win control of Tunis, but he proved quite ungrateful and no more willing to pay tribute than his predecessor. Thereupon Pedro III determined to avenge this betrayal by supporting the rebellion of Ibn al-Wazir, the governor of Constantine, who promised to surrender to him the small port of Collo. This would afford a valuable base for future expansion in Tunisia, but it was also located conveniently for a descent upon Sicily, should that become feasible. Both objectives were inextricably bound up together.

Charles of Anjou, meanwhile, was busily preparing a fleet for the conquest of the Byzantine empire. To ward off the expected assault, Emperor Michael VIII Paleologus accepted the reunion of the Greek and Latin churches proclaimed at the Council of Lyons in 1274. For the time being, the papacy compelled Charles of Anjou to lay aside his plans. Some years later, however, a French pope, Martin IV, fell in with his designs and excommunicated Michael VIII, thereby destroying the union of the churches. Charles of Anjou concluded an alliance with Venice and with Philip of Courtenay, the son of the last Latin emperor of Constantinople; the Angevin fleet assembled in the port of Messina was to sail for Constantinople in April 1282, there to be joined by the Venetian fleet. The Byzantine empire was doomed, or so it seemed.

Yet Charles of Anjou's enemies had not been inactive. Resentment of Angevin rule was especially intense among the Sicilians who were susceptible to conspiracy and rebellion. Legend attributed the responsibility for organizing a conspiracy to Giovanni da Procida, a former servant of Frederick II, who had been named chancellor by Pedro III at whose court he had taken refuge. Although historians question the tale of his travels to the various courts of Europe to enlist aid against the Angevins, there seems very little doubt that a conspiracy was fomented by Byzantine and Aragonese agents. Contact between the Byzantine and Aragonese courts appears to have been limited, but both clearly stood to profit from the downfall of Charles of Anjou. While Pedro III could bide his time, probably until the Angevin fleet sailed away to Constantinople, Michael VIII had no such option. He had to contrive the wreck of the expedition before it left Sicilian waters.

The Byzantine empire was saved by the revolt known as the Sicilian Vespers. While the citizens of Palermo, celebrating the Easter holiday, were on their way to Vesper services on 31 March 1282, a French soldier began to abuse a Sicilian woman; angered by this outrage, the townsmen rushed to arms and massacred the French. The uprising quickly spread to other towns, and within a month the Sicilians had exterminated the French and their sympathizers and wrecked the fleet at Messina, thereby blasting Charles of Anjou's hopes for the conquest of Constantinople.

Pedro III watched these developments carefully but without revealing his intentions. His neighbor, Philip III, assuming that those intentions were false, warned him that if his fleet attacked the Angevins, France would declare war. Pedro III reiterated his plan to go on crusade, but Pope Martin IV professed not to be deceived and refused his request for crusade indulgences and subsidies, saying that he could expect no favors from the Holy See so long as he refused to renew the homage and fealty pledged by his predecessors.

After making his will and entrusting the kingdom to the care of his oldest son, Pedro III set sail on 6 June 1282, with a fleet of about 200 ships of all sizes and about 15,000 men. His destination was known only to himself. When asked what he proposed to do, he replied, as Desclot relates, "If my left hand knew what the right hand had to do, I would cut it off myself." The fleet sailed directly to Minorca where additional supplies were taken on board, and the ship captains opened their sealed orders to discover that they were to proceed to Collo on the North African coast. When he arrived at Collo on 28 June he learned that his ally, Ibn al-Wazir, had been defeated and killed and that the city of Constantine had been taken by the emir's forces. Realizing that the capture of Constantine would be a costly and prolonged effort, the king again asked Martin IV to grant crusading indulgences and subsidies to support his African venture, but the pope sent a sharp response, refusing the request and again questioning his motives.

In the meantime the citizens of Palermo asked the pope to recognize their commune, but he denounced them as traitors to their legitimate sovereign. Denied papal protection, they turned at last to Pedro III and offered sovereignty over their island to him. According to Bernat Desclot, the king justified his acceptance on the grounds of his wife's claims to Sicily and also because the pope had refused to aid his campaign in Africa. His barons agreed that to return home empty-handed, without having increased his dominions, would be a cause of great shame. Once more the fleet lifted anchor and sailed to Trapani on the western coast of Sicily, arriving on 30 August 1282. Pedro III entered Palermo on 4 September and was received with great joy and acclaimed as king. He promised to uphold and safeguard the "good laws and customs" of King William "the Good" who had ruled at the close of the twelfth century. Upon the appearance of the Catalan fleet before Messina, Charles of Anjou who had been besieging the port withdrew to the mainland. Pedro III now had the whole of Sicily firmly in his grasp, and his forces began to harass Angevin shipping in the straits and to execute raids on the Calabrian coast.

As expected, Pope Martin IV, overlord of the kingdom of Naples and Sicily, refused to admit Pedro III's rights, and on 9 November excommunicated him as a usurper who had seized the throne belonging of right to Charles of Anjou. The king of Aragon ignored the papal censure and designated his second son, Jaime, as heir to the kingdom of Sicily. Since the reconquest of the island was bound to be difficult, Charles of Anjou, presuming on the chivalrous character of his adversary, challenged him to single combat, accusing him of treachery and injustice. Both rulers recognized that a prolonged military conflict was bound to entail extraordinary financial burdens and believed that a duel offered an easy solution. In retrospect it seems highly unlikely that either man would have surrendered his holdings on the basis of a judgment by battle, but by persuading Pedro III to leave the scene of conflict at a crucial moment, Charles of Anjou gained a subtle victory. The duel was to take place in the comparatively neutral city of Bordeaux, belonging to King Edward I of England.

Leaving the government of Sicily in the hands of his wife and son, Pedro III returned to Aragon, and then, accompanied by three knights and a horsetrader, traveled in disguise to Bordeaux. Edward I was unwilling to guarantee the security of the combatants and temporarily yielded the city to Philip III and Charles of Anjou. On the pretext of bearing a message from the king of Aragon, Pedro III, without identifying himself, summoned Edward's seneschal to meet him outside the city. When asked about the situation in Bordeaux, the seneschal declared, as Desclot reported in his Crònica (104), that the two French kings "will do all in their power to cause his (Pedro III's) death or to capture him. Therefore I advise him not to come here for any reason in the world, for the king of France and King Charles are not come here for a battle, but to betray him." Pedro III, consequently, asked to be shown the field of combat and "then gave spurs to his horse and rode over the field." He raised his helmet, revealing himself to the seneschal, and asked him to draw up a charter testifying to his appearance. Having thus satisfied his honor, he hastily returned to Aragon, evading all efforts to capture him.

The Crusade against Aragon

Pope Martin IV, his most tenacious opponent, now brought all the weapons of the church to bear against him. Having already excommunicated the king and imposed an interdict on his kingdom, the pontiff now deposed him and released his subjects from their oath of allegiance (21 March 1283). A few months later (27 August) he offered the kingdoms of Aragon, Valencia, and Catalonia to Charles of Valois, second son of the king of France. Philip III accepted on his son's behalf on 2 February 1284, and the pope solemnly invested Charles as king of Aragon on 5 May. In order to stimulate the conquest of Aragon the pope proclaimed a crusade on 4 June, offering to all who participated the plenary indulgence customarily granted to those who engaged in crusades against the infidels. He also permitted the king of France to use ecclesiastical revenues to finance the campaign. In that the crusade against Aragon was directed against a Christian prince whose chief fault was his political opposition to the papacy, the expedition can only be viewed as a perversion of the crusading ideal.

As the church readied its might to overwhelm him, Pedro III faced another no less serious challenge from the recalcitrant nobles of Aragon. Unlike the Catalans, the landlocked Aragonese saw little profit in the conquest of Sicily and were opposed to any military involvement with the papacy and France. They also charged the king with failure to observe the traditional liberties, customs, and laws of Aragon. Like so many of their contemporaries in other kingdoms, they were reacting against the king's effort to strengthen his power with the collaboration of the legists and by the application of the principles of Roman law. When they confronted him with their complaints at Tarazona in September 1283, he rebuffed them, whereupon the nobles promptly organized a Union to defend their rights and privileges.

Threatened by the uncertain prospect of civil war and foreign invasion, Pedro III prudently yielded and "with a good heart and free will" accepted the list of demands presented by the nobles and towns at the cortes of Zaragoza in October. The Privilegio general embodying these demands was comparable to Magna Charta in its attempt to restore the balance of rights and duties traditionally existing between the king and his subjects. After confirming the fueros, usages, and customs of Aragon, Pedro III agreed that the justicia "should judge all pleas that come to the court, with the counsel of the ricos hombres, mesnaderos, knights, infanzones, citizens, and good men of the towns, according to the Fuero" (MHDE, II, 897). In order to effectuate his promise to take counsel with the nobles and citizens concerning his wars and other matters touching the community, he pledged to "hold a general court of the Aragonese once each year in the city of Zaragoza." In addition, he promised to appoint only natives of the realm as judges, to abandon his attempt to introduce the Catalan tax known as the *bovatge*, to accept other restrictions on the kinds of taxes he could collect, and to limit the military obligations of the nobility. The latter swore to uphold their privileges by whatever means were necessary, and by means of their Union endeavored to hold the king to his promises. For more than half a century their Union remained a source of great difficulty for the sovereign and at times acted as a real check upon his authority.

Journeying to Valencia, Pedro III confirmed the privileges of that realm and promised that in the future his successors would come to the city for the confirmation of privileges within a month of their accession. At a meeting of the Catalan *corts* in Barcelona in December he confirmed the usages of Catalonia, abolished the tax on salt and other new taxes, and limited the *bovatge* to those places where it had been paid in the past. Although he was a sovereign very much inclined to personal rule, he promulgated two laws that became the basis of Catalan constitutionalism. The first of these, *Una vegada l'any*, briefly describes the composition of the *corts*, its essential function, and provides for an annual convocation: "Once a year at that time which seems to us most expedient, we and our successors will celebrate in Catalonia a general court of the Catalans, in which, with our prelates, religious, barons, knights and townsmen we will treat of the good estate and reformation of the land. We shall not be obliged to celebrate this court, if we should be prevented by any just reason" (*MHDE*, II, 952). The *corts* was not convoked every year thereafter, but the principle of frequent convocation was confirmed by his successors. The law *Volem, statuim*, provided that general constitutions should be enacted with the consent of the three estates: "We wish, we establish and we ordain that if we and our successors wish to make any general constitution or statute in Catalonia, we shall do so with the approbation and consent of the prelates, barons, knights and townsmen of Catalonia or of the greater and wiser group (*maior et sanior pars*) of those summoned" (*MHDE*, II, 95). In effect the king recognized that the *corts* had an essential role to play in government, not merely by advising him on matters of policy, but by deliberating with him and enacting with him fundamental legislation binding on all. In no other European country at so early a date was the legislative function of parliament so clearly acknowledged.

In spite of his domestic difficulties and the hostility of the pope, the Angevins, and the king of France, Pedro III's lieutenants were pressing the war in Sicily with considerable success. Early in 1284 his fleet seized Malta and the adjacent islands and also won a major naval battle in the bay of Naples on 5 June, capturing Charles of Salerno, the son and heir of Charles of Anjou; he remained a prisoner and a pawn in diplomatic maneuvering until 1288.

In the meantime Pedro III was actively seeking allies to aid him in turning back the expected French invasion, but his negotiations with Edward I of England and Rudolf of Hapsburg, the Holy Roman Emperor, led nowhere and the promise of a subsidy from the Byzantine Emperor Andronicus II was never fulfilled. Mutual hostility to France, based on several factors, made natural allies of Sancho IV and Pedro III, but in the long run their alliance, concluded in February 1285, proved fruitless. Sancho IV's paramount concern was that his nephews, the *infantes* de la Cerda, who were in Pedro III's custody, should never be liberated lest they challenge his rights to the Castilian throne. Philip III of France, however, as the uncle of the *infantes*, had already given proof of his intent to uphold their rights. The establishment of a French presence in Navarre, following the marriage of his son Philip to Queen Jeanne in 1284, not only thwarted Castilian and Aragonese desires to annex that kingdom, but also constituted a very real threat to them. There was every reason to expect that Castile would support Aragon during the coming crusade, but at the crucial moment, the Banu Marin landed at Tarifa and resumed their assault upon the Castilian frontier, so that Pedro III had to meet the French entirely alone.

The deaths of Charles of Anjou and Martin IV early in 1285 momentarily dampened Philip III's spirit, but he did not abandon his preparations for the invasion of Aragon. Accompanied by his sons and the papal legate, he advanced into Rousillon in June, where King Jaume of Majorca, Pedro III's brother, welcomed him; Perpignan and other towns recently occupied by Pedro III, who expected treachery from his brother, were forced to open their gates. Entering Catalonia, the French besieged Gerona by land and sea and reduced it to submission after three months on 7 September. In the meantime, the Catalan fleet, summoned from Sicily, routed the French fleet near San Feliu de Guíxols.

At the same time pestilence swept through the French army, and Philip III, falling victim to it, ordered a retreat. He died at Perpignan in October 1285, and his lieutenants promptly surrendered Gerona and other places to the Aragonese.

Pedro III did not long survive his enemies. While preparing an armada to occupy the kingdom of Majorca in retaliation for his brother's betrayal, he fell ill and died on 11 November 1285; he was buried in the Cistercian abbey of Santes Creus. In the words of the poet Dante, "D'ogni valor portó cinta la corda"—"He was girded with the cord of every worth" (*Purgatorio*, VII, 112–114). On the basis of Desclot's testimony, Soldevila believes that as a condition of receiving final absolution, Pedro III offered to restore Sicily to the papacy, but Sobrequés has thrown serious doubt on this hypothesis. A surrender such as this, after so much toil and after achieving an apparent victory over his enemies, would appear to be incredible. Under his leadership the crown of Aragon for the first time played a major role in European affairs, but his successors were constrained to battle mightily during the next twenty years to retain the island kingdom, and more than a century was to pass before the Aragonese banners were implanted in the mainland kingdom of Naples.

The Repulse of the Marinids

While the French were invading Aragon, Sancho IV had to defend Castile against a new invasion from Morocco. From the beginning of his reign his position was somewhat tenuous. His resistance to his father had lessened the prestige and authority of the monarchy, and in order to gain supporters he had made many promises that he subsequently refused or was unable to fulfill. His claims to the throne were not undisputed, and he had reason to be fearful of a French attack; moreover, he had been excommunicated, and an interdict had been laid on the kingdom. The pope also refused to legitimize his marriage to Maria de Molina, his cousin, so that any children born to her would be regarded as illegitimate and denied the right to inherit the throne. His contemporaries called him Sancho *el bravo*, a name testifying to his strength of will and his determination to overcome all opposition.

His immediate task was to protect his southern frontier against an expected attack by the Banu Marin; ultimately he hoped to gain control of the straits of Gibraltar so that future invasions from Morocco would be impossible. Abu Yusuf, the Marinid emir who had supported

Alfonso X during his son's rebellion, now sent to inquire Sancho IV's future intentions. He replied, in the words of the *Crónica de Sancho IV* (1), with characteristic boldness, saying that "he had bread in one hand and a cudgel in the other, and if anyone should attempt to take the bread, he would strike him with the cudgel." This challenge was answered by the emir who thereupon crossed the straits to Tarifa in April 1285 and laid siege to Jerez. His columns spread destruction far and wide in the vicinity of Medina Sidonia, Carmona, Ecija, and Seville, but failed to seize any important town or fortress. Meanwhile, Sancho IV engaged the Genoese, Benedetto Zaccaria, to provide twelve ships to protect the mouth of the Guadalquivir, and a Castilian fleet of about 100 ships was assembled in the straits to relieve Jerez or to sever the emir's communications with Morocco. When Sancho IV advanced with his army from Seville to Jerez, challenging Abu Yusuf to battle, the latter lifted the siege and withdrew to the safety of Algeciras (2 August).

As the French were beginning their invasion of Aragon at this time, Sancho IV was anxious to come to the aid of Pedro III and therefore made peace with the Marinids in October. Abu Yusuf dictated terms to Sancho IV that seem exaggerated, but are probably accurate in some details. The emir's conditions of peace, as recorded by Ibn Abi Zar, were "that you not attack any Muslim territory, nor any of their ships, nor do injury to my subjects or others either on land or sea. In your country you will be my servant, in whatever I may command you or forbid you. If Muslims journey through your land for trade or to earn their living, they will not be impeded by day or night, nor will any tribute be demanded of them; you will not interfere between Muslim kings, not even by one word and you will not ally yourself with any of them in war" (*Rawd al-Qirtas*, II, 672–673). It is not likely that Sancho IV bore this arrogant tone with equanimity, for, in fact, he had compelled Abu Yusuf to give up his campaign and had obtained a substantial indemnity from him for damages caused to his kingdom. It would also seem that Muhammad II of Granada had a deep distrust of the Banu Marin and was perhaps thinking of allying himself with Sancho IV against them. When Abu Yusuf died early in the next year his son Abu Yaqub (1286–1307) made peace with Granada, restoring all the towns hitherto occupied, with the exception of Ronda and Guadix and the ports of Algeciras and Tarifa that would enable the Marinids to pass freely from Morocco into Spain in the future. After renewing the pact with Castile, he retired to Morocco where rebellious tribesmen required his attention. Thus the peninsular frontier remained quiet for several years.

Given the failure of the French crusade, Sancho IV had no need to hasten to Pedro III's side, but in the ensuing years his diplomatic talents were tried to the utmost because of pressures to choose an alliance with either Aragon or France. Opinion within his court was divided, for there were advantages to both proposals. In the first years of his reign the most influential personage in his entourage was Lope Díaz de Haro, lord of Vizcaya, a man of extraordinary ambition, who had supported Infante Sancho's claims to the throne; now, perhaps as a reward, the king gave him extensive authority over the royal household and finances, as well as custody of all the royal fortresses in Castile. In this way Lope Díaz acquired control over the essential powers of the monarchy. His foreign policy, favoring a continuing alliance with Aragon, was determined in part by his hostility to the longtime foes of his house, the Lara family, who supported the *infantes* de la Cerda and enjoyed close ties with the French court. Alvaro Núñez de Lara, outspoken in his opposition to Lope Díaz, roused the Castilian nobility against him and joined forces with the Portuguese Infante Afonso in launching attacks on Castilian territory.

Afonso of Portugal, an unruly prince, was for many years a disturber of the peace. Already he had challenged the right of his brother, King Dinis, to rule, but his fallacious arguments won little support. Dinis and Sancho IV began a joint campaign against their rebellious subjects but came to terms with them in December 1287. Dinis was reconciled with his brother and offered sound advice to the king of Castile: pointing out the grave error Sancho had committed in entrusting so much authority to Lope Díaz, he warned that "if anything should happen to the king, it was doubtful whether his son Infante Fernando would inherit, and that . . . his brother Infante Juan, son-in-law of [Lope Díaz] would have an eye for the kingdom. . . . When King Sancho heard these words, he realized that what the king of Portugal told him was the truth" (*Crónica de Sancho IV*, 4).

As Sancho IV strove to recover his power, his relationship with Lope Díaz deteriorated steadily until it broke down completely. While discussing with his council the possibilities of an alliance with France or

Aragon, the king demanded that Lope Díaz return all the castles he held. In a rage Lope "put his hand on his dagger, and with the dagger drawn and his hand held high, went toward the door where the king was. . . . The king's men . . . struck him with a sword, cutting off his hand, and the hand fell to the ground with his dagger; then, though the king did not command it, they struck him on the head with a mace, and he fell down dead" (*Crónica de Sancho IV, 5*). The king's brother Juan was saved from harm in the melee but was promptly imprisoned. As a result of this tragedy, Sancho IV was again master of his own house and, at the urging of the queen, turned away from Aragon to France. Now, however, his principal rivals, the *infantes* de la Cerda, so long secluded in the castle of Játiva, found an active champion in the person of the new king of Aragon.

The Sicilian Dilemma

Upon the death of Pedro III, his son Alfonso III (1285–1291) inherited the bulk of the Aragonese dominions; a second son, Jaime, designated as heir to Sicily, was proclaimed and crowned as king at Palermo. The brothers exchanged a pledge of mutual support, but it proved to be extraordinarily difficult to fulfill.

At the time of his father's death Alfonso III was enroute to Majorca, intent upon occupying that kingdom as a punishment for the support given by King Jaume to the French during their invasion of Aragon. Both Majorca and Ibiza submitted without difficulty and were formally annexed in perpetuity to the crown of Aragon. The tributary Muslim kingdom of Minorca was occupied in 1286 in reprisal for its treacherous attitude during the recent crusade.

Upon returning from Majorca, Alfonso III proceeded to Zaragoza where he was crowned in April 1286 by the bishop of Huesca, acting in the name of the archbishop of Tarragona. Although he pledged to uphold the laws and customs of Aragon, the Aragonese nobility, who had formed a Union in defense of their rights during his father's reign, were determined to exercise a greater voice in his affairs. They protested at first that he used the royal title and functioned as king, prior to his coronation. Now that he was crowned, they demanded that he admit to his council and his household only persons approved by them in the *cortes*; but he rejected these demands as impertinent and as an unwarranted intrusion upon his prerogative. Failing to bend him to their will, the unionists sent ambassadors to treat with his potential enemies and threatened to recognize the French prince, Charles of Valois, as king. Alfonso III's external relations were already quite grave and, not willing to run the risk of a full-scale civil war, he yielded to the Union, granting two privileges on 28 December 1287. He promised to convene

a general court of the Aragonese in the city of Zaragoza once each year on the feast of All Saints in the month of November. And those who assemble in the said court shall have power to elect . . . councilors for us and our successors . . . with whose counsel we and our successors will govern and administer the kingdoms of Aragon, Valencia, and Ribagorza. . . . The said councilors may be changed, all or part of them, when it pleases the court. [*MHDE*, II, 933–934]

The king also promised not to arrest, torture, or execute any noble without sentence having first been pronounced by the *justicia* of Aragon, "with the counsel and consent of the court of Aragon, or the greater part of it, summoned and assembled in the said city of Zaragoza." As security for the fulfillment of these pledges he agreed to turn over sixteen castles to the nobility and by anticipation released his subjects from their oath of allegiance, should he or his successors fail to observe the privilege. The king's surrender was unavoidable, but in more favorable political circumstances his successors were able to ignore and eventually to revoke the *Privileges of the Union*.

In spite of the Union's challenge to royal supremacy, Alfonso III's most compelling concern was the unfinished business of his father's reign. Together with his brother Jaime, he had to face the hostility of the pope, the king of France, and the Angevins. He hoped to persuade the pope to lift the ecclesiastical censures imposed on Aragon, to abandon his support of Charles of Valois, the designated papal candidate for the Aragonese throne, and to recognize Jaime as the legitimate king of Sicily and a papal vassal. Alfonso III had an apparent advantage, since Charles of Salerno, king of Naples and son of Charles of Anjou, was his prisoner. The combination of forces aligned against him was formidable, however, and was capable of destroying him and his brother. King Edward I of England, offering to serve as mediator, arranged a conference at Oléron in July 1287 to propose a definitive settlement; but papal insistence that Jaime immediately withdraw from Sicily as a precondition to peace talks thwarted these efforts.

The formation of a Franco-Castilian alliance in July 1288 made the Aragonese position even more precarious. In their anxiety to secure an undisputed hold on the throne for themselves and their children, whom the papacy still refused to legitimize, Sancho IV and his queen, Maria de Molina, had concluded that an accommodation with France was necessary. Not only would it remove French opposition to the papal legitimation of their marriage and their offspring, but also the constant threat of French intervention on behalf of the *infantes* de la Cerda. Thus, in return for a renunciation of claims to the Castilian throne by the *infantes*, Sancho IV agreed to give them joint rule over Murcia and Ciudad Real as an independent realm; he and Philip IV also made a mutual pledge of military assistance against their common enemy, Aragon. Once Alfonso III learned that Castile had turned against him, he released the *infantes* from the castle of Játiva in September 1288 and proclaimed Alfonso de la Cerda, then eighteen, as king of Castile. By accepting the royal title, Alfonso forfeited any share in Castilian territory as offered by Sancho IV and also the support of the king of France. Border warfare between Aragon and Castile commenced immediately.

A month later Alfonso III met Edward I at Canfranc and as a first step toward the resolution of the Sicilian impasse agreed to liberate Charles of Salerno; but the pope remained adamant in his opposition to the Aragonese presence in Sicily. Alfonso III now realized the absolute necessity of disentangling himself from Sicily in order to assure the permanence of his dynasty in Aragon. With Jaime's authorization to make a separate peace, he attended a conference held under the auspices of Edward I at Tarascon in February 1291. While the pope lifted all ecclesiastical censures and revoked the donation of the kingdom of Aragon to Charles of Valois, Alfonso III pledged his loyalty to the Holy See and also promised to withdraw all support from his brother in Sicily. Although Jaime was now left entirely to his own devices, he had shown great tenacity and skill in retaining control of the island, and his chances of survival seemed good. The pact saved Aragon from a potentially disastrous conflict, and from that point of view it was a satisfactory compromise. Only a few months later, however, on 18 June 1291, Alfonso III died suddenly, and the peace of Tarascon remained inoperative.

The Conquest of Tarifa

His younger brother, Jaime II (1291–1327), as the oldest surviving son of Pedro III, now hastened from Sicily to claim the dominions of the crown of Aragon; but he had no intention of yielding Sicily and virtually repudiated the treaty of Tarascon. In preparation for the struggle he knew would follow, he sought an early rapprochement with Sancho IV of Castile. The two rulers, meeting in November 1291, pledged mutual aid against their enemies. Sancho IV offered to mediate between France and Aragon, and Jaime II abandoned the cause of the *infantes* de la Cerda. As an indication of future aspirations the two kings marked out spheres of influence and possible conquest in North Africa, with Morocco being allotted to Castile, and Algeria and Tunis to Aragon. Moreover, Jaime II promised to assist Castile in the impending conflict with the Moroccans.

For Sancho IV the alliance was concluded at a most opportune time, for his truce with the Marinids had expired, and preparations for war were in progress. Muhammad II of Granada, fearing the consequences of a successful Moroccan invasion, renewed the payment of tribute as a sign of vassalage to Castile but remained ready to take advantage of any unexpected circumstance. The Genoese admiral Benedetto Zaccaria, again in Castilian service, won a signal victory over the Moroccan fleet in August 1291, but this did not prevent the Marinid emir, Abu Yaqub, from landing in Spain a month later and ravaging the countryside.

In the following spring, Sancho IV and Muhammad II, determined to deprive the Moroccans of easy access to the peninsula, laid siege to the port of Tarifa, which, together with Algeciras, was one of the keys to control of the straits. The town capitulated to Sancho IV who made his entrance on 13 October 1292, but Muhammad II, angered that it was not restored to him, shifted alliances once more. Visiting Abu Yaqub at Tangier, he asked forgiveness for past hostility and appealed for aid against Castile. Moroccan and Granadan forces consequently besieged Tarifa in 1294, but Alfonso Pérez de Guzmán, who, by his heroism gained the sobriquet, *el bueno*, successfully held off the attack until the arrival of Castilian and Catalan ships forced the besiegers to retire. The conquest and defense of Tarifa was the first step toward closing the gates of the peninsula to future invasions from Morocco.

In the meantime the alliance between Castile and Aragon was seen to rest upon a shaky foundation, and collapsed. In his efforts to mediate between France and Aragon, Sancho IV tried to persuade Jaime II to accept conditions of peace which he considered detrimental to his best interests. Thus Jaime II repudiated the alliance in 1294 and thereafter abandoned the policy of accommodation with Castile. Sancho IV, an energetic ruler, a brave warrior, and a patron of scholars, died on 25 April in the following year. His nine-year-old son, Fernando IV (1295–1312), succeeded him.

The Settlement of the Sicilian Question

Not long after, Jaime II came to terms with his principal opponents. Although he had been determined to preserve the union of Aragon and Sicily, circumstances gradually forced him to realize that he could not overcome the steady opposition of the papacy, France, and Naples. In the end he adopted the policy which earlier led his brother to sign the treaty of Tarascon. The treaty of Anagni, signed on 12 June 1295, required him to renounce his rights to Sicily and to compel his younger brother, Federico, who had been acting as his lieutenant, to leave the island. He also had to restore the kingdom of Majorca to his uncle, Jaume, to hold as a fief of the crown of Aragon. In return for yielding Sicily, Pope Boniface VIII promised to invest him with the islands of Sardinia and Corsica, traditionally fiefs of the Holy See. For Jaime II the treaty of Anagni was a total, but undoubtedly necessary, capitulation. By abandoning Aragon's hard-won rights to Sicily he gained a secure title to his throne and no longer had to fear French attempts, possibly in conjunction with Castile, to deprive him of it. Although Sardinia and Corsica might be considered adequate compensation for Sicily, strong Genoese and Pisan interests in the islands would have to be overcome by force. For the time being, however, Jaime II shifted his attention from the central Mediterranean to peninsular affairs.

His younger brother, however, instead of leaving Sicily as the treaty stipulated, was proclaimed as King Federico III, and all the efforts of Pope Boniface VIII to induce him to withdraw were unavailing. The exasperated pontiff called upon Jaime II and Charles II of Naples to expel him. As an inducement to accept this reversal of roles, the pope formally invested Jaime II with title to Sardinia and Corsica and appointed him papal gonfalonier. Aragonese and Angevin forces, united in a strange alliance, launched an assault against Sicily in 1298, but Jaime II was unable to disguise his lack of enthusiasm for the war and soon returned to Aragon. The evident impossibility of expelling Federico III forced the pope to negotiate, and peace was concluded at Caltabellota in August 1302. Federico III was recognized as king of Trinacria, a title intended to limit his rights to Sicily and to exclude any

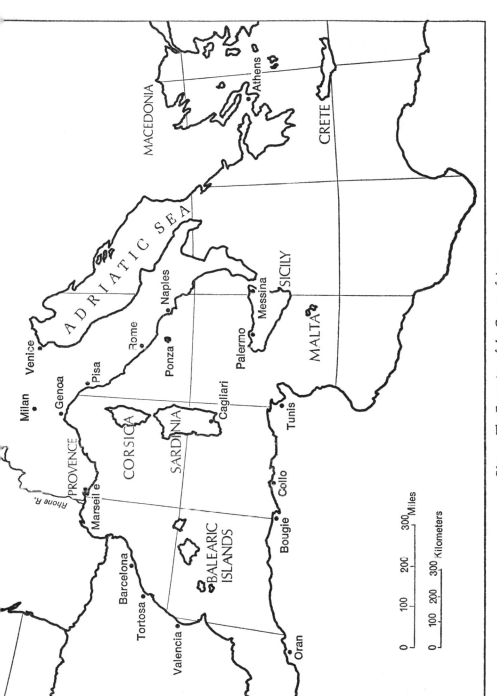

Map 7. The Expansion of the Crown of Aragon

claim to the mainland kingdom of Naples. After his death the island would be united with Naples under Angevin rule, but in spite of this provision he and his descendants retained possession of Sicily. The peace of Caltabellota brought an end to the twenty-year struggle between Aragon and her enemies. On the whole, the Aragonese dynasty, with immediate control or title through its three branches to all the major islands in the western Mediterranean, namely, Majorca, Sicily, Sardinia, and Corsica, emerged satisfactorily.

Federico III reaped an unexpected profit from the exploits of the Catalan Company in the eastern Mediterranean. Formed by contingents of *almògavers*, the light-armed Catalan and Aragonese soldiery who had enabled Pedro III and his sons to withstand all efforts to dislodge them from Sicily, the Company entered the service of the Byzantine Emperor, Andronicus II, who needed troops to turn back the Turks threatening Byzantine positions in Anatolia. Under its German commander, Roger de Flor, the Company set out on its first campaign in the spring of 1304, marching through Anatolia to Philadelphia, Magnesia, Ephesus and the Cilician Gates, the entrance to the Taurus mountains. In every encounter with the Turks they were victorious, but reports of their ravages and brutality terrorized friend and foe alike. Recalled to Constantinople and quartered in the Gallipoli peninsula, they became a menace to the empire itself. When the emperor's son assassinated Roger de Flor in 1305, the Company under the leadership of Berenger de Entenza declared war on the empire. They successfully repelled all efforts to drive them out of Gallipoli and carried out far-reaching attacks along the coasts; after exhausting the resources of the peninsula, they crossed into Macedonia in 1307 where they continued their destruction. Three years later they entered the service of Walter of Brienne, duke of Athens, but when he tried to dismiss them they turned against him and killed him in battle on the river Cephissus in 1311. Occupying the duchy, they parceled out lands among themselves and so brought their wanderings to an end. Mindful of their allegiance to Federico III, they acknowledged his sovereignty; the duchy survived for more than seventy years as the most remote outpost of Catalan culture and influence. Among the conquered Greeks, however, the memory of Catalan terror and brutality persisted for centuries thereafter.

The adventures of the Catalan Company did not directly benefit Jaime II of Aragon. After freeing himself from the Sicilian encumbrance, he redirected his policy and his ambition to Spain itself, seeking to break through the barriers by which Castile had excluded Aragon from any further expansion in the peninsula. Only toward the close of his reign did he return to the pursuit of imperialistic designs in the Mediterranean.

Anarchy in Castile

The minority of Fernando IV offered Aragon an opportunity to achieve territorial gains at Castilian expense. The years of the minority were full of anarchy, but the queen mother, Maria de Molina, a woman of great prudence and strength of character, guarded her son's person and his throne against his many enemies. His uncle, Juan, who had never displayed fraternal affection or loyalty for Sancho IV, as one might have expected, hoped to make himself king; in justification of his claims, he alleged that Fernando IV was illegitimate, since the marriage of his parents had not been validated by the papacy. Families mindful of high-handed treatment by Sancho IV were ready to oppose his son, as was Dinis of Portugal, who hoped to secure an advantageous modification of the frontier. Jaime II linked together all the enemies of the child-king in a plan to dismember Castile, proposing that León, Galicia, and Asturias be allotted to Infante Juan, the central regions of Castile, Toledo, and Andalusia to Alfonso de la Cerda, and Murcia to Aragon. The Aragonese frontier thus would be contiguous to that of Granada, and Jaime II could consider the prospect of reopening the reconquest successfully; for the moment, however, he deemed it preferable to have the alliance of Muhammad II. The projected partition of Castile, if it had been carried out, would have restored the equilibrium among the peninsular states that had been upset by the union of Castile and León and Fernando III's rapid conquest of Andalusia.

The allies invaded Castile from all directions in 1296. Dinis occupied the zone between the Coa and the Duero, while Jaime II marched triumphantly through Murcia, seizing all the principal cities. Muhammad II simultaneously besieged Tarifa, but Guzmán el bueno steadfastly held him off. The first breach in the coalition came in the following year when Dinis made peace at Alcañices; Castile yielded possession of Moura, Serpa, and the district of Riba-Coa to him, thereby completing the peninsular frontiers of Portugal. The withdrawal of Portugal now enabled Maria de Molina to thwart her son's other enemies; she also persuaded the pope to legitimate her children, thereby removing any legal pretext for rebellion. When Fernando IV came of age in 1301, however, he showed little gratitude for her labors and quickly became estranged from her.

Aragonese claims to Murcia were submitted in 1304 to the arbitration of King Dinis, Infante Juan, and the bishop of Zaragoza. They decreed that the greater part of Murcia should be restored to Castile, in conformity with earlier treaties between the two kingdoms, but Jaime II was allowed to retain Alicante, Elche, Orihuela, and the lands north of the river Segura. Alfonso de la Cerda was persuaded to renounce his claims to the Castilian throne in return for the cession of several towns and fortresses.

Jaime II was still effectively denied direct access to Muslim territory, but by promising to act against Granada in concert with Castile he expected to profit territorially in the future. He concluded an alliance for that purpose with Fernando IV in December 1308. Although previous treaties between the two kingdoms reserved the whole of Granada for Castilian conquest, Fernando IV now allotted one-sixth, namely, the great port of Almería and its dependencies, to Aragon. The adventuresome course of Muhammad III (1302–1309), who succeeded his father as king of Granada, aroused domestic opposition to his rule and encouraged Christian intervention at this time. Earlier in 1306, taking advantage of strife among the Marinids he seized the Moroccan port of Ceuta; not only would it protect his rear against possible treachery by the Marinids, but it would also enable him to prevent the Castilians from gaining control of the straits. The Marinids, however, blockaded his forces in Ceuta, and a rebellion at home resulted in his overthrow and the accession of his brother, Abu-l-Juyush Nasr (1309–1314). Jaime II sent Catalan ships to aid the Marinids in recovering Ceuta, but he was unable to induce them to join the war against Granada.

The Christians began their offensive in late July 1309 by besieging Algeciras and Almería. Castilian troops achieved the only success of the campaign, the capture of Gibraltar in August. An old man among those evacuating the fortress poignantly expressed the plight of the Spanish Muslims when he said to the king:

My Lord, why do you drive me hence? When your greatgrandfather King Fernando took Seville he drove me out and I went to live at Jerez, but when your grandfather Alfonso took Jerez he drove me out and I went to live at Tarifa, thinking that I was in a safe place. Your father King Sancho came and took Tarifa and drove me out and I went to live here at Gibraltar, thinking that I would not be in any safer place in the whole land of the Moors . . . but now I see that I cannot remain in any of these places, so I will go beyond the sea and settle in a place where I can live in safety and end my days. [*Crónica de Fernando IV*, 17]

The loss of Gibraltar, one of the keys to the straits, induced King Nasr of Granada to conclude a treaty with the Marinids, ceding Algeciras and other fortresses to them, in return for reinforcements. The siege of Algeciras continued listlessly until mid-January 1310 when Fernando IV reluctantly withdrew; Jaime II also retired from Almería. The campaign failed partly because of poor organization and ineffective coordination between armies and fleets, partly because of a lack of enthusiasm among some of the Castilian nobility. Whereas Jaime II had nothing to show for his labors, Fernando IV did have possession of Gibraltar, though it was lost in 1333. Nasr renewed his homage and fealty to Castile and the payment of tribute, in addition to surrendering several castles and paying an indemnity. Shortly, however, he was faced with widespread rebellion and appealed to his lord, Fernando IV, for assistance. While preparing for war, the king fell ill and died suddenly on 9 September 1312 at the early age of twenty-eight.

His infant son, Alfonso XI (1312–1350), aged precisely one year and twenty days, succeeded him. For thirteen years the kingdom again had to endure the travail of a royal minority. After the death of the child's mother in 1313, his grandmother, Maria de Molina, stepped forward once more to defend the throne and to guard the king's person. The *cortes* in 1315 recognized her as regent along with her son Pedro and her brother-in-law, Infante Juan. While she endeavored to curb disorder and to pacify disgruntled elements, Pedro took advantage of the civil war in Granada, seizing several fortresses, ostensibly in support of King Nasr who was overthrown by his cousin, Ismail I (1314–1325); but in 1319 Pedro and Infante Juan were defeated and killed in battle. The Muslims gained no territory as a result of their victory, but the disappearance of the princes reopened the struggle for power in Castile.

Several members of the royal family, including Juan Manuel, a grandson of Fernando III and a figure famous in the history of Castilian literature, clamored for a share in the regency. The death of Maria de Molina in 1321 removed the only person capable of containing the contending factions. Disorder became general as the self-proclaimed regents effectively divided the realm among themselves. A contemporary graphically described the deplorable anarchy that spread through the kingdom:

All the magnates and knights lived off the robberies and seizures they committed throughout the land and the regents, so that each of them might have their support, consented to it. . . . All the towns were divided into factions . . . and tried as much as possible to oppress one another. . . . In some towns . . . certain working men, in the name of a commune, rose up and killed those who oppressed them and seized and destroyed all their goods. In no part of the realm was justice done in accordance with law, and the land reached such a state that men did not dare to travel on the highways unless armed and in a numerous company so they could defend themselves against robbers. . . . Besides this the regents imposed many illegal tributes . . . and for these reasons there was a great depopulation of the towns. [*Crónica de Alfonso XI*, 37]

This unhappy state of affairs came to an end in 1325 when Alfonso XI reached his majority at the age of fourteen. Despite his youth, he soon displayed an uncommon ability to blunt the opposition of his relatives. In the same year a conspiracy resulted in the murder of Ismail I of Granada and the proclamation of his son, Muhammad IV (1325–1333), as a puppet king controlled by the conspirators.

Jaime II and the Conquest of Sardinia

King Dinis of Portugal, one of the most capable of the medieval sovereigns, also closed his days in 1325. His career was distinguished by an intensive development of the economy and the merchant marine, the affirmation of royal authority against the challenges of the church and the nobility, and the encouragement of literature and scholarly pursuits. A fine lyric poet, he fostered the use of the vernacular as the official language and founded a university at Lisbon in 1290, though town-and-gown conflicts forced him to remove it to Coimbra in 1308. His last years were marked by bitter conflict with his oldest son, Afonso, and only the timely intervention of the saintly Queen Isabel averted a violent clash between father and son; yet, in spite of promises of fidelity and concessions made, there was no peace. When Dinis died in January 1325 he still regarded his son, Afonso IV (1325–1357), as his enemy.

Within two years Jaime II followed Dinis to the grave. In the closing years of his reign, especially after the failure of his attempt to conquer

Almería, he took up once more a number of projects intended to extend Aragonese influence and power in the Mediterranean. He assiduously cultivated Aragonese interests in North Africa, where the rulers of Tlemcen, Bougie, and Tunis, usually hostile to one another, paid him tribute and guaranteed his subjects freedom of trade and the right to establish warehouses and settlements in the principal seaports. His designs in the eastern Mediterranean were even more ambitious. After the downfall of the crusader kingdom of Jerusalem in 1291, Jaime II persuaded the sultan of Egypt to grant him a general protectorate over all the Christians in his dominions, including Palestine and Syria. The prospect of becoming king of Cyprus with a claim to the defunct kingdom of Jerusalem led him to contract marriage in 1315 with Marie de Lusignan, sister and heiress of King Henry II of Cyprus and Jerusalem. The marriage proved to be unhappy, especially since the bride failed to give her husband a male heir, and the Cypriot barons, always adverse to absentee rulers, chose a nephew of Henry II to suceed him in 1324. Thus Jaime II's dream of adding another crown to his dominions came to naught.

On the other hand he successfully annexed the island of Sardinia which, together with Corsica, he had been promised in the treaty of Anagni as compensation for his renunciation of Sicily. His subsequent involvement in peninsular affairs and the war against the Muslims caused him to postpone for more than twenty years any action to take possession of the islands. Though perhaps he evinced a lack of enthusiasm for the enterprise, Catalan merchants clearly recognized the commercial importance of the islands and favored a prompt occupation, even though this was bound to provoke the hostility of Pisa and Genoa, who had long-standing interests there.

Preparations for the conquest of Sardinia, an island dominated by the Pisans, were begun in earnest in 1323. The Aragonese fleet, commanded by the king's son Alfonso, sailed for Sardinia in June. After long sieges the two principal Pisan strongholds on Sardinia, Iglesias and Cagliari, surrendered in February and July 1324; the Pisans were entirely expelled from the island by 1325. The establishment of Aragonese rule in Sardinia hastened the decline of Pisa and initiated a long war for commercial supremacy in the western Mediterranean between Aragon and Genoa.

Jaime II did not live to see that conflict. He died on 3 November 1327 after a reign of thirty-six years and was succeeded by his son, Alfonso IV (1327–1336). After overcoming the initial difficulties that confronted him, Jaime II emerged as one of the most respected sovereigns of his day. His clear perception of his responsibilities and his genuine respect for law gained for him the sobriquet, the Justiciar.

CHAPTER 17

The Straits, the Mediterranean, and Civil War

The Fourteenth Century

The middle years of the fourteenth century were filled with violent upheaval caused by domestic and foreign wars, family hatreds, the plague, and changing social conditions. As Alfonso XI's minority came to an end, Castile resumed its position of predominance in peninsular affairs and under his energetic leadership attempted once again to gain control of the straits of Gibraltar. The kingdom of Granada maintained its traditionally ambiguous posture, skillfully maneuvering to avoid destruction either by Castile or Morocco. It is worthy of note that in spite of their resentment of Castilian ascendancy, the other Christian states joined in the common defense against the Muslim threat. After the death of Alfonso XI, the reconquest ceased to be the primary concern of the Castilian monarchy, as there seemed no compelling urgency to complete it, and so it was left in suspension for a hundred and fifty years. A major factor distracting attention from it was a brutal civil war between Pedro the Cruel and his half-brother Enrique of Trastámara, who, through murder, ascended the throne and made the fortunes of his family.

The civil conflict embroiled all the peninsular states, and France and England as well. Violence and ferocity characterized the Portuguese kings, Afonso IV and Pedro, and Pedro IV of Aragon, too. His long reign illustrates the dual role of Aragon as a Mediterranean power and a peninsular state. While engaging in a war with Genoa for commercial supremacy in the western Mediterranean, he also pursued the dream of territorial aggrandizement in the peninsula. His arrogance and brutality prompted the Aragonese nobility to resurrect the Union as a means of curbing royal power, but he crushed it once and for all. During most of this period, the kingdom of Navarre, ruled by the French house of Evreux, was only minimally involved in peninsular affairs, for King Carlos II found that meddling in French politics, with the possibility of gaining the throne, was a more attractive prospect.

The spread of the Black Death contributed to the general turbulence of the age. The people were devastated and demoralized, and social and economic relationships were rudely upset, with a consequent lessening of respect for public authority.

The Three Alfonsos

At the beginning of the second quarter of the fourteenth century the three principal Christian kingdoms were ruled by Alfonso XI of Castile, Afonso IV of Portugal, and Alfonso IV of Aragon, whose fortunes were soon intertwined by marriage and politics. In ending his minority on his own initiative in 1325, Alfonso XI acted boldly and disconcerted his opponents. His cousin, Juan Manuel, a born conspirator, hoped that his daughter's betrothal to the king would enable him to direct royal policy; but the king was not to be dominated so easily. When it suited his purpose, Alfonso XI broke the engagement and married the daughter of Afonso IV. By so doing he hoped to allay potential hostility from that sector and to secure Portuguese collaboration in his projected campaign against the Moors, who had taken advantage of his minority to ravage the Castilian frontiers. Angered by this rebuff, Juan Manuel fled to Aragon and attempted to draw Alfonso IV into his intrigues; but he declined to become involved and married Alfonso XI's sister, Leonor, promising military support against the Moors. In view of the failure of his schemes, Juan Manuel pledged homage to Alfonso XI in 1329, but his loyalty always rested on a shaky foundation. Two years later, Alfonso de la Cerda too pledged himself to Alfonso XI, thereby abandoning once and for all his pretensions to the Castilian throne and terminating a dynastic dispute of long standing.

The fate of the kingdom of Navarre, so long linked with that of France, was also resolved at this time. Ever since the marriage of Jeanne of Navarre and Philip IV of France, the kingdom had been administered by a governor appointed by the French king. The absence of the sovereign for so many years encouraged upheaval and conflict with the governor who was regarded as a foreigner. Upon the death of

Louis X (1314–1316), who had inherited both France and Navarre from his parents, the question of succession was raised. His seven-year-old daughter Jeanne was shunted aside by her uncle Philip V (1316–1322), who denied the right of females to inherit the French crown and also usurped her rights to Navarre and the counties of Champagne and Brie. Both he and his brother, Charles IV (1322–1328), employed the title king of Navarre, though neither visited the kingdom to be crowned nor to take the customary oath to uphold Navarrese liberties. When Philip VI of Valois (1328–1350) succeeded to the French throne, he retained Champagne and Brie, but he yielded all rights to Navarre to Jeanne II (1328–1349). In the meantime she had married Philip of Evreux, a grandson of Philip III. The Navarrese, having endured usurpers overly long, invited Jeanne and her husband to take possession of the kingdom that was rightfully theirs. In a solemn assembly held in the cathedral of Pamplona in March 1329, they swore to guard and preserve the laws and customs of Navarre and not to appoint "foreigners nor our familiars who are not natives born in the kingdom of Navarre, to any office or service." The union of Navarre with the French crown was terminated, but the house of Evreux was French and could not remain disinterested in French affairs nor in the possibility of recovering the lost counties of Champagne and Brie.

Meanwhile Alfonso XI launched his drive against the Moors, planning a major assault upon Granada in conjunction with Aragon and Portugal. His first campaign in 1327 resulted in the capture of several fortresses in the western sector of the kingdom of Granada and several additional strongholds in that area fell in 1330. These victories frightened Muhammad IV, king of Granada, who journeyed to Morocco to enlist the aid of the Marinid Emir Abu-l-Hasan (1331–1351). Responding enthusiastically, he sent an expeditionary force to Spain under the command of his son who gained a triumph of the first order when he captured Gibraltar after a siege of five months in June 1333. Alfonso XI's efforts to relieve the fortress and to recover it once it surrendered were impeded by continued unrest and conspiracy among the nobility as well as by difficulties with his neighbors. The return of the Marinids and their occupation of Gibraltar displeased influential elements among the Granadan nobility, however; denouncing Muhammad IV for having invited these intruders into the peninsula, they assassinated him and proclaimed his brother Yusuf I (1333–1354) king in his stead. A general peace among Castile, Granada, and Morocco was concluded shortly thereafter. Alfonso IV, whose fleet had taken part in recent naval engagements in the straits, resented Alfonso XI's presumption in trying to include Aragon in the pact and insisted upon making a separate settlement.

The lack of cordiality in Alfonso XI's relations with Aragon was more than matched by open hostility with Portugal. Alfonso XI made no secret of his lack of feeling for his Portuguese wife (the daughter of Afonso IV) and publicly flaunted his relationship with Leonor de Guzmán, who bore him several illegitimate children, including Enrique of Trastámara. Believing his daughter to be dishonored by her husband, Afonso IV plotted against him with Juan Manuel; their alliance was sealed by the marriage of the king's son Pedro and Juan Manuel's daughter. Alfonso XI tried to prevent the bride from leaving Castile, giving his enemies further cause to hate him. As it turned out, Pedro fell madly in love with Inés de Castro, a beautiful lady in his betrothed's entourage, and so began a tale that ended in tragedy. Warfare irrupted shortly as the Castilians invaded the Algarve and the Portuguese ravaged Galicia.

Despite the urgings of Juan Manuel, Alfonso IV of Aragon preferred to remain aloof from these intrapeninsular conflicts. History has bestowed upon him the sobriquet, the benign, which, while attesting to his affability, also suggests a lack of decision. His forces had repulsed Granadan attacks upon the frontier, and he had aided Castile in the defense of the straits, but his primary concern was to uphold Aragonese rights in Sardinia. His father had entrusted him with the occupation of the island, but the Genoese regarded this as an intrusion upon their interests and encouraged the Sardinians to revolt. A long naval war between Genoa and Aragon to determine commercial hegemony in the western Mediterranean as well as the future of Sardinia began, and continued well into the next reign.

To some extent Alfonso IV's ability to restrain Genoese intervention in Sardinia was hampered by domestic opposition to his attempt to effect a partial partition of the realm. Upon his accession he had confirmed, as his father before him had done, the indissoluble union of the Aragonese kingdoms, but his attempt to circumvent that declaration threw the kingdom into confusion. His heir was his son Pedro, by his first wife, Teresa de Entenza, who had died in childbirth. His second wife, Leonor of Castile, demanded that some provision be made for her son, Ferran. Succumbing to her insistence, Alfonso IV announced in

1332 his intention to cede the city of Tortosa to Ferran with the title of marquess. Ferran's patrimony was increased by the addition of Alicante, Elche, Orihuela, Albarracín, and some other towns, chiefly in the kingdom of Valencia. The citizens of Valencia were most outspoken in protesting this dismemberment of the crown of Aragon in contravention of the law of the land and the rights of the heir to the throne; they also objected that it left Valencia open to Castilian intervention and possible absorption. Rather than acquiesce, they declared their readiness to die in defense of the union of the realms. Queen Leonor was furious at their remonstrances and upbraided her husband saying: "My Lord, my brother Alfonso, king of Castile, would not consent to this but would behead them all." The king replied: "My Lady, our people is free and is not so subjected as the people of Castile, for they regard us as their lord and we regard them as good vassals and companions" (*Chronique de Pierre IV*, I, 48). Contrary to the opinion of some Catalan historians, these remarks ought not to be interpreted so much as a commentary upon the differing constitutional structures of the two kingdoms, but simply as a reflection upon the differing personalities of the kings of Aragon and Castile.

Thwarted in her ambitions for her son, Queen Leonor directed a bitter hatred toward her stepson who responded in kind. When the king died on 24 January 1336, Pedro IV (1336–1387), then sixteen years of age, attempted to arrest the queen, but she succeeded in making her escape to Castile. Known to history as "the Ceremonious," Pedro IV, like so many of his contemporaries, was a cruel man, lacking in scruples, but concerned to justify his acts according to the letter of the law. He was endowed with great energy, pertinacity, and shrewdness and displayed an avid interest in cultural activities. At his coronation in the cathedral of Zaragoza he placed the crown upon his own head, declaring that it would prejudice his rights if he received it from a prelate. His animosity toward his stepmother led him to align himself with Juan Manuel and Afonso IV, the enemies of the king of Castile.

The Battle of Salado

Reports of Moroccan preparations for a new offensive convinced the kings of Aragon and Portugal to put their quarrels with Castile aside, at least temporarily, and to join in defense of the peninsula. They recognized that their own kingdoms could not be secure so long as they were threatened by the possibility of invasion from North Africa. The lessons of the past emphasized the importance of closing the straits once and for all, especially now when the Marinids, who already held Gibraltar and Algeciras and had recently completed the conquest of the kingdoms of Sijilmassa and Tlemcen in the southern and eastern extremities of Morocco, were dreaming of reconstituting the Almohad empire straddling the straits.

[Abu-l-Hasan] sent his *alfaquis* throughout all his realms to proclaim that God had given him power in the kingdoms overseas . . . because he wished to serve Muhammad . . . and in this Muhammad showed great friendship for him . . . and that he wished to pass over the sea, to serve the law of Muhammad by conquering and seizing the land of the Christians. [*Crónica de Alfonso XI*, 239]

In the fall of 1339 his son was defeated and killed in battle, but in the following spring the Moroccan fleet destroyed a combined Castilian and Aragonese fleet in the straits, enabling him to transport a sizeable army into Spain. Then with the help of Yusuf I he began the siege of Tarifa in June.

Meantime, Alfonso XI was assembling his forces and asking the pope for crusading indulgences and financial aid. Many knights, hoping to win fame on the battlefield, came to help him from Navarre, Aragon, France, and other northern countries. Pedro IV supplied ships, but Afonso IV personally led his contingents to the host. As the Christian forces advanced, the Muslims gave up the siege of Tarifa and prepared for battle on the banks of the nearby river Salado. Gil de Albornoz, the archbishop of Toledo, gave the customary blessing to the Christian soldiers and in the words of the *Poema de Alfonso XI* (1533–1534), declared to the king:

Hoy salvades vuestra alma	Today you will save your soul
Honraredes la santa ley	You will honor the holy law
E ganaredes tal fama	And you will win such fame
Como nunca hobo rey.	As no king ever had.

And to the knights:

Fijosdalgo castellanos	Noble Castilians,
Hoy podedes a Dios servir	Today you can serve God
Agora cabalgar, hermanos,	Now ride forth, brothers,
E non temades morir.	And do not fear to die.

Once the battle was joined on 30 October 1340 Afonso IV routed the wing commanded by Yusuf I, while Alfonso XI scattered the Moroccans. The fighting was bloody, but the Christians gained a decisive victory and took immense booty, including the emir's harem. Comparing the battles of Salado and Las Navas de Tolosa, the royal chronicle, reflecting an intense Castilian national feeling, pronounced the former more worthy of praise "because men of the kingdoms of Castile and León won it," while an international force was responsible for the latter victory. This interpretation ignores the valiant contribution of Afonso IV of Portugal and of other non-Castilians. In any case the battle of Salado was a decisive blow to Moroccan ambitions in the peninsula, and even though the war continued for some years thereafter, the Marinids were never again able to mount a major offensive in Spain. As the battle triumphantly brought to a close the struggle of more than a generation for dominance in the straits and delivered Spain from the threat of Moroccan invasion, it marked a significant turning point in the history of the reconquest.

Elated by his triumph, Alfonso XI sent a solemn embassy to Avignon to present the trophies of war to the pope and to ask continued spiritual and financial support for the war against Islam. Resuming the offensive in the following year, he captured Alcalá de Benzayde, Rute, Priego, Benameji, and Matrera to the northwest of Granada. With the help of money sent by the pope and the king of France, and ships from Portugal, Aragon, and Genoa, he began the siege of Algeciras, one of the chief ports giving the Moroccans access to the peninsula, in August 1342. Among the distinguished knights who participated in the siege were Philip of Evreux, king of Navarre, who died in 1343, the count of Foix, and the earls of Derby and Salisbury. Alfonso XI's victory over the Moroccan and Granadan forces on the river Palmones in November 1343 in effect guaranteed that no relief would reach Algeciras. Eventually the defenders could no longer withstand the pressure of the siege and, with the authorization of the emir of Morocco, surrendered on 26 March 1344. Peace was concluded with the emir who still retained Gibraltar, Ronda, and Marbella, and with Yusuf I of Granada who resumed the payment of tribute to Castile.

The impetus to continue the offensive was strong, however, and in the afterglow of the fall of Algeciras the theologian, Alvaro Pelayo, in his *Speculum regum*, dedicated to Alfonso XI, urged him to carry the war to Africa:

Africa, where once the name of Christ was revered, but where Muhammad is exalted today, belongs to you by right. The . . . kings of the Goths, from whom you descend, subjected Africa to the faith. . . . Take it, as the other western lands, for it is yours by hereditary right. Because it is yours, subject it to the faith. *[UKS, II, 515]*

The king himself informed the pope that the conquest of Africa belonged to him and to his royal right and to no one else. He realized, of course, that an invasion of Africa could not be undertaken until he had gained complete control of the Spanish side of the straits. As the truce with the Muslims expired, he prepared for the renewal of war, and in August 1349 he began the siege of Gibraltar, the *clavis potissima* of his kingdom. The Black Death, that scourge of the fourteenth century, ravaged his camp, however, and he fell victim to it, dying on 27 March 1350, at the early age of thirty-nine. If he had lived longer, he might very well have captured that fortress, and he might have invaded Africa, but his death halted the reconquest until the time of Ferdinand and Isabella. "When the Moors . . . in . . . Gibraltar learned that King Alfonso was dead they ordered that no one should dare to make any movement against the Christians. . . . They said . . . that a noble king and prince of the world died that day and that both Christian and Moorish knights were greatly honored by him" (*Crónica de Alfonso XI*, 339).

Though "a great warrior against the Moors and their wicked sect," and "the equal of the emperor in the Spains," Alfonso XI also took steps to strengthen the monarchy by imposing stricter and more direct control upon the towns and also by resolving much of the confusion in the administration of justice. The royal legacy unfortunately included much more. His only legitimate child, Pedro the Cruel (1350–1369), succeeded him, but Alfonso's ten illegitimate children by Leonor de Guzmán caused great sorrow to the realm in future years.

Pedro IV and the Aragonese Union

Pedro IV of Aragon did not participate personally in the crusade of Salado and the subsequent campaigns against the Muslims because of his preoccupation with several other matters of more immediate concern to him. He did supply ships to prevent the Marinids from dominating the straits, but the likelihood of making any significant territorial gains for Aragon seemed remote. The Mediterranean interests of the crown of Aragon required a greater investment of his energy and resources.

Almost from the beginning of his reign Pedro IV planned to reincorporate Majorca into the crown of Aragon. Jaime I had bestowed the kingdom of Majorca, together with the county of Rousillon and the lordship of Montpellier, upon his second son Jaume II. Pedro III compelled Jaume to admit that he held the kingdom as a fief of Aragon, but when Jaume was found to be favoring France during the Sicillian Vespers Pedro decided to seize the kingdom. This was accomplished in 1285, but the treaty of Anagni signed ten years later required the restoration of Majorca to Jaume II, who renewed his pledge of homage and fealty to Aragon. Jaume's son Sanç (1311–1324) succeeded him; but when Sanç willed the kingdom to his nephew Jaume III (1324–1343), Jaime II of Aragon briefly but vainly tried to prevent it.

When King Philip VI of France began to encroach upon the lordship of Montpellier, Pedro IV saw an opportunity to profit. Irritated by Jaume III's delay in declaring his vassalage, he summoned Jaume to his court, knowing full well that the need to defend Montpellier would make it difficult if not impossible for him to come. When Jaume III failed to answer the summons, he was condemned as a contumacious vassal, and his fiefs were confiscated in February 1343. Pedro IV promptly sailed to Majorca where he was welcomed by the citizens who recognized that there were substantial advantages to a reunion with Aragon. He promised to guard their privileges and to call a general *corts* every five years. Aragonese troops also overran Rousillon, capturing Perpignan, the chief city, after a strong resistance. The king proclaimed the perpetual union of Majorca and Rousillon to the crown of Aragon in March 1344. Unable to prevent the confiscation of his dominions and finding himself a fugitive, Jaume III sold his rights to Montpellier in 1348 to France. With a fleet provided by Queen Joanna I of Naples he made a landing on Majorca but was defeated and killed in the battle of Llucmajor on 25 August 1349. His son, Jaume IV, was captured and imprisoned until he made his escape in 1362. Hoping to recover Majorca, he married the queen of Naples, but his death in 1375 ended the male line of his family. From 1344 the kingdom of Majorca formed an integral part of the crown of Aragon and was never again separated from it.

In the course of the struggle, Pedro IV had occasion to suspect the loyalty of his brother, Count Jaume of Urgel, procurator general of the realm and, as the king had no sons, heir presumptive. The king's attempt to deprive him of that status raised a serious constitutional issue and caused the revival of the Union of Aragon. Announcing his desire to name his daughter, Constança, as heir to the throne, Pedro IV consulted with experts in canon and civil law, the majority of whom told him there was no reason why she could not inherit the realm. Therefore he proclaimed her as heir in March 1347 but promised that he would not arrange for her marriage without the consent of the *cortes*. There were many, of course, including the king's brother, who argued that females had been excluded from the succession by the wills of Jaime I and Alfonso IV. They could also point to France where the Valois dynasty had replaced the Capetians precisely by excluding females from the succession.

The king now insisted that Jaume give up his post as procurator general, a position traditionally held by the heir to the throne, and that he not reside in Valencia, Barcelona, Zaragoza, or other major cities. Unwilling to give up his rights, Jaume went to Zaragoza where he appealed to the nobles and cities of Aragon to gather in defense of the laws and customs of the realm. The response was substantial; only Teruel, Daroca, Calatayud, and Huesca, of the chief Aragonese cities, refused to join the Union that was now reorganized. The Union elected a number of conservators, including Jaume of Urgel, and struck a seal and invited the king to attend the *cortes* at Zaragoza. Pedro IV's troubles were multiplied when the nobles and towns of Valencia formed a Union and invited his stepbrother Ferran to become their leader.

Pedro IV was still preoccupied with the overthrow of Jaume III and did not come to Zaragoza until August 1347. At the meeting of the *cortes* the Unionists tried to prevent the procurators of towns which had not joined the alliance from taking their seats, but the king insisted that they be allowed to do so. He excused himself for not having held the *cortes* in Aragon since the beginning of his reign and expressed his willingness to attend to their petitions. The Unionists demanded that he confirm the privileges of the Union granted by Pedro III and Alfonso III, requiring the annual summoning of the *cortes* and the nominating of royal counselors by the Union. All non-Aragonese were to be excluded from the council. Although he remonstrated that their demands were unreasonable and dishonorable, the king finally capitulated, confirming the Union, revoking his recognition of his daughter as heir to the throne, and restoring Jaume as procurator general and heir. Alleging the need to deal with the problems of Sardinia, he dissolved the *cortes* in October, promising to summon it again in May.

Thus he was able to escape from a hostile situation and return to Catalonia where he expected to find substantial support. As he entered Catalan territory he exclaimed "O, blessed land, O, loyal people!" Just a month after his dissolution of the *cortes*, his brother Jaume died suddenly, and the king was suspected of having poisoned him, something not improbable, but never proved. His death deprived the Unionists of their leader, but they were not prepared to submit tamely to the crown.

After having assured himself of Catalan loyalty at the *corts* of Barcelona, Pedro IV entered the kingdom of Valencia whose Unionists had formed an alliance with the Aragonese Union. His opponents met him at Murviedro and forced him to recognize his stepbrother Ferran as procurator general and heir to the kingdom of Valencia; he also had to confirm the Valencian Union, allowing it to choose a *justicia* with the same powers as the *justicia* of Aragon, and to exclude certain persons from his council. His attempt to escape from Murviedro was thwarted by the citizens who sent him under guard to Valencia in March 1348. In the midst of the confusion and the celebrations proclaiming the triumph of the Union, the king and queen were compelled to dance among the populace, who left him in no doubt that he was their prisoner. The Black Death struck the city in May, causing the Unionists to disperse; Pedro IV was also able to regain his freedom, as no one dared to hold him in the city where he might die of the plague.

In the meantime the royalist party in Aragon was growing steadily and preparing a counterattack against the Union. In a battle fought at Epila, southwest of Zaragoza, on 21 July, the royalists gained a complete victory. The king's stepbrother Ferran was wounded but escaped to Castile; many other Unionists were killed. As the king made his way to Zaragoza, the citizens humbly sent to tell him that they were at his service. Much to their surprise he ordered the execution of only thirteen persons as guilty of *lèse majesté*. But he was implacable in his determination to stamp out the Union for all time to come. Convening the *cortes* at Zaragoza in August, he formally condemned all the acts of the Union, ordering its privileges, documents, and books to be burned and its seal to be broken; he used his own dagger to cut one of the documents to shreds. Then, granting a general pardon, he promised to uphold the laws and to guarantee due process before inflicting penalties of imprisonment, exile, or death. The role of the *justicia* was defined and strengthened. Though he continued to be appointed by the king, he would act as judge in litigation between the king and his subjects, with authority to punish royal officials or counselors who violated the law, and to interpret doubtful points in the law; his judgment was final. If he proved to be incompetent or corrupt, the *cortes* could compel his removal from office. In effect the Aragonese were protected against the possibility of tyranny by the strengthening of the *justicia*'s office, and to that extent the Union curbed the king's inclination to arbitrary rule.

The plague caused Pedro IV to terminate the *cortes* and to return to Valencia where the Union was beginning to fall apart. The royal forces defeated the rebels outside the city in December 1348. Pedro's treatment of the Valencian rebels contrasted sharply with that meted out to the Aragonese. He contemplated destroying the city by fire and then sowing it with salt, but his counselors dissuaded him from that Draconian measure. In a more moderate vein, he revoked the city's privileges and declared that he would restore only those that suited him. A general pardon, with some notable exceptions, of living and deceased members of the Union whose property was confiscated, was granted. When he entered Valencia he caused the bell that had been used to summon the Union to meetings to be melted down and then poured down the throats of the leaders. He commented that it was only just that those who had made the bell "should taste of its liqueur." By terror he succeeded in reducing the entire region, and as a result the Union, as organized opposition to the crown, ceased to exist in Aragon and Valencia. Though he allowed the *justicia* to adjudicate litigation between the crown and the nobility, he showed little inclination to summon the *cortes* in Aragon or Valencia with any degree of regularity thereafter.

Pedro IV's difficulties with the Union were compounded by the outbreak of revolt on the island of Sardinia in 1347. The defeat of the Aragonese governor-general by the rebels induced the Genoese to intervene, in the hope of extending their dominion over the island. To counter Genoa, Pedro IV entered an alliance with her traditional enemy, Venice, in 1351. A combined Venetian and Aragonese fleet defeated a Genoese fleet at Pera near Constantinople on 13 February 1352, and in August of the following year the Aragonese routed another Genoese fleet near Alghero on the Sardinian coast. These defeats contributed to Genoa's eventual decline as a major maritime power, but the Sardinians continued their rebellion and seemed well on the way to winning complete control of the island. Consequently, Pedro IV personally led an expedition to Sardinia in 1354 and after a lengthy siege was able to force the surrender of Alghero. With the hope of achieving a general pacification he summoned the prelates, nobles, and townsmen of Sardinia to a *curia generalis* at Cagliari in March 1355. Opposition continued, however, and he returned to Catalonia in September without really having subdued the island. The rebels' resistance to Aragonese power until the very end of the reign placed a heavy strain upon his resources.

Pedro the Cruel

While attempting to deal with the Sardinian revolt, Pedro IV had to engage in a much more serious war with his new neighbor to the west, Pedro of Castile, a man generally known to history as the Cruel because of his many executions of members of his family and leading nobles. Several authors, attempting to rehabilitate his memory, have argued that his executions were appropriate punishment for traitors and that he might more properly be called the *Justiciar*. The suggestion that he may have been mentally unbalanced seems exaggerated and, in any case, cannot be proven. He exhibited the same brutality as other fourteenth-century kings, such as his father and the kings of Aragon and Portugal, who with equal justice might also be called Cruel. Even so, his executions do seem excessive. The nearly twenty years that followed his accession at age sixteen were filled with hatred and civil war, as the kingdom of Castile was torn asunder, until he met a horrible death at the hands of his brother.

The reign began inauspiciously when the Queen Mother, Maria of Portugal, after years of humiliation and silent suffering, avenged herself upon her rival, Leonor de Guzmán, whom she ordered imprisoned and then executed. This act angered Leonor's sons, Alfonso XI's bastards, Enrique, count of Trastámara, and Fadrique, master of the military Order of Santiago, but there was little they could do to prevent it. The queen's collaborator in this drama of vengeance was her cousin, Juan Alfonso, lord of Alburquerque, formerly tutor to King Pedro and now his chancellor. He was detested because of his Portuguese background, his great riches, and his undoubted influence with the king. His presumption was revealed at the *cortes* of Valladolid in 1351 when he tried to obtain the lion's share of a proposed, but never effected, division of the *behetrías* among the nobility.

The *cortes*, prompted by the devastation wrought by the Black Death in recent years, also enacted the *Ordenamiento de menestrales*, a law similar in intent to the *Statute of Laborers* enacted by the English parliament in the same year. The shortage of labor resulting from the plague encouraged workingmen to demand higher wages, while artisans offered their goods for sale at higher prices. Reacting against this, the ordinance attempted to compel workers to accept wages at the same level as before the plague, and it also tried to fix prices at that level. As these measures favored the landlords and employers, they produced among the lower classes an intense discontent that manifested itself in violent form in the ensuing years.

Alburquerque thought to strengthen his hold over the king by arranging for the king's marriage to Blanche, daughter of the duke of Bourbon, but before she reached Castile, Pedro had fallen madly in love with Maria de Padilla. The marriage to Blanche was solemnized in June 1353, but two days later the king abandoned his wife and returned to the arms of his mistress. Various explanations have been offered for his rejection of his wife, but the simplest seems to be that he preferred Maria de Padilla. Blanche never saw him again; she was imprisoned in the *alcazar* of Toledo. The king's scandalous behavior not only displeased the French and the papacy, but it also had significant consequences on the internal politics of Castile.

Realizing that his ascendancy was ended, Alburquerque retired to the safety of his estates in Portugal, where he died a year later, apparently poisoned by his physician. The family of Maria de Padilla profited from her relationship with the king to obtain a number of principal offices in the royal household. The royal bastards, led by Enrique of Trastámara, favored the Padilla influence initially, but now that Alburquerque was out of the way, they came forward in defense of Blanche of Bourbon's rights as wife and queen. A number of towns also championed her. In the circumstances, the king decided to conciliate his opponents; but hostilities resumed shortly, and reached a climax in September 1356 when he forced his opponents to surrender at Toro. The opposition was dispersed and dissolved. The queen mother retired to her native country; Pedro's brother, Enrique of Trastámara, went to Aragon; Fadrique, the master of Santiago, submitted fully. Blanche of Bourbon remained in confinement, and Maria de Padilla continued to enjoy the king's favor.

The Castilian-Aragonese War

In the very year that he affirmed his independence, Pedro the Cruel embarked upon a ferocious war with Aragon. At the beginning of his reign he had concluded an alliance with Pedro IV, but their relations cooled rapidly. The Castilian Pedro was offended by the protection extended to Enrique of Trastámara, exiled in Aragon, while Pedro IV took equal umbrage at the favor shown to his half-brother Ferran, once the leader of the Valencian Union and now an honored exile in the Castilian court. There was also an aggressive streak in Pedro of Castile, a determination to establish his predominance in the peninsula and to defend his sovereignty against real or fancied challenges to it. The principal reason for the war that followed seems to have been his desire to recover that part of the kingdom of Murcia annexed by Jaime II at the beginning of the century and to restore the frontier there as it had existed in the time of Alfonso X. A pretext for war was found when some Genoese ships, sailing in Castilian waters near Cádiz, were seized by the Catalans. Pedro the Cruel, who witnessed the act, protested vigorously, demanding the liberation of the Genoese. Upon the rejection of his protest, Pedro ordered the arrest of all Catalan merchants in Seville and demanded the restoration of Alicante, Orihuela, and other Murcian towns ceded to Aragon in 1304. When this challenge was denied, the war was on.

The Castilians launched an energetic assault on the frontiers of Valencia and Aragon and seized Tarazona in March 1357. A papal legate endeavored to bring about a settlement, but Pedro the Cruel would not abide by a truce for very long and consequently incurred sentence of excommunication. Meantime both sides sought allies. Enrique of Trastámara and other discontented Castilian nobles had aligned themselves with Aragon from the beginning, but Pedro the Cruel could count upon the alliance of Granada and Portugal. Muhammad V (1354–1391), who ascended the throne after the assassination of his father, Yusuf I, proved to be a faithful ally of the king of Castile through all his vicissitudes.

King Pedro of Portugal (1357–1367) was a man very much in the mold of his Castilian namesake and, like him, is known to history as the Cruel. His love affair with Inés de Castro has become the subject of legend and poetry, but it is chiefly important as an illustration of the violence of the age. She came to Portugal as lady-in-waiting to Juan Manuel's daughter, Constanza, who was to marry Pedro, at that time heir to the throne. The scandal of his illicit love affair caused King Afonso IV to banish Inés from court; but after Constanza's death in 1345, she returned to live openly with Pedro, and her brothers began to enjoy an inordinate influence in public affairs. Convinced that the

Castro family was becoming too powerful, Afonso IV apparently commissioned three of his knights to assassinate Inés in 1355. Pedro, beside himself with rage, revolted but was induced to make peace before the year was over. His relations with his father remained outwardly peaceful until he died in 1357. Pedro gained fame in his lifetime as a popular king who danced in the streets with his people and shared their pleasures; but he was also known as a ruler who meted out justice with alacrity and brutality without mercy. He agreed to an alliance with Castile in 1360, giving up a number of Castilian refugees to the mercies of Pedro the Cruel, in exchange for the assassins of Inés de Castro who had fled to Castile. In his presence they were horribly murdered as their hearts were ripped out of their bodies. He then convened an assembly of the chief men of his kingdom and revealed that he had secretly married Inés years before. Her body was exhumed and removed to a sumptuous tomb at Alcobaça where all solemnly acknowledged her as queen.

These grotesque events were matched by a series of executions carried out about this time by Pedro of Castile. Suspecting his brother Fadrique, master of Santiago, of treasonable activity, he executed him in 1358. He also planned to arrest his cousin, Ferran, but Ferran fled to Aragon and threw himself upon the mercy of his half-brother, Pedro IV. Ferran's mother, Leonor, and his brother, Juan, were not so fortunate and fell victim to the king's wrath. Juan's execution was especially brutal. Believing falsely that the king would give him the lordship of Vizcaya, he entered the royal palace at Bilbao unarmed and was struck down by maces wielded by the king's men. The royal chronicler, Pedro López de Ayala, reported that "when he fell to the ground dead, the king ordered him to be thrown out the window into the plaza, and shouted to the Vizcayans assembled in the street: 'Here is the lord of Vizcaya you asked for.' "

During all this the king continued to wage war against Aragon. Sailing along the Valencian coast in 1359 he seized Guardamar, threatened Barcelona, and then Ibiza before returning home. Enrique of Trastámara invaded Castile meanwhile and defeated the Castilians; infuriated, Pedro countered by executing his illegitimate brothers, Juan and Pedro. He avenged himself to some extent in April 1360 when he defeated Enrique at Nájera. Through the intervention of the papal legate, Castile and Aragon agreed to a peace settlement in May 1361 that provided for the restoration of conquests. Enrique of Trastámara was excluded from the treaty and had to retire to France.

In the same year, Blanche of Bourbon, queen of Castile, aged twenty-five, a prisoner for the previous eight years, was executed by her husband. Her rival, Maria de Padilla, aged twenty-eight, died a natural death in July. Early in 1362 the king summoned the *cortes* to Seville and announced that ten years before he had secretly married Maria de Padilla and produced witnesses to the ceremony. The assembly accepted the king's word and acknowledged the rights of his four children by Maria de Padilla to inherit the throne.

Pedro utilized the cessation of hostilities with Aragon to intervene in the affairs of the kingdom of Granada, where his ally, Muhammad V, was deposed by his half-brother, Ismail II (1359–1360); he in turn was overthrown by his cousin, Muhammad VI (1360–1362). Responding to Muhammad V's plea for help in recovering his throne, Pedro ravaged the kingdom of Granada. As opposition to the usurper mounted he foolishly fled to Seville to throw himself on the mercy of the king of Castile. But Pedro lacked the knightly virtues; seeing Muhammad VI as an enemy, he struck him with his lance, crying out, as López de Ayala tells us, "Take that, because of your evil pacts with the king of Aragon." As he fell, the Moor replied: "O, how little chivalry you display!" Thirty-seven of his followers were killed at the same time. Muhammad V was now restored to the throne in close alliance with Castile.

In the meantime Castile and Aragon prepared to resume hostilities. While Pedro IV joined forces with Enrique of Trastámara, Pedro the Cruel sought alliances with England and Navarre. Carlos II, known as "the Bad" (1349–1387), succeeded his mother as ruler of Navarre, but his principal interest was the recovery of estates in France which he alleged had been unjustly taken from his family by the Valois kings; from time to time he also put forward claims to the French throne, arguing that his mother's rights had been unjustly denied. An active and untrustworthy conspirator, for a brief moment during the crisis of 1356–1358 he enjoyed considerable power and influence in France. He collaborated with the leaders of the Estates-General, who tried to take advantage of the captivity of the king of France after the battle of Poitiers, to dominate the government. He also achieved notoriety of sorts by leading the nobility in crushing the *jacquerie* or peasant uprising in 1358. His influence and that of the Estates declined rapidly thereafter, and the conclusion of peace between France and England in 1360 lessened his opportunities in France. He had given little attention to Navarre but now began to meddle in the troubled politics of the peninsula, promising to support Castile against Aragon.

Pedro the Cruel, with his customary energy, invaded Aragon and after a short siege captured Calatayud in September 1362. In the following year his forces seized Tarazona and other towns, opening the road to Zaragoza, but he turned instead to the south, taking Teruel, Segorbe, and Murviedro. Once more the papal legate intervened and persuaded the two kings to accept a new peace treaty in June 1363; any expectation, however, that it might serve as the basis for a perpetual peace proved to be vain indeed. As an immediate consequence of the treaty, Pedro IV, evidently with Castilian encouragement, executed his half-brother, Ferran, who had advanced some pretensions to the Castilian crown. The king of Aragon also executed Bernat de Cabrera, until then one of his most faithful counselors, apparently because he favored peace with Castile and opposed the growing ambition of Enrique of Trastámara. Thus the peace treaty was promptly forgotten as soon as both sides had repaired their losses, and preparations were again made for war. Carlos II, who bore his loyalties lightly, this time pledged his support to Aragon.

As the year drew to a close, Pedro the Cruel invaded the kingdom of Valencia, taking Alicante, Elche, Denia, and other towns, and besieged Valencia, but he withdrew upon the approach of Pedro IV and Enrique. He returned to the offensive in the following year, without much success, but in 1365 he captured Orihuela. The conflict, however, seemed more and more to be purposeless and, without a decisive military victory on one side or the other, there seemed to be no way of bringing it to an end.

The Triumph of Enrique of Trastámara

Compelled to wage a defensive war during all these years, Pedro IV realized the need to obtain substantial military assistance in order to turn the tide in his favor. For this reason he and Enrique of Trastámara negotiated with King Charles V of France and contracted for the services of the French general Bertrand du Guesclin and a force of mercenary troops, who were to be paid 300,000 gold florins. This sum was payable in equal parts by the pope and the kings of France and Aragon. The agreement was intended not only to assist Aragon in the war with

Castile, but to rid France of the bands of mercenaries who, ever since the treaty of 1360 ending hostilities between France and England, had been spreading ruin and destruction throughout the country.

With these forces, Enrique of Trastámara invaded Castile early in 1366 and was proclaimed king at Calahorra. As supporters began to flock to Enrique's standard from all sides, Pedro retreated rapidly from Burgos to Toledo to Seville and then to Portugal, where he discovered that his counterpart was unwilling to help him. Hastening to La Coruña in Galicia, he took ship to Bayonne and then journeyed overland to Bordeaux; there he concluded an alliance with the Black Prince, Edward of Wales, heir to the English throne, in September 1366. In return for help in expelling the count of Trastámara, Pedro promised to give the Black Prince Bilbao, Castro Urdiales, and several other places along the Bay of Biscay.

The king and the Black Prince invaded Castile, passing through Navarre. Although Carlos II had promised Enrique to prevent their passage, he did nothing to oppose them, and he also defaulted on his pledge to fight personally on Enrique's side in the ensuing battle. In response to a challenge from the Black Prince, Enrique charged his brother with the murder of queens, princes, and nobles, and justified his own assumption of royal power in these words:

Believing that God showed his mercy to them to deliver them from such a hard and dangerous master . . . the prelates, knights, magnates, cities and towns of the realm all came to us and of their own volition accepted us as their king and lord. This is not to be wondered at because when the Goths, from whom we are descended, ruled the Spains, they did likewise, taking as king the one whom they believed could best govern them. This custom was observed for a long time in Spain and it is still the custom today. . . . Therefore we believe we have a right to this kingdom because it was given to us by the will of God and of all the people, and you ought not to disturb us for any reason. [MHDE, II, 987–988]

But the issue was to be settled not by words but by force of arms.

The combined English and Castilian forces met Enrique and Bertrand du Guesclin at Nájera on the borders of Castile and Navarre on 13 April 1367, and gained a resounding victory. Count Enrique fled from the field while du Guesclin and many others were captured. Pedro wanted to execute all the Castilian rebels who had fallen into his hands, but the Black Prince opposed this, partly for chivalrous sentiments, chiefly because he preferred to collect ransom from the prisoners. The tenuous alliance between the victors was strained on this account, and Edward, finding himself ill, and seeing that the king lacked the wherewithal to pay for his services, soon withdrew to Bordeaux. Left to his own resources, Pedro set out to punish traitors by his usual means and to assure himself of the loyalty of the towns by demanding hostages, but his hold on the kingdom was extremely shaky.

Pedro IV of Aragon made a truce with Castile in August and remained aloof thereafter, but he began negotiations with England, France, and Navarre to gain the best possible advantage from the eventual resolution of the Castilian civil war. Enrique of Trastámara, on the other hand, was determined to continue the struggle to the finish. Obtaining reinforcements in France, he entered Castile again in September and received recognition as king from the *cortes* of Burgos. Córdoba, Jaén, Palencia, Valladolid, and other cities aligned themselves with him, though Galicia and Asturias continued to support the king. As Enrique advanced upon Toledo, Pedro retreated to Andalusia.

In the early months of 1369, Pedro decided to relieve Toledo and marched northward to Montiel, a fortress belonging to the Order of Santiago. Enrique and du Guesclin, who had recently come from France, moved south and easily defeated Pedro in the battle of Montiel on 14 March 1369, but he escaped to the temporary security of the fortress. Realizing that he had few supplies to sustain a lengthy siege, he decided to try to make his escape and secretly offered du Guesclin, Soria, Almazán, Atienza, and other towns, together with 200,000 gold coins, if he would help him. But du Guesclin informed Enrique of the bribe offered him, and Enrique promised to match it if he would betray the king. Judging that Enrique's chances of ultimate success were greater than Pedro's, he agreed to do so, and arranged for the king to be brought to his tent in the dead of night.

The historian López de Ayala recounted the dénouement in this way. When Enrique entered the tent, he "found King Pedro there. He did not recognize him because it was a long time since they had seen one another. One of Monsieur Bertrand's men said 'Here is your enemy.' But King Enrique asked if it was he and . . . King Pedro said twice, 'I am he, I am he.' Then King Enrique recognized him and struck him in the face with a dagger and both of them . . . fell to the ground and while they were on the ground King Enrique struck him again and again. King Pedro died on 23 March . . . at the age of thirty-five." Concluding his account of the reign, López de Ayala commented:

He killed many people in his kingdom, wherefore all the ruin that you have heard above came upon him. Let us say now, therefore, what the Prophet David said: "And now, O ye kings, understand; receive instruction, ye who rule the earth." For this judgment was great and full of wonder and dread. [*Crónica de Pedro*, 1369, 8]

Geoffrey Chaucer's Monk found the murder of the king an apt illustration of the fickleness of fortune:

> O noble, o worthy Petro, glorie of Spayne,
> Whom fortune heeld so hy in magestee,
> Wel oughten men thy pitous deeth complayne!
> Out of thy lond thy brother made thee flee;
> And after, at a sege, by subtiltee,
> Thou wirt betrayed, and lad un-to his tente,
> Wher-as he with his owene hond slow thee,
> Succeding in thy regne and in thy rente!
>
> ["The Monk's Tale," *The Canterbury Tales*]

The contemporary French historian, Jean Froissart, expressed his horror at the murder and at the disrespect shown to the dead body which was left lying on the ground for three days, exposed to public mockery.

With the death of Pedro the Cruel, his brother ascended the throne as Enrique II (1369–1379). The Trastámara dynasty, an illegitimate branch of the Burgundian house which had ruled Castile since the twelfth century, now took possession of the crown; but as all of Castile's neighbors turned against the king and tried to despoil his conquest, many long years had yet to elapse before the new dynasty was secure.

CHAPTER 18

Government, 1212–1369

The Political Structure of the Peninsula

As a result of the rapid reconquest in the thirteenth century all the Christian kingdoms, with the exception of Castile, reached the frontiers they were to retain until modern times. Territorial expansion created kingdoms with marked internal differences of language, customs, laws, religion, and race. Each region strove to defend and to preserve its identity and its peculiar institutions and to resist any royal effort to achieve uniformity in administration. Regionalism not only complicated and weakened the internal organization of kingdoms, but also thwarted attempts to bring about the union of kingdoms with one another. The Leonese concept of empire, expressing the unifying aspirations of an earlier epoch, no longer had any meaning and was largely forgotten. The name *Hispania* or *España* survived, however, as a remembrance of Roman and Visigothic times and as a symbol of the unity hopefully to be attained in the future.

The kingdom of León-Castile held a predominant position in the peninsula because of its location and extension over the great central *meseta*. The union of the two kingdoms in 1230, after a separation of more than seventy years, placed their joint resources at the disposal of one sovereign who was able to carry out a broad expansion along a frontier stretching across the heart of the peninsula. Thus the richest fruits of the reconquest, including Murcia, Jaén, Córdoba, and Seville, fell to the united kingdom, and the Muslim state of Granada was clearly marked for annexation at some future time. No partition of the realm took place after 1230, but during the reigns of Alfonso X and Fernando IV there were serious proposals to break up the agglomeration of territories (Galicia, Asturias, León, Castile, Toledo, Extremadura, Murcia, Andalusia) for the benefit of the *infantes* de la Cerda.

By the middle of the thirteenth century the expansion of Portugal into the Alentejo and the Algarve was completed. Possession of the Algarve was disputed by Alfonso X, but he yielded Castilian rights there in 1267 and also agreed to the establishment of the Portuguese-Castilian frontier along the river Guadiana from Elvas to Ayamonte on the Atlantic Ocean. Thirty years later the line was modified to give Portugal possession of Moura and Serpa, east of the Guadiana, and the district of Riba-Coa. The frontier remained stable thereafter.

Little need be said of the kingdom of Navarre whose growth was checked by the expansion of Castile and Aragon in the twelfth century. The successive French dynasties that ruled Navarre in the thirteenth and fourteenth centuries all had possessions in France, but there was no legal tie connecting these lands with Navarre.

The most complex of all the Christian states was the crown of Aragon, whose initial constituents were the kingdom of Aragon, an inland state located along the Ebro river with its seat at Zaragoza, and the principality of Catalonia centered about the port of Barcelona. While Aragon tended to be dominated by a landed aristocracy jealous of their privileges, Catalonia, bordering the Mediterranean, had a growing mercantile population with a more cosmopolitan outlook. Linguistic differences also posed a difficult barrier to the assimilation of the Catalans and Aragonese. In the thirteenth century the dominions of the crown of Aragon were increased by the conquest of the Balearic Islands, the kingdom of Valencia, the kingdom of Sicily, and, in the fourteenth century, Sardinia, and a portion of the kingdom of Murcia north of the river Segura, taken from Castile. Jaime I partitioned the realm, creating a separate kingdom of Majorca, including the lordship of Montpellier and the county of Rousillon, for his second son; from 1285 to 1298 Majorca was reunited to the crown of Aragon, but then regained its independence for a period until the final reincorporation in 1344. Montpellier, however, passed into French hands. Sicily was separated from Aragon after 1295, but continued to be ruled by a younger branch of the Aragonese dynasty; for most of the fourteenth century the king of Sicily was acknowledged as sovereign by the Catalans settled in the duchy of Athens. Jaime II in 1319 formally decreed the indissolubility of the union of Aragon, Catalonia, and Valencia. This principle was vigorously affirmed by Pedro IV who resisted attempts to partition the realm for the benefit of his stepbrother.

As the Christian states pressed the reconquest, Muslim power was contracted to lower Andalusia, where the kingdom of Granada came into being in the second quarter of the thirteenth century. With its capital in the palace of the Alhambra the kingdom included the inland towns of Guadix, Antequera, and Ronda, and the seaports of Almería, Málaga, Gibraltar, and Algeciras. During much of this period Gibraltar and Algeciras were occupied by the Marinids, giving them easy access to the peninsula. Castile had possession of Gibraltar from 1310 to 1333 and annexed Algeciras in 1344. Granada was a vassal state of Castile from 1246 onward, owing an annual tribute, though the tie was often broken.

Kingship

In the thirteenth and fourteenth centuries the idea of kingship was greatly influenced by the revival of Roman law with principles that encouraged sovereigns to believe they were endowed with nearly absolute authority. Most rulers claimed to receive their power directly from God and did not admit in theory any human limitation on their authority. Reflecting this view, the *Siete Partidas* (II, 1, 5) set forth an exalted concept of the monarch:

Kings . . . are vicars of God, placed over the people to maintain them in justice and truth in temporal matters, in the same way as the emperor in his empire. . . . The king is put upon the earth in place of God to render justice and to give each one his right; wherefore he is called the heart and soul of his people. As the soul resides in man's heart and the body lives and is sustained by it, so justice, which is the life and sustenance of the people, resides in the king. . . . As the heart is one and as all the other members receive from it unity in one body, so also all the people of the kingdom . . . ought to be one with the king, to serve him and to aid him. . . . The king is the head of the kingdom, and as the senses, by which all the members of the body are directed, originate in the head, so also all ought to be directed and guided by the commandment originating with the king, who is lord and head of all the people of the realm. . . . He is the soul and the head, and they are the members [of the body politic].

The *Partidas* emphasized that the king possessed all the rights and powers of the emperor in his empire, but the lawyers and theorists were quick to deny that the universal dominion attributed to the emperor in Roman legal texts gave him any authority in Spain. The historian Lucas of Túy expressed it quite simply: "the king of the Span-iards is subject to no temporal empire"; and in the *Espéculo de las leyes* (I, 13) the king declared: "by the grace of God we have no superior in temporal matters." Early in the fourteenth century, Alvaro Pelayo argued in the *Speculum regum* that kings indeed were subject to the emperor, but "the kings of Spain are excepted from this rule . . . because they have ripped their kingdoms out of the jaws of the enemy" (*UKS*, II, 522).

The rejection of any external temporal superior included also the pope, even though his authority was admitted in the spiritual realm. Infante Juan Manuel noted, in his *Libro de los Estados* (II, 36), that "the pope has full power in spiritual matters . . . and all Christians are bound to keep and observe his spiritual commandments. He also has great power in temporal affairs, but as to what that power is and how great it is, I know little, for I come from Castile and the kings of Castile and their kingdoms are not subject to any other land in the world; therefore let those who belong to the empire and who are affected by this, look to it." Despite this disclaimer, in some instances the papacy did have temporal power over peninsular realms: Portugal and Aragon were both vassal states of the papacy which indeed intervened decisively in the temporal affairs of both kingdoms. The tendency, however, on the part of the Portuguese and Aragonese kings was to shake off any sort of feudal dependency and to refuse to pay the annual tribute symbolizing it.

Within the peninsular kingdoms, royal authority was limited in practice by the older tradition emphasizing the mutual rights and responsibilities of the king and his people. Despite the legal precept "what pleases the prince has the force of law," often quoted by the legists, the people insisted that the king abide by the law and uphold their customary rights and privileges. The frequent meetings of the *cortes* provided a forum for protest against arbitrary royal behavior, but its influence tended to fluctuate. From time to time, said Alvaro Pelayo, in the *Speculum regum*, kings became "wrathful, furious, cruel and proud because of their royal dignity, when, following the example of Christ, the king of kings, they ought to be kind, tractable, humble and human, for they are men and not Gods" (*UKS*, II, 521). Although he argued that it was preferable to tolerate a tyrannical king and to ask God to humble his heart, rather than to bring about worse conditions by actively opposing him, the Portuguese, Castilians, and Aragonese occasionally took up arms as the most effective means of checking a king who abused his authority.

The king of Granada inherited from the caliphs absolute authority in spiritual and temporal affairs and, unlike the Christian kings, was not subject to any institutional limitations, but assassination and deposition were more frequently used there to get rid of unpopular rulers.

Succession to the throne was hereditary in all the peninsular states, but the Christians also admitted the principle of primogeniture; this, while guaranteeing an orderly succession, also raised the possibility of confusion and turmoil during several minorities (Jaime I, Enrique I, Fernando IV, Alfonso XI). Alfonso X was the first to clarify the rules of succession, but his attempt to exclude collateral lines was challenged successfully by his son Sancho, who overrode the right of representation alleged on behalf of his nephews, the *infantes* de la Cerda. The right of females was recognized in Castile, though Berenguela chose to yield her claims to her son, Fernando III; when Pedro IV, on the other hand, designated his daughter as heir to the Aragonese throne, the opposition was so vociferous that he had to abandon the plan, and thereafter females were effectively excluded. Female rights of inheritance came into play most often in Navarre, where Thibault of Champagne became king in 1234 after the death of his uncle. When his grandniece Jeanne married Philip IV in 1284, the crowns of Navarre and France were united until 1328. Their granddaughter, Jeanne, was deliberately excluded from the French succession, but the Navarrese accepted her and her husband, Philip of Evreux as rulers. The Evreux dynasty ruled Navarre until the middle of the fifteenth century.

The ordinary rules of succession were thrust aside when Afonso III, with the blessing of the papacy, expelled his brother from the Portuguese throne; and when Enrique of Trastámara declared that the Castilians, rejecting his brother's tyranny, had, in conformity with Gothic custom, elected him as their king. Violence was employed most often to determine the succession in the kingdom of Granada; there the crown changed hands through armed rebellion, assassination, or both in 1309, 1314, 1325, 1333, 1354, 1359, 1360, and 1362. The survival of the Nasrid dynasty in these vicissitudes is testimony to the strength of the hereditary principle.

The making of a king began when his vassals pledged their allegiance, and it reached its climax in a solemn coronation. When Fernando III died, Lucas of Túy reported that his son Alfonso X declared to the assembled prelates and nobles, "I am now the king" and they replied, "We know certainly that you are the first-born son of your father and ought to receive the government of the kingdom." Mounted on a horse, he was led through the streets of Seville as heralds proclaimed to the crowds: "Behold your king! Do him reverence and honor and obey him, because he is your king and the prince of all the Spaniards!" Not all the Castilian kings were crowned, but the text of a ceremonial composed for the coronation of Alfonso XI in 1332 is extant. The *Crónica de Alfonso XI* (100) relates that, on this occasion, the king and queen attended mass celebrated by the archbishop of Santiago in the monastery of Las Huelgas de Burgos: "At the offertory . . . the archbishop and bishops blessed them . . . and . . . the archbishop anointed the king on the right shoulder with blessed oil. . . . Then the archbishop and bishops blessed the crowns resting on the altar. . . . The king went up to the altar alone and took his crown of gold and of very precious stones and put it on his head, and then taking the other crown, he put it on the queen's head." After mass, the day was given over to feasting, jousting, and other courtly entertainment.

The coronation of the kings of Aragon took place at Zaragoza with the archbishop of Tarragona as celebrant; but Pedro IV, who published ordinances regulating the ceremony of anointing and coronation, crowned himself, "since it would be a prejudice to the crown if we were crowned by the hand of a prelate."

The ceremonies surrounding the accession of the kings of Granada were much like those employed in Christian Spain. The new monarch swore to defend Islam, the kingdom, and his subjects, and received an oath of allegiance from the palace functionaries and then from the populace. As a symbol of sovereignty, he assumed an honorific name, but he did not take the caliphal title; rather he was content to call himself *amir al-muslimin*, that is, ruler of the Muslims. The title *sultan* also came into use, though it appears as early as the eleventh century. From the time of the founder of the dynasty, Ibn al-Ahmar (the Red), the color red was considered a special symbol of the monarchy and was used not only in clothing and chancery documents but even in the great palace called the Alhambra (*al-Hamra*, the Red).

The King's Council

As royal responsibilities increased, the rudimentary administrative apparatus of the *curia regis* of earlier times became more complex. A greater differentiation of functions led to the development of certain departments of state and an increase in the number of officials, many of whom were legists or *letrados*, trained professionally in Roman law.

The duties of palatine officials are described in several sources including Afonso III's *Regimento da Casa Real* published in 1258, the *Siete Partidas*, and the *Leges Palatinae* drawn up by Jaume III of Majorca and adopted in 1344 by Pedro IV of Aragon. The chief officer of the household, supervising its activities and its accounts was the *mayordomo mayor* (*mordomo mor*, *majordom*), usually a distinguished noble. His subordinates included the chamberlain (*camarero mayor*, *camerlenc*) who cared for the royal bedchamber and its appurtenances; the butler (*repostero*, *reboster*), and the steward (*despensero*) who saw to the victualing of the household, and the chaplain who cared for the spiritual welfare of the king and his court. With the exception of the last, most of these posts were held by noblemen. Although their duties were primarily domestic in nature, the distinction between the private and public affairs of the king was never absolute so that the principal household officers ordinarily participated fully in the deliberations of the king's council concerning affairs of state.

The public offices of the council were often, but not always, filled by legists or other professionals. Secretarial, judicial, and financial functions were somewhat more clearly separated than in the past. The preparation of royal documents, the guarding of the royal seal, and the preservation of the archives continued to be the task of the chancellor and his subordinates; but as the chancellorship was often a purely honorary title held by prelates (for example, the archbishop of Santiago for the kingdom of León, the archbishop of Toledo for Castile, the archbishop of Braga for Portugal, the archbishop of Tarragona for Aragon), the bulk of the administrative work fell upon the notaries and other permanent members of the staff. By the beginning of the fourteenth century the use of a great seal and of a privy seal (*sello de la poridad*) was common in all the Christian states.

The judicial functions of the royal council were regularly assigned to judges expert in the law (*adelantado mayor*, *justicia*, *alcaldes de corte*), whose activities will be discussed more fully below. Similarly attention will also be given to those officials responsible for the keeping of accounts (*mayordomo mayor*, *mestre racional*) and the collection of taxes (*almojarife mayor*, *batlle general*).

The military and naval commanders also held positions of influence in the royal council. The *alferez mayor*, usually a great noble, served as commander-in-chief of the army and as the king's standard-bearer, and the *almirante* (a post created by Fernando III in preparation for the siege of Seville) had full responsibility for the fleet.

In sum, the chief personages of the royal council in the western kingdoms were the *mayordomo*, the chancellor, the *adelantado mayor*, the *almojarife mayor*, the *alferez*, and the *almirante*; in Aragon, after the reform of Pedro IV, there were four principal officers: the *majordom*, the chamberlain, the chancellor, and the *mestre racional*. Together with their subordinates, they counseled the king on both foreign and domestic affairs, dispatched communications in his name, received and expended his income, and adjudicated lawsuits. From time to time, especially when the business at hand was of greater significance, for example, preparation for war, discussion of treaties or marriages, the king summoned an expanded council including archbishops, bishops, abbots, and magnates to advise him.

The central administration of the kingdom of Granada evidently continued the traditions inherited from preceding Muslim regimes, but especially that of the Almohads. Unlike the Christian rulers who continued to be peripatetic monarchs without fixed capitals, the kings of Granada usually resided in the palace of the Alhambra where the principal administrative bureaus were also located. The head of the administration was the *wazir*, a prime minister, whose broad powers, extending to all foreign and domestic affairs, were equivalent to those of the *hajib* under the caliphs of Córdoba. If the sovereign were weak, the *wazir* was in a position to dominate him, so it is not surprising that more than one *wazir* was assassinated.

The Cortes

The most important institutional development of this period unquestionably was the emergence of the parliament or *cortes*. The convocation of parliamentary assemblies reflected the changes that had been taking place in the social and political structure of the Hispanic kingdoms since the twelfth century, especially the rise of towns and of a self-conscious urban population, jealous of their rights and privileges. Some towns in Catalonia and in the recently reconquered zones were prominent as centers of trade and industry, though many of them in the western kingdoms were more important because of their responsibility for the administration of extensive territories lying beyond their walls and because of the substantial military forces they supplied to the armies of the reconquest.

In earlier times kings frequently consulted with the bishops and magnates, but the great innovation of the thirteenth century was the summoning of townsmen to these meetings. The *cortes* thus represented a natural expansion of the great council, as the term itself, the plural of *corte*, suggests. It was also a sign of a growing belief in the organic structure of society composed of three estates or classes, who, in solemn assembly with the king, constituted the fullness of the kingdom acting as one, as a legal person. The common opinion that the king required the consent of his subjects before imposing new taxes to meet the rising costs of government, or to implement fundamental changes in law or government was a principal reason for the summoning of the *cortes* in all the peninsular kingdoms. The assembly gave the members of the estates a unique opportunity to make their grievances known to the king and to urge governmental reform; in that sense it had an inherent potential to act as an effective limitation on the king's authority.

The summoning of representatives of the towns to join with the prelates and magnates in counseling the king occurred earlier in the Iberian peninsula than elsewhere in Europe, the first certain instance being the *curia* convened by Alfonso IX at León in 1188. Other assemblies were held in 1202 and 1208, and it seems likely that the Castilian kings also convoked the estates at least from the second quarter of the century. For example, the *Chronique latine des rois de Castille* (40) tells us that, on the occasion of Fernando III's marriage in 1219, "a celebrated *curia* was held at Burgos, to which many magnates and knights and the chief men of the cities were summoned." Thus, although it has usually been stated that the first meeting of the Castilian *cortes* took place at Seville in 1250, this seems to mark the culmination, rather than the beginning of a period of development. After the union of the kingdoms the *cortes* of León and Castile were usually convened jointly, though occasionally, as in the reign of Alfonso XI, separate meetings were held in order to divide and weaken possible opposition to royal policy; from the middle of the fourteenth century onward, however, the *cortes* was a joint assembly of the two kingdoms. The earliest recorded *cortes* in Portugal, attended by bishops, nobles, and "good men" of the towns, met with Afonso III at Leiria in 1254; further study may reveal prior gatherings.

The *cortes* also appeared early in the thirteenth century in the crown of Aragon, but given the federal character of that state, each of the constituent elements, namely, Aragon, Catalonia, and Valencia, developed its own parliament. Majorca was represented in the Catalan *corts* and, despite the promises of Pedro IV, never had a separate parliament. An assembly of prelates, nobles, and "prudent men" of Catalonia and Aragon, convened by the papal legate at Lérida in 1214 to deal with the problems of Jaime I's minority, may be the earliest meeting of three estates of the crown of Aragon, but it is not certain that the "prudent men" were sent by the towns. The royal chronicle stated that each town was represented by ten syndics, but this testimony is too late to be accepted without question. On the other hand, there can be no dispute about the nature of an assembly at Tortosa in 1225, attended by the archbishop of Tarragona, the bishops, nobles, and citizens of Catalonia to give aid and counsel for the king's projected campaign against the Muslims. As the evidence is unequivocal, this may be taken as the first certain meeting of the three estates of Catalonia in a *curia generalis* or *corts*. The first meeting of the *cortes* in Aragon was probably held at Almudafar in 1227; the archbishop, the bishop of Huesca, the barons, knights, and citizens of several towns were present. Pedro III summoned the first *corts* in the kingdom of Valencia in 1283, and Alfonso III convoked the first general *cortes* including all the states of the crown of Aragon six years later. The origins of the *cortes* of Navarre are the most obscure of any in the peninsula; the first meeting may have been the assembly held in 1253 to pledge allegiance to the new king.

In all the Christian states, with the exception of Aragon, the *cortes* consisted of the three estates (later called *brazos*, *cambras*, or *estaments*), namely, the prelates, nobles, and townsmen, but regularity in composition did not characterize every meeting. The archbishops, bishops, abbots, priors, masters of military Orders, and proctors of cathedral chapters were often summoned, but in general only the archbishops and bishops customarily attended; in Aragon they appear not to have constituted a regular element in the *cortes* until after 1301. The lower clergy were seldom present, as it was generally accepted that the voice of the bishop was that of the ecclesiastical estate. The nobility, that is, the magnates (*ricos hombres*, *barons*), summoned individually, and the knights (*caballeros*, *milites*) formed another estate, except in Aragon; there the barons and knights met separately, so that the *cortes* consisted of four estates. Later attempts by the crown to divide the nobility of Catalonia and Valencia into two estates, with the intention of weakening them, were unsuccessful.

Representatives of the towns formed the third estate. All cities and towns, independent of every lord and possessing their own municipal organization directly subject to the crown, were summoned or were eligible to be summoned. It is likely, however, that not all those summoned always sent representatives. The documents seldom indicate the number of towns summoned or in attendance, but 100 towns sent 201 representatives to the Castilian *cortes* in 1315. Elsewhere the number of towns was smaller, so that only about twelve towns regularly attended the *cortes* in Aragon and Catalonia.

Town representatives in the thirteenth century were described in various ways, for example, as *cives, probi homines* in Catalonia, *boni homines, omnes buenos, los de la tierra, personeros* in Castile and Portugal. By the end of the century the Roman legal term *procurator* (or in Catalonia, *sindicus*), used to designate one empowered to represent an individual or a corporation in a court of law, had gained general acceptance in all the Christian kingdoms. Various legal texts equate it with *personero*, so there is every reason to believe that town representatives, at least from the middle of the century if not before, had the status and functions of *procuratores*. As such, they received and presented to the assembly letters of credentials (*cartas de personería*) authorizing them to act in the name of the town and to bind it in advance by their actions. The legal capability of the *procurator* and the binding force of his consent is emphasized in Jaime II's writ of summons ordering the towns to choose representatives "endowed with full power (*plena potestas*) to treat, to do, to consent, to confirm each and every thing that will be done in the *corts*." Royal insistence that representatives have full powers was intended as a safeguard against any later attempt by a town to repudiate the actions taken by its procurator.

Though the evidence is not clear, it seems likely that town representatives were elected in the same manner as other municipal officials. The Castilian towns agreed in 1295 that when they had to send "good men" to the *cortes*, they would send *los mejores del logar*, which probably meant the most talented rather than the most aristocratic. The counselors and the council of 100 of Barcelona met in the Dominican monastery in 1305 to confirm and ordain their syndics and proctors, but little is known of the means employed. The number of representatives varied from time to time, but two seems to have been most common; obviously the number did not correspond to population size. At the *corts* of Barcelona in 1283, for example, there were four representatives from Barcelona, Lérida, Gerona, and Tortosa, three from Tarragona, and two from Vich and several smaller towns. The towns remunerated their representatives, while the king assumed responsibility for assuring the availability of lodgings. The Castilian *procuradores* in 1302, and on several other occasions, demanded a guarantee of protection in going to and from the *cortes* as well as during the sessions.

The prerogative of summoning the parliament belonged exclusively to the king or, in case of a minority, to the regents. The king's presence was essential to the legality of the assembly. The members of his family and the officers of his court also usually attended. Letters of summons indicated the purpose, place, and date of the meeting. The Castilian *cortes* met frequently in the late thirteenth and early fourteenth centuries, sometimes as often as every three or four years; during the two royal minorities of the period it met almost annually, and the *cortes* of 1313 asked that meetings be held every two years. Thus the *cortes* seemed well on the way to developing into a vigorous institution, but Alfonso XI, once he attained his majority, tended to view it with suspicion, convening it at irregular intervals and then usually in regional rather than plenary sessions. Meetings usually lasted a few weeks or a month, and occasionally longer, and were held in centrally located towns such as Burgos, Valladolid, or Madrid. Royal palaces or cathedral or monastic cloisters served as assembly halls.

Pedro III pledged in 1283 to convene the Catalan *corts* each year, but Jaime II, after confirming this principle on more than one occasion, modified it in 1301 by declaring that the assembly should meet every three years. In response to the demands of the Union, Pedro III in 1283 and Alfonso III in 1287 agreed to summon the Aragonese *cortes* to Zaragoza every year, but Jaime II stated in 1307 that he would call it only every two years, in the city that seemed most convenient. Pledges of this sort were never observed consistently, but Jaime II did summon the Catalan *corts* eleven times during his reign of twenty-seven years, and Pedro IV summoned it more than thirty times in fifty-one years.

The proceedings of the *cortes* are sometimes described in the royal chronicles; those of Jaime I and Pedro IV offer the fullest record of some sessions. In his opening address, the king set forth the reasons for convocation and the problems to be resolved and perhaps requested a subsidy. Each estate was entitled to respond, if only to ask his permission to withdraw to deliberate upon his proposals. The estates met separately for this purpose, but there is very little information concerning the procedures followed in the course of their deliberations. Meanwhile the king's council reviewed and prepared answers to the petitions presented by the estates; the Castilian *cortes* of 1351 protested that the council omitted certain words in a petition presented to the king. The Catalans reserved the grant of a subsidy to the king until they had received a response to their demands for redress of grievances, but this did not become the rule in the other states. Once the subsidy was voted and the petitions were approved, the session was closed and the members were allowed to return home. Texts (*cuadernos*) containing the petitions and royal responses were sent to the towns so that they would have a record of the principal actions taken.

There were few rules defining the competence of the *cortes*, but it could intervene in matters relating to the succession, legislation, taxation, and other aspects of foreign and domestic policy. The extent of its potential competence was revealed by Pedro III in 1283 when he declared that the Catalan *corts* should meet annually to consider "the good estate and reformation" of the realm. Alvaro Pelayo in his *Speculum regum* stressed essentially the same principle when he said:

Kings expedite the chief business of their kingdoms according to their own minds or with a few advisers when they ought rather to summon, concerning this, the greater part of the kingdom, that is, their subjects, since it concerns them and "what touches all ought to be approved by all." [*UKS*, II, 522]

The king of Aragon upon his accession was expected to convoke the *cortes* in each of his realms to take an oath to uphold the laws and privileges of his subjects; the *cortes* in the other peninsular states was not always insistent on this point, but the Castilian *cortes* established and confirmed the authority of the regents during two minorities, and it also recognized the rights of royal children to the throne.

There is considerable diversity of opinion concerning the legislative role of the Castilian *cortes*. Martínez Marina, imbued with the principles of the French revolution, neatly separated the powers of government, assigning the executive to the king and the legislative to the *cortes*; Colmeiro, on the contrary, argued that the *cortes* was only a consultative body and that the power of legislation belonged exclusively to the king. Piskorski's view that the *cortes*, at least until the end of the fourteenth century, collaborated with the king in the making of law seems to accord more closely with the facts. Whereas the principles of Roman law gaining currency in the thirteenth century encouraged the king to think of himself as the source of law and as the sole legislator, an older medieval tradition that expected the king customarily to enact laws with the advice and consent of bishops and barons provided the basis for the effective participation of the *cortes* in legislation. This tradition is reflected in Alfonso X's publication of ordinances in 1258 with the counsel of prelates, nobles, and townsmen: "What they have set down, I have granted that it should be held and observed throughout my realms" (C£C, I, 55).

The *cortes* participated in legislation chiefly by submitting petitions touching on nearly every aspect of public administration, namely, the royal household, justice, tolls, coinage, the economy, the status of Muslims and Jews, and so on. The bulk of the documentation pertaining to the *cortes* consists of the petitions and the king's responses enacting them into law. The principle was laid down in 1305 and again in 1313 that laws promulgated in the *cortes* could only be abrogated or repealed by the *cortes*, but this was never strictly observed. From time to time more formal and systematic legislation, prepared by the legists in the royal court, was enacted; for example, Alfonso XI promulgated the *Ordenamiento de Alcalá* in 1348 "with the counsel of the prelates, magnates, knights and good men who are with us in these *cortes*" (C£C, I, 500).

The legislative functions of the Catalan *corts* were spelled out in precise terms by Pedro III, in 1283, when he declared that no "general constitution or statute" was to be enacted without the consent of the estates. As this pronouncement invested the *corts* with a share in legislation and denied the king the right to legislate solely on his own authority, it is rightly regarded as one of the essential foundations of Catalan constitutional government. Jaime II declared in 1299 that if any constitution required interpretation he would summon four barons, four knights, four citizens, and four legists to advise him, and if further clarification were necessary, he would submit the question to the next meeting of the *corts*. He and his successors pledged not to grant privileges in contravention of the enactments of the *corts*. In effect a law made in the *corts* could only be changed or abrogated with its consent.

The parliaments of Valencia and Aragon also participated in legislation by exercising the right of petition. The *Privileges of the Aragonese Union*, for many years regarded as the fundamental law of the realm, were granted by Pedro III and Alfonso III in response to petitions. Moreover, Jaime I thought it necessary to promulgate the *Code of Huesca*, a codification of Aragonese law, in the *cortes* of 1247. The permanent character of the enactments of the *cortes* was emphasized by Alfonso III in 1289 in an assembly of all the realms of the crown of Aragon, when he declared that the king alone could not abrogate the acts of the *cortes*. Very little is known of the legislative role of the Navarrese *cortes*, but the king and the *cortes* appointed a commission in 1330 to revise the traditional *fueros*. In Portugal the petitions of the *cortes* had the force of law when approved by the crown, though the king frequently ignored or infringed these enactments without the consent of the *cortes*.

The most important function of the *cortes* in all the peninsular states, and the principal reason for the frequency of its meetings, was to give consent to the king's request for taxation. As his ordinary revenues were of a fixed and permanent nature, they no longer sufficed to meet the needs of an expanded administration, a greater military establishment, a more resplendent court, more complex relations with foreign powers, and so forth. But the king could not levy taxes arbitrarily; he had to ask his subjects for subsidies and, since the clergy and nobility were frequently exempt, this request was made usually but not exclusively of the third estate. The prelates and magnates were sometimes asked to consent to the imposition of taxes on their dependents.

As a device for increasing their income, kings often resorted to the debasement of the coinage, but this evoked strong opposition from the people who offered to pay a regular tax (*moneda, monedatge, monetágio*) in return for preservation of a stable coinage. For example, responding to Jaime I's pledge to guarantee the Aragonese coinage in perpetuity, the *cortes* of 1236 declared that "every person living in a house worth the sum of ten gold pieces or more in the towns, villages and castles of our dominion, shall be bound every seven years to give you and your heirs one *maravedi*" (*MHDE*, II, 949). The concession of a similar tribute to Afonso III of Portugal by the *cortes* of 1254 has already been mentioned. In the kingdom of Castile *moneda forera* was a regalian right which the king could not give up to anyone, but there is reason to believe it became a permanent tribute not requiring the consent of the *cortes* at regular intervals. On this point, Alvaro Pelayo complained in the *Speculum regum*, that kings "change the coinage for temporal gain to the prejudice of the people and without their approval" (*UKS*, II, 521).

From time to time the king asked the *cortes* for other subsidies to be used for specific purposes; for example, Jaime I obtained Catalan consent to the levying of the *bovatge*, a tax on livestock, for his campaigns against the Muslims, but his attempt to introduce the tax into Aragon was rebuffed on the ground that it was unknown there. Pedro III assured the Catalans in 1283 that he would not attempt to impose new taxes without their consent. Years later the *corts* of 1358 granted Pedro IV a tax (*fogatge*) to be levied on each hearth or household; the census taken for that purpose has come down to us. The *servicios* frequently requested by the kings of Castile were usually intended to pay the military stipends owed to the nobles for their participation in the reconquest. Alfonso X affirmed more than once the obligation to seek the consent of the *cortes* before levying taxes, and the principle was repeated in the *cortes* of 1307, 1315, and 1329: "If perchance I should need any taxes, I shall have to ask for them" (*CLC*, I, 187, 274, 428).

Taxes were usually granted for a fixed term of a year or two, but there were exceptions. Alfonso X obtained a *servicio* every year for as many years as his quest for the imperial crown required, though that turned out to be no more than two years. The *cortes* in 1277 also voted to give him a tax for life, in lieu of all other tributes, and his son obtained a levy for ten years, enabling him to avoid summoning the *cortes* for much of that time. The *cortes* tried to prevent abuses in the collection of taxes and often demanded that Jews, Muslims, nobles, churchmen, or other high officials not be appointed as tax collectors, but that they be chosen from the incorruptible citizens of the towns. During the minorities of Fernando IV and Alfonso XI (1308, 1315, 1317), the *cortes* asked for an accounting of the king's revenues before approving a subsidy. Merriman argued that the failure of the Castilian *cortes* to make redress precede supply was a fundamental weakness, but it is not apparent in the period under review.

The appointment of commissions by the Catalan *corts* in 1289, 1291, and 1299 to supervise the collection of taxes eventually gave birth to the *Generalitat*, one of the fundamental political institutions of Catalonia. In 1323, for example, the *corts* granted the king a subsidy for two years, the money to be collected by persons designated by the syndics of the towns. Money collected was to be deposited in the Dominican monasteries of Barcelona and Lérida, under keys held by several persons. The king and his subordinates were thereby effectively excluded from the collection and distribution of the sums in question. The *corts* of 1359 appointed twelve deputies and twelve auditors of accounts, four from each estate, to administer the money collected. The agency which thus came into being, hesitantly and temporarily at first, began to acquire a permanent character in the latter half of the fourteenth century. The name given to it was *Diputació del General de Catalunya* or simply *Generalitat*, an agency representing, as did the *corts*, the totality of Catalonia. In the last century of the medieval era the *Generalitat* wielded great power and influence as a permanent agency of the *corts*, capable of exercising a constant supervision and control of the king's actions.

Aside from participation in legislation and taxation, the *cortes* of the several kingdoms displayed an active interest in internal administration and in the conduct of foreign relations. They constantly demanded that the king guard their charters and privileges, assure justice to everyone, remove wicked officials, restrain the financial activities of the Jews, intervene in the economy by regulating prices or wages, check the alienation of crown lands, and so forth. From the reign of Pedro III until that of Pedro IV, the Aragonese Union tried to control royal policy by appointing members of the royal council; during the minority of Fernando IV the Castilian *cortes* made a similar attempt to place several townsmen in the council.

From the early thirteenth century until the middle of the fourteenth, the *cortes* of the Hispanic kingdoms passed through a time of vigorous growth and development. Summoned in part to help the king meet his need for money, the *cortes* soon provided his subjects with a forum in which to defend their rights and to express their views on public issues. The role of the *cortes* was never clearly defined and depended to a certain degree upon the character of the monarch, the political circumstances in which he found himself, and the ability of the estates to present their views effectively. Insofar as the king bowed to their demands, corrected abuses, and defended their *fueros*, the *cortes* served as a useful limitation on royal power and the tendency toward absolutism given such strong impetus by the revival of Roman law. On the whole, one may say that during this time the Hispanic kingdoms were developing a form of parliamentary government equal to or in advance of that of any other European country.

Territorial Administration

As a consequence of the great expansion of the Christian states in the thirteenth century, the territorial administration was modified to meet new circumstances. In the twelfth century the development of lordships and municipalities in the western kingdoms resulted in the breakdown of the counties, and the counts became military tenants holding fortresses or districts in vassalage to the crown. They did not entirely disappear, but new circumscriptions of a much larger geographical extent were established. In the kingdom of Castile these included the *merindades* of Castile, León, Asturias and Galicia, usually administered by a *merino mayor;* Andalusia, administered by the *adelantado de la frontera;* Murcia and the Basque provinces of Alava and Guipúzcoa by an *adelantado mayor.* In Portugal, from the reign of Afonso III, officials with the title of *meirinho mor* appear with responsibility for extensive regions identified by river boundaries, for example, Além Douro, Aquém Douro, Entre Douro e Minho, Entre Douro e Mondego, Entre Douro e Tejo and so on. The office of *meirinho mor de Portugal* appears in 1235, though it seems to have disappeared in the reign of Dinis. According to the *Siete Partidas, merino mayor* and *adelantado mayor* were equivalent terms and in practice were used interchangeably. The *adelantado mayor,* who was comparable to the Roman *praeses provinciae,* had administrative and judicial powers in the region assigned to him, though in frontier zones his principal responsibility was military defense. The post was usually given to great nobles, but as they often tended to abuse their authority, the *cortes* of 1295 pointedly demanded that only men who would love justice should be appointed. Each of them was assisted by a number of subordinate *merinos;* Castile, for example, was subdivided into seventeen *merindades.*

The federative character of the crown of Aragon necessitated a somewhat more complex territorial administration. The king was represented in each of the constituent states by a procurator general, who usually functioned during the king's absence; for this reason the office assumed a more or less permanent character in Valencia and Majorca. The heir to the throne ordinarily received the title *procurador general de tots les regnes* (sometimes also called lieutenant-general) with viceregal authority. His role was comparable to that of the governor-general of Navarre who had full responsibility for the government of the realm, especially during the years when the king was an absentee ruler.

The basic unit of territorial administration in Catalonia and Majorca was the vicariate (*vegueria*) governed by a vicar (*veguer*) appointed by the king, and directly responsible to the procurator general. The vicar maintained the public peace, administered justice, summoned troops to war, and to a certain extent supervised municipal administration. Under Jaime II Catalonia was divided into eighteen vicariates while Majorca consisted of two, one for the city of Palma, the other embracing the rest of the island. The *justicias* in Valencia and Aragon exercised similar functions. In the thirteenth century the Aragonese towns were grouped in *juntas* for mutual defense, under the direction of royal officials known as *sobrejunteros*, whose task was to prevent crime, to arrest criminals, to execute judicial sentences, and to collect fines. There were *sobrejunteros* in Zaragoza, Huesca, Teruel, Jaca, Tarazona, and in the counties of Ribagorza and Sobrarbe. The title was also used to designate officials serving in the districts of the kingdom of Navarre.

In all the Christian kingdoms large areas were given as lordships to bishops, monasteries, nobles, and military Orders. The lordship of the archiepiscopal see of Compostela was one of the largest, and its administrator, the *pertiguero mayor*, was important enough to be listed among the subscribers to royal charters. In Andalusia and throughout the southernmost sector of the peninsula, the military Orders held extensive lordships; there too the nobility acquired vast estates. As one might expect, all lords tried to expand and consolidate their lordships, though this tendency was never wholly successful. Within his domains the lord administered justice, collected tributes, required military service, and so on, but the king reserved the right to hear appeals and to intervene in specific cases, especially if the lord's agents failed to carry out their duties.

Detailed studies of the administration of the kingdom of Granada are still lacking, but it seems evident that with some modifications the organization of the Almohad period continued. Within the limited extent of the kingdom, the governors were appointed by the sovereign and were directly responsible to the *wazir*. Substantial territories, including major cities, however, were held as lordships with near independence of the king. In the thirteenth century the *arraeces* (*al-rais*) of the Ashqilula family controlled Guadix, Comares, and Málaga and frequently followed policies at variance with those of the king. In addition the kings of Granada in the late thirteenth and fourteenth centuries ceded parts of their territory, namely, Algeciras, Gibraltar, Ronda, and Marbella, to the Marinid rulers of Morocco in return for promises of assistance against Castile. Thus the territory directly under the control of the king of Granada was rather small.

The Municipalities

In the thirteenth and fourteenth centuries the municipalities reached the height of their development and influence upon public affairs, chiefly through their action in the *cortes*. But they also began to undergo fundamental internal transformations and were brought more closely under royal control. Besides the older towns between the Duero and the Tagus and great cities such as Toledo, Lisbon, Zaragoza, and Barcelona, the metropolises of Muslim Spain, namely, Seville, Córdoba, Murcia, and Valencia, were also now incorporated into the Christian kingdoms.

During the thirteenth century the democratic character of the towns in the western kingdoms gradually disappeared while the social gap between the urban aristrocracy and the lower classes widened. Honored by royal privileges and exemption from tributes, the *caballeros villanos* constituted an urban patriciate of wealthy and distinguished families; they controlled municipal administration and excluded both the lower orders and the rural population from any real participation in it. Through a small council, usually of twenty-four *regidores*, sometimes elected but often appointed by the king for life, the aristocrats dominated the town, assuming the functions and responsibilities of the citizen assembly (*concejo*) which met only on rare occasions.

The trend toward municipal oligarchy was accompanied, among the aristocratic families, by intensive and sometimes violent rivalry of the kind that encouraged increasing royal intervention. Alfonso X's attempt to impose the *Fuero Real* as a uniform code of law supplanting the older *fueros* encountered much opposition, but the monarchy had greater success in sending officials (*jueces de salario, veedores*) to remedy abuses and to resolve factional disputes. The next step was to transform them into permanent representatives of the crown. During the reign of Alfonso XI these officials, known as *corregidores*, were sent to those towns requesting them, ostensibly to work together with the local *alcaldes* to maintain law and order. *Corregidores* eventually were sent to all the cities of Castile and Portugal and superseded the ordinary officials of municipal administration. In this way the autonomy of the towns was gradually destroyed.

The Castilian towns influenced the public life of the kingdom not only by their participation in the *cortes*, but also through *hermandades* organized to defend their mutual interests. Examples of regional brotherhoods or associations of towns can be found as early as the beginning of the thirteenth century, but by the close of the century their impact was felt throughout the realm as all the towns were grouped in two or three provincial *hermandades*. For example, in 1282 the towns of Castile, León, Galicia, Extremadura, and Andalusia joined the prelates and nobles in support of Infante Sancho "because of the many illegalities, injuries, assaults, killings, imprisonments and illegal tributes . . . imposed upon us by King Alfonso contrary to God and justice and law and to the great injury of all the realms" (*MHDE*, II, 936). While the *hermandad* in this instance was directed against the abuse of power by the king, during the minority of Fernando IV the towns organized themselves to maintain law and order and to uphold the rights of the king as well as their own. For the same reason, the *hermandad* was formed in 1315 during the minority of Alfonso XI:

Considering the many evils and injuries and aggravations that we have received until now from powerful men because the king is so small . . . we all together make this pledge and agreement and brotherhood that we will love and cherish one another and will all be of one heart and will, to guard the sovereignty and service of the king and all the rights that he ought to have and to guard our bodies and all that we have . . . and we will live in peace and quiet so that when our king comes of age he will find the land well ordered and richer and better settled for his service. [*CLC*, I, 248–249]

Emphasizing mutual support and collaboration, the *hermandades* usually provided for an annual assembly attended by two representatives from each town; they also employed a common seal and attempted to keep a common treasury. Organized in time of crisis, supposedly they were to remain in existence until the end of time, but once the crisis passed, they usually dissolved. They were, however, an effective means of defending urban rights and privileges against infringements either by the king or by the magnates.

Municipal government in the crown of Aragon evolved toward

greater autonomy in the thirteenth century, though under the domination of a small number of aristocratic families. The continued presence of royal officials, moreover, facilitated intervention in the towns whenever the king deemed it necessary. Aside from the king's representative, the effective agency of government in the towns of Aragon, Catalonia, and Valencia was a small council; the general assembly (*concejo, consell*) of all the citizens met infrequently. Barcelona, which developed a remarkable commercial activity and attained a high degree of prosperity, received a series of privileges from Jaime I, culminating in the charter of 1274, which delineated the essential features of a self-governing municipality, and became the model for other Catalan towns. The *veguer* represented the king, but day-to-day administration was entrusted to a small council of five *consellers* elected annually. A larger council, called the *consell de cent*, because it was composed in theory of 100 "men of probity" (*prohoms*) elected each year, was summoned as the need required to discuss major problems.

In the Aragonese towns the *justicia* or *zalmedina* representing the king was freely appointed by him, though at times the citizens presented a list of candidates, one of whom was selected by the king. Executive authority ordinarily was exercised by a council (*cabildo*) of "sworn men" (*jurados*) elected annually in representation of the different parishes in the town; later they were chosen by the out-going *jurados*. Those who had served as *jurados* usually were ineligible to serve again until three or four years had passed. In Valencia a council of six *jurats* directed municipal business under the presidency of the royal *justicia*.

The towns in the kingdom of Granada did not enjoy autonomy, as their officials were still appointed by the sovereign. Very little change seems to have taken place in the functions of the *sahib al-madina*, who continued to be responsible for maintaining law and order, the *qadi* who settled lawsuits in accordance with the Koran, and the *muhtasib* who guaranteed the use of authentic weights and measures.

The Law and the Administration of Justice

In the thirteenth and fourteenth centuries Roman law began to offer a serious challenge to the old, popular, customary law of the *fueros*. The rediscovery of Justinian's *Code*, the *Digest*, and the *Institutes* in the twelfth century opened an entirely new world of law to thousands of students who flocked to Bologna and Montpellier to study. Upon returning home, Spanish students easily found employment in the courts of kings and bishops and tried to apply the principles of Roman law to contemporary conditions. Under their influence the Spanish kings attempted to impose uniformity upon the legal structure and to develop a common, royal, territorial law. The injection of much of the substance of Roman law into the legal system met with stiff opposition, however, from the people who insisted that the traditional laws and customs could not be displaced.

Rulers approached the task of achieving a common law from several directions. On the one hand they tried to extend the use of the more substantial *fueros*, such as those of Cuenca, Teruel, and Jaca. Fernando III had the Visigothic Code translated into Castilian under the title of *Fuero Juzgo* and gave it to the newly conquered cities of Andalusia as their municipal code, in the hope that it could become the basis for a common royal law. Jaime I in 1247 promulgated the *Code of Huesca*, a systematic arrangement of the traditional laws of Aragon compiled by Vidal de Canellas, bishop of Huesca. It became the basis of Aragonese common law and the nucleus of the collection known as the *Fueros de Aragón*. The Catalans, meanwhile, insisted upon the preservation of their *Usages*, and the king, in response to their vigorous objection to the use of Roman law, declared in 1251:

that the Roman and Gothic laws, the *Decreta* and *Decretales* [Canon Law] shall not be received, admitted, cited or alleged in secular cases nor shall any legist dare to serve as an advocate in the secular courts except in his own suit. . . . In every secular case allegations shall be made according to the *Usages of Barcelona* and the approved constitutions of the place where the suit lies; in defect thereof one shall proceed according to the natural sense. [*MHDE*, II, 263]

About this time, Pere Albert, a canon of Barcelona, wrote the *Commemorationes*, a commentary on feudal and seigneurial customs contained in the *Usages*. Jaime I was more easily able to create a territorial law based primarily upon Roman law in the kingdom of Valencia; in a general assembly held in 1240 he promulgated the *Fori regni Valentie*, later translated into Catalan as the *Furs de Valencia*.

Fernando III's plan to draw up a uniform code of law for his kingdom was carried out by his son Alfonso X. Very early in his reign he published the *Fuero Real* and gave it to a number of towns as their municipal law, with the apparent hope that it would gradually replace the older *fueros*. A more ambitious work was the *Fuero* or *Espéculo de las leyes*, a general code of law in five books, inspired chiefly by Roman law and dealing not only with private law but also with public law. Opposition to royal attempts to impose this new law upon the realm forced the king to retreat and to confirm the traditional customs of nobles and townsmen. The *Fuero Viejo*, a compilation of customs concerning the nobility, was probably put together following this conflict, though in its present form it dates from the middle of the fourteenth century. The *Libro de los fueros de Castilla*, a collection of more than 300 articles dealing with Castilian customs, was also compiled about the middle of the thirteenth century. In the meantime the jurists used the *Fuero de las leyes* as the foundation for the development of the far more ample code known as the *Siete Partidas*. In its final form it was completed early in the fourteenth century, and in 1348 Alfonso XI declared that it should have legal force as a supplement to the other sources of law. A unique monument to the legal development of medieval Europe, the *Partidas* is more than a code of law; not only does it cover the entire body of law, but it also provides philosophical and theological justification and explanation for specific problems of law. In view of its comprehensive character it gradually supplanted other sources as the principal body of law in the kingdom of Castile. During the reign of King Dinis it was translated into Portuguese and was widely used in his kingdom. Through the *Partidas*, Roman influence upon the legal systems of the peninsula steadily increased until the older law was completely overwhelmed.

Among the other important legal compilations of this period are the *Leyes del estilo*, dating from the end of the thirteenth century and containing material relative to the procedures of the Castilian royal court. The *Ordenamiento de Alcalá*, promulgated by Alfonso XI in 1348, established an order of precedence among the different legal systems in the realm, giving first place to the *Ordenamiento* itself, followed by the *fueros* of the towns and of the nobility, and then by the *Siete Partidas*. The ordinances and constitutions of the *cortes* of the several kingdoms also contributed to the general body of law. The territorial customs of Navarre were gathered in the *Fuero general de Navarra* in the thirteenth century and gained general acceptance as a legal authority; Philip of Evreux, after consultation with lawyers and others, in 1330 published an *amejoramiento*, modifying the *Fuero general* in various places. Important collections of local laws included the *Customs of Tortosa* and the *Customs of Lérida*, both compiled in the thirteenth century. In the kingdom of Granada the law continued to be based primarily upon the Koran and the interpretations of the Malikite school. Ibn Lubb (d. 1380) published an important collection of *fatwa* or opinions of learned jurisconsults.

From the thirteenth century onward the administration of justice was clearly recognized as a fundamental responsibility of the state rather than as a private concern of contending parties. The king, as the representative of the state, was described by Vidal de Canellas as the source of jurisdiction, and in practice he and those whom he designated dispensed justice. There continued to be some confusion between general administration and the administration of justice, but professional jurists or legists (*letrados, sabidores de derecho*) played an increasingly important role in the tribunals.

The king functioned as the chief judge, but the need for greater specialization and professionalism in the royal court was acknowledged. Alfonso X tried to establish a permanent *tribunal de corte* consisting of himself, a chief justice (*adelantado mayor, justicia mayor, sobrejuez*), and a number of *alcaldes de corte*. The chief justice was authorized to act in the king's place and to hear major pleas and appeals from lower courts. The several *alcaldes de corte* were assigned to hear suits in the principal territorial divisions of the realm, namely in Castile, León, Extremadura. A chief complaint of the nobility was that there should be judges of noble birth in the king's court to hear their suits in accordance with the principle of trial by peers; the king was obliged to satisfy this charge and to assure the nobles that they would be tried by their own, rather than by upstart legists of inferior social rank. Though the composition of the king's court was altered from time to time, the concept of a special royal court was maintained, and by the close of the fourteenth century it received the name of *audiencia*. Similar developments took place in Aragon, Portugal, and Navarre.

In the course of the thirteenth century the *justicia* of Aragon began to acquire the jurisdiction that eventually gave him a rather unique position among the judges of the peninsula. Julián Ribera thought this office was borrowed from the Muslims in the early twelfth century and that it corresponded to the Muslim *sahib al-mazalim* or lord of injustices, but Giménez Soler demonstrated the falsity of this view, pointing out that the *justicia* originally was a judge in the royal court, appointed at will by the king to hear specific cases. The nobility, however, began to protest the increasing prominence in the royal court of men trained in Roman and canon law, and Jaime I, at the *cortes* of Exea in 1265, bowed to their insistence that the *justicia* should be a knight with jurisdiction over disputes among the nobles or between them and the king; he was expected to pronounce sentence in accordance with the traditional *fueros* of the realm rather than Roman or canon law. Pedro III and Alfonso III in their *Privileges* granted to the Union in 1283 and 1287 reaffirmed the *justicia's* role and functions. Although Pedro IV crushed the Union, at the *cortes* of Zaragoza in 1348, he confirmed the *justicia's* position as chief judge with authority to interpret the *fueros* of Aragon and to bind royal officials and judges to his interpretations. He could also hear appeals in which officials were charged with violation of the *fueros*. The *justicia* continued to be appointed by the king and was removable by him, but the tendency was to allow him to remain in office for life, and so to enhance his independence and judicial authority.

The officers responsible for territorial and municipal administration (*adelantados mayores, merinos mayores, sobrejunteros, vegueres, alcaldes, zalmedinas*) also dispensed justice, as did lords in their lordships, though the crown tried to limit them; in Aragon, however, lords retained civil and criminal, high and low justice, with the right to punish crimes by death, mutilation, or exile. Appeals could be carried from seigneurial, municipal, and territorial courts to the royal court. In Castile the crown tended to supplant municipal *alcaldes* by sending royal justices to hear specific suits; from the middle of the fourteenth century the royal justices began to receive permanent responsibility for the administration of justice in the towns. In the kingdom of Granada the municipal *qadi* continued to function as the ordinary judge in most cases.

Court procedures were modified under the influence of Roman law. Ordeals and purgation as forms of proof were eliminated, though the nobility continued to settle many of their disputes by means of the judicial duel. The new procedures were described by Jacopo Ruíz in his book, *Flores de las leyes* and by Fernando Martínez in his *Margarita de las leyes*. Once summoned, the litigants had to appear in court personally or through their procurators. Exceptions could be presented, challenging the competence of the court or the capacity of the procurators, but when these had been cleared away, the charge was made and answered by the defendant; replies and counterreplies could also be offered. The entire process was written rather than oral. Oftentimes the testimony of witnesses was taken by court-appointed inquisitors in the locality where the dispute originated. The record of their inquest was opened and read and, on the basis of its findings, judgment was pronounced. The litigants could also present documentary evidence, and the judge, rather than being a spectator, intervened actively by interrogating the parties and the witnesses. His judgment closed the case, but, in accord with Roman legal practice, it could be appealed to a higher court. In criminal cases the accusatory procedure of Germanic law was replaced by the inquest carried out by public officials to discover those who had committed crime. This reflected the abandonment of the idea that crime was a private concern; as it was now considered a violation of the peace of the realm punishable by the crown, royal officials initiated the arrest and punishment of criminals. The searching nature of the inquest, however, and the possibility of its producing false accusations made it an unpopular procedure and prompted the Aragonese nobles to demand of Pedro III in 1283:

that an inquisition never be conducted against anyone in any case; but if an inquisition is conducted, and judgment has not been given, let no judgment be given on account of it . . . but if sentence has been given, let it not be executed.   [MHDE, II, 897]

Torture was used to obtain confessions, and the penalties meted out to criminals were of the harshest sort, including death, mutilation, lashings, confiscation, exile, and infamy. For all that, the notion that men were entitled to due process of law before condemnation was reiterated many times in all the Christian states, as this pledge of Alfonso XI in 1325 indicates:

I agree indeed not to order anyone to be killed, arrested, mutilated, nor anything of his to be plundered or seized until he has first been summoned and heard and convicted by custom and law.   [CLC, I, 384]

Financial Administration

As the types of revenue multiplied and the necessities of the crown grew, so did the administration of finance become more complex. Serious studies of the subject are lacking, however, partly because of the difficulties created by the haphazard survival of financial records. In the western kingdoms the *mayordomo mayor* had the primary responsibility for keeping the king's accounts, while the *almojarife mayor*, who was very often a Jew, had charge of the collection of taxes. Given frequent complaints of maladministration and the demands of the *cortes* to be shown royal accounts, and the king's own need to have a more accurate record of income and expenses, numerous accountants (*contadores*) were employed, and some attempt was made to encourage greater efficiency in the treasury. In the crown of Aragon the *magister rationalis* or *mestre racional* was the chief financial officer, heading a rather complex bureaucracy; in each of the constitutent states a general bailiff (*batlle* or *bayle general*) supervised the collection of taxes. The king usually contracted with tax farmers who guaranteed to pay a specified sum into his treasury every year, but as the tax farmers frequently were Jews the *cortes* demanded that only Christians, natives of the region in which they were to act, should be allowed to collect taxes. Throughout the peninsula an army of tax collectors (*merinos, cogedores, almojarifes, batlles*) labored with varying success to fill the royal coffers, but their efforts, especially to collect arrears of taxes, elicited strong protests from reluctant taxpayers.

Customary revenues included personal services, and dues of a seigneurial character, a land tax (*terratge, infurción, martiniega*) paid as a sign of lordship, and the right to hospitality (*yantar, cena*); these were usually paid in coin, though numerous exemptions were allowed. The crown also received a share in the profits of mines and salt pits, whose exploitation was leased to private persons. Tolls levied on roads and bridges and on migratory flocks of sheep (*servicio y montazgo*) and customs duties (*diezmo, almojarifazgo*) on imports and exports, usually at the rate of ten percent of value, were also important sources of revenue. The *alcabala* (*al-qabala*), a sales tax of five per cent, became general under Alfonso XI, who collected it with the consent of the *cortes* to finance his military operations against the Moors; but it eventually became a permanent tax, levied without specific authorization by the *cortes*, and enjoyed a long history thereafter. The *sisa*, varying from one to three per cent, was another burden imposed upon the consumer in the marketplace. An exceedingly unpopular tax, levied initially by Sancho IV, it was abolished after his death by his widow, who sought thereby to win support among the towns; however, it was subsequently revived. Other revenues included judicial fines, chancery fees, and poll taxes paid by Muslims and Jews. From the time of Fernando III the Castilian kings collected a third of the tithe owed to the church and, after some protest, the papacy finally authorized the use of the *tercias reales*, as the third was called, to finance the reconquest. The annual tribute owed by the king of Granada, which Fernando III set at one-half the revenues of the kingdom or 300,000 *maravedís*, was a substantial sum, though payment was frequently interrupted.

The increasing services performed by the royal government and the needs of the reconquest compelled the Christian rulers to seek additional sources of income. From time to time they borrowed money or obtained forced loans (*emprestitos*) from the towns, but the usual means of obtaining extraordinary income was to request the concession of a subsidy (*servicio, donatiu, peitia, questia*) by the *cortes*.

The tribute owed to Castile was the major factor in the financial considerations of the kings of Granada. Though the amount was later reduced, it remained a heavy burden and necessitated the imposition of numerous illegal taxes, that is, taxes not sanctioned by the Koran. The jurisconsults fortunately recognized the necessity for these taxes and issued legal opinions justifying them. A wide variety of taxes were levied on the value of real property and on the production of vineyards and groves; customs duties of ten per cent were imposed on merchandise, and there were other tributes on livestock and agricultural products.

Military Organization

The structure of royal armies (*hueste, fonsado*) in the campaigns of the thirteenth and early fourteenth centuries remained essentially the same as before. The king summoned his own household guards (*mesnaderos*) and his great vassals who served in return for the stipends (*soldadas*) or benefices (*prestimonia, honores*) they received. Many of the subsidies granted by the *cortes* were intended precisely to pay the magnates for their services. The great lords were accompanied by their own vassals fulfilling their obligation to serve; the towns also sent their militia, under the command of the *juez* bearing the town standard. The obligations of the towns were specified in their *fueros,* it sometimes meant that footmen owed limited service. Cavalry forces, because of greater mobility, had greater utility. Urban cavalry, especially from the frontier towns, often went out on raiding expeditions (*cabalgada*) of their own. The military Orders of Calatrava, Santiago, Alcantára, Avis, the Hospital, the Temple, and after the suppression of the Templars early in the fourteenth century, the Orders of Christ and Montesa, performed valuable services both by garrisoning positions exposed on the frontier and by maintaining troops ready for immediate combat. Alfonso X founded the Order of Santa Maria de Cartagena to defend the Murcian frontier, but it languished and soon was merged with Santiago.

The several elements mentioned above served as units under their own commanders whose efforts were coordinated by the royal *alferez* or *senyaler*. The Orders of Calatrava and Santiago did make some attempt to provide for united action and a single command when their knights went into battle. While cavalry remained the predominant element in the army, light-armed footsoldiers known as *almògavers* (*almugawar*) gained renown in the war of the Sicilian Vespers and subsequently, as the Catalan Company, ravaged much of Turkey and Greece before settling at Athens. Their discipline and success in withstanding cavalry gave a new importance to infantry forces.

The Granadan armies of this period consisted of regular troops, whose names were inscribed in registers and who were paid for their services. There were also some volunteers who wished to participate in the holy war as a means of gaining merit. Some Christians were incorporated into the army, as in times past they had served the Almoravids and the Almohads. One of the principal, and most dangerous elements, was the troop sent by the Marinid emir of Morocco to aid the king of Granada. The commander of these forces (*shaykh al-guzat*) was usually a distinguished Marinid noble who used his power to intervene in Granadan politics at will; for this reason Muhammad V suppressed the office. During the reign of Ismail II, Ibn Hudhail wrote a treatise on warfare and military organization, but it apparently presented an ideal with little basis in reality.

The use of naval forces was much more common during this period than before. Jaime I was able to call upon his own subjects in Catalonia to provide the fleet necessary for the conquest of Majorca, and subsequently Catalan fleets made possible the creation of an empire in the western Mediterranean. Pedro IV published ordinances in 1354 regulating the organization of the fleet, the disciplining of the crew, the responsibilities of the admiral (*almirall*), and the like. The Castilian fleets were first brought into play for the conquest of Seville, when Fernando III summoned Ramón Bonifaz, whom he named *almirante*, to gather ships from the Cantabrian ports. Though Alfonso X later built shipyards at Seville, the Castilians continued to have need of Genoese and Catalan vessels in the battle of the straits. The Portuguese also began to build up their naval strength, though they too had to rely upon foreign assistance. King Dinis summoned the Genoese Manuel Pezagno to Portugal as his admiral with responsibility for developing a royal fleet. The kings of Granada, of course, could call upon the services of many coastal towns as well as Moroccan ports for naval forces.

CHAPTER 19

Society and the Economy, 1212–1369

The Social Structure

Several major changes affected the population of the peninsula during the thirteenth and fourteenth centuries. The remarkable success of the reconquest resulted in the incorporation of large numbers of Muslims and Jews into the Christian states. Many Muslims, however, preferred to leave their ancestral homes to settle in Granada or even to withdraw to North Africa. Vast areas, consequently, were left open to Christian immigrants from the north, whose settlements were concentrated in Andalusia, Alentejo, and the Algarve; the least change occurred in Valencia and Murcia where thousands of Muslims remained. The colonization of Andalusia resulted in the depopulation of many villages in Old Castile whose inhabitants moved on in search of opportunities hitherto denied them. Colonists tended to cluster in the large southern cities, while the Muslims remained chiefly in the rural areas. Colonization continued without interruption until the Black Death struck in 1348 causing an extraordinary decline in the total population.

Attempts to estimate the size of the population are hazardous, but there are some records for this period that provide statistics on which calculations can be based. Vicens Vives, who did the most to encourage studies of this kind, believed that the total Hispanic population doubled in the two hundred years from 1130 to 1340, for this was a time of general economic expansion and population growth throughout Europe, and Spain shared in it. He estimated the population of Castile, the largest of the peninsular states, at about the middle of the thirteenth century, to be four or five million people, including about 300,000 Muslims and Jews. Yet he did not consider this comparable to northern European population growth because of Castile's slow economic development. Even less attention has been given to demographic studies in Portugal, though most recently Oliveira Marquês utilized military recruitment records to study the thirteenth-century population. He did not attempt to estimate numbers, but the total probably would be less than one million. The area of greatest density lay between the Duero and the Miño rivers, the older regions of Portugal. The Algarve, of course, was settled in the thirteenth century, but there was no corresponding depopulation of the north as occurred in Castile. The population of the kingdom of Granada was quite dense because of the settlement there of thousands of Muslims who abandoned their homes in Christian territory. Ibn al-Khatib remarked in mid-fourteenth century that there were no empty or uninhabited spaces. At the Council of Vienne in 1314, Aragonese envoys informed the pope that there were 200,000 people in the kingdom of Granada, though it is not known on what that figure was based.

For the crown of Aragon there are a number of statistical records that scholars have used to advantage. On the basis of the census of households of 1359, the population of Catalonia has been estimated at about 450,000 people, including about 18,000 Jews and 9,000 Muslims located mostly in the south. Vicens Vives believed that the population had dropped from about 500,000 in the thirteenth century because of emigration to Valencia, Majorca, Sicily, Sardinia, and Greece. The estimate for Valencia is about 300,000, for Aragon about 200,000, and for Majorca about 45,000. This would give a total population of one million in the crown of Aragon. Taking all the figures together and recognizing that some are guesses and that all are subject to correction, the population of the peninsula during this period was probably about 6,200,000 or 7,200,000.

This total was undoubtedly diminished by the great plague (la gran mortandad) that ravaged Europe in 1348 and succeeding years. The plague struck the coastal areas of Valencia and Catalonia in May of that year, spreading destruction. Pedro IV reported that three hundred people died each day in the city of Valencia; he was at the time being restrained by the Union at Valencia, and because of the dangers of the plague was able to regain his liberty, but as he moved to the interior the plague continued to impede his progress, striking Teruel, Zaragoza, and other towns. The plague spread over the peninsula, carrying death to Castile, León, Extremadura, Portugal, and Granada. Ibn al-Khatib, while not mentioning the plague specifically, referred to the brevity of life in Granada and to the increasing number of lepers in Málaga, the chief port of the kingdom; the sores which spread over the body probably seemed similar to those of leprosy. Ibn Khatimah (d. 1369) wrote a treatise concerning prevention of the contagion. No respecter of persons, the plague touched all classes in society, in the country and urban areas, and recurred thereafter many times in the late fourteenth century. The population of Catalonia, one of the regions most severely afflicted, apparently declined to about 350,000 in 1378, a drop of nearly one quarter of the population, a factor which contributed to the political decline of Catalonia in the fifteenth century. Whether the same proportions died elsewhere in the peninsula cannot be ascertained, but the loss of life had obvious effects upon the economy. Much agricultural land was abandoned, and the surviving workers, taking advantage of the shortage of labor, demanded higher wages, promoting in turn governmental attempts to control wages and prices. Pedro IV in 1349 instructed his officials to consult with town governments to set wages, which had risen four or five times; Afonso IV also tried to regulate wages in the same year, and in 1351 Pedro the Cruel promulgated the *Ordenamiento de menestrales* fixing wages for artisans and rural workers. None of these measures was especially effective, but all of them were highly unpopular.

With the exception of foreign merchants, mainly Genoese, who settled in port cities such as Lisbon, Seville, and Málaga, and on Majorca, the ethnic composition of the population remained comparatively unchanged. The most important change for the Christian kingdoms was the inclusion within their borders of large numbers of Muslims and Jews. On the other hand, there do not seem to have been large indigenous settlements of Christians in the kingdom of Granada, and the number of Jews there apparently was small. It has been estimated that there were about 300,000 Muslims in Andalusia in the middle of the thirteenth century, settled chiefly in rural areas in dependence on Christian landlords. Because of the continued pressure of Castilian forces, from the fall of Seville until the middle of the fourteenth century there was a steady emigration to Granada or Morocco. According to the *Primera Crónica General* the Muslims who evacuated Seville in 1248 included 100,000 who withdrew to Ceuta and 30,000 who retired to Jerez. How accurate these figures are, no one can tell. Muslims greatly outnumbered Christians in Murcia and Valencia and constituted a very real threat to the conquerors. After suppressing the revolt of the Valencian Muslims in 1248, Jaime I decided to drive them out of the kingdom; as they left, his lieutenants collected a coin from each one to the total of 100,000. Even though that many may have been expelled, thousands remained behind; it was estimated in 1272 that there were only 30,000 Christians in the kingdom of Valencia as against 200,000 Muslims, and in 1337 the archbishop of Tarragona, noting that there were in the kingdom "as many mosques as churches," urged the expulsion of the Muslims as a grave threat to Spain. There was also a very heavy concentration of Muslims in lower Aragon and in Majorca, but there were very few in Catalonia. Altogether Sobreques suggested that about half the population of the crown of Aragon were Muslims. The Muslims of Portugal were found mainly in the Algarve, but there are no estimates of their numbers.

The *mudéjares* were a protected people whose liberty was clearly circumscribed. An indeterminate number were slaves (usually described in documents as *moros*) held by nobles, bishops, monasteries, convents, military Orders, non-nobles, and so on, and employed either in cultivating the soil or in household services. Most Muslims lived in the country, but there were important communities (*al-jama*) in the major cities, where some of the separate districts (*morerías*) in which they lived have retained a physical identity until today. When they initially surrendered, the Moors were guaranteed protection of their persons and property, subject to the payment of tribute to their new rulers, and were allowed to govern themselves and to resolve their own disputes according to their own law (*çuna, azuna,* or *sunna*). In 1255, for example, Çabah, son of Hamlet Abençabah, *alcayad* of the Moors of Morón and *adelantado de los vieios e de la Aliama*, made a pact with the Christians concerning justice and the payment of tributes. *Los vieios* evidently were a council of *shaykhs*, old or wise men primarily responsible for governing the community, and the *alcayad* or *adelantado* was their leader. In the thirteenth century legal compilation known as *Vidal Mayor*, the chief judge of the Muslim community (*çavalachen*, or *sahib al-jama*) could be summoned to the Christian court if he failed to do justice, and judgment would then be given according to Muslim law. A small collection of *leyes de moros* originating in one of the Castilian communities in the early fourteenth century, and dealing with marriage, sales, homicide, sharecropping, and the like, is extant.

The Moors enjoyed religious liberty, but the principal mosques usually were taken from them and converted to Christian use. In the *Siete*

Partidas the point was made that the Moors ought not to have any mosques in Christian cities, and those once belonging to them were claimed for the king who could give them to whomever he wished. Pope Clement V forbade the muezzin to summon the faithful to prayer by chanting the customary verses from the Koran; nor were the Moors permitted to invoke the name of the prophet publicly or to go on pilgrimage to the tombs of holy men. These restrictions soon were echoed by the church councils held in the course of the fourteenth century. The *Siete Partidas* (VII, 25, 2) declared that Christians should "labor by good words and suitable preaching to convert the Moors to our faith and to lead them to it not by force or by pressure . . . for the Lord is not pleased by the service that men give him through fear." No one was to prevent a Moor from becoming a Christian, but on the other hand no Christian was allowed to become a Muslim. If he did so, he would lose his inheritance, and if he was found in Christian lands "let him die for his error." These legal principles point up the fact that there were numerous conversions and reconversions among Moors and Christians living along the frontier. Christians captured by the enemy were able to regain their freedom by embracing Islam, though Moorish captives remained slaves even though they were baptized. A Christian renegade who returned to his own country usually found it wise to return to his original religion, and the same was true for Muslims.

Restrictions imposed upon the Moors occupy a substantial place in the records of the *cortes*, of church councils, and in the law codes. As early as 1252 the Castilian *cortes* enacted legislation concerning Moorish dress, and in later years this was further elaborated and imitated in the other Christian realms. Moors, for example, were required to wear their hair cut short round about without a forelock, but their beards were to be long as required by their law. They were forbidden to wear brightly colored clothing (red, vermillion, green) or to have white or gilded shoes. They could not live in Christian houses, nor employ Christians in their service, nor give their children to be nursed by Christian women. They could not purchase lands from Christians, but if they did so they had to pay tithes to the church. A Moor who made so bold as to sleep with a Christian virgin was to be stoned, while she lost half her goods for the first offense and all of them for the second. If the culprit were a married woman, she was left to the mercy of her husband who could burn her or throw her out or do whatever he wanted with her.

The situation of the Jews in Christian Spain was analogous to that of the Muslims. Estimates of their numbers have varied widely and have tended to be exaggerated. Amador de los Rios suggested that there were about 1,000,000 Jews in Castile around 1300, and on the basis of the census of 1365–1370 Abadal estimated about 18,000 Jews in Catalonia. Other estimates for the mid-thirteenth century give Catalonia 25,000, Aragon 20,000, Valencia 10,000, and Majorca 5,000. Yitzhak Baer has been perhaps most cautious in trying to determine the number of Jews in the peninsula. The Jewish communities were undoubtedly the largest and most prosperous in Europe, but even in Toledo where the Jews were especially numerous there were no more than about 400 families at the end of the thirteenth century. In Zaragoza and Barcelona there were about 200 families, and perhaps 250 in Valencia. There were few Jews in Portugal and probably not many in Aragon. Baer estimated about 3,600 families in Castile and about the same number in the crown of Aragon. Even if one assigned an average of six persons to each family the total would not reach 45,000, a figure which seems quite low and at variance with the other estimates given above.

Jews were settled chiefly in the towns where they inhabited their own quarters (*juderías, call dels jueus*) and governed themselves. The *aljama* (Hebrew: *kahal*) or council of old and wise men (*viejos, adelantados, mukademin*) was responsible for the direction of affairs. The king usually designated a *rab mayor* with primarily judicial authority over the Jews of several provinces. The community was subject to the payment of most of the taxes owed by the Christians, but they also paid thirty *dineros* monthly in memory of the thirty pieces of silver paid to Judas for the betrayal of Christ, or as Fernando IV put it, "in memory of the death of our Lord Jesus Christ when the Jews put Him on the cross." At times the Jews had to endure arbitrary impositions; their representatives were summoned to court from time to time to accept the king's latest demands. In litigation, Jews appeared before their own judge (*dayyan*), but in suits with Christians a Christian judge usually presided, and the Jews were required to swear an extremely lengthy oath before the proceedings began.

Within limits, Jews enjoyed religious liberty. The restrictions imposed upon them are summed up in the *Siete Partidas* (VII, 24, 1) which explains that "the reason that the church, emperors, kings and princes permitted the Jews to dwell among them and with Christians is because they have always lived, as it were, in captivity, as it was constantly in the minds of men that they were descended from those who crucified our Lord Jesus Christ." Jews were guaranteed freedom of worship and were not to be summoned to court on the Sabbath, but they could not erect new synagogues nor enlarge old ones without royal permission. The Jews of Córdoba apparently planned to build a large, new synagogue with the approbation of Fernando III, but the bishop and chapter protested and appealed to the pope who prohibited it. The *Partidas* (VII, 24, 4) also reminded Christians of the sanctity of the synagogue: "Because a synagogue is a place where the name of God is praised, we forbid any Christian to deface it or remove anything from it or take anything out of it by force."

Like the Muslims, Jews were obliged to wear distinctive dress, usually a yellow badge or six-pointed star on front and back. The decrees of the Fourth Lateran Council of 1215 on this matter apparently were inoperative in most of Spain. Neither Jaime I nor Fernando III enforced them; the king of Castile protested that many of his Jewish subjects preferred to emigrate to Muslim Spain rather than wear the mark of ignominy. The repetition of this decree by church councils throughout the thirteenth and fourteenth centuries seems to indicate that the civil authorities made little attempt to enforce it. Jews were forbidden by law to own Christian slaves, to have intercourse with Christians, to proselytize among them or to harass a fellow Jew who became a Christian. Christians were not allowed to use force to convert the Jews, as Innocent IV reminded Thibault of Champagne when commending the Jews of Navarre to his protection in 1246.

In spite of the pope's admonition the Dominican friars of the kingdom of Aragon, under the leadership of Ramon de Penyafort, a great canon lawyer and papal adviser, began to preach to the Jews in circumstances which modern missiologists would not condone. By order of Jaime I, the Jews were compelled to sit in their synagogues on Fridays and listen to the exposition of the Christian faith by members of the Dominican Order. The friars also persuaded the king to sponsor a disputation between Rabbi Moses ibn Nahman of Gerona and Fray Pablo Christiani, a converted Jew. Two years later, in 1265, the friars convinced the king to summon the rabbi before his court on the charge of having uttered words in vituperation of the Catholic faith. The rabbi protested that the king and the friars had given him license to speak freely, but in order to placate the Dominicans Jaime I ordered him banished for two years.

Christian rulers usually ignored papal demands that they not employ Jews as envoys or officials with authority over Christians, especially when their services were useful and even essential. Jewish financiers, physicians, and scholars were prominent in all the royal courts of this period. Members of the Ravaya, Portella, and Ibn Yahia families held high positions in Aragon, while men such as Abraham el Barchilón and Samuel ha-Levi served the Castilian kings. Such service was apt to be hazardous, however; Samuel ha-Levi, treasurer of Pedro the Cruel for many years, ultimately fell victim to the king's wrath and was subjected to torture and death because he would not reveal the location of his supposedly immense store of riches. The presence of Jews in the royal court, their role in the management of finance, their work as tax farmers and as money lenders led to frequent complaints by the *cortes* to the effect that only Christians should be allowed to collect taxes, that interest should be kept to a reasonable limit and so forth. From time to time protests gave way to assaults upon Jewish communities; for example, in 1321 bands of shepherds from southern France, stimulated by crusade preaching, crossed the frontier with the announced intention of driving the Muslims from Granada, but instead they pillaged and burned the Jewish quarter in Tudela. Attacks upon the Jews took on a special intensity following the Black Death, as Christians easily laid the blame for that catastrophe at the door of the Jews. During the Castilian-Aragonese war of the 1350's many Jewish settlements on the frontier were plundered and in the ensuing Castilian civil war, the *juderías* of Nájera, Miranda de Ebro, and Toledo were sacked and burned. In the course of the next century the status of the Jews underwent a radical transformation.

In the thirteenth and fourteenth centuries Europeans conceived of society as hierarchically organized and constituted by several orders or estates (*estaments, estados*) of men. The individual existed as a member of an estate and followed the way of life and enjoyed the juridical condition distinctive to it. These ideas, summarized in the *Partidas*, were partly the result of scholastic interest in categorization and partly due to the revival of the Roman law concept of *status* or juridical condition. Infante Juan Manuel thought it useful to describe the principal classifications of contemporary society in his *Libro de los estados*. The classic division recognized three orders or estates: the nobles, whose characteristic function was warfare, theoretically in defense of the community; the clergy who prayed to God to protect His people; and the workers who cultivated the fields or labored in the towns. The idea that the three estates when assembled in parliament represented the community of the realm was generally accepted.

From the twelfth century onward increasing self-consciousness among the nobility led to the belief that all members of the military class from the king to the simplest knight were bound together in a fraternity known to contemporaries as the order of chivalry or knighthood. As the young noble passed from childhood to adolescence, he was entrusted to the care of an experienced warrior (*amo*) who trained him in the profession of arms and whom he served as a squire (*escudero*, or shieldbearer; *donzell*, or young lord). If he performed some notable feat, the young man might be knighted on the field of battle, but the ceremony tended to be given greater solemnity and religious significance, as the order of knighthood was compared to the priesthood. The aspirant for knighthood prepared himself for the step he was about to take by the vigil of arms, placing his weapons and gear upon the altar and spending the night in prayer and meditation. On the following day he received the accolade (*espaldarazo*) or blow on the shoulders with the flat of a sword which symbolized his admission into the order of knighthood. Kings often received knighthood soon after accession and then in turn knighted many of their vassals. The practice fell into disuse in Castile, until revived by Alfonso XI who received the order in a unique way:

In the church of Santiago he watched all night while his weapons lay on the altar. On the morrow the archbishop . . . said mass and blessed his weapons. The king armed himself with all his weapons . . . taking them from the altar of Santiago, not receiving them from any other person. The king drew near to the statue of Santiago on the altar and caused it to give him a blow on the cheek. In this way King Alfonso received knighthood from the Apostle Santiago. [*Crónica de Alfonso XI*, 99]

As this example suggests, a special bond of loyalty and friendship was created between the new knight and the one who knighted him. For this reason the future Sancho IV was said to have refused to receive knighthood from his older brother Fernando de la Cerda, choosing instead to be knighted by his uncle Pedro III.

The theory of knighthood was elaborated in the *Partidas*, in the writings of Juan Manuel, who spoke of it as a "manera de sacramento," and by the great Catalan writer, Ramon Llull in his *Llibre de la Orde de Cavallería*, written around 1275; Llull's work became standard in the later Middle Ages and was published in English by William Caxton in the sixteenth century. All of these works describe the qualities or virtues which the knight ought to possess: courage, loyalty, generosity. While recognizing the knight's quest for personal glory and fame, they also emphasized his responsibility to use his arms for the service of the Christian community. Llull put it in the book cited above, "the knight should be a lover of the common good because chivalry was instituted for the common utility of the people." This marked the culmination of a long process of civilizing the warrior class by directing their bellicose energy to justifiable ends. The Peace and Truce of God, still promulgated in Catalonia in the thirteenth century, royal efforts to curb private warfare, the encouragement of the Christian warrior's sense of responsibility to the community, especially by his participation in the war against the infidels, were among the means used to achieve that goal. For some, the military Orders exemplified the highest form of Christian chivalry, and they do not seem to have lacked recruits; but for those who were unwilling to assume the burden of asceticism entailed by membership in the Orders, Alfonso XI in 1330 founded the secular Order of the Scarf (*Banda*) to encourage the practice of the *menester de caballería*, the trade of chivalry.

Knighthood in theory linked all members of the noble class, but there were very real differences in rank, wealth, power, and influence within that body. All nobles profited considerably by the conquest of so much Muslim territory in the thirteenth century, but the economic, social, and political gap between the magnates and the knights was broadened. The magnates (*ricos hombres, barons*), whose numbers were relatively small (about 100 families in Castile, 30 in Portugal, 20 in Aragon, 25 in Catalonia) included many older houses, as well as many newer ones originating among younger branches of the royal family, or among men whose extraordinary talent brought them to prominence. Even in the higher ranks the nobility was still open to new blood, to men of ability who rendered valuable services to the crown and could therefore claim the appropriate reward. Noble titles were the exception in the western kingdoms, but in Catalonia the titles of marquess, count, and viscount were commonly used.

The power and influence of the magnates rested upon their consciousness of a common interest and their status as the king's natural counselors and as the principal defenders of the realm. Intermarriage and close family ties with the ecclesiastical hierarchy and with the military Orders were also important as were the immense lordships they acquired in the Alentejo, the Algarve, Andalusia, Extremadura, Aragon, and Valencia, and to some extent Majorca, Sicily, and Sardinia. Whereas Catalan lords usually held estates in fief and owed typical feudal services, elsewhere in the peninsula lands were often held in full ownership (*juro de heredad*). The magnates received the bulk of their income from tenant rents and services, but in the west they were also paid *soldadas* in return for their annual military service. They tried to increase their holdings by purchases, exchanges, marriages, and additional gifts from the crown. From the close of the thirteenth century some of them began to entail their estates, declaring them indivisible and heritable only by the first-born son of each generation. Entailed estates (*mayorazgo*) concentrated enormous amounts of land in the hands of comparatively few people, and forced younger sons to seek a future in the military Orders or to fall into the ranks of the lower nobility.

The nobles were exempt from direct taxation and were entitled to be judged by their peers in the king's court. When their privileges were threatened by the steady growth of royal power in the thirteenth century, they reacted strongly and, because of the greater wealth at their disposal, were able to challenge the monarchy more effectively than at any time in the past. By the middle of the fourteenth century the magnates were beginning to reside permanently at the royal court where they could exercise an immediate influence upon policy and attempt to control the essential organs of government.

The petty nobility or knights (*caballeros, infanzones, hidalgos*) were much more numerous but much less wealthy and powerful. Many were the younger sons of magnates or their descendants; most of them were vassals either of the king or of the magnates. Only in Aragon were they recognized as an estate entitled to be summoned to the *cortes*. So long as the reconquest was still in progress they had the opportunity to enrich themselves by booty or the acquisition of lands. Once that enterprise slackened, they had little to do and many tended to vegetate on their small rural estates, collecting meager rents from their tenants over whom they exercised jurisdiction of a varying sort. The privileges of exemption from direct taxation and trial by their peers were substantial enough to encourage many townsmen to seek admission to the ranks of the nobility. For many, achievement of the status of *hidalgo* was a goal eagerly and persistently pursued.

The aristocracy in the kingdom of Granada claimed descent from the thirty-six families traditionally said to have come from Arabia at the time of the conquest, though in fact there had been considerable mixture of Arabian, Berber, and indigenous Hispanic stock since then. Blood ties and tribal relationships were especially strong, and rivalries and jealousies existing between tribes were perpetuated from one generation to the next. Blood feuds often disturbed the peace of the cities and country areas and were a basic cause of the chronic instability of the kingdom. In the thirteenth century the Banu Ashqilula were one of the most influential families because of the assistance they gave to Ibn al-Ahmar in founding the kingdom, and later because of their opposition to his successors. Many Granadan nobles ordinarily resided in cities, though they possessed extensive country estates.

The clergy existed as an estate whose members were exempt from direct taxation and justiciable in their own courts. The higher clergy were summoned to the *cortes* to speak on behalf of the entire body. From a social and economic point of view there were vast differences between the lower clergy and the men who held the major sees and abbeys, the masterships and *encomiendas* of the military Orders. Bishops and abbots often were related to the royal family or leading noble houses, while the lower clergy usually came of humbler stock. Despite a non-noble background, education and demonstrated ability as theologians, jurists, clerks, and so on, enabled many men to rise in the ecclesiastical hierarchy. The bulk of the clergy serving urban and rural parishes, however, usually shared the life style, the aspirations, and tribulations of the people among whom they lived.

The urban population increased substantially during the thirteenth and fourteenth centuries, in part because of the conquest of the great southern cities, in part because of the general expansion of commercial and industrial activity. Class distinctions within the cities also became more pronounced. The urban aristocracy, composed of wealthy merchants and bankers (known as *ciutatans honrats* in Catalonia, and in the west as *caballeros villanos* or *ciudadanos*) dominated the political life of the cities and usually represented them in the *cortes*. Many obtained the privilege of nobility from the crown. Factionalism was common among them and was one of the reasons why the king deprived cities of their earlier autonomy. Professional men, such as lawyers, notaries, physicians, and well-to-do craftsmen (*menestrales*), formed an intermediate group. The craftsmen were the largest single element

in the urban population and possessed a high degree of self-consciousness, stimulated by their organization in guilds and the location in the
same street of the houses and shops of those in the same craft. Craftsmen in Muslim cities lived under very similar conditions. In the twelfth
and early thirteenth centuries, by their participation in the general assembly of citizens, they had a real voice in municipal government in
Christian Spain, but as that body was summoned less frequently, they
were effectively silenced and practically disfranchised. As time passed,
they developed a strong antipathy to the oligarchs who controlled the
cities and also to the Jews. The urban population continued to grow
because of the influx of peasants who gained rights of citizenship after
residence of a year and a day. Many of them were unskilled laborers
who formed a proletariat in dependence upon the aristocrats and the
craftsmen.

In spite of the growth of urban society the greater number of people
continued to live in rural areas. Sobreques estimates the peasant population to have been about three or four million around the beginning
of the thirteenth century. The advance of the reconquest and the opening of new regions for colonization in the south continued to encourage
a spirit of freedom and adventure among the peasantry, but by the
middle of the fourteenth century the peasant's right to move freely was
under serious challenge.

In the central *meseta* between the Duero and the Tagus and in some
parts of the Algarve, Andalusia, and Valencia, free proprietors living in
towns or villages and owning small parcels of land in the immediately
adjacent countryside were numerous. Many other freemen in these
areas had no land of their own and worked for others. The most indi-
vidualistic and independent freemen were perhaps the shepherds whose
numbers increased with the expansion of the sheep industry.

Among the older groups of freemen were the *hombres de behetria*
who had settled particularly in old Castile and northern Portugal. By
the thirteenth century the right which their ancestors had enjoyed of
commending themselves to the protection of any lord they pleased had
been circumscribed. The inhabitants of certain villages did retain the
right to choose their lord freely (*behetría de mar a mar*), but most
often they had to do so among the members of a specific noble family
(*behetría de linaje*). This served only to encourage bitter rivalry and
contention among members of these families (*deviseros*), who asked
Pedro the Cruel in 1351 to divide the *behetrías* among them. With that

intention in mind he ordered the compilation of the *Becerro de Behe-trías*, a volume recording the extent of these lordships and their obligations to the crown and to their lords; the division, however, was not carried out.

In the northern regions of Galicia, Portugal, Castile, Aragon, and Catalonia, most peasants were tenant farmers, economically and juridically dependent upon their lords. Known variously as *iuniores de heredad* or *de cabeza* (Galicia and Portugal), *solariegos* (Castile), *villanos de parada* (Aragon), or *homes propis e solids* (Catalonia), they were commended to their lords to whom they owed rents and services. As they abandoned their ancestral homes to seek a better life in the south, their lords reacted by attempting to impose heavier burdens upon them and to bind them more closely to the soil. The *Siete Partidas* and other Castilian legal texts affirmed the right of peasants to move freely, taking their movables with them, but in Aragon and Catalonia lords were especially adamant in their opposition. Pedro III in 1283 confirmed the right of a Catalan landlord to demand payment of a redemption by any tenant who wished to leave the land. The lord could set the amount impossibly high and if the tenant left without his consent he could call upon royal officials to arrest him. The problem of the *payeses de remensa*, as peasants subject to redemption were called, became exceedingly grave after the destruction caused by the plague. In the kingdom of Granada many peasants worked in the fields as sharecroppers or as shepherds.

During the years of progress in the reconquest the supply of slaves in both Christian and Muslim Spain was good, as many of those who had the misfortune to be captured in war were sold into slavery. Many Christian lords and religious houses owned Muslim slaves who performed household services or worked in the fields. Granada obtained slaves from Christian Spain and also from Africa. The slave trade also seems to have flourished on both sides of the frontier and indeed throughout the Mediterranean. The pope and other prelates, such as the bishop of Barcelona in 1244, forbade anyone, under pain of excommunication, to sell Christians into slavery.

The Economy

The thirteenth and fourteenth centuries, at least until the impact of the Black Death, were a time of substantial economic growth throughout Europe. Commerce and industry continued to expand and to flourish, providing not only the necessities but an ever-increasing supply of luxuries for a greater number of people. Commercial enterprise linked Europe in an economic unity it had never known before, as products of north, south, east, and west, of the Christian and Muslim worlds, circulated freely and abundantly. Spain was not apart from these developments. In one way or another her people shared in the rising standard of living, suffered from inflation, flocked to the cities in search of new opportunities, and journeyed to distant lands to trade.

The most consequential development within the peninsula was the colonization of vast areas in the south by the Christian conquerors. The settlement of the Algarve, Andalusia, Murcia, Valencia, and Majorca was carried out under the direction of the king, but with differing intensity and characteristics in each region. The *Repartimientos* of Seville, Murcia, Valencia, and Majorca, now extant, record the distribution of lands and houses to nobles, prelates, military Orders, and ordinary people who collaborated in the reconquest. The work of distribution usually was done by a group of officials appointed by the king, who, in case of disputes concerning boundaries, summoned local people, including Muslims, to bear witness.

Given the rapidity of the reconquest, the Christians were concerned primarily to provide for military occupation of the principal cities and strongholds. Only after the great revolt against Alfonso X in 1264 was the Muslim population of Andalusia uprooted and a systematic colonization begun. For purposes of defense much of the rural area was ceded in the form of large estates to nobles and military Orders whose effective political power thereafter was greatly enhanced. These lands generally were given over to the cultivation of olive trees or to the grazing of sheep and were scantily populated, for most workers usually lived in the towns or villages. Many were hired on an annual basis, but others found work only day by day or seasonally; lacking any real security they were confronted constantly by the specter of starvation. The details of the colonization of southern Portugal are not as well known, but it seems that the nobles and military Orders obtained great estates there and that settlements were much more intensive in the Algarve than in the Alentejo.

The colonization of Murcia was undertaken only after Jaime I suppressed the revolt there in 1266. The *Repartiment* indicates that he settled about 10,000 Catalans and Aragonese; Alfonso X later settled Castilians there, but the Muslim population in the country areas remained predominant. Much the same situation prevailed in Valencia. The Moors were ousted from the cities and other strategic places, and Christian settlers were brought in. The king usually gave small holdings of a house, an orchard, a vineyard, and a few acres (*jovadas*, the amount of land plowed by a team of oxen in a day) to individual proprietors who usually prospered because of the fertility of the soil and the availability of a supply of cheap Moorish labor. In the inland rural areas larger grants were made to the nobles, and there the Moorish peasantry continued to cultivate the land as in the past. Small holdings were also characteristic of the Christian colonization of Majorca.

The scanty information available indicates that the king of Granada and the chief Moorish lords held much of the *vega* or lowland, where they maintained country houses and gardens; even so, many farms (*alqarya*, or *alquería*) were held by small proprietors. Sharecropping was common in Granada and also in lower Aragon, Valencia, and Murcia. In the *meseta* where people clustered in towns or villages and cultivated the outlying lands, an individual proprietor's holdings often were scattered and did not form a compact unit. Hired men with teams of oxen (*yugueros, quinteros*) were frequently employed on a yearly basis, receiving a fifth of the harvest or a fifth of the seed sown, in addition to food for themselves and their animals. Laborers usually had to walk long distances to work, getting up very early in the morning and returning home late in the evening. By the thirteenth century those who worked on the harvest often were paid in coin, and vineyard workers sometimes received a ration of wine. The *Ordenamiento de menestrales* of 1351 reflected a view held no doubt by most employers, namely, that wine and the siesta were not conducive to productivity, and forbade both.

In the mountainous regions of Galicia, Portugal, upper Aragon, Navarre, and Catalonia, where great estates had been formed in earlier times, tenant farmers often lived in isolated farmhouses (*casal, caserío*) surrounded by granaries, corrals, and small parcels of land or else in tiny hamlets (*aldeas, lugares, llocs*) with their lands lying out beyond. In addition to labor services, tenants owed an annual rent (*infurción, cens*) of varying amount, a portion of the harvest (in Catalonia their heaviest burden), and in Castile, a fixed payment known as *martiniega* or *marzadga*, payable on St. Martin's Day or in March. These obligations were converted into monetary payments by the thirteenth century. Tenants in Catalonia were subject to the so-called "evil usages" described in an earlier chapter; elsewhere they were expected to pay fees for marriages, inheritances, and the like. The burden of these obligations was not excessive, as some were seldom if ever collected. The tenant usually had security in his holding and could bequeath it to his heirs or alienate it to someone else; his main complaint was that his lord was attempting to deprive him of his right to leave the land when he wished to do so.

Agricultural production was generally diversified in the northern regions, but in the center and south greater reliance was placed upon the cultivation of a single item. In the northern mountains dairy farming was common, while in the *meseta* wheat, barley, and rye were grown. Vineyards were found in many parts of the peninsula, and the wines of La Rioja, Porto, La Mancha, and Jerez were beginning to acquire a renown beyond the immediate area of production. The popularity of wine was attested in the *Partidas* which noted that "men love it very much." The Muslims too retained a fondness for wine that had distinguished their ancestors; Ibn al-Khatib related the tale of a man who, on his deathbed, called upon Allah to assure him of a goodly supply of the wines of Málaga in Paradise. The production of olives was intensive in Andalusia and Murcia, but surprisingly Granada had to import olive oil, as well as wheat and barley. On the other hand, the kingdom's supply of fruits, figs, raisins, almonds, and so forth was ample. Sugar cane was cultivated in the Mediterranean lowlands around Motril and Almuñécar, and there was a certain amount of cotton production in the valley of the Guadalquivir. The Christian conquest seems, however, to have resulted in a decline in the cultivation of sugar cane and cotton in Andalusia. Oranges, the distinctive product of Valencia, were widely distributed throughout the peninsula and were exported abroad.

The techniques of production appear not to have changed substantially, though like so many other questions relating to the history of medieval Hispanic agriculture, this needs intensive investigation. Glick recently studied the techniques of irrigation developed in earlier times in the kingdom of Valencia and still in use after the Christian conquest. So important was irrigation that a tribunal had to be established to resolve disputes concerning the use of water. Even today the eight members of the tribunal gather every Thursday at the door of the cathedral to dispense justice and to impose fines upon those guilty of misusing the irrigation system.

Contention concerning the use of woodland was also commonplace.

Peasants and townsmen had need of wood for firewood and building, and the *cortes* set down penalties for those who deliberately set fires in the woods or wantonly cut down trees. Rulers also tried to preserve woodland, not only as a hunting ground, but also as a supply of raw material for shipbuilding. For this reason and also to establish a barrier against coastal sands that threatened farmland, Dinis of Portugal planted an extensive pine forest near Leiria. The extent of woodland in the medieval centuries was considerable, and the denuding of the countryside, which strikes one today as a dominant feature, did not begin on a large scale until the sixteenth century.

The Castilian economy of the thirteenth and fourteenth centuries was based especially upon the raising of sheep and the production of wool. As the reconquest opened up vast areas in Extremadura, Lower Aragon, and Andalusia for pasturage, many men found sheep-raising more profitable than the cultivation of the soil. Sheep-raising in the mountains of Ronda was also a major element in the economy of the kingdom of Granada, and both Christians and Muslims profited from raids on one another's flocks along the frontier. As the European population continued to increase, the demand for woolen goods also rose and encouraged the expansion of sheep-raising. Woolen cloth was manufactured chiefly in the towns of Flanders and Italy, but England and Castile supplied the bulk of the raw material.

By the beginning of the fourteenth century Castilian wool was a principal item of export, and the sheep-raising industry was organized throughout the realm under royal direction. At that time there were perhaps, as Vicens Vives suggested, a million and a half sheep in Castile. Lopez proposed the theory that Genoese merchants, fearing the possibility that the supply of raw wool from England might be cut off, introduced the merino sheep from North Africa to Castile around 1280. By breeding merino sheep with the native sheep they were able to produce an animal giving wool of such high quality that it was readily acceptable on the international market.

The distinctive characteristic of Castilian sheep-raising was the system of *trashumancia*, the annual migration of sheep from north to south to escape the rigors of winter. As the number of flocks grew, and nobles, prelates, military Orders, and monasteries began to draw increasing profit from them, the king endeavored to regulate and tax them. Whether the king or the sheepmen were mainly responsible for creating the national sheep-raising organization known as the *mesta* is uncertain. Klein argued that Alfonso X imposed a *servicio* on migratory sheep in 1269 and organized the *mesta* in 1273 to collect it more efficiently; but Bishko pointed out that the king's charters to the *mesta* in 1273 are in confirmation of earlier privileges; therefore he believes that the *mesta* probably originated between 1230 and 1265. In the late twelfth and early thirteenth centuries local *mestas* (so-called from the small commons where sheep were rounded-up) were adequate for regulating pasturage, but with the development of migration on a large scale an agency with a broad territorial base was necessary to defend the interests of the sheepmen. As the flocks from Galicia and Asturias migrated southward to the Tagus and Guadiana valleys, they traversed the lands of *concejos* and military Orders who tried to impose tributes upon every head of sheep and otherwise to impede their progress. The crown naturally had an interest in preventing and adjudicating the inevitable conflicts that arose; moreover, a king such as Alfonso X, hard-pressed for money in a time of inflation, saw the possibility of increasing his revenues substantially by the regular taxation of migratory sheep. The *mesta* therefore served both the king and the sheepmen.

The "Honorable Council of the *Mesta* of the Sheepmen of Castile" controlled all migratory sheep and the routes (*cañadas*) they followed from north to south. Twice-yearly meetings were held, one in the south in January-February, the other in the north in September-October, to resolve issues and to elect officers. The king appointed the chief officer, the *alcalde entregador*, who with his lieutenants (*alcaldes de cuadrilla*), was responsible for the settlement of conflicts that might arise among the sheepmen, or between them and the landlords through whose fields the sheep passed. It was absolutely essential that the sheepwalks be kept open.

There were three principal sheepwalks or *cañadas*. One extended from León southward through Zamora and Salamanca to Plasencia, Cáceres, Mérida, and Badajoz. Another ran from Logroño on the Navarrese border through Burgos, Palencia, Segovia, and Avila to Bejar, and then into Extremadura; an eastern branch of this route came from Soria to Talavera and then southward to the Guadalquivir valley. The third route began in the hills about Cuenca and passed through La Mancha to Andalusia or Murcia. The *cañadas* were about 150 to 350 miles long and about 250 feet wide; they were marked when they adjoined cultivated ground, but this was a frequent cause of contention with landlords. Flocks were usually quite large, often of 1,000 or more head; they traveled about 15 to 18 miles daily in enclosed land and about 5 to 6 miles in open fields where they could graze more freely. Leaving the south in mid-April, they were clipped and shorn enroute to the north. By August they had completed the journey and were soon ready to return to the south. The king's tax, the *servicio y montazgo*, was also collected on the trip. Shepherds accompanying the flocks were usually hired for the year from June 24, the feast of St. John.

While the sheepmen dominated the central *meseta*, cattlemen were the principal beneficiaries of the distribution of conquered lands in Andalusia. There, as Bishko has pointed out, cattle ranching became the dominant feature of the economy. Cattle ranching, one of the unique characteristics of medieval Spain, had begun to develop in the late eleventh and twelfth centuries in the lands of the central *meseta*. Many small ranchers who were settled in the towns had herds of from 40 to 100 head of cattle that they pastured in the municipal ranges, subject to the control of the town government. In Andalusia, on the other hand, the cattlemen were usually great lords with herds sometimes as large as 1,000 head or more; the military Orders also herded cattle and appointed a *comendador de las vacas* to take charge of them. A hybrid of domestic types, the range cattle were tough and aggressive but valuable for their beef and their hides. Sometimes the cattle were driven overland, as much as 400 miles, from summer pastures in the north to winter ones in Andalusia, usually following the *cañadas* used by the *mesta*. Small ranchers often joined in shareholding arrangements for extensive drives of this kind. The cowboys (*vaqueros*), like the shepherds, usually were freemen hired for the year and were paid either in coin or in a certain number of calves. The *cantigas* of the Archpriest of Hita illustrate the life and habits of the cowboys and cowgirls he encountered in the vicinity of Madrid, Segovia, and Guadalajara.

Bishko, who has described the essential features of the cattle-ranching industry, has also pointed out that the dress and equipment of the cowboys, and the techniques such as the spring round-up, the branding of calves, and the fall cutting out of beef for slaughter, were all subsequently transplanted to the New World. Most interestingly, he has emphasized that the historical antecedents of bullfighting are to be found in the techniques used to herd cattle on the open range in medieval Castile.

Recognizing the importance of the sheep and cattle industries, the kings of Castile, at least from the time of Alfonso VIII, prohibited the export of sheep, horses, and mules. In so many different ways these types of livestock provided the backbone of the Castilian economy.

The increasing production of raw wool supplied the peninsula with an essential material for the development of a native textile industry and also with a valuable commodity for export to Flanders and Italy, the two great wool-manufacturing centers in Europe. As one might expect, a woolen industry began to develop in the Castilian towns along the routes of the *mesta*, for example, in Segovia, Zamora, Avila and Soria, and also in Córdoba and Murcia. Even more important was the woolen industry of Catalonia, centered in Barcelona and other towns; by the fourteenth century there were thousands of workers, many of them French or Italian, producing woolen cloth in houses and shops all over Catalonia. Raw wool was imported from Castile and Aragon, and the finished product was then exported to Italy, northern Europe, and Africa.

Other important textiles were cotton and silk, produced in Valencia, and in Málaga and Almería and other towns of the kingdom of Granada. There were also many local industries producing for essentially local consumption.

The expansion of trade gave impetus to the development of the shipbuilding industry, especially in Catalonia, where Barcelona constructed dockyards large enough for thirty ships. Alfonso X ordered the construction of shipyards in Seville, and Dinis encouraged the development of the industry at Lisbon. In the kingdom of Granada, Almería retained its old prominence as a shipbuilding center.

As industrial activity increased, the artisans began to organize themselves into confraternities and guilds. The former were primarily religious and social in character, intended to provide for sick brethren, the burial of the dead, and the care of widows and orphans of members. But there was also a strong trend toward organization for the defense of their common economic interests. The guilds tried to monopolize the crafts, to eliminate competition, and to exclude nonguildsmen from participation. The kings of Castile tended to react in a hostile manner to any manifestation of guild organization. Thus Fernando III in 1250 condemned *confradías* and *ayuntamientos malos*, believing that they diminished his authority and worked to the detriment of the towns. He permitted only those associations devoted to the care of the poor, the sick, and the dead. Even so, it was difficult to prevent the formation of guilds or to restrict associations of workers to strictly religious or social activities. In Aragon, guilds encountered similar opposition from the crown and from the *cortes,* but in Catalonia guild organization developed and flourished, no doubt because the industrial middle class was more powerful there than elsewhere in the peninsula. Thus the crown, instead of opposing the guilds, confirmed their right to exist, and in 1337 Pedro IV granted the towns the right to establish and to regulate the guilds. The organization of guilds was essentially the same as elsewhere in Europe and was based upon the three traditional ranks of masters, journeymen, and apprentices. The guild's statutes, confirmed by the city government, set down the conditions for advancement from one rank to another, determined the methods and techniques of production, and regulated sales to the public.

Weekly town markets held in the *plaza mayor* or at the gates of the town provided an opportunity for merchants, artisans, farmers, and sheepherders to offer their goods for sale. Sheep, cattle, pigs, bread, fish, fruits, clothing, and similar products changed hands, but this was primarily local and retail trade. From the thirteenth century onward the great fairs (*ferias*) of Castile began to make their appearance, first in Andalusia where the Genoese found it convenient to purchase raw wool for shipment to Italy. Alfonso X established two fairs to be held annually at Seville, the one extending for fifteen days before and fifteen days after Pentecost, and the other for the same length of time at Michaelmas; Dinis established many fairs throughout Portugal. The growth of fairs was slow, however, because kings were not inclined to favor a free market and tended to limit the number of fairs and to regulate closely those that did exist. Fairs established by royal charter attracted buyers and sellers from a much wider area than the weekly town markets and offered a greater variety of goods for sale; wholesale transactions were usually more important than retail. Those who participated were under the protection of the crown and of the town government; but the town levied a fee for the rental of space for tents and shops and another for police protection, and the king collected sales taxes. In view of the extraordinary inflation in Castile and Portugal in the middle of the thirteenth century both Alfonso X and Afonso III established maximum prices for most goods sold and prohibited merchants from entering agreements to fix prices at higher levels.

The international trade of Castile and Portugal developed slowly because neither kingdom was yet producing a sufficiency to supply its own essential needs for food and clothing, and the demand for peninsular products was limited. In the thirteenth century the kings of both realms imposed restrictions on the export of *cosas vedadas*, namely, sheep, horses, cattle, goats, pigs, gold, silver, cereals, Moors, and so on. Clearly these products were in limited supply and were regarded as essential to the domestic economy. On the other hand, both kingdoms imported food products, arms, and especially cloth from Flanders, and luxuries of all types. Although there are indications of the presence of Portuguese and Castilian merchants in England, Flanders, and France early in the thirteenth century, peninsular trade was primarily in the hands of foreign merchants and was carried in foreign ships. The weak position of the two kingdoms is suggested by decrees of Afonso III and Alfonso X requiring foreign merchants to bring into the country goods of equal value to those exported. Only in the later thirteenth century did a native merchant marine, capable of competing effectively for a share in the carrying trade, develop in either Castile or Portugal.

The Genoese enjoyed an especially prominent position in the trade of both kingdoms. Fernando III in 1249 gave them commercial privileges in the newly conquered city of Seville, and within a few years they also had important colonies in Cádiz, Jerez, Murcia, Cartagena, and Lisbon. The Genoese admiral Manuel Pezagno helped to develop the Portuguese merchant fleet, training native seamen and supervising the construction of ships. The Genoese also supplied naval power to prevent the Moroccans from controlling the straits of Gibraltar. In the long run that benefited both Castile and Portugal, because Genoese and Venetian fleets were encouraged to venture out of the Mediterranean into the Atlantic, visiting the ports of both kingdoms. From the end of the thirteenth century the Venetian Flanders Fleet usually stopped at Seville and Lisbon, and the Genoese regularly brought necessities to those ports and picked up cargoes of wool and olive oil.

The Castilian and Portuguese merchant marine operated most successfully in the Atlantic Ocean rather than the Mediterranean. From the beginning of the thirteenth century the Cantabrian ports of Santander, Castro Urdiales, Laredo, and San Vicente de la Barquera began to participate in the carrying trade in a significant way. They developed first as fishing ports, but soon became involved in the export of iron from the Basque country and the import of cloth from Flemish towns such as Cambrai, Douai, Ghent, and Ypres; they also transported wine from Bordeaux and other places in Gascony to England. These four Cantabrian ports in 1296 joined with San Sebastián, Fuenterrabia, Bermeo, and Guetaria to form the *hermandad de las villas de la marina de Castilla con Vitoria*, also known as the *hermandad de las marismas*. Its purposes were to free the towns from the obligation of paying tolls to the bishop of Burgos; to escape from the jurisdiction of the *almirante de Castilla*, whose headquarters were in Burgos; to monopolize the export of iron; and to defend their common interests against competition from Gascon and Portuguese shipping.

Encouraged by King Dinis, the Portuguese merchant marine developed quickly. Significant evidence of this is a contract, confirmed by the king in 1293, whereby merchants engaged in trade with the ports of Seville, La Rochelle, Brittany, Normandy, England, or Flanders, created a *bolsa de comércio*, that is, they agreed to contribute for each of their ships to a common fund to cover risks of loss and to provide credit for those in need. The conflict with the Gascons and the Castilians in the Bay of Biscay led to diplomatic intervention and eventually amicable settlement.

In the course of the fourteenth century, trade between the Atlantic ports of the peninsula and northern Europe became regular. For example, Edward III in 1351 concluded a treaty with the *hermandad de las marismas* guaranteeing the protection of their merchant ships in his ports. He entered a similar engagement in 1353 with the merchants and mariners of Lisbon and Porto, giving them safe-conduct for themselves and their goods and allowing them to trade in any of his ports, subject only to the payment of the same tolls as the natives. In Flanders both Castilians and Portuguese established colonies at the end of the thirteenth century under the protection of the counts. The Castilian colony in Bruges was one of the most important because of the expansion of the wool trade and the growing demand for Castilian wool. Charles V of France in 1363 also assured his protection to Castilian merchants who established important colonies at Rouen, Bordeaux, and Bayonne as those cities came into French possession. Wool, iron, and wine were the principal cargoes carried by Castilians and Portuguese to the north. They brought back the finished textiles of the Flemish towns as well as miscellaneous items, such as furs, knives, mirrors, tools, and so forth.

The maritime commerce of Catalonia developed more swiftly than that of Castile or Portugal as the Catalans created a great commercial empire in the Mediterranean in the thirteenth and fourteenth centuries. In earlier times Genoese and Pisans had carried Catalan goods abroad, but in 1227 Jaime I issued a decree requiring goods to be carried in ships of Barcelona. The conquest of Majorca two years later, carried out largely with Catalan ships, marked the coming of age of the Catalan merchant marine. The Catalans first developed trade relations along the coast northward to Languedoc and Provence; Montpellier, held as a lordship by the kings of Aragon for most of this period, served as a strategic base for dominating the trade of the area. By the close of the thirteenth century, Sicily provided an advanced position for trade with the Italian mainland and North Africa. Early in the next century an additional outpost was established on Sardinia. The Genoese, however, resented the Catalan presence there and in the Tyrrhenian Sea which they regarded as their own. The Catalans seldom intruded into the Adriatic due to Venetian hegemony there, but by the middle of the fourteenth century they established themselves at Pera, a suburb of Constantinople, as well as on Crete, Cyprus, and Rhodes. They even had a colony in the Crimean peninsula, which gave them access to the gold, silk, slaves, and spices brought from the Far East. In exchange for these goods and Sicilian wheat and Sardinian silver, they exported woolen cloth of medium quality, as well as olive oil, rice, Valencian oranges, and other fruits.

From the earliest times, the Catalans engaged in trade with the Muslim lands of the Mediterranean Sea, even though this was illicit trade, frequently condemned by the papacy and by local bishops. Those who sold iron, arms, wood, bread, and similar contraband to the Muslims were subject to excommunication, but the frequency with which absolutions were given to violators indicates that the ban was seldom observed. Catalan merchant colonies were established at Alexandria in Egypt as early as 1264, and by the fourteenth century the Catalans had commercial hegemony in the city. From Majorca and Sicily they were also able to dominate the trade relations of Tunis and the neighboring Muslim states of Bougie and Tlemcen. Jaime II in 1301 was so bold as to require the emir of Tunis to pay half the customs duties collected at that port into the Aragonese treasury. From these coastal positions the Catalans tapped the resources of the interior, namely, the Sudan, the Sahara, and Uganda, importing cotton, linen, spices, and slaves.

The Catalans were also involved in trade with Castile and the kingdom of Granada. The principal ports of the latter realm were Almería and Málaga; Al-Shaqundi mentions that Christian merchants of all nations frequented Almería and maintained factories there. Málaga too was continually visited by Christian and Muslim vessels, which, according to Ibn Batuta, loaded cargoes of figs, almonds, and fruits for export throughout the Mediterranean. The Catalans who had settled in Seville after its conquest participated in this trade, but they were outnumbered by their archrivals in the western Mediterranean, the Genoese. Conflict with the Genoese in Castilian waters was one of the reasons for the outbreak of war between Castile and Aragon in the middle of the fourteenth century. Coupled with the naval wars with Genoa for control of Sardinia, it helped to bring about the decline of Catalan overseas trade in the following century. Although the Catalans visited the Canary Islands in the later fourteenth century, and Jaume Ferrer sailed along the west coast of Africa as far as Rio de Oro in Senegal in 1346, the Catalans played a negligible role in the fifteenth-century explorations in the Atlantic. This is clearly attributable to their failure to overcome Genoese hegemony, particularly in Seville and Lisbon.

In those foreign ports where the Catalans had important colonies, they usually acquired extraterritorial privileges. In Alexandria, Damascus, and Beirut, for example, they inhabited quarters set apart from the rest of the city and were governed by their own consuls who adjudicated their lawsuits and defended their interests before the Muslim authorities. The consuls were appointed by the king of Aragon, but in 1266 Jaime I allowed the city of Barcelona to name consuls in foreign ports.

In the crown of Aragon itself the merchants engaged in overseas trade began to organize guilds or associations known as consulates to protect their mutual interests. Jaime I in 1257 allowed the good men of the sea (*pro homs de la ribera*) to draw up ordinances regulating maritime customs in the waterfront district of Barcelona. A charter given by Pedro III in 1283 to the merchants and seamen engaged in maritime trade in Valencia was the foundation of the Consulate of the Sea in that city. It provided for the annual election at Christmastime by the *probi homines maris* of two consuls, who would preside over the guild and also settle any disputes that might arise. Pedro IV chartered similar organizations in Majorca in 1343 and in Barcelona in 1347. The ordinances, charters, and constitutions of these associations were gathered together about 1370 in the *Llibre del Consolat del Mar*, the most comprehensive code of maritime law in the Mediterranean, used not only in the crown of Aragon but also in Italy and in the ports of southern France. The formation of consulates was mainly in response to the desire of merchants engaged in maritime trade to have at hand a tribunal composed of judges who knew the custom of the sea and who would resolve conflicts in accordance with it. The consulates therefore enjoyed a distinct form of judicial jurisdiction.

From their contacts with Italian maritime practice, Catalan merchants adopted various forms of trading organization. The earliest of these used in the thirteenth century was the *commenda* or *comanda*, an arrangement whereby a merchant commended his goods to the master of a ship who sold them in foreign ports in return for a commission. The association lasted only for the length of the sea voyage. In the fourteenth century two or more merchants formed an association called a *societas maris* for a specific enterprise; while one or more of the participants might remain at home, another might travel with the cargo, taking the responsibility for disposing of it and purchasing another for the return voyage. Profits were shared at the end of the voyage in accordance with the extent of one's investment of capital or labor. Once the journey was completed, the *societas* was dissolved. Only in the fifteenth century did more permanent forms of association, such as the trading company, make their appearance.

From Carolingian times, silver was the standard coinage used in most of western Europe, but the expansion of international trade brought gold to the fore once again. In the middle of the thirteenth century the Italian cities began to issue gold coins, and the gold florin of Florence, weighing about 3.5 grams, became the most widely accepted money in the Mediterranean world. Silver coinage minted at Jaca or Barcelona by order of the king was long in use in the crown of Aragon; the temptation to tamper with it in time of economic change was great, but Jaime I, among others, pledged to maintain it intact for life. The need for a money readily acceptable in international exchange no doubt induced Pedro IV in 1346 to cause the minting of gold florins at Perpignan. Gold money had long been in use in Muslim Spain, and the gold *maravedí* of Alfonso VIII, which later circulated in Castile and Portugal, imitated the money of the Almoravids. In petty transactions pennies of copper and silver alloy were most commonly used. There were frequent devaluations of the coinage during this period, and gold tended to be restricted in its circulation. By the time of Pedro the Cruel the silver *real* was becoming the ordinary medium of exchange in the kingdom of Castile.

The increasing circulation of money and the greater variety of coins in use provided considerable profit for moneychangers. From the accumulation of profits they also were able to lend money, though the church had a long-standing tradition of opposition to the taking of interest or usury. In the kingdoms of Castile and Portugal, Jewish moneylenders dominated the trade in the thirteenth and fourteenth centuries. The *Fuero Real* allowed an annual rate of 33⅓ per cent interest; but excessive rates were reason for the constant outcry against the Jews and eventually provoked the pogroms of 1391. In Catalonia, the emerging middle class supplanted Jewish moneylenders, and a number of important banking families came into existence, such as that of Pere Descaus; he and others lent money to the king, to the church, to municipalities, and to private persons, and on the whole they flourished until the great financial collapse of 1381. Thereafter the great private banks (*taulas*) gave place to other types of banking institutions.

CHAPTER 20

Religion and Culture, 1212–1369

Apogee and Decline

Medieval civilization attained its apogee in the thirteenth century, but then entered upon a time of change in which older values and ideas were challenged, debated, and sometimes rejected. The fortunes of the papacy graphically illustrate this point. The popes of the thirteenth century achieved a great triumph in their long struggle for supremacy over the secular power, but their humiliation at the hands of the French king at the close of the century marked a significant change in relationships between the spiritual and temporal powers. The long residence of the popes at Avignon for most of the fourteenth century, moreover, damaged their prestige and authority. In the realm of the spirit, the era opened with the advent of the mendicant Orders who tried to recall men to apostolic simplicity, but the church seemed to have become mired in worldly complications and excessively concerned with money and the letter of the law. An insistent cry for reform began to be heard, though seldom heeded, and the populace, finding little consolation in ecclesiastical juridicism, clamored for a more profound spirituality. In different parts of Europe this led some to mysticism and others to heresy.

The thirteenth century was the age of universities and the age of synthesis. The *studia generalia* at Paris and Bologna were models for similar institutions established in Spain and in other countries. The universities were the principal intellectual centers of the time, where scholars attempted to organize, analyze, and systematize the principal bodies of knowledge. St. Thomas Aquinas achieved a synthesis of theology and Aristotelian ideas, but the trend toward rationalism evoked protest from those who wished to re-emphasize the importance

487

of religious faith. The fourteenth century therefore became a battle-ground between the Thomists and the members of the Augustinian school, whose principal spokesmen were Duns Scotus and William of Ockham.

Latin continued to be the language of the professional, clerical, and scholarly class, but vernacular languages were being used more frequently as vehicles of literary expression. This was the age of Dante and Chaucer, two of the greatest poets of the Middle Ages, who did so much to mold the languages of their respective countries. It was in its use of the vernacular that the culture of Christian Spain, so long overshadowed by that of al-Andalus, finally came into full bloom. Muslim Spain, unhappily, experienced a cultural decline, relieved only occasionally by the appearance of a truly exceptional writer such as Ibn al-Khatib.

The Church

The ties between the papacy and the church in Spain were especially close during the thirteenth and fourteenth centuries, as the centralization of authority in Rome reached its fullest development. As the possessor of the *plenitudo potestatis*, the pope freely intervened in secular affairs, by deposing kings and threatening others with excommunication and interdict, usually on the grounds that the monarch had in some way violated the liberties of the church. The papacy also actively encouraged the reconquest by conceding crusading indulgences and portions of ecclesiastical revenue to finance campaigns. In the spiritual sphere, the volume of appeals to the papal *curia* steadily increased, as did papal appointments to ecclesiastical benefices and taxation of the clergy. For the most part the Spanish church was submissive to the papacy, though from time to time there were protests, similar to those heard elsewhere, against papal taxation and papal provisions.

The reconquest of the Algarve, Andalusia, Valencia, Murcia, and the Balearics necessitated some modification of the ecclesiastical structure of the peninsula. Although the territory added to the Christian states easily constituted a third of the peninsula, comparatively few bishoprics were restored, and only two ecclesiastical provinces were created. The bishoprics in question were Silves in the Algarve (1255), Badajoz (1255), Córdoba (1236), Baeza (1228), transferred to Jaén (1248), Medina Sidonia (1261), transferred to Cádiz (1267), Seville (1248), Cartagena (1250), Valencia (1238), and Majorca (1232).

Seville formed a province, but its territory was narrowly circumscribed, including only the suffragan sees of Cádiz and Silves, though the latter was later subordinated to Lisbon. Zaragoza was elevated to metropolitan rank in 1318 with only Pamplona and Calahorra dependent upon it.

The delimitation of provincial boundaries was the cause of frequent conflict among the metropolitans who seem to have been endowed with strong imperialistic ambitions. Jealous of rivals, they were anxious to subject the newly conquered areas to their own control. When it was to their advantage they favored the restoration of boundaries as they had existed in the Visigothic era, but at other times they invoked political changes as justification for ignoring the ancient boundaries or for not restoring sees. Thus, of the new bishoprics, Badajoz was subject to Santiago, but the ancient see of Mérida was not restored because its metropolitan rank had been transferred to Santiago. Jaén and Córdoba, though anciently subject to Seville, were included in Toledo's jurisdiction. Toledo also claimed supremacy over Valencia, as once having belonged to the province of Cartaginensis, but the king of Aragon insisted that Valencia be submitted to the archbishop of Tarragona. The metropolitans of Toledo and Tarragona also disputed possession of Cartagena, but the pope resolved the issue by making it an exempt bishopric. Majorca, claimed by Tarragona and Barcelona, was similarly exempted. The extension of provincial boundaries into more than one kingdom further complicated these arguments. Santiago, for example, had jurisdiction over the sees of central and southern Portugal, while Braga had similar rights over the sees of Galicia, excepting Santiago. Tarragona, and later Zaragoza, had jurisdiction over Pamplona in Navarre and Calahorra in Castile. Rulers usually opposed the intervention of a foreign metropolitan in the affairs of their bishoprics, so that in the long run metropolitan rights could seldom be enforced.

The touchy question of the primacy was definitively settled in favor of Toledo, largely through the persistence of Archbishop Rodrigo Jiménez de Rada, who obtained confirmation of his rights from Gregory IX in 1239. Even so, squabbles continued as the other metropolitans occasionally refused to acknowledge Toledo's superiority. Trivial controversies also arose when one archbishop entered another province with his cross of office borne on high, as a sort of challenge to the other's authority. In these instances the pope generally had to intervene to restore the peace.

The convocation of provincial councils and diocesan synods, encouraged by the Fourth Lateran Council of 1215, was considerably more frequent than in times past. The papal legate, Cardinal Jean d' Abbeville, on visiting all the peninsular realms in 1227–1229, admonished the bishops to convoke councils frequently. Among the more notable Councils were those of Tarragona in 1242, Peñafiel in 1302, and Valladolid in 1322. Conciliar decrees reveal a wide range of concerns, such as the defense of the church's liberties against encroachments by the crown or other secular persons, ecclesiastical jurisdiction, the life and habits of the clergy, the administration of the sacraments, the instruction of the faithful in the Our Father and the Creed, pastoral problems such as marriage, adultery, rape, gambling, sorcery, relations with Jews and Muslims, and so on.

Technically the bishops were elected by the cathedral chapter, but the liberty of the canons (members of the chapter) in this regard was steadily circumscribed by the king and by the pope. On the one hand, the king claimed the right to authorize an election and often nominated the candidates, especially for newly reconquered sees, and the chapter was expected to elect them without further ado. In general the pope confirmed royal nominations, though occasionally, as in the case of Fernando III's nomination of his son Felipe as bishop of Osma, he rejected it on the grounds of defect of age. In other instances, when the canons could not agree upon a candidate, the controverted election was appealed to the pope. Sometimes an inquiry was ordered to determine whether a valid election had taken place, but from the time of Innocent IV onward the pope frequently set the election aside and ordered the canons to choose his own nominee. As time passed, papal intervention became more and more common.

The relationship between the bishop and the chapter, who constituted his council, was not always harmonious. Many chapters were reformed and given a tighter organization in the thirteenth century, but the division of revenues between the bishop and the canons was a frequent source of controversy. Bishops and chapters did collaborate in the major task of cathedral-building. Those of Santiago, León, Burgos, Toledo, Tarragona, Lérida, Valencia, and others erected during the thirteenth century, were built in the newly developed Gothic style.

Appointment to ecclesiastical benefices such as canonries, chaplaincies, rectorships, and so forth became more and more frequently a right reserved to the papacy. The *Siete Partidas* (I, 16, 1) simply stated contemporary belief and frequent practice: "The pope has the power to give . . . all the benefices of the Holy Church to whomever he wishes and in whatever bishopric he wishes." Thirteenth-century rulers obtained from the pope the right to nominate men to certain benefices in the newly reconquered bishoprics; they also asked the pope to favor members of the royal family or faithful servants with appointments. Spanish clerics in the papal service, such as Cardinal Pelayo Gaitán, the leader of the Fifth Crusade, and Cardinal Gil de Albornoz who restored order in the papal states, all used their influence to obtain appointments for their protégés. Clerics serving in the *curia* at Avignon were given Spanish benefices as a means of providing them with income; eventually plurality of benefices and absenteeism became common and evoked protest. The *cortes* of 1329, for example, asked Alfonso XI to complain to the pope concerning the appointment of foreigners to Castilian benefices on the ground that these appointments brought positive evils in their train, namely, the king's secrets were revealed abroad, and the wealth of the kingdom was taken abroad. The king promised to take appropriate action, but in fact nothing was done.

Conciliar decrees suggest something of the lives and habits of the clergy. From time to time they were admonished to reside in their parishes and were instructed in their responsibilities to their parishioners. As unlettered men were not supposed to be ordained, a *magister scholarum* was given responsibility for clerical education in each diocese. Many of the clergy holding important positions were well educated, and some of them were masters trained in the universities, but the level of education among those serving in urban and rural parishes evidently was not always very high. Yet as the poet Gonzalo de Berceo (d.c. 1250) implies, piety was not dependent upon education. He tells of a simple, unlearned priest who said mass in honor of the Virgin Mary every day because he did not know how to say any other:

> Era un simple clerigo pobre de clerecía
> Diçie cutiano missa de la Sancta Maria,
> Non sabia deçir otra, diçiela cada dia,
> Mas la sabia por uso que por sabiduría.
> *[Milagros de Nuestra Señora, 220]*

When the bishop heard of this he became exceedingly angry and, denouncing the "idiota, mal clerigo probado," forbade him to say

mass; but the Virgin appeared to the bishop in a dream and commanded him in the sternest tones to allow the priest to continue offering mass in her honor. More than likely there were many other clergy
who knew not much more about the mass than this one. Perhaps on
this account, Berceo, himself a parish priest, attempted in another of
his poems, *Del Sacrificio de la Misa*, to instruct the faithful in the
meaning of the mass, showing how it fulfilled the sacrifice of the Old
Testament and explaining the purposes of each of the prayers and
actions of the ceremony.

The *cortes*, however, frequently complained that the clergy wasted
their time on gambling, fighting, drinking, and similar pursuits. Celibacy continued to be a problem as the canons forbidding the clergy to
cohabit with women or to give church property to their children indicate; the *cortes* demanded that clerical concubines be compelled to
wear distinctive dress so that good Christian women could avoid their
company. Juan Ruíz, the Archpriest of Hita (d.c. 1351), no model of
virtue in this respect, tells of his own *amores* and justifies them by
quoting Aristotle:

> Como dise Aristoteles, cosa es verdadera,
> El mundo por dos cosas trabaja: la primera
> Por aver mantenencia; la otra cosa era
> Por aver juntamiento con fembra plasentera.
> Si lo dixiese de mio, seria de culpar;
> Diselo gran filosofo, non so yo de rebtar;
> De lo que dise el sabio non debemos dubdar . . .

> As Aristotle truly says,
> The world strives for two things, the one
> To gain sustenance, the other
> To make love with a pretty girl.
> If I'd said that, I'd be to blame.
> A great philosopher said it;
> It's not for me to challenge him.
> We shouldn't doubt what a wise man says.
> [*Libro de Buen Amor*, 71-72]

In another place he mockingly describes the reaction of the clergy of
Talavera to a decree of the archbishop of Toledo forbidding them
under pain of excommunication to live with women. Vexed, to say the
least, the clergy proposed an appeal to the king because, although

clerics, they were his natural and loyal subjects and he would understand the weakness of their flesh:

> Appellasemos del papa antel rey de Castilla.
> Que maguer que somos clerigos, somos sus naturales.
> Servimosle muy bien, fuemos siempre leales,
> Demas que sabe el rey, que todos somos carnales,
> Creed se ha de adolecer de aquestos nuestros males.
>
> [*Libro*, 1696–1697]

The notion of appealing to the king of Castile against the pope and the archbishop is interesting and, allowing for poetic license, probably reflects an intensification of national sentiment and a growing discontent with the centralization of authority in Avignon.

The clergy enjoyed a centuries-old privilege of exemption from direct taxation, but increasing governmental costs impelled both popes and secular rulers to levy taxes upon the clergy. From the beginning of the thirteenth century the papacy taxed the clergy to support crusades to the Holy Land, though this money was often diverted to the reconquest as, for example, when Honorius III allowed money collected for the Fifth Crusade to be used in the war against the Moors. Kings reasoned, no doubt, that they could use clerical wealth for the same purpose, and at least from the time of Alfonso VIII the clergy were asked to make regular contributions. Fernando III claimed a third of the tithe for the reconquest, and the papacy, despite the continuing protests of the Spanish clergy, eventually authorized the collection of the *tercias reales*, as this tax was called, for limited periods of time. In practice it became a permanent levy. It is noteworthy that the Council of Peñafiel in 1302 urged all the bishops to publish Boniface VIII's bull *Clericis Laicos* (1296) forbidding taxation of the clergy without papal consent.

The continued acquisition of property of all kinds by ecclesiastical institutions became an ever-more serious problem as rulers saw the sources of taxable income steadily diminished. From time to time inquests were carried out to recover royal domain lands which had passed into the hands of the church. Dinis of Portugal was especially persistent in his efforts to curtail the accumulation of real property by ecclesiastical institutions. He decreed in 1286 that within a year all lands acquired by the church since the beginning of his reign should be sold to private persons; five years later he expressly forbade anyone entering a religious Order to give it his property. Those wishing to make gifts to the church were permitted to sell a third of their landed property to laymen and then to contribute the proceeds to the church. Despite such stringent measures, this was a never-ending struggle.

Church claims to jurisdiction over the clergy and their goods also provoked constant controversy with the civil authorities. According to the Council of Valladolid (1322) "ecclesiastical is known to be distinct from secular jurisdiction, and the one ought not to impede the other, but rather to assist it. Yet certain secular judges, disregarding the statutes of the canons enacted concerning this, injuriously compel clerics and other ecclesiastical persons to appear in judgment before them concerning their goods and personal suits" (CMCH, III, 558). As exact limitations on ecclesiastical jurisdiction were impossible, clerical and secular judges often charged one another with usurpation of jurisdiction. In general, clergy accused of crime were justiciable in church courts, but in civil cases involving clerics and laymen, it appears that the suit was often heard in the defendant's court. The church's claim to jurisdiction over certain types of cases was also cause for conflict; for example, the cortes in 1299 declared that "no one shall be summoned before ecclesiastical judges in pleas concerning inheritances, but rather shall be summoned before secular judges" (CLC, I, 141). The complaint was made in 1345 that "prelates and their vicars and archpriests intervene in hearing pleas that ought to be heard by us (the king) and by our judges and they impose sentence of excommunication on those who do not wish to consent to this" (CLC, I, 491). Thus it seems that so long as an independent system of church courts existed, conflict was unavoidable.

One of the consequences of the development of an urban civilization was the appearance of new religious Orders dedicated primarily to work among the urban classes. The thirteenth was the century of the mendicant Orders, the Franciscans and Dominicans. Abandoning the principle of stability so characteristic of Benedictine monasticism, they were organized on an international basis as associations of individuals rather than as congregations of monasteries. Exempted from episcopal jurisdiction, they proved to be especially effective instruments of papal policy and gained fame as teachers, preachers, and missionaries.

Reacting against the materialism of the bourgeoisie, St. Francis of Assisi (d. 1226) preached poverty and within a few years attracted an army of followers from all parts of Europe. He made a pilgrimage to

Santiago de Compostela in 1213–1214, and a few years later the first province of his Order was established in Spain. Among the distinguished recruits was St. Anthony of Padua (d. 1231), a native of Lisbon, who won renown as a preacher in Italy. Though kings and the people generally welcomed the friars, the bishops and secular clergy tended to view them with hostility because of the special privileges they had received from the papacy. For example, the cathedral chapter of Porto in 1233 denounced the friars as "thieves, heretics, and false prophets," but the burghers recognized the worth of the Franciscans, and the pope intervened to guarantee their peaceful settlement in the city.

St. Dominic de Guzmán (d. 1221), the founder of the Order of Preachers, was a native of Castile, who studied at Palencia, then emerging as a university. After becoming a canon of the cathedral of Osma and helping to restore community life there, he was sent by Alfonso VIII, along with his bishop, Diego, on a diplomatic mission to Denmark. Discovering the extent to which the Albigensian heresy had spread throughout Languedoc, he decided to devote himself to preaching in that area and in 1216 obtained papal approval for his Order. The constitutions he drafted have a markedly democratic character, providing for representative government to a certain extent; perhaps this may reflect his own knowledge and experience of the Castilian municipal government. Emphasizing theological study as prerequisite to effective preaching, he sent his friars to study at the newly developing universities. Houses were established early in the Iberian peninsula, and St. Ramon de Penyafort (d. 1275), who served as master general of the Order from 1238 to 1240, was only one of many Spaniards who enlisted in Dominican ranks.

Franciscans and Dominicans played an important role in the development of missions to the Muslim world in the thirteenth and fourteenth centuries, but the task was fraught with difficulty and danger. St. Francis had to give up his own plan to work as a missionary among the Spanish Muslims, and five friars sent to Morocco in 1219 were promptly executed by the caliph. Despite this, Pope Honorius III ordered Rodrigo Jiménez de Rada, archbishop of Toledo, to send Dominican and Franciscan friars to Morocco and to consecrate a bishop for the community. In this connection it may be noted that the archbishop commissioned Mark, one of the canons of his cathedral, to make a new Latin translation of the Koran, as an essential tool for the missionary effort. Although one Muslim writer reports that Fernando III made an agreement with the caliph allowing Christians in Morocco to worship freely and guaranteeing the safety of Muslims who embraced the Christian religion, this seems improbable, as there is ample evidence that missionaries were unwelcome and often were martyred.

St. Ramon de Penyafort took an active interest in the missions to Islam and established friaries in Tunis and Murcia where the brethren could study Arabic in preparation for their work. On his request, St. Thomas Aquinas, a fellow Dominican, wrote the *Summa contra Gentiles*, a treatise on natural theology intended to equip missionaries for debate and argumentation with the Muslims. St. Pedro Pascual (d. 1300), consecrated bishop of Jaén in 1296, labored as a missionary among the Andalusian Muslims until he was captured by a raiding party; he was imprisoned at Granada where he probably died a natural death, though legend has it that he was beheaded. His writings include a refutation of Islamic belief entitled *Impugnación de la secta de Mahoma*, and treatises on the commandments, the Creed, and the Lord's Prayer. The most famous missionary was Ramon Llull (d. 1315) whose activities will be discussed below.

The new emphasis upon missionary work among the Muslims marks a significant turning point in Christian attitudes toward Islam, but armed hostilities continued to typify most clearly the relationships between the two religions. Consequently, the military Orders of Calatrava, Santiago, Alcántara, and Avis were still responsible for the defense of the frontiers and still constituted the vanguard of Christian armies. By the middle of the fourteenth century, as the reconquest slowed and the Orders had less to do, they became increasingly involved in domestic politics and abandoned the simplicity that had characterized them in the early years of their existence. Considering the vast estates and material resources in their possession, the crown began to exercise a direct control over the election of the masters of the Orders. Alfonso XI went so far as to cause the election of his bastard Fadrique, as master of Santiago, thereby setting a pattern for the future.

When Pope Clement V, under pressure from the king of France, suppressed the Order of the Temple in 1312, two new Hispanic Orders were created in its stead. Both Jaime II of Aragon and Dinis of Portugal declared that they found no truth in the charges of heresy, blasphemy, and immorality hurled against the Templars, who had rendered valuable services in the reconquest. The monarchs especially opposed, as constituting a grave danger to the crown, the papal plan to cede the vast estates of the Temple to the Order of the Hospital. In response to Jaime II's pleas, Pope John XXII formally established the Order of Montesa in 1317, giving it all the lands of the Temple and the Hospital in the kingdom of Valencia, though the property of the Templars elsewhere in the crown of Aragon was yielded to the Hospitallers. The pope created the Order of Christ in 1319 and endowed it with all the property of the Temple in the kingdom of Portugal. Both Orders were affiliated with Calatrava and Cîteaux.

Among the perils of warfare along the frontiers the possibility of capture, imprisonment, or enslavement with little hope of eventual liberation or survival was one of the most serious. In order to ransom Christians held captive by the Moors, St. Peter Nolasco, a native of Languedoc, founded the Order of Our Lady of Mercy (Mercedarians); Jaime I aided the Order in establishing houses in the kingdom of Valencia, and St. Ramon de Penyafort drew up its constitutions. The French Order of the Trinity, dedicated to the same purpose, was also active in the peninsula.

The zeal of the mendicants, as well as of the older, more established religious Orders, the Benedictines, Cistercians, and others, evidently began to wear thin by the fourteenth century. Relaxation of the monastic rule, comfortable living, concern for material possessions typified many religious communities. Thus the Archpriest of Hita commented upon clerical acquisitiveness:

> Yo vi a muchos monges en sus predicaciones
> Denostar al dinero et a sus tentaciones
> En cabo por dinero otorgan los perdones,
> Assuelven el ayuno, ansi fasen oraciones.

> I heard many monks in their preaching
> Condemn money and its temptations.
> But for money they grant pardons,
> Dispense the fast and offer prayers. [*Libro de Buen Amor*, 503]

Even in the thirteenth century, Airas Nunes (d. 1250), a cleric of Compostela, wrote caustically of his search for truth in religious houses:

> Nos moesteyros dos frades rregrados
> A demandey e diseron-m' assy:

Non busquedes uos a uerdad' aqui,
Ca muytos anos auemos passados
Que non morou nosco, per boa fe.
E d'al havemos mayores coydados.
E en Cistel, hu uerdade soya
Sempre morar, diseron-me que non
Moraua hy, auya gram sazon
Nen frade d'y ia a non conhocia. . . .

In the houses of the friars
I inquired but they said to me,
Don't look for truth here.
Many years have passed now
Since she dwelt with us
And we have greater cares.
And among the Cistercians
Where truth always used to dwell,
They told me she lived there no more,
Nor did the brothers know her.

[*Cancioneiro da Biblioteca Nacional*, IV, 203]

The same poet's comment that neither was truth likely to be found on the pilgrimage to Compostela is a reflection of a growing scepticism about religion and the role of the church in society. This led many to break entirely with the church and to repudiate hierarchical authority. Despite preaching, excommunication, interdict, and a crusade, the Albigensian heresy continued to flourish in Languedoc, and the Waldensian movement was by no means dead. The pilgrimage to Compostela apparently served as a route whereby these heresies penetrated into the western part of the peninsula. As early as 1216 heretics appeared in the city of León, prompting Lucas of Túy to write a treatise against them, *De altera vita fideique controversiis adversus Albigensium errores*. Papal letters to the bishops of Burgos and Palencia also reveal the presence of heretics in those dioceses. Fernando III evidently enacted an edict against heretics, though it is no longer extant; in any case the *Siete Partidas* (VII, 26, 2) provided the death penalty for obdurate heretics.

Given its proximity to Languedoc, the center of Albigensianism, Catalonia was more seriously affected by the heresy, as Pedro II's introduction of the death penalty in 1197 suggests. Jaime I excluded heretics from the protection of the Peace of God, and explicitly forbade laymen to dispute about the Catholic faith on pain of being suspected of heresy; nor was it permitted to have a Bible in the vernacular. Bishops were commanded to conduct inquisitions in their dioceses to determine whether heresy was present. Pope Gregory IX's bull in 1232 ordering Archbishop Espàrec of Tarragona to appoint Dominican friars as inquisitors marked the beginning of the activities of the papal inquisition in the crown of Aragon. A decade later, at the Council of Tarragona, Archbishop Pere d'Albalat, elaborating on the work of Ramon de Penyafort, laid down rules for determining whether one was guilty of heresy, the penalties to be imposed, and the formulas for abjuration.

The search for a deeper spiritual experience gave impetus to many popular, quasi-monastic movements that spread through Europe in the fourteenth century. Though orthodox in origin, they often encountered hostility from the ecclesiastical authorities who feared laymen preaching or teaching the Gospel. Moreover, fantasies and aberrations of one sort or another characterized some of these groups, who were known by various names, for example, *fraticelli*, Apostolic Brethren, Beghards, and Beguines. The Councils of Tarragona in 1292 and 1317 enacted legislation against "false apostles" and "Beguines" and prohibited the use of theological books in the vernacular. In his *De planctu ecclesiae*, Alvaro Pelayo charged the Beghards with belief in the possibility of attaining perfection and impeccability in this life and of being entirely free of obedience to any human authority. He denounced them as hypocrites who neglected to observe any monastic rule and wandered idly about, taking advantage of the people's charity toward the mendicant Orders. Numbers of them appearing in Catalonia and Valencia were punished by the bishops and inquisitors. Popular groups of this sort holding radical, unorthodox views of society were viewed as a real threat to the church's leadership and authority, and as there seemed no way of assimilating them into the mainstream of Christianity, they were persecuted.

The Universities

From the cathedral schools founded in the twelfth century for the purpose of educating the clergy, there emerged the first peninsular Universities at Palencia and Salamanca. These schools were nearly contemporaneous with those founded at Paris and Bologna, usually considered the first universities. For the most part, the peninsular universities owed their foundation to royal initiative and adopted the student university organization characteristic of Bologna.

Both Rodrigo Jiménez de Rada and Lucas of Túy recorded Alfonso VIII's decision to summon learned men, masters of theology and the liberal arts, from Gaul and Italy to Palencia. No date can be assigned for the foundation of the University, but there is evidence of the presence of foreign masters in the city from the last quarter of the twelfth century. Decline apparently set in, probably after the king's death, and the University had to be resurrected by Fernando III and Bishop Tello, who planned to establish faculties of arts, theology, and canon law; but unfortunately, the University seems to have died out by mid-century. The University of Salamanca was brought into being by Alfonso IX of León quite early in the thirteenth century; Fernando III strengthened it, and Pope Alexander IV in 1255 granted its graduates the license to teach anywhere in Christendom. The University flourished and, along with Paris, Oxford, and Bologna, was singled out by the Council of Vienne in 1312, as one of the major universities where Arabic, Hebrew, and Chaldean should be taught. Alfonso X laid the basis for the University of Valladolid, which came to replace that of Palencia, though it did not receive a papal charter until 1346. Sancho IV intended to establish a University at Alcalá, but it did not really come into existence until the sixteenth century.

Since the University of Montpellier in southern France, distinguished for legal and medical studies, lay within the dominions of the Aragonese kings, it attracted students from Catalonia, Aragon, and Valencia. Not until 1300, therefore, did Jaime II establish a University in his peninsular territories, at Lérida, with faculties of arts, law, and medicine, but its history was filled with controversy and rivalry with the Universities founded by Pedro IV at Perpignan (1350) and Huesca (1354). King Dinis, in response to the request of his bishops, established a University at Lisbon in 1290, but it too had an erratic history. By 1308 it was transferred to Coimbra, because of town and gown conflicts, but Afonso IV returned it to Lisbon in 1338 and then back to Coimbra in 1355. The peripatetic character of the University contributed nothing to its prestige, and it had to be reorganized later in the century. None of the peninsular universities had the international character and influence of Paris and Bologna, and Spanish students continued to go abroad to study, especially theology, although there were masters of theology teaching in the houses of study maintained by the mendicant Orders in university towns. Cardinal Albornoz, for instance, founded the College of St. Clement at Bologna for Spanish students of law and theology.

Among other types of schools were the grammar schools in the towns, such as one described by Berceo:

> Tenie en essa villa, ca era menester
> Un clerigo escuela de cantar e leer.
> Tenie muchos criados a letras aprender,
> Fijos de bonos omnes que querien más valer.
>
> Because there was need, a cleric in this town
> Had a school of chant and reading.
> He set many pupils to learn their letters
> The sons of good men, with high aspirations.
> [*Milagros de Nuestra Señora*, 354]

Schools of this sort provided students with the fundamentals necessary for university education.

The university curriculum was similar to that elsewhere in Europe. The arts course was based principally upon the study of Aristotelian philosophy; legal studies utilized Gratian's *Decretum*, Justinian's Code, and the work of the glossators and commentators. The theologians studied the Bible, Peter Lombard's *Sentences*, and the writings of Thomas Aquinas, Duns Scotus, and William of Ockham.

Theological and Religious Writings

Several Spanish scholars taught at the Universities of Bologna and Paris and made significant contributions to the study of canon law, philosophy, and theology. Among the important canonists, noted for their glosses or commentaries, were Laurentius Hispanus, who taught at Bologna before he became bishop of Orense (d. 1230); Vincentius Hispanus, also a master at Bologna, and archbishop of Braga (d. 1248); Joannes Hispanus de Petesella, and Bernardus Compostellanus. The most famous of the Spanish canonists was Ramon de Penyafort, who was appointed by the pope to codify the immense body of canon law that had grown up since the twelfth century. The fruit of his labors was the collection entitled *Decretales Gregorii IX*. He also wrote a *Summa de casibus penitentialibus*, a handbook for confessors. Among the philosophers, Petrus Hispanus (d. 1277), a native of Portugal, taught at Paris and Siena and was elected as Pope John XXI in 1276,

His *Summulae logicales*, a treatise on logic, remained in use in the schools for more than three hundred years.

The Dominican friar, Ramon Martí (d. c. 1286), is best known for his controversies with the Jews. Having learned Arabic and Hebrew at the Dominican house in Murcia, he gained public attention by participating in the disputation with Jewish rabbis held at Barcelona in 1263; the king also named him to a commission to scrutinize Jewish texts. His dissatisfaction with the oral disputation probably induced him to set to work on his major treatise, the *Pugio fidei contra Judaeos*, a defense of Christian belief against the Jews. The first part, dealing with natural religion and refuting the arguments of philosophers and non-believers, is entirely lacking in originality, as Martí plagiarized heavily from St. Thomas's *Summa contra Gentiles*. The last two parts, drawing upon both the Scriptures and the Talmud, are more truly the author's own work and are directed to the Jews in order to demonstrate that Christ was the Messiah and fulfilled the Messianic prophecies. Martí's book had considerable influence upon later anti-Jewish polemists and even Blaise Pascal (d. 1662) found it useful for his apology for the Christian religion.

Martí's concern for the conversion of the Jews was one task on the contemporary Christian agenda, but in the minds of many it was by no means the most important. Arnau de Vilanova (d. 1311), a man of far greater talent, insisted that the most urgent need was to reform Christian society itself. After studying medicine at Naples and Montpellier and teaching at the latter University for many years, Arnau became known as the most brilliant physician of his day. He attended Pedro III on his deathbed and thereafter served Jaime II both as physician and as diplomatic envoy to the papal and the French courts. His voluminous medical writings reveal a knowledge of both the Greek and Arabic physicians and, having studied the oriental languages with Ramon Martí, he was able to translate Arabic medical texts. His principal work is a *Commentary on the Regimen Salernitanum*, a treatise on hygiene; others include the *Breviarium practicae a capite usque ad plantam pedis*, a handbook of medical practice from head to toe; a sort of "how to stay young" manual entitled *De Conservanda iuventute et retardanda senectute*, and brief treatises on leprosy, epilepsy, sterility, poisons, and so forth.

Arnau also was widely known as a disciple of the apocalyptic visonary, Joachim of Flora (d. 1202), and he was in contact with the leaders of the Spiritual Franciscans. He made so bold as to predict the coming of the Antichrist around 1345 and the proximate end of the world. With this in mind, he exhorted the pope, the cardinals, the kings of Aragon and France, to reform themselves, the church and society, and to return to the pure spirituality that had characterized the early Christian centuries. In expressing these views he engaged in diatribe and invective, especially against the Dominicans, but against the other clergy too, accusing them of abandoning their original ideals and of giving themselves up to greed, pride, hypocrisy, vanity, lying, and fraud. He denounced the theologians for presuming that only they were properly equipped to interpret the scriptures; God's revelation, he argued, was not so obscure that simple men could not understand it. No doubt this reflected the educated layman's impatience with the learned subtleties of the theologians, who in their turn, told him to stick to his medicine and not to meddle in matters beyond his ken. But Arnau was also reacting against the application of Aristotelian rationalism to faith, and he accused the Dominicans of preferring the study of the *Sentences* of Peter Lombard or the *Summa* of Thomas Aquinas to the Bible. Not too many years later, William of Ockham attacked the Thomistic synthesis on similar grounds.

Arnau set forth his views in a host of writings, many of them in the vernacular. Best known among them is the *De adventu Antichristi et fine mundi*. The theologians of the University of Paris condemned his opinions in 1299, and Boniface VIII, while engaging him as his physician, admonished him to say nothing more about the end of the world. Arnau was unable to do so and continued his propaganda and also indulged in the interpretation of the dreams of his most steadfast supporter, King Federico III of Sicily. After Arnau's death a theological commission at Tarragona in 1316 condemned a number of his propositions. Though he failed to persuade the pope or anyone else to implement his ideas, no doubt because they often smacked of fantasy, his plea for reform was authentic. It was the voice of many who were discontented with the role of the church in society, who found it difficult to recognize in that powerful institution the church founded by Christ, and who were troubled by the subordination of the laity to the clergy and the tendency to identify the church with the clerical estate.

Arnau de Vilanova did not fit the mold typical of thirteenth-century theologians; nor did Ramon Llull (d. 1315), whose agitated career bears a certain external resemblance to Arnau's. An extraordinary man, Llull was a theologian and philosopher, a mystic and missionary, a novelist and poet, a propagandist and preacher, and in the end, a martyr. Born in Majorca of the lesser nobility, he spent a dissolute youth in the court of Jaime I, until he experienced visions of Christ and determined to change his way of life. Devoting himself to asceticism and study, he prepared for his principal goal, the conversion of the Muslims to Christianity. To this end he made three specific pledges: to offer his life, if necessary, to convert the infidels; "to write books, some good and others better, against the errors of the infidels"; and to urge the pope and the kings to found schools where men might learn Arabic in preparation for the mission to Islam. To these ideals he remained entirely faithful for more than forty years.

As one who was self-taught in the scholastic disciplines, Llull worried about his ability to achieve the second of his aims, but he tells us that God illumined his mind and made known to him the principles of his *Art major*. Soon after, he achieved his first success when he persuaded Jaume II of Majorca to found the college of Miramar for the study of the Arabic tongue; unfortunately, this venture failed, though it is not clear why. Llull was an indefatigable traveler and visited Rome, Paris, Montpellier, Barcelona, Cyprus, and many other parts of the Mediterranean world, trying to convince the pope, the kings, the Franciscans, and the Dominicans of the need to carry out his missionary plans and his proposals for the recovery of the Holy Land. He also read his *Art* to the scholars at the University of Paris and from time to time visited Bougie and Tunis to debate with Muslim scholars. All the while, he was writing, and more than 250 works poured from his pen, with many others having been attributed to him. But apart from his success in convincing the Council of Vienne to establish chairs of oriental languages at the universities and his conversion of some Muslims, he failed and expressed his melancholy in the beautiful poems *Cant de Ramon* and *Desconhort*. In *Desconhort* he lamented:

> E.s eu ayso tractan trenta ans, ha verament
> No.u ay pogut obtenir, perque n'estay dolent
> Tant, que.n plore soven e.n son en languiment.

> I have labored so for thirty years and truly
> I have obtained nothing. I am so sorrowful
> that I often weep and am despondent.   [*Obras literarias*, 1096]

He made his last missionary journey to Tunis in 1315, where according to later legend he was stoned to death.

Llull wrote in Arabic and Catalan and translated some of his works from one language to the other, while his disciples prepared Latin versions. Here mention can be made of only a few of his voluminous writings, though it can be said that, no matter how they may be classified, there is a unity of theme and purpose to all and that is Llull's lifework: the conversion of the Muslims. While standing in the mainstream of the Augustinian tradition exemplified in his own time chiefly by Franciscan scholars, he also made use of Aristotelian doctrine as expounded by the Dominicans. He sought to develop a rational and systematic exposition of Christian belief so that the Muslims would of necessity accept it. He saw no contradiction between faith and reason, though he recognized that there were elements of faith that reason could not comprehend. There is a strong rationalistic tendency in his writing, motivated by his overwhelming desire to prove to the Muslims by necessary reasons the truth of Christianity, but this is always tempered by his mysticism. Believing that truth was one and that reason could be used to explicate the truths of faith, he denounced the Latin Averroists who separated philosophy and theology and propounded the theory of the double truth. In books such as the *Disputatio Raymundi et Averroistae*, he rejected the notion that there could be contradictory truths known through faith and reason.

In his desire to achieve a rational explanation of Christianity, he developed the principles of his *Art*, which he believed God had made known to him. The *Short Art of Finding Truth* (*Art abreujada d'atrobar veritat*), written early in his career, was the primitive version, which he elaborated and completed in 1308 as the *Ars magna generalis ultima*. This was an attempt to show the unity of knowledge, to demonstrate that there were certain general principles common to all bodies of knowledge, and that the particular principles of each could be deduced from the general principles. In order to demonstrate practically how this could be done, he devised a mechanical system of revolving concentric rings, each bearing certain fundamental concepts, which could be brought into combination with one another. Among the most important concepts were nine attributes of the divinity, namely, goodness, greatness, eternity, power, wisdom, will, virtue, truth, and glory. By combining them with others, one could proceed from general to particular principles, resolve questions and realize the truth of the Christian faith. Though Llull lectured on his *Art* at the University of Paris, he seems not to have been able to convince many of its utility, but centuries later Leibniz took up some of his ideas.

Among Llull's other works one may note the *Book of the Gentile and the Three Wise Men* (*Llibre del gentil e dels tres savis*), in which a Jew, a Christian, and a Muslim discuss their religious beliefs in the presence of a pagan. In the exhortation entitled *Liber de fine* he proposed the recovery of the Holy Land, suggesting that a tenth of ecclesiastical income be used for the purpose and that the Orders of the Temple and the Hospital be united under the control of the king of Jerusalem. Drawing upon his own experiences as a knight and a courtier, he also wrote the *Book of the Order of Chivalry* (*Llibre del Orde de la Cavalleria*), depicting the ideal of Christian knighthood. The *Doctrina pueril*, dedicated to his son, expounds Llull's views on education; the *Felix de las meravillas del mon* or *Book of the Wonders of the World*, a sort of popular encyclopedia, treats of God, the angels, the elements, plants, metals, animals, man, and man's destiny in heaven or hell.

Perhaps the most famous of Llull's works is his novel, *The Book of Evast and Blanquerna*, a religious romance, charming, utopian, and at times offering autobiographical glimpses. The protagonist, Blanquerna, the long-awaited son of very devout parents, Evast and Aloma, upon attaining manhood, resists their desire that he marry and instead becomes a hermit. Thereafter he successively becomes a monk, an abbot, a bishop, and at last is even elected pope. In each of these roles he seeks to reform himself and the world about him and Llull has ample opportunity to discourse upon the virtues that ought to characterize those in different states in society, namely, those who are married, those in religious life, and so on. After setting forth his program for the church, Blanquerna renounced the papacy to return again to the eremitical life. In his solitude the hermit composed the *Book of the Lover and the Beloved* (*Llibre d'amic e amat*) and the *Art de Contemplació*, mystical treatises in which life is perceived as a continual striving for union with God. As a mystic, Llull stands in the Franciscan tradition, but the influence of Islamic Sufism is apparent in these writings which form the concluding portion of the novel. A gifted poet, Llull closed the work with the powerful hymn of praise to God:

> Sènyer, ver Déus, rey gloriós,
> Qui ab vós volgués hom unir!

Membre-us dels vostres servidors
Qui per vós volen mort sufrir.

O Lord, true God, glorious King,
Who wished to join man to yourself,
Be mindful of your servants
Who wish to suffer death for you.   [*Obras literarias*, 578]

In these brief lines is contained all the hope of Ramon Llull.

Standing more firmly in the theological mainstream was the Portuguese Franciscan, Alvaro Pelayo, also called Alvaro Pais (d. 1353). After studying at Bologna he became a member of the papal *curia* and was named penitentiary by Pope John XXII. In 1333 he was appointed bishop of Silves in the Algarve but seems to have become involved in controversy with Afonso IV concerning ecclesiastical immunities. Later, he retreated to Seville where he died. His principal writings are the *Collyrium fidei contra hereses*, a description and refutation of various heresies and heretics; the *Speculum regum*, a sort of mirror of princes, dedicated to Alfonso XI of Castile, whom he exhorted to defend the faith against Muslims, Jews, and heretics, to expel the Moors from Spain, and to conquer Africa.

Alvaro is best known, however, for his *De planctu ecclesiae*, a lamentation and denunciation of abuses in the church, and a defense of the papal theocracy. Deploring the current status of the church, he spared no class and attributed many evils to the greed of the papal *curia* itself. He attacked usurers and clerics keeping concubines, and reproached the friars for their pride, idleness, incontinence, and ambition. He charged that friars serving as inquisitors often condemned victims in order to get their money and spend it for their own pleasure. Even the peasants, whom one tends to regard with sympathy, had their share of sins. He noted, for example, that they often came to church but remained outside during mass, entering only at the elevation in order to see the Body of Christ, but not to receive it. They too, he said, violated the matrimonial bond and kept themselves from their wives so as not to have children whom they could not support.

The main thrust of Alvaro's book is to champion the absolute authority of the pope against recent challenges by secular rulers, especially the emperor and the king of France, and by polemists such as Marsiglio of Padua, author of the *Defender of the Peace*. Although the church has as its purpose a spiritual goal, that is, the salvation of all men, Alvaro saw it as a highly visible and material organization, requiring a hierarchical order of authority, laws, and property. At the head of this body stood the pope, the vicar of Christ, Godlike (*quasi Deus*) in his power and authority, which he received from God and exercised without limitation by any other human being or institution. The plenitude of papal power extended to the temporal sphere and to the temporal authority, for as the pope had care and governance over souls, this also included bodies. The church thus embraced the state and by its sanction justified and legitimated secular rulership. The Holy Roman Emperor was considered a papal vicar to whom other kings (excepting the Spanish rulers) were subordinated.

Alvaro skillfully pulled together the many elements out of the controversies of the past that supported his defense of the papal monarchy, but he failed to recognize that the idealized structure he depicted no longer existed. Already many canonists were questioning papal absolutism and developing the conciliar theory of church government, and the secular rulers and their lawyers not only repudiated the idea that they were subordinate to the Holy Roman Emperor, but also that the pope had any power over them in temporal affairs. In sum, Alvaro's arguments were highly anachronistic and did not take into account the changed circumstances of the fourteenth century.

Vernacular Prose Literature

The authors discussed above represent, at least in a broad sense, the ecclesiastical, scholastic tradition of the thirteenth and early fourteenth centuries. Yet another, more secular, tradition of learning was developing simultaneously and found its expression in the vernacular languages, rather than in Latin, the language of the church and the university. Appearing in private charters in the twelfth century, the vernacular a hundred years later was widely used in public documents and recognized as a suitable instrument for expressing the subtleties of the law and the beauties of literature. By using it for public affairs, kings made the vernacular respectable and stimulated and patronized a new secular, vernacular culture. The Romance languages included Portuguese spoken both in Portugal and Galicia, and, from the reign of King Dinis, usually employed in royal charters; Castilian, with its regional variants, throughout the central *meseta*; Aragonese in Aragon proper and Catalan in Catalonia, Valencia, Murcia, and the Balearic Islands. The federative character of the crown of Aragon resulted in the retention of Latin as the official language into the fourteenth century, though private documents were issued in the vernacular, and eventually the royal court also employed either Aragonese or Catalan in dealing with the inhabitants of those distinct territories. In any case, by the beginning of the fourteenth century the vernacular had come into its own, in all parts of the peninsula, as the language of literature and the courts.

Fernando III was the first peninsular ruler to employ the vernacular generally in public documents and to encourage the translation of important texts, such as the Visigothic Code, known under its Castilian title as the *Fuero Juzgo*. Toledo continued to enjoy renown as a center of scholarly pursuits, and a new generation of translators gathered there under the patronage of Archbishop Rodrigo Jiménez de Rada; but their translations were mostly of philosophical works turned into Latin. Thus Michael Scot (d. c. 1235) translated various works of Aristotle, Avicenna, and Averroës, and Herman the German, later bishop of Astorga (d. 1272), translated Averroës. Even so, the impetus given by the king to the development and use of the vernacular produced magnificent results during the reign of his son.

Alfonso X, the Learned, truly a scholar on the throne, had a major impact upon nearly every aspect of late thirteenth-century cultural life. Menéndez Pidal suggested that he wished to educate his people and extended his interest to every branch of knowledge useful for this purpose. The work achieved by the king and his collaborators was presented in the vernacular so that it could have the widest possible audience, attracting laymen as well as clerics, but this did limit its influence in northern Europe. As the king's favorite residence was at Seville, much of this work was done there, and he planned to establish in the city an "estudio general" for the study of both Latin and Arabic, but the project did not succeed. His educational plans included the completion of a work begun at his father's direction, that is, the *Setenario*, a vernacular encyclopedia dealing with the seven liberal arts, and fundamental Christian beliefs and practices. Reflecting no doubt the king's personal interests, many of the translations were of scientific works, especially those concerned with astronomy or astrology, for example, the *Libros del saber de Astronomia*, a collection of fifteen Arabic treatises. On his orders the *Alfonsine Tables*, charting the movement of the planets and the stars, were compiled on the basis of older Arabic studies amplified by new observations.

In addition to scientific treatises and a volume on chess (*Libro de ajedrez, dados e tablas*), collections of maxims and moral tales were translated. These had great vogue in the thirteenth century and influenced the many books purporting to offer counsel and instruction to princes. Among these "mirrors of princes" one should note the *Llibre de Saviesa* or *Book of Wisdom,* a Catalan work attributed to Jaime I, though certainly not by his hand; it is a mixture of proverbs, aphorisms, and words of wisdom drawn chiefly from Arabic sources. Of somewhat the same character is the *Castigos e Documentos* purportedly by Sancho IV, though it has been pointed out that it bears a striking resemblance to Juan García de Castrogeriz's adaptation of Giles of Rome's *De regimine principum.*

The influence of oriental fables is best seen in the writings of Infante Juan Manuel (d. 1348), one of the outstanding figures of Castilian literature. A grandson of Fernando III and a nephew of Alfonso X, he led an active political life, seeking self-aggrandizement, and was often at odds with the king. In the midst of his intrigues, conspiracies, and rebellions he found time to compose a large number of books, some of which have enduring value. Conscious of his role as writer and artist, he deliberately strove to develop a cultivated prose style and displayed an uncommon concern for the integrity of his works. So that they would be preserved for posterity he deposited them in a monastery at Peñafiel, and advised his readers who encountered faulty and distorted copies done by careless scribes to consult the originals. In sum, Juan Manuel was both self-conscious and self-confident and was willing to be judged by his contemporaries and by future generations. On the whole, the judgment has been highly favorable.

The best known of his books is the *Libro de los enxemplos del Conde Lucanor et de Patronio,* the masterwork of fourteenth-century Castilian prose, according to Menéndez Pelayo. A collection of tales and fables derived from Arabic, Jewish, and Christian sources, it resembles in form the *Decameron* of Boccaccio, written about fifteen years later. Count Lucanor, a young noble of great honor and renown, it seems, is frequently asked to give advice about many different kinds of problems, and calls upon the wisdom of his faithful counselor, Patronio, who responds by telling a little story containing a moral and revealing a deep knowledge of human nature. Giménez Soler has pointed out that Count Lucanor personifies Juan Manuel, who in several instances expresses regret for the destruction and wrong caused by the many civil wars in which he engaged, and often alludes to his uneasy relations with Alfonso XI. An example of this is the story of two horses that could never be put in the same stall because they fought continually; yet when they found themselves in a corral with a lion, symbolizing the sultan of Morocco, they joined forces against the common foe. Juan Manuel's purpose was to offer guidance and counsel to others, even to the unlearned, and the sincerity and the seriousness of his intent, distinguishes his work from Boccaccio's. He does not attack the church, the clergy, the monks, or the friars, nor does he make a mockery of love and sex. Indeed, his concern not to cause shame to his readers, even in the tale of the philosopher who "entered a street where wicked women lived" seems almost Victorian in its puritanism.

The age-old theme of the taming of the shrew is one of the many stories found in the work. A young man newly married to a girl of exceedingly bad temper, determined to reduce her to docility. After the wedding when the young couple were left alone to eat, the bridegroom addressed himself to his dog, demanding that it bring water so he could wash his hands; when the dog failed to respond, he killed it; for similar unwitting disobedience he killed his favorite horse while his bride looked on in growing fear and horror. When, at last, he turned to her and demanded water, she responded with alacrity, and on the morrow, when her friends and relations came to visit, she revealed her complete submission by warning them not to waken her sleeping husband: "Don't make any noise; don't speak in a loud voice, lest he kill us all."

The influence of Ramon Llull on Juan Manuel is evident in the *Libro del caballero et del escuder*, a treatise on chivalry similar to Llull's book, and also in the *Libro de los estados*, a description of the principal orders in society, reminiscent of *Blanquerna*. In the *Libro de los estados*, a Christian from Castile instructs and counsels a pagan prince and his father, demonstrating the falsity of Islam and Judaism and convincing them, as men of sense and reason, to become Christians. Juan Manuel emphasized, however, that no one should be compelled to accept religion "because involuntary and forced services do not please God." He makes the same point when speaking of the wars between Christians and Moors:

There is war between Christians and Moors and there will be until the Christians have recovered the lands that the Moors have taken from them by force; there would not be war between them on account of religion or sect, because

Jesus Christ never ordered that anyone should be killed or forced to accept His religion. . . . The reason why God consented that the Christians should receive so much evil from the Moors was so that they would have just cause for making war against them and so that those who died in the war, having fulfilled the commandments of Holy Church, would be martyrs. [*Libro de los estados,* I, 30]

After describing the life of Christ and the basic tenets of Christianity, he discussed the ranks in society, both lay and ecclesiastical, in order to show that a Christian, no matter his social status, could be saved or damned, depending upon his deeds.

Juan Manuel's minor works include a treatise on hunting and falconry and a chronicle in which he briefly notes contemporary events. With Alfonso X and his collaborators, he ranks as one of the principal molders of the medieval Castilian tongue.

Poetry

In the twelfth century, Provençal lyric poetry was known throughout the Christian states, but nowhere was it received more enthusiastically than in Catalonia. Due to the similarity of the language, poetry in Catalan proper was slow to develop, and Ramon Llull, writing in the late thirteenth century, is the first truly important Catalan poet. In the westernmost part of the peninsula, lyric poetry in the Galician-Portuguese language, but often in the form and style of Provençal poetry, was being written at the end of the twelfth and the beginning of the thirteenth century. Three great *Cancioneiros* were compiled, the earliest on the orders of King Dinis, himself a distinguished lyric poet who holds a secure place in the history of Portuguese literature. Among the 2,000 poems by 200 poets there are love songs similar to the Andalusian *kharjas,* in which a young girl tells her mother of the friend with whom she has fallen in love; love poems in the style of the troubadours, like the *alba,* a lament for the coming of dawn when the lovers will have to part; poems of abuse and insult; and religious poems, especially in praise of the Virgin Mary.

The most famous hymns to the Virgin are the *Cantigas de Santa Maria,* a collection of 400 poems, written for the most part by Alfonso X in the Galician-Portuguese tongue, and accompanied by music to which they were to be sung. Describing himself as Mary's troubadour, the king sings her praises and relates in verse miracles performed through her intercession, as for example, the story of the abbess who was saved from the shame of having her pregnancy discovered. The following lines simply praise the Virgin who conceived God's Son, contrary to nature, and rose to heaven because she did His will:

> Salue te, que concebiste
> Mui contra natura
> E pois teu Padre pariste
> E ficasti pura
> Virgen e por en sobiste
> Sobre la altura
> Dos ceos porque quisisti
> O que El queria.   [*Cancioneiro da Biblioteca Nacional*, II, 318]

The king also wrote love songs and songs of abuse, many of them commenting upon current events or the disloyalty of his vassals and friends.

In the early thirteenth century the *mester de clerecía*, a form of Castilian lyric poetry written by clerics began to flourish. The poets distinguished it from the *mester de ioglaría*, the popular songs of the wandering minstrels, pointing out that it consisted of four-line strophes with a single rhyme and counting fourteen syllables to the line. Examples of this type of poetry are the *Libro de Apolonio*, a tale of Byzantine origin, and the *Libro de Alexandre*, presenting the adventures of Alexander the Great in medieval dress. The poetry of Gonzalo de Berceo (d. c. 1250), already mentioned, is also typical. A secular priest who lived in the tranquil vicinity of the monastery of San Millán de la Cogolla, he composed in verse the lives of San Millán, Santo Domingo de Silos, and Santa Oria, hymns in praise of our Lady (*Loores de Nuestra Señora*), her miracles (*Miraglos*) and her sorrows (*Planto*). Written in the common tongue (*en roman paladino, en qual suele el pueblo fablar a su vecino*) to instruct his people and to encourage their devotion, his poetry is unaffected and simple, with an innocent beauty, as in these lines asking San Domingo to show favor to him and to intercede with the creator for him:

> Quierote por mi misme, padre, merced clamar,
> Ca ovi grant taliento de seer tu ioglar.
> Esti poco servicio tu lo quieras tomar
> Et quieras por mi Gonzalo al Criador rogar.
> [*Vida de Santo Domingo de Silos*, 775]

A monk of San Pedro de Arlanza, writing about the middle of the thirteenth century, composed the epic *Poema de Fernán González* in the style of the *mester de clerecía*. A tale of war and battles recounting the deeds of the tenth-century count of Castile, the *Poema* (156) reveals a passionate affection for that region:

> Pero de toda Spanna Castiella es mejor
> Por que fue de los otros comienço mayor.

In sharp contrast to the naive faith of Berceo, stands the cynical Archpriest of Hita, Juan Ruíz (d.c. 1351), whom Gerald Brenan has called "one of the greatest poets of the Middle Ages, the equal of Chaucer." While imprisoned by the archbishop of Toledo, probably because of his immoral habits, he composed his *Book of Good Love* (*Libro de Buen Amor*), a collection of poems on the theme of love, treated mockingly, humorously, and at times with great sensitivity. Knowing full well the scandalous character of his work, he protested that by revealing the deceptions and wiles of the "loco amor del mundo," his book of good love would help his readers attain salvation. With this in mind, he was careful, after describing love affairs and sexual adventures, to insert admonitions and prayers, exhorting his readers. Despite his protestations no one can seriously believe that he intended to write a book of moral counsel. His lament upon the death of Trotaconventos, the old woman whom he employed as his go-between in making advances to young ladies, reveals a capacity for more than frivolous sentiment. Bitter is his reproach of Death:

> Non catas sennorio, deudo, nin amistad,
> Con todo el mundo tienes continua enemistad,
> Non hay en ti mesura, amor, nin piedad,
> Si non dolor, tristesa, pena e gran crueldad.

> You care not for lordship, debt or friendship.
> You bear constant enmity for the whole world.
> You have no courtesy, love or pity
> But only sorrow, sadness, pain and great cruelty.

> [*Libro de Buen Amor*, 1522]

Similarly, the poet's hymns to the Virgin have a beauty and sincerity not unlike that of Berceo. With all its variety, its satire, irony, humor, low comedy, piety, and religiosity, Menéndez Pelayo hailed the *Libro de Buen Amor* as the "Human Comedy" of the fourteenth century and the comic epic of the Middle Ages.

Historiography

In the first half of the thirteenth century historians continued to use Latin for their work, but thereafter the vernacular came into its own, and historiography in the language of the people flourished in abundance and high quality as nowhere else in Europe.

The greatest historian of medieval Castile was Rodrigo Jiménez de Rada, archbishop of Toledo (d. 1247), friend and counselor of Alfonso VIII and Fernando III. Encouraged by the latter, he wrote *De rebus Hispaniae*, the first true history of Spain, whose influence upon later historiography has been profound. After briefly noting the peopling of Europe, he traced the rise of the Visigoths, the Muslim conquest, and Christian reconquest, emphasizing the deeds of the rulers of Asturias, León, and Castile, whom he regarded as continuators of the Gothic tradition. His history ends in 1237 and is particularly valuable for the events of his own time which he witnessed or in which he participated. He used all the earlier Latin chronicles as well as Arabic sources, reworking the material to his own purpose and striving to present it in an elegant and, at times, poetic style. He also wrote histories of the Romans, Ostrogoths, and other Germanic tribes, and a history of the Arabs from Muhammad to the twelfth century, the first work of its kind in western Europe.

His contemporary, Lucas, bishop of Túy (d. 1249), is the author of a *Chronicon mundi*, extending from creation to the conquest of Córdoba in 1236; written on the request of Queen Berenguela, it is inferior in style and historical sense to the archbishop's work. The anonymous *Latin Chronicle of the Kings of Castile*, covering the reigns of Alfonso VIII and Fernando III to 1236 is valuable primarily for its accuracy and attention to detail. One should also note Gil de Zamora's *Liber illustrium personarum*, a biographical dictionary with useful data concerning contemporary figures, and his *Liber de preconiis Hispaniae*, a book extolling the glories of Spain. The principal Latin history for Aragon and Catalonia is the *Gesta veterum comitum Barcinonensium et regum Aragonensium*, compiled by the monks of Ripoll and extending in its two redactions from the ninth century to 1276 and to 1304.

Vernacular historiography began to appear, chiefly through the impetus given by Alfonso X. His collaborators wrote two major histories, a *General Estoria* or universal history, extending only to the birth of Christ, and an *Estoria de España*, also known as *Primera Crónica General*, a national history of Spain down to the death of Fernando III. It utilizes all the earlier sources, borrowing the general framework of Archbishop Rodrigo's history, but it also includes material taken from many epic poems, some of which are no longer extant. The incorporation of this type of literary material sets it apart from all other historiographical works.

In order to continue the tradition initiated by his great-grandfather, Alfonso XI ordered chronicles of Alfonso X, Sancho IV, and Fernando IV to be written. The author of the *Tres Crónicas*, as they are called, may have been the chancellor, Fernán Sánchez de Valladolid; the first of the three presents many chronological problems especially in the earlier chapters. Somewhat earlier, Jofre de Loaysa continued the chronicle of Archbishop Rodrigo to 1305; though Jofre wrote in Castilian, only a Latin version made at his request survives. There are two principal sources for the reign of Alfonso XI, the *Poema de Alfonso XI*, a detailed, accurate narrative written in his praise, and a lengthy *Chronicle*, written perhaps by Juan Núñez de Villazán; unfortunately neither work goes beyond the fall of Algeciras in 1344.

Aside from the writings of Ramon Llull, the greatest works of Catalan literature in this period are the "four pearls," that is, the chronicles of Jaime I, Bernat Desclot, Ramon Muntaner, and Pedro IV. The autobiographical form in which the *Chronicle of Jaime I* is presented was a distinct novelty, and the first-person narrative, full of color and anecdote, lends an extraordinary interest to the book. Written in a simple, rather naive style, it covers nearly the entire life of the king, though there are few who would hold that it is indeed the work of his hand. More than likely he entrusted the task to his secretaries and from time to time supplied them with material and personal observations. Bernat Desclot's *Chronicle* begins with the union of Aragon and Catalonia in the twelfth century and treats fully the reigns of Jaime I and Pedro III. Little is known of the author, who seems to have been a knight in the service of the latter ruler; he is well-informed and evidently had access to chancery documents. His work is a major source for the story of the Sicilian Vespers and in general is exact and impartial, and endowed with literary grace.

Perhaps most interesting of all is the *Chronicle* of Ramon Muntaner (d. 1336), a Catalan nobleman who took part in the wars in Sicily and in the subsequent adventures of the Catalan Company in Greece. His chronicle extends from the birth of Jaime I to the coronation of Alfonso IV in 1327. Muntaner is full of passion and energy, enthusiasm and vivacity, and an unbounded love of Catalonia. Pedro IV, the last of the four, was a patron of scholars who strongly encouraged the use of the vernacular and commissioned the translation into Catalan of many patristic and classical works. The *Chronicle of San Juan de la Peña*, in Latin, Catalan, and Aragonese versions extending to 1336, was composed on his orders. Much more valuable, however, is the *Chronicle of Pedro IV*, presented as the king's autobiography and covering the reigns of his father and grandfather and of himself to 1366 and from 1374 to 1380. The author appears not to have been the king but Bernat Dezcoll, who worked under his direction. The book is full of detail, dialogue, anecdote, and throughout conveys the royalist point of view.

King Dinis of Portugal commissioned the translation of several of the legal and literary treatises composed at the court of Alfonso X, including the *Estoria de España*. Also on his orders, Gil Pérez translated the Arabic history of al-Razi (d. 955), and the text was incorporated into the *Crónica general de 1344* or *Segunda Crónica general*. This history which purports to continue and elaborate upon the work of Alfonso X, extends to the fall of Algeciras in 1344. Lindley Cintra, who published the Portuguese version believes it to be anterior to the Castilian, and suggests that the author was Count Pedro de Barcelos (d. 1354), King Dinis's son. The count is known as the author of the last two of the four *Livros de Linhagens* or *Books of Lineages* that have come down to us. The oldest of these, the *Livro Velho*, is not much more than the listing of names of noblemen, and the same is true for the second book. Count Pedro, however, endeavored to do considerable investigation of documents and other sources "so that the nobles of Portugal might know of what lineage they came and of what immunities, honors, monasteries and churches they were natural lords." Interwoven with genealogical material are legends and stories about the Greeks and Romans, King Arthur and his knights, and so forth. Aside from literary interest, the work is of paramount importance for the history of the nobility, though the genealogies are not always certain.

Arabic Literature

As a consequence of the great reconquest of the thirteenth century many scholars and scholarly families abandoned al-Andalus, thereby hastening the advent of cultural decadence. The precarious existence which the kingdom of Granada was compelled to lead did not allow the tranquility, prosperity, and sense of confidence in the future so often essential to study. For this reason García Gómez has called the period an epilogue in the history of Spanish Muslim literature.

The most distinguished man of letters of the epoch was Lisan al-Din ibn al-Khatib (d. 1374), royal *wazir*, poet, historian and physician. Many of his numerous works have been lost and of those that are extant many remain unedited. Among the more important are a treatise on the plague of 1348–1349, a biographical dictionary, and above all a history of the kings of Granada extending to 1369 and recording events in which he participated. He unfortunately ran into disfavor with the King, Muhammad V, and went into exile to Morocco where he was later assassinated. One of his pupils, who also served as *wazir*, Ibn Zamrak (d. 1393), was perhaps the outstanding poet of the age and, as García Gómez has noted, his work has been edited with greater luxury than that of most poets, that is, many of his verses form part of the decoration of the walls of the Alhambra.

Although not a native of al-Andalus, Ibn Khaldun (d. 1406) deserves mention here because his family came originally from Spain, leaving after the fall of Seville, and for several years he served at the court of the king of Granada. He aroused the jealousy of Ibn al-Khatib, however, and retired from the scene and eventually ended his political career in the service of the sultan of Egypt. His great work is the *Book of Examples* (*Kitab al-Jbar*), a species of universal history, which reveals him as one of the most important students of the philosophy of history. In the introduction to this work, he attempted to determine general principles that explain the rise and fall of civilizations. Civilizations, kingdoms, or states pass through the same cycle of birth, growth, maturity, decline, and death as human beings, and nowhere was this process better illustrated than in the history of al-Andalus. The other parts of his history record the development of Islam in the eastern world and in the west; the sections dealing with the Berber tribes in North Africa and the kingdom of Granada are particularly valuable.

Among the historians whose works Ibn Khaldun used, one should mention Ibn Abi Zar, the author of the *Rawd al-Qirtas*, a confused and often inaccurate history of Morocco and of al-Andalus, extending to 1326. Much more valuable is the work of another Moroccan author, Ibn Idhari, whose great compilation of history, *Al-Bayan al-Mugrib*, extending almost to the end of the thirteenth century is detailed and precise, based upon many earlier works now lost. Little is known of the author, though he can be praised for his objectivity and completeness.

Although the literary output of the Granadan period is small, the Alhambra, that magnificent palace standing high above the city on the flanks of the Sierra Nevada, will always remain as a reminder of the luxury and refinement of the Nasrid court. Built mainly in the middle of the fourteenth century as a palace and a center of governmental offices, it was also a fortress; its defensive character reveals the fundamental malaise of Granadan society, its turning inward, its insecurity, its hesitancy and uncertainty about the future, and its sense of inevitable doom.

On the other hand, the *mudéjares* living under Christian rule were contributing to the rapprochement of Muslim and Christian civilizations. This blending of two worlds is illustrated by the so-called *al-jamiado* literature, such as the *Poema de Yusuf*, written in Arabic characters but in the Aragonese dialect, and by *mudéjar* art, as in the *alcazar* of Seville, a Moorish palace built for the Christian King, Pedro of Castile.

Jewish Literature

In the Jewish community the controversies aroused by the teaching of Maimonides continued into the thirteenth century, and the reaction to his rationalism contributed to the development of the mystical movement known as cabalism. This was bound up with popular hostility to the Jewish aristocracy who enjoyed power and influence in the royal courts but who frequently had abandoned their religious beliefs. Todros ben Judah Halevi (d. c. 1306), the principal Jewish poet of the age, himself a courtier of long experience, reveals the scandalous behavior of his friends and colleagues in his verses; but he also speaks harshly of them, charging them with having forgotten the law of Moses, of not knowing the Hebrew tongue, and of giving themselves up to the study of Christian lore and the use of the Castilian language. One is reminded of Alvaro of Córdoba's complaint concerning the Mozarabs of the ninth century.

The denunciation of immorality and irreligion among the Jewish aristocracy is particularly biting in the *Book of Splendor* (*Sefer ha-Zohar*), written by Rabbi Moses de León around 1280. The book had great influence upon the cabalist movement, and Baer has noted similarities in theme, though not in doctrine, to the Franciscan Spirituals and other followers of Joachim of Flora's apocalyptic visions. Messianic expectations ran high at the close of the thirteenth century, but their failure may have prompted Rabbi Abner of Burgos to accept the Christian religion around 1320. Known thereafter as Master Alfonso de Valladolid, he engaged in a continuing polemic with the Jews, and in his chief work, *The Teacher of Righteousness* (*Mostrador de Justicia*), extant in Castilian and Hebrew, he tried to prove that Jesus Christ was the Messiah and that Christianity was superior to Judaism. One of those opposing him was Shem Tob of Carrión, known in the history of Castilian literature as the author of the *Proverbios morales*, pithy verses intended to convey moral instruction. They were also known widely in Hebrew until the end of the Middle Ages.

PART V

~~~~

The Struggle for Peninsular Union

1369—1479

Quien bastará a contar e relatar el triste e doloroso proceso de la infortunada España y de los malos en ella acaescidos?

Who is able to tell and relate the sad and dolorous story of unhappy Spain and the evils that have befallen her?

<div align="right">

Fernán Pérez de Guzmán,
Generaciones y Semblanzas, 34

</div>

CHAPTER 21

The Early Trastámaras

The New Dynasties

The half-century following Enrique of Trastámara's triumph on the field of Montiel in 1369 witnessed important dynastic changes. His own family, after winning the Castilian throne, fought off the attempts of the neighboring states to drive them out, and then embarked upon a campaign to unify the peninsular realms under Trastámaran control. Marriage was the primary instrument of their policy, though from time to time they used armed force to achieve their objectives. The expansion of the dynasty also meant the expansion of Castile and resulted to some extent in the Castilianization of the other kingdoms. In this sense the Trastámaras were the agents whereby Castile was able to realize, at least in part, her traditional ambition to dominate the peninsula.

The Trastámaran effort to subdue Portugal by marriage and conquest provoked a strong reaction, firing sentiments of Portuguese nationality. A new dynasty, the house of Avis (like the Trastámaras an illegitimate branch of the Burgundian family installed in the twelfth century), came to power as the champions of Portuguese independence and, as a defense against Castile, established an alliance with England that would become traditional over the next several hundred years. By the beginning of the fifteenth century the house of Avis set Portugal on the course that ultimately led to the establishment of her overseas empire. The Trastámaras had greater success in Aragon, where the male line, uninterrupted since the twelfth century, faltered early in the fifteenth. Candidates for the throne abounded, but the election of a member of the Trastámara family eventually led to the union of Aragon and Castile by virtue of the marriage of Ferdinand and Isabella.

Throughout this period the kingdom of Granada continued tributary to Castile, and although there was always a certain amount of border warfare, no significant advance of the reconquest took place.

Enrique II: Securing the Throne

Enrique II (1369–1379), who gained the Castilian throne by murdering his brother Pedro at Montiel, was faced with the difficult task of defending what he had won against the *petristas*, the partisans of the dead king, and against foreign enemies. In his efforts to overcome domestic opposition and the possibility of encirclement by his neighbors who sought to deprive him of his throne or at least to dismember his kingdom, he continued to rely upon the mercenaries led by Bertrand du Guesclin. He also counted upon the support of King Charles V of France with whom he concluded a treaty of alliance in November 1369; the pact provided for the loan of Castilian ships to France for use against England, but because of his own needs Enrique II was not immediately able to supply them.

Though most of the realm accepted him as king, the *petristas* held out in several fortresses along the frontiers of Portugal, Navarre, and Aragon. Most importantly Martín López de Córdoba, master of Calatrava, who held in his custody two bastards of Pedro the Cruel and a large portion of the royal treasure, resisted at Carmona near Seville. For the moment the *petristas* lacked a candidate for the throne to oppose Enrique II, but they soon found one in King Fernando of Portugal (1367–1383), whose claims were based on his descent from Sancho IV of Castile. Sending a fleet to blockade Seville, Fernando personally invaded Galicia and occupied Túy, La Coruña, and other towns. Pedro IV, meantime, charged that Enrique of Trastámara reneged upon his promise to give him Molina, Soria, Atienza, and Almazán in return for his help in winning the throne, alleging that "it was agreed and stipulated by the general *cortes* that no place in the kingdom of Castile should be given up or yielded to us." Thereupon he set about organizing the diplomatic encirclement of Castile, winning from Fernando of Portugal the promise that if he became king of Castile, he would cede both Murcia and the other disputed places to Aragon; Carlos II of Navarre also entered the alliance and took the opportunity to annex Logroño and Vitoria. Muhammad V of Granada, an erstwhile ally of Pedro the Cruel, ravaged Andalusia and seized Algeciras in July 1369;

ten years later, rather than allow the Christians to recover it, the Muslims destroyed and abandoned it.

In order to counter his enemies Enrique II sent troops to defend the southern frontier against Granada while he entered Galicia; Fernando did not await his coming but prudently retreated, yielding his recent conquests. Enrique II pursued him into Portugal, taking Braga and Bragança, before returning to Castile. In the spring of the next year he paid off the mercenaries who were returning to France and rewarded du Guesclin with the lordship of Molina, Soria, Atienza, and Almazán; two years later, however, du Guesclin, anxious to terminate his involvement in Spain, sold these rights to the king. The departure of the mercenaries was not entirely lamented, for they had caused great destruction to both friend and foe since their coming to Spain. Many of the disorders prevailing in the realm were attributable to them; in response to complaints of the *cortes* on this account, the king authorized the organization of a *hermandad* of cities to curb bandits, brigands, and other malefactors. The king's concessions of privileges, rents, and lordships, whereby he gained the nickname Enrique *de las mercedes*, had much to do with the creation of a powerful nobility whose arrogance and lawlessness also contributed to the turmoil of the times and eventually became a serious threat to the monarchy itself.

The tide began to turn in Enrique II's favor when Muhammad V of Granada, recognizing the wisdom of withdrawing from the conflict while he was undefeated, decided in May 1370 to conclude an eight-year truce. In the summer, the Castilian fleet, commanded by the Genoese Ambrosio Boccanegra, broke the Portuguese blockade of Seville, thus preparing the way for peace. The treaty, signed in March 1371, provided for Fernando's marriage to the Castilian princess Leonor who would receive as her dowry Ciudad Rodrigo and other frontier towns; but when Fernando changed his mind and decided to marry Leonor Téllez de Meneses, whom he forced to separate from her husband, the Castilian towns which were to have been his remained in Enrique II's hands. After making peace with Portugal, Enrique II turned to Carmona, the only important town still resisting him. Realizing that his situation was hopeless, Martín López de Córdoba surrendered in May on condition that he and Pedro's bastards be given safe-conduct out of the realm. The pledge was not honored, however; on the king's orders he was brutally beheaded, and Pedro's children were imprisoned. Leonor López de Córdoba later recounted that, as her father was being led away to the place of execution, Bertrand du Guesclin, who had betrayed King Pedro to his death, said to him: "Did I not tell you that your activities would end like this?" But he replied: "Better to die loyally as I do, than to live, as you do, having been a traitor" (text in Joaquín Guichot, *Don Pedro I de Castilla* [Seville, 1878], 267–268).

Carlos II of Navarre in November agreed to allow his claims to Logroño and the other border fortresses he had seized to be decided by papal arbitration; not surprisingly, the decision favored Castile. As the encirclement of Castile, which he had labored so hard to bring about, was now broken, Pedro IV also accepted a preliminary peace in January 1372. Enrique II's position seemed firm and secure.

At this point, however, Trastámaran rights to the Castilian throne were challenged by John of Gaunt, duke of Lancaster, a younger son of King Edward III of England, whose intervention involved Castile and Portugal more directly in the Hundred Years' War than before. Edward III, who was old, and the Black Prince, who was ill, had remained aloof from peninsular affairs after the battle of Nájera; both recognized the inadvisability of engaging in any action against Castile without strong military support from Aragon. John of Gaunt, on the other hand, an extremely ambitious person, in September 1371 married Constanza, the oldest daughter of Pedro of Castile; early in the following year her sister Isabel married John's brother, Edmund, earl of Cambridge. John and Constanza now claimed the Castilian throne and were formally recognized as king and queen by Edward III and the English parliament. John hoped to arouse Aragon and Portugal to renew the struggle against Castile, but Pedro IV was wary of entangling himself in an alliance of this kind. Fernando of Portugal was more amenable and agreed to collaborate militarily with John of Gaunt whom he acknowledged as king of Castile.

Well aware of these developments, Enrique II took steps to discomfit his opponents. In response to a French appeal he sent a fleet in 1372 to assist in the siege of La Rochelle, a port held by the English on the west coast of France. The Castilian rout of an English fleet sent to relieve the city compelled the defenders to surrender in September. The fall of La Rochelle impeded John of Gaunt's plans, but it also assured Castilian domination of the Bay of Biscay and greater ease of communication with the markets in Flanders. In recent years the English had caused great difficulty for Castilian merchant ships passing through the channel enroute to Flanders.

Heartened by his fleet's successes, Enrique II decided to forestall any hostile action and late in 1372 invaded Portugal, taking Viseu and then moving southward to Lisbon, now blockaded by his fleet. Seeing that there was no hope of English assistance, Fernando made peace in March 1373 and promised to supply a few ships to aid France and Castile against England in the next two years. A pair of marriages between members of the two royal families were intended to strengthen the pact. Soon after, John of Gaunt set out with a large army from Calais, intending ultimately to invade Castile, but by the time he reached Bordeaux in the fall of 1373 he had lost most of his troops and had to abandon his plans. Enrique II turned the tables on the English by entering Gascony to besiege Bayonne in June 1374, but the failure of the French to come to his aid forced him to return home.

Meanwhile he reaffirmed peaceful relations with Navarre, regaining definitive possession of Logroño and Vitoria, and marrying his daughter to Carlos, heir to the Navarrese throne. The marriage foreshadowed the eventual establishment of the Trastámaran dynasty in Navarre. Pedro IV also made a firm treaty in April 1375, yielding all claims to Castilian territory and marrying his daughter, Leonor, to Juan, heir to the Castilian throne. This marriage proved to be particularly significant, because Fernando de Antequera, the child born of the union, eventually was elected king of Aragon, thereby installing the Trastámaran dynasty in that kingdom. By means of these treaties Enrique II succeeded in preserving the territorial integrity of his kingdom and prepared the way for the future aggrandizement of his family.

Castile continued to provide naval forces to assist the French in the Hundred Years' War. The Castilians destroyed a large English fleet at Bourgneuf in 1375, and two years later a combined Franco-Castilian fleet ravaged the English coastline, burning and sacking Rye, Lewes, Rottingdean, Folkestone, Portsmouth, Dartmouth, Plymouth, and the Isle of Wight. In the midst of these troubles Edward III breathed his last, leaving the throne to his grandson Richard II, who was under age. John of Gaunt, as the new king's uncle, assumed major responsibility for directing the conflict with France and Castile, and to that end endeavored to stir up Aragonese and Navarrese opposition to Castile. As usual Pedro IV was quite cautious and would not commit himself, but Carlos II, a conspirator till the last, elaborated a plan to assassinate the king of France, to introduce the English into Normandy, and to re-cover lands lost to Castile. Apprised of these developments, Enrique II took the initiative and sent his troops into Navarre in July 1378; as they advanced to Pamplona and Viana, Carlos II pleaded for peace. The treaty signed in March 1379 re-established the frontiers between the two kingdoms and provided for perpetual peace among France, Castile, and Navarre; as surety that the Navarrese would abide by its terms, Enrique II obtained custody of Tudela, Viana, Estella, and other major fortresses for ten years. In sum, the treaty delivered the king of Navarre, bound hand and foot, to Castile.

Two months later on 30 May 1379 Enrique II died at the early age of forty-six. His final advice to his son was "always be a friend to the Royal House of France, from whom I received great assistance." The first of the Trastámaras gained a crown and succeeded in keeping it, partly because of his own abilities, partly because of the failure of his enemies to unite against him. By seeking marital alliances with the other peninsular states he secured his family's rights to the Castilian throne and prepared the way for the eventual union of the greater part of the peninsula by his descendants.

The Defense of Portuguese Independence

During the next decade Juan I (1379-1390), the new king of Cas-tile, endeavored to acquire the Portuguese throne and to overcome John of Gaunt's pretensions to Castile, but only in the latter effort was he successful. Though faithful to his father's policies, his poor health made it difficult for him to deal effectively with the problems confront-ing him and to dominate the nobility who had risen to power in the civil war. In response to the demands of the cortes in the summer of 1379 he undertook a review of all privileges granted by his father and tried to put his finances in order by eliminating superfluous expendi-tures. In the following year anti-Semitic feelings which had been build-ing up for a long time, but especially since the Black Death ravaged the country, caused the king to enact an ordinance against the Jews re-quiring them to live in ghettos and suppressing the autonomous Jewish tribunals that handled cases involving Jews accused of crime. These actions marked the beginning of a new phase of hostility toward the Jews that reached a climax just a year after the king's death in the most vicious pogrom in the history of Spain.

All the peninsular realms were confronted at this time by the difficult questions raised by the Great Western Schism. After a residence at Avignon for seventy years, the papacy was restored in Rome, but soon after the death of Pope Gregory XI in 1378 a grave crisis occurred. The new pontiff, Urban VI, proved to be so overbearing and tactless that the cardinals, before the summer was over, abandoned him, declaring his election null and void because of the pressures put upon them by the Roman mob. Branding him a usurper, they then elected another pope who called himself Clement VII and eventually established himself at Avignon. Thus the unity of Christendom was rent for forty years. In deciding which of the rival candidates to support, secular rulers were guided chiefly by political rather than canonical considerations. Charles V of France pronounced at once in favor of Clement VII while England declared for Urban VI.

The peninsular rulers were subjected immediately to pressures from both pontiffs and from the king of France, but they preferred not to commit themselves until they had the opportunity to investigate the situation more fully. Because he was fearful of upsetting the delicate balance of peaceful relationships only recently established with his neighbors, Enrique II maintained his neutrality until his death; he advised his son to seek good counsel "since it is a questionable and highly dangerous affair." Similarly, Pedro IV, in spite of the urgings of his son and of the Dominican preacher, St. Vincent Ferrer, refused to take sides, though he enjoyed the advantage of controlling appointments to benefices without papal interference; he remarked that he "did not allow their bulls to be obeyed in our land."

His attitude was also influenced by his ambitions in Sicily and Sardinia. His family ties with Sicily were especially strong, as his daughter was married to King Federico IV (1355–1377), and he himself was married to Federico's sister. When the king of Sicily died, his daughter Maria was the rightful heiress, but Pedro IV claimed the kingdom as his own, arguing that females were excluded from the succession by testamentary dispositions of previous rulers. The Roman pontiff, as feudal overlord of Sicily, rejected his reasoning and refused to invest him as king, causing him to maintain a neutral posture during the schism in the expectation that sooner or later his support would be of sufficient necessity to prompt the pope to grant him investiture. In the meantime, recognizing that the Sicilians were exceedingly jealous of their independence, Pedro IV appointed his second son, Martin the Humane, as his vicar-general in Sicily, reserving for himself the title of king as long as he lived; the Sicilian throne eventually would pass to Martin's son Martin the Younger, who was married to Maria, the heiress whose rights had been brushed aside (1380). In this way the Sicilians were assured of their autonomy within the crown of Aragon and the eventual restoration of their full independence. One of the unexpected benefits accruing to Pedro IV as a result of his assumption of the crown of Sicily was recognition of his sovereignty by the Catalans settled in the duchies of Athens and Neopatria in Greece (1382).

The Roman pope also opposed Pedro IV's efforts to pacify Sardinia and encouraged Genoese support of the rebellious islanders. Genoese preoccupation with her wars with Venice, however, did not permit her to intervene in Sardinia on a large scale. Pedro IV therefore was able to regain the allegiance of the leading Sardinian nobles by 1381 and to impose a reasonably stable government upon the island until his death.

Carlos II of Navarre also followed a policy of neutrality during the schism. Fernando of Portugal initially declared in favor of Clement VII, but Juan I of Castile convened an assembly of prelates at Medina del Campo in the fall of 1380 to discuss the issue and to hear arguments on behalf of the rival pontiffs. As the assembly finally inclined to Clement VII, the king in the following spring formally declared Castile's submission to the Avignon obedience. Although he emphasized that his decision was based upon a thorough inquiry and evaluation of the two elections, it was also prompted by the revival of the Anglo-Portuguese combination and a recognition of the importance of the French alliance.

The king of Portugal had been following a very devious policy. While professing support for the Avignon pope and negotiating the marriage of his daughter to Juan I's son, he was also dealing secretly with John of Gaunt, and in July 1380 concluded an alliance with him against Castile. An English expeditionary force commanded by Edmund, earl of Cambridge, would be sent to join the Portuguese in an assault upon the neighboring realm. When he discovered these plans, Juan I committed himself unequivocally to the Avignon pope and began an invasion of Portugal in June 1381. His fleet routed the Portuguese fleet off Saltes, but was unable to prevent the earl's arrival at Lisbon in July. At that point Fernando announced his transfer of allegiance to the Roman pope. The ensuing campaign was poorly conducted, and the Portuguese soon became disgusted by the outrages committed by their English allies. Fernando, as erratic as ever, decided to make peace with Castile and as a consequence also returned to the obedience of the Avignon pope. For the time being, John of Gaunt's peninsular ambitions were thwarted, but this was due in very large measure to the refusal of the English parliament to lend him substantial support.

The peace settlement between Castile and Portugal in August 1382 provided for the marriage of Fernando's daughter and heiress, Beatriz, to Juan I's second son, but it was quickly modified and assumed a far greater significance than originally intended. As the queen of Castile died in September, Juan I was now eligible to remarry and proposed to wed Beatriz of Portugal. Not only would the marriage disrupt the Anglo-Portuguese alliance once and for all, but it would also unite the crowns of Castile and Portugal, something the Portuguese were not likely to view with equanimity. Fernando, in poor health and fearful of his approaching end, favored the match in that it would protect his daughter from the machinations of his relatives who, considering that there was no precedent for female succession, might be tempted to seize the throne. Yet he was concerned to preserve the integrity and independence of Portugal. Thus, while the marriage contract stipulated that Beatriz should inherit the crown and that Juan I should be called king of Portugal, the Queen Mother Leonor would act as regent until a child born to the royal couple reached the age of fourteen and assumed the government in his or her own right, whereupon Beatriz and Juan I would no longer call themselves king and queen of Portugal. The union of Castile and Portugal would be averted, unless Beatriz died without children and no other legitimate members of the Portuguese royal family were alive; only then would Juan I be allowed to assume the crown of Portugal in his own right, an eventuality that seemed quite remote. The betrothal of the royal couple took place in April 1383.

The situation changed rapidly after Fernando's death on 22 October 1383. As he lay dying, he lamented "God gave me this realm to maintain it in law and justice, but by my sins I have behaved in such wise that I will have to give Him a very poor accounting." His son-in-law Juan I, ignoring the pledges given in the marriage agreement, announced his intention to assume the Portuguese crown and to take possession of the kingdom; there were some in his council who opposed this, however, arguing, as López de Ayala noted, that "he should first wait until he knew the will of the people of the kingdom of Portugal."

Although he could count upon the support of many of the Portuguese nobility, the mass of the people were not disposed to submit willingly. Organizing the resistance, the citizens of Lisbon persuaded João, master of the military Order of Avis, an illegitimate son of King Pedro, to assume the title Defender of the Realm. Through the force of circumstances, this young man became the champion of Portuguese independence and the founder of a new and brilliant dynasty.

Entering Portugal late in the year, Juan I assumed direction of the government and laid siege to Lisbon in March 1384. While João of Avis exhorted the citizenry to resist, a remarkable guerrilla leader, Nun'Alvares Pereira, harassed the Castilian army, and Portuguese ships broke the Castilian blockade of the port; but the principal factor in bringing the siege to an end was the plague which decimated the Castilians, killing the best captains and many of the troops. With very great reluctance Juan I had to withdraw in September.

The estates of Portugal, recognizing the importance of having a king to oppose Juan I, met in the royal palace at Coimbra in March 1385 to consider the claims of several candidates. López de Ayala reported that "there were legists there who said that since King Fernando of Portugal died without legitimate children who could inherit the kingdom, the people of the realm could legally elect a king to rule and govern them." They argued that Beatriz was illegitimate because her father's marriage to Queen Leonor was invalid, and they also rejected the rights of João and Dinis, the sons of King Pedro by Inés de Castro, on the grounds of illegitimacy and also because of their collaboration with the Castilians. João of Avis, on the contrary, "came of the lineage of kings and had proved himself a good defender of the realm." The estates, therefore, declared him worthy of advancement to the "royal honor, status and dignity . . . so that we may not be destroyed by our enemies and that the church may not fall into the hands of schismatics." João I (1385–1433) was proclaimed and crowned king of Portugal on 11 April; the estates asked him to choose his counselors wisely, to convoke the cortes annually and not to make war or peace or contract marriage without their consent. Moving swiftly, he appealed to England for help and began to expel the Castilians and their allies from fortresses and towns.

In view of this unfavorable turn of events Juan I, faced with the choice of giving up all claims to Portugal or of attempting a new invasion, opted for the latter. As he crossed the border in the summer of 1385 and advanced toward Lisbon, João I called upon him "in the name of God and St. George . . . not to destroy the land of Portugal"; but he replied that he was the rightful king as the Portuguese well knew and "God will aid me in my good right." Determined to submit the issue to the judgment of God, the two kings joined battle at Aljubarrota, south of Leiria, late in the afternoon of 14 August. Displaying exceptional generalship, João I and Nun'Alvares Pereira turned the day into a rout; Juan I fled to Santarém and then to the coast where he took ship to Seville, leaving the flower of his army dead on the field. The battle of Aljubarrota solidified Portuguese independence and enhanced the prestige of João I, who gained fame and honor comparable to that of Afonso Henriques, the founder of the kingdom. The victory also represented a triumph of the bourgeoisie of Lisbon, Porto, Evora, and other towns where the people, unlike so many of the nobility, had opposed Castilian intervention from the start. Froissart commented that João I "so won the favor and love of the whole kingdom of Portugal that all those who before the battle had dissembled upon meeting him, now came to Lisbon to offer their oath and homage to him, saying that . . . he was indeed worthy to wear the crown. Thus the king remained in the favor of his people and especially of the whole community of the realm." Many Portuguese nobles, however, went into exile to Castile where they played a prominent role in the political activities of the fifteenth century. In commemoration of his victory, João I erected on the site the magnificient monastery of Batalha and entrusted it to the Dominican friars.

Juan I's humiliation encouraged John of Gaunt to revive his claims to the Castilian throne. Aided by the conclusion of a formal alliance between England and Portugal in May 1386, he also attempted to enlist the aid of Aragon and Navarre, but Pedro IV and Carlos II preferred to remain neutral. Sailing from Plymouth in July with 7,000 men, John landed at La Coruña and then occupied Compostela and Orense; but he found little popular enthusiasm for his cause and wasted the summer months in petty skirmishes. The king of Castile had no wish to commit the issue to a pitched battle and so maintained a purely defensive posture. In the meantime he denounced the intruders before the *cortes* in 1386:

The English people, ever since they became Christians, have often rebelled against the Church, as in the killing of St. Thomas of Canterbury and in the killing of other martyrs in that island. They also have always been supporters and partisans of schisms in the Church of God even until now; wherefore God imposed certain tributes and signs upon them, so that men might always be mindful of their sins. . . . The English have always supported the most unjust wars that have taken place among Christians, not fearing God nor caring for anything, but only wanting to do things with pride and arrogance. [CLC, II, 351]

Emphasizing that his own legitimate title to the crown came through his mother by descent from Fernando de la Cerda (and implicitly branding as usurpers Sancho IV and all his successors), he declared that "a man ought to labor and to die for his land. . . . We are bound to strive unto death for the defense and honor of our kingdoms."

João I, meanwhile, renewed his alliance with John of Gaunt, promising to marry his daughter Philippa. Together they invaded Castile in the spring of 1387 but met with little success; John of Gaunt seems already to have abandoned any real hope of obtaining the Castilian crown and returned to Bayonne in September, after agreeing to the basic terms of peace. In the treaty signed at Bayonne early in the next year, he renounced his rights and those of his wife to the Castilian throne, in return for an indemnity and an annual pension. The projected marriage of his daughter Catherine (Catalina de Lancaster) to Enrique, prince of Asturias, Juan I's oldest son, was intended to unite the descendants of Pedro the Cruel and Enrique of Trastámara and to harmonize their rights to the throne. A general truce in 1389 among France, England, Castile, and Portugal for all practical purposes ended the direct participation of the peninsular kingdoms in the Hundred Years' War.

A Time of Equilibrium

In the next few years several changes in the ruling houses helped to bring about an equilibrium among the peninsular kingdoms. Both Carlos II of Navarre and Pedro IV of Aragon died in January 1387. Both had remained aloof from the recent conflict involving England, France, Castile, and Portugal, and both had professed neutrality in the matter of the schism. Much of Carlos II's career was spent in France in opposition to the Valois dynasty, but his incessant intrigues led nowhere and gained him the reputation of being a treacherous person. His son, Carlos III (1387–1425), known by contrast as the Noble, was a man of far different character. A peaceful king, he preferred to maintain good relations with all his neighbors and especially with Juan I of Castile whose sister he married; not surprisingly he followed the Castilian lead in recognizing the Avignon pope.

Pedro IV, in his long reign of fifty years, overcame the challenge of the Union of Aragon and bolstered royal power; but though he fought tenaciously to subjugate Sardinia and successfully regained Sicily for the crown of Aragon, his ambitions to acquire territory at Castilian expense remained unfulfilled. A cultivated and erudite king, he brought many scholars and artists to his court and founded the University of Perpignan; with the collaboration of Bernat Dezcoll, he also wrote a chronicle of his reign. Comparing himself with King David, who overcame so many trials with the help of God, he declared:

We also have had wars not only with neighboring kings . . . but also with our own people who chose their captains from our own blood, that is, our brothers. But as the goodness of the Creator delivered David from the hand of Saul, king of the Philistines, and from the hand of Absalom, and from the people who rose against him, so the mercy of the Lord has delivered us and our kingdoms from the hand of all our enemies. [*Chronique de Pierre IV*, Prologue, 4]

His last years were clouded with controversy with his son, however, and they were unreconciled when he died.

Promptly abandoning his father's policy of neutrality in the schism, Juan I (1387–1396) of Aragon recognized Clement VII of Avignon as the legitimate pontiff. Otherwise, he proved to be more inclined to the pleasures of hunting, music, literature, and art than to the business of government and allowed his wife and her friends an excessive influence in affairs so as to evoke strong protest from the *cortes*. Through his indecision the Acciajuoli family was able to seize the duchy of Athens in 1388, thereby ending the history of the Catalan Company begun earlier in the century; nor did he deal more effectively with the recurrent problems of Sardinia and Sicily. His delay in sending forces to Sardinia nearly enabled the rebels to expel the Catalans from the island. The king's younger brother, Martin the Humane, endeavored to secure firm control of Sicily for the benefit of his son, Martin the Younger and his bride, Maria; but he had to overcome the opposition of the Sicilian barons who appealed to the Roman pontiff for support. As Martin's resources were strained and Juan I was slow to send reinforcements, the rebellion continued for several years.

Juan I of Castile, meantime, was trying to repair his fortunes and to reinforce the weakened foundations of the monarchy. The *cortes* adopted a more aggressive tone, demanding the reform of abuses and also the right to inspect the king's accounts; in response he acted prudently, avoiding any unfortunate confrontation with the assembly. He still retained the faint hope of conquering Portugal and even briefly entertained the notion of abdicating the Castilian throne, so that his chances of winning the allegiance of the Portuguese might be improved; his counselors, however, wisely dissuaded him from such a reckless course. In any case his Portuguese aspirations were dashed when he was killed by a fall from his horse on 9 October 1390.

This untimely event brought his twelve-year-old son Enrique III (1390–1406) to the throne. The dynasty's rights, fortunately, had been secured by the recent settlement with John of Gaunt; otherwise the minority might have resulted in a renewal of the attempt to drive the Trastámaras out. The formation of a regency council agitated the realm during the several months that Archbishop Pedro Tenorio of Toledo, Duke Fadrique of Benavente, the king's uncle, and other prelates and nobles strove to gain power. The *cortes,* summoned in January 1391 to consider the question, decided that a broadly representative council including the archbishop, the duke, and other nobles, together with thirteen procurators of the towns, should be established; but the council's powers were restricted, and no individual member was allowed to act by himself. As these arrangements satisfied no one, the *cortes* in the next year decided to implement the hitherto ignored will of Juan I that provided for a smaller council; the rivalry of prelates and nobles continued, however, and the kingdom came close to civil war.

The disastrous massacre of thousands of Jews in Castile and Aragon in the year 1391, an event with profound consequences for the future of Hispanic society, added to the turbulence. Hostility toward the Jews had often been manifested in the past, chiefly because of their involvement in money-lending and tax-farming. Complaints about Jewish usury and Jewish tax collectors occur again and again in the records of the *cortes.* Though the crown usually promised to attend to those complaints, Jews continued to figure prominently in the management of royal finances. The miseries attendant upon the Black Death and the wars of the latter half of the fourteenth century encouraged the populace to lay the blame for their troubles at the door of the Jews.

The pogroms of 1391 were initiated by the violent preaching of

Fernando Martínez, archdeacon of Ecija, who had been admonished by the king as early as 1378 to curb his tongue, but nothing really was done to stop him. He now took advantage of the royal minority and the rivalry among the king's councilors to abandon all restraint in his harassment of the Jews. Aroused by his preaching, the people of Seville assaulted the ghetto in June and killed perhaps as many as 4,000 people. In the ensuing months the Jews of Carmona, Ecija, Córdoba, Jaén, Ubeda, Cuenca, Burgos, Madrid, Logroño, and other towns suffered the same fate. The contemporary historian Pedro López de Ayala commented that

All this was done out of a thirst for plunder rather than piety. The people also wanted to do the same to the Moors living in the cities and towns of the kingdom, but they didn't dare to do so, because they were fearful that Christians held captive in Granada or overseas might be killed.   [Crónica de Enrique III, 1391, 20]

Jewish communities in the neighboring kingdom of Aragon did not escape; in July the Jews of Valencia were plundered and murdered, and their synagogue was turned into a church. Though the city council of Barcelona took steps to safeguard the ghetto, the mob broke in and killed the Jews. Similar outbreaks occurred in Tarragona, Gerona, and other towns. The regency council in Castile and the king of Aragon protested the massacres, but no effective protection was afforded to any of the Jewish communities, and few of those who committed these atrocities were ever punished.

Hispanic Jewry scarcely survived this gravest crisis in its history. Thousands were dead, while untold numbers saved themselves from murder by accepting baptism; only a remnant of the once flourishing Jewish community remained. In the fifteenth century the conversos, as those who converted to Christianity were called, aroused the jealousy of the old Christians who resented their success in obtaining important positions in church and state and accused them of secretly continuing to live as Jews. Their fate was left to the mercies of the Inquisition, while those who had remained Jews were expelled from Spain, just a century after the great pogroms of 1391.

Discord and confusion in the government came to an end in August 1393 when Enrique III, not yet fourteen, assumed personal power. Though troubled with poor health throughout his reign, he proved to be an effective ruler who closely guarded his authority and succeeded in containing the ambitions of men such as his uncle, Fadrique of

Benavente, whose struggle to control the crown and its resources fore-shadowed developments in the next century. On the whole, Enrique III's relations with the neighboring states were peaceful, though strained from time to time. Although he disclaimed any rights to the Portuguese throne and pledged not to support anyone else who might challenge João I, misunderstandings did lead to the outbreak of hostilities in 1396; after some years of desultory warfare the truce was renewed in 1402.

About the same time, the basis for a long-standing dispute between Castile and Portugal concerning the Canary Islands was being laid. The Fortunate Islands, as they were known in ancient times, were rediscovered at the end of the thirteenth century by Genoese seamen. With the support and encouragement of Afonso IV, Genoese ships sailed to the islands in 1341, thereby giving Portugal a claim to lordship. Pope Clement VI, however, gave investiture of the islands in 1344 to Luis de la Cerda, a great-grandson of Alfonso X, thus evoking a protest from Portugal. But de la Cerda did nothing to establish his rights, and visitations of the islands by various fleets later in the century failed to lead to permanent settlement. Some Castilians who sailed from Seville in 1393 to visit the Canaries, upon returning home, informed the king "how easy it would be to conquer the islands, and how little the cost, if that were his pleasure." With the king's support the Norman adventurers Jean de Bethencourt and Gadifer de la Salle sailed from La Rochelle in 1402 and after landing on the island of Lanzarote began the process of colonization and Christianization. Within a few years colonies were established on the islands of Fuerteventura, Gomera, and Hierro, but the "customs of France and Normandy," according to Bethencourt's disposition, ruled the colonists. The chaplains who accompanied the initial expedition, Pierre Boutier and Jean le Verrier, wrote an account of the settlement. Meanwhile, Bethencourt returned to Spain and did homage to Enrique III, thereby giving Castile a claim in direct conflict with Portugal. Many years elapsed before the dispute was resolved.

The peaceful relations established between Castile and England, following the settlement with the duke of Lancaster, gave way to conflict on the high seas with the increase of piratical activities. As Englishmen began to prey upon Castilian shipping, raiding the coasts of Galicia and interfering with trade to Flanders, the Castilians responded in kind. Pedro Niño, count of Buelna, whose adventures were recounted by Gutierre Díez de Gámez in his *Victorial de caballeros,* raided the channel coast and even sailed into the mouth of the Thames; a truce was concluded, however, soon after the king's death in 1406. Piracy was also a serious problem in the Mediterranean and prompted reprisals from both Castile and Aragon against Bona, Tetuán, and other ports along the North African coast.

In the meantime, the succession to the throne became a question of crucial importance in the kingdom of Aragon after the unexpected death of Juan I as the result of a fall from his horse on 19 May 1396. As he had no surviving sons, the regular transfer of power from father to son was interrupted, and his younger brother, Martin the Humane, then absent in Sicily, was recognized as king (1396–1410). Little did anyone then realize that within a few years the dynasty would default altogether in providing male heirs and a Trastámaran would be seated on the throne. Martin's rights were immediately challenged by Count Mateu de Foix, who argued that his wife, Jeanne, daughter of the deceased king, was entitled to rule. In rebuttal, the estates of the realm pointed out that females were excluded from the succession and that, by the will of Pedro IV, Martin was the rightful heir. The count's attempt to advance his wife's claims by force was vigorously repelled, and he was obliged to withdraw to his own estates. Meanwhile, leaving his son Martin the Younger to continue the pacification of Sicily, Martin stopped at Avignon to consult Pope Benedict XIII concerning the resolution of the schism.

The continuance of the schism for nearly twenty years was recognized by most thoughtful Europeans as a grave and intolerable scandal. The theologians of the University of Paris proposed several means of ending it, including the abdication of the rival popes, the arbitration of their claims, or the summoning of a general council. Although the Avignon Pope, Clement VII, died in 1394, his cardinals insisted on perpetuating the schism by electing Pedro de Luna, a member of a distinguished Aragonese family, who took the name Benedict XIII. Hoping to induce both the Roman and Avignon popes to resign, the French government sought the support of England, Castile, and Aragon; Enrique III decided to collaborate, but the death of Juan I of Aragon created uncertainty as to the position his brother would take. When Martin visited Avignon in April 1397, perhaps because his wife, Maria de Luna, was related to the pope, he was completely won over to Benedict XIII's cause. Bolstered by Aragonese recognition, Benedict

XIII unhesitatingly rejected the proposals of the French, English, and Castilian envoys that he resign; the Roman Pope, Boniface IX, responded in like manner.

The French therefore officially withdrew obedience from Benedict XIII in July 1398 and sent troops to besiege him at Avignon. An assembly of the Castilian clergy convened by the king at Alcalá de Henares in December also repudiated the Avignon pope, but Martin the Humane remained steadfast in his allegiance and sent a fleet up the Rhone to aid the pope against the French. As it became clear that the withdrawal of obedience would not bring the schism to an end, Enrique III renewed Castilian allegiance to Benedict XIII in April 1403, and the French followed suit a month later. The king of Castile became more insistent, as time passed, on the need to end the schism by the abdication of the two pontiffs, but diplomatic efforts toward that end were unsuccessful.

While the schism was the subject of gravest concern to Enrique III and his colleagues, the growing threat of the Ottoman Turks to eastern Europe also demanded their attention. While the Turks occupied the Balkan peninsula and encircled Constantinople, the fate of the Byzantine empire hung in the balance; but the disastrous failure of the crusade of Nicopolis to stop the Turks in 1396 pointed up the need for extraordinary efforts to organize a coalition of powers hostile to them. Western Christians took heart when they learned that the Tartar leader, Tamurlane, was overrunning Anatolia and threatening the Turks from the rear. In order to obtain information about him and to incite him to join forces with the Christians against their common foe, Enrique III sent an embassy to him. The Castilian envoys witnessed Tamurlane's great victory at Angora in 1402, a successful attack that slowed Turkish expansion for the next quarter century. Tamurlane in turn sent representatives to Castile, and in May 1403 Enrique III again dispatched ambassadors to the east. Upon reaching Tamurlane's capital at Samarkand in August 1404 they were entertained royally, but were quickly dismissed and sent home when the conqueror fell into his last illness. Nothing came of these missions, but the *Historia del gran Tamorlan,* an account of the journey written by Rúy González de Clavijo, one of the envoys, expanded western knowledge of the east. When the Turks resumed their offensive in the next generation, Spanish Christians again had to consider a possible response.

Ever since the conclusion of a truce in 1370 Castile and Granada maintained an exceptionally long period of peace, interrupted only occasionally by minor border incidents. In the meantime Muhammad V took advantage of dissension in Morocco to intervene in the affairs of the Marinid dynasty and to expel the Moroccan garrison from Gibraltar, thereby effectively terminating a long-standing alliance. One of the victims of these diplomatic changes was Ibn al-Khatib, the *wazir* of the king of Granada, who, upon losing favor, fled to Morocco where he was later assassinated. As al-Maqqari said, he was "the phoenix of the age, the prince of the poets and historians of his time and the model of the *wazirs*." One may well lament his passing, for he was the last Muslim author to write about the contemporary history of Granada. After the death of Muhammad V and the brief reign of his son Yusuf II (1391–1392), the latter's son Muhammad VII (1392–1408) came to power. A bellicose ruler, who judged Enrique III to be weak, he refused to pay the usual tribute and invaded Murcia in 1405, and though repulsed, returned to the fray in the following year. Angered by these irruptions into Castilian territory, Enrique III summoned the *cortes* to prepare for war, but fell ill and died on Christmas Day 1406.

His death brought to the throne his two-year-old son Juan II (1406–1454), whose reign was the longest in the history of the dynasty. The minority was also quite lengthy, lasting thirteen years, but on the whole it was a time of comparative tranquility, owing largely to the wisdom of the king's uncle, Fernando, who shared the regency with the Queen Mother, Catalina de Lancaster. Harsh moments passed between them, but factionalism was minimized in April 1407 when they agreed to divide the administration, Catalina retaining the north while Fernando assumed responsibility for Toledo, Extremadura, Murcia, and Andalusia.

As he was particularly anxious to prosecute the war with Granada, Fernando sent a fleet to drive off the ships sent by the sultans of Tunis and Tlemcen to blockade the straits. The Castilians also engaged the enemy in several border clashes, capturing Zahara in late September 1407. Muhammad VII responded vigorously to these attacks, but when he died in May 1408, his brother, Yusuf III (1408–1417), obtained a truce for two years. At the end of that time Fernando launched a major assault against Antequera, one of the chief fortresses to the northwest of Málaga. A few days after the siege was begun late in April 1410, a Muslim relieving force from Archidona was turned aside, and the blockade of the city was tightened. A general assault on 16 September induced the defenders to surrender, on condition of being allowed to leave, taking their movables with them. The capture of Antequera was the most important achievement in the reconquest since Alfonso XI's victory at Salado. The truce granted to the Muslims in November terminated this phase of the reconquest and opened a long period of peace between the two kingdoms, but if other events had not interposed, Fernando, known thereafter as Fernando de Antequera, might have resumed the war and carried it much further.

The Compromise of Caspe

Fernando de Antequera's career changed abruptly when he was elected king of Aragon in succession to Martin the Humane. The latter, and his son Martin the Younger, king of Sicily, after achieving the pacification of Sicily, concentrated their attention on the perennial disorders in Sardinia. Sailing there in November 1408, Martin the Younger routed the viscount of Narbonne who was trying to occupy the island. Martin's death in July 1409, however, not only ruined his triumph but immediately complicated the problem of the succession in both Sicily and Aragon. As the Catalan historian Turell expressed it in his *Recort* (109) "the entire victory was turned to sorrow . . . for on that day the honor and prosperity of the Catalan nation was lost." By his wife Maria of Sicily who died in 1401 and by Blanca of Navarre whom he married in 1402, young Martin had no legitimate children, nor did his father have any other children who might inherit his kingdom. Although Martin the Humane personally inclined to allow his son's bastard, Federico, to succeed him, he realized that there was great antipathy to that idea among his subjects. Acceding to their wishes, therefore, he married Margarita de Prades in September 1409 in the hope of begetting a new heir.

Pope Benedict XIII took an active part in counseling the king and eventually in resolving the problem of the succession in a manner which he hoped would be favorable to his own cause. About this time the schism took a new turn when the Roman and Avignon cardinals, despairing that their respective popes would ever willingly abdicate, took matters into their own hands and summoned a General Council to Pisa in 1409. Deposing both popes, they elected Alexander V, and on his death in 1410, John XXIII. This failed to resolve the schism, however, for neither of the deposed pontiffs would step aside. Though abandoned by France and many of his other supporters, Benedict XIII continued to enjoy the recognition of Castile and Navarre and was given a warm welcome to Aragon by Martin the Humane when he decided to establish his residence there. João I of Portugal, who hitherto had recognized the Roman pope, now transferred his allegiance to the Pisan John XXIII. The schism had now become a triangular affair and was apparently as far from settlement as ever.

Meanwhile, Martin the Humane died on 31 May 1410, without children and without making an unequivocal decision among the many possible heirs to the throne. Although he designated Jaume, count of Urgel, as governor-general, a post usually held by the heir, he also made it plain that he did not really favor him as his successor. Martin was the last king in direct succession from Ramon Berenguer IV and Petronila, whose betrothal in 1137 had effected the union of Aragon and Catalonia. The union was thrown into a grave crisis but, in spite of the very real differences between Catalans and Aragonese, it survived.

A number of candidates now put forward their claims to the crown. Aside from Martin's grandson, Federico, who had little support, the most important were Jaume of Urgel and Fernando de Antequera. The former was a great-grandson of Alfonso IV and was married to a daughter of Pedro IV. Fernando's mother Leonor, a daughter of Pedro IV, was Martin's younger sister. Among other candidates, Louis III, duke of Calabria, an Angevin, alleged a claim through his mother, a daughter of Juan I; Alfonso, duke of Gandia, and later his son by the same name, and his younger brother, Juan, count of Prades, argued their rights as grandsons of Jaime II. Despite the number of possibilities, the contest was essentially between Jaume of Urgel and Fernando de Antequera; parties favoring one or the other appeared immediately in the several constituent states of the crown of Aragon.

The interregnum, lasting two years, was a time of disorder especially in Aragon and Valencia, where the Luna and Urrea, Vilaregut and Centelle families resumed old quarrels in the name of rival candidates for the throne. The *Generalitat* of Catalonia appointed twelve commissioners to maintain order and summoned a parliament to Barcelona. The Catalans urged that an assembly of all the estates of the crown of Aragon should be convened to deal with the question of the succession. In the spring of 1411 the Aragonese estates gathered at Calatayud, but the archbishop of Zaragoza, who favored Fernando de

Antequera, thwarted the plan for a convocation of a general *cortes*, lest it decide for another candidate. The assassination of the archbishop soon after by members of the Luna family supporting Jaume of Urgel cost the count dearly among the Aragonese. In response to the appeals of his partisans, Fernando sent troops into Aragon and Valencia to preserve order.

While Catalonia remained relatively calm, factionalism was rampant in Aragon and Valencia. Rival parties met in rival parliaments in 1411 at Alcañiz and Mequinenza in Aragon, at Vinaroz and Traiguera in Valencia. The Catalans (whom Turell praised, by contrast, for preserving order during the interregnum) assembled at Tortosa and entered into contact with the Aragonese parliament at Alcañiz, which was dominated by the partisans of Fernando de Antequera. As the idea of bringing about a meeting of all the realms was not entirely acceptable, Pope Benedict XIII intervened and suggested that the decision be left to a number of God-fearing men who knew the law and the affairs of each kingdom. Taking up this proposal, representatives of Aragon and Catalonia met at Alcañiz in February 1412 to appoint a commission for this purpose.

Nine persons, three from each of the realms, with full powers to elect a king, were chosen to meet at Caspe, a fortress on the Ebro river belonging to the Hospitallers. The commissioners included the bishop of Huesca, a Carthusian monk, and a lawyer from Aragon; the archbishop of Tarragona, and two lawyers from Catalonia; and Vincent Ferrer, the famed Dominican preacher, another Carthusian monk, and another lawyer from Valencia. As six votes were necessary for election, and six of the commissioners were definitely hostile to the count of Urgel, the outcome seemed certain. Moreover, Fernando de Antequera was already triumphant in Aragon, and his supporters had recently defeated the opposition in Valencia. Benedict XIII and Vincent Ferrer were also committed firmly to his cause. Not surprisingly, the decision of the nine announced on 28 June 1412 was in favor of the Trastámaran candidate.

The Compromise of Caspe, as this determination is called, has aroused strong objection from modern Catalan historians who have denounced it because it represented the triumph of the Trastámaras and of Castile. Vicens Vives has pointed out, however, that the decision was reached by a group of men who knew what they wanted and were able to argue effectively that this was the best solution at that time. Fernando's juridical rights were not necessarily the best, but from a political point of view his election was the obvious thing to do, if the crown of Aragon was to remain united and to be delivered from civil war. The Catalans, divided among themselves, had no candidate and failed to act decisively on behalf of anyone, including the count of Urgel. The Compromise was the only realistic solution.

The Trastámaran dynasty, established on the Castilian throne hardly fifty years before, now in the person of Fernando I (1412–1416), took possession of the crown of Aragon. In conformity with custom he convened the *cortes* to Zaragoza in August and there swore to defend and uphold the liberties of his people. At Lérida he gave similar pledges to the Catalans. Turell noted:

> He was elected king by means of a pact and is bound to safeguard the liberties of the people which he first swore to uphold before taking possession. The first kings on earth made what laws they pleased, granting them as a matter of favor, but kings who are elected find things already ordained and . . . have to safeguard them and . . . on those conditions they accept the sovereignty, and by the same reason their successors are obliged to observe the same things. [*Recort*, 117]

The Catalans were to become increasingly insistent upon the contractual nature of kingship described above.

Jaume of Urgel, after some hesitation, pledged homage to the king, but simultaneously began to plot his downfall. With vague promises of help from the duke of Clarence, a son of King Henry IV of England, and from some French lords, the count raised the standard of rebellion in the spring of 1413. Deserted almost immediately by his allies, he was forced to take refuge in the castle of Balaguer, where Fernando I besieged him for two months until he surrendered in October. Rather than execute him as a traitor, Fernando I proved to be quite benevolent, sentencing the count to life imprisonment and confiscation of property. In celebration of his triumph the king was solemnly crowned at Zaragoza in February 1414; at that time he designated his oldest son, Alfonso, duke of Gerona, and named his second son, Juan, as his lieutenant general in Sicily. In the years of the interregnum Sicily and Sardinia were disturbed by rebellions, but the king successfully imposed his authority upon them. He took the precaution of obtaining investiture of both islands from Pope Benedict XIII in 1412, and to avert the possibility that Sicily might break away from the crown of Aragon he formally declared the perpetual union of the two realms. His interest in the Mediterranean continued the policy of his predecessors and prepared the way for the remarkable career of his son Alfonso in Italy.

In the last two years of his life Fernando I was preoccupied with the scandalous prolongation of the schism by the three claimants to the papal office. In order to end this situation the Holy Roman Emperor Sigismund persuaded the Pisan Pope, John XXIII, to convoke a General Council at Constance in 1414, inviting all the rulers and prelates in Europe to attend. Fernando I, as king of Aragon and co-regent of Castile, had an important role in the termination of the schism, as the two realms under his government provided the most substantial support for Benedict XIII. After the Council of Constance in 1415 deposed John XXIII and accepted the abdication of the Roman Pope, Gregory XII, the only remaining obstacle to union was Benedict XIII, who made it clear that he did not intend to resign. Sigismund proposed a meeting with the pope and the king of Aragon at Perpignan in September, but, the pope remained obstinate in his refusal to yield. While he realized the futility of this position and hesitated to apply pressure, Fernando I at last, in January 1416 formally announced the withdawal of obedience from Benedict XIII. Feeling betrayed, Benedict XIII instructed the envoys of the king of Aragon to say to him, "You have sent me, who made you, into the desert." He also declared Fernando I deposed and excommunicated him, though these measures had no effect. Castile followed the Aragonese lead, but Catalina de Lancaster was not entirely in accord and subsequently renewed support for the deposed pontiff.

Fernando I died on 2 April 1416 before he could see the conclusion of the affair. He had reigned only four years and had not had the opportunity to display fully his exceptional talents as a diplomat and a ruler, but he had made a good beginning in Aragon, and he had preserved peace in Castile during the minority of his nephew. His efforts to aggrandize his family, however, were the cause of grief and anarchy in Castile in the next thirty years.

The Conquest of Ceuta

Several months before the death of Fernando I of Aragon the Portuguese inaugurated their great work of overseas expansion and discovery. By the middle of the thirteenth century they completed the reconquest of their territory and began to develop a flourishing maritime trade with northern Europe. The signing of a truce in 1411 freed Portugal from any anxiety about a possible revival of a Castilian threat to her independence. Beckoned by the proximity of North Africa and encouraged by civil war among the Marinids, Portugal was ready to embark on her first overseas adventure. Both Aragon and Castile, by a treaty in 1291, had marked out zones of future expansion in North Africa but had done nothing to translate ambition into reality.

The Portuguese chose as their objective the city of Ceuta, a port guarding the eastern end of the straits of Gibraltar and long a point of embarcation for Muslim armies invading Spain. Diffie suggests that João I and his advisers took this step to stake a claim in Africa and to counter recent signs of Castilian interest, such as the sack of Tetuán in 1400 and the acceptance of Bethencourt's homage for the Canary Islands. Portugal ran some risk in challenging Castilian expansion into the Atlantic, but the situation was still tentative, and the possibility of success was great. During the minority of Juan II, Castile was not ready to take any further action herself nor to prevent Portugal from doing so. The initiation of this enterprise has been attributed traditionally to the desire of the king's three sons, Duarte, Pedro, and Henrique—the future Henry the Navigator—to participate in some noble feat of arms before receiving knighthood. While it may be true that notions of chivalry influenced the king, territorial ambitions were paramount.

Preparations for the expedition commenced in secret in 1412. Portuguese envoys to Sicily stopped at Ceuta to reconnoiter the situation of the place. Money was obtained from bankers and also by the debasement of the coinage. Ships were gathered from all the ports of the Cantabrian and Atlantic coasts, and troops were recruited not only in Portugal but abroad. These intense preparations were carried out without any public announcement of their purposes. Several European rulers expressed their concern, but they were assured privately that they had nothing to fear. As a diversionary move, João I defied the duke of Holland, alleging grievances relative to trade, but secretly informed him that the expedition would not be directed against him.

Just before the fleet set sail, the queen, who had done much to animate the warriors, died, and there were some who thought the enterprise should be postponed. Too much time, effort, and money had been invested, however, and on 25 July 1415 the fleet of about 200 ships sailed from Lisbon. Landing at Ceuta on the morning of 21

August, the Portuguese repulsed the Muslims who attempted to oppose them and broke into the city. By the end of the day, it was in their hands. Knighting his sons in the mosque of Ceuta, the king also rewarded Pedro and Henrique for their gallantry by investing them with the titles duke of Coimbra and duke of Viseu respectively. After leaving a garrison to hold the city João I sailed for home in September. Portugal now had her first base in Africa from which she could carry out further penetration of the continent or possibily even launch an assault upon Gibraltar across the straits.

The fall of Ceuta, greeted with applause in Christian Europe, spread alarm and consternation throughout the Muslim world. Yusuf III, king of Granada, was especially disturbed by the Portuguese intrusion into Morocco where he had been meddling for some years, even to the point of installing a rebel prince as sultan. Death prevented him, however, from taking any action against them. His young son, Muhammad VIII (1417–1419, 1427–1429), was promptly overthrown by the Banu al-Sarraj, a family commonly known to the Castilians as the Abencerrajes. Muhammad IX (1419–1427, 1429–1445, 1447–1453), who came to power with their help, tried to organize a coalition with the Marinids and the Hafsids of Tunis to expel the Portuguese, but Prince Henry successfully defended Ceuta, thereby preserving the opportunity for further activity in North Africa.

CHAPTER 22

The Hegemony of
the Trastámaras

Anarchy, Expansion, and Discovery

In the sixty years following the death of Fernando de Antequera the ideal of peninsular union came close to realization, though turmoil threatened to destroy monarchy in Castile and Aragon. The Trastámara family continued their policy of aggrandizement by marriage, and through their several branches dominated Castile, Aragon, Sicily, and Navarre. The acquisition of the Navarrese throne was only temporary, and a series of marriages with the Portuguese royal family failed at this time to lead to the union of Portugal and Castile. The acquisition of Naples, on the other hand, completed the work begun by Pedro III in the late thirteenth century, but it also enmeshed the Aragonese in the politics of Renaissance Italy. Royal absenteeism, coupled with economic difficulties, caused great disaffection in Catalonia, leading to revolution and an attempt to overthrow the dynasty and to terminate the union with Aragon.

In Castile the members of the Trastámara family abused their relationship with the king and contributed to the near anarchy that prevailed there. The ineptitude of the Castilian kings greatly diminished the prestige of the monarchy and encouraged incessant rivalries among the nobility seeking to control the crown's resources. Dominated by favorites, the kings were unable to rule effectively or to curb the depredations of the nobles. Palace intrigues and revolts also undermined the kingdom of Granada and prepared the way for its final downfall.

Portugal suffered from similar disorders, though to a lesser degree. Especially important for the future were the remarkable strides made by the Portuguese in exploring the west coast of Africa and in venturing out into the Atlantic as far west as the Azores, making voyages that led eventually to the discovery of the route around Africa to India and China and the explorations of the Americas.

The Trastámara family fortunately was capable of producing competent leaders as well as ineffectual ones. Thus the union of Catalonia and Aragon was preserved, disorder and civil war were checked, and the authority of the monarchy in Castile was restored. This was essentially the achievement of Ferdinand and Isabella, whose marriage united their respective kingdoms and gave a new sense of purpose and direction to their people.

Alfonso V and Juan II

The death of Fernando de Antequera produced important changes in the political situation of Aragon and Castile. While he was king of Aragon and co-regent in Castile, with Catalina de Lancaster, there was a certain unity of direction to the public affairs of both realms. His successor as king of Aragon and Sicily was his son, Alfonso V, known as the Magnanimous (1416–1458). In Castile, Catalina continued as sole regent for her son until her death in 1418. The *cortes* in the next year declared the fourteen-year-old king of age. Alfonso V and Juan II, representing the Aragonese and Castilian branches of the Trastámara family, were very different from one another, though both were lovers of good literature and patrons of scholars, men in whose reigns the influence of the Italian Renaissance began to be felt in the Iberian peninsula. There the resemblance ended. Alfonso V was a man of vigor and action, a prudent and skilled diplomat who spent more than half his forty-two years as king in Italy, where he acquired the kingdom of Naples and displayed even more wide-ranging territorial ambitions. Juan II was a man of weak character and will who had neither aptitude nor interest for government. In his *Generaciones y Semblanzas* (33), Fernán Pérez de Guzmán, after noting that the king sang and danced very well, commented: "He did not wish to involve himself nor to labor one single hour in the governing of his realm." Consequently, his reign of forty-eight years was a time of continuous disorder and rivalry among the magnates.

More than blood bound the kings of Castile and Aragon to one another. Not only were they first cousins, but also brothers-in-law, twice over. Alfonso V married Maria, sister of the king of Castile who married Maria, sister of the king of Aragon. In addition, Alfonso V had two younger brothers Juan and Enrique, usually called the *infantes* of Aragon, though they were among the most powerful of the Castilian magnates, and it was in Castile that they had their principal resources and their chief interest. Juan in 1420 married Blanca, daughter of Carlos III of Navarre and heiress to the throne. Enrique was master of the military Order of Santiago and married Juan II's sister Catalina, receiving the march of Villena as her dowry. These estates made him probably the richest landowner in the kingdom. The several marriages linking the two branches of the family and the liberal endowments in Castile which Fernando I had arranged for his younger sons contributed in very large measure to the confusion of Juan II's reign. The history of Spain for the next forty years or so is very much the history of the interlocking relationships among these people.

Just before he died, Fernando I withdrew obedience from Pope Benedict XIII, though many of the Aragonese clergy still favored him. Determined, however, to collaborate with other European monarchs in terminating the schism, Alfonso V sent his representatives to the Council of Constance, as did the ever-vacillating Catalina de Lancaster.

The Castilians and Aragonese disagreed as to the procedures to be followed in the Council, but they eventually acquiesced in its major actions, namely, the deposition of Benedict XIII and the election of Martin V in 1417. Intransigent to the end, Benedict XIII continued to maintain his rights to the papacy until his death at Peñíscola in 1424. A handful of followers elected a canon of Barcelona as Pope Clement VIII, but he resigned in 1429; the schism, fortunately, had ended long before that.

Alfonso V's accession to power was not received with universal enthusiasm. Both the Aragonese and the Catalans expressed displeasure at the presence in his entourage of so many Castilians. In both states there was a long-standing opposition to foreign officials, that is, to Catalans in Aragon, to Aragonese in Catalonia. The king responded to the demand that he oust all the Castilians from his service by pointing out that they were former counselors of his father and that it would be unjust to them to turn them out of doors. The differing views of royal power held by the king and his subjects were made plain at the *corts* of Tortosa in 1419. The assembly emphasized the principle of ministerial responsibility by calling for the confirmation of appointments to the royal council in the *corts*, and by declaring that no royal disposition contrary to the *Usages of Barcelona* should have legal force. While he was willing to listen to these proposals and to implement some of them, Alfonso V did not intend to allow his authority to be unduly circumscribed. As he was anxious to be on his way overseas, the issue was not resolved.

His purpose was to restore order in Sardinia and Sicily and to chastise the Genoese who had been harassing Catalan shipping. Sailing to Sardinia in May 1420, he was able to overcome the rebels and to persuade the viscount of Narbonne, in return for a goodly sum of money, to give up all claims to the island. The king then decided to occupy Corsica, awarded to Aragon by the papacy in 1295, though none of his predecessors had established effective possession. The Genoese, who usually dominated Corsica, strenuously opposed him and forced him to abandon the undertaking in January 1421.

An extraordinary invitation sent to Alfonso V by Queen Joanna II of Naples served also to speed his departure from Corsica. Her position was extremely precarious, as her rights to the throne were disputed by Louis III of Anjou, backed by Pope Martin V. The queen's counselors persuaded her to summon Alfonso V to her aid and to adopt him; as she was well beyond child-bearing age, he could be assured of eventual succession to the throne. Accepting the offer, he hastened to Naples in July 1421 where he was formally designated as heir to the throne with the title duke of Calabria and lieutenant-general of the realm.

Discomfited for the moment, the Angevins had to give up their attempt to seize Naples. Alfonso V also won an important victory over the Genoese fleet and, by threatening to acknowledge Benedict XIII once more as pope, he won recognition as heir to the Neapolitan throne from Martin V. All this was very deceptive. Within a few months, Alfonso V found himself surrounded by enemies united only by their common determination to get rid of him: Martin V, fearful of a renewal of the schism; Joanna II, changeable as ever and frightened by the king's readiness to seize power; Louis of Anjou, who saw him as a rival for the throne, and the Genoese who wished to prevent any further Aragonese aggrandizement in the central Mediterranean. When the people of Naples revolted, Alfonso V was shut up in the Castello nuovo, but the arrival of a Catalan fleet in June 1423 enabled him to escape and to recover control of the city. The queen and her supporters fled, but she revoked her adoption of him and recognized Louis of

Anjou as her heir. At this point Alfonso V decided to return home to attend to the interests of his subjects and also to come to the aid of his brothers.

In his absence his wife Maria acted as his lieutenant in Aragon, administering justice and obtaining money from the estates to support his activities. But neither the Aragonese nor the Catalans were happy. The former in 1423 protested the king's long absence and only as an exception admitted that the *cortes* could be assembled without him. The Catalan *corts* meeting in 1421 and 1423 continued to defend their traditional liberties against any potential abuse by the crown. They expressed their views succinctly in the principle: "the fruit of the laws is in their observance; otherwise they are made in vain."

Meanwhile, Alfonso V's brothers, Juan and Enrique, were engaged in an intense rivalry as each tried to gain control of the Castilian government. When Juan went to Navarre in July 1420 to celebrate his marriage, Enrique decided to seize power by force. Breaking into the royal palace at Tordesillas, in an unprecedented affront to the king's majesty, he took Juan II into custody. This coup d'etat opened a disastrous period in the history of Castile. For the moment, Infante Juan was disconcerted and unsure what counteraction to take, but in November the king escaped from Enrique's clutches.

The person chiefly responsible for this turn of events was Alvaro de Luna, a grandnephew of Pope Benedict XIII, who steadily gained a complete ascendancy over the king's mind and will. His success in liberating the king marked the beginning of his struggle against the *infantes* of Aragon and the advancement of his own fortunes. Before his death the power of the Castilian monarchy was fully vested in his hands, and the king was little more than a puppet whom he manipulated at will. Fernán Pérez de Guzmán described the effects of their relationship in these words:

The principal and original cause of the troubles in Spain was the remiss and negligent attitude of the king and the avarice and excessive ambition of Alvaro de Luna, but this is not to excuse the avarice of the great lords. . . . Seeing that the king was more to be ruled than to rule, they believed that whoever among them became his master would govern him and the kingdom and would be able to increase his estates.   [*Generaciones y Semblanzas, 3*]

Suárez Fernández has pointed out that the struggle between Alvaro de Luna and the *infantes* of Aragon was one between members of the nobility motivated by different political objectives. Juan and Enrique typified those who believed that the preservation of their privileged status depended upon their controlling the resources and power of the government. Alvaro de Luna, on the other hand, fought for the personal supremacy of the monarch, seeking to free the crown from limitations imposed by the nobility or by the townsmen in the *cortes*. From this time on, the importance of the *cortes* and the number of towns summoned to its meetings began to diminish. While a proponent of the untrammeled authority of the crown, Alvaro de Luna intended, of course, that he should be the one to exercise it; the king's lack of will made it possible for him to do so.

Skillfully playing off the *infantes* against one another, Alvaro ordered Enrique's arrest in the spring of 1422 on charges of treasonable correspondence with the king of Granada. His estates were confiscated and distributed in such a manner as to gain for Alvaro the largest possible number of supporters. As his own reward he accepted the office of constable of Castile, with command of all the military forces of the realm.

With great indignation Alfonso V denounced Alvaro de Luna for "usurping and appropriating to himself the administration and government both of the king's person and of his kingdoms . . . not allowing him to rule his kingdoms nor to know his subjects." Demanding Enrique's release from prison, he threatened to invade Castile. The third brother, Juan, was glad enough to have Enrique out of the way for the time being and was disinclined to cooperate. Together with his wife Blanca (1425–1441) he succeeded to the throne of Navarre upon the death of Carlos III on 7 September 1425, and the Trastámara dynasty thus captured its third peninsular crown. While pleased to have the royal title, Juan was little interested in Navarre and was content to leave its administration to the queen. But as the thirst to command in Castile was always uppermost in his mind, he yielded to the insistence of Alfonso V and joined him in compelling Alvaro de Luna to liberate Enrique. Then, setting out to destroy Alvaro's extraordinary influence, Juan prevailed upon the king to dismiss him from court in September 1427. In the ensuing months, however, Juan discovered that he could not give effective direction to the government. The king was unwilling to trust him; the nobility were restless and difficult to control and unhappy because the *infantes* of Aragon "had such a large place in the affairs of the kingdom that there was little room for them." As it soon became apparent that no one could replace Alvaro de Luna, he was summoned to court again in February 1428. Juan had failed miserably and Alvaro, now sure of his position, decided to counterattack. On his urging, Juan II courteously invited Juan of Navarre to return to his own realm, "as it was not seemly that there be two kings in one kingdom."

Though he acceded to this request, Juan was deeply offended and appealed to Alfonso V to help him crush the inordinate pride of Alvaro de Luna. Both sides prepared for war and only narrowly averted a clash of arms in June 1429. Realizing that his own subjects were unwilling to finance his intervention in Castile, especially when it seemed evident that Alvaro had won the Castilian nobility over to his side, Alfonso V agreed to a five-year truce in 1430. This ended the first stage in the struggle between the *infantes* of Aragon and Alvaro de Luna who, for the time being, was clearly in the ascendant.

The truce enabled Alvaro to undertake a campaign against the Muslims in the hope of enhancing his authority by the glory of a victory in the reconquest. For twenty years Castile and Granada had remained at peace, but recent upheavals in the Muslim kingdom caused a rupture. Muhammad VIII, who had been driven from power eight years before, recovered the throne in November 1427, forcing his rival, Muhammad IX (known as *el rey izquierdo*, the left-handed), into exile. Just two years later, however, with the help of the Hafsids of Tunis, Muhammad IX returned to overthrow his opponent and to begin the second stage of his reign (1429–1445). Lest there be any further attempt to seize the crown, he ordered the execution of Muhammad VIII. Juan II of Castile and Alvaro de Luna favored Muhammad IX's efforts to regain the crown, but when he refused to pay tribute and aligned himself with Aragon, they decided to bring him down and threw their support to Yusuf IV (1430–1432), a grandson of Muhammad VI. In the spring of 1431 incursions into the *vega* of Granada, preparatory to a major campaign were begun, and on 1 July Juan II and Alvaro de Luna won a considerable victory over the enemy at La Higeruela, about three miles from the capital. Instead of pressing their advantage, however, they retired from the field, leaving the continuance of the war in the hands of the frontier commanders. With Castilian backing, Yusuf IV was able to gain control of the western part of the kingdom and even to enter Granada in January

1432, but three months later he was assassinated. Muhammad IX promptly recovered control of the city and continued the war of border skirmishes until a truce was concluded in 1439.

Portugal Overseas

While the Castilians were expending their energies in fruitless political intrigues and rivalries, the Portuguese were making significant advances in the colonization of the Atlantic islands and the exploration of the west African coast. The person mainly responsible for these enterprises was Henry the Navigator, the third son of King João I. As administrator of the military Order of Christ he was heir to a long crusading tradition, but there was little to be done in Portugal since the completion of the reconquest. Henry's participation in the conquest of Ceuta probably heightened his desire to find an effective means of overcoming the Islamic world, though he was aware that crusading theory had undergone considerable change since the thirteenth century. Propagandists talked not only about the conquest of Islam, but also about the conversion of the Muslims. The desire to win the Muslims to Christianity no doubt ranked high among the reasons for his explorations, but the hope of establishing contact with Prester John, a legendary Christian prince first mentioned in the twelfth century, also was important. Initially believing that he was in Asia, the Latins who traversed the region from Palestine to China failed to discover any trace of him; now it seemed that he might be found in Ethiopia where Coptic Christians were numerous. The Latins dreamed of launching an offensive against Islam from several directions in conjunction with Prester John. Henry also hoped to develop Portuguese trade in Africa and to open an alternate route to India around Africa; since no one imagined that Africa extended as far south as it does, the likelihood of developing the route seemed especially good. By diverting traffic from the Mediterranean, Portugal stood to profit immensely.

Henry did not personally lead any expedition for colonization or exploration. Settling at Sagres in the Algarve, he devoted his life to study and to the organization of fleets, the gathering of ships, captains, pilots, sailors, cartographers, and others who might be useful to his enterprise. The Portuguese had long since learned the techniques and skills of seamanship in the active maritime trade they carried on with northern Europe, and they knew how to use and to adapt to new purposes the caravel, a three-masted square-rigged ship. Henry was quite willing to engage the services of Italians and other foreigners who might be helpful, but the Portuguese were his principal lieutenants. We are fortunate in having in Gomes Eannes de Azurara's *The Discovery and Conquest of Guinea*, an account of the expeditions sent forth by the Navigator until 1448.

Prince Henry's expeditions were directed to the island groups: the Canaries, Madeira, and the Azores, and to the west coast of Africa. The Canaries, inhabited by fierce natives, the Guanches, were visited numerous times in the fourteenth century, and Afonso IV laid claim to them. Colonization began early in the fifteenth century with the expedition led by Jean de Bethencourt under Castilian patronage. The Portuguese were unwilling to allow the Castilians to take possession of the islands without some challenge, especially as it seemed likely that they might use the islands as a base for intervention in Africa itself. Thus in 1425 and again in 1427 Prince Henry sent expeditions to colonize the Grand Canary, as yet unoccupied by Europeans; but the natives put up a stiff resistance and the effort had to be abandoned. Juan II of Castile also protested, and when Pope Eugene IV ceded the islands to Portugal in 1435, the protest was carried to the Council of Basel, with which the pope was then at odds; as a consequence, the pope advised the Portuguese that the matter was still open. Henry continued his interest in the islands, but a final settlement of the question of ownership was not reached until 1479, when Castile's rights were confirmed.

Madeira was known in the middle of the fourteenth century but was uninhabited. João Gonçalves Zarco and Tristão Vaz Teixeira, on a voyage to the west in 1415, touched the island of Porto Santo and in the next year, Madeira; with Bartolomeu Perestrelo they began colonization in 1420. Sugar cane planted there quickly became a major export not only to Portugal but to all the chief ports of Europe. Madeira wine came into prominence in the sixteenth century.

Located directly west of Portugal, at a distance of 800 miles are the Azores, a group of islands recorded on fourteenth-century maps. Under Prince Henry, systematic exploration began, perhaps as early as 1427. Four years later Gonçalo Velho visited the islands and returned several times thereafter. By 1439 seven islands were known, but effective colonization began only in 1445.

The exploration of the African coast was a matter of much greater consequence and was much more time-consuming. In the late thir-

PORTUGAL

Lisbon

Lagos

Alcácer Seguir — Ceuta
Tangier
Arzila — Melilla
Fez

AZORES

MADEIRA

ATLANTIC OCEAN

CANARY
ISLANDS

PALMA
HIERRO GOMERA TENERIFE
GRAN CANARIA
LANZAROTE
FUERTEVENTURA

Cape Non

Cape Bojador

AFRICA

Arguim

CAPE
VERDE
ISLANDS

Cape Verde

0   250   500 Miles

0   250   500 Kilometers

Map 8. The Overseas Expansion of Portugal

teenth century, Genoese voyagers apparently sailed southward along the coast but never returned. For years after, seamen did not dare to sail beyond Cape Non, but Prince Henry made this one of his prime objectives. Gil Eannes, after passing Cape Non, rounded Cape Bojador in 1434 and in the next year sailed to Angra dos Ruivos; in 1436 the Portuguese reached Rio de Oro. These expeditions overcame the fears that had long restrained men from venturing to the south, but the distance still to be traveled around Africa was immense.

For about four years Prince Henry curtailed his expeditions to participate in an attempt to broaden the Portuguese position across the straits of Gibraltar. João I, the conqueror of Ceuta, died on 14 August 1433, forty-eight years to the day since his triumph over the Castilians at Aljubarrota. He bequeathed to his son Duarte (1433–1438) a firmly independent kingdom with territorial ambitions in Africa.

Temperamentally inclined more to study than to action, Duarte would probably not have pursued further overseas adventures had it not been for the insistence of Infante Fernando who, we are told, wishing to emulate the bravery displayed by his older brothers in the conquest of Ceuta, proposed an assault upon Tangier. If the city were taken, the Portuguese would have effective control of the southern shore of the straits of Gibraltar, thereby countering Castilian claims put forward in the Council of Basel. Prince Henry strongly supported the project, and the *cortes* in 1436 voted a subsidy, though with reluctance, and the pope granted the usual crusading indulgences. Duarte vacillated, especially when his brothers Pedro and João expressed their opposition on account of the costs and the danger, but he finally gave his approval. Henry and Fernando sailed from Lisbon in August 1437, though they lacked the number of men and ships originally planned. Landing at Ceuta early in September, they advanced overland to the west to besiege Tangier, but the Moors cut them off from their ships and continually harassed them. As matters steadily went from bad to worse, Henry realized that he had no choice but to surrender and did so on 16 October. The terms of the capitulation allowed his army to depart, but he had to agree to the surrender of Ceuta and, until the city was turned over to the Moors, to Fernando's being held hostage. The imprisoned *infante* urged the king to accept the treaty so that he could recover his liberty, and his brothers Pedro and João supported his plea. The count of Arraiolos, constable of Portugal, who had participated in the expedition, argued, however, that Ceuta should never be surrendered, even in order to liberate a prince of the blood. Prince Henry, while lamenting the necessity to leave his brother in captivity, was unwilling to give up Ceuta. The archbishop of Braga also urged this view, arguing that only the pope could authorize the abandonment of the city. As the majority of the *cortes* assembled at Leiria in 1438 also rejected surrender, the troubled and tormented king bowed to their decision. Thus Portugal retained Ceuta, because reasons of state demanded it, and Fernando remained a prisoner at Fez where he was worked as a slave until his death eleven years later.

The expedition to Tangier was a disaster that caused deep grief to the king and especially to Henry, who indeed bore the chief responsibility for it, and whose efforts to ransom his brother in later years were in vain. Soon after, Duarte fell victim to the plague and died on 9 September 1438, leaving the throne to his six-year-old son, Afonso V (1438–1481). The regency was entrusted to the Queen Mother Leonor, a sister of Alfonso V of Aragon.

Alfonso V, Master of Naples

Ever since his departure from Naples in 1423 the fortunes of war had turned against Alfonso V, as Queen Joanna II's forces recovered all the places held by the Aragonese. The question of the succession, however, continued to agitate the minds of many, and several Neapolitan lords, opposed to Louis of Anjou, whom the queen had named as her heir, encouraged Alfonso V to return. Sailing for Sicily in May 1432, he never returned to Spain again. Soon after his reappearance in the Neapolitan kingdom the situation changed significantly when the queen broke wtih Louis of Anjou and again adopted Alfonso V (4 April 1433). Unwilling to accept an Aragonese succession, Pope Eugene IV, as suzerain of Naples and Sicily, set about organizing an anti-Aragonese league with Florence, Venice, and Filippo Maria Visconti, duke of Milan and lord of Genoa. Alfonso V, disheartened and apparently preparing to return to Spain, suddenly saw his chances greatly enhanced when Louis of Anjou died in November 1434; but when the queen died in the following February, her last act was to disinherit Alfonso V and to name Louis's brother, René of Anjou, as heir to the kingdom of Naples.

Determined to secure the kingdom in spite of her betrayal and the opposition of the people, Alfonso V sailed to Gaeta in May 1435 to begin what he thought would be a triumphal advance to Naples. But Genoa, the long-time enemy of the crown of Aragon, sent a fleet to relieve the city; near the island of Ponza on 5 August the king was defeated and captured, together with his brothers Juan and Enrique and the most distinguished of his barons. This disaster seemed to ensure René's triumph, but at the moment of his greatest humiliation, Alfonso V was able to achieve a remarkable diplomatic success.

As a prisoner he was taken to Genoa and then to Milan where he was turned over to Duke Filippo Maria Visconti. In the course of their conversations Filippo Maria came to see Alfonso V as a potential ally with whose assistance he could attain hegemony in northern Italy. Concluding an alliance on 8 October against their mutual enemies, they also agreed to the effective partition of Italy between them. The region north of Bologna was reserved as Visconti's sphere of influence and conquest, and Alfonso V's rights to Naples against René of Anjou were recognized. The king renounced claims to several outposts on Corsica and agreed to aid Visconti against the *condottiere* Francesco Sforza. After the *cortes* of Aragon, Valencia, and Catalonia paid a substantial ransom of 30,000 ducats, Alfonso V was liberated in February 1436.

Deeply offended by this treaty, the Genoese threw off the Visconti lordship and joined a coalition with Florence, Venice, Pope Eugene IV, and Sforza against the king and the duke. In the meantime, the Aragonese seized Gaeta, and the struggle for Naples began in earnest. As the pope was hostile, Alfonso V sought support and recognition from the prelates assembled in the Council of Basel, whose relations with the pope had steadily worsened. When Eugene IV transferred the Council to Ferrara and later to Florence a handful of prelates remaining at Basel declared him deposed and elected an anti-pope Felix V in 1439. They also authorized Alfonso V and Visconti to conquer the papal states, but the king hoped only to persuade Eugene IV to acknowledge him as the lawful king of Naples. After capturing several cities and fortresses, his troops began the siege of Naples in November 1441. René defended it as best he could but fled at last, allowing the city to surrender on 1 June 1442. In the next nine months Alfonso V eliminated all vestiges of opposition. As he was completely master of the kingdom, there was no course left for the pope but to recognize him. Receiving investiture as king of Naples, Alfonso V pledged homage and fealty to the pope on 14 June 1443 and broke off all relations with the Council of Basel.

Henceforth, Naples was the seat of Alfonso V's government, and by virtue of that fact he became embroiled in the turbulent world of Italian politics. His continued absence from Spain was a cause of increasing annoyance there, as his subjects became more and more truculent in their dealings with Queen Maria who was acting in his stead. The *cortes* in the several kingdoms complained of the levying of taxes for foreign wars and protested that there were serious domestic problems that required the king's prompt personal attention. Though he assured them that he would return soon, the continually shifting situation in Italy caused him to postpone his departure indefinitely.

When Filippo Maria Visconti died in August 1447, he named Alfonso V as heir to the duchy of Milan, giving him an exceptional opportunity to extend his authority to the north and to dominate the entire peninsula. But the Milanese, refusing to accept him, proclaimed a republic, and called upon Francesco Sforza to defend them against their enemies. As the champion of Milanese independence it did not take Sforza long to have himself recognized as duke of Milan in 1450, thus nullifying Alfonso V's ambitions there. Four years later all of the principal Italian powers concluded the peace of Lodi whereby a balance of power and comparative calm were maintained for the next forty years.

The Ascendancy of Alvaro de Luna

In the seven or eight years after the conclusion of a truce between Aragon and Castile in 1430, Alvaro de Luna was able to govern the realm very much as he wished. Juan II showed no disposition to deprive him of power, and the towns assembled in the *cortes* were docile and ready to do whatever was asked of them. At first the men of the great noble houses believed that they would share power with the constable, but as his personal rule became more and more evident, they grew hostile. Not only did Alvaro accumulate vast estates and riches for his own benefit, but he also filled important offices with friends and relatives; his brother, a man of ill repute, was appointed, for example, to the archbishopric of Toledo.

The absence of the *infantes* of Aragon in Italy during these years freed Alvaro de Luna from any potential restraints that they might have imposed on his dominance. Upon regaining their liberty after being captured with Alfonso V at Ponza, however, they returned to

Spain and resumed their efforts to topple the constable. Pedro Carrillo de Huete recorded a new challenge to Alvaro's supremacy issued by disaffected nobles in 1438; they urged the king "to rule your realms in your own person . . . without the interference of any other person." He retorted sharply that "the king has all the laws under him, having them not from men but from God whose place he holds in all temporal matters; he is not bound to judge according to the opinions of men but . . . according to his conscience. . . . I cannot and ought not to be judged in this by any person" (*Crónica*, 231).

In spite of these protestations Juan II was soon persuaded to banish Alvaro from court for six months in October 1439. Juan of Navarre now endeavored to act as the chief royal counselor, but Juan II tried to avoid him, even moving from one town to another for that purpose. Ties between the royal houses of Castile and Navarre were drawn tightly, however, when Enrique, prince of Asturias, heir to the Castilian throne, married Blanca, daughter of Juan of Navarre in 1440. By this union, the king of Navarre hoped to assure himself of a continuing influence over Castilian policy even in the next reign.

The return of Alvaro de Luna to court after his brief exile revived the struggle for power. The *infantes* of Aragon drew up an indictment charging him with "usurping your royal power and wishing to subordinate everything to himself and to make himself monarch of your realms." Thus once more in July 1441, through the combined opposition of Juan of Navarre, Prince Enrique, and Queen Maria, the constable was ordered to retire to his estates, this time for six years.

An oligarchy of nobles headed by Juan of Navarre now controlled the government. Juan II was a virtual prisoner, and the institution of kingship was perhaps never so much humiliated as in these years. Juan of Navarre's situation changed slightly in 1441 upon the death of his wife, Queen Blanca; their son, Carlos, prince of Viana, rightfully was entitled to rule as king of Navarre, but in accordance with his mother's expressed wish he did not take the royal title in his father's lifetime. Navarre continued to serve as a base for Juan's Castilian activities, but his relations with his son gradually deteriorated.

Enrique, prince of Asturias, a young man with all his father's defects of character, was already under the influence of Juan Pacheco, an ambitious nobleman, who saw himself as Alvaro de Luna's eventual successor. With the intent of undermining Juan of Navarre, they proclaimed themselves champions of monarchy and encouraged the constable to return to the king's side in 1444.

Withdrawing to his own kingdom, Juan of Navarre prepared to take the offensive. Joined by his brother Enrique and many Castilian nobles, he advanced into the heart of Castile to meet the forces of the king, the prince, and the constable. In a great battle fought at Olmedo on 19 May 1445, the royalists won a complete victory, while Juan fled in disorder to Navarre and Enrique died shortly of wounds received. Alvaro de Luna's supremacy and authority to dispose the affairs of the kingdom as he wished now seemed assured. Enrique's death also enabled him further to enrich himself and his supporters. As his own special prize he obtained the mastership of Santiago, one of the richest lordships in the kingdom, which he had long coveted. The march of Villena, also vacated by Enrique's death, escaped his grasp, however, for he had to share the spoils with the prince of Asturias and his coterie. Juan Pacheco was named marquess of Villena, and his brother Pedro Girón received the mastership of Calatrava, previously held by the king of Navarre's illegitimate son.

Alvaro de Luna quickly discovered that the prince and his mentor, the marquess of Villena, were powerful competitors for influence with the king. He also inadvertently created a new focus of opposition when, after the death of Queen Maria, without consulting Juan II, he arranged his second marriage to Isabel of Portugal. Although Juan II was "very displeased, as he was dominated entirely by the constable, he could not avoid doing what he wanted." Isabel proved to be a strong-minded woman who developed an intense dislike for the constable and soon became one of his most implacable enemies. Thus in the years following the battle of Olmedo, the kingdom of Castile was filled with a bewildering complex of conspiracies, intrigues, shifting alliances, and clashes of arms, all directed toward the destruction of Alvaro de Luna.

Prince Enrique and the marquess of Villena alternated between rebellion and reconciliation, each time demanding a higher price for their submission. From time to time they sought alliance with Juan of Navarre, while other Castilian nobles invited Alfonso V to return from Italy and join in an offensive against the constable. Alvaro displayed a remarkable ability to circumvent his enemies and to sow discord among them and, so long as the king continued in his customary negligence, he seemed able to withstand all the assaults on his position. The chorus of protest against the constable grew ever louder, however, as these lines of the marquess of Santillana illustrate:

> Desterraste lealtad
> de los lymites yspanos
> roca de seguridad
> de los reyes castellanos. . . .

> You banished loyalty
> From the bounds of Spain,
> The rock of security
> Of the Castilian kings. . . . [CC, I, 499]

If Alvaro de Luna had retired at this time, he might have averted the disaster that soon befell him, but he was tenacious of power and refused to step aside.

At last Queen Isabel convinced her husband to order Alvaro to retire to his estates; but when he delayed his departure, in effect refusing to obey the royal command, the king ordered his arrest at Burgos in April 1453. A selected body of lords and legists, after reviewing his purported crimes, concluded that as "he had usurped the royal crown and ruled as a tyrant . . . he ought to be beheaded." Juan II ordered the execution "so that he might be a witness and example for others . . . and so that all may recognize that the king, their natural lord, has the place of God on earth" (*Crónica de Juan II*, 1452, 2–3). The beheading of the constable took place in the main square of Valladolid on 2 June 1453, calling to mind these prophetic lines of the marquess of Santillana:

> De tu resplandor, o Luna
> Te ha priuado la fortuna.

> Of your brightness, o Moon,
> Fortune has deprived you. [CC, I, 497]

Alvaro de Luna, "the most powerful man in the whole history of Spain, among those who have not worn a crown," was endowed with great talent and skill in diplomacy and government, but his eclipse of the king and his effective usurpation of royal authority, lessened the prestige of the monarchy and encouraged assaults upon it.

"In killing the constable, the king killed himself." Such, at least, was the opinion of the author of the *Crónica de Alvaro de Luna*. Obsessed by the execution of the man who had so long guided his life, Juan II was unable to govern by himself and followed his victim to the grave on 20 July 1454. Castile lay impoverished, her government in ruins, her people divided, and her future prospects dim indeed. Accepting his father's legacy was Enrique IV (1454–1474) at whose side stood Juan Pacheco, marquess of Villena, ready to assume the mantle laid down by Alvaro de Luna.

Afonso V of Portugal

With somewhat less intensity, a similar struggle for power was taking place in the neighboring kingdom of Portugal. Queen Leonor, designated as regent for her son, Afonso V, encountered strong opposition from those who feared that her brothers, the *infantes* of Aragon, might begin to meddle in Portuguese affairs. At the *cortes* in 1438 the proposal was made that she share the regency with the king's uncle, Pedro, duke of Coimbra, an accomplished soldier and diplomat, who had traveled widely in Europe. Though he was supported by Lisbon and by other towns, his ambitions were disputed by his half-brother Afonso, count of Barcelos, a bastard son of João I. Henry the Navigator suggested a compromise, allowing the queen to retain guardianship of her son and control of the finances, while Pedro took responsibility for the defense of the realm, but this proved unacceptable. The *cortes* meeting at Lisbon in December 1439 in the absence of the queen and the count of Barcelos, decided to recognize Pedro as the sole regent. Deprived of power, Queen Leonor appealed to her brothers, but their promises of aid were never fulfilled, and Pedro successfully undercut them by entering a secret alliance with Alvaro de Luna. Rather than await seizure and imprisonment by the regent, the queen fled to Castile where she died in 1445.

Accepting the situation, the count of Barcelos submitted to Pedro as regent and in 1442 was given the title duke of Bragança; in this way the foundations of a future dynasty were laid. When Afonso V came of age in January 1446, he asked Pedro to continue governing the realm and he married Pedro's daughter Isabel; but the duke of Bragança, assuming the role of chief royal counselor, set out to destroy his rival, spreading rumors and accusations of the worst sort, including the suggestion that Pedro had poisoned his brother Duarte. As his friends and supporters were deprived of their offices, Pedro soon realized that he had been effectively isolated; rather than submit meekly, he refused the king's order to give up his arms and prepared for war. As he advanced toward Lisbon, hoping to gain popular support for his cause, the king and the duke came out to meet him at Alfarrobeira. There he was defeated and killed on 24 May 1449. The Bragança family took advantage of their triumph to secure money, lands, and titles for themselves and their friends, and for many years thereafter they were the most powerful family in the kingdom.

Henry the Navigator remained aloof from these intrigues and in 1441 resumed his explorations of the African coast. His captains sailed as far south as Cape Branco and Rio de Oro where they seized some natives and brought them back to Portugal. In the next few years voyages were made to the mouth of the Senegal river which was thought to be one of the branches of the Nile. By 1444 Cape Verde was reached. Four years later Henry's men began the construction of a fort on the bay of Arguim. This, the first European settlement on the west coast of Africa, quickly became an important trading post, supplying gold and slaves to the homeland. Azurara's chronicle recording these expeditions terminates in this year, and it is possible that Henry was obliged either for want of funds or because of the conflict within the royal family to desist from his activities for a while. His efforts to gain papal recognition of his rights to colonize the Canary Islands not already settled by the Castilians came to naught, but Pope Nicholas V did confirm the monopoly on trade to the Guinea coast already given him by the crown. In 1455 the Venetian Alvise de Cadamosto, in Henry's service, made a voyage to Madeira and the Canaries and then southward along the coast to the Senegal, and vividly recounted the curiosities and hazards of exploration.

The Offensive against Islam: East and West

The exploration of the African coast, important as it was for the future, was overshadowed in the minds of men by the rising power of the Ottoman Turks. Their capture of Constantinople in 1453 bringing the Byzantine empire to an end had a profound impact upon the European conscience and prompted Pope Calixtus III to summon the rulers of the west to participate in a crusade to stop the Turkish menace. The response to his appeal was scant, but in their several ways the Christian rulers of Spain took action against the Muslim world. The results achieved, however, were slight and hardly compensated for the loss of Constantinople.

Enrique IV, the new king of Castile, began his reign auspiciously by announcing his intention to go to war against the kingdom of Granada. After the disasters of his father's reign he attempted to conciliate the factions among the nobility and to maintain peace with Aragon and Navarre. He repudiated his wife, Blanca of Navarre, however, and married Juana of Portugal so as to effect an alliance with Afonso V. Given internal tranquility and peaceful relations with the other Christian kingdoms of the peninsula, he could take the offensive against Granada. He frankly saw the war as a means of diverting the nobility from the intrigues to which they had grown accustomed. In appealing to the pope for crusade indulgences his ambassadors declared that once the kingdom of Granada had been conquered the Castilians could then deal with the Turks.

The condition of the kingdom of Granada had worsened steadily since the truce of 1439. A series of coups kept the realm in a state of confusion and encouraged external intervention. Muhammad IX was overthrown by his nephew Muhammad X (1445–1447) "the lame," but the Abencerrajes threw their support to still another candidate, Yusuf V, who also was favored by Castile. Even so, Muhammad IX regained power in 1447 and accepted as co-ruler his cousin Muhammad XI (1448–1454). When the former died in 1453, the Abencerrajes ousted the latter and proclaimed Sad (1454–1464), a grandson of Yusuf II. At this point, Enrique IV decided to intervene.

The Castilian invasion began in the spring of 1455 with great enthusiasm among the nobility. The size of the royal army gave promise of a decisive blow against the enemy, but the king avoided any direct confrontation with opposing forces and contented himself with the devastation of the countryside. He expected that by destroying the basis of the Granadan economy, the kingdom would collapse, but the nobles found this style of campaigning unsatisfying for it gave them no opportunity to cover themselves with glory in the clash of arms. In the next two years the king adhered to the same strategy, amid mounting criticism from the magnates. After 1458 he left his frontier captains, the duke of Medina Sidonia, and the marquess of Cádiz, to continue the war of raids and devastation. Their most significant accomplishment was the capture of Gibraltar in 1462. A truce was concluded in the next year and the frontier was stabilized, but the prestige of the monarchy was compromised by the king's failure to meet the enemy face to face on the field of battle. An irreparable breach between him and many of the great lords of the realm had been opened.

The papal appeal to a crusade evoked a positive response from Afonso V of Portugal who began to prepare actively, but it soon became apparent to him that other rulers were disinclined to attempt the recovery of Constantinople. Deciding to direct his attack on a Muslim base closer to home, he selected Alcácer Seguir on the west coast of Africa as his objective. In late September 1458 he sailed from Setúbal and was joined by Prince Henry; landing at Alcácer on 21 October, they drove the defenders back, breached and scaled the walls, and by the end of the day forced the enemy to surrender and to evacuate the city. The king of Fez attempted to recover possession and pressed the city about until January 1459, and returned again in the summer, but the Portuguese successfully defended the city. Alcácer Seguir, the second Portuguese conquest in Morocco, whetted the king's appetite, but several years passed before he returned. His uncle, Henry the Navigator, died on 11 November 1460, bringing to a close an extraordinary period in Portuguese overseas activity.

The papacy expected much more direct participation in the anti-Turkish crusade from Alfonso V of Aragon. As king of Naples and Sicily he occupied a pivotal position in the Mediterranean and was heir to a long tradition of interest in the Balkan peninsula. As the Turks were expanding their rule there, he entered into contact with the Albanians and Hungarians and expressed his concern for the fate of Constantinople; but he did nothing to save the city nor did he respond afterwards to any of the papal appeals for action. He probably realized that his situation in Italy was not so firm as to allow him to challenge the Turks directly. Moreover, like other contemporary rulers his objectives were those which would bring substantial advantages to himself and to his subjects. Thus instead of attacking the Turks, he organized an army and a fleet and declared war against Genoa, the chief obstacle to Catalan domination of the western Mediterranean. His forces were engaged in the siege of Genoa when he died on 27 June 1458.

Juan II of Aragon and Navarre

Alfonso V left the kingdom of Naples to his illegitimate son Ferrante (1458–1494), while Aragon, Sardinia, and Sicily passed to his younger brother Juan of Navarre. Though already sixty years of age. and threatened with blindness, Juan II (1458–1479) was still vigorous and ambitious. As king of Navarre and now of Aragon, he still retained an intense interest in Castilian affairs and aimed to unify all the peninsular states in his own immediate family. He had numerous allies among the Castilian nobility, many of whom were disgusted by Enrique IV's strategy in the war with Granada; others were resentful of the great influence of the marquess of Villena. As a counterweight to them all, Enrique IV elevated to high office a number of young men of humble origin; of them, Beltrán de la Cueva had the most interesting future. Many of the disgruntled magnates formed an alliance with Juan II in April 1460, demanding the restoration of his Castilian estates. This, coupled with his treatment of his oldest son and presumed heir, Carlos of Viana, resulted in a rupture between the two kingdoms.

Juan II's relations with Carlos of Viana had deteriorated to such a point that Navarre came to the verge of civil war, and Alfonso V, while still alive, had had to mediate the quarrel. Hostilities resumed when Juan II refused to designate his son as heir to all his dominions or to appoint him as lieutenant-general. Taking an active interest in these developments was the king's second wife, Juana Enríquez, who undoubtedly hoped to arrange the succession of her son, the future Ferdinand the Catholic. Matters came to a head in December 1460 when the king arrested Carlos and charged him, falsely as it later turned out, with treasonable correspondence with Enrique IV. On learning of the prince's imprisonment, Enrique IV prepared an invasion of Navarre.

The Catalans were also provoked by Juan II's action. They had learned to dislike him before his accession and were ready to seize any occasion to oppose him. Catalonia was in the throes of an economic and social crisis and ready for revolution. Not only were the *payeses de remensa*, or peasants bound to the soil, agitating for deliverance from the oppression of their landlords, but the lower classes in the towns were trying to break the grip of the oligarchy of rich men on municipal government. When the king refused to liberate the prince, the *Generalitat* issued a call to arms, "declaring that kings ought to rule by laws the peoples commended to them . . . and if any king wishes to do anything . . . greatly injurious and prejudicial to his realms, his subjects are obliged and bound to warn him against it" (*MHDE*, II, 974). The response was enthusiastic. When Enrique IV simultaneously invaded Navarre, Juan II bowed to the opposition, liberating his son on 25 February 1461 and agreeing to negotiate a settlement with him.

The outcome of these discussions was the Capitulation of Vilafranca del Panadés, dated 22 June 1461. Noting that "there is an inestimable good deriving from the regulated order and peace of the republic, which is based principally on the uniformity and concord between the head and the body and its members" (*MHDE*, II, 903), the *Generalitat* requested the king to recognize Carlos as his heir and lieutenant-general in Catalonia for life; if he should die, his stepbrother Ferdinand would take his place. Juan II agreed and also promised not to enter Catalonia without the consent of the *Generalitat*, but he retained the right to summon the *corts* and to appoint officials. If he failed to observe the terms of the pact, he absolved the Catalans in advance from their oath of allegiance. The Capitulation was a humiliation for him and compromised his sovereignty, but it did not bring peace. The Catalans were rushing headlong into revolution, as the great lords set out to crush the *payeses* and the municipal oligarchy attacked their enemies among the small merchants, artisans, and workingmen. The sudden death of Prince Carlos at Barcelona on 23 September, moreover, immediately raised the suspicion that he had been poisoned by his father.

This, coupled with Juan II's machinations with France convinced the Catalans of his treachery. By virtue of a treaty of alliance with Louis XI of France, signed at Bayonne in May 1462, he obtained military and financial aid, to be used to crush the Catalans; but he allowed the French to occupy Rousillon and Cerdagne as a pledge of repayment. No doubt Louis XI was hopeful of annexing the counties to France in perpetuity. The two kings also agreed to a settlement of the long-disputed succession to the kingdom of Navarre. Prince Carlos had designated his older sister Blanca as his heir, but Juan II preferred to leave the kingdom to his other daughter Leonor and her husband Gaston, count of Foix. Louis XI also supported this arrangement. Blanca, however, willed her rights to Navarre to her former husband, Enrique IV of Castile, thereby setting the stage for Castilian intervention.

The Catalans were infuriated when they learned of the treaty of Bayonne. When the king entered Catalonia at the head of an army, in violation of the Capitulation, the *Generalitat*, charging him with having "conceived hatred and rancor toward the principality," denounced him and his supporters as "enemies of the republic of the said principality." Then on 12 August the *Generalitat* proclaimed, as lord of the principality, Enrique IV, the nearest direct descendant of Pedro IV. Though gratified by this action, Enrique IV hesitated briefly before sending troops to the frontier in support of the Catalan revolt. In the meantime the Catalans forced Juan II to abandon the siege of Barcelona, but despite this setback he did not lose heart and soon achieved a diplomatic triumph of considerable importance. With the purpose of detaching Enrique IV from the Catalans he proposed that the differences between Castile and Aragon be submitted to the arbitration of Louis XI, the Spider King, who presented himself as the friend and ally of both. In his decision, rendered at Bayonne in April 1463, he required Enrique IV to renounce all claims to Catalonia and to withdraw his forces from Navarre, except for the district of Estella. In return he would receive an indemnity as partial compensation for his expenses.

Enríquez del Castillo recorded the feeling of betrayal expressed by the Catalan ambassador at the Castilian court: "We thought . . . that we would be protected, but we are destroyed, that we would be defended, but we are ruined . . . now we are put to the knife by the one who ought to protect and defend us" (Crónica, 50). Rather than acquiesce, the Catalans sent envoys to Louis XI, suspecting that he would be willing to play a double game against Juan II; but when he proposed to incorporate Catalonia into his dominions, they backed off. They then offered the principality to Pedro, constable of Portugal, who had been forced into exile after the defeat and death of his father, Pedro, duke of Coimbra, at the hands of Afonso V. Though Pedro was proclaimed at Barcelona in January 1464, he was no match for Juan II who began the systematic conquest of the principality.

The Downfall of Enrique IV

Meanwhile, Enrique IV began to realize that he had also been betrayed by the marquess of Villena, who posed as his most faithful counselor, but who used his position for personal gain and at Bayonne gave away solid claims to Catalonia and Navarre. As a rival to Villena, Enrique IV began to shower titles and riches upon Beltrán de la Cueva, whose steady rise reached its culmination when he was appointed master of Santiago, a post long desired by the marquess. Beltrán, or so it seemed, would fill the role of Alvaro de Luna as a buffer between the king and the nobility.

Angered by these developments, Villena broke with the king and, assembling his allies at Burgos in September 1464, published a manifesto condemning the king's mismanagement and the abuses of his officials and the excessive power of Beltrán de la Cueva. Charging that Infanta Juana, the heiress to the throne, born two years before, was illegitimate and that Beltrán was her real father (for this reason they called her in derision, *la Beltraneja*), they demanded that the king recognize his younger brother, Alfonso, a boy of eleven years, as heir and that he also be given the mastership of Santiago. The basis for the charge of illegitimacy made against her was the admitted relative impotence of the king, whose marriage to Blanca of Navarre had been nullified on that ground; but he had also spent six years of married life with Juana of Portugal before the *infanta* was born. Her legitimacy will always remain in doubt, though no convincing proof to the contrary has ever been presented; the king's behavior unfortunately did little to uphold her good name or that of her mother.

Within a month, Enrique IV acceded to the demands of the nobles, recognizing his brother as heir and entrusting him to the custody of the marquess of Villena. He also consented to the appointment of a commission to reform his government and to Beltrán's renunciation of the mastership of Santiago. Early in the next year, however, he changed his mind and repudiated his pledges. The nobles, therefore, gathered at Avila on 5 June 1465 and deposed the king:

They caused a platform to be erected in a great plain outside the city and placed on top of it an effigy seated in a chair, which they said represented the person of the king. . . . They accused the king specifically of four things: that he deserved to lose the royal dignity, and therefore Alonso Carrillo, archbishop of Toledo, removed the crown from the effigy's head . . . that he deserved to lose the administration of justice, and . . . the count of Plasencia removed the sword that it held aloft . . . that he deserved to lose the government of the kingdom, and . . . the count of Benavente removed the scepter that it held in its hand . . . that he deserved to lose the throne and seat of kingship, and Diego López de Zúñiga with harsh and brutal words, knocked the effigy out of the chair. [Enriquez del Castillo, *Crónica*, 74]

In his stead the magnates proclaimed Alfonso as king, throwing Castile into civil war; but in spite of the weaknesses of Enrique IV, the mass of the people remained loyal to him. Villena also discovered that he could not command the full support of the magnates, who resented his self-seeking. By the next year he turned again to negotiation and proposed to abandon Alfonso of Avila, if the king would oust Beltrán de la Cueva from court and agree to the marriage of Infanta Isabella with Pedro Girón, master of Calatrava, and brother of the marquess. "Thinking that he could recover his estate," the king agreed, but Girón's sudden death in May 1466 saved Isabella from a match which she regarded with undisguised loathing.

The civil war continued despite renewed efforts by the king to placate his enemies; nor did a royalist victory over the rebels at Olmedo in August 1467 bring peace to the troubled land. The death of Alfonso of Avila from the plague in July 1468, however, changed the entire situation. Deprived of their pawn, the rebellious magnates planned to proclaim the king's sister Isabella as queen, but she would not allow herself to be used in that way. Instead she sought power through an accommodation with her brother, with whom she concluded a pact at Los Toros de Guisando on 18 September 1468. Enrique IV recognized her as the legitimate heir to the throne, and she agreed "to marry the one whom the king decided and determined, with the consent of the Infanta . . . and not with any other person." The princess's marriage now became the principal question to be resolved; but while the king and Villena proposed Afonso V of Portugal as a suitable husband, Isabella preferred to marry her cousin, Ferdinand of Aragon. She realized that the Aragonese marriage, uniting two branches of the Trastámara family, would also bring the two realms under joint rule, but a marriage with Afonso V, a widower, who already had a son to inherit the kingdom of Portugal, would not result in a union of kingdoms and would probably contribute further to the weakening of monarchy in Castile. Urged on by her counselors, the archbishop of Toledo and Bishop Pedro de Mendoza, she decided to marry Ferdinand without awaiting her brother's consent.

Ferdinand was the son of Juan II, who favored the marriage because it would eventually achieve the union of Castile and Aragon, something he had long contemplated. He also expected some immediate advantage in the form of Castilian support against his enemies, the Catalan rebels and Louis XI of France. Though Pedro of Portugal, whom the Catalans had chosen as their ruler, died in June 1466, they steadfastly refused to surrender and invited René of Anjou, pretender to the thrones of Naples and Sicily, to rule over them. Louis XI supported René, chiefly because he hoped through his triumph to gain a permanent, legitimate title to Rousillon and Cerdagne. In order to counter the French and the Angevins, Juan II entered into alliances with Charles the Bold, duke of Burgundy, and Edward IV of England, both staunch opponents of the king of France; he also took an active part in bringing about the marriage of Ferdinand and Isabella, so as to cut off the possibility of Castilian aid to France.

Without the consent of her brother, who was absent in Andalusia, but supported by a forged papal dispensation presented by the archbishop of Toledo, Isabella was married to the prince of Aragon at Valladolid on 19 October 1469. Her hope that Enrique IV would accept the *fait accompli* was in vain. Feeling betrayed, he denounced the marriage as a violation of the pact of Guisando which was thereby nullified. In October 1470 he solemnly declared that Juana was his true daughter and the proper heir to the throne and arranged her betrothal to a younger brother of Louis XI; but the prince's death soon after undermined the potential Franco-Castilian alliance. Meanwhile, anarchy spread throughout the realm as magnates, townsmen, and others aligned themselves under the banners either of Juana or Isabella.

As the struggle progressed, Isabella was fortunate in receiving substantial help from her father-in-law, Juan II. His fortunes, it turned out, improved immeasurably when René of Anjou's son died, an occurrence that left the Catalan rebels without effective military leadership. Royalist forces besieged Barcelona, the last stronghold of the resistance, and forced its surrender in October 1472. With that, the Catalan revolt was at an end. Avoiding vindictiveness, Juan II swore to uphold Catalan liberties and to pardon his enemies. Having recovered the principality, he tried now to enlist Catalan aid in expelling the French from Roussillon and Cerdagne; though he was able to make a triumphal entrance into Perpignan in 1473, the French recovered possession two years later, so that the future of the two counties was left for his descendants to resolve.

Juan Pacheco, marquess of Villena, a skillful manipulator of power and influence and one of the most ambitious men of his time, who had gained for himself the richest prize of all, the mastership of Santiago, died in October 1474. Two months later on 11 December, Enrique IV, the man whose interests he always purportedly served, followed him to the grave, without altering his judgment concerning the succession. His reign was a tragedy, for the decline of royal authority and prestige which had characterized his father's rule continued unchecked, allowing the arrogance of the aristocracy to expand beyond all limits.

The Accession of Ferdinand and Isabella

Immediately after her brother's death Isabella was proclaimed as queen of Castile, but her right to rule was challenged by the partisans of the dead king's daughter, Juana. There were also some who asserted that females could not inherit the throne and that Ferdinand was entitled to rule as the nearest male representative of the Trastámara family. This issue was submitted to the judgment of the archbishops of Toledo and Seville who confirmed the principle of female succession, but allowed Ferdinand to share in the exercise of royal authority and not to be a mere prince consort. In the meantime Juana's supporters arranged her betrothal to Afonso V of Portugal who prepared to invade Castile in defense of her rights.

Afonso V had distinguished himself recently by exploits in Africa which had gained him the nickname "the African." Sailing from Lisbon in August 1471, he assaulted the town of Arzila on the Moroccan coast, some miles southwest of Tangier. After a siege of three days the defenders surrendered on 24 August and, shortly after, the populace of Tangier, fearing to be caught from behind, evacuated the city, which was promptly occupied by the Portuguese. As a consequence, the Portuguese now controlled the southern shore of the straits of Gibraltar from Ceuta to Tangier.

When Afonso V invaded Castile in the spring of 1475 he found little effective support and would have withdrawn if Isabella had yielded Galicia or León to him, but she was unwilling to dismember the realm. Ferdinand routed the Portuguese at Toro in March 1476, thereby assuring his wife's rights to the throne. As many of Juana's partisans hastened to make peace with Isabella, the king of Portugal decided to make a personal appeal for help to Louis XI of France. He sailed from Lisbon in September, passing through the straits of Gibraltar to southern France and then traveling overland to Tours, where he met Louis XI. His pleas were in vain, for the king of France, involved in a struggle with the duke of Burgundy, could not commit himself to a cause which showed little possibility of success, and indeed formally acknowledged Isabella's rights to the throne in November 1478.

A few months later, on 19 January 1479, Juan II, now over eighty years of age, breathed his last, leaving the kingdom of Aragon, with Valencia, Catalonia, Majorca, Sardinia, and Sicily to his son Ferdinand. His daughter Leonor inherited Navarre, but she died in February, leaving the kingdom to her grandson, Francisco (1479–1483). Juan II lived a very full life, overcoming extraordinary obstacles in his efforts to further the fortunes of his family and to unify the peninsula.

Afonso V, meanwhile, disheartened by his failure to enlist the aid of Louis XI, returned home and concluded the treaty of Alcáçovas on 4 September 1479 with Ferdinand and Isabella. Renouncing all claims to the Castilian throne on Juana's behalf, he also gave up any claim to the Canary Islands. In return, Ferdinand and Isabella recognized Portugal's rights in Africa, and promised not to undertake any enterprise there without Portuguese consent. Juana rejected the proposal that she marry a Castilian prince, though she was free to do so, for her marriage to Afonso V had never been solemnized; she preferred to retire to a convent in Lisbon where she died in 1530, still styling herself queen. Afonso V, full of melancholy, was preparing to abdicate when he died on 28 August 1481.

The accession of Isabella as queen of Castile in 1474, of Ferdinand as king of Aragon in 1479, and of João II as king of Portugal in 1481 opened a new era in the history of the peninsula. Under the direction of these energetic sovereigns, the institution of monarchy recovered its luster, the reconquest was completed, the route to India by way of the Cape of Good Hope was opened, and the new world was discovered.

CHAPTER 23

Government, 1369–1479

The State

In the later medieval centuries western Europeans became aware once again of the ancient concept of the state as described by Aristotle in his *Politics* and as exemplified by the Roman empire. Declaring man to be both a social and a political animal, Aristotle argued that government and the state consequently derive from man's very nature. Late medieval theologians and publicists, following this lead, recognized the state as a natural institution and rejected the older Christian view that government came into existence as a result of man's wickedness due to original sin and required the justification and sanctification which only the church could give. These arguments gave the state an existence independent of and separate from the church; no longer was the state subordinate to the church or in need of its sanction.

In late medieval Spain the state was conceived as a political community endowed with its own juridical personality, distinct from that of the ruler. Kings themselves distinguished between "the estate of the realm" and "the royal estate" and acknowledged that the interests and needs of the state were of paramount importance. As justification for their actions, they often spoke of "the good of my realms" or "the service of my realms." The commissioners of Caspe in 1412 emphasized that they were acting "for the profit and good estate of the republic." Terms commonly employed to describe the state were kingdom (*reyno*), republic (*cosa pública*), mystical body (*cuerpo místico*), or body politic (*cuerpo político*). The term "royal crown" (*corona real*) was also used frequently to express the sum of the rights, powers, and privileges of the state and government. Theorists preferred to use the image of the human body to illustrate the nature of the state, as in this letter of Diego de Valera to Juan II:

> The princes joined together with their subjects and natural born citizens are like a human body; just as one cannot cut off any member without great pain and injury to the body, so no subject can be destroyed without great loss and damage to the prince. . . . If matters continue as they have, how many members will be cut off, and if they are, tell me, my lord, what will become of the head? [*Crónica de Juan II*, 1441, 4]

In effect, the health of the body politic required concord and unity between the mutually dependent head and members; as parts of one body, they ought to love, honor, and cherish one another. Yet the whole was greater than any of the parts; for this reason the Catalans in 1461 branded Juan II as an enemy of the republic and principality of Catalonia, for they believed that loyalty to the state transcended loyalty to individual lords, or even to the person of the king.

An intensification of patriotic and national feeling in the fifteenth century emphasizes this point. Love of the fatherland is evident in many texts, as, for example, in Joan Margarit de Pau's exaltation of "the fortunate, glorious and most loyal nation of Catalonia"; in Juan I's statement that a "man ought to labor and die for his homeland"; and in the marquess of Santillana's exclamation "O my fatherland! O Spain!"

Castilian poets and publicists, by identifying the Castilian with the Hispanic or Spanish nation and by calling their king "rey d'España" were consciously asserting claims to peninsular supremacy. Rodrigo Sánchez de Arévalo, for example, commented that "the first and indeed the chief kingdom of Spain is the one today called Castile and León, which occupies the center of Spain and from which, down to the present time, the kings of the other kingdoms have come" (Maravall, *El Concepto de España en la edad media*, 464). In the same vein, Alfonso de Cartagena emphasized that the kings of Castile were commonly known throughout Europe as kings of Spain; he argued further that they were heirs of the universal Hispanic monarchy of the Visigoths and that, as such, "the conquest of that region overseas in Africa, previously known as Tingitania and today as Benamarin [Morocco] and of the adjacent islands . . . the Canary Islands" belonged to them (*MHDE*, II, 628). Thus traditional Leonese aspirations to hegemony over the whole of Spain were restated, but also extended to Africa. The Leonese idea of empire, however, does not seem to have been the principal inspiration for the tendency to exalt the king as "the new Caesar, the new Augustus" or to proclaim him "the exalted peer of the emperor." The imperial ambitions suggested by this kind of language seem to be born rather of a new admiration for the ancient Roman empire stimulated by the humanist revival of the classics.

While the Castilians were evidently hopeful of dominating and unifying the peninsula, the Portuguese in fact were making greater progress toward the creation of an extrapeninsular empire by their colonization of the Atlantic islands, by the exploration of the west African coast, and by the conquest of several important coastal fortresses. Similarly, the Aragonese empire, a confederation of kingdoms, was strengthened by Pedro IV's recovery of Majorca and Sicily and Alfonso V's conquest of Naples. The frontiers of the kingdom of Castile, on the contrary, were expanded only slightly by the conquest of several places, including Antequera, Archidona, and Gibraltar.

Kingship

Two principal theories of royal power were expressed in the late Middle Ages. The one stressed the divine origin of the king's authority and his responsibility to God; the other, while admitting that all power comes from God, emphasized, however, that the king received his power immediately from the people to whom he was also accountable. The theory of divine-right monarchy with its implications of royal absolutism was expressed no more clearly than in the *cortes* of Olmedo in 1445 following Juan II's victory over the rebellious *infantes* of Aragon. The *cortes* stated that divine law

expressly commands and forbids anyone to dare to touch the king and prince as one who is anointed by God, nor even to comment or to say anything evil about him nor even to think it in spirit; rather he should be held as God's vicar . . . no one should dare to oppose him, because those who resist the king evidently wish to resist the ordinance of God.   [C£C, III, 458]

Repeating phrases already used by Juan II, the *cortes* declared that the laws are beneath the king who cannot be judged by men "because he does not have his power from men, but from God, whose place he holds in temporal affairs." Some years later, Enrique IV made the same arguments, affirming that "kings rule in the place of God on earth . . . to resist the earthly power of kings is to resist God who appointed them to their place."

The royal responsibility to God was a serious one, though kings often had to be reminded of it. Thus the marquess of Santillana warned Afonso V that "kings, chosen by God, ought to uphold the laws, because he entrusted them to them;" and he noted that those kings were virtuous "who were obedient to the law." Yet if a king were negligent, was it licit to admonish him, or to oppose him by force, or to depose him? Pedro González de Mendoza, later archbishop of Toledo, tried to dissuade the nobles from rebelling against Enrique IV by arguing that

Every kingdom is like a body, of which we hold the king to be the head; but if it is infirm due to any illness, it would seem the better wisdom to provide the medicines that reason dictates than to cut off the head, which nature forbids. . . . If kings are anointed by God on earth, one cannot believe that they are subject to human judgment. . . . Sacred Scripture expressly forbids rebellion and commands obedience to kings, even though they may be unworthy, because . . . the devastations that divided kingdoms suffer are greater than those they suffer from an unsuitable king.   [Fernando del Pulgar, *Crónica*, 1]

On the other hand, Diego de Valera in letters to Juan II and Enrique IV pointedly reminded them of various Old Testament kings who were anointed, but deposed nonetheless, and of thirteen Gothic kings who died at the hand of their vassals on account of evil government. Without necessarily approving rebellion and deposition, he implied that such was the common fate of unworthy kings. Enrique IV suffered that fate when he was deposed in 1465.

The argument that the king was responsible to the people rested on the belief that he received his authority from them, usually through some form of an election. The most recent examples of elections were those of Fernando I of Aragon, João I of Portugal, and Enrique II of Castile. Royal elections were held to be of great antiquity, as Enrique II noted when he declared that the Goths anciently had chosen their kings, as the Castilians did now in his case. Similarly, Carlos of Viana recounted how the eighth-century Navarrese and Aragonese, because of dissension among themselves, gathered at Sobrarbe to redact their *fueros* and then to elect a king who would swear to uphold them. Juan Ximénez de Cerdán, *justicia* of Aragon, explained that besides electing a king, the people also elected a *justicia* to act as judge between them and the king. The story of an ancient royal election was later embellished by the addition of an oath purportedly taken by the Aragonese nobility to their king: "We who are as good as you . . . elect you as king on condition that you guard our liberties, and if not, not." While apocryphal, the story does reflect the contractual theory of monarchy current in some circles.

The theory was expounded most systematically by Francesch Eiximenis in his *Regiment de la Cosa Pública*. Declaring that men existed originally as free individuals, Eiximenis goes on to explain how they determined to organize themselves into a community and to elect persons to rule over them to further the common good. "Communities never give power over themselves absolutely to anyone, but always under certain pacts and laws." The ruler is chosen for the welfare of the community, but if he pursues his own interests, he separates himself from the community and becomes a tyrant and an enemy. There seems no doubt that these doctrines provided the basic justification for the Catalan revolt of 1461.

Influenced perhaps by the Catalan example, by the teaching of Eiximenis and of Alfonso de Madrigal, who declared that the people always retain the right to elect and to correct their ruler, the Castilian *cortes* of 1469 declared that "the office of king . . . is to rule . . . and to rule well, because the king who rules badly does not rule, but destroys." The responsibility of the king is a burdensome one:

Your task is to keep watch, guarding over your subjects while they sleep, for you are their hireling (*merescenario*) for your subjects pay you wages for this, part of their fruits and the profits of their industry, and they serve you faithfully with their persons in time of your necessities, so as to make you more powerful, so that you may relieve their necessities and take away their cares. Your highness should take note that you are indeed obliged by a tacit contract (*contrato callado*) to keep and maintain them in justice. [*CLC*, III, 767]

Ineffectual royal government prompted outcries against the theory of divine-right monarchy and encouraged the partisans of popular sovereignty. But the factiousness and gross self-interest of the nobility in opposing the crown aroused a longing for the restoration of firm royal power. That, in the end, helped the doctrine of royal absolutism triumph over the idea of a constitutionally limited monarchy.

Hereditary right and primogeniture continued to regulate the succession, though the establishment of the Trastámara dynasty in Castile and the Avis dynasty in Portugal resulted from revolutionary action and the temporary suspension of these principles. In both cases Enrique II and João I claimed election by the people, but the most formal election was that of Fernando de Antequera as king of Aragon by the commissioners of Caspe. Aside from these exceptions the throne usually passed from father to son, though Juan of Navarre, who acquired that throne by marriage, succeeded his brother as king of Aragon. In the three minorities of Enrique III and Juan II of Castile and Afonso V of Portugal, a council of regency, including the queen mother and other members of the royal family and the chief men of the realm, assumed responsibility for the government. Female rights were urged in several instances, but the only woman to ascend the throne in her own right was Isabella the Catholic.

The ruler was proclaimed by the assembled magnates who pledged fealty, while he swore to uphold the liberties of his subjects. The ceremony of anointing and coronation seems to have fallen into disuse, except in Aragon. Juan I who crowned himself and his wife at Las Huelgas de Burgos apparently was the last Castilian king to be crowned; the pope authorized the coronation of the Portuguese kings in a bull of 1428, but it was never used. In the royal intitulation all dominions were listed in order of precedence; thus Catalonia, a mere principality, was listed after the kingdoms of Aragon, Valencia, Majorca, and Sicily. In imitation of French custom, the heir to the throne usually received a distinctive title; for example, Pedro IV in 1351 designated his oldest son as duke of Gerona, while Juan I created the title prince of Asturias in 1388 for the heir to Castile, and Carlos III of Navarre in 1423 named his grandson prince of Viana.

The succession in Granada remained within the Nasrid family, though the relationships among the several kings have only recently been clarified. Sons, brothers, uncles, and nephews occupied the throne, sometimes by virtue of designation by the previous ruler, most often as the result of a palace intrigue directed against the incumbent monarch. Conspiracy and rebellion were the most effective counterweights to the tendency to royal despotism.

The Royal Council

From the late thirteenth century, rulers were convinced by the increasing complexity of affairs of the need to create a council separate and distinct from the group of officials who ordinarily attended them; but the new council did not begin to receive definitive form until the late fourteenth century. After his humiliation at Portuguese hands in 1385, Juan I acceded to the request of the cortes that he establish a consejo real independent of his household (casa del rey) and of the judicial tribunal (audiencia) created by his father. The council was conceived as a body permanently representing the *cortes*, as it was to be composed of twelve persons chosen equally from the three estates. The townsmen expected that they would have the same opportunity as the prelates and magnates to advise the king regularly on major issues of policy; but within two years the four procurators representing the towns were replaced by four legists who were defenders of royal authority. The *consejo* was intended to deal with "*todos los fechos del regno,*" that is, with all aspects of government, and it became the principal organism of the administration. The number of members fluctuated continually throughout the fifteenth century, especially during the minorities and the ascendancy of Alvaro de Luna. Nearly every important prelate and magnate claimed the right to participate in its deliberations so that each might further his own interests. Thus the council became rather unwieldy and did not always act for the advantage of the crown. Only under Isabella the Catholic was it transformed into a truly effective instrument of royal power.

Similar organisms functioned in the other Christian states. Pedro IV and the later kings of Aragon continued to rely upon a council composed of the chief officers of administration. João I, however, in response to a request of the *cortes* in 1385 created a representative council including prelates, nobles, townsmen, and legists. The council helped to determine policy, to control the administration and to draft legislation.

The officials who ordinarily formed the king's court and household, performing a variety of public or private functions, were essentially the same as in the past; among them were the chancellor and notaries, the *mayordomo mayor*, the head of the household, the chamberlain, and the financial, judicial, and military officers. Some of these positions were held by distinguished prelates and magnates on an honorific basis. In the kingdom of Granada, the *wazir*, a man noted for his learning and culture, continued to serve as the chief royal counselor, and as a buffer between the king and the other household officers. But oftentimes the hostility of the nobility was directed at him rather than the king; consequently a *wazir* such as Ibn al-Khatib could easily and rapidly lose favor and be dismissed from office.

The Cortes

In the late medieval era the *cortes* as an instrument of representative government had a checkered history. In times of crisis rulers perceived its utility as a body theoretically representing the realm and capable of expressing popular support of royal policy. At the same time the *cortes* became aware of its strength and could impose some limits upon the king's freedom of action, but once the crisis passed its influence tended to wane. In the course of the fifteenth century the Castilian *cortes* declined rapidly, and the monarchy began to deal with it more and more arrogantly. Parliaments in the other kingdoms did not deteriorate to the same degree, but they all suffered from a malaise of the spirit.

Each of the peninsular realms possessed a parliament composed of three estates (*estados, estaments, brazos*). The Aragonese knights formed a fourth estate, but an attempt by the Catalan knights to separate themselves from the other nobility in 1388 encountered stiff opposition and failed. The kings of Aragon occasionally convened the estates of all their realms in *cortes generales*, and they also summoned parliaments in their overseas dependencies; at times they met with small groups of prelates, nobles, and townsmen in informal assemblies, called *parlaments*.

The number of prelates and nobles in attendance at any session of the *cortes* was relatively small. The Castilian ecclesiastical estate included about twenty persons, but in the other kingdoms, about ten to fifteen. While about twenty magnates and perhaps as many knights attended the Castilian *cortes*, these numbers would be halved elsewhere. Castilian prelates and nobles attended the *cortes* irregularly in the fifteenth century and ceased to come at all after 1538. As most of them claimed membership in the royal council, they were in daily association with the king and could directly influence his policy; furthermore as they were also exempt from taxes, there was little reason for them to participate in parliamentary sessions where the chief business was the voting of taxes. As a result the Castilian *cortes* of the fifteenth century frequently included only townsmen.

The number of Castilian towns represented also declined; forty-nine large and middle-sized towns were represented in 1391, but the number steadily decreased until by 1480 only seventeen were recognized as having a "vote in the *cortes*." One of the principal reasons for this decline was that many cities once directly dependent on the crown were now held in lordship by bishops or magnates who, henceforth, claimed to speak for their townsmen; these towns therefore were no longer summoned. Besides, many towns traditionally summoned viewed attendance as a burden and neglected to send representatives, and made little objection when the king no longer summoned them. The towns that continued to attend came to regard this as a cherished privilege, rather than a right or a duty, and were unwilling to share it with other cities. And yet decisions taken in the *cortes* were binding on all the towns, whether they were represented or not.

The decline in attendance suggests that the towns had come to see the *cortes* as an essentially passive body, whose sole purpose was to hear and approve policies and proposals presented by the crown and to give perfunctory consent to the request for taxes. Suárez Fernández, speaking harshly of the decadence of the *cortes* in the fifteenth century, emphasized that it lacked any truly representative character. Not only were few towns in attendance, but whole regions such as Galicia, Asturias, Extremadura, and the Basque provinces had no representation at all. Furthermore, the representatives acted solely on behalf of the urban oligarchy, leaving the small merchants, artisans, and peasants without any real voice.

In the other kingdoms the number of towns represented in the parliament remained steady or increased. About twenty attended in Aragon and Navarre, eighteen in Catalonia, and about thirty in Valencia.

In earlier times, town representatives (*procuradores*, or in Catalonia, syndics) seem to have been elected by the general assembly of citizens; but from the late fourteenth century they were either designated by the town council or chosen by lot from lists drawn up by the council, or else municipal officials served in rotation. Juan II and Enrique IV named the procurators to represent Castilian towns on various occasions, prompting the protest of the *cortes*, though in vain. Whatever the method of selection, the rank and file of the citizenry seem to have been excluded from participation. The Castilian *cortes* of 1430, for example, declared that no workingmen (*labradores*) or "men of humble condition" (*omnes de pequenna manera*) could serve as representatives; the number of procurators from each city was also limited to two. In the crown of Aragon each city usually sent one, though Barcelona, Zaragoza, and Valencia claimed the right to send five; but no matter how many representatives were sent, each city had only one vote. Their expenses were paid by the cities, but in 1422 Juan II of Castile agreed to pay them from his treasury; thereafter, as their independence certainly was compromised, they could be described as paid agents of the crown.

Representatives were expected to present letters of procuration giving them full or sufficient power (*plena potestas, poder bastante*) to act upon matters of service to the king and the kingdom. Martin the Humane's summons to the Catalan towns in 1405, requiring them to send syndics "endowed with full power" to consider "the conservation of the tranquil state of the principality," was typical. The town of Sahagún in 1402 authorized its procurators "to treat and ordain and consent to those matters that fulfill the service of our lord the king . . . which the procurators of the cities and towns . . . of his realms do and ordain and consent to and grant . . . on this account we will grant it, hold it and keep it firmly." Though it has often been said that the procurators carried an imperative mandate strictly limiting their actions to specific matters spelled out in advance by their towns, there is scant evidence of this. Extant letters of procuration are stated in general terms and indicate that the consent of the representatives given in the *cortes* would bind their constituents. Nor is there any evidence that the king gave the towns a detailed description of the business he proposed to transact thereby enabling them to prepare a narrowly defined mandate; the royal summons usually referred vaguely to the need to undertake certain affairs of service to God and the crown. It is true that Barcelona from 1387 onward, and later other Catalan towns, appointed a group of twenty-four, the so-called *vintiquatrena de cort* (eight patricians, eight merchants, four artisans, and four workingmen) to maintain continuing contact with their syndics and to counsel them while the *corts* was in session.

The *cortes* met fairly often, usually about every two or three years, during the late fourteenth and early fifteenth centuries. In response to a request of the *cortes* of 1385, João I convened annual parliaments for several years, but it was generally found that annual sessions were too burdensome for everyone. In the later fifteenth century, meetings in all the kingdoms were held irregularly. The principal cities continued to serve as the usual locale. Sessions lasted weeks or months and, in some instances in the crown of Aragon, even a year or more; but lengthy meetings seldom accomplished anything of importance and frequently were marked by quarreling between the king and the estates or among the estates themselves.

At the opening session, with the prelates seated to the right of the king, the nobles to the left, and the townsmen directly in front, the king or one of his lieutenants pronounced a discourse setting forth the reasons for convocation. The continued absence of Alfonso V in

Naples posed a constitutional problem for the Aragonese *cortes*, who protested that no valid assembly could be held without him; but having made the objection, the assembly then agreed to proceed with the business at hand. A prelate (in Castile, the archbishop of Toledo; in Catalonia, the archbishop of Tarragona), a noble (the lord of Lara in Castile; the lord of Moncada in Catalonia), and a townsman (from Burgos, Zaragoza, Barcelona, or Lisbon) responded to the royal address. In general they spoke their minds freely, though usually prefacing any strong dissent or criticism with some expression of respect for the king's majesty. Toledo persistently challenged Burgos's claim to speak on behalf of the assembled Castilian towns, but the issue was usually resolved as it had been in 1348 when Alfonso XI declared that Burgos should speak, as he spoke for Toledo.

Following the opening session, the powers given to the urban representatives were verified by *habilitadores* appointed for the purpose. In Catalonia and the other states of the crown of Aragon each estate chose a small number of *tractadors* to meet with the king's counselors to consider the means of dealing with the business before the assembly. The deliberations of the Catalan and Aragonese *cortes* are known in some detail because many of the records kept have survived, but the internal workings of the Castilian *cortes* are illuminated only by occasional references in the chronicles. The *cuadernos* drawn up at the conclusion of the assembly record royal responses to petitions or ordinances enacted, but they do not ordinarily describe the manner in which the estates conducted their affairs.

The competence of the *cortes*, as the Castilian assembly of 1419 pointed out, extended to those "general and difficult matters" which the king had to resolve. These included the recognition of a new king or the heir to the throne or the regulation of a royal minority. The Portuguese estates assembled in 1385 elected João I as king, and parliaments in Aragon and Catalonia designated the commission that elected Fernando de Antequera. The Castilian and Portuguese *cortes* also participated in discussions concerning the regencies for Enrique III, Juan II, and Afonso V. Occasionally they were also called upon to swear to uphold treaties concluded by the king.

The right of the Catalan *corts* to share in the legislative function had been guaranteed by Pedro III in 1283. The fifteenth-century jurist Jaume Callis restated the law saying, "the lord king, count of Barcelona, cannot make any constitution or statute in Catalonia without the approval and consent of the prelates, barons, knights and citizens of Catalonia, the greater and wiser part of those summoned." For the same reason he declared that the principle "what pleases the prince has the force of law" was limited in Catalonia. "The king in his chamber can issue a pragmatic if it pleases him, provided that it does not contradict the general constitutions of Catalonia . . . because what is enacted by the *corts* in a general assembly cannot be revoked except by a general assembly" (Both quotations from Callis are cited by F. E. de Tejada, *Las doctrinas políticas en la Cataluña medieval*, 183–184). A plan for the codification of the many laws enacted by the Catalan *corts* was approved in 1413. Similarly the compilation of the usages, observances, *fueros*, and *actos de corte* promulgated by the Aragonese parliament was authorized in 1427. In the preamble to his *amejoramiento* of the *Fuero general de Navarra* in 1418, Carlos III declared that as his predecessors had done, so he too "had enacted some *fueros* and ordinances with the consent of the three estates of the realm."

The bulk of the laws enacted in the Castilian *cortes* are in the form of ordinances containing royal responses to petitions presented by the townsmen, though occasionally also by the nobles and prelates. In addition, the crown promulgated ordinances regulating the administration of justice, the chancery, military obligations, and the like, with the counsel and consent of the *cortes*, no major ordinance was enacted in the fifteenth century, however, and that may be, as Suárez Fernández pointed out, a sign of decadence in the institution. The crown tended to issue charters contradicting the enactments of the *cortes*, prompting the assembly of 1379 to demand that the king declare "that what is done by the *cortes* or by *ayuntamientos* cannot be undone by such charters, but only by the *cortes*" (*CLC*, II, 299). Though he responded vaguely at the time, Juan I pledged in the *cortes* of 1387 that no charter contrary to the law was to be obeyed and that "valid *fueros* and laws and ordinances not revoked by others are not to be prejudiced except by ordinances made in the *cortes*" (*CLC*, II, 371). Yet the right of the Castilian *cortes* to share in legislation was always rather tenuous, as a pragmatic sanction issued by Juan II in 1427 illustrates: "By my own action and absolute royal power (*de mi propio motu . . . e poderio real absoluto*) I establish . . . by this my charter which I wish to be held and kept as law and to have the force of law, just as if it had been enacted in *cortes*" (*MHDE*, II, 219). In effect, while acknowledging the legal force of the ordinances enacted in the *cortes*, he obviously believed that he could legislate without that body, and both he and his son did so with increasing frequency. The Portuguese *cortes* also protested against the derogation of ordinances enacted in the *cortes*, but Afonso V declared in 1451 that he would alter the laws made in the *cortes* "whenever the case required it."

From the king's point of view the most important activity of the *cortes* was the granting of a subsidy. His obligation to ask consent before levying any extraordinary tax was well recognized, though not always observed. The Castilian *cortes* in 1391, for example, asked the regents "not to levy any tribute other than that granted by the *cortes*," and two years later they asked that no tax be levied "unless the three estates are first summoned and assembled." The Catalan *corts* usually emphasized that the subsidy (*donatiu*) was granted without prejudice to their liberties and not as an obligation, but out of their own generosity. They also reserved the concession of the tax until the king answered their petitions. The money was usually granted for a specific term and purpose, as for example, in 1407 when the Castilian *cortes* asked the regents to swear that the subsidy "would not be spent on anything other than this war" against the Moors; obviously the money was not always used as intended. Although the assembly often haggled over the amount requested, protesting the poverty of the people, some kind of grant was always forthcoming. Juan I showed his accounts to the Castilian *cortes* in 1386 in justification of his request for funds, and in the following year the assembly demanded to see them. Complaints of abuses by tax collectors prompted the *cortes* of 1386 to appoint officials to receive and expend the tax voted to the crown, but this important step toward exercising control over royal finance was never developed beyond this point. In the fifteenth century Juan II and Enrique IV were not especially scrupulous about asking consent before collecting taxes or using the money for purposes other than those for which it was granted.

In Catalonia, on the other hand, the collection and expenditure of taxes voted by the *corts* was entirely under the control of the *Diputació del General* or *Generalitat*. Originating at the end of the thirteenth century, this body, composed of three deputies, one for each estate, and three auditors, had developed into a permanent deputation of the *corts*, with a fixed residence in Barcelona. Through its control of taxes it enjoyed great power and influence and was able to raise armies and organize fleets for the service of the crown. But in the fifteenth century, under the Trastámaras, the *Generalitat* also assumed the role of defender of Catalan liberties. Fernando I, in the *corts* of 1413, recognized the right of the *Generalitat*, as an organ permanently representing the *corts* and the community, to guard the observance of the constitutions, usages, *capitols de cort*, and other laws of the principality; should he violate them, it could remonstrate with him. In the reign of Juan II, the *Generalitat* used its authority to direct the rebellion against him. On the request of the *corts* in 1460 the deputies formed a council with members of the municipal government of Barcelona to represent the principality in seeking redress of grievances. From then until the king triumphed in 1472 the council effectively governed Catalonia, raising taxes, organizing armies, and maintaining the struggle against him.

The *cortes* of Zaragoza in 1412 established an Aragonese *Diputación del reyno*, consisting of eight deputies, two from each of the four estates to control the collection and disbursement of taxes; in 1461 it was entrusted with responsibility for guarding against violations of the law by royal officials. A *Diputació* with similar functions was created in Valencia in 1419 with six members, two from each estate. The Navarrese *Diputación* originated in the fifteenth century but did not become a permanent body with a definitive organization until 1501.

Territorial Administration

Territorial administration changed little in the late Middle Ages, save for the growth of lordships exempt from the jurisdiction of royal officials. Castile continued to be divided into several large areas, each administered by an *adelantado mayor* or *merino mayor*, whose functions were primarily judicial; the *adelantado mayor de la frontera* in charge of Andalusia and his counterpart in Murcia, who were usually great lords, were also responsible for military defense; in Murcia the Fajardo family obtained what amounted to an hereditary right to the office. Portugal was divided into similar circumscriptions, as was Navarre; to the five *merindades* formed in the fourteenth century (Pamplona, Tudela, Estella, Sangüesa, and Ultrapuertos), Carlos III added Olite in 1407.

In the crown of Aragon the office of lieutenant-general took on a nearly permanent character because of the prolonged absence of Alfonso V, who delegated his wife Maria or his brother Juan to act in his stead, with essentially viceregal authority. In each of the constituent states the king was usually represented by a governor-general. Aside from this, Aragon proper was divided into six administrative districts (Zaragoza, Huesca, Jaca, Sobrarbe, Exea, and Tarazona), each under a *sobrejuntero*, in Catalonia there were fourteen vicariates (Rousillon, Cerdagne, Pallars, Manresa, Osona, Gerona, Barcelona, Vilafranca, Cervera, Tárrega, Lérida, Montblanch, Tarragona, and Tortosa), and two on Majorca. In the kingdom of Valencia there were four *governacions* (Valencia, Játiva, Castellón, and Orihuela) each administered by a *portant-veus* or lieutenant of the governor-general.

An extraordinary increase in the number and extent of lordships held by prelates, magnates, and military Orders took place in the late medieval centuries. Despite continued opposition to the alienation of the royal domain and the formation of new lordships, and attempts to recover royal lands already given away, at the close of the fifteenth century about two-thirds of each of the realms was held in lordship. The growth of lordships resulted to a very great degree from the king's need to win and retain the support of the nobility, but as a consequence the resources of the crown were greatly depleted. Not only were rural estates alienated, but even more importantly so were towns long dependent directly upon the monarchy; the capacity of the nobility to resist royal authority therefore was considerably enhanced, and their appetite for additional concessions became insatiable. The process continued throughout the fifteenth century, even though Juan II in the *cortes* of 1442 declared that, if he alienated any place without reason and without the consent of the realm, the people would be justified in resisting their new lord. The nature of a lordship was indicated in a royal charter of 1453 conferring on the widow of Alvaro de Luna "in hereditary right, for ever and ever, the towns . . . with their fortresses, lands, justice, civil and criminal jurisdiction, high and low justice, *merum et mixtum imperium*, rents, tributes and rights belonging to the lordship of those places."

João I of Portugal displayed great generosity in ceding to his supporters many of the estates confiscated from his enemies. Fernão Lopes declared that the constable Nun'Alvares Pereira was rewarded so fully for his services to the new dynasty that "he held half the kingdom"; this obviously was an exaggeration, but he did hold the counties of Ourém, Barcelos, and Arraiolos as well as eighteen cities and towns. All this was inherited by his daughter and her husband, Afonso, the first duke of Bragança, a bastard son of the king. João I also gave substantial lordships to his sons.

From time to time the crown was able to recover some of the lands given away, or to acquire others by marriage or inheritance. Thus Alfonso XI acquired Alava in 1332, and Juan I obtained the lordship of Vizcaya, long held by the great family of Haro. The kings of Aragon recovered the lordship of Albarracín on the eastern frontier next to Castile in 1365, and the county of Urgel in 1433. João I, in order not to reduce the monarchy to a state of permanent penury and weakness, planned to repossess many of the crown lands alienated early in his reign, but it was left to his son, Duarte, to promulgate the so-called *lei mental*, the law his father had in mind, on April 8, 1434. This declared that lands granted by the crown were indivisible and transmissible by hereditary right to the first-born male heir, and in default of such an heir, should escheat to the crown. Nevertheless, Afonso V proved to be as prodigal in giving away royal lands as his Castilian contemporary Enrique IV, and the task of recovering alienated crown lands was left to João II and Ferdinand and Isabella to carry out.

Little can be added to what has already been said in a previous chapter concerning the territorial administration of the kingdom of Granada. There are even fewer materials available for the fifteenth century, though it seems that the magnates held large estates and towns in lordship in much the same way as their neighbors in Castile.

The Municipalities

Two major changes in municipal government had taken place in the thirteenth and early fourteenth centuries. On the one hand, the urban aristocracy of wealthy merchants, bankers, landowners, and speculators gained effective control of the government; but at the same time the crown began to intervene readily, often by reserving the right to appoint members of the municipal council (*ayuntamiento, consell, cabildo*), or by dispatching special officials (*corregidores*) with authority to override any decision of the council. The council, numbering six, eight, twelve, or twenty-four (for example, *los veinticuatro* of Seville), replaced the old popular assembly of citizens.

Innumerable disturbances in the towns in the later medieval centuries eventually led to a major reform in the system of choosing town officials. As João I noted, the electoral system encouraged the formation of factions that used pressure and force to secure the election of unworthy persons, thereby touching off riots and tumults. He and other rulers came to realize the need to put an end to urban discord and dissension. The solution adopted in all the Christian states was the process known as *insaculación*, a form of drawing lots. The names of persons from each social class considered suitable for public office were recorded; when offices had to be filled, the names of eligible candidates were jotted on slips of paper and placed in bags (*saco*), one for each class; an appropriate number of names was then drawn from each bag to fill the available positions. The purpose of this system was to eliminate the party struggles so characteristic of the past, and, by giving all classes a share in government, to end the domination of the urban oligarchies. João I in 1391 ordered all the Portuguese towns to adopt the process. In Aragon, where experience showed, according to Alfonso V, that the "process of the sack" helped to avert sedition, discord, and destruction, it was adopted at Játiva in 1427, Zaragoza in 1442, and Gerona in 1457.

The conflict between classes was perhaps nowhere more bitter than in Barcelona. The ruling oligarchy of bankers, capitalists, speculators, and other extremely wealthy men, known collectively as the *biga*, came under attack from a number of leading merchants who were supported by the mass of craftsmen and workers. The *busca*, as the popular party was called, charged the oligarchs with abuse of power, the ruination of municipal finances, and the like. A syndicate (*sindicat dels tres-estaments*) uniting merchants, artisans, and workers, formed to exert political pressure on the oligarchs, was recognized by Alfonso V in 1453. Two years later the governor-general of Catalonia, acting on the king's orders and in response to the demands of the syndicate, promulgated a general reform of the city government. The *Consell de cent* was increased to 128 members (*jurats*), 32 from each *estament* or class, namely, the patricians (*ciutadans honrats*), merchants, artisans, and workers. A smaller commission known as the *trentenari*, composed of eight members from each class, acted as a standing deputation of the *Consell* and watched over the activities of the executive board of five *consellers*. The five, who were chosen annually by twelve electors drawn equally from the *estaments*, included two patricians, one merchant, one artisan, and one worker. Ferdinand the Catholic, in 1498, introduced *insaculación* for the election of all these officials. The reform helped to bring internal peace to the city by allowing all classes a voice in public affairs.

Similar unrest had prompted Fernando I to reform the government of Zaragoza in 1414. In place of a town council (*cabildo*), consisting of twelve *jurados* elected from the wards of the city, there would be five *jurados* chosen indirectly to represent five classes based on income. The king directly appointed the *zalmedina* or chief judge and a number of subordinate officials.

The Castilian kings, from the time of Alfonso XI, appointed the *regidores* in groups of six, eight, and so on, who tended to supplant the larger municipal council. Occasionally, the king also appointed the *alcaldes* or magistrates and the *alguacil* or constable. In Madrid, for example, the *regidores* nominated four persons for the office of *alcalde* and two for *alguacil*; the king chose two of the former and one of the latter. Juan I reminded the people of Seville to observe the ordinances concerning the election of their *alcaldes*; otherwise, he threatened to appoint them himself as Alfonso XI had done. The *alcaldes* apparently were remiss in fulfilling their duties as numerous complaints against them indicate. Burgos complained, for example, in 1395 that its *alcaldes* were not hearing pleas at the fixed hours of the day but were attending to their own affairs; in 1432 Juan II had to require them to reside in the city for at least six months. Friction between *regidores* named by the king or by the lord of a town and the officials elected by the citizens was common; for example, the *regidores* of Sepúlveda ("who, on my behalf, are to supervise and regulate the affairs of the council") appointed by Leonor of Navarre, who held the town in lordship, complained in 1397 that the *alcaldes* and other officials were meeting in council without them. A communal revolt, soon after, resulted in the overthrow of the *regidores*, but by 1401 Leonor regained control and appointed six of them, four from the ranks of the local aristocracy of knights and squires and two from the tax-paying citizens (*pecheros*).

When internal disorder became unmanageable, the crown sent a *corregidor* to the city. Enrique III reportedly sent *corregidores* to all the cities of his realm which, consequently, feared him greatly. Killings, robberies, burnings, and similar outrages perpetrated by urban factions caused Juan II to send *corregidores* to restore order, but often they abused their authority so much as to create greater division in the city than before. The *corregidores* were decidedly unpopular because they entirely supplanted all other municipal officials and, as representatives of royal power, were not especially concerned to preserve the rights and privileges contained in municipal *fueros*. The *cortes* of 1419 asked that *corregidores* be required to remain in the city for fifty days after the termination of their appointment to answer charges that might be brought against them. The *cortes* of 1435 demanded that they be sent only to those cities which asked for them, that they be natives of the region, that they serve for only one year, and that the king, rather than the city, pay their salaries. Abuses of authority by the *corregidores* were commonplace during the turbulent reigns of Juan II and Enrique IV, but Ferdinand and Isabella transformed them into effective instruments for controlling the towns.

After Alfonso XI reached his majority the *hermandades* or associations of towns that had been formed in times of crisis to defend municipal liberties were dissolved. Enrique II revived the *hermandad* in 1370 as a means of extending his rule throughout the kingdom of Castile, but it was only after Aljubarrota that Juan I decided to make significant use of it. At the *cortes* in 1386 he reorganized it, requiring each city to maintain a force of cavalry and infantry to pursue criminals and malefactors. The organization subsequently fell into desuetude, but it was revived again in the time of Juan II and Enrique IV. The insistent demands of the *cortes* that the *hermandad* be maintained reflect the faith which the towns had in its efficacy as a means of preserving law and order. Ferdinand and Isabella revived it in 1474 as the *Santa Hermandad*, and in their hands it became a truly effective body.

The absence of documentation makes it impossible to detect significant changes in the municipal administration of the kingdom of Granada. The names of a number of officials are known, and one can surmise that they continued to have essentially the same responsibilities as in the past.

The Law and the Administration of Justice

In the later Middle Ages the expansion of royal law over the entire territory of the state continued without letup. The need to systematize the abundance of charters, privileges, ordinances, and constitutions in which the law was embodied was recognized and, to some extent, met.

In Castile the basic legal texts were the *Ordenamiento de Alcalá* and the *Siete Partidas*, whose influence grew steadily. But there were also numerous ordinances issued in the *cortes*; these, if they were to have any real utility, had to be set in some sort of topical arrangement. Both Juan II and Enrique IV, in response to the request of the *cortes*, promised to carry out the task, but, as with so many other things, nothing was done until Ferdinand and Isabella came to power.

Responding to a similar need, João I initiated work on a compilation of Portuguese law, but it was not completed until 1446 during the minority of Afonso V. Known as the *Ordenações Afonsinas*, it was divided into five books dealing with the crown, the church, the nobility, civil law, and penal law.

The *Fuero general de Navarra* and the *amejoramientos* promulgated by Philip of Evreux in 1330 and by Carlos III in 1418, together with local *fueros*, constituted the essential body of Navarrese law. The *Fueros de Aragón* dating from 1247 continued in vigor, but new books were added, including the laws enacted by Pedro IV, Juan I, and Martin in the *cortes* down to 1404. The jurists also elaborated a substantial body of commentary and interpretation of the *Fueros*; around 1361, for example, Jacopo del Hospital published his *Observantiae regni Aragonum*, giving a resumé and exposition of each title in the *Fueros*. A century later, in 1437, the *justicia*, Martín Díez de Aux, prompted by the request of the *cortes* of 1427, published a collection of the usages, customs, ordinances, and acts of the *cortes*, entitled *Observantiae Consuetudinesque regni Aragoniae*. The *Constitucions de Cathalunya*, including the usages, constitutions, *capitols*, and *actes de corts*, was published after the *corts* of 1413 asked Fernando I to order the compilation and translation of all the dispersed sources of Catalan law. Many distinguished jurists also wrote commentaries on the law; Jaume Callis (d. 1434), for example, wrote a treatise on the *corts* entitled *Curiarum extravagatorium rerum* and another on royal finance, *Margarita fisci*; Tomas Mieres, around 1445 published his *Apparatus super Constitutionibus Curiarum generalium Cathalonie*.

Several Hispano-Muslim legal texts have come down to us, including notarial formulae and a collection of legal opinions compiled by Ibn Asim (d. 1452). In addition, the fourteenth-century *Leyes de moros* and the *Suma de los principales mandamientos y devedamientos de la ley y la sunna*, composed in 1462 by Isa Jabir, contain Muslim law in the Castilian language for the use of the *mudéjares*.

The principal innovation in the administration of justice was the establishment of the Castilian *audiencia* by Enrique II in 1371. A reorganization of the earlier *tribunal de corte*, it was intended to serve as the chief royal court, but as it often sat in the rooms of the chancery it was usually called in the fifteenth century the *chancillería*. The *audiencia* consisted of a number of auditors (*oidores*) who rendered justice in the king's name and from whose sentences no appeal was permitted; also several *alcaldes de corte* were assigned to hear suits from specific regions where they had their origins (for example, Castile, León, Extremadura, Toledo, Andalusia), and an *alcalde de los fijos-dalgo* had jurisdiction over pleas involving the nobles. The composition of the *audiencia* varied over the years, and its utility was lessened by the fact that it did not have a permanent residence. Juan I tried to remedy this in 1387 by providing that sessions should be held at certain fixed places in the heart of the realm, easily accessible to everyone (at Madrid, Alcalá de Henares, Olmedo, Medina del Campo); but even that measure was not executed. The tribunal was settled at Segovia in 1390 for a short time, but in 1442 Juan II declared that it should sit at Valladolid; there, in the reign of Ferdinand and Isabella, it eventually found a permanent residence. In Portugal the *Casa de Justiça da Corte*, presided over by a *regedor e governador*, had essentially the same functions, but it also followed the king.

The *justicia*, appointed by the king from the ranks of the knights, continued to be the supreme judge in the kingdom of Aragon. He sat in judgment of suits among members of the nobility or between the king and the nobles, and declared what the law was, in case of doubt or dispute; he could also prevent other judges from proceeding with a trial if it was alleged that the process was contrary to the *fueros*. Anyone believing that a judge unjustly threatened his life, property, or rights, could appeal to the *justicia* to suspend a trial or the execution of a sentence. The appellant gave surety (*firma de directo*) that, after the justicia had completed his inquiry, he would accept his sentence and if necessary indemnify his opponent for all damages resulting from an unjust charge. Similarly, anyone fearing violence at the hands of judges or other agents of the court could appeal to the protection of the *justicia*; if the appellant was already in prison the *justicia* could remove him to another prison where he could be safeguarded until his case was resolved. This process was known as *manifestación*.

For his own delinquencies the *justicia* was answerable to the *cortes*, and in 1390 the *cortes* named four inquisitors, one for each *brazo*, to inquire into alleged abuses. The *cortes* in 1461 declared that a commission of this sort should be chosen annually. The *justicia* held office for life and was removable only by the joint action of the king and the *cortes*, but Alfonso V forced Juan Ximénez Cerdán to renounce the office in 1420, and in 1439 he ousted Martín Díez de Aux on the charge of corruption. In spite of these blows, the character of the office remained essentially the same, and the *cortes* undertook to re-affirm its traditional jurisdiction.

The lesser courts continued to function much as before, and the procedures adopted from Roman law were more widely used. In general there was a tendency for local law to give way to royal terri-torial law. In the kingdom of Granada, the *qadi* apparently enjoyed the prestige anciently associated with his office and was expected to be a man of virtue, one who knew religious law and the traditions of Islam and would judge prudently.

Financial Administration

As financial administration in all the kingdoms tended to be chaotic, the kings of Castile and Navarre attempted some reforms. In Castile, royal accountants or *contadores mayores* were given primary respon-sibility in this area. In the reign of Juan II two *contadores mayores de hacienda* were charged with the administration of the king's ordinary revenues, their collection and disbursement, the keeping of the books in which they were recorded (*libros de asiento*) and those books in which alienated income was noted (*libros de lo salvado*). Two other *contadores mayores de cuentas* were responsible for keeping the king's accounts; they also had judicial authority in litigation involving these matters. From 1436 onward, they were supposed to reside permanently in Valladolid in the *Casa de las Cuentas*. As with so many other insti-tutions, Ferdinand and Isabella found it necessary to reform this one.

Carlos II of Navarre in 1365 founded the *Cámara de Complos*, or chamber of accounts, whose four auditors had authority to inquire into all matters touching royal revenue and to act in a judicial capacity in all pertinent disputes. In Aragon the *mestre racional* continued to function as the chief financial officer of the crown, but the collection and disbursement of the sums voted by the parliament was controlled by the *Diputación* or *Generalitat*. On the local level there were fre-quent protests of extortion and other abuses by tax collectors and tax farmers.

Royal financial needs in an age of exceptional luxury, peninsular warfare, and overseas expansion were extraordinary, though the sources of income tended to be narrow. The exemption of the clergy and nobility from most taxes lessened the base of taxable wealth, and alienations deprived the king of many traditional types of revenue, including rents and services from estates on the royal domain. For other sources of income, the crown depended upon land taxes, hospitality, profits from mines and salt pits, *moneda forera* or *monedatge*, judicial fines, chancery fees, *tercias reales*, tolls, *servicio y montazgo*, customs duties, sales taxes, and subsidies voted by the *cortes*. The *alcabala*, a sales tax exploited by Alfonso XI at the rate of five per cent, was increased to ten per cent, and was levied annually without authorization by the *cortes*. The *sisa*, a tribute obtained by giving the consumer less weight or quantity than he paid for, with the balance reserved for the treasury, was an extremely unpopular tax. Pedro IV prohibited it in 1372, but it reappeared in Aragon in 1429. Despite an earlier ban in Castile, it continued to be levied there as well.

Customs duties levied at frontier posts were one of the most lucrative sources of royal income. Enrique III and Juan II established a network of customs houses along the frontiers of Aragon and Navarre to control the flow of merchandise. In Aragon, in the fifteenth century, there were 179 customs houses (*tablas*), each directed by a collector (*cullidor*) who was responsible to a regional supervisor (*sobrecullidor*). In both Aragon and Catalonia the subsidies voted by the *cortes* were often raised from the customs, and their collection and eventual disbursement were controlled by the *Diputación* or the *Generalitat*. For this reason, customs duties were known as *generalidades* or *drets de la generalitat*. At other times the subsidies were apportioned among households (*fogatge*). In Castile the *servicios* authorized by the *cortes* were levied upon the towns, where registers (*padrones*) were drawn up to record the names of those who were subject to payment. Most often the money was collected by tax farmers (*arrendadores*), and there were frequent outcries from those who claimed exemption for one reason or another. The *cortes* in 1387 attempted to impose a tax upon everyone, excusing no one, but the nobles and clergy protested, and the king eventually had to resort to other means.

The most common means of obtaining money in emergency was the forced loan (*emprestito*): for example, in 1382 Juan I wrote to several citizens of Murcia telling them that he had great need of money because he had expended all his income; having decided to impose an *emprestito*, he specified the sums he expected each one to contribute, but although he promised repayment from the *moneda* or *alcabala* to be collected in the next year, he made no pledge to pay interest. The *Diputación* in Aragon and the *Generalitat* in Catalonia obtained loans, promising to pay interest and guaranteeing repayment from the anticipated future income from customs duties or other sources; as the lender was repaid by means of a *censo* or rent from this income, such loans were called *censales* (or *violaris*). Similar in character were the Castilian *juros*, granted for life or in perpetuity as repayment of debts contracted by the crown; these concessions became so numerous in the fifteenth century as to bring the monarchy to the verge of financial disaster.

The payment of the annual tribute to Castile was the principal factor in the finances of the kingdom of Granada. Ibn al-Khatib estimated the annual revenue at about 560,000 *dinars* in the middle of the fourteenth century, while at the time of the Christian conquest a hundred years later, it was estimated at about one million silver *reales*. One-fourth or one-fifth of the total revenue was usually payable as tribute to Castile. Impositions on landed property, vineyards, livestock, agricultural production, customs duties, and the poll tax were the chief sources of revenue.

Military Organization

In the late Middle Ages military organization was somewhat more refined and disciplined than in the past. Pedro IV had created the post of captain-general in 1344, but in the western kingdoms command of the armies, under French influence, was entrusted to a constable. João I owed his throne in large measure to his constable, Nun'Alvares Pereira; Juan I introduced the office into Castile in 1382, but it was Alvaro de Luna who made it a position of exceptional importance; Navarre adopted it in 1430. While the constable was commander-in-chief under the king, the defense of the Granadan and Murcian frontiers continued to be the major charge of the *adelantados de la frontera*. They were aided by the military Orders who often supplied castellans (*alcaide, castlán*) and garrisons for many of the principal fortresses. By the close of the medieval era, as armies moved into battle, they were divided into major divisions called *batallas* and these in turn were subdivided into smaller units (*quadrillas*, each commanded by a *quadrillero*). When the army was *en marche, adalids* were appointed to direct the movement of troops along the most suitable route and to locate campsites.

Most of the magnates served as heavily armed cavalry and constituted a major element in the army. But there were also lightly armed cavalry (*jinetes*) whose importance was sometimes much greater, in that they were able to move with the greatest rapidity to strike the enemy when he least expected it. Infantry forces (*peones, omes a pie*) enjoyed a role of ever-increasing importance as the medieval centuries drew to a close; they included archers, lancers, and *ballesteros* or crossbowmen whose accuracy often wreaked havoc among the enemy.

The magnates continued to serve in fulfillment of their pledge of vassalage to the crown and in return for fiefs in Catalonia or for *soldadas*, sums paid them from the royal treasury, in the western kingdoms. Many vassals rendering military service received from their lords an *acostamiento*, that is, food, clothing, and lodging. After the battle of Aljubarrota, Juan I attempted to give new importance to the traditional obligations of military service, by requiring all males between the ages of 20 and 60, both clerics and laymen, to be armed with specific equipment in accordance with their income and to be prepared for periodic reviews (*alarde*). This was the first serious attempt to establish a permanent military force of citizens ready at all times to answer the royal summons to war.

Undoubtedly the most significant change in the art of war in the later Middle Ages was the greater use of gunpowder. Its employment rendered all men, no matter how heavily armed, quite vulnerable and also made possible the destruction of castle walls hitherto considered impregnable. Rudimentary cannons were employed in the thirteenth-century sieges of Niebla and Algeciras, but their effectiveness was quite limited; by the fifteenth century, however, Fernando I made use of cannon with great success in the siege of Balaguer. Catapults and mangonels were still used as types of artillery; siege towers made of wood were pushed up against castle walls to enable troops to gain entrance, and attempts also were made to undermine the walls. Artillerymen and sappers consequently played a major role in late medieval military operations.

Naval forces figured prominently in the wars of the late Middle Ages. Castilian and Portuguese fleets frequently engaged one another in combat off Lisbon and Seville, and encounters between Christian and Muslim fleets in the straits were common. Castile, in addition, sent ships to aid the French against England in the Hundred Years' War. The Catalan navy had grown steadily in size and importance since the overseas expansion of the thirteenth century, and the reconstruction of the shipyards at Barcelona in the late fourteenth century favored continued development. But the constant wars with Genoa took a significant toll, and Alfonso V's defeat and capture by the Genoese in the naval battle of Ponza emphasized Catalan naval decline.

Types of ships used included sailing vessels of heavy tonnage (*naos, naus*), capable of carrying large numbers of troops and strong enough to ram smaller ships and to wreck them. Galleys (*galeras, uixers*) were even more valuable because they were not dependent on the wind for mobility.

CHAPTER 24

Society and the Economy, 1369–1479

The Social Structure

In the last century of the medieval era there were no substantial external additions to the peninsular population nor were there vast colonizing movements as in the past. The frontiers remained comparatively stable, and the number of those uprooted by the reconquest was slight, though there seems to have been a fairly steady emigration of Muslims to North Africa. But the days when thousands of Berbers crossed the straits to settle in the peninsula were over. Colonies of foreign merchants were found in all the principal cities, but most had originated and had enjoyed their greatest growth in the previous century. The indigenous population suffered a precipitate decline in the middle of the fourteenth century as a result of the Black Death, and the recurrence of plague, especially in Catalonia, retarded the process of recovery. The consequent economic hardship encouraged hostility between classes and particularly toward the Jews.

The population grew, but the rate of growth apparently was less than that for northern Europe. The statistical evidence consists of several censuses taken for tax purposes in the crown of Aragon in the late fourteenth and fifteenth centuries and a census of 1482 for Castile. One can only guess the size of the population in Portugal and Granada. The Castilian census of 1482 listed 1,500,000 households or about seven to eight million people, an increase of less than 100 per cent over the estimated population of the middle of the thirteenth century, and well below the rise of 200 per cent in the rest of Europe. The largest numbers were concentrated in Andalusia, especially in the cities. Seville counted 75,000 inhabitants, Córdoba, 35,000, and Murcia, 25,000. Several other towns such as Toledo, Valladolid, and

Medina del Campo had substantial numbers ranging from 20,000 to 25,000.

The impact of the pestilence was more evident in the crown of Aragon, particularly in Catalonia, where the population dropped from 350,000 to 270,000 between 1378 and 1497. The decline was also evident in cities. Barcelona in the course of the century fell from 38,000 people to 20,000. In Valencia, on the other hand, the total at the close of the fourteenth century was about 300,000, and the city of Valencia rose from 40,000 in 1418 to 75,000 in 1483. Aragon had about 200,000 people in 1429 and 250,000 in 1496; about 20,000 lived in the city of Zaragoza. The population of Majorca seems to have remained stable at about 50,000. The total for the crown of Aragon then would be about 870,000 at the end of the fifteenth century. Navarre had about 100,000 inhabitants, Portugal perhaps a million, and Granada perhaps 300,000. Taking all these figures together, the population of the peninsula at the close of the medieval era was probably about nine or ten million.

The number and condition of the *mudéjares* probably changed very little in the last century of the medieval era, because the Christians conquered few new areas and made no attempt at wholesale conversion or expulsion of the Muslims. It is true that persons living on the frontier occasionally converted from one religion to another and sometimes back again for reasons of convenience, but these were exceptions. The *mudéjares* were found mainly in the southern sections of the peninsula, in the Algarve, Andalusia, Murcia, Valencia, lower Aragon, and the Balearic Islands. Restrictive legislation received new emphasis from Catalina de Lancaster, regent for Juan II of Castile, who made a serious effort to enforce the law and to make it more stringent. Muslims were required to wear a bright yellow capuche with a blue moon on the right shoulder and, in the towns, to live in enclosures (*morerías*), thus limiting their contact with Christians; nor could they hold public office, engage in trade, or in various professions. Most of them, however, were settled in rural areas, and many of them were held as slaves. Martin of Aragon also enacted legislation intended to restrict their freedom of movement or their emigration from his kingdom; moreover, he forbade any public manifestation of the Muslim religion and would not allow the muezzin to summon the faithful to prayer. He also curtailed their judicial autonomy by ordering their lawsuits to be heard by royal judges. The Council of Tortosa in 1429 repeated all the traditional ecclesiastical laws against Muslims and Jews, and the *cortes* frequently expressed its hostility toward non-Christians. By the time of Enrique IV, however, the Castilian laws against the *mudéjares* were allowed to lapse, while the king displayed an affinity for Muslim dress and surrounded himself with a Moorish guard. Enríquez del Castillo mentioned that the nobility, in their hostility to the king seized upon this and piously expressed their shock at his scandalous behavior: "In offense against the Christian religion, his highness ordinarily has with him a band of Moorish infidels, enemies of the holy Catholic faith, who rape Christian women and commit many other grave injuries, without being punished" (*Crónica*, 64). They eventually used this as one pretext for his deposition. A certain cultural assimilation resulting from the coexistence of Christians and Moors is illustrated by the *mudéjar* laws written in Castilian and other literary remains using Arabic script but the Romance languages.

The Jews of Spain, who had always encountered greater enmity than the *mudéjares*, entered upon their final agony in 1391, when religious tolerance, so long practiced in the peninsula, was strained to the breaking point. The general upheaval of society resulting from the plague, the civil wars and their attendant destruction, the oppression by the nobility, and economic stagnation, encouraged a spirit of despair and misery among the people, who gladly vented their frustrations upon the scapegoat, the Jews. Stirred by the preaching of the archdeacon of Ecija, Fernando Martínez, the mob plundered and burned the Jewish community of Seville in June 1391; from thence the destruction spread rapidly to the other towns of Andalusia, Valencia, Aragon, Catalonia, and the Balearic Islands. Aside from the destruction of property and of human life, the massacres forced many to flee to Granada or to Portugal, or else to save themselves by converting to Christianity. The conversions following the pogroms of 1391 marked a decisive turning point in the history of Hispanic Jewry, but it is difficult to determine the number of converts. Vicens Vives suggested that of 200,000 Castilian Jews, about one-half became Christians; 25,000 were killed or fled, leaving 75,000 as the remnant of a once-flourishing community. In the years preceding 1492 he estimated that the Jewish population in Castile doubled to 150,000, with about 30,000 in Aragon.

The conversions of 1391 in general are easily explicable as a consequence of an immediate and real fear of death, but as the years passed conversions continued when that fear was no longer so great. Converts included not only the poor and the ignorant, but men of prominence, wealth, and education. Among the most notable was Solomon Halevi, who assumed the name Pablo de Santa Maria (d. 1435) and eventually became bishop of Burgos; in order to convince the Jews that Jesus was the Messiah who fulfilled all the prophecies, he composed the *Scrutinium sacrarum scripturarum*. His son, Alfonso de Cartagena, tried to achieve the same purpose in his *Defensorium unitatis christianae*. While Halevi's conversion was in response to his intellectual development, in other cases the opportunity for fame, fortune, and power was an important consideration, especially among those whose Jewish faith was only a veneer. Moreover, the Jews suffered a terrible psychological blow in 1391 and, in their questioning of God's favor, succumbed to many influences. St. Vincent Ferrer, the great Dominican preacher, gained thousands of converts among the Jews of Aragon and Castile, who probably were moved by his magnetic personality, fear of the crowds, and the increasing pressures of the secular and ecclesiastical authorities.

So that the Jews could not contaminate the faith of the recent converts, Catalina de Lancaster promulgated an "Ordinance on the enclosure of the Jews and Moors" at Valladolid in 1412. Reviving and codifying all the previous legislation, the ordinance required Jews to wear a distinctive yellow garment and to live in ghettos that were enclosed and locked at night, so that they could have no relationships with Christians. Henceforth the Jewish community was subject to the judicial jurisdiction of local Christian judges. Jews, and Moors too, were not permitted to be tax farmers, moneylenders, physicians, surgeons, or apothecaries; nor could they employ Christian servants, or Christian nurses for their children, nor visit Christians who were ill, nor take supper with Christian friends. No Jew was to prevent another from receiving baptism. Although the law was never fully enforced, the list of disabilities burdening the Jews was considerable and was sufficient to convince an individual that his life would be easier if he embraced the Christian faith.

Pope Benedict XIII, the last of the Avignon popes, hoping to take advantage of the new climate to convert the Jews, in November 1412 commanded the Jewish communities of Aragon and Catalonia to send delegations to his residence at Tortosa for instruction in the Christian religion. The ensuing disputation between Christian advocates and Jewish rabbis commenced in February 1413 and with various interruptions continued until April 1414. The principal Christian spokesman was a *converso*, Jerónimo de Santa Fe, formerly known as Joshua Halorki, who had been converted by Vincent Ferrer; on the other side, Rabbi Joseph Albo of Daroca was one of the leading exponents of Jewish beliefs. The arguments centered on the Christian contention that Jesus was the Messiah, who fulfilled all the Jewish prophecies; but despite the insistence of the Christians the Jews steadfastly refused to agree. From that standpoint the debate ended inconclusively, but even during the course of the arguments and in the months immediately following, many Jews announced their readiness to become Christians. Moreover, urged on by the pope, Fernando I of Aragon enacted a series of ordinances in 1415 similar to those published at Valladolid in 1412 to restrain the Jews. In that sense, the disputation of Tortosa was seen as a triumph for Christianity, and the Jews indeed wondered whether they had been abandoned by their God.

The oppressive legislation directed against the Jews was either abolished outright or allowed to lapse in the second quarter of the fifteenth century. In this more relaxed atmosphere many *conversos* resumed familiar relationships with their Jewish friends and relations and began again to visit the synagogues and to observe the Jewish law and customs, though often in secret. For this reason the *conversos* came under strong suspicion among the old Christians, who were especially resentful of upper-class Jews who had converted in order to retain their power and wealth as royal counselors, treasurers, and tax collectors. Men of this sort wore their religious convictions lightly and were regarded by contemporaries as neither good Jews nor good Christians. A popular outbreak in Toledo in 1449, in which *conversos* were attacked and despoiled of their property revealed the extent of hostility toward them. In derision they were called *marranos*, or swine, and the notion that Christian blood was made impure by intermarriage with *conversos* or Jews soon became widespread. In the latter part of the century, Christians seeking important positions in the church or admission to religious Orders were obliged to prove the purity of their blood (*limpieza de sangre*) by demonstrating that their genealogy was untainted by Jewish ancestry.

The revival of hostility toward the Jews and *conversos* was intensified during the civil disorders of the reign of Enrique IV and prepared the way for the eventual establishment of the royal inquisition by Ferdinand and Isabella. As early as 1451, Juan II obtained papal authorization to establish an episcopal inquisition to deal with *conversos* accused of Judaizing. Furthermore, Alfonso de Espina, a Franciscan friar, launched a broad attack upon both *conversos* and Jews in his *Fortalitium fidei*, a vast work in which he urged the need for an inquisition to deal with Judaizing heretics whom he charged with the denial of the immortality of the soul and the continued practice of circumcision. He also denounced the Jews more harshly than any previous polemicist, accusing them, among other things, of desecrating the host. Alfonso de Oropesa, head of the Order of San Jerónimo, in his *Lumen ad revelationem gentium*, adopted a more moderate tone, though he argued the necessity of excluding Jews from public office and of isolating them from the *conversos* so they could not encourage their Judaizing. As for the *conversos*, he said that there were many who were backsliders and that some of the resentment of the old Christians against them was justified; for this reason he urged that the bishops establish an inquisition to punish the Judaizers. In this way he believed that much of the disorder and rioting in the cities could be suppressed. The dissident nobles in 1465 demanded that the king take action against the Jews by reviving the Ordinances of 1412 and by organizing the inquisition against the *conversos*, but Enrique IV lacked the will to carry out any kind of policy. Thus the last few years of his reign saw a steady rise in racial and religious tensions leading directly to Pope Sixtus IV's bull of 1478 authorizing Ferdinand and Isabella to appoint inquisitors in the kingdom of Castile to deal with *conversos* suspected of the Judaizing heresy. With that, a new chapter in the religious history of Spain was opened, and the definitive solution of the Jewish question was not too far off.

The hierarchic and corporate structure of society expressed by the term "estates of the realm" did not change significantly in the late Middle Ages. Nobles, clergy, and townsmen continued to constitute the three estates traditionally summoned to the *cortes*, though they did not in fact include all classes in society. In his *Regiment de Princeps*, Francesch Eiximenis spoke of a threefold division of society, namely, *maiors, mitjáns,* and *menors*. The first group, the great men, included the barons, bishops, priors of military Orders, abbots, counts, viscounts, knights, and the urban patricians—whose wealth was so enormous that they easily entered the ranks of the aristocracy. The middle class consisted of most public officials, jurists, physicians, merchants, bankers, and artisans, while the *poble menut*, the little people, were the urban proletariat and the peasantry. This schema was not the same as that of the estates assembled in the *cortes*, but it was a more realistic division based upon actual wealth and power. As the rich became richer and the poor, poorer, the gulf between classes widened, intensifying hostility between them.

The principal changes in the status and character of the nobility were the displacement of old families by new ones, the transformation of the great lords into courtiers residing with the king rather than on their estates, the extraordinary aggrandizement of a few great families, and the depression of the petty nobility.

Continuing civil upheavals, especially in Castile and Portugal, contributed to the decline and destruction of older noble houses and the appearance of new ones who owed their advancement to their support of successful aspirants to royal power. Both Enrique II and João I rewarded their followers with lands and revenues, thereby creating a new nobility; though the number of great houses was quite small, they controlled a tenth of the land in the peninsula. For their benefit, the older titles of count and viscount were revived, and the titles of duke and marquess were introduced in imitation of French practice. The magnificence of the great lords is implied in the term *los grandes*, an expression used by Juan II in 1451 that eventually passed into English usage as "grandees." Some grandees held estates of truly fabulous extent. Alvaro de Luna, so hated by the others, was lord of about 100,000 persons living on his estates, while the marquess of Villena controlled about 25,000 square kilometers with about 150,000 dependents. In order not to dissipate the accumulated power and wealth of the family, the magnates created entailed estates (*mayorazgos*), which passed in their entirety to the first-born son and his descendants. Thus enormous wealth of all kinds was concentrated in the hands of very few families.

By becoming courtiers, living regularly with the king and accompanying him on his travels, the magnates were able to participate directly and continuously in the government of the realm and to use the agencies of government to advance their own private interests. As possessors of vast estates, allied by marriage and common aims, controlling the chief offices of state and royal revenues and fortresses, and commanding the services of numerous vassals, they were the dominant force in the political life of Castile and Portugal in the fifteenth century. If royal policy did not suit them, they were able to challenge the king on the field of battle if necessary, and if they disagreed among themselves, they did not hesitate to resort to arms to solve their difficulties. In sum, the magnates, particularly in Castile, were the cause of terrible disorder; the monarchy could not counterbalance them by an appeal to the middle class, for it was weak and ineffective and apt to be pro-aristocratic. On the contrary, the presence of a powerful middle class in Catalonia aided the crown in holding the nobility in check. It is also true that Alfonso V's intervention in Naples provided an outlet for the bellicose energies of both the Aragonese and Catalan nobles who might otherwise have attempted to challenge the king.

By their intimate association with the king and his court, the magnates acquired a more sophisticated outlook and adopted a more cultured style of life. Their manners and language became more refined and their clothing and food more sumptuous and luxurious. Many of them were persons of good taste who lived in splendid opulence, indulging in feasts, dances, and other elaborate forms of entertainment, collecting books, patronizing scholars and poets, and oftentimes writing books and treatises themselves. Indeed, the principal literary works of this period were authored by members of this courtly society.

The ideal of chivalry continued to be held up before them by an abundance of literary works, such as Alfonso de Cartagena's Doctrinal de caballeros. The man who would be the perfect knight could also learn much from the story of Galahad and the quest for the Holy Grail, the adventures of Lancelot, and the contemporary novel of chivalry, Tirant lo Blanc. Interest in the noble deeds of earlier generations inspired genealogical works such as the Portuguese Livros de Linhagens. Knights wishing to emulate the chivalric prowess of the heroes of romance could do so in the many fashionable and popular tournaments.

Membership in the order of chivalry theoretically linked in a common brotherhood the king and all the aristocrats from the most powerful magnates down to the simplest knights who possessed little more than horse and arms. Many members of the petty nobility, however, who were dependent upon the revenues of their estates for sustenance, were impoverished; some had to abandon their condition as hidalgos or members of the noble class in order to survive, but most preferred to retain their dignity and honor in the midst of poverty, rather than defile themselves by engaging in trade or crafts. Here is the model of the broken-down knight caricatured by Cervantes in Don Quixote.

Despite the example of poverty-stricken knights, the ascendancy of the nobility and their dominance of nearly every aspect of life created a pro-aristocratic mentality in the kingdom of Castile. Disdain for manual labor, a desire to share in the esteem enjoyed by the nobles, and especially to be exempt from taxation, caused many men to aspire to the privileged status of *hidalguía*. The concession of noble rank to wealthy townsmen and status-seekers of all sorts soon came to be seen as an abuse. The *cortes* of 1432 complained that many taxpayers were knighted so that they could be exempt from taxation; Juan II agreed that they should not enjoy that privilege unless they had horse and arms and held land from the crown. Some years later he also agreed to stop the abuse of conferring knighthood by mail and stipulated that in the future he would personally grant it only by his own hand. Protests and complaints continued, however, and friction between townsmen and nobles residing in the towns became particularly intense. The nobles were accused of fomenting urban disorders, of monopolizing the offices of municipal government, while not being obliged to contribute to the taxes required by the towns or by the king.

Lacking any contemporary Muslim historical accounts, it is difficult to speak of social conditions in the kingdom of Granada in the fifteenth century. Christian sources, however, indicate that a noble family known as the Abencerrajes, or Banu al-Sarraj, played a prominent role in politics. They were responsible for a number of coups resulting in the deposition of rulers and were able to use the numerous sons and brothers of rulers for their own purposes. By thus encouraging partisan strife they hastened the downfall of the kingdom.

Although the clergy traditionally were said to form an estate distinct from the others, Eiximenis quite properly included the bishops, abbots, and heads of military Orders among the *maiors*, the aristocracy. At no time did the higher clergy more truly belong to the aristocracy than in the fifteenth century. As they were drawn for the most part from the families of the king and the magnates, their mentality and their style of life was essentially that of the noble class. They were courtiers, politicians, and warriors fully capable of competing with the secular magnates on their own terms. Though pledged to a life of celibacy, many ignored their vows and tried to provide estates for their illegitimate children. It even seemed possible that some ecclesiastical positions might become hereditary; Pedro Girón, for example, was succeeded as master of Calatrava in 1466 by his eight-year-old son, Rodrigo, and it is conceivable that the mastership could have become the hereditary possession of the Girón family, if the Catholic kings had not intervened.

Urban society was frequently and bitterly torn by conflict between the ruling oligarchy and the rest of the population. The "rich citizens" (*rics homens ciutatans*), as Eiximenis called them, were few in number but extremely wealthy. In the past their families had accumulated a great deal of money and capital chiefly by trade and commerce. Vicens Vives has pointed out that the Catalan urban patricians of the fifteenth century were losing confidence and were no longer ready to take the risks involved in trade, and invested their money instead in land, country estates, annuities, and other more permanent and regular sources of income. They owned mills, shops, forges, ovens, and the like, which they rented to others. Most of them lived in sumptuous palaces in the cities and controlled city government, often attempting to transform public offices into hereditary ones. Their wealth, refinement, and sophistication, and their ancestry enabled them to share with the nobility in the leadership of the realm. For this reason Eiximenis placed them among the *maiors*.

The merchants engaged in commerce and industry constituted the principal element in the middle class (*mà mitjana*), and though quite well-to-do they did not yet have the social standing and prestige of the patricians. In Catalonia wealthy merchants usually were shipowners and bankers, but in Castile, where a significant mercantile middle class was just beginning to develop, they were mainly engaged in the manufacture and sale of woolen goods. Professional men such as lawyers and notaries shared in the wealth and influence of the merchants for whom they provided useful and indispensable services. The artisans formed the largest number of citizens, and most still maintained their own shops, but those in the textile industry were increasingly dependent upon the rich merchants to purchase their goods and to distribute them to the ordinary consumer. In Catalonia many artisans rented mills, forges, and shops from the patricians. In most parts of the peninsula artisans were deprived of any effective voice in city government and agitated frequently against the oligarchs. Both economic and political considerations were at the root of the conflict between the Catalan *biga*, the oligarchy of wealthy merchants and patricians, and the *busca*, the middle and lower-middle class merchants and artisans and the urban proletariat allied with them. In Portugal the mercantile classes expanded in numbers and riches in the late Middle Ages because of the growth of overseas trade. But when the artisans became more insistent on having a voice in city government, the merchants or "honored citizens" protested that these men of lower rank (*baixa mão*) "do not have the knowledge or the maturity to govern the common weal."

The malaise of the times also left its mark upon the peasantry. The number of free proprietors in Castile declined steadily, partly because of the cession of large parts of the royal domain to the magnates. Free peasants, formerly dependent directly upon the crown, were now subjected to nobles who tried to impose new burdens upon them. Some abandoned the land and took up residence in the towns, while others borrowed from Jewish moneylenders in order to meet their obligations; in the end many were forced into the ranks of tenants or hired labor. In Aragon, free proprietors began to settle in the towns, renting their lands to others. The condition of hired workers changed little, though their attempts to secure higher wages following the Black Death were unavailing. A plan to divide the *hombres de behetría* among the Castilian nobles, in order to curb controversies, was proposed in 1371, but was not carried out; in general these freemen were more closely subjected to their lords and bound to the soil.

From the close of the fourteenth century the *payeses de remensa*, that is, the Catalan peasants bound to the soil, began to agitate for their liberty. The "evil usages" to which they were subject were condemned as contrary to Christian teaching, as well as natural law. Juan I and Martin the Humane proposed to abolish such burdens, but the nobility were opposed, and in the *corts* of 1413 and 1432 the peasant agitation, which was becoming steadily more violent, was denounced. Alfonso V in 1455 finally proclaimed the abolition of the "evil usages" and redemption, but failed to enforce his decree. The issue was confused by the outbreak of civil war in 1462, at a time when both King Juan II and his opponents sought the support of the *payeses*, who consequently gained an effective liberty; but it was not until 1486 that Ferdinand and Isabella formally confirmed the freedom of the *payeses de remensa*—their right to leave the land without paying a redemption—

and abolished the "evil usages." About a sixth of the population, or 50,000 people were affected.

Slavery continued to flourish, principally in the frontier zones, where those captured by Christian or Muslim forces were often reduced to that status. The problem of slavery took on a far-reaching dimension when Portuguese expeditions sent by Henry the Navigator to explore the west coast of Africa began to seize the natives and bring them back to Portugal to be sold as slaves. The chronicler, Azurara, noting the moving spectacle when the first slaves were brought to Portugal as booty, justified it as a chivalric enterprise that brought honor and glory to the knights who participated; the slaves also benefited, he argued, as the Portuguese would teach them the Christian religion and various trades and in general would treat them quite well. Such elaborate explanations no doubt seemed necessary in view of the extraordinary increase in the number of slaves.

The Economy

In the closing century of the medieval era the economy of the western kingdoms, Castile and Portugal, expanded with the development of the wool trade and the beginnings of exploration and colonization in the Atlantic islands and the west coast of Africa. On the other hand, the Catalan economy, which had flourished in the thirteenth and early fourteenth centuries, sharply contracted due to a combination of factors, including the recurrence of plague, the ensuing shortage of manpower, the exhaustion brought on by continuing rivalry with Genoa, the collapse of private banks, and the loss of initiative and enterprise by Catalan merchants who became wary of risk-taking. Economic decline did not affect the other states of the Aragonese confederation to the same degree, and Valencia in fact prospered as never before in the fifteenth century. But at the time of the marriage of Ferdinand and Isabella, Castile was in a generally better economic position than the crown of Aragon.

Although agriculture remained the foundation of economic life, governments generally made little conscious effort to regulate and direct its development. From time to time, in response to petitions presented in the cortes, the crown issued decrees concerning the relations between peasants and landlords, the levying of tributes on agricultural property and so forth, but not much was done to develop and improve the techniques of agricultural production. Production more than likely fell off because of the plague and the destruction of crops during the civil wars. The plague hit Catalonia more severely than elsewhere and returned at regular intervals in the fifteenth century, causing a chronic shortage of agricultural labor. This resulted in the abandonment of cultivated land and continuing conflict between peasants and their landlords who tried to increase their burdens and to deny their right to leave the land freely.

The shortage of labor was also acute in Portugal as the *Lei das Sesmarias* promulgated in 1375 by King Fernando makes clear. Noting that a great deal of land was uncultivated, to the detriment of the people, and that the decline in the production of wheat and barley resulted in starvation for many, the king ordered agricultural proprietors to cultivate all their arable land and to distribute it to those who would work it in return for reasonable rents and services. Uncultivated lands would be given by the civil authorities to those who would cultivate them, and able-bodied farm workers would be compelled to work. In spite of the law, many workers left the land to take service in the houses of the wealthy or powerful, or to seek their fortunes in the cities, while others simply turned to begging as a way of life. Emigration to Madeira and the Azores in the fifteenth century also lessened the agricultural population on the mainland.

In other parts of the peninsula, where the ravages of the plague were not so great, the difficulties facing agricultural production in the middle of the fourteenth century were eventually overcome. Galicia, the Basque country, Andalusia, Murcia, Granada, and Valencia continued to grow the staple crops: wheat, olive oil, grapes, rice, oranges, figs, raisins, and so forth. As the Canary Islands, Madeira, and the Azores were settled and exploited, they began to produce sugar cane in substantial quantities for export to the mainland. The vineyards that eventually made Madeira wine famous were also cultivated in the late fifteenth century.

In the central *meseta* an extraordinary expansion of the sheep-raising industry took place. The depopulation caused by the Black Death has been urged as the principal reason for this development, but the rivalry between France and England in the Hundred Years' War would seem to have been more decisive. At the beginning of the war Edward III imposed an embargo on the shipment of wool from England to Flanders, and though he eventually lifted it, the supply of English wool to the Flemish weavers was always uncertain; the Flemings consequently were glad to receive shipments of Castilian wool. As the demand for raw wool also rose in Catalonia and Italy, the number of Castilian sheep nearly doubled over the total from the thirteenth century, reaching the approximate figure of 2,700,000 in 1467.

The activities of the sheep-raising industry continued to be regulated by the *Mesta*, about whose organization we are more fully informed by the ordinances promulgated by Ferdinand and Isabella in 1492. Given the large number of sheep, the royal tax (*servicio y montazgo*) upon them now constituted a major portion of the crown's revenue. The great lords who often owned flocks of 20,000 to 40,000 sheep easily overwhelmed the smaller sheepherders and dominated the organization. At the two annual meetings of the *Mesta* about 200 to 300 members, a tenth of the total, usually attended; at least 40 were necessary for a quorum. The meetings dealt with internal organization and difficulties, continuing conflicts with farmers and others, and the election of officers. More than likely, as Vicens Vives argues, they were elected directly, rather than by lot as Klein suggested, though the latter practice became the rule after 1492; the king continued to appoint the *alcalde entregador*. Sheep grouped in flocks of at least 1,000 head continued to make the annual journey over the *cañadas* from north to south and back again. As remarkable as was the growth of sheep-raising in the late Middle Ages, it achieved even higher levels in the reign of the Catholic kings and their successors.

Cattle ranching also developed rapidly, though on a lesser scale, in Andalusia, Alentejo, and the Algarve. There were still many comparatively small ranchers in the *concejos* of the central *meseta*, but the number of herds over 100 head increased substantially. It was, however, in the south that cattle ranching became a distinctive way of life and the most prominent industry. The estates of the great southern lords were given over to cattle ranching, and the municipalities were beginning to assign lands for grazing purposes. At the close of the fifteenth century the Andalusian towns were also requiring the registration of brands and earmarks of cattle in a *libro de marcas y señales* kept by a town scribe. Bishko has emphasized that many characteristics of Latin American cattle ranching were in the process of development in late medieval Castile. Cattle were sold for their beef and hides at the annual fairs held at Seville, Evora, Córdoba, Cáceres, Segovia, Avila, and other towns. The importance of beef in the daily diet of the peninsular peoples, in contrast to those of northern Europe, was such that the papacy in conferring spiritual benefits upon those who contributed to the support of the crusade against the Moors also granted exemption from the laws of abstinence from meat.

Domestic needs for horses, cattle, and sheep evidently remained substantial, so that Juan I in 1390 and Enrique IV in 1462 renewed the long-standing prohibition against the export of these types of livestock.

As sheep-raising developed and expanded, a native Castilian woolen industry almost inevitably came into existence. Its importance is reflected in a petition presented to Juan II by the *cortes* in 1438, asking that the export of Castilian wool and the import of foreign wool be prohibited. The Castilian weavers obviously wanted to reserve for themselves good, cheap, raw wool, but the *Mesta* opposed their petition because the sheep-raisers were anxious to sell their product at the highest price on the international market. For the moment, the king sided with them, but in 1462 Enrique IV allowed the export of only one-third of the total production of raw wool; this represented a triumph for the native woolen industry.

The manufacture of woolen cloth was the most important industrial activity carried on in the towns of Catalonia, especially Barcelona, Tortosa, and Gerona. Raw wool was imported from Castile and from the Maestrazgo in Aragon, and from time to time English wool was also used or woven with native wool. Woolen goods were exported to Naples, Sicily, Sardinia, Corsica, Syria, Egypt, and North Africa. In the fifteenth century, however, the Catalan woolen industry declined, chiefly because of foreign competition. English woolens began to supplant Catalan wool in the Italian markets and even in Valencia, partly because of a desire for cloth of a finer quality than that which the Catalans were able to produce. Attempts to develop a silk industry in Barcelona were no more successful. In Valencia the production of cotton and silk was of greater importance than that of wool.

Aside from textiles, shipbuilding continued to be a major industry in the ports of Portugal, the Cantabrian coast, Seville, and Barcelona, where an abundance of wood and iron was available or within easy access. Iron mining was carried out on a large scale in the Basque regions around Bilbao, and as the Catalans began to exploit the iron deposits in the Pyrenees, the production of iron goods attained considerable importance in Catalonia in the late fourteenth century. The so-called Catalan forge was developed there and was eventually widely used in western Europe.

Within the towns many small craftsmen were engaged in a variety of trades, but their efforts to organize guilds to defend their economic interests encountered the opposition of the Castilian kings. In the crown of Aragon, on the contrary, the guilds developed steadily and became highly specialized. They regulated the distribution of raw material and the standards of production; inspectors visited the shops to see to it that standards were maintained, that work was done only on the appointed days during regular hours, and that legitimate prices were charged. Fines could be imposed for any violations. The guild master who maintained his own shop and had his own trademark (senyal)—registered with the town authorities and transmissible to his heirs—attained that status by demonstrating his capacity in a public examination. The requirement of an examination seems to have been introduced at a comparatively late date, the earliest instance being 1389; some guilds such as the dyers did not adopt it until the close of the fifteenth century. Fees were also charged for admission to membership in the guild, except for the sons of masters. In some guilds, the number of new masters admitted yearly was quite limited—in the case of the pharmacists, to two.

Journeymen, who worked for a daily wage, whence their name, were hired in public places set aside for that purpose; in general their situation was tolerable, but in the fifteenth century they attempted to form guilds of their own to defend themselves against the oppression of the masters. Apprentices were even more completely at the mercy of their masters. Although the normal working day extended to about ten hours, there were frequent abuses on the part of masters who also often ignored the prohibition against working on Sundays and holy days. Toward the close of the fifteenth century the traditional guild system began to receive competition from the domestic system whereby individual entrepreneurs employed the services of workmen, outside the guild structure and its regulations, to produce goods in their own homes or shops; the entrepreneur, who supplied the raw material, also assumed the responsibility for distributing the finished product. The artisans, no matter their talent, became hired labor, dependent upon the emerging capitalist for materials and wages.

Aside from local markets, the most important trading activity in Castile took place in regional fairs, where the volume of goods exchanged and the number of merchants attending steadily increased. For this reason magnates often established markets and fairs in the hope of being able to profit from fees and tributes imposed upon those who attended; but as this ran counter to the interests of the crown, whose revenues were prejudiced thereby, the cortes of 1430 explicitly forbade the establishment of fairs except by royal privilege.

From the middle of the fifteenth century the fairs of Medina del Campo became the most widely known in Castile, attracting merchants from many other countries. This was due principally to the crown's decision to concentrate both the wool trade and the money trade at that point; there, tributes owed the crown by the flocks of the Mesta could be most conveniently collected, and raw wool could be sold or exchanged for luxury goods imported from northern Europe. Money was changed there, loans were arranged, and letters of exchange were made payable in Medina del Campo. After 1450 the city became the financial capital of Castile; its importance continued to grow in the time of the Catholic kings who tried to centralize economic life there even more fully.

Great annual assemblies of merchants at the fairs of Medina del Campo, Valladolid, Segovia, and other towns, were not common in the crown of Aragon. There the volume of commercial traffic was substantially greater and was carried on in the principal cities in public buildings erected for that purpose. In the halls of the llotge, a building with a pillared arcade similar to an Italian loggia, merchants met daily to buy and sell either directly or through brokers (corredors d'orella). The llotge of Barcelona was a magnificent structure in the florid Gothic style, built between 1350 and 1392; the llotges of Valencia and Palma de Mallorca also reflected the riches and power of the mercantile class. It is worthy of note, however, that the erection of these imposing edifices occurred during a time of economic contraction.

Castilian and Portuguese overseas commerce expanded rapidly in the fifteenth century. The increasing demand for wool enabled Castile to broaden already existing commercial contacts with Flanders. The fleets from the Cantabrian ports, which had long been engaged in carrying wine and iron to the north, increased both the volume and number of their cargoes of wool. An association of merchants (universidad de mercaderes) at Burgos, mentioned for the first time in 1443, endeavored to organize the transport of raw wool from the interior to the Cantabrian ports and to control its shipment overseas.

This resulted in rivalry between Castilians and Basques, or more explicitly between Burgos and Bilbao, the Basque city which had begun to attain prominence in the late fourteenth century. In 1453 the merchants of Burgos, for example, tried to assure preferential treatment in the export of wool to Santander rather than Bilbao. In Flanders, whither the raw wool was carried, Castilian merchants, and Catalans too, had been active since the fourteenth century. A guild of Castilian merchants, dominated by those from Burgos, was organized in Bruges in 1441; the Basques did not wish to be represented by it, however, and ten years later secured recognition of their separate guild from Philip the Good, duke of Burgundy. The Catholic kings later attempted to organize more efficiently the shipment of raw wool from Burgos, where they created a *consulado* in 1494, to Bilbao and thence to Flanders.

Portuguese trade with northern Europe was encouraged by privileges given to foreign merchants by João I in 1386; he lifted the old requirement that they bring to Portugal goods of equal value to those exported. Earlier King Fernando encouraged the development of a native merchant marine and revived the association for naval insurance authorized by Dinis in 1293. In Lisbon and Porto the merchants contributed to a common fund to be used to indemnify losses of ships at sea. The king, who maintained twelve merchant ships of his own, and was a member of this *companhia de navios*, also contributed to the fund. João I's alliance with England laid the basis for the development of regular trade relations between the two countries, in rather sharp contrast to the relations between England and Castile. Ever since Enrique II threw in his lot with France, supplying her with naval warships to be used against the English, the latter did all in their power to exclude the Castilians from the North Sea and to impede their progress through the channel. Only in the time of the Catholic kings were harmonious relations re-established.

Both Castile and Portugal maintained trade relations with the Hanseatic League, an organization of immense importance in the fifteenth century. Bruges, where colonies of Castilians and Portuguese were settled, was a major market and distribution center for the League. But the League's ships began to venture into the Atlantic, sailing as far south as the Cantabrian ports and even to Lisbon, with cargoes of wheat, fish, furs, and other northern products to be exchanged for iron, wool, and the like. Oliveira Marquês has studied the contacts between the Hansa and Portugal in the fifteenth century. Conflicts arose almost inevitably in the Bay of Biscay, centering upon control of the commerce of La Rochelle, where the Cantabrian towns had long had the upper hand; a peace settlement in 1453 decided the issue in favor of the Castilians. One consequence of this relationship was the adoption of the *kogge* or *coca*, a ship that was heavy, broad, and rounded at bow and stern, commonly used by the Hansa towns, and capable of carrying larger cargoes than any of the ships ordinarily used in southern Europe.

Partly because of the great competition for the carrying trade in the Atlantic area, the Basques and the Portuguese turned their attention to the western Mediterranean. During the first half of the fifteenth century, because of the wars between Genoa and the crown of Aragon, they were able to take over much of the carrying trade, but they also brought into the area goods from northern Europe and the Atlantic regions. The Genoese never lost their influential position in Lisbon and Seville and continued to supply both Castile and Portugal with necessities and luxuries. As the pressure of the Turks became more severe in the eastern Mediterranean, interfering with Christian trade there, the Genoese became more aggressive in the western Mediterranean and by the end of the fifteenth century were able to turn back the competition of the Basques and the Portuguese.

The zone offering the greatest opportunities for the future of both Castilian and Portuguese trade was the Atlantic Ocean. From the middle of the fifteenth century effective colonization of the Canary Islands, Madeira, and the Azores was begun, and these colonies were soon able to export goods to the mother countries. The Castilians soon found an extensive market in Flanders for sugar from the Canary Islands, while the Portuguese supplied the wants of the Mediterranean world. Portugal's continuing need for wheat and other cereals could now be met by the production of Madeira and the Azores. The exploration of the African coast opened entirely new economic horizons for Portugal, as gold and slaves in ever-increasing quantities were obtained from Arab merchants who brought them from the interior to the coastal factory established at Arguim after 1448. In exchange, the Portuguese offered the varied products of Europe and Morocco, especially cloth and horses. On the southern coast of Portugal, African goods were carried to Lagos, a great commercial emporium that rivaled in importance Lisbon and Porto.

In contrast to the growth of Castilian and Portuguese trade, Catalan commerce declined sharply for a number of reasons. The impact of the plague, more severe than in other regions, the investment of capital in land rather than in maritime enterprise, the failure of the banks, the depletion of gold and silver reserves, and the loss of nerve, all contributed. Naval wars with Genoa for dominance in the western Mediterranean hastened the decline of the Catalan merchant marine; Alfonso V's defeat and capture in the naval battle of Ponza in 1435 manifested this to the whole world. The growth of piracy in the Mediterranean, a practice in which the Catalans did their full share, also ultimately worked to their disadvantage. Not only did piracy encourage reprisals and the destruction of ships, but it also ruined friendly relations with Egypt where the Catalans had long dominated the commercial life of Alexandria. Restrictive measures were imposed upon the Catalan colony there and also in Tunis. The expansion of the Turks in the eastern Mediterranean curtailed Catalan trade with the Byzantine empire, but as it also compelled the Genoese and Venetians to seek compensation in the west, the Catalans were hard pressed to keep up with them. The Catalans also lost their ascendancy along the coast of southern France; Marseille replaced Barcelona as the chief distributor of spices in the region, as the great French capitalist, Jacques Coeur, endeavored to exclude the Catalans. Finally, Catalan trade also suffered to some extent from the Portuguese exploitation of the west coast of Africa. Goods that might have been carried northward through Africa to the Mediterranean coast for sale to Catalan merchants were diverted instead to the western coast and the Portuguese.

The one region in the crown of Aragon that continued to prosper in the fifteenth century was Valencia. Although the kingdom shared to some extent in the restrictions on overseas commerce that afflicted Catalonia, Valencian rice, oranges, and sugar continued in demand and enabled Valencia to overcome the economic crisis. The city of Valencia also supplanted Barcelona as the financial capital of the crown of Aragon.

Alfonso V tried to counteract the decline in several ways. He pursued a protectionist policy, forbidding the shipment of goods from Majorca (1419) or Catalonia except in native ships; in order to encourage their use, freight charges were reduced to some extent. The Catalans profited from these measures and were able to supply cloth and wheat to the kingdom of Naples and to participate more actively in the slave trade. Slaves came not only from North Africa, but also from the eastern Mediterranean and could be obtained at Crete, Naples, Palermo, Genoa, and Venice. In spite of these signs of recovery, the Catalan economy was hard hit by the civil war that took place during the reign of Juan II and, at the close of this era, Catalonia's claims to maritime hegemony in the western Mediterranean no longer had any substance.

Progress in the technical organization of trade continued, despite other weaknesses. By the close of the fifteenth century, partnerships were more numerous, and the company or association of several persons engaged in a commercial enterprise for a fixed term, usually of five years at the maximum, was becoming common. Maritime insurance was also developed, in imitation of Italian practice. The earliest references to it are contained in Pedro IV's constitutions of 1340, and the municipal ordinances of Barcelona in 1438 gave substantial attention to it, as may be seen in the *Consolat del Mar*; the city enacted definitive ordinances regulating insurance practice in 1484. The letter of exchange came into widespread use in the fourteenth century; the first true letter of exchange issued in the peninsula refers to an exchange between Majorca and Barcelona. Others subsequently were drawn on Bruges, Florence, Valencia, and other cities. The letter of exchange became general in Castile in connection with the fairs of Medina del Campo.

The economic decline of Catalonia was hastened in part by the failure of the principal private banks in 1381. Business activity was immediately paralyzed, municipal finances were undermined, capital became scarce, and Barcelona lost its status as one of the principal financial centers of the Mediterranean. The pogroms of 1391 were an indirect consequence of the economic crisis, signaled by the collapse of the banks. In addition, the monarchy turned to foreign bankers for loans; the Florentines and Genoese replaced the Catalans as the creditors of the king. Having lost confidence in private banks, a number of Catalan towns established their own banks. Of these, the most famous was the *Taula de Canvi* founded by the city of Barcelona in 1401 after appropriate studies and recommendations had been made by a committee of merchants and citizens. A municipal bank, whose officers were chosen by the city government, it became the depository for municipal funds as well as for those of private persons. The earliest extant ordinances regulating the bank date from 1412. Since it was in the hands of the ruling oligarchy of the city, the bank inclined to conservative policies; by restricting the flow of capital for investment, it failed to contribute to the economic recovery of the principality.

Hamilton's studies of prices and wages in the crown of Aragon during this era reflect the crisis afflicting the region. From 1340 to 1380 there was a sharp rise, which Vicens Vives attributes to the fact that the supply of goods was less than the demand, just as the supply of labor was less than the demand. From 1380 to 1420 prices and wages were unstable, but this time of adjustment was followed by a period of relative calm until 1460. For most of the reign of Juan II, prices and wages were subject to violent change, generally tending upward, due largely to the disorder caused by the civil war.

CHAPTER 25

Religion and Culture, 1369–1479

A Time of Upheaval

Upheaval in nearly every aspect of life was the principal characteristic of the last century of the Middle Ages. Protests against the established order and authorities occurred in most parts of Europe, taking the form of peasant revolts, proletarian uprisings, aristocratic revolutions, dynastic quarrels, and ecclesiastical rebellions. Brutality and violence were common in everyday life among all classes, though the weak usually were the victims of the strong. Public documents as well as literary works are full of protest against the abuse of power, the failure to do justice and to love one's neighbor as Christians were supposed to do, and the prevalence of the seven deadly sins.

The tone of the times is perhaps best illustrated by the challenge to papal authority from both within and without the church. Secular rulers, buoyed by the growing spirit of nationalism, repudiated as foreign the intervention of the omnicompetent and all-pervasive papal bureaucracy and tried to transform the church within their frontiers into a national institution. The conciliarists, borrowing elements from secular practice, simultaneously proposed a theory of limited, constitutional government for the church. The papacy eventually overcame this threat, but the persistent cry for the reform of the church in head and members was an unfortunate victim of the struggle.

Not only was there increasing distress over abuses of ecclesiastical authority and the evidence of vice in the lives of many churchmen, but there was also a more radical attack upon the doctrinal foundations of the church. Echoes of the heresies propagated in England by John Wycliffe and in Bohemia by John Hus, were eventually heard even in Spain. The growth of magic and witchcraft, moreover, reflected widespread dissatisfaction with the traditional practices of the Christian religion.

The Latin and vernacular literature of the times, often providing a commentary on the problems of society, continued to draw its fundamental inspiration from the chivalric and scholastic traditions; but the first influences of the Italian Renaissance can also be detected. The introduction of the ideas of the Italian humanists, who sought to recapture the spirit of classical literature and to pattern their lives on the classical ideal, marked a major turning point in the development of Spanish literature.

The Church

The outbreak of the Great Western Schism, leaving the faithful, as it did, without identifiable leadership, was the cause of great confusion in the church. Pedro López de Ayala voiced the common feeling of dismay when he asked, "Who is the pope?"

> Uno disen de Roma, do era ordenado,
> De todos los cardenales por papa fue tomado . . .
> Disen los cardenales otrosi su entincion.
> Non fue como deuia fecha la eleccion
> Ca ouo en ella fuerça e publica ymprision . . .

> They say the one in Rome, where he was ordained
> And received as pope by all the cardinals . . .
> The cardinals say their intention was otherwise.
> The election was not made as it ought to be
> For it was done with force and popular pressure . . .
>   [Rimado de Palacio, 198]

Professing to be a simple man, he urged the summoning of a council:

> E segunt me paresce, maguer non so letrado
> Si Dios por bien touiese que fuese acordado
> Que se fisies concilio segunt es ordenado
> El tal caso como este alli fuese librado.

> It seems to me, though I'm not learned,
> If it pleases God that it be agreed
> That a council be held, as is ordained,
> An affair such as this can be resolved.   [Rimado de Palacio, 215]

Though he seems to have believed that the secular powers could hasten the end of the schism, their actions tended to perpetuate it. At first the peninsular rulers remained neutral, but within a few years—chiefly for reasons of friendship and alliance with France—Castile, Aragon, and Navarre declared for the Avignon pope. Portugal, under João I who wished to affirm his independence of Castile and his alliance with England, after initially vacillating adhered steadfastly to the Roman cause. Even after the Council of Constance assembled in 1415 to bring this scandalous situation to an end, Castile and Aragon hesitated for more than a year before abandoning the Avignon pope. The resolution of the schism brought in its train the problem of conciliarism, that is, the idea that a general council representing the whole body of the faithful is the supreme authority in the church. While individual churchmen such as Juan of Segovia were staunch conciliarists, the kings and their kingdoms refused to follow the Council of Basel when it deposed Pope Eugene IV in 1438 and elected an antipope. For reasons connected with his political ambitions in Italy, Alfonso V of Aragon flirted briefly with the Council, but, on the whole, Europe was tired of schisms and conciliarism.

The fragmentation of authority resulting from the schism strengthened the national character of the church in different countries. Royal insistence that papal letters not be published nor enforced without prior royal consent illustrates the attempt to subordinate the church to royal control. The exercise of jurisdiction by foreign bishops was also curtailed, as for example, when Benedict IX of the Roman line in 1390 raised Lisbon to archiepiscopal status, removing it from the jurisdiction of Compostela and subordinating to it the sees of Evora, Lamego, and Guarda, formerly suffragans of the Galician archbishopric. Other Castilian bishoprics also were deprived of territorial jurisdiction in Portugal; though Martin V in 1423 ordered the restoration to the see of Túy of Portuguese districts once pertaining to it, in fact, diocesan boundaries thereafter seldom extended beyond national frontiers. All this was simply a manifestation of the Portuguese desire for independence of Castile in every respect.

The territorial structure of the church in the peninsula otherwise was modified very little, but overseas expansion did necessitate the establishment of bishoprics at Fuerteventura in the Canary Islands (1423) and at Ceuta (1421) and Tangier (1468). In addition, Henry the Navigator, as administrator of the Order of Christ, received spiritual jurisdiction over the zones being explored and colonized in west Africa and in the Atlantic islands.

Provincial councils and diocesan synods seem to have been held with reasonable frequency; occasionally national councils were convened, chiefly to deal with the problems of the schism. The most important of these were the Council of Palencia in 1388 presided over by Cardinal Pedro de Luna, and that of Tortosa in 1429, under the presidency of Cardinal Pierre de Foix, at which the submission of the antipope Clement VIII was received. The Council of Aranda, held in 1473 by Archbishop Alfonso Carrillo of Toledo, provided that provincial councils should be held biennially and diocesan synods annually.

Papal and royal intervention practically terminated the free election of bishops. A disputed election in Toledo in 1375, for example, enabled the pope to reject the rival candidates and to transfer the bishop of Coimbra to the archiepiscopal see. In other instances the crown was able to obtain papal appointment of members of the royal family to important bishoprics, for example, Juan de Aragon, bastard of Juan II, who was named archbishop of Zaragoza in 1458.

In his *Loores de los claros varones de España* (401), Fernán Pérez de Guzmán commented that kings "ought not to intervene in the elections of prelates, for they are temporal lords and have nothing to do with spiritual matters. They ought only to command and admonish the clergy to elect a good and virtuous person and allow them to carry out their election freely." The reservation of bishoprics and other benefices for members of the *curia* unfortunately entailed the problems of absenteeism and pluralities. A grotesque example of this sort is the case of Cardinal Jorge da Costa, a supporter of Afonso V, who was allowed to hold at one and the same time the archbishoprics of Braga and Lisbon, the bishoprics of Evora, Porto, Viseu, Silves, and Ceuta, as well as the abbacies of Alcobaça and of eleven other Cistercian and Benedictine monasteries, the priorships of ten houses of canons regular, the deanships of seven cathedral chapters, and other miscellaneous benefices in Castile, Navarre, and Italy. From all these he derived a huge income which enabled him to live in great pomp in Rome. Given this example, it is not surprising that the satirical poem, *La danza de la muerte*, accused prelates of failure to perform their duties, of giving themselves up to the enjoyment of the riches and pleasures of this world, and of spending their time "in the king's court and not in church." As López de Ayala remarked: "Aman al mundo mucho, nunca cuydan morir"—"They love the world very much and have no care of death."

Papal provisions to bishoprics and other benefices continued to grow beyond all measure in this period, as the popes steadily elaborated conditions under which appointments were reserved to the Holy See. López de Ayala suggested that anyone who wanted a bishopric had only to present the cardinals with fine drinking cups emblazoned with their arms:

> Quien les presenta copas buenas con sus sennales
> Rrecabdara obispados e otras cosas tales.   [Rimado, 228]

The cry of protest against papal provisions was heard constantly. The cortes in 1377, 1390, and 1396 demanded that no one not a native of the kingdom of Castile be allowed to hold a bishopric or other benefice there. Not only were the churches poorly served and parishes abandoned, but income from benefices was taken out of the kingdom. What counted in all this was money; the accumulation of benefices enabled the incumbent to live well and, if he also took some responsibility for the performance of the duties connected with his living, or hired someone to do so, that was all to the good. A decree of the Synod of Tarragona in 1372, requiring those appointed to benefices to be ordained within a year so that they could fulfill the duties of their office, points this up. The Synod of Palencia in 1388 required residency on the part of beneficed clerics and also tried to curb plurality of benefices. In spite of all the protest, however, the crown did little to prevent papal provisions, chiefly because the papacy was willing to share the spoils.

In view of the crassness of these transactions it is not surprising that the spiritual caliber of the clergy left much to be desired. Although the prelates were well-educated men, usually coming from noble families, their lives were often spent at court and were characterized by the dissolute manners of the lay nobility. Men such as Archbishop Alfonso Carrillo were notorious for incontinence, as were other bishops and masters of the military Orders. Conciliar decrees required that only worthy persons should be ordained (Tortosa, 1429) or those who could speak Latin (Aranda, 1473), but López de Ayala noted that by paying the bishop, one could be ordained without a rigorous examination. Many priests were even ignorant of the words of consecration:

> Non saben las palabras de la consagracion
> Nin curen de saber nin lo han a coraçon.   [Rimado, 223]

Their moral habits were a scandal in a lax age. Both the councils and the *cortes* inveighed against clerical unchastity; the *cortes* of 1380, for example, demanded that the children of the clergy be denied rights of inheritance and that clerical concubines (*barraganas*) be obliged to wear a yellow cloth on their dresses so they would not be mistaken for properly married women. In the same vein, López de Ayala denounced those "ministers of Satan" and their lady friends:

En toda la aldea non ha tan apostada
Como la su mançeba, nin tan bien afeytada. . . .

In the whole village there is no one so well situated
Nor so well made up as his [the priest's] mistress. . . .
[*Rimado*, 227]

The charge was made at the *cortes* of Braga in 1401 that women kept by the clergy "were dressed and gowned as well or better than the wives of laymen" and for this reason many girls chose to take up with clerics, friars, and monks rather than legitimate husbands. The laity were no longer devout and deprecated liturgical services celebrated by concubinary clergy and refused to confess to them. Fifty years later, at the *cortes* of Santarém, it appeared that nothing had changed and that government efforts to compel the clergy to put away their concubines had failed. Fines imposed upon them were regarded as a normal expense of their lives, and royal officials pocketed the money as merely another perquisite. The complaints of the *cortes* in all the Hispanic realms indicate that the clergy, because of their dissolute character, were rather widely discredited. The sense of neglect and irresponsibility conveyed by these examples is not relieved by the following confession and exhortation of the Council of Aranda in 1473 (Canon 12): "Some clerics of our province . . . after the reception of the priestly order, disdain to celebrate the sacrament of the Eucharist. . . . We command the clergy . . . to celebrate the mass devoutly at least four times a year. . . . Moreover, we exhort the prelates of our province . . . to celebrate at least three times a year" (*CMCH*, IV, 677). If this is a reflection of common practice, then it would seem to be testimony to a wholesale abandonment of spiritual responsibilities by bishops and priests.

Monastic observance also seems to have been quite relaxed. The abbot depicted in *La danza de la muerte* lived in comfort and disdained penitential garb, while the Franciscan friar, "a subtle master, wise in all the arts," was haughty and proud. The decay of the monasteries is attributable in part to the increasing number of commendatory abbots, who usually were not monks, nor did they reside in the monastery, nor care much about the life within its walls. For them the monastery's importance was financial: the commendatory abbot received that portion of the monastery's income traditionally set aside for the sustenance of the abbot. The accumulation of property of all kinds, which was ordinarily exempt from taxation, made the monasteries extraordinarily wealthy and encouraged the pope or the king to name commendatory abbots as a convenient means of rewarding faithful service.

But without a resident abbot, himself professed in accordance with the rule of the Order and prepared to direct and guide the monks, it is little wonder that strict observance of the rule in many monasteries was a thing of the past. Stories of feasting, incontinence, idleness, hunting, and other mundane activities reveal the extent to which the monks had departed from the practice of poverty, chastity, and obedience. The fact that noble families often placed their younger sons and unmarried daughters in monasteries under family patronage also weakened monastic life. Finally, the growth of nationalism tended to undermine the supervisory structures of such international Orders as Cîteaux, whose system of visitations and whose annual general chapter were intended to preserve uniform observance of the rule in all abbeys pertaining to the Order.

Only one new religious community of importance was founded during this period, namely, the Order of San Jerónimo, confirmed by Gregory XI in 1373, with its principal seat in the monastery of Guadalupe, and following the rule of St. Augustine.

The military religious Orders of Calatrava, Alcántara, Santiago, Avis, Christ, and Montesa were rapidly tending toward secularization. Without any further justification for their existence since the abandonment of the reconquest, they were deeply involved in the political upheavals in the Hispanic realms, in part because so many of the knights belonged to the noble houses contending for power. The traditional ascetic practices of prayer, fasting, chastity, and the use of simple clothing, were gradually ignored or abandoned. In view of the power and resources at the disposal of the Orders, the crown became intensely concerned to control them. Thus, for example, Juan I of Castile obtained papal permission to name the masters of Santiago, Calatrava, and Alcántara, if those offices fell vacant during his reign. Fernando de Antequera in 1409 obtained papal appointment of his son Enrique as master of Santiago, a post later held by Alvaro de Luna and the marquess of Villena, as part of the spoils of the struggle for power. In Portugal João I, named master of Avis at age seven by his father, entrusted the administration of the Order of Christ to his son Henry the Navigator and that of Avis and Santiago to his son Fernando. In all these instances the traditional right of the members of the Orders to elect their leaders was overridden. Moreover, the kings of Aragon and Portugal endeavored to free the branches of Calatrava and Santiago in their kingdoms from any dependence upon the parent Orders in Castile. These actions foreshadowed the eventual annexation to the crown, in perpetuity, of the masterships of the military Orders.

The pilgrimage to Santiago and pilgrimages to the many shrines of the Virgin continued to be popular expressions of piety. The shrine of Our Lady of the Pillar in Zaragoza began to attract attention in the fifteenth century and received the first of its papal privileges from Calixtus III (himself the former Alfonso de Borja, member of an old Valencian family) in 1453. Religious drama also seems to have become a popular form of devotion, although the first extant text of a play, the *Auto de los Reyes* dates only from the end of the fifteenth century. But Canon 19 of the Council of Aranda in 1473 reveals that the performance of religious drama during the mass had long been customary and had reached the point of abuse. The Council declared that on the feasts of the Nativity, of Sts. Stephen and John, and of the Holy Innocents, as well as others, "while divine services were being celebrated, theatrical plays, masques, shows, spectacles, and many other dishonest and diverse fictions were introduced into the churches. There were tumults and disgraceful songs, and derisive words were spoken so that the divine office was impeded and the people ceased to be devout" (*CMCH*, IV, 679). Henceforth these "dishonest representations" were forbidden.

Perhaps these religious dramas were performed at times in the spirit of irreverence that characterized such parodies as Suero de Ribera's *Misa de amor* or Diego de Valera's *Letania de amor*. Much more serious was the recrudescence of magic and sorcery and the occasional appearance of heresy. Literary texts are full of references to divination, auguries, enchantments, conjuring, necromancy, the invocation of the devil, the power of the evil eye, and so on. The inquisitor general of Aragon, Fray Nicolás Eymerich, O.P. (d. 1399), denounced astrologers and necromancers and also brought about the condemnation of

Fray Ramón de Tárrega, O.P. (d. 1371), a convert from Judaism, who was charged with errors relating to the mass, and authorship of a treatise on the invocation of demons. Eymerich's principal work, the *Directorium Inquisitorum*, a manual for inquisitors, is a mine of information concerning the inquisition in Catalonia.

In the fifteenth century there is notice of the heresy of the *fraticelli* at Durango in Vizcaya; the inquisition condemned and burned a number of the heretics, but their leader, Alfonso de Mella, O.F.M., escaped to Granada where the Muslim authorities eventually executed him. On an entirely different level, Pedro Martínez de Osma (d. 1481), an erudite professor of theology at the University of Salamanca, was accused of holding the views of John Wycliffe and John Hus concerning confession and indulgences; his book *De confessione* was burned, and he was compelled to make a public recantation. Aside from this, there were no widespread heretical movements in the peninsula.

The popular longing for spiritual sustenance, which at times led to heresy, is nowhere better illustrated than in the missionary career of the Dominican friar, St. Vincent Ferrer (d. 1419). No one was more successful than he in summoning men to repentance and conversion. His renown was such that he was chosen as one of the delegates to resolve the succession to the throne of Aragon through the Compromise of Caspe. He tried to persuade Benedict XIII to resign in order to end the schism, but when he refused, Vincent advised the king of Aragon to repudiate Benedict for the good of the church. Vincent's missionary travels took him through much of Spain and also into Italy, France, Burgundy, and Brittany where he died. Crowds swarmed to hear him preach, and thousands promised to amend their lives; heretics returned to the orthodox faith, and many Jews were converted to Christianity. In Castile he persuaded the regents for Juan II to order Jews and Moors to live apart from Christians, especially so that new converts from Judaism or Islam would not relapse.

More than 300 extant texts containing notes or summaries of his sermons reveal a vibrant and expressive style, laced with stories calculated to win the attention of his listeners and to point out a moral. One example intended to illustrate the Second Commandment may be cited: "Once upon a time a man went to confession and the confessor asked him: Have you ever sworn in the name of God? By God's Head, No! When asked by the priest why he swore, he replied lamely: It is the custom." Without attempting to estimate the steadfastness of those who were moved by Vincent Ferrer's works to change their habits and to strive for the good, it must be recognized that his extraordinary success resulted from his response to a deeply felt human need in a time of spiritual turmoil and confusion.

Theological and Philosophical Studies

In the last century of the medieval era, some of the older peninsular universities achieved greater stability than before, while others continued to flounder, and some new ones were founded. The University of Salamanca, with faculties of arts, medicine, and law, to which Benedict XIII, and later Martin V, added theology, was the most prestigious in the peninsula. The College of St. Bartholomew, the oldest residence for students at the University, was founded in 1401. The Universities of Valladolid and Seville had a tenuous existence while Alcalá, projected by Sancho IV, had long since died out; Pius II's establishment of a chair of grammar there in 1445 did foreshadow the eventual development of the University in the sixteenth century. The foundation of a Franciscan house of studies (1476) and a secular college (1477) marked the beginning of the University of Sigüenza.

The Portuguese University, which had moved from Lisbon to Coimbra to Lisbon and then in 1355 back to Coimbra, returned to Lisbon in 1377, where it remained until a final migration in 1437 brought it back once again to Coimbra. In the crown of Aragon, the University of Lérida retained its pre-eminence despite several competitors. The Universities of Huesca and Perpignan, founded by Pedro IV, were never viable, and the former died out by the middle of the fifteenth century. Alfonso V chartered the Universities of Gerona (1446) and Barcelona (1450), and Sixtus IV gave a charter to the University of Zaragoza (1474). As early as the fourteenth century the Valencian city council expressed interest in establishing a university, but it did not come into being until chartered by Alexander VI in 1500.

The caliber of the universities varied considerably, depending upon the number of faculties, the capability of the professors, financial support from the crown or the cities, facilities for students, and so forth. University government was patterned upon the student university plan originated at Bologna, but was modified by the enactment of additional statutes over the course of two hundred years.

Three major intellectual traditions are discernible in this epoch, namely, Llullist, Scholastic, and Humanist. The continuation of Ramon

Llull's work by numerous disciples was a unique development which set Spain, and particularly the crown of Aragon, apart from the rest of Europe. The scholastics in the main were divided into three differing schools of thought, following respectively Thomas Aquinas, Duns Scotus, and William of Ockham. From the second half of the fifteenth century humanist influences from Italy, based upon a new interest in Platonism, began to have an effect upon philosophical studies.

The Llullist movement was a popular movement of Franciscan friars, secular clergy, merchants, and artisans especially in Valencia, Majorca, and Catalonia. The kings of Aragon favored the development of Llullism, perhaps as Carreras suggests, because they regarded it as a sort of national philosophy. In any case Pedro IV in 1369 gave a privilege for a Llullist school at Alcoy in Valencia, and in 1392 Juan I did the same for a school at Barcelona. The tendency of the Llullists of the fourteenth century to be linked with the spiritualist and apocalyptic elements among the Franciscans created suspicion concerning the orthodoxy of the movement and of Llull's doctrines. The popular character of the movement and the fact that so many of Llull's writings were in the vernacular also contributed to the hostility with which professional theologians and philosophers viewed Llullism.

The inquisitor, Nicolás Eymerich, mentioned above, was the sternest opponent of Llullism, seeing it as the antithesis of his own intellectual tradition based upon Aristotle and Thomas Aquinas. Declaring that Llull had propagated unorthodox views, he persuaded Pope Gregory XI in 1376 to censure a number of propositions drawn from Llull's writings. In general, he attacked Llull for an excessive reliance upon human reason, and for failure to be precise in speaking of God, the Trinity, and Christ's divine and human natures. But Eymerich's harshness and inflexibility evoked protest from a number of quarters, and Pedro IV forced him to leave the kingdom. Thereafter the inquisitor tried to destroy Llullism in a number of treatises, for example, *Dialogus contra Lullistas*. He was particularly bothered by the fact that he had to carry on this disputation with merchants, tailors, shoemakers, and others of that kind, rather than theologians like himself.

In the meantime the kings of Aragon and the cities of Valencia and Barcelona petitioned the pope to conduct a more thorough inquiry into Llull's writings. This was done finally in 1419, and a definitive sentence was published declaring that there was nothing unorthodox in Llull's work. The Llullist movement continued to thrive thereafter, and Alfonso V issued several privileges for the establishment of schools dedicated to teaching Llull's *Art*. The city council of Palma de Mallorca in 1481 chartered a school to which Ferdinand the Catholic later gave university status.

Llullism also had an impact in Portugal, where a school was established at Lisbon. More important evidence of Llull's influence, however, is found in the anonymous *Corte imperial*, dating from the end of the fourteenth or the beginning of the fifteenth century. Couched in allegorical form, it reveals the imperial court of Christ, the heavenly emperor, before whom all the nations and peoples of the world appear. The substance of the work is a debate between the church militant and the Muslims, Jews, pagans, and schismatic Christians; in the course of it the author demonstrates by Llull's evident and necessary reasons the truth of the Christian religion and of the specific claims of the Catholic church.

A Catalan professor at the University of Toulouse, Ramon Sabunde (or Sibiuda), also influenced by Llull's ideas, composed a *Liber creaturarum* in the latter part of the fifteenth century with the intent of demonstrating that by the observation of nature one could come to an understanding and acceptance of the essential doctrines of Christianity. The importance he attributed to knowledge acquired by experience and especially by the experience of each individual within himself foreshadowed significant developments of modern philosophy and psychology.

While Sabunde may be regarded as one of Llull's intellectual heirs, Anselm Turmeda (d. 1425/30) has been called the "Anti-Llull." A native of Majorca and a Franciscan, he completed his university studies at Lérida and Bologna but then rejected the Catholic faith and fled to Tunis where he became a Muslim. The emir of Tunis held him in high regard, and after his death the populace venerated him as a holy man. Turmeda wrote an extraordinarily popular book of proverbs, but of much greater importance is his *Disputa de l'Ase*, written in Catalan, though extant only in a sixteenth-century French version. Marked by scepticism, rationalism, and sarcastic commentary on the clergy and the church, the book takes the form of a dialogue between Anselm and an ass concerning the question: Is man superior to the animals? The ass, assisted by insects and other "dumb beasts," demonstrates that man by his vanity, stupidity, and madness is clearly inferior. In the Muslim world, Turmeda, known as Abd Allah, enjoyed great renown as the author of an Arabic treatise, *A Refutation of the Partisans of the Cross*, in which he proposed to present clear and decisive proofs drawn from natural reason, and easily comprehensible by anyone, of the truth of Islam and the falsity of Christianity. In effect, Turmeda turned the tables and tried to provide Islam with a system of apologetics based upon Llullian principles.

The popular character of the Llullist movement contrasts sharply with the scholastic tradition so closely linked to the university system. Within that tradition there were wide divergences of opinion, as the careers of several distinguished Spanish theologians and philosophers suggest. Among them Juan de Torquemada, O.P. (d. 1468) holds a prominent place as representative of conservative theology. He is not to be confused with his nephew, Tomás, also a Dominican, who later gained notoriety as the inquisitor-general in the reign of Ferdinand and Isabella. After becoming a master of theology at Paris, Juan was summoned to Rome by Eugene IV and named a cardinal. He participated in the Councils of Basel and Florence and also found time to write about forty books. His great masterpiece was the *Summa de ecclesia*, in which he vigorously defended the papal monarchy against the conciliarists, rejecting the notion that a general council was in any way superior to the pope. Seeing the church in biblical terms as a flock of sheep being guided to salvation by the supreme shepherd, he emphasized that the plenitude of power in the church belonged to the pope, who transmitted power to the lower ranks of the hierarchy. The pope also had authority in the temporal sphere insofar as he had need to protect the faith, to correct sins, to maintain peace in the Christian community, and to guard church property. Though he did not have the right to exercise royal or imperial jurisdiction, he could excommunicate and depose kings or emperors, if the good of the church required it. Though he presents a traditional view of papal power, it has been pointed out that Torquemada moved away from the extreme hierocratic claims of the papalists of the thirteenth and fourteenth centuries and that he is a forerunner of the theory of indirect power expressed by Bellarmine and others in the sixteenth century. In another treatise, *Opusculum ad honorem Romani imperii*, he defended the univeralist claims of the Holy Roman Empire against the arguments of royalist lawyers and others, such as his countryman, Rodrigo Sánchez de Arévalo, who held that the kingdoms of France and Spain had no temporal superior. In this respect, Torquemada's views were decidedly anachronistic, but his defense of the papacy and its unique role in the church proved to be a major weapon in the struggle against conciliarism.

Alfonso de Madrigal, el Tostado (d. 1455), one of the most learned men in Spain, differed with Torquemada on the question of church government and on some minor issues. A Franciscan friar, he became professor of moral philosophy and then of sacred scripture at the University of Salamanca; though he stood with the conciliarists at the Council of Basel, he opposed the deposition of Eugene IV, to whom he pledged obedience. He was named bishop of Avila in 1449. His voluminous writings include biblical commentaries, sermons, books of piety, and a treatise on the pagan gods, inspired by a similar work of Boccaccio. His writings reflect the transition from the medieval form, characterized by the dry, scholastic method, to the more expansive Renaissance form, filled with classical allusions and oratorical flourishes. His views on church government were set forth principally in his *Defensorium trium conclusionum* and *De optima politia*. He argued that democracy was the preferable form of government and that a general council adequately represented the whole body of the faithful and could command obedience from all, including the pope. He believed that the universal church was infallible in those matters necessary to salvation, though individual popes were not, and some had indeed fallen into error and heresy. It was the unwillingness of men like el Tostado to take the radical way in opposing the pope—to the point of deposition—that caused the conciliar movement to fail.

Rodrigo Sánchez de Arévalo (d. 1470) was even more extreme in his concept of papal power than Torquemada. He gained fame initially as a skilled orator and diplomat in the service of the king of Castile and later of the popes, who rewarded him with a number of bishoprics, including that of Zamora. His chief work, the *De monarchia orbis*, is a thoroughgoing defense of a universal papal monarchy. Although he denied the sovereignty of the Holy Roman Emperor over the kingdoms of France and Spain and so prompted a response from Torquemada, he attributed to the pope an authority greater than that conceived by Torquemada; he believed the pope had universal authority in both the spiritual and temporal realms and could intervene directly and frequently in the affairs of secular rulers. He also wrote a *Suma de politica*, a treatise on good government; the *Vergel de los principes*, a mirror of princes; and the *Speculum humanae vitae*, a moral treatise on the ranks in secular and ecclesiastical society, which enjoyed enormous popularity throughout Europe. His *Historia Hispanica*, traces peninsular history down to the reign of Juan II, in the light of St. Augustine's providential view of history.

No truly great philosopher emerged in this period, though Fernando de Córdoba (d. 1486), who reflects the influence of the humanist revival of Platonism, astounded contemporaries by the breadth of his knowledge, his skill in disputation, and his command of languages. The great promise which he seemed to offer, however, was only partially fulfilled. Though he had little but contempt for Ramon Llull, like him, he sought to develop the general principles of universal knowledge; his influence and success were clearly inferior, however, to that of the great Catalan thinker.

Vernacular Literature and the Dawn of the Renaissance

Vernacular literature flourished during the last century of the medieval era, as whatever hesitation concerning the suitability of the common tongue for expressing profound or sublime thoughts was dissipated. The use of the vernacular is testimony to the extent of literacy among the laity, many of whom, especially nobles and townsmen, were among the principal writers of the time. The themes of vernacular literature were typically medieval, but at the end of the fourteenth century one can perceive the first influences of the Italian Renaissance in Catalonia and gradually thereafter in Castile, Navarre, and Portugal.

The Italian humanists, from the time of Petrarch (d. 1374), were moved by a love and enthusiasm for the literature of the ancient classics, to study and correct and edit them and to translate them into the vernacular so that the newly discovered ideas could be disseminated as widely as possible. Humanist influence in Spain was focused not in the universities which continued to be closely bound up with scholasticism and the medieval tradition, but rather in the courts of kings and great nobles. One of the consequences was that theology and philosophy no longer dominated the world of knowledge; the more humanistically oriented subjects, grammar and rhetoric, gained the ascendancy.

Although the vernacular literature burgeoned and served as a vehicle for spreading humanist ideas, in the long run the humanists could only regard it, along with medieval Latin, as barbarous and uncouth. Thus, by the time of Ferdinand and Isabella, writers were turning away from the vernacular and were writing in Latin, consciously patterning their work upon classical models. The effects upon Catalan literature in particular were unfortunate, for it began a steady decline thereafter, though other factors, such as the political hegemony of Castile contributed to the decline.

In the latter part of the fourteenth century numerous Latin works were translated into the vernacular, oftentimes under the patronage of kings or magnates, such as Pedro IV and Juan I of Aragon, João I of Portugal, and Juan Fernández de Heredia, grand master of the Order of the Hospital. The works selected for translation included St. Augustine's *City of God*, Gregory the Great's *Moralia*, Boethius's *Consolation of Philosophy*, but pagan classical writings, for instance, Cicero's *De officiis*, Seneca's *De beneficiis*, were also translated. In the fifteenth century translations continued to appear and included now not only ancient works such as Eusebius's *Ecclesiastical History*, translated by el Tostado, but the writings of Italian humanists, especially Boccaccio, whose *Decameron*, *Corbaccio*, and Latin treatises were turned into Catalan or Castilian. Dante, whose influence had not been so great, was more widely appreciated after Andreu Febrer made a Catalan translation of the *Divine Comedy* in 1429; Enrique de Villena did a partial translation into Castilian.

The impact of the Renaissance was most strongly felt during the reigns of Alfonso V of Aragon, Juan II of Castile, and Duarte of Portugal. Alfonso V, totally captivated by the Renaissanse, made his court at Naples one of the greatest centers of literature and learning in Europe. Every humanist of any consequence, men such as Lorenzo Valla and Aeneas Silvius Piccolomini, enjoyed his patronage at one time or another. Catalan and Castilian writers visited his court, imbibed new ideas, learned new styles, and returned home to propagate them. Juan II of Castile, though a total failure as a statesman, was a distinguished patron of poets and scholars, a ruler whose court became an important literary center, spreading Renaissance classicism and humanism not only throughout Castile, but also into the neighboring kingdoms. Prince Carlos of Viana, heir to the throne of Navarre, developed acquaintance with Italian humanists during his stay at Alfonso V's court and even tried his hand at translating Aristotle's *Ethics*. In Portugal, Duarte and his brother Pedro were open to humanism and encouraged translations of classical authors, especially Cicero, Seneca, and Aristotle. All of this prepared the way for the triumph of the Renaissance in the reign of Ferdinand and Isabella.

Vernacular Prose Literature

In the last quarter of the fourteenth century the medieval tradition was still quite vigorous, and few authors had yet been affected by classicism or humanism. A characteristic representative of the medieval tradition is Francesch Eiximenis (d. 1409), a Franciscan friar who spent many years in Valencia. Like Ramon Llull, the only Catalan writer who surpassed him in literary output, he chose to write consistently in the vernacular, for he believed that it was his mission to instruct the people at large in the essential principles of Christian morality. With this in mind he planned to write a kind of encyclopedia, a didactic work to guide the Christian man in all his activities. Only four books of El Crestià (The Christian) are extant; the first three are expositions of doctrinal and moral questions, while the twelfth book El Dotzé, also known as Regiment de Princeps, contains his views on government. He had already expounded them some years earlier in his Regiment de la Cosa Pública, dedicated to the town council of Valencia. His conception of political society was essentially Christian, and he hoped that men, by living in accordance with the Christian moral law, could transform society. In the practical sphere he favored a limited monarchy in which the several estates would have the opportunity to participate. His other works include a treatise on angels and another on the virtues and responsibilities of women.

The first Catalan, or Hispanic writer, to reflect humanist influences was Bernat Metge (d. 1413), a royal servant, who while forced to spend some time in prison wrote Lo Somni (The Dream). The first of its four dialogues concerns the spirituality and immortality of the soul and reveals a certain materialism and skepticism on Metge's part. The other dialogues include comments upon contemporary events, as when the ghost of Juan I tells that he has to spend time in purgatory because of his attitude in the matter of the schism; and a diatribe against women, and a concluding eulogy of celebrated women of the past.

The work of the Castilian author, Enrique de Villena (d. 1434) curiously reflects the transition from the medieval to the Renaissance era. To his contemporaries he was ineffectual and inept, a judgment justified no doubt by his willing dissolution of his marriage on the grounds of impotence, so that his wife could become the mistress of Enrique III, who then rewarded him with the mastership of Calatrava. In contrast to most of his fellow nobles, Villena was entirely preoccupied by study and had no inclination for chivalrous activity. His interest in the occult gained him a reputation as a magician, and later legend had it that he made a pact with the devil. There is little foundation for this, other than the fact that Juan II ordered his books to be burned after his death. Of those that survive, his treatise on the evil eye (*Tractado del aojamiento*) evoked Menéndez Pelayo's comment that if the rest were as ridiculous as this one, then there was little loss to science. The man entrusted with burning Villena's books was Fray Lope de Barrientos (d. 1469), a bishop of Segovia, Avila, and Cuenca in succession, who used some of them to compose treatises of his own on chance, prophecy, divination, augury, magic, interpretation of dreams, and the like. His most important book, the *Tratado de la divinanza*, concludes with a condemnation of these practices as abhorrent to the Christian religion.

Villena was also a gourmet, a role which Fernán Pérez de Guzmán summarized simply: he ate a great deal. Villena wrote a book on the culinary arts, entitled *Tractado del arte de cortar del cuchillo*, the art of cutting with a knife; in it he discoursed on the proper manner of setting and serving at table. In the classical vein he composed an allegory on a pagan theme, though with distinctive Christian overtones, called *Los doce trabajos de Hercules*. Each of the twelve labors symbolizes the triumph of virtue over vice, as in Christian moral tales. Villena also contributed to the stimulation of interest in the classics by making the first complete translation in any romance language of Vergil's *Aeneid*.

Just a few years after Villena's death, Alfonso Martínez de Toledo, Archpriest of Talavera (d. c. 1466), published one of the most vivid and entertaining books of the epoch, *El Corbacho*. A skillful mix of the old and the new, it is presented as a book of moral instruction, especially for those who had not yet tasted the bitterness of the world. Dividing his work into four parts, he condemns foolish love, the "loco amor" of which the Archpriest of Hita had spoken a century before; he then reveals the vices of women, whom he accuses of being promiscuous, envious, inconstant, two-faced, disobedient, vain, liars, detractors, gossips, and so forth, each of these characteristics is illustrated by an appropriate story. Part three is a discourse on the habits and qualities of men who are choleric, sanguine, phlegmatic, or melancholic, and in the last part he tells of fortunetellers, astrologers, diviners, and the like. The Archpriest was influenced by Boccaccio's *Corbaccio* and by various Catalan writers, and his list of feminine vices is much the same as that given by Andreas Capellanus in the twelfth-century *Art of Courtly Love*. What makes the book real and alive, however, is the author's astute observation of human frailty and his ability to capture the sounds of popular speech, with all its vigor, color, and extravagance. The book is at times realistic, ironical, satirical, and comical, and a valuable picture of contemporary life and customs.

Several members of the Avis dynasty displayed an affinity for literature and made significant contributions to the development of Portuguese prose. João I encouraged literary endeavors and translations and even wrote a book on hunting. His son Duarte ranks with the greatest Portuguese writers and showed an uncommon concern for the proper and exact use of language. His chief work, *The Loyal Counselor* (*Leal Conselheiro*) is concerned with right conduct and draws together materials from numerous sources, including Cicero, Gregory the Great, and Thomas Aquinas. In his work, the king shows himself to be truly worthy, essentially honest, truthful, and just. Pedro, duke of Coimbra (d. 1449), his younger brother, composed the *Livro da virtuosa bemfeitoria* on the basis of Seneca's *De beneficiis*, but added elements from Christian moralists. Both Pedro and Duarte gave impetus not only to the development of Portuguese prose literature, but also to the introduction of humanist ideas and interests.

Denunciations of women and essays on morality were typical of the medieval literary tradition, and so too was the romance of chivalry. A number of romances derived from French originals were in circulation, for instance, the quest for the Holy Grail, *Demanda do Santo Graal*, and *Amadis de Gaula*, the earliest version of which dates from the fourteenth century. Indigenous to Spain are two Catalan romances, *Curial e Guelfa*, written about the middle of the fifteenth century, and the greatly superior, *Tirant lo Blanc*, written by the Valencian noble, Joanot Martorell (d. c. 1460). The perfect knight, Tirant is yet a man of flesh and blood, whose adventures carry him to England, Sicily, the Byzantine empire, and Barbary, overcoming enemies and exemplifying the ideals of chivalry. *Tirant* differs from other romances in its strong realism and its reference to historical events and personages. Drawing heavily on the adventures of the Catalan Company in Sicily and Byzantium, the author presents Tirant as the champion of the faith against the Turks who were besieging Constantinople. While reflecting the traditional spirit of chivalry, *Tirant* also includes elements of humor and caricature, typical of the new age. In *Don Quixote*, Cervantes spared *Tirant* from destruction, along with *Amadis*, because its elegant style surpassed other books of chivalry.

Historiography

Some of the finest prose literature of this era was concerned with contemporary historical events. The bare-bones annals and chronicles of earlier times gave place to more detailed narratives, often characterized by description of personalities, inquiry into motivation, and assessment of consequences. Universal history survived to some extent, and Alfonso X's *General Chronicle* served as the foundation for the third and fourth *General Chronicles* compiled in the first half of the fifteenth century. The major historical works of the period are centered upon the reigns of individual monarchs, but there are also a number of chronicles of the deeds of leading personages. At the close of this period the vernacular gave way to Latin as the language of historical writing, thus marking the final triumph of classicism.

Pedro López de Ayala (d. 1407), has been called the first Castilian humanist and certainly ranks as one of the great Castilian authors of this era. Soldier, diplomat, and statesman, in his youth he followed Pedro the Cruel but abandoned him in 1366 for Enrique II and thereafter loyally served Juan I and Enrique III; the latter named him chancellor of Castile. With all these preoccupations he still found time to compose chronicles of the reigns of these monarchs covering the years from 1350 to 1395. The *Chronicle of Pedro the Cruel*, because of the dramatic nature of the revolutionary upheaval, has attracted the greatest interest; López de Ayala depicts the king as a cruel, hard personage, but otherwise strove to be objective in his account of events. The *Chronicle of Juan I*, dealing with the attempted conquest of Portugal, is also of great importance and elegant style. Taken in all, the four chronicles constitute an extremely valuable record presented by one who was a perceptive observer and a major participant in many of the events described. His style is vivid and moving, and his historical judgment is, on the whole, quite sound. López de Ayala was also a poet of some ability. His *Rimado de Palacio*, already mentioned, is a long didactic poem, lamenting the immorality of the times, the evils arising from the Great Schism, abuses in government, and so forth. Written in *cuaderna vía*, it is the last manifestation of the *mester de clerecía*.

His nephew, Fernán Pérez de Guzmán (d. c. 1460), was active in pubic affairs during the reigns of Enrique III and Juan II, but his opposition to Alvaro de Luna eventually hastened his retirement. He has left us one of the most interesting and important works of the time, a collection of sketches, *Generaciones y Semblanzas*, of the leading figures of the early fifteenth century: Enrique III, Fernando de Antequera, Catalina de Lancaster, and so many other prelates, nobles, and courtiers whom he knew personally. In each instance he describes the individual's physical appearance and his moral character and habits, as well as his principal achievements. Of his uncle he said, in chapter seven: "He was tall and thin, of handsome person, a man of great discretion and authority, wise in counsel both in peace and war. He loved the sciences very much and gave himself to the study of books and histories. . . . He loved women very much, more so than was proper for such a wise knight as himself." Pérez de Guzmán also wrote poetry, though not of very high quality, for example, *Loores de los claros varones de España*, a long poem in praise of kings, princes, prelates and other great men of Spain from ancient times to the fifteenth century.

The long and detailed *Chronicle of Juan II*, covering the first half of the fifteenth century, was begun by Alvar García de Santa Maria, but was then retouched and revised by others, until Lorenzo Galíndez de Carvajal made the final revision in the early sixteenth century. It is distinguished by its harmonious style and an appreciation of the significance of historical events. Given the extraordinary importance of Alvaro de Luna during the reign, it is not surprising that he should be the central figure in the *Crónica del Condestable*, attributed to Gonzalo Chacón, one of his dependents, who set out to glorify him and to justify his actions in every way.

The historical works relating to Enrique IV reveal the same heated passions that marked political events. His chaplain, Diego Enríquez del Castillo (d. 1480) wrote a *Chronicle of Enrique IV*, as a defense of the king and a denunciation in bitter terms of those who betrayed him; seldom does the author suggest that the king was the cause of his own misfortunes. Alfonso de Palencia (d. 1490), on the other hand, was extremely hostile to the king in his *Gesta Hispaniensia*, a work in

elegant Latin, whose appearance ushered in Renaissance historiography. Mosén Diego de Valera (d. c. 1488), a nobleman whose
chivalrous adventures had taken him as far as Bohemia, where he
participated in the Hussite Wars, was also highly critical of the king in
his *Memorial de diversas hazañas*. Finally, one of the king's favorites,
Miguel Lucas de Iranzo was the subject of a *Chronicle* written by
Pedro de Escabías covering the period from 1458 to 1471; it is important as a description of the customs of a great lord and his entourage and of events in Andalusia where he spent most of his time.

Fernão Lopes (d. c. 1460), one of the greatest Portuguese writers,
is generally recognized as the father of Portuguese historical writing.
Appointed royal chronicler by Duarte, he set out to write the history
of all the kings of Portugal and for this purpose carefully searched the
royal archives in Lisbon as well as those of many monasteries and
churches for documentation appropriate to his purposes. Unfortunately, only his *Chronicles of Pedro 1, Fernando, and João 1* are extant,
but they reveal him as an historian of great capability. His data are
presented intelligently, with a concern for accuracy, and his judgments
and interpretations are always balanced and sensible. In 1454 he was
succeeded in his post by Gomes Eannes de Azurara or Zurara (d.
1474), who lacked Lopes's archival training, and is not so much an
historian as an enthusiastic biographer of the house of Avis. His
Chronicle of João 1 is full of praise for the king who defended Portuguese independence and initiated Portuguese expansion in Africa by
the conquest of Ceuta. The *Chronicle of the Discovery and Conquest
of Guinea* is the major account of Henry the Navigator's explorations
and colonizations in Africa and the adjacent islands. One might also
mention Frei João Alvares's *Chronicle of the Infante Fernando*, a
description by an eyewitness of the capture and imprisonment of the
prince after the disastrous campaign at Tangier. Finally, Rui de Pina
(d. c. 1523), using materials gathered and composed by Fernão Lopes,
compiled chronicles of the Portuguese kings from Sancho I to Afonso
IV, and wrote the *Chronicles of Duarte, Afonso V, and João II*, thereby
concluding the medieval cycle.

Historical writing in the crown of Aragon is clearly inferior to
Castilian and Portuguese production and also to the works of the
great Catalan historians of the thirteenth and fourteenth centuries.
Three Catalan works must be noted. In the first half of the fifteenth
century Pere Tomic composed the *Histories e conquestes dels reys*

d'Aragó e comtes de Catalunya, from creation to the first years of Alfonso V; it was later extended to the reign of Ferdinand the Catholic, but in comparison to the Castilian chronicles, it is jejeune indeed. Gabriel Turell used it as the foundation for his *Recort,* written in 1476, and notable otherwise for the important information concerning Barcelona and the Catalan constitution in the fifteenth century. *La Fi del Comte d'Urgell,* a political pamphlet, rather than a history as such, is important for its discussion and defense of the rights of the count of Urgel to the throne of Aragon against the intrusion of the Trastámaras.

Italian humanists, enjoying the patronage of Alfonso V in his court at Naples, were encouraged to record his activities and policies in Italy. Lorenzo Valla (d. 1457), famous for his exposition of the falsity of the Donation of Constantine, composed a life of Fernando de Antequera, *Historia de Ferdinando Aragoniae rege,* while Antonio Beccadelli, called Panormita, from Palermo, his birthplace, wrote *De dictis et factis Alphonsi regis Aragonum,* a history of Alfonso V; Bartolomeo Fazio also honored the king with his *De rebus gestis ab Alphonso V.*

Finally, the reign of Juan II of Aragon was chronicled by Gonzalo García de Santa Maria, *Vita Johannis secundi Aragonum regis,* and the king's son, Carlos de Viana, wrote the *Crónica de los reyes de Navarra,* extending down to the accession of Carlos III.

Poetry

By the middle of the fifteenth century the medieval poetic tradition was giving way to classical and humanist influences. The popular poetry of the *juglares* and troubadours disappeared, as did Galician lyric poetry and the *mester de clerecía.* Moreover, poetry was separated from music, that is, it was no longer sung, but recited. The new poets were courtiers and noblemen, using new meters, and sprinkling their verses with allusions to Greek and Roman mythology and history. Courtly love was no longer a dominant theme, though love poetry continued to abound; satire, especially political satire, became much more common. Though the quantity of poetry preserved is considerable, a great deal of it is dull, trivial, and frivolous, and yet there were some truly great poets in this epoch.

A sizeable collection of poetry from the late fourteenth and early fifteenth centuries is contained in the *Cancionero de Baena,* compiled by Juan Alfonso de Baena on the command of Juan II. The ablest of the poets represented there, Alfonso Alvarez de Villasandino (d. 1425), a court poet who wrote for pay, exemplifies a major change in lyric poetry. His earliest poems were in Galician, hitherto regarded as the most suitable language for lyric expression, but he gradually abandoned it and by the end of his days was using a mature Castilian, from that time on used by all the best lyric poets.

With Juan de Mena (d. 1456) we have the first humanist among Castilian poets. Secretary of Latin Letters to Juan II, he spent some time in Italy where he imbibed the spirit of the Renaissance, and learned the new meters being employed there. His greatest poem, the *Laberinto de Fortuna,* is an allegory full of classical allusions and clearly shows the influence of Dante. His purpose was to counsel Juan II, whom he addressed as "the great king of Spain, the new Caesar." Typical are these verses (stanza 230) urging "the new Augustus," "the light of Spain," to strike fear in the hearts of evildoers, so that justice may not be trampled to the ground:

> Sanad vos los reynos de aqueste recelo
> O principe bueno, o novel Agusto,
> O lumbre de España, o rey mucho justo,
> Pues rey de la tierra vos fizo el del cielo;
> E los que vos siruen con malvado celo,
> Con fanbre tirana, con non buena ley,
> Fazed que deprendan temer a su rey.
> Porque justicia non ande por suelo.   [CC, I, 175]

Without doubt the greatest lyric poet of the time was Iñigo López de Mendoza, marquess of Santillana (d. 1458). Active in politics and a determined enemy of Alvaro de Luna, he was also a bibliophile who accumulated a vast library in his palace at Guadalajara. Though apparently he did not know Latin, he was influenced by the humanist spirit and especially by Dante and Petrarch. His works include didactic and allegorical poems, sonnets, love poems, religious poems, and others on contemporary political events. Among these last, *La comedieta de Ponza* is a reflection on the misfortunes of princes as illustrated by the defeat and capture of Alfonso V in the naval battle of Ponza. The *Doctrinal de privados,* inspired by the career and downfall of Alvaro de Luna, is an admonition to those who might be tempted to imitate the constable in his quest for power and riches. Santillana's best-known and best-loved poems are ten *serranillas,* songs of encounters with mountain girls and shepherdesses. Among them, the most frequently cited is the sixth, describing his meeting with a beautiful cowgirl of Hinojosa, who stands in a green field full of roses and flowers:

Moça tan fermosa
Non vi en la frontera
Como una vaquera
De la Finojosa.
En un verde prado
De rosas e flores
Guardando ganado
Con otros pastores
La vi tan graciosa
Que apenas creyera
Que fuesse vaquera
De la Finojosa.

A prettier girl
I've not seen on the frontier
Than a cowgirl
Of Hinojosa.
In a green field
Full of roses and flowers
Watching her flock
With other shepherds
I saw one so graceful
I could hardly believe
She was a cowgirl
Of Hinojosa.   [CC, I, 573]

Jorge Manrique (d. 1478) is, on the whole, a minor poet, but he will always be remembered for one outstanding poem, *Coplas por la muerte de su padre*, an elegy written in 1476 on the death of his father, Rodrigo Manrique, master of Santiago. Though his reflections on death are borrowed from the common medieval store, he infused them with a very deep sense of his personal sorrow and loss. After noting the passing glory of Juan II, Alvaro de Luna, and others, the poet comments that knights win eternal life, not through the accumulation of riches, but through their labors against the Moors; and then Death summons his father, who shed so much pagan blood, to his reward (stanza 36):

El biuir que es perdurable
No se gana con estados
            mundanales,

Ni con vida deleytable,
En que moran los pecados
                    ynfernales;
Mas los buenos religiosos
Gananlo con oraciones
                    y con lloros,
Los cavalleros famosos
Con trabajos y aflicciones
                    contra moros.   [CC, II, 233]

In the thirteenth and fourteenth centuries Galician-Portuguese was acknowledged as the most fitting language for lyric poetry, but by the end of the fourteenth century Portuguese poets were beginning to write in Castilian, and in this way classical and humanist influences appeared in Portuguese poetry. This transition is clearly marked in the career of Infante Pedro (d. 1466), whom the Catalans chose as their king. After writing a few short lyrics in Portuguese he turned to Castilian, and this long remained the language of poetry. The *Cancioneiro* of García de Resende (d. 1536) includes many poems from the middle of the fifteenth century, but there is no Portuguese poet to compare with Santillana.

Catalan poetry was long bound to the Provençal tradition and was given new life, at least for a time, when Juan I founded the *Consistori de la Gaya Sciensa* at Barcelona in 1393, to encourage prize competition among poets. Enrique de Villena, who reorganized the *Consistori* for Fernando I in 1413, described it in his *Arte de trovar*. Royal patronage, however, could not elevate mediocre poetry above the commonplace. During the reign of Alfonso V the spirit of Catalan poetry began to change under Castilian and Italian influence. The poets of Catalonia proper remained steadfast in the earlier tradition, but a new school of poets centered at Valencia were receptive to new ideas, and these are the poets who are most highly regarded today.

Among them, Jordi de Sant Jordi (d. 1430), a Valencian noble who served Alfonso V in Italy, has left eighteen exquisite poems revealing Petrarchan influence. *Estramps*, the loveliest of them, celebrates the beauty of his beloved, whose image he will bear with him to the grave:

Jus lo front port vostra bella semblança
De què mon cors nit e jorn fa gran festa,
Que remirant la molt bella figura
De vostra faç m'és romasa l'empremta

Que ja per mort no se'n partrà la forma
Ans, quan serai del tot fores d'est segle
Cells que lo cors portaran al sepulcre
Sobre ma faç veuran vostre signe.

Beneath my brow I bear your lovely face
On which my body feasts by night and day.
For contemplating your lovely form
The memory of your face will remain with me,
Nor will it depart even at death.
But when I leave entirely this world
Those who bear my body to the grave
Will see your sign upon my face.   [LCA, IV, 48]

The greatest poet of the Catalan language was Ausiàs March (d. 1459), a Valencian noble, who, after brief service under Alfonso V, retired to his estates where he led an outwardly tranquil existence. His poetry, however, reveals the intense torments he suffered within his being as he was torn between passion and lust and a desire for pure love. In his *Cants d'Amor* he dwells on the nature, characteristics, and difficulties of love. Love involves the entire person, body and soul, and, as he shows in his *Cants de Mort*, is only changed by death which removes its physical and sensual aspects. As a remembrance and contemplation of the beloved, love is now spiritual; but the most complete love, truly pure, truly spiritual, is the love of God, the theme of his *Cant spiritual*. The influence of Dante, Petrarch, Aristotle, and Thomas Aquinas on his poetry has been pointed out; by reason of its highly abstract character and its avoidance of imagery, it has been called poetry of ideas. The spectre of Death looms large in his poetry, as suggested by these lines describing the weakening of his senses, the ebbing of the strength of his body and his mind:

Cobrir no puc la dolor qui.m turmenta
Veent que Mort son aguait me descobre
Io li graesc com sa intenció m'obre
Volent del mon traure.m sens dar-me empenta
Car tot primer virtut del cos m'ha tolta.
Ia mos cinc senys non senten lo que solen
Los a part dins de gran por ja tremolen
L'enteniment de follia tem volta.
La velledat en Valencians mal prova
E no sé com io faça obra nova.

I can't conceal the sorrow that torments me
Seeing that Death reveals his snare for me.
I thank him when he works his will on me
Wishing to take me from the world without giving me a push
For he's already taken all the strength from my body.
My five senses no longer feel as they used to.
Those within are trembling out of great fear
And understanding has turned to madness.
Old age sits not well on Valencians
And I don't know how to do something new.   [*LCA*, IV, 59–60]

The last important Catalan poet is Jaume Roig (d. 1478), a Valencian physician in the service of the queen of Aragon. His *Spill* or *Llibre de les Dones* is a terrible satire on women, whom he represents as full of sin and aberration; even the wise Solomon was deceived by their counsel into worshiping a strange god:

Per mala sort
En tot malguany
Jo.m fiu Déu strany
Per llur consell
Fiu, déu novell
E l'adorí
Apostatí
Contra mon ús:
No.n vull dir pus.

Through bad luck
In all misfortune
I trusted a strange God.
By their counsel
I trusted a new God,
I adored him
And apostasized
Contrary to my law:
I will say no more.   [*LCA*, IV, 90]

Though realistic and sordid, the poem is a diverting spectacle written by a man with an eye for the absurd and ridiculous in human life.

Epilogue

Avreis la monarchia de todas las Españas y reformareis la silla inperial de la inclita sangre de los godos donde venis.

You shall have rulership over all the Spains and you shall reform the imperial throne of the noble race of the Goths, from whence you come.

Diego de Valera, Doctrinal de Principes, Prologue

The Catholic Kings and
the Perfect Prince

Spain and Portugal

After more than a century of upheaval and violent change, the Middle Ages came to a close. As characteristic signs of the transition from the old to the new, historians have pointed to the emergence of national monarchies, the development of capitalism, the discovery and exploration of the New World and the Far East, the triumph of Renaissance classicism and humanism, and the disintegration of Christian unity.

In the Iberian peninsula the beginning of the modern age was heralded by the advent of "the Catholic Kings," Ferdinand and Isabella, and their Portuguese counterpart, João II, "the Perfect Prince." Overcoming the challenges of the past, they restored the power and prestige of the monarchy in their respective kingdoms and were able to play a more effective role in the general affairs of Europe. Most importantly, Ferdinand and Isabella by their marriage united Aragon and Castile, a giant step toward the unification of the entire peninsula. The fall of Granada, the last Muslim stronghold in Spain, in 1492, not only brought the centuries-old reconquest to a finish, further advancing the cause of unification, but also marked the end of the history of medieval Spain. The seemingly irresistible trend toward peninsular union was thwarted, however, by the failure of a series of marriage alliances to unite Portugal to Castile and Aragon. Thus, by the accidents of history the political structure of the peninsula was finally settled with the permanent separation of Portugal from her eastern neighbors, now known collectively as Spain, the name once given to the whole peninsula.

657

The new age was distinguished in other ways. Abandoning the medieval policy of religious tolerance or coexistence, the Catholic kings expelled the Jews and Muslims who would not accept the Christian religion. In this way the concept of a nation united in religious belief and suffering no deviation from orthodoxy was rooted firmly in the peninsular mind. The exploration of the west coast of Africa begun in the days of Henry the Navigator reached a triumphal climax when the Portuguese rounded the Cape of Good Hope and opened the route to India. But Columbus's discovery of America forced the Portuguese to share the world overseas with Spain. While these new vistas were being opened, the outbreak of hostilities between France and Spain, harkening back to the thirteenth-century struggle over Naples and Sicily, established the central theme of western European history for much of the sixteenth century.

The Yoke and the Arrows

The marriage of Ferdinand and Isabella in 1469 prepared the way for the union of the two most powerful Hispanic kingdoms. If Isabella had chosen to marry Afonso V of Portugal, however, the subsequent history of the peninsula, of Europe, and of the New World would undoubtedly have been very different. The union of Castile and Portugal seemed, on the face of it, to be more logical than the union of Castile and Aragon, because the similarity of laws, customs, institutions, and languages was greater. The establishment of the Castilian Trastámaras in Aragon since the beginning of the fifteenth century, on the other hand, attracted Isabella to that kingdom, an attraction strengthened by the disparity in age, looks, and abilities between Afonso V and Ferdinand. While not intending to exclude an ultimate union with Portugal, Isabella's choice determined that the new Spain would be composed of Castile and Aragon, rather than Castile and Portugal.

When she began her reign in 1474, she was a young woman of twenty-three, already giving evidence of high intelligence, will power, and energy, as well as a sense of purpose and great political wisdom. Ferdinand, her junior by a year, was equally skilled in politics and diplomacy and experienced in government, having been appointed at the age of fifteen to govern Sicily on behalf of his father. When Juan II died in 1479, Ferdinand inherited the realms of Aragon, Sicily, and Sardinia, while his sister Leonor, countess of Foix—and, upon her death, her grandson Francisco Febo (1479–1483)—obtained Navarre. Ferdinand is reckoned as II of Aragon and V of Castile.

The royal marriage effected an essentially personal union of the two kingdoms. The unity and solidarity of the king and queen found expression in several ways, for example, in the title "the Catholic Kings" given them by Pope Alexander VI in 1494; in the device of the yoke and the arrows which they adopted as their arms, and in the motto, *tanto monta, monta tanto*, symbolizing their basic equality. Yet there was no fusion of the two realms; each retained its distinctive institutions and laws. Moreover, Isabella, as queen proprietress of Castile, held the power of final decision in the affairs of that kingdom, though Ferdinand, during her lifetime, was allowed to share the royal power and title with her; in Aragon he was sovereign, and Isabella simply his queen consort. But the king and queen trusted and complemented each other in so many ways that one can properly speak of their joint rulership.

Of the two kingdoms, Castile, by virtue of its central position in the peninsula, the greater extent of its territory, its more numerous population, and its currently more vigorous economy, assumed a natural hegemony. To some extent this was suggested by the fact that in the royal intitulation Castile and León took precedence over Aragon and Sicily. Soldevila emphasized that Ferdinand, as a member of a Castilian dynasty, favored Castilian ascendancy and contributed to the process of Castilianizing the Catalan administration. On the contrary, Elliott argued that Ferdinand was a Catalan by his upbringing and did not sacrifice Catalan liberties or interests to those of Castile. Coming to power after the constitutional struggles of the reign of Juan II, he took care to strengthen the Catalan concept of a contractual state. Promulgating the constitution *Observança* in the *corts* of 1481, he acknowledged the traditional limitations on royal power and charged the *Generalitat* with the task of guarding against any infringement of Catalan liberties by himself or by any royal official. According to Vicens Vives, Ferdinand, more than Isabella, favored a pluralistic rather than an integrated monarchy; but while preserving the traditional liberties of the states of the crown of Aragon, he also affirmed royal power more solidly than before.

The New Monarchy

Ferdinand and Isabella and João II of Portugal (1481–1495) typified the new generation of sovereigns coming to power in western Europe in the closing years of the fifteenth century. Historians have used the term "new monarchy" to describe the governments forged by these rulers, but the extent to which their methods and policies were new has been disputed. Many of the political principles by which they conducted their affairs derived from an earlier time and were set forth some years later by Machiavelli in his book The Prince. The greatest responsibility of the new monarchs was the preservation of the state. "Reason of state," that is, all those ideas and principles relating to the survival and continued functioning of the state, became the customary justification for royal actions. Duplicity, secrecy, treachery, cruelty, and violence, indeed any means whatsoever, could be used in defense of the state. Royal policy, therefore, could often be immoral or amoral. Contemporaries, however, frequently praised or applauded the efforts of their rulers, partly because the contrast with the disorder and indiscipline of the immediately preceding age was so great. By restoring law and order, by crushing the arrogance of the aristocracy, the sovereigns won the enthusiastic support of their subjects, who then experienced a new sense of greatness, a new feeling of hope and pride in their nation.

João II, a monarch endowed with exceptional intelligence and fortitude, is known to posterity as the "Perfect Prince," one with a clear perception of the needs of the state and the resolution to fulfill them. His motto, Polla ley e polla grey, "For the law and the people," emphasized his intent to render justice strictly and to uphold the interests of the community of the realm against those of the privileged orders. Distressed by his father's prodigality, he resolved to recover royal rights and prerogatives and to reduce the nobility to submission. Summoning the cortes in 1481, he listened attentively to popular complaints against the excesses of nobles and prelates. In response, he directed royal officials to correct abuses in administration in aristocratic lordships, and he entrusted territorial government to his own professionally trained officers, rather than to the magnates.

What especially provoked the enmity of the nobility, however, was his insistence on receiving from each of them a pledge of homage and fealty which they considered to be demeaning, and his order requiring the confirmation of all grants of regalian rights made by his predecessors. The consequent review of royal charters was bound to result in the recovery of rights and properties by the crown. The king's brother-in-law, Fernando, duke of Bragança, the wealthiest man in the kingdom, realizing that he would surely lose from the proposed review, only with the greatest reluctance agreed to present his charters. In the meantime, the king's spies discovered that the duke had been in correspondence with Ferdinand and Isabella. Convinced that the duke and his brothers were conspiring to overthrow him and to deliver his realm to the Castilians, João II ordered Fernando's arrest on the grounds of treason. Royal justices speedily found him guilty, and he was beheaded in the public square of Evora in June 1484, as an example to others; his vast estates were confiscated for the benefit of the crown. Yet his brother-in-law, the duke of Viseu, a nephew of Afonso V, was not cowed, and prepared to avenge the execution. His plan to assassinate the king was discovered, however, by royal spies, and he was summoned, all unawares, to Alcácer where the king murdered him with his own hand. His estates were given to his younger brother Manuel, duke of Beja, who eventually succeeded to the throne as Manuel I (1495–1521). By these means, João II effectively crushed the Portuguese nobility, who long hesitated to challenge the monarchy again.

The Catholic kings, once the war of succession was terminated in 1479, carried out a similar restoration of order and enforced a new respect for royal authority. By offering amnesty to rebels and conferring numerous honorific titles without authority, they tried to attract the support of the nobles. But at the same time, they compelled them to submit to the law, to give up royal estates and revenues illegally usurped, to cease their private wars, and to allow the destruction of castles erected without royal permission.

A major source of aristocratic strength were the military Orders which had long since deviated from their original purpose of waging war against the infidels. Dominated by noble famiiles, they had participated in the civil wars of the fifteenth century, often in opposition to the crown, using their formidable resources to further aristocratic ambitions. With papal approbation, the Catholic kings were able to annex the administration of the Orders to the crown, following the deaths of the masters of Calatrava (1489), Santiago (1493), and Alcántara (1494). The *Consejo de las Ordenes* was created in 1495 to administer the Orders in the name of the king and queen. Pope

Hadrian VI in 1523 incorporated the masterships to the Spanish crown in perpetuity. From the fourteenth century, the Portuguese kings controlled the Orders, usually by entrusting the administration to their sons. João II named his son Afonso as master of Avis and Santiago, while Manuel, duke of Beja, held the mastership of Christ. After he became king, Manuel I recommended in his will that the masterships be incorporated to the crown in perpetuity; this was authorized by a papal bull in 1551. Thus, institutions created with the support of the monarchy in the late twelfth century to serve the needs of the king and the kingdom were again turned to that purpose.

Ferdinand and Isabella also made use of an older medieval institution, the *hermandad*, to curb the increase in criminal activity encouraged by the collapse of royal authority in the previous reign. In the past, towns in different regions of Castile formed brotherhoods to defend their mutual interests, especially against the nobility. The *Santa Hermandad* was constituted in the *cortes* of 1476 under the authority of the crown; the *Consejo de la Santa Hermandad*, whose members were appointed by the king and queen, was responsible for its activity. A military force of as many as 2,000 mounted troops, supplied and maintained by the towns, provided the essential power of the brotherhood, guaranteeing the security of the highways and suppressing brigandage. Persons charged with specific crimes, for example, rape, housebreaking, rebellion, murder, robbery, and arson, were brought to trial before local *alcaldes de la hermandad*, who meted out swift punishment to strike terror into the hearts of malefactors. So well did the *hermandad* do its work that within a few years the towns themselves asked that it be dissolved, partly because of the cost of its upkeep. But the king and queen recognized the value of a standing army that could be used also in the wars against Granada and only agreed to dismantle the *hermandad* and dissolve the *Consejo* in 1498. An exceptional tribunal, its very effectiveness made it unpopular with those who helped to bring it into being.

While the *hermandad* was created as an emergency measure, more lasting reforms were effected in the ordinary institutions of government. The mainspring of government was the royal council (*Consejo Real*), reorganized in 1480. No longer dominated by the magnates who, in the past, tried to use it for their own advantage, it was composed of a prelate, three knights, and eight or nine legists, who by their training in Roman law and their social origin could be expected to give the fullest support to royal authority. As a matter of general policy the king and queen, and João II too, preferred to entrust their affairs to men drawn from the petty nobility or the bourgeoisie, while allowing the magnates a primarily decorative role in the royal court. The council advised the monarchs on all affairs touching the kingdom of Castile; the royal secretary who acted as the link between the crown and the council was a highly influential personage. The *Consejo de Aragón*, of similar composition, was responsible for Aragonese affairs, but it should be noted that its members resided with the king, usually in Castile, rather than Aragon.

In the early years, Ferdinand and Isabella relied heavily upon the *cortes*, as theoretically representing the estates of the realm, to support their reforms. From 1482 to 1498, however, the *cortes* of Castile was not summoned at all, partly because the crown, by the more efficient collection of taxes, was not dependent financially upon the subsidies voted by this assembly. The convocation of the *cortes* on several occasions after 1498 was prompted by the need for money to pay the bills arising from the conquest of Granada and the Italian wars. The Castilian *cortes* in any case was only a shadow of the past, for the prelates and magnates now seldom attended, and only eighteen towns with two representatives each presumed to speak for the third estate. Each of the states of the crown of Aragon retained its parliament, though Ferdinand summoned them as infrequently as possible. Thus while Isabella summoned the Castilian *cortes* only nine times, he called the Catalan *corts* seven times and usually endeavored to control the choice of representatives, at least indirectly. João II found popular support in the *cortes* for his antiaristocratic policy, but he convened it only four times in fourteen years; Manuel I summoned the *cortes* four times too, but in the space of twenty-six years, and he did not hesitate to levy taxes without parliamentary consent. By infrequent convocation and careful manipulation, the *cortes* was subordinated to the power of the crown in all the peninsular states. In many ways it seemed an anachronism surviving from the medieval era.

Factionalism in the Castilian towns prompted Ferdinand and Isabella to declare their intention in 1480 to send *corregidores* to all the towns as permanent royal representatives with judicial and administrative authority. As a result, the towns lost much of their ancient autonomy, but they did enjoy greater internal peace. Royal intervention in the Aragonese towns was not so direct, though Ferdinand did attempt to break the hold of small cliques on municipal government. By introducing the lottery system in elections and by participating in the preparation of lists of candidates, he was able to influence the choice of officials. João II and Manuel I dominated the Portuguese towns in much the same way, by sending royal *corregidores* to supplant locally elected magistrates. In response to long-standing petitions, Manuel I also ordered a review of all urban charters (*forais*); his purpose was not to confirm traditional liberties, but to revise and standardize the tributes owed by the towns to the monarchy.

Considering the great territorial extension of the kingdom of Castile, Ferdinand and Isabella established two supreme tribunals of justice, the *chancillería* of Valladolid, surviving from the late fourteenth century, and a new one at Ciudad Real (1494), later transferred to Granada (1505). These courts had jurisdiction over north and south respectively, with the Tagus as the boundary. To facilitate the administration of justice, the *cortes* of 1480 authorized the jurist Alonso Díaz de Montalvo to assemble a collection of the fundamental laws of the realm; this was promulgated in 1484 as the *Ordenanzas reales de Castilla*. Ferdinand published a new edition of the *Constitucions i altres drets de Catalunya* in 1495 and reissued the *Fueros y observancias del reino de Aragon* in 1496. Manuel I also gave attention to judicial reform, reorganizing the royal tribunals in Lisbon, and he also appointed a commission to revise the law code. The definitive edition, known as the *Ordenações Manuelinas* was published in 1521.

The recovery of royal estates and the more efficient collection and administration of taxes increased royal income prodigiously and made the crown less dependent upon concessions by the *cortes*. The economic policies of the Catholic kings and of their Portuguese counterparts moreover, while not the result of any elaborate theory, were intended to increase the wealth of the monarchy. Thus the export of gold and silver was forbidden; measures were taken to protect domestic industry against foreign competition; shipbuilding was encouraged, and the shipment of native products in native ships was required; the Aragonese guild system was imported to Castile, and a *consulado* was established at Burgos to regulate the wool trade. Although Ferdinand liberated the *payeses de remensa* by the Sentence of Guadalupe in 1486, allowing the Catalan peasants to freely dispose of their holdings, royal policy was not generally favorable to small farmers nor to agriculture. The magnates, in spite of royal efforts to recover domain lands, still retained possession of vast estates, often given over in Castile to cattle-ranching and sheep-raising. The sheepmen's organization, the *Mesta*, dominated by the aristocracy, was highly favored by the crown, which derived from it one of its most important and regular sources of income. The extraordinary growth of the sheep industry ultimately worked to the detriment of Castilian agriculture and made famine a very real and ever-present threat.

As Ferdinand and Isabella consolidated their power in the secular realm, they also gave thought to the necessity of subordinating the church to their authority. The experience of recent years had taught them that wealthy bishops, by joining with the lay nobility, could undermine and very nearly destroy monarchy. As the most effective means of countering this threat, they proposed to control the appointment of bishops, but when they approached Pope Sixtus IV on the subject, he turned a deaf ear. Only in 1482 did he concede, quite reluctantly, a limited right to nominate bishops, subject to papal approval. Still, Ferdinand and Isabella persisted and persuaded Innocent VIII in 1486 to grant them the right of appointment (*patronato*) over all the principal benefices in the kingdom of Granada then being conquered. Subsequent concessions by Alexander VI and Julius II extended this right to all ecclesiastical benefices in the New World. By granting the Catholic kings this type of control over the church, the papacy averted the possibility of a violent confrontation such as later occurred elsewhere during the Protestant Reformation. The revenues of the church were also made more readily available to the crown. Alexander VI in 1494 allowed the monarchy to collect the *tercias reales*, or third of the tithe, in perpetuity. The issuance of the bull of crusade granting indulgences to those who contributed to the support of the wars against Granada became more frequent; even after the fall of Granada, money was obtained for projected crusades against the Muslims of North Africa.

The Portuguese kings, through the Order of Christ, exercised authority over the ecclesiastical organization of the new lands being explored and colonized in the West. But their relations with the papacy were strained in part because of a long-standing prohibition against the publication of papal bulls in Portugal without royal consent (*beneplácito régio*). João II, who was particularly insistent on this, eventually decided to adopt a more conciliatory attitude and to allow the free publication of papal documents; but in return Innocent VIII granted a crusading bull in support of the king's projected plans in Africa; besides the usual indulgences, the bull also granted the crown considerable financial advantages. On the other hand, the king did not give up his right to supervise and intervene, if necessary, in the workings of ecclesiastical courts, a subject of continuing controversy.

Ferdinand and Isabella also effectively carried out the reform of the church and uprooted abuses entrenched for more than three hundred years. Fray Hernando de Talavera encouraged Isabella to favor reform and especially to appoint to bishoprics only men of upright moral character and learning, thereby greatly improving the caliber of the Spanish episcopate. When Talavera was named archbishop of Granada in 1492, his post as confessor to the queen was taken by the Franciscan, Francisco Jiménez de Cisneros. In spite of bitter and sometimes violent opposition he reformed the houses of his Order in Spain and with the queen's backing also began the reform of other monastic Orders. Realizing the need for a truly educated clergy, he established the University of Alcalá de Henares in 1508 and by generous patronage made it one of the most important centers of theological study in western Europe. Though not a humanist, Cisneros welcomed humanists to the University and spurred their collaboration in the publication of the Polyglot Bible, printing the Greek, Hebrew, Aramaic, and Latin texts in parallel columns. Through his efforts the laxity of the past was checked, and a deeper spirituality was encouraged among the people. This helped the Spanish church to ride out the storm of the Protestant Reformation with a minimal degree of upset.

Ferdinand and Isabella raised up Castile and Aragon which had fallen on hard times, suffering from the miseries of civil war, and created a new confidence in the future that enabled Spain to develop an empire and to dominate European politics in the sixteenth century. In the same way, João II was able to direct the attention of his countrymen to the exciting prospect of overseas discovery and the foundation of a world-wide empire. The pessimism and depression of the earlier years was dissipated as Spain and Portugal moved fully into a period of political, cultural, and economic renaissance.

The Conquest of Granada

The fame of Ferdinand and Isabella and the enthusiasm they inspired among their subjects was due in large measure to their conquest of the kingdom of Granada. Since the middle of the fourteenth century the reconquest had remained in abeyance, as wars among the Christian states and civil wars assumed a greater and more immediate importance. Occasional campaigns against the Muslims were undertaken, resulting in the conquest of Antequera (1410), the victory at La Higeruela (1431), and the seizure of Gibraltar (1462); but for the most part the kings of Castile were content to receive tribute from Granada and to maintain the truce, despite frequent border clashes and raids. In these circumstances the kingdom of Granada seemed destined to survive for centuries.

The Catholic kings proclaimed their intention, however, to recover the lands they rightfully believed to be theirs and to expel the intruders, as their ancestors had long hoped to do. The papacy supported the enterprise with crusading indulgences and financial benefits, because victory over western Islam would counterbalance the extraordinary success of the Muslims in the eastern Mediterranean after the fall of Constantinople. In addition to the *tercias reales*, the crown also borrowed from bankers. The armies were generally better organized and equipped than in the past and made use of artillery on a larger scale than before. During the course of the conflict, footsoldiers, the famed Spanish infantry of the sixteenth century, came into their own as the backbone of the army.

A series of frontier incidents ruptured the truce that Ferdinand and Isabella concluded with the king of Granada, Abu-l-Hasan Ali (1464–1485), in 1478. The Muslim seizure of Zahara in December 1481 and the capture of Alhama in the following February by the Castilians marked the beginning of the struggle that would continue for the next decade. The Granadans soon found themselves at a disadvantage because of discord within the royal family. The king's son Abu Abd Allah, known to the Christians as Boabdil, was incited to revolt by the Abencerrajes and was proclaimed as King Muhammad XII (1482–1492). His father had to flee to Málaga. But in order to win adherents to their respective factions, the rival kings determined to oppose the Castilians as vigorously as possible. Abu-l-Hasan Ali won a resounding victory over them in the mountains of Málaga in March 1483, but Boabdil was much less fortunate; he was defeated and captured at Lucena a month later, and so his father was able to regain possession of Granada. In return for his freedom, Boabdil pledged homage and fealty to the Catholic kings and promised to collaborate with them against his father.

By sowing dissension among the Muslims, Ferdinand believed that he had won a signal diplomatic triumph that would work ultimately to the benefit of the Castilian kingdom. He was now inclined to turn his attention to other affairs, especially in Italy, but Isabella insisted that the moment was propitious for the final conquest of the kingdom. From 1484 onward, the Castilians commenced an unremitting aggression, chiefly through sieges, with the clear intent to destroy the kingdom of Granada. The extraordinary confusion there could only benefit the Castilians. Boabdil, who had returned to Granada, was forced to flee again to Castile. His uncle, Muhammad ibn Sad, known as el Zagal, seized control of the government and deposed his brother Abu-l-Hasan Ali who died later in the year 1485. For two years el Zagal, or Muhammad XIII (1485–1487), was the effective ruler of the kingdom of Granada.

During that time, the Castilians carried out a three-pronged offensive. In the southwest their objective was Ronda; once the city fell in May 1485, the adjacent mountainous region was also occupied, and the road to Málaga, the economic center of the kingdom, was laid open. Simultaneously Castilian troops moved into the *vega* of Granada, the breadbasket of the realm, ravaging it and seizing Loja in May 1486. In the interim, Boabdil and el Zagal decided to present a united front against the infidels, but Boabdil was taken prisoner again at Loja and compelled to renew his vassalage to the Catholic kings who promised to give him a duchy in the eastern sector of the kingdom of Granada. Returning once more, he resumed the struggle with his uncle for control of the capital. The Castilians, meanwhile, pressed relentlessly onward, taking Velez Málaga on the coast in April 1487 and forcing Málaga itself to surrender in August. The loss of the whole southwestern sector cost el Zagal greatly in prestige and popular support, so that he had to retire to Almería, leaving Granada in the hands of his nephew.

The energy and resources expended in the campaigns of 1486–1487 were substantial, so much so that the Castilians could mount only a limited offensive in 1488. Even so, an extensive area on the southeastern coast stretching down toward Almería submitted to them. In the following year the king and queen concentrated their strength on the siege of Baza, one of the key fortresses leading to Granada from the east. After six months the city surrendered and el Zagal, concluding that further resistance was futile, made his submission, yielding to the

Catholic kings the whole southeastern region, including Almería and Guadix. Though treated courteously and granted a lordship, he eventually retired to Morocco. Boabdil had agreed in 1487 to surrender Granada to Ferdinand and Isabella in return for a lordship in this newly conquered zone, but he now refused to carry out the bargain. Fired up in their resolve to resist, the people of Granada compelled their king to lead them, whether he would or no. The outcome was, of course, inevitable.

During 1490 the Castilians ravaged the *vega* of Granada in preparation for the siege of the capital which they began in the following spring. Building Santa Fe, a military headquarters directly west of Granada, Ferdinand and Isabella were able to sever the city's communications with the outside. As the months passed, the defenders were confronted with the spectacle of eventual starvation. Boabdil, rather than suffer that fate, secretly opened negotiations and agreed to the terms of capitulation on 25 November 1491. The Castilians took possession of the Alhambra on the night of 1–2 January 1492 and entered the city on the next morning. Ferdinand and Isabella made their triumphal entry on 6 January. The Moors were allowed to retain their houses and mosques, to practice their religion freely, and to be governed by their own magistrates; if they wished to emigrate to Africa, they could do so, and ships were readied to carry them there. Boabdil, the last of the Nasrid dynasty and the last Moorish king in Spain, set out for Las Alpujarras where he was to enjoy a lordship under the sovereignty of Castile, but in the next year he retired to Morocco where he died many years later.

The Imposition of Religious Uniformity

The fall of Granada, marking the end of Muslim domination in Spain, was greeted with general rejoicing in Europe, but it brought in its train the grave problem of assimilating a mass of people who were culturally and religiously alien to the Christian majority. The religious toleration of earlier times was no longer practicable when the number of non-Christians was so great as to be considered a danger to the state. In order to weld the community into one nation under their leadership, the Catholic kings sought to impose religious uniformity and to eradicate fundamental distinctions among their subjects. The unity and integrity of the state seemed to demand the end of religious diversity.

The existence of large numbers of Jews and *conversos* in their dominions had already posed the problem of religious uniformity for the Catholic kings. The thousands of Jews who had converted to Christianity following the pogroms of 1391 were always suspect in the popular mind of Judaizing and were resented for their prominence in public affairs. An insistent clamor to punish *conversos* whose loyalty to the faith was questioned began to be heard in the land, prompting Pope Sixtus IV to respond favorably to the petition of the Catholic kings for the establishment of an inquisition in their realms (1 November 1478).

The Spanish Inquisition was essentially a royal institution directed and controlled by the *Consejo de la Suprema y General Inquisición* created in 1483. In this respect it differed from the papal inquisition established in the thirteenth century to deal with heresy; the papal inquisition had functioned somewhat in the crown of Aragon, but it had little to do elsewhere in the peninsula. The Spanish Inquisition was primarily a Castilian agency whose authority was extended, despite vociferous protest, to the crown of Aragon as well. The *Consejo* was the only institution common to both Castile and Aragon; through it the king and queen controlled the appointment of inquisitorial officials, issued them instructions, regulated their activities and paid their salaries. The first inquisitor-general, Fray Tomás de Torquemada, O.P., gained world-wide notoriety as a symbol of the arbitrary suppression of religious dissent so often associated with the inquisition.

All the worst features of the medieval inquisition were to be found in the Spanish Inquisition. It operated secretly; the accused were not given the names of their accusers; torture was used to obtain confessions; those convicted were subject to confiscation of property for the benefit of the state, as well as exile, imprisonment, or burning at the stake. The execution of convicted heretics was carried out in a solemn ceremony called an *auto da fe*, an act of faith intended as a public manifestation of the community's acceptance of orthodoxy. As the problem of heresy in the usual sense was minimal, the chief business of the Inquisition was the searching out and punishment of false *conversos*. This was done with a persistence, thoroughness and heartlessness that shocked Pope Sixtus IV himself. His remonstrances, however, were of no avail. The Inquisition gave official sanction to the spirit of religious intolerance that had been growing ever stronger in the later Middle Ages, and it served as a forewarning to the Jews of their inevitable destruction.

Just a few months after the surrender of Granada, on 30 March 1492, an edict was issued ordering the Jews to accept baptism as Christians within four months or to leave the kingdom. While many agreed to be baptized, the lot of *conversos* was not as attractive as it had seemed a century before. Consequently most Jews elected to go into exile. Estimates of their numbers vary from the extremes of 150,000 to 800,000 or even greater; Vicens Vives believes that the first figure is the most reasonable one. The departure of the Jews depleted the financial resources of the kingdom, and it also represented the loss of business acumen so necessary to the vitality of the state. The Jews scattered throughout the Mediterranean, establishing new communities of Sephardim, as they were known, and long retaining their Castilian or Catalan speech.

João II agreed to admit the Jews into Portugal for a limited time, provided that they paid a poll tax; although they would have to leave at the end of eight months, he promised to provide transportation to Africa. Filling his treasury with money collected from the exiles, he then failed to facilitate their departure, allowing them to be assaulted by the mob and reduced to slavery. He even seized the younger children of Jewish families and transported them to the island of Santo Tome where he expected them to colonize it and to learn the Christian religion, uncontaminated by their parents. This cruelty was surpassed by his successor Manuel I, who issued an edict in December 1496, expelling the Jews from Portugal unless they converted to Christianity; those who remained in the realm by the following October were threatened with confiscation and death. He too ordered the seizure of Jewish children so that they could be reared as Christians. When the Jews tried to leave the realm, strenuous efforts were made to convert them by force; once having accepted Christianity, the king promised not to inquire into their religious opinions for twenty years. In this way he tried to achieve religious uniformity without losing the talents and resources of the Jewish community.

Besides the Jews, there remained the Muslims, who, in the kingdom of Granada, had been guaranteed freedom of worship. Hernando de Talavera, the first archbishop of Granada, learned Arabic and instructed his clergy to do so, so that they could preach to the Moors, but his policy of seeking converts through discourse was bound to be slow and perhaps ultimately unsuccessful. Cisneros, now archbishop of Toledo, favored more expeditious methods, and when visiting Granada in 1499 achieved notable success in effecting mass conversions; but he also ordered the burning of the Koran and other Arabic books, gravely irritating the leaders of the Muslim community, who condemned this as a violation of the capitulation.

The Muslims rose in revolt in the city, and Cisneros discovered that his life was in jeopardy. Royal forces fortunately were able to crush the uprising, but the vengeance with which the rebels were punished prompted about 50,000 to accept baptism in order to avoid further trouble. The aggressiveness of Christian missionaries provoked a violent reaction in the next year as the Muslims from Ronda to Almería took up arms in defense of their liberty. Once again the revolt was put down, but the king and queen now decided to publish an edict on 11 February 1502 requiring all Muslims to accept the Christian religion or to leave the kingdom. Most of them chose to become Christians rather than abandon their ancestral lands, but they bore their religious opinions lightly and were never trusted thereafter. The problem of assimilating the *moriscos*, as they were called, was not entirely solved until the final expulsion early in the seventeenth century.

The Routes to India and the New World

If the conquest of Granada and the attempt to impose religious uniformity signaled the close of the medieval era, the Portuguese discovery of the route around Africa to India and the Spanish discovery of America marked the beginning of the modern age. With the resources of the crown at his disposal, João II continued the overseas activities of Henry the Navigator, developing facilities along the coast to exploit the gold, ivory, and slaves to be had in Africa. Rumors to the effect that Prester John ruled somewhere in central Africa prompted him to send out two Arabic-speaking adventurers, Pedro de Covilhã and Afonso Paiva, in search of him. From Alexandria in Egypt they traveled to the Gulf of Aden, where they separated, Paiva going to Ethiopia and Covilhã to India. After visiting Calicut and Goa, Covilhã returned to Cairo in 1490 where he learned that Paiva had died. Deciding to finish the mission, he journeyed to Ethiopia where he was well received by the emperor, who would not allow him, however, to leave. Other Portuguese emissaries found him still living there in 1520. In the meantime he had sent word of his travels to Lisbon, confirming the king's hope that India could be reached by sailing around Africa.

Portuguese expeditions had already sailed as far south as Cape Cross on the west African coast, and the king was determined to round the continent and find the way to India. In August 1487 he sent Bartolomeu Dias with two ships to make that fateful passage. Sailing southward beyond Walfisch Bay, Dias was driven farther south by strong winds, so that when he turned eastward he had already passed the southern tip of Africa. After landing at Mossel Bay on the Indian Ocean, he continued northward to the Great Fish River where he decided to turn back. On the return journey he passed the Cape of Storms, as he called it, and reached Lisbon in December 1488. Elated by this voyage, the king named the cape, the Cape of Good Hope, because it marked the end of the long years of striving southward and the beginning of the advance on India.

While the Portuguese were planning further ventures in that direction, the Genoese mariner, Christopher Columbus, sailed westward across the Atlantic to the New World, giving Spain claim to a vast, uncharted empire. Columbus offered his services initially to João II who was not convinced by his calculations and geography that India could be reached by the journey to the west. Nor were Ferdinand and Isabella prepared to back him when he approached them in 1484; but after a futile effort to persuade the English king to support him, he returned to Castile and at last gained royal financial aid. With his three ships he set out in August 1492, sailing westward from the Canaries to the West Indies, landing on San Salvador on 12 October. After visiting several other islands, he sailed for home convinced that he had reached the islands off the Asian continent. Bad weather compelled him to put in to Lisbon in May 1493; but João II received his story of having reached Asia with extreme skepticism. Ferdinand and Isabella, however, were overjoyed by the news and prepared to finance additional voyages.

While doubting Columbus's report, João II decided to lay claim to the area he had discovered. The Catholic kings, as a countermeasure, appealed to Pope Alexander VI who issued four bulls in April–May 1493 confirming Spanish rights to the newly discovered lands and drawing an imaginary line of demarcation from the north to the south pole, a hundred leagues west of the Azores. Though willing to accept the principle of demarcation, João II suggested that the line be pushed two hundred and seventy leagues farther west. The ensuing negotiations between Spain and Portugal resulted in the treaty of Tordesillas, signed on 7 June 1494, setting the line where the king of Portugal indicated. The pact proved to be a great boon to Portugal because it subsequently guaranteed her rights to Brazil.

As the century came to a close, Vasco da Gama completed the long-hoped-for journey from Portugal around Africa to India and back in the two years 1497–1499, while Columbus continued his exploration of the Caribbean islands. The full discovery of the New World and the circumnavigation of the earth, revealing for the first time the true size and configuration of the globe, were not far off.

A European Empire

The revelation of the vast world beyond the European continent wrought extraordinary changes in man's ways of thought and action, but it did not distract the rulers of Spain and Portugal from the pursuit of commonplace, but nevertheless, fundamental goals closer to home. Both the Spanish and Portuguese sovereigns were hopeful of unifying their realms by a series of marriages between their families. The marriage of the Castilian Infanta Isabel to João II's son and heir, Afonso, might have achieved that aim eventually, but the prince died suddenly as a result of a fall from his horse in 1491. His father, one of the great kings of Portugal, followed him to the grave on 25 October 1495, leaving the throne to his cousin Manuel of Beja. Known as the Fortunate King, Manuel I (1495–1521) presided over the expansion of Portugal throughout the globe, but he also aspired to unite and dominate the peninsula. For this reason he married Infanta Isabel, but her death in 1498 and that of her son two years later destroyed these illusions. Manuel I then married Maria, another daughter of the Catholic kings, but the long-desired union of Spain and Portugal was achieved only at the end of the sixteenth century, and it proved to be an ephemeral one.

Peninsular unification also demanded the recovery of the counties of Rousillon and Cerdagne occupied by the French during the Catalan revolt, and the incorporation of Navarre. As the French had designs on Navarre and were also about to reassert Angevin claims in southern Italy, the traditional alliance between France and the Castilian Trastámaras was jettisoned. In order to protect their interests, primarily those of Aragon, Ferdinand and Isabella set about the diplomatic encirclement of France by arranging marital alliances with England and the empire. This was the purpose of the marriage of their daughter Catherine of Aragon first to Arthur and then to Henry VIII, both sons of

King Henry VII of England. For the same reason, their oldest son and heir-presumptive, Juan, was married to the daughter of the Emperor Maximilian; but the high hopes the Catholic kings had for their son were dashed when he died in 1497 at the early age of nineteen.

In the meantime, Charles VIII of France, anxious to concentrate on the conquest of Naples, agreed in 1493 to restore Rousillon and Cerdagne to Aragon. They remained in Spanish hands until finally recovered by France a hundred and fifty years later. When Charles VIII invaded Italy in 1494 with the intention of resurrecting Angevin claims to Naples, ruled by the descendants of Alfonso V, he expected Ferdinand to remain neutral. But Ferdinand had his own designs on Naples and joined with other powers in opposing the French. The details of that struggle lie beyond the scope of this book; suffice it to say that by 1504 Ferdinand's armies had driven out all opposition and incorporated the kingdom of Naples into the Spanish dominions. The scene was now ready for the great wars between France and Spain in the sixteenth century.

The triumph of Spanish arms in Naples occurred in the same year as the death of Isabella the Catholic, on 26 November 1504. By the rules of inheritance Castile passed to her daughter Juana, and her inept husband, Philip of Hapsburg, son of the emperor; the union of Castile and Aragon consequently was dissolved, at least temporarily. But Philip's death two years later and the announced insanity of Juana *la loca* enabled Ferdinand to act as regent on her behalf and to resume the government of a united Spain. His final achievement was the annexation of Navarre in 1512, dispossesing his grandniece, Catalina (1483–1512), and thwarting French intervention there. When he died on 23 January 1516, the crowns of Spain passed to his grandson, the Hapsburg prince, Charles I of Spain and V of the Holy Roman Empire.

By then the long travail of medieval Spain was done. But the aspirations of the past were only partially fulfilled. The reconquest was finished, and the greater part of the peninsula was united under one ruler; but Portugal remained independent. The infidels were driven out or, if not, were forced to conform to the dominant Christian majority; but could one say that the destruction of the Muslim and Jewish communities, which had contributed so much to the making of medieval Spain, truly helped to restore the *salus Spanie* of which Pelayo had spoken centuries before? The Hispanic empire of León was no more, scarcely even a memory, but the peoples of Spain and Portugal were transforming in another way the legacy received from the Romans and Visigoths. By their own valor, they were gaining a new empire overseas, one their ancestors never dreamed of, and in the person of Charles V the imperial ambitions of Alfonso X and Pedro III would be realized. Medieval Spain, so long isolated and turned in upon itself, through the far-flung empires of modern Spain and Portugal, stood astride the world at the opening of the sixteenth century.

Genealogical Charts,
Bibliography,
and Index

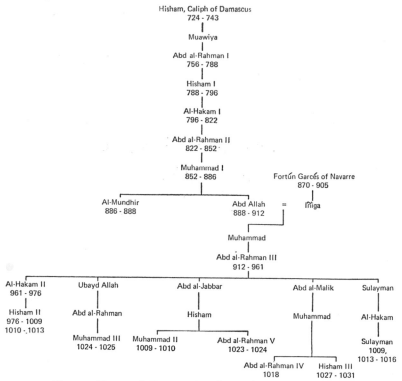

Chart 1. Umayyad Emirs and Caliphs of Córdoba, 756–1031

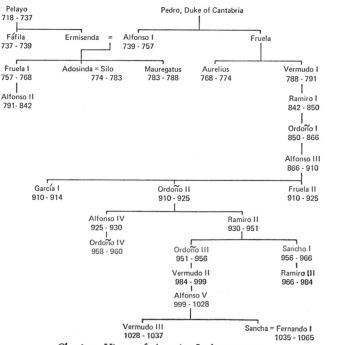

Chart 2. Kings of Asturias-León to 1037

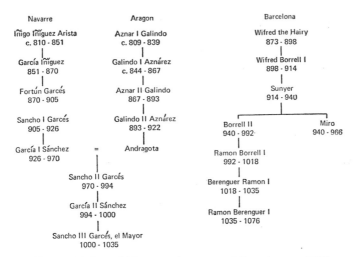

Chart 3. Rulers of Navarre, Aragon, and Barcelona to 1035

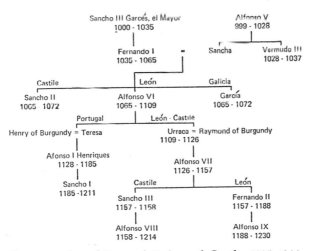

Chart 4. Rulers of Portugal, León, and Castile, 1035–1214

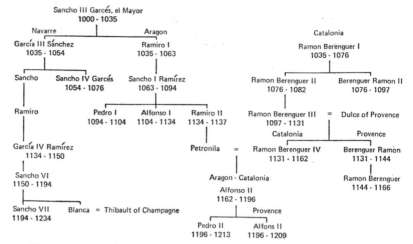

Chart 5. Rulers of Navarre, Aragon, Catalonia, and Provence, 1035–1214

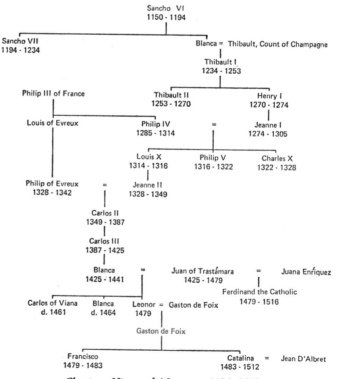

Chart 6. Kings of Navarre, 1194–1512

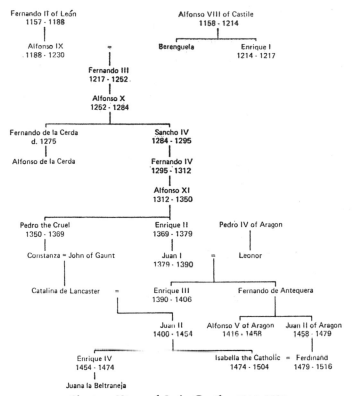

Chart 7. Kings of León-Castile, 1214–1504

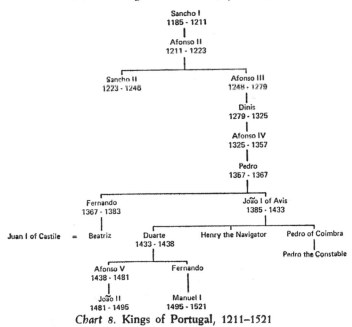

Chart 8. Kings of Portugal, 1211–1521

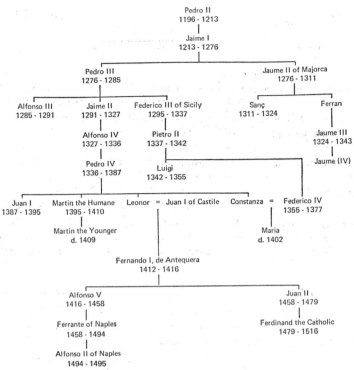

Chart 9. Kings of Aragon, 1213–1516

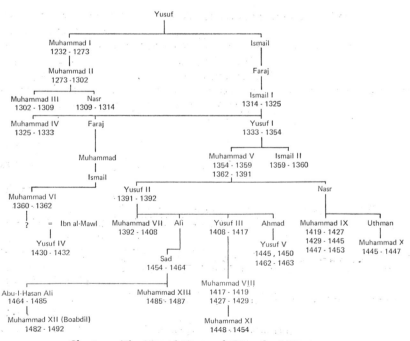

Chart 10. The Nasrid Kings of Granada, 1232–1492

Bibliography

The first section of this bibliography lists materials that can be consulted for the whole of medieval Spanish history as well as for specific themes or periods. The following six sections correspond to the parts into which the book is divided. Under each section are listed the principal sources and modern works relating chiefly, though not always exclusively, to that chronological period. I have tried to include those books and articles of the greatest utility for the study of medieval Spanish history and upon which my own work rests.

ABBREVIATIONS

AHDE: Anuario de Historia del Derecho Español.
AHR: American Historical Review.
BAE: Biblioteca de Autores Españoles.
CHE: Cuadernos de Historia de España.
ES: España Sagrada.
MGH: Monumenta Germaniae Historica.
MGH Auct. Antiq.: Monumenta Germaniae Historica. Auctores Antiquissimi.
MGH Legum Sectio: Monumenta Germaniae Historica. Legum Sectio.
MGH SS: Monumenta Germaniae Historica. Scriptores.
PL: J. P. Migne. Patrologia Latina. 222 vols. Paris, 1844–1864.
RH: Revue Hispanique.
RSJB: Recueils de la Société Jean Bodin.

GENERAL WORKS

Bibliographical Guides

Oliveira Marquês, A. H. *Guia do estudante de história medieval portuguesa.* Lisbon, 1964.
Sánchez Alonso, Benito. *Fuentes de la historia española e hispano-americana.* 3d ed. 3 vols. Madrid, 1952.
———. *Historia de la historiografía española.* 2 vols. Madrid, 1941–1944.

Atlases

Salinas y Bellver, Salvador. *Atlas histórico general de España.* 7th ed. Madrid, 1961.
Vicens Vives, Jaime. *Atlas de historia de España.* Barcelona, 1956.

General Histories

Spain

Ballesteros, Antonio. *Historia de España y su influencia en la historia universal.* 8 vols. in 9. Barcelona, 1918–1941.

Menéndez Pidal, Ramón, ed. *Historia de España.* In course of publication. Vol. I.1, *España prehistórica* (Madrid, 1947); Vol. I.2, *España protohistórica* (1952); Vol. I.3, *España preromana* (1954); Vol. II, *España romana* (1935); Vol. III, *España visigoda* (1940); Vol. IV, *España musulmana* (1950); Vol. VI, *España cristiana, 711–1035* (1956); Vol. XIV, *España cristiana: Crisis de la reconquista* (1966); Vol. XV, *Los Trastámaras de Castilla y Aragón en el siglo XV* (1964).

Merriman, R. B. *The Rise of the Spanish Empire.* 4 vols. New York, 1918.

Soldevila, Ferran. *Historia de España.* 3 vols. Barcelona, 1952–1954.

Valdeavellano, Luis G. de. *Historia de España.* 1 vol. in 2. 2d ed. Madrid, 1952.

Aragon and Catalonia

Chaytor, H. J. *A History of Aragon and Catalonia.* London, 1933.

Soldevila, Ferran. *Història de Catalunya.* 3 vols. Barcelona, 1962.

Zurita, Gerónimo. *Anales de la Corona de Aragón.* Ed. Angel Canellas López. 2 vols. Zaragoza, 1967.

Muslim Spain

Dozy, Reinhart. *Histoire des musulmanes d'Espagne.* Ed. E. Lévi-Provençal. 3 vols. Leyden, 1932.

——. *Récherches sur l'histoire et la littérature en Espagne pendant le moyen âge.* 3d ed. 2 vols. Leyden, 1881. Reprint, 1966.

——. *Spanish Islam.* Tr. F. G. Stokes. London, 1913.

Sánchez Albornoz, Claudio. *La España musulmana según los autores islamitas y cristianos medievales.* 2 vols. Buenos Aires, 1946.

Watt, W. Montgomery. *A History of Islamic Spain.* Edinburgh, 1965.

Navarre

Clavería, Carlos. *Historia de Navarra.* Pamplona, 1971.

Portugal

Almeida, Fortunato de. *História de Portugal.* 6 vols. Coimbra, 1922–1929.

Diffie, Bailey. *Prelude to Empire: Portugal Overseas before Henry the Navigator.* Lincoln, Neb., 1960.

Herculano, Aleixandre. *História de Portugal desde o começo da monarchia até o fim do reinado de Afonso III.* 8th ed. by David Lopes. 8 vols. Lisbon-Paris, n.d.

Oliveira Marquês, A. H. *History of Portugal.* Vol. I. *From Lusitania to Empire.* New York, 1972.

Peres, Damião, ed. *História de Portugal.* 9 vols. Barcelos, 1928–1958.

Genealogy

Caetano de Sousa, António. *História genealógica da Casa Real portuguesa*. Ed. M. Lopes de Almeida and C. Pegado. 12 vols. Coimbra, 1946–1954. *Provas.* 4 vols. in 10, 1946–1952.

Fernández de Bethencourt, Francisco. *Historia genealógica y heráldica de la monarquía española*. 10 vols. Madrid, 1897–1920.

Interpretive Works

Castro, Américo. *The Spaniards: An Introduction to their History*. Tr. W. F. King and S. Margaretten. Berkeley, Cal., 1971.

Lapeyre, Henri. "Deux interpretations de l'Histoire de l'Espagne: Américo Castro et Claudio Sánchez Albornoz," *Annales* (Sept.–Oct. 1965), 1015–1037.

Maravall, J. A. *El Concepto de España en la edad media*. 2d ed. Madrid, 1964.

Menéndez Pidal, Ramón. *The Spaniards in their History*. Tr. W. Starkie. New York, 1950.

Sánchez Albornoz, Claudio. *España, un enigma histórico*. 2 vols. Buenos Aires, 1957.

Vicens Vives, Jaime. *Approaches to the History of Spain*. Tr. J. C. Ullman. Berkeley, Cal., 1970.

Special Topics

Government and Law

Caetano, Marcello. *Lições de História de direito português*. Coimbra, 1962.

Carlé, Maria del Carmen. *Del Concejo medieval castellano-leonés*. Buenos Aires, 1968.

Colmeiro, Manuel. *Introducción a las Cortes de los Antiguos Reinos de León y Castilla*. 2 vols. Madrid, 1883–1903.

Font Rius, J. M., "Origenes del regimen municipal de Cataluña," *AHDE*, 16 (1945) 388–529; 17 (1946) 229–585.

———. "Les Villes dans l'Espagne du moyen âge: L'histoire de leurs institutions administratives et judiciares," *La Ville. RSJB*, VI (1954) 263–296.

Gama Barros, Henrique da. *História da administração pública em Portugal nos séculos XII a XV*. 2d ed. by Torquato de Sousa Soares. 11 vols. Lisbon, 1945–1954.

García Gallo, Alfonso. *Manual de Historia del Derecho español*. 3d ed. 2 vols. Madrid, 1967.

Giesey, Ralph. *"If Not, Not": The Oath of the Aragonese and the Legendary Laws of Sobrarbe*. Princeton, 1968.

Guglielmi, Nilda. "La curia regia en León y Castilla," *CHE*, 23–24 (1955) 116–267; 28 (1958) 43–101.

La Fuente, Vicente de. *Estudios críticos sobre la Historia y el Derecho de Aragón*. 3 vols. Madrid, 1884–1886.

Martínez Marina, Francisco. *Teoría de las Cortes*. 3 vols. Madrid, 1813.

Merêa, Paulo. *O Poder Real e as Côrtes*. Coimbra, 1923.

Merriman, R. B. "The Cortes of the Spanish Kingdoms in the Later Middle Ages," *AHR*, 16 (1911) 476–495.

O'Callaghan, Joseph F., "The Beginnings of the Cortes of León-Castile," *AHR*, 74 (1969) 1503–1537.

Piskorski, Wladimir. *Las Cortes de Castilla en el período de tránsito de la edad media a la moderna, 1188–1520*. Barcelona, 1930.

Sánchez Albornoz, Claudio. *Estudios sobre las instituciones medievales españolas*. Mexico City, 1965.

———. *Investigaciones y documentos sobre las instituciones hispanas*. Santiago, Chile, 1970.

Suárez Fernández, Luis. "Evolución histórica de las hermandades castellanas," *CHE*, 16 (1951) 6–78.

Valdeavellano, Luis G. de. *Curso de historia de las instituciones españolas: De los orígenes al final de la Edad Media*. Madrid, 1968.

Van Kleffens, E. N. *Hispanic Law until the End of the Middle Ages*. Edinburgh-Chicago, 1968.

Society and the Economy

Baer, Yitzhak. *A History of the Jews in Christian Spain*. 2 vols. Philadelphia, 1961.

Cagigas, Isidro de las. *Los Mozárabes*. 2 vols. Madrid, 1947–1948.

———. *Los Mudéjares*. 2 vols. Madrid, 1948–1949.

Castro, Armando. *A Evolução econômica de Portugal dos séculos XII a XV*. 9 vols. thus far. Lisbon, 1964– .

Glick, Thomas F. *Irrigation and Society in Medieval Valencia*. Cambridge, Mass., 1970.

Heiss, Alois. *Descripción general de las monedas hispano-cristianas*. 3 vols. Zaragoza, n.d.

Klein, Julius. *The Mesta: A Study in Spanish Economic History, 1273–1836*. Cambridge, Mass., 1920.

Oliveira Marqués, A. H. *Daily Life in Portugal in the Late Middle Ages*. Tr. S. S. Wyatt. Madison, Wis., 1971.

———. *Introdução a história da agricultura em Portugal*. 2d ed. Lisbon, 1968.

Rau, Virginia. *Estudos de História: Mercadores, Mercadorias, Pensamento Económico*. Lisbon, 1968.

Sánchez Albornoz, Claudio. *En torno a los orígenes del feudalismo*. 3 vols. Mendoza, 1942.

Simonet, Francisco. *Historia de los Mozárabes de España*. Madrid, 1897–1903.

Valdeavellano, Luis G. de. "Les Liens de vassalité et les immunités en Espagne," *Les Liens de vassalité et les immunités*. *RSJB*, I, 2d ed. (1958) 223–256.

Verlinden, Charles. "Les Conditions des populations rurales dans l'Espagne médiévale," *Le Servage*. *RSJB*, II, 2d ed. (1959) 169–220.

———. *L'Esclavage dans l'Europe médiévale*. Vol. I. *La Péninsule ibérique: France*. Bruges, 1955.

———. "Le Grand Domaine dans les états ibériques chrétiens au moyen âge," *Le Domaine. RSJB*, IV (1949) 177–208.

———. "Quelques aspects de l'histoire de la tenure au Portugal," *La Tenure. RSJB*, III (1938) 231–244.

Vicens Vives, Jaime. *An Economic History of Spain*. Tr. F. M. López Morillas. Princeton, 1969.

———. *Historia social y económica de España y América*. 4 vols. Barcelona, 1957–1958.

The Church

Almeida, Fortunato de. *História da Igreja em Portugal*. 4 vols. Coimbra, 1910–1926.

Cocheril, Maur. *Études sur le monachisme en Espagne et au Portugal*. Lisbon-Paris, 1966.

García Villada, Zacarías. *Historia eclesiástica de España*. 5 vols. Madrid, 1929–1936.

Goñi Gaztambide, José. *Historia de la bula de la cruzada en España*. Vitoria, 1958.

Menéndez Pelayo, Marcelino. *Historia de los heterodoxos españoles*. 2 vols. Madrid, 1956.

Lomax, Derek W. *La Orden de Santiago, 1170–1275*. Madrid, 1965.

López Ferreiro, Antonio. *Historia de la Santa A. M. Iglesia de Santiago de Compostela*. 11 vols. Santiago, 1898–1909.

O'Callaghan, Joseph F., "The Affiliation of the Order of Calatrava with the Order of Cîteaux," *Analecta Sacri Ordinis Cisterciensis*, 15 (1959) 161–193; 16 (1960) 3–59; 255–292.

Orlandis, José. *Estudios sobre instituciones monásticas medievales*. Pamplona, 1971.

Pérez de Urbel, Justo. *Los monjes españoles en la Edad Media*. 2d ed. 2 vols. Madrid, 1945.

Vázquez de Parga, Luis, J. M. Lacarra, and J. Uría. *Las peregrinaciones a Santiago de Compostela*. 3 vols. Madrid, 1948–1949.

Literature and Learning

Ajo y Saínz de Zuñiga, C. M. *Historia de las universidades hispánicas*. 7 vols. thus far. Madrid 1958– .

Carreras y Artau, Tomás and Joaquin. *Historia de la Filosofía española: Filosofía cristiana de los siglos XIII al XV*. 2 vols. Madrid, 1939–1943.

Cruz Hernández, Miguel. *Historia de la Filosofía española: Filosofía hispano-musulmana*. 2 vols. Madrid, 1957.

Husik, Isaac. *History of Medieval Jewish Philosophy*. New York, 1966.

Menéndez Pidal, Ramón. *Poesía árabe y poesía europea*. Madrid, 1938.

Molas, Joaquin, and Josep Romeu, *Literatura Catalana Antiga*. 4 vols. Barcelona, 1961–1964.

Nykl, A. R. *Hispano-Arabic Poetry*. Baltimore, 1946.

Rubió y Lluch, A. *Documents per l'història de la Cultura catalana mig-eval.*
2 vols. Barcelona, 1908–1921.

Saraiva, António José. *História da cultura em Portugal.* 2 vols. Lisbon, 1950–
1955.

Tejada, F. E. de. *Las doctrinas políticas en Cataluña medieval.* Barcelona, 1950.

——. *Las doctrinas políticas en Portugal en la Edad Media.* Madrid 1943.

Source Collections

Narrative and Literary Collections

Biblioteca de Autores Españoles. 203 vols. thus far. Madrid, 1846 ff.

*Crónicas de los Reyes de Castilla desde Alfonso el Sabio hasta los Católicos,
Don Fernando y Doña Isabel.* Ed. Cayetano Rosell. BAE, vols. 66, 68, 70.
Madrid, 1875–1878.

Poetas castellanos anteriores al siglo XV. Ed. T. A. Sánchez, P. J. Pidal, F.
Janer. BAE, vol. 57. Madrid, 1895.

Schott, Andreas, ed. *Hispania Illustrata.* 4 vols. Frankfort, 1603–1608.

Documentary Collections

Aguirre, José Sáenz de, ed. *Collectio maxima Conciliorum omnium Hispaniae.*
4 vols. Rome, 1693–1694.

Los Códigos Españoles. Ed. Antonio de San Martín. 12 vols. Madrid, 1872–
1873.

*Colección de documentos inéditos del Archivo General de la Corona de
Aragón.* Ed. Prospero de Bofarull et al. 41 vols. Barcelona, 1847–1910.

Colección de documentos inéditos para la historia de España. Ed. Martín
Fernández de Navarrete et al. 112 vols. Madrid, 1842–1895.

Colección de documentos para el estudio de la historia de Aragón. Ed. Eduardo
Ibarra. 12 vols. Zaragoza, 1904–1920.

Constitucions y altres drets de Catalunya. 3 vols. Barcelona, 1588.

*Cortes de los antiguos Reinos de Aragón y de Valencia y Principado de Cata-
luña.* 25 vols. Madrid, 1896–1919.

Cortes de los antiguos Reinos de León y Castilla. 5 vols. Madrid, 1861–1903.

Documentos medievais portugueses. Ed. Rui Pinto de Azevedo. *Documentos
Régios,* Vol. I. Lisbon, 1945–1962. *Documentos Particulares,* Vol. III. Lisbon,
1940.

Erdmann, Carl. *Papsturkunden in Portugal.* Berlin, 1927.

Flórez, Enrique. *España Sagrada.* 51 vols. Madrid, 1754–1759.

Font Rius, J. M. *Cartas de población y franquicia de Cataluña.* 2 vols. Madrid-
Barcelona, 1969.

Fueros, Observancias y Actos de Corte del Reyno de Aragón. Ed. Luis Parral.
2 vols. Zaragoza, 1907.

González, Tomás. *Colección de Cédulas, cartas patentes, provisiones, reales
ordenes y documentos concernientes a las Provincias Vascongadas.* 6 vols.
Madrid, 1829–1833.

Kehr, P. F. *Papsturkunden in Spanien.* 2 vols. Berlin, 1926.

Lévi-Provençal, Évariste. *Inscriptions arabes d'Espagne*. Leyden-Paris, 1931.
Memorial Histórico Español. 49 vols. Madrid, 1851–1948.
Muñoz y Romero, Tomás. *Colección de fueros municipales y cartas pueblas de los reinos de Castilla, León, Corona de Aragón y Navarra*. Madrid, 1847.
Portugalliae Monumenta Historica. Ed. Aleixandre Herculano and Joaquim da Silva Mendes Leal. 5 vols. Lisbon, 1856–1897.
Villanueva, Jaime. *Viaje literario a las iglesias de España*. 22 vols. Madrid, 1803–1852.

General Narrative Sources

Christian

Anales Toledanos I, II, III. ES, 23, 381–401.
Carlos of Viana, *Crónica de los reyes de Navarra*. Ed. José Yanguas. Pamplona, 1843.
Chronique latine des rois de Castille. Ed. L. Barrau-Dihigo. Bordeaux, 1913.
Crónica de Cinco Reis de Portugal. Ed. A. Magalhães Basto. 2 vols. Porto, 1945.
Crónica de 1344 que ordenó el Conde de Barcelos don Pedro Afonso. Ed. Diego Catalán and Maria Soledad. Madrid, 1971.
Crònica general de Pere III el Cerimoniós. Ed. A. J. Soberanas Lleó. Barcelona, 1961.
Crónica geral de Espanha de 1344. Ed. L. F. Lindley Cintra. 3 vols. Lisbon, 1951–1961.
Crónica latina de los reyes de Castilla. Ed. Maria Desamparados Cabanés Pecourt. Valencia, 1964.
Crónicas dos sete primeiros reis de Portugal. Ed. Carlos da Silva Tarouca. 3 vols. Lisbon, 1952–1953.
Gesta Comitum Barchinonensium. Ed. L. Barrau-Dihigo and J. Massó Torrents. Barcelona, 1925.
Lucas of Túy. *Crónica de España*. Ed. Julio Puyol. Madrid, 1926.
Orosius, Paul. *Historiarum Libri Septem*. PL, 31, 635–1174.
Primera Crónica General. 2d ed. by Ramón Menéndez Pidal. 2 vols. Madrid, 1955.
Rodrigo Jiménez de Rada. *De rebus Hispaniae* in *Opera*. Ed. Francisco Lorenzana. Madrid, 1793. Reprint, Valencia, 1968.
Tomic, Pere. *Històries e Conquestes dels Reys d'Aragó e Comtes de Catalunya*. Barcelona, 1534. Reprint, Valencia, 1970.
Turell, Gabriel. *Recort*. Ed. J. Casas Carbó and J. Massó Torrents. Barcelona, 1894.

Muslim

Al-Himyari. *Kitab al-Rawd al-Mitar*. Tr. Pilar Maestro González. Valencia, 1963.
———. *La péninsule ibérique au moyen âge*. Ed. and tr. E. Lévi-Provençal. Leiden, 1938.

Al-Hulal al-Mawsiyya. Crónica árabe de las dinastías almorávide, almohade y benimerin. Tr. Ambrosio Huici. Tetuán, 1952.

Al-Maqqari. *Analectes sur l'histoire et la littérature des Arabes d'Espagne.* Ed. R. Dozy et al. 5 vols. Leyden, 1855–1860.

——. *The History of the Mohammedan Dynasties in Spain.* Tr. Pascual de Gayangos. 2 vols. London, 1843.

Al-Marrakushi. *Histoire des Almohades.* Tr. E. Fagnan. Algiers, 1893.

——. *The History of the Almohades.* Ed. Reinhart Dozy. Leyden, 1881.

——. *Kitab al-Muyib fi Taljis ajbar al-Magrib: Lo Admirable en el resumen de las noticias del Magrib.* Tr. Ambrosio Huici. Tetuán, 1955.

Ibn Abi Zar. *Rawd al-Qirtas.* Tr. Ambrosio Huici. 2 vols. Valencia, 1964.

Ibn al-Athir. *Annales du Maghreb et de l'Espagne.* Tr. E. Fagnan. Algiers, 1901.

Ibn Idhari. *Al-Bayan al-Mugrib.* Tr. Ambrosio Huici. 2 vols. Tetuán, 1953.

——. *Al-Bayan al-Mugrib. Nuevos fragmentos almorávides y almohades.* Tr. Ambrosio Huici. Valencia, 1963.

——. *Histoire de l'Afrique et de l'Espagne.* Ed. Reinhart Dozy. 2 vols. Leyden, 1848–1851.

——. *Histoire de l'Afrique et de l'Espagne.* Tr. E. Fagnan. 3 vols. Algiers, 1901–1930.

Ibn Khaldun. *Histoire des Berberes et des dynasties musulmanes de l'Afrique septentrionale.* Tr. Baron de Slane. 4 vols. Paris, 1852–1856.

——. *The Muqaddimah: An Introduction to History.* Tr. Franz Rosenthal. 3 vols. New York, 1958.

PART I: THE VISIGOTHIC ERA

Narrative Sources

Garvin, J. N. *The Vitas Sanctorum Patrum Emeritensium.* Washington, 1946.

Idatius. *Continuatio Chronicorum Hieronymianorum ad annum CCCCLVIII.* MGH Auct. Antiq., XI. Chronica Minora, II, 1–36.

Ildefonsus of Toledo. *Liber de viris illustribus.* PL, 96, 195–206.

Isidore of Seville. *Chronicon.* MGH Auct. Antiq., XI. Chronica Minora, II, 424–481.

——. *Historia de Regibus Gothorum, Wandalorum, et Suevorum.* MGH Auct. Antiq., XI. Chronica Minora, II, 267–303.

——. *History of the Kings of the Goths, Vandals, and Suevi.* Tr. G. Donini and G. Ford. 2d ed. Leyden, 1970.

John of Biclaro. *Chronicon.* MGH Auct. Antiq., XI. Chronica Minora, II, 211–220.

Julian of Toledo. *Historia Galliae temporibus Wambae.* PL, 96, 759–809.

Nock, F. C. *The Vita Sancti Fructuosi.* Washington, 1946.

Victor of Tunis. *Chronicon.* MGH Auct. Antiq., XI. Chronica Minora, II, 184–206.

Literary and Documentary Sources

Barlow, Claude. *The Iberian Fathers.* 2 vols. Washington, 1969.

Braulio of Zaragoza. *Epistolario*. Ed. José Madoz. Madrid, 1941.

El Código de Eurico. Ed. Alvaro D'Ors. Madrid, 1960.

Concilios Visigóticos e Hispano-Romanos. Ed. J. Vives, T. Marín Martínez, and G. Martínez Díez. Madrid, 1963.

Fructuosus of Braga. *Regula monachorum; Regula monastica communis*. PL, 87, 1099–1130.

Isidore of Seville. *Etymologiarum sive Originum Libri XX*. Ed. W. M. Lindsay, 2 vols. Oxford, 1911.

——. *The Letters*. Ed. and tr. G. B. Ford. 2d ed. Amsterdam, 1970.

——. *Opera*. PL, 81–85.

Lex Romana Visigothorum. Ed. G. Haenel. Berlin, 1849.

Liber Judiciorum, in *Leges Visigothorum*. Ed. K. Zeumer. MGH Legum Sectio, I, t. I, 33–456.

Martínez Díez, Gonzalo, ed. *La Colección canónica hispana*. Madrid, 1966.

Modern Works

Abadal, Ramón de. *Del reino de Tolosa al reino de Toledo*. Madrid, 1960.

——. *La batalla del adopcionismo y la desintegración de la iglesia visigoda*. Barcelona, 1949.

Bidagor, Ramón. *La iglesia propia en España*. Rome, 1933.

Díaz y Díaz, Manuel, ed. *Isidoriana: Estudios sobre San Isidoro de Sevilla en el XIV centenario de su nacimiento*. León, 1961.

D'Ors, Alvaro. "La territorialidad del derecho de los visigodos," *Estudios Visigóticos*, 1 (1956) 91–124.

Fontaine, Jacques. *Isidore de Seville et la culture classique dans l'Espagne wisigothique*. 2 vols. Paris, 1959.

García Gallo, Alfonso. "Nacionalidad y territorialidad del derecho en la época visigoda," *AHDE*, 13 (1936–41) 168–264.

Katz, Solomon. *The Jews in the Visigothic and Frankish Kingdoms of Gaul and Spain*. Cambridge, Mass., 1937.

King, P. D. *Law and Society in the Visigothic Kingdom*. Cambridge, 1972.

Lear, F. S. "The Public Law of the Visigothic Code," *Speculum*, 26 (1951) 1–23.

Lynch, C. H. *St. Braulio, Bishop of Saragossa: His Life and Writings*. Washington, 1938.

Merêa, Paulo. *Estudos de direito visigótico*. Coimbra, 1948.

Murphy, F. X. "Julian of Toledo and the Fall of the Visigothic Kingdom in Spain," *Speculum*, 27 (1952) 1–27.

Prado, Germán. *Manual de la litúrgia hispano-visigótica o mozárabe*. Madrid, 1927.

Sánchez Albornoz, Claudio. "El aula regia y las asambleas políticas de los godos," *CHE*, 5 (1946) 5–110.

——. *Ruina y extinción del municipio romana en España y las instituciones que le reemplazan*. Buenos Aires, 1943.

——. *El stipendium hispano-godo y los origenes del beneficio prefeudal.* Buenos Aires, 1947.

Thompson, E. A. *The Goths in Spain.* Oxford, 1969.

Ziegler, Aloysius. *Church and State in Visigothic Spain.* Washington, 1930.

PART II: THE ASCENDANCY OF ISLAM

Sources

Muslim

Abd al-Hakam. *History of the Conquest of Spain.* Ed. and tr. J. H. Jones. London, 1858.

Ajbar Machmua. Colección de Tradiciones. Crónica anónima del siglo XI. Ed. and tr. Emilio Lafuente y Alcántara. Madrid, 1867.

Al-Khushani, *Historia de los jueces de Córdoba.* Ed. and tr. Julián Ribera. Madrid, 1914.

Crónica anónima de Abd al-Rahman III al-Nasir. Ed. and tr. E. Lévi-Provençal and E. García Gómez. Madrid-Granada, 1950.

Fath al-Andalusi. Historia de la conquista de España. Tr. J. González. Algiers, 1899.

Ibn al-Qutiyya. *Historia de la conquista de España de Abenalcotía el Cordobés.* Ed. and tr. Julián Ribera. Madrid, 1926.

Ibn Hawkal. *Configuración del mundo: Fragmentos alusivos de Magreb y España.* Tr. Maria Roman i Suay. Valencia, 1971.

Ibn Hayyan. *Al-Muktabis: Chronique du régne du calife umaiyade Abd Allah a Courdoue.* Ed. Melchor Antuna. Paris, 1937.

Isa al-Razi. *Anales palatinos del califa de Córdoba al-Hakam II.* Tr. Emilio García Gómez. Madrid, 1967.

Christian

Agobard of Lyons. *Liber adversum dogma Felicis Urgellensis. PL,* 104, 29–70.

Alcuin. *Adversus Felicis Haeresin libellus ad abbates et monachos Gothiae missus; Contra Felicem Urgellitanum Episcopum Libri VII; Contra epistolam sibi ab Elipando directam Libri IV. PL,* 101, 87–300.

Alvarus of Córdoba. *Confessio; Epistolae; Indiculus Luminosus; Carmina. PL,* 121, 397–565.

——. *Vita Eulogii. PL,* 115, 705–720.

Annales Regni Francorum. MGH SS, I, 112–218.

Barrau-Dihigo, L. "Notes et documents sur l'histoire du royaume de León," *RH,* 10 (1903) 349–454; 16 (1907) 539–564.

Chronicle of 754. Continuatio Hispana. MGH Auct. Antiq., XI, *Chronica Minora,* II, 323–368.

Chronique de Moissac. MGH SS, I, 280–313.

Crónica de Alfonso III. Ed. Zacarías García Villada. Madrid, 1918.

Crónicon Albeldense. ES, 13, 417–466.

Einhard. *Life of Charlemagne.* Ed. H. W. Garrod and R. B. Mowat. Oxford, 1925.

Eulogius of Córdoba. *Memoriale Sanctorum Libri III, Documentum Martyriale, Epistolae, Liber apologeticum martyrum. PL,* 115, 731–870.

Floriano, Antonio. *Diplomática española del período astur.* 2 vols. Oviedo, 1949–1951.

Modern Works

Muslim Spain

Castejón Calderón, Rafael. *Los juristas hispano-musulmanes desde la conquista hasta la caída del califato de Córdoba.* Madrid, 1948.

Imamuddin, S. M. *The Economic History of Spain under the Umayyads, 711–1031.* Dacca, 1963.

Irving, T. B. *Falcon of Spain: A Study of Eighth-Century Spain with special emphasis on the Life of the Umayyad Ruler Abdurrahman I.* 2d ed. Lahore, 1962.

Lévi-Provençal, Evariste. *Histoire de l'Espagne musulmane, 711–1031.* 3 vols. Paris-Leiden, 1950–1953.

Monés, Hussain. *Essai sur la chute du califat de Cordoue en 1009.* Cairo 1948.

Sánchez Albornoz, Claudio. "Itinerario de la conquista de España por los musulmanes," *CHE,* 10 (1948) 21–74.

Christian Spain

Abadal, Ramón de. *Catalunya Carolingia.* 3 vols. Barcelona, 1926–1955.

Barrau-Dihigo, L. "Étude sur les actes des rois asturiens, 718–910," *RH,* 46 (1919) 1–192.

——. "Les origenes du royaume de Navarre d'aprés un théorie récente," *RH* 7 (1900) 141–222.

——. "Les premiers rois de Navarre," *RH,* 15 (1906) 614–644.

——. "Récherches sur l'histoire politique du royaume asturien, 718–910," *RH,* 52 (1921) 1–360.

Colbert, Edward. *The Martyrs of Córdoba: A Study of the Sources.* Washington, 1962.

Cotarelo, Armando. *Historia crítica y documentada de la vida de Alfonso III el Magno.* Madrid, 1933.

David, Pierre. *Études historiques sur la Galice et le Portugal de VIe au XIIe siècle.* Lisbon-Paris, 1947.

Floriano, Antonio. *Estudios de historia de Asturias.* Oviedo, 1962.

Martínez Díez, Gonzalo, "Las instituciones del reino astur a través de los diplomas (718–910)," *AHDE,* 35 (1965) 59–168.

Pérez de Urbel, Justo. *Historia del condado de Castilla.* 3 vols. Madrid, 1945.

Ramos Loscertales, J. M. *El reino de Aragón bajo la dinastía pamplonesa.* Salamanca, 1961.

Sage, Carleton. *Paul Albar of Córdoba.* Washington, 1943.

Sánchez Albornoz, Claudio. *Despoblación y repoblación del valle del Duero.* Buenos Aires, 1966.

——. *Estampas de la vida en León durante el siglo X.* 4th ed. Buenos Aires, 1947.

——. *Investigaciones sobre historiografía hispana medieval (siglos VIII al XII).* Buenos Aires, 1967.

Sánchez Candeira, Alfonso. *El regnum-imperium leonés hasta 1037.* Madrid, 1951.

PART III: A BALANCE OF POWER: FROM THE FALL OF THE CALIPHATE TO LAS NAVAS DE TOLOSA

Sources

Muslim

Abu Bakr of Tortosa. *Lámpara de los príncipes.* Tr. M. Alarcón. 2 vols. Madrid, 1930–1931.

Al-Idrisi. *Description de l'Afrique et de l'Espagne.* Ed. and tr. R. Dozy and M. J. de Goeje. Leiden, 1864–1866.

Avempace (Ibn Bajja). *El régimen del solitario.* Ed. and tr. Miguel Asín. Madrid, 1946.

Averroës (Ibn Rushd). *Tahafut al-Tahafut.* Tr. S. van den Berg. 2 vols. Oxford, 1954.

García Gómez, Emilio. *Cinco poetas musulmanes.* Buenos Aires, 1935.

——. *Las jarchas romances de la serie árabe en su marco.* Madrid, 1965.

——. *Poemas arábigo-andaluces.* 2d ed. Buenos Aires, 1942.

——. *Todo Ben Quzman.* 3 vols. Madrid, 1972.

Ibn Abdun. *Seville musulmane au début du XII siècle.* Tr. E. Lévi-Provençal. Paris, 1947.

Ibn Hazm. *A Book containing the Risala known as the Dove's Neck Ring about Love and Lovers.* Tr. A. R. Nykl. Baltimore, 1931.

——. *El Collar de la Paloma: Tratado sobre el amor y los amantes.* Tr. E. García Gómez. Madrid, 1952.

Ibn Sahib al-Sala. *Al-Mann bil-Imama.* Tr. Ambrosio Huici. Valencia, 1969.

Ibn Said. *Moorish Poetry: A Translation of the Pennants, An Anthology Compiled in 1243.* Tr. A. J. Arberry. Cambridge, 1953.

Ibn Tufayl. *Hayy ibn Yaqzan.* Tr. L. E. Goodman. New York, 1972.

Lévi-Provençal, Evariste. "Les Mémoires de Abd Allah, dernier roi ziride de Grenade," *Al-Andalus,* 3 (1935) 232–344; 4 (1936) 29–145; 6 (1941) 1–63.

——. "Un recueil des lettres officielles almohades," *Hesperis,* 28 (1941) 1–80.

Jewish

Benjamin of Tudela. *The Itinerary.* Ed. and tr. M. N. Adler. London, 1907.

Halevi, Judah. *The Kuzari: An Argument for the Faith of Israel.* Tr. H. Hirshfeld. New York, 1964.

Ibn Daud, Abraham. *Sefer ha-Kabbalah: Libro de la tradición.* Tr. Jaime Bages. Valencia, 1972.

Ibn Gabirol, Solomon. *The Kingly Crown.* Tr. Bernard Lewis. London, 1961.

Maimonides, Moses. *The Guide of the Perplexed.* Tr. S. Pines. Chicago, 1963.

Christian

Cantar de Mio Cid. Ed. Ramón Menéndez Pidal. 3 vols. Madrid, 1954.

Chronica Adefonsi Imperatoris. Ed. Luis Sánchez Belda. Madrid, 1950.

Chronica Gothorum. Ed. Monica Blöcker-Walter, *Alfons I von Portugal* (Zürich, 1966), 151–161.

Crónica de la población de Avila. Ed. A. Hernández Segura. Valencia, 1966.

Crónica Najerense. Ed. Antonio Ubieto Arteta. Valencia, 1966.

De Expugnatione Lyxbonensis: The Conquest of Lisbon. Ed. and tr. C. W. David. New York, 1936.

González Palencia, Angel. *Los mozárabes de Toledo en los siglos XII y XIII.* 2 vols. Madrid, 1926–1928.

Historia Compostelana. ES, 20, 1–598.

Historia Silense. Ed. Justo Pérez de Urbel and Atilano González Ruíz-Zorrilla. Madrid, 1960.

Liber Maiolichinus de Gestis Pisanorum illustribus. Ed. Carlo Calisse. Rome, 1904.

Mansilla, Demetrio. *La Documentación pontificia hasta Inocencio III (965–1216).* Rome, 1955.

Pérez de Urbel, Justo. *Sampiro: Su crónica y la monarquía leonesa en el siglo X.* Madrid, 1952.

Petrus Alphonsi. *Dialogus; Disciplina clericalis. PL,* 157, 535–672.

———. *The Scholar's Guide.* Tr. J. R. Jones and J. E. Keller. Toronto, 1969.

Rassow, Peter. "Die Urkunden Kaiser Alfons VII von Spanien," *Archiv für Urkundenforschung,* 10 (1928) 327–458; 11 (1930) 66–137.

Stern, S. M. *Les chansons mozarabes.* Palermo, 1953.

Urena, Rafael. *Fuero de Cuenca.* Madrid, 1935.

Modern Works

Muslim Spain

Asín Palacios, Miguel. *El Islam cristianizado: Estudio del sufismo a través de las obras de Abenarabí de Murcia.* Madrid, 1931.

Bargebuhr, Frederick. *The Alhambra: A Cycle of Studies on the Eleventh Century in Moorish Spain.* Berlin, 1968.

Le Tourneau, R. *The Almohad Movement in North Africa in the Twelfth and Thirteenth Centuries.* Princeton, 1969.

Millás Vallicrosa, J. M. *La poesía sagrada hebraico-española.* 2d ed. Madrid, 1948.

Pérès, Henri. *La poésie andalouse en arabe classique au XIe siècle.* Paris, 1937.

Christian Spain

Biggs, Anselm. *Diego Gelmírez: First Archbishop of Compostela.* Washington, 1949.

Bishko, C. J. "Count Henrique of Portugal, Cluny and the Antecedents of the *Pacto Sucessório,"* *Revista Portuguesa de História,* 13 (1970) 155–188.

———. "Liturgical Intercession at Cluny for the King-Emperors of León," *Studia Monastica,* 3 (1961) 53–76.

———. "Peter the Venerable's Journey to Spain," *Petrus Venerabilis, 1156– 1956.* Ed. G. Constable and J. Kritzeck. Rome (1956) 163–76.

Calzada, Luciano de la. "La proyección del pensamiento de Gregorio VII en los reinos de Castilla y León," *Studi Gregoriani,* 3 (1948) 1–87.

Defourneaux, Marcelin. *Les français en Espagne aux XIe et XIIe siècles.* Paris, 1949.

Erdmann, Carl. *Das Papsttum und Portugal im ersten Jahrhundert der Portugiesischen Geschichte.* Berlin, 1928.

García Gallo, Alfonso. "El Concilio de Coyanza: Contribución al estudio del derecho canónico español de la alta edad media," *AHDE,* 20 (1950) 275– 633.

González, Julio. *Alfonso IX.* 2 vols. Madrid, 1944.

———. *Regesta de Fernando II.* Madrid, 1943.

———. *El reino de Castilla en la época de Alfonso VIII.* 3 vols. Madrid, 1960.

Huici, Ambrosio. *Las grandes batallas de la reconquista.* Madrid, 1956.

Lacarra, J. M. "La reconquista de Zaragoza por Alfonso I," *Al-Andalus,* 12 (1947) 65–96.

Lewis, Archibald. *The Development of Southern French and Catalan Society, 718–1050.* Austin, Texas, 1965.

Llorca, Bernardino. "Derechos de la Santa Sede sobre España: El pensamiento de Gregorio VII" *Miscellanea Historiae Pontificiae,* 18 (1954) 79–105.

Menéndez Pidal, Ramón. *La España del Cid.* 4th ed. 2 vols. Madrid, 1947.

———. *El imperio hispánico y los cinco reinos.* Madrid, 1950.

O'Callaghan, J. F. "The Foundation of the Order of Alcántara, 1176–1218," *The Catholic Historical Review,* 47 (1962) 471–486.

———. "*Hermandades* between the Military Orders of Calatrava and Santiago during the Castilian Reconquest, 1158–1252," *Speculum,* 44 (1969) 609– 618.

———. "The Order of Calatrava and the Archbishops of Toledo, 1158–1252," in *Studies in Medieval Cistercian History Presented in Honor of Jeremiah F. O'Sullivan.* Spencer, Mass. 1971.

Peres, Damião. *Como nasceu Portugal.* 4th ed. Porto, 1955.

Pérez de Urbel, Justo. *Sancho el mayor de Navarra.* Madrid, 1950.

Pescador, Carmela. "La caballería popular en León y Castilla," *CHE,* 33–34 (1961) 101–238; 35–36 (1962) 56–201.

Powers, J. F. "The Origins and Development of Municipal Military Service in the Leonese and Castilian Reconquest, 800-1250," *Traditio,* 16 (1970) 91– 113.

————. "Townsmen and Soldiers: The Interaction of Urban and Military Organization in the Militias of Medieval Castile," *Speculum*, 46 (1971) 641–655.

Soldevila, Ferran. *Ramon Berenguer IV*. Barcelona, 1955.

PART IV: THE GREAT RECONQUEST AND THE BEGINNINGS OF OVERSEAS EXPANSION

Sources

Muslim

Al-Shaqundi. *Elogio del Islam español*. Tr. E. García Gómez. Madrid, 1934.

Hoernerbach, Wilhelm. *Spanische-Islamische Urkunden aus der Zeit der Nasriden und Moriscos*. Berkeley-Los Angeles, 1965.

Ibn al-Khatib. *Correspondencia diplomática entre Granada y Fez*. Ed. Melchior Gaspar Remiro. Granada, 1916.

————. *Islamische Geschichte Spaniens*. Tr. W. Hoernerbach. Zurich, 1970.

López Ortiz, José. "Fatwas granadinas," *Al-Andalus*, 6 (1941) 73–127.

Tratados de legislación musulmana. *Memorial Histórico Español*, 5 (1853) 1–449.

Christian

Chronicles

The Chronicle of James I, King of Aragon. Tr. J. Forster. 2 vols. London, 1883.

Chronique catalane de Pierre IV d'Aragon. Ed. Amédée Pagès. Toulouse, 1941.

Crónica de D. Diniz, rei de Portugal. Ed. Carlos da Silva Tarouca. Coimbra, 1947.

Crònica de Jaume I. Ed. J. M. de Casacuberta and E. Bague. 9 vols. Barcelona, 1926–1962.

Crónica del rey don Alfonso X. BAE, 66 (1875) 3–66.

Crónica del rey don Alfonso XI. BAE, 66 (1875) 173–392.

Crónica del rey don Fernando IV. BAE, 66 (1875) 93–170.

Crónica del rey don Sancho IV. BAE, 66 (1875) 69–90.

Desclot, Bernat. *Chronicle of the Reign of King Pedro III of Aragon*. Tr. F. L. Critchlow. 2 vols. Princeton, 1928–1934.

————. *Crònica*. Ed. M. Coll i Alentorn. 5 vols. Barcelona, 1949–1951.

Loaysa, Jofre de. *Crónica de los reyes de Castilla*. Ed. and tr. A. García Martínez. Murcia, 1961.

Lopes, Fernão. *Crónica de D. Pedro I*. Ed. Damião Peres. Barcelos, 1932.

López de Ayala, Pedro. *Crónica de don Pedro I*. BAE, 66 (1875) 393–614.

Muntaner, Ramon. *The Chronicle of Muntaner*. Tr. Lady Henrietta Goodenough. 2 vols. Hakluyt Society Publications. Series 2, nos. 47, 50. London, 1920–1921.

————. *Crònica*. Ed. Enric Bague. 2d ed. 9 vols. Barcelona, 1927–1952.

Pina, Rui de. *Crónica de D. Dinis*. Porto, 1945.

Documents

Becerro. *Libro famoso de las behetrías de Castilla.* Ed. Fabián Hernández. Santander, 1866.

Benavides, Antonio. *Memorias de Fernando IV de Castilla.* 2 vols. Madrid, 1860.

Burriel, Antonio. *Memorias para la vida del santo rey don Fernando III.* Ed. Miguel de Manuel Rodríguez. Madrid, 1800.

Finke, Heinrich. *Acta Aragonensia: Quellen zur deutschen, italeinischen, französischen, spanischen Kirchen- und Kulturgeschichte aus der diplomatischen Korrespondenz Jaymes II.* 3 vols. Berlin, 1903–1933.

Fori antiqui Valentiae. Ed. Manuel Dualde Serrano. Madrid-Valencia, 1950–1967.

Fuero general de Navarra. Ed. P. Ilarregui and S. Lapuerta. Pamplona, 1869.

Los Fueros de Aragón. Ed. Gunnar Tilander. Lund, 1937.

García Gallo, Alfonso. "El libro de leyes de Alfonso el sabio," *AHDE,* 21–22 (1951–52) 345–528.

Huici, Ambrosio. *Colección diplomática de Jaime I.* 2 vols. in 4. Valencia, 1916–1919.

Llibre del Consolat de Mar. Ed. Ferran Valls i Taberner. 2 vols. Barcelona, 1930–1933.

Mansilla, Demetrio. *La documentación pontificia de Honorio III.* Rome, 1965.

Penyafort, Ramon de. *Diplomatario.* Ed. J. Rius Serra. Barcelona, 1954.

Rubió i Lluch, Antonio. *Diplomatari de l'orient català.* Barcelona, 1947.

Siete Partidas, in *Los Códigos Españoles,* II–V.

Usatges de Barcelona. Ed. R. d'Abadal and F. Valls Taberner. Barcelona, 1913.

Vidal Mayor. Traducción aragonesa de la obra In excelsis Dei Thesauris de Vidal de Canellas. Ed. Gunnar Tillander. 3 vols. Lund, 1956.

Vincke, Johannes. *Documenta selecta mutuas civitatis arago-cathalaunicae et ecclesiae relationes illustrantia.* Barcelona, 1936.

Literature and Theology

Alfonso X. *Cantigas de Santa Maria.* Ed. Real Academia de la Historia. 2 vols. Madrid, 1889.

———. *Setenario.* Ed. K. H. Vanderford. Buenos Aires, 1945.

Alvaro Pelayo. *De planctu ecclesiae libri II.* Venice, 1560.

———. *Speculum regum.* Ed. Richard Scholz. *Unbekannte Kirchenpolitische Streitschriften aus der Zeit Ludwigs des Bayern* (1327–1354). 2 vols. (Berlin, 1914), II, 514–529.

Arnau de Vilanova. *Obres catalanes.* Ed. J. Carreras Artau. Barcelona, 1947.

Berceo, Gonzalo de. *Milagros de Nuestra Señora.* 3d ed. A. G. Solalinde. Madrid, 1944.

———. *Vida de Santo Domingo de Silos.* BAE, 57 (1895) 39–64.

Cancioneiro da Biblioteca Nacional. Antigo Colucci-Brancuti. Ed. E. Paxeco Machado and J. P. Machado, 8 vols. Lisbon, n.d.

Castigos y documentos del rey don Sancho IV. Ed. Agapito Rey. Bloomington, Ind., 1952.

Gil de Zamora. *De Preconiis Hispaniae.* Ed. Manuel de Castro y Castro. Madrid, 1955.

Juan Manuel. *Obras.* Ed. J. M. Castro y Calvo and M. Riquier. Madrid, 1955.

Llibre de Saviesa del rey don Jaime I. Ed. J. M. Castro y Calvo. Madrid, 1946.

Llull, Ramon. *Obras literarias.* Ed. M. Batllori and M. Caldentey. Madrid, 1945.

——. *Opera omnia.* Ed. Ivo Salzinger. 10 vols. Mainz, 1721–1742.

López de Ayala, Pedro. *Rimado de Palacio. BAE,* 57 (1895) 423–476.

Martí, Ramon. *Pugio fidei adversus Mauros et Judaeos.* Paris, 1651.

Pedro Pascual. *Obras.* Ed. J. Armengol Valenzuela. Rome, 1905–1908.

Penyafort, Ramon de. *Summa de penitentia.* Rome, 1603.

Poema de Alfonso XI. Ed. Yo Ten Cate. Madrid, 1956.

Poema de Fernán González. Ed. A. Zamora Vicente. Madrid, 1946.

Ruíz, Juan, Archpriest of Hita. *Libro de Buen Amor.* Ed. Julio Cejador. 2 vols. Madrid, 1960.

Modern Works

Aragon

Atiya, Aziz. *Egypt and Aragon: Embassies and Diplomatic Correspondence 1300–1330.* Leipzig, 1938.

Burns, Robert I. *The Crusader Kingdom of Valencia.* 2 vols. Cambridge, Mass., 1967.

Dufourcq, Charles. *L'Espagne catalane et le Maghrib aux XIIIe et XIVe siècles.* Paris, 1967.

Giménez Soler, Andrés. *La Corona de Aragón y Granada.* Barcelona, 1905.

Giunta, Francesco. *Aragonesi e Catalani nel Mediterraneo.* 2 vols. Palermo, 1953–1959.

Gubern, Ramón. *Pere el Cerimoniós i els sues fils.* Barcelona, 1960.

Martínez Ferrando, J. Ernesto. *Els descendants de Pere el Gran.* Barcelona, 1957.

Masía de Ros, Angeles. *La corona de Aragón y los estados del norte de Africa: Política de Jaime II y Alfonso IV en Egipto, Ifriquía y Tremecen.* Barcelona, 1951.

Peers, E. Allison. *Fool of Love: The Life of Ramon Lull.* London, 1946.

Salavert, Vicente. *Cerdeña y la expansión mediterránea de la corona de Aragón, 1297–1314.* Madrid, 1956.

Schlumberger, Gustave. *Expédition des almugavares ou routiers catalanes en Orient.* Paris, 1902.

Setton, Kenneth. *Catalan Domination of Athens, 1311–1388.* Cambridge, Mass., 1948.

Smith, Robert. *The Spanish Guild Merchant: A History of the Consulado, 1250–1700.* Durham, N.C., 1940.

Wieruszowski, Helene. *Politics and Culture in Medieval Spain and Italy*. Rome, 1971.

Castile and Granada

Arie, Rachel. *L'Espagne musulmane au temps des Nasrides (1232–1492)*. Paris, 1973.

Ballesteros, Antonio. *Alfonso X el Sabio*. Murcia, 1963.

Carlé, Maria del Carmen. "Mercaderes en Castilla, 1252–1512," *CHE*, 21–22 (1954) 146–328.

Daumet, Georges. *Mémoires sur les relations de la France et la Castille de 1255 à 1320*. Paris, 1913.

Gaibrois de Ballesteros, Mercedes. *Historia del reinado de Sancho IV de Castilla*. 3 vols. Madrid, 1922.

Giménez Soler, Andrés. *Don Juan Manuel*. Zaragoza, 1932.

González, Julio. *Las conquistas de Fernando III en Andalucía*. Madrid, 1945.

Gorosterratzu, Javier. *Don Rodrigo Jiménez de Rada*. Pamplona, 1925.

Iung, Nicholas. *Un Franciscain Théologien du Pouvoir pontifical au XIVe siècle: Alvaro Pelayo*. Paris, 1931.

Keller, J. E. *Alfonso X el Sabio*. New York, 1967.

Ladero Quesada, Miguel Angel. *Granada: Historia de un país islámico, 1232–1571*. Madrid, 1969.

Linehan, Peter. *The Spanish Church and the Papacy in the Thirteenth Century*. Cambridge, 1971.

Mansilla, Demetrio. *Iglesia castellano-leonesa y curia romana en los tiempos del rey san Fernando*. Madrid, 1945.

O'Callaghan, J. F. "The Cortes and Royal Taxation during the Reign of Alfonso X of Castile," *Traditio*, 27 (1971) 379–398.

Procter, Evelyn. *Alfonso X of Castile*. Oxford, 1951.

——. "The Towns of León and Castile as Suitors before the King's Court," *English Historical Review*, 74 (1959) 1–22.

Sánchez Albornoz, Claudio. *La curia regia portuguesa: Siglos XII–XIII*. Madrid, 1920.

PART V: THE STRUGGLE FOR PENINSULAR UNION

Sources

Aragon

Beccadelli, Antonio. *De dictis et factis Alphonsi V*. Pisa, 1485.

Carbonell, Pere Miquel. *Chroniques d'Espanya*. Barcelona, 1547.

Coroleu, José. *Los dietarios de la generalidad de Cataluña*. Barcelona, 1889.

Fazio, Bartolomeo. *De rebus gestis ab Alphonso V*. Lyons, 1560.

Marineo Siculo, Lucio. *Historia regum Aragoniae*. Zaragoza, 1509.

Pasquier, Felix. *Lettres de Louis XI relatives a sa politique en Catalogne de 1461–1473*. Foix, 1895.

Safont, Jaume. *Dietari de la Diputació del General de Catalunya, 1454–1472*. Ed. M. Mitjà. Barcelona, 1950.

Salas Bosch, Xavier de. *La Fi del Comte d'Urgell*. Barcelona, 1931.
Valla, Lorenzo. *Historia Ferdinandi regis Aragoniae*. Paris, 1521. Reprint. Valencia, 1970.

Castile

Barrientos, Lope de. *Refundición de la Crónica del Halconero*. Ed. J. de Mata Carriazo. Madrid, 1946.
Boutier, Pierre, and Jean le Verrier. *The Canarian or Book of the Conquest and Conversion of the Canarians in the year 1402 by Messire Jean de Bethencourt*. Ed. and tr. R. H. Major. Hakluyt Society Publications. Series 1, no. 46. London, 1872.
Carrillo de Huete, Pedro. *Crónica del Halconero de Juan II*. Ed. J. de Mata Carriazo. Madrid, 1946.
Crónica de Alvaro de Luna. Ed. J. de Mata Carriazo. Madrid, 1946.
Díez de Gámez, Gutierre. *The Unconquered Knight: A Chronicle of the Deeds of Pero Niño, Count of Buelna*. Tr. J. Evans. New York, 1928.
Enríquez del Castillo, Diego. *Crónica del rey don Enrique IV*. BAE, 70 (1875) 99–222.
Escabías, Pedro de. *Hechos del Condestable Miguel Lucas de Iranzo*. Ed. J. de Mata Carriazo. Madrid, 1946.
González de Clavijo, Rúy. *Narrative of the Embassy to the Court of Timour*. Tr. C. R. Markham. Hakluyt Society Publications. Series 1, no. 26. London, 1859.
López de Ayala, Pedro. *Crónicas de los reyes de Castilla: Enrique II, Juan I y Enrique III*. BAE, 68 (1875) 1–257.
Memorias de don Enrique IV de Castilla. Madrid, 1835–1913.
Palencia, Alonso de. *Crónica de Enrique IV*. Tr. A. Paz y Melia. 5 vols. Madrid, 1904–1909.
Pérez de Guzmán, Fernán. *Crónica de Juan II*. BAE, 68 (1875) 276–695.
———. *Generaciones y Semblanzas*. BAE, 68 (1875) 697–719.
Pulgar, Fernando del. *Claros Varones de Castilla*. Ed. R. B. Tate. Oxford, 1971.
Valera, Diego de. *Memorial de diversas hazañas*. Ed. J. de Carriazo. Madrid, 1941.

Granada

Carriazo, Juan de Mata. "Cartas de la frontera de Granada," *Al-Andalus*, 11 (1946) 69–130.
Gaspar y Remiro, Mariano. "Documentos árabes de la corte nazari de Granada," *Revista de Archivos, Bibliotecas y Museos*, 21 (1909) 330–339, 531–535; 22 (1910) 260–269, 421–431; 23 (1911) 127–148, 411–423.
Gaspar y Remiro, Mariano, J. M. Caparros, and C. Espejo, "Documentos para la historia del reino granadino," *Revista del Centro de Estudios históricos de Granada*, 2 (1912) 18–39.
Ibn Hudhail. *L'ornement des ames et la devise des habitants d'el Andalus*. Tr. Louis Mercier. Paris, 1936.

Lafuente Alcántara, Emilio. *Inscripciones árabes de Granada*. Madrid, 1859.
Seco de Lucena, Luis. *Documentos árabigos-granadinos*. Madrid, 1961.

Portugal

Alvares, João. *Crónica do Infante Santo Dom Fernando*. Ed. Mendes dos Remedios. Coimbra, 1911.
Azurara, Gomes Eannes. *Crónica de descobrimento e conquista da Guiné*. Ed. J. de Bragança. 2 vols. Oporto, 1937.
——. *The Discovery and Conquest of Guinea*. Tr. C. R. Beazley and E. Prestage. Hakluyt Society Publications. Series 1, no. 95. London, 1896.
Lopes, Fernão. *Crónica de Dom Fernando I*. Ed. Damião Peres. 2 vols. Barcelos, 1933–1935.
——. *Crónica de Dom João I*. Ed. António Sérgio. 2 vols. Porto, 1945–1949.
Magalhães Godinho, Vitorino de. *Documentos sobre a expansão portuguesa*. 3 vols. Lisbon, 1943–1956.
Monumenta Henricina. Ed. M. Lopes de Almeida et al. 6 vols. Lisbon, 1960.
Pina, Rui de. *Crónica del rei Dom Afonso V*. Ed. G. Pereira. 3 vols. Lisbon, 1901–1902.
——. *Crónica del rei Dom Duarte*. Ed. G. Pereira. Lisbon, 1901.

Literature and Theology

Cancionero Castellano del siglo XV. Ed. R. Foulché-Delbosc. 2 vols. Madrid, 1912–1915.
Cartagena, Alonso de. *Defensorium unitatis christianae*. Ed. Manuel Alonso. Madrid, 1943.
Duarte. *Leal Conselheiro*. Ed. J. Piel. Lisbon, 1942.
Eiximenis, Francesch. *Regiment de la Cosa Pública*. Ed. Daniel de Molins de Rei. Barcelona, 1928.
Eymerich, Nicolás. *Directorium Inquisitorum*. Rome, 1585.
Madrigal, Alonso de. *De optima politia*. Venice, 1615.
March, Auziàs. *Les Obres*. Ed. Amédée Pagès. 2 vols. Barcelona, 1912–1915.
Martínez de Toledo, Alfonso. *Arcipreste de Talavera: Corbacho*. Ed. J. González Muela. Madrid, 1970.
Metge, Bernat. *Obres*. Ed. Martin de Riquier. Barcelona, 1959.
Michaelis de Vasconcelos, Carolina. *Cancioneiro de Ajuda*. 2 vols. Halle, 1904.
Monaci, Ernesto. *Il Canzionere Portoghese della Biblioteca Vaticana*. Halle, 1876.
Pedro, Duke of Coimbra. *Livro da virtuosa bemfeitoria*. Ed. Joaquim Costa. Porto, 1940.
Pérez de Guzmán, Fernán. *Loores de los claros varones de España*, in *Cancionero castellano del Siglo XV*. I, 706–752.
Roig, Jaume. *Llibre de les Dones o Spill*. Ed. Francesc Almela. Barcelona, 1928.
Sánchez de Arévalo, Rodrigo. *Suma de la política*. Ed. Juan Beneyto Pérez. Madrid, 1944.

Torquemada, Juan de. *Summa de Ecclesia.* Venice, 1561.
Turmeda, Anselm. *Disputa de l'ase.* Ed. Marcel Olivar. Barcelona, 1928.

Modern Works

Aragon

Batlle, Carmen. "La ideología de la Busca: La crisis municipal de Barcelona en el siglo XV," *Estudios de Historia Moderna,* 5 (1955) 165–196.

Boscolo, Alberto. *I Parlamenti di Alfonso il Magnanimo.* Milan, 1953.

Carrère, Claude. *Barcelone, centre économique, a l'époque des difficultés, 1380–1462.* 2 vols. Paris, 1967.

Dualde, Manuel, and José Camarena. *El Compromiso de Caspe.* Zaragoza, 1971.

Hamilton, Earl. *Money, prices and wages in Valencia, Aragon and Navarre (1351–1500).* Cambridge, 1936.

Rubió y Cambronero, Ignacio. *La Deputació del General de Catalunya en los siglos XV y XVI.* 2 vols. Barcelona, 1950.

Sobreques, Santiago. *La alta nobleza del norte en la guerra civil catalana de 1462 a 1472.* Zaragoza, 1966.

———. "Los origenes de la revolución catalana del siglo XV: Las cortes de Barcelona de 1454–1458," *Estudios de Historia Moderna,* 2 (1952) 1–96.

Usher, A. P. *The Early History of Deposit Banking in Mediterranean Europe: Banking in Catalonia.* Cambridge, Mass., 1943.

Vicens Vives, Jaime. *Els Trastámares.* Barcelona, 1956.

———. *Fernando el Católico, Principe de Aragón, Rey de Sicilia, 1458–1478.* Madrid, 1952.

———. *Monarquía y revolución en la España del siglo XV: Juan II de Aragón.* Barcelona, 1953.

Castile

Daumet, Georges. *Etude sur l alliance de la France et de la Castille au XIVe et au XVe siècles.* Paris, 1898.

Ferrara, Orestes. *Un pleito sucesorio: Enrique IV, Isabel de Castilla y la Beltraneja.* Madrid, 1945.

Macdonald, Inez. *Don Fernando de Antequera.* Oxford, 1948.

Marañon, Gregorio. *Ensayo biológico sobre Enrique IV de Castilla.* Madrid, 1930.

Russell, P. E. *English Intervention in Spain and Portugal in the Time of Edward III and Richard II.* Oxford, 1955.

Sitges, J. B. *Enrique IV y la excelente señora . . . doña Juana la Beltraneja.* Madrid, 1912.

Suárez Fernández, Luis. *Castilla, el Cisma y la crisis conciliar, 1378–1440.* Madrid, 1960.

———. *Estudios sobre el régimen monárquico de Enrique II de Castilla.* Madrid, 1956.

——. *Juan J, rey de Castilla*. Madrid, 1956.

——. *Nobleza y monarquía: Puntos de vista sobre historia castellana del siglo XV*. Valladolid, 1959.

——. *Relaciones entre Portugal y Castilla en la época del Jnfante don Enrique*. Madrid, 1964.

Trame, Richard. *Rodrigo Sánchez de Arévalo: Spanish Diplomat and Champion of the Papacy*. Washington, 1960.

Navarre

Castro, J. R. *Carlos JJJ el Noble, rey de Navarra*. Pamplona, 1967.

Portugal

Albuquerque, Luis. *Jntrodução a História dos descobrimentos*. Coimbra, 1962.

Beazley, Raymond. *Prince Henry the Navigator*. London, 1895.

Oliveira Marquês, A. H. *Daily Life in Portugal in the Late Middle Ages*. Madison, Wis., 1970.

——. *Hansa e Portugal na idade media*. Lisbon, 1959.

Peres, Damião. *História dos descobrimentos portuguêses*. Porto, 1943.

Pérez Embid, Florentino. *Descubrimientos del Atlántico y la rivalidad castellano-portuguesa hasta el tratado de Jordesillas*. Madrid, 1948.

Prestage, Edgar. *The Portuguese Pioneers*. London, 1933.

Rogers, Francis. *The Travels of the Jnfante Dom Pedro of Portugal*. Cambridge, Mass., 1961.

EPILOGUE: THE CATHOLIC KINGS AND THE PERFECT PRINCE
Sources

Alvares, Francisco. *The Prester John of the Jndies*. Ed. C. F. Beckingham and G. W. B. Huntingford. 2 vols. Cambridge, 1961.

Barros, João de. *Asia*. Ed. Antonio Baião. Coimbra, 1932.

Bernáldez, Andres. *Historia de los reyes católicos, don Fernando y doña Jsabel*. Ed. Manuel Gómez Moreno and J. de Mata Carriazo. Madrid, 1962.

Gois, Damião de. *Chrónica do Principe Dom João*. Ed. Gonçalves Guimarães. Coimbra, 1905.

Llorca, Bernardino. *Bulario pontifício de la Jnquisición española en su período constitucional, 1478–1525*. Rome, 1949.

Pina, Rui de. *Crónica del rei Dom João JJ*. Ed. Alberto Martins de Carvalho. Coimbra, 1950.

Pulgar, Fernando de. *Crónica de los reyes católicos, don Fernando y doña Jsabel*. Ed. J. de Mata Carriazo. 2 vols. Madrid, 1943.

Resende, García de. *Chrónica de el rei dom João JJ*. 2 vols. Lisbon, 1902.

Torre, Antonio de la. *Documentos sobre relaciones internacionales de los reyes católicos*. 4 vols. Barcelona, 1949–1951.

Torre, Antonio de la, and Luis Suárez Fernández. *Documentos referentes a las relaciones con Portugal durante el reinado de los reyes católicos.* 3 vols. Valladolid, 1958–1963.

Valera, Diego de. *Doctrinal de Principes. BAE,* 116 (1959) 173–202.

Modern Works

Azcona, Tarsicio de. *Isabel la Católica. Estudio crítico de su vida y su reinado.* Madrid, 1964.

Boxer, C. R. *The Portuguese Seaborne Empire, 1415–1825.* New York, 1969.

Caro Baroja, Julio. *Los moriscos del reino de Granada.* Madrid, 1957.

Cepeda Adán, José. *En torno al concepto del estado en los reyes católicos.* Madrid, 1956.

García Oro, José. *La reforma de los religiosos españoles en tiempo de los reyes católicos.* Valladolid, 1969.

Ladero Quesada, Miguel Angel. *Castilla y la conquista del reino de Granada.* Valladolid, 1967.

——. *Los mudéjares de Castilla en tiempo de Isabel I.* Valladolid, 1969.

Lea, H. C. *A History of the Inquisition of Spain.* 4 vols. New York, 1906–1907.

Llorente, Miguel de la Pinta. *La inquisición española.* Madrid, 1948.

Lunenfeld, Marvin. *The Council of the Santa Hermandad: A Study of the Pacification Forces of Ferdinand and Isabella.* Coral Gables, Fla., 1971.

Moreno Casado, José. *Las capitulaciones de Granada en su aspecto jurídico.* Granada, 1949.

Reglá, Juan. *Estudios sobre los moriscos.* Valencia, 1964.

Sanceau, Elaine. *The Perfect Prince: A Biography of the King João II.* Barcelos, 1959.

Torre, Antonio de la. *Los reyes católicos y Granada.* Madrid, 1946.

Vicens Vives, Jaime. *Historia crítica de la vida y reinado de Fernando el católico.* Zaragoza, 1952.

Index

Abadal, Ramon d', 78, 257, 273, 464
Abbadids, *see* Banu Abbad
Abbasids, 100, 101, 103, 106, 109, 114, 118, 119, 138, 208, 260, 339, 343
Abd al-Aziz, governor of al-Andalus, 93-94
Abd al-Malik, son of Almanzor, 129, 131
Abd al-Malik, king of Zaragoza, 219
Abd al-Malik ibn Habid, 161
Abd al-Rahman I, emir of Córdoba, 100-103, 138
Abd al-Rahman II, emir of Córdoba, 107, 109-110, 140, 146, 156, 158
Abd al-Rahman III, caliph of Córdoba, 115-119, 121-122, 124, 132, 138-139, 141, 144, 146, 149-151, 153, 157-158, 160, 162
Abd al-Rahman IV, caliph of Córdoba, 133
Abd al-Rahman V, caliph of Córdoba, 133, 319
Abd al-Rahman, son of Almanzor, *see* Sanjul
Abd al-Rahman al-Ghafiqi, governor of al-Andalus, 98
Abd al-Wahid, Almohad caliph, 338
Abd Allah, emir of Córdoba, 114-115, 117, 138-139, 162
Abd Allah, son of Almanzor, 129
Abd Allah, king of Granada, 209 210; *Memoirs,* 204, 324
Abd Allah ibn Yasin, 208
Abencerrajes (Banu al-Sarraj), 548, 568, 612, 667
Abraham el *Barchilón,* 466
Abu Bakr of Tortosa, *Light of Princes,* 325
Abu Ishaq, emir of Tunis, 384
Abu Yahya, king of Majorca, 341-342
Abu Yaqub, Marinid emir, 392, 397
Abu Yaqub Yusuf, Almohad caliph, 237, 241, 260
Abu Yusuf Yaqub b. Abd al-Haqq, Marinid emir, 364, 373, 375, 376, 380, 391, 392
Abu Zakariyya, emir of Tunis, 343, 347, 351, 352
Abu Zayd, governor of Valencia, 338, 341, 343, 345
Abu-l-Hasan Ali, king of Granada, 667-668
Abu-l-Hassan, Marinid emir, 409, 412
Abulcasis, 161
Administration, financial, 68-69, 146-147, 174-175, 277-278, 454-456, 599-601

Administration, territorial, 28-30, 61-63, 142, 170-171, 267-269, 445-447, 591-593
Adoptionism, 186-187
Adrianople, battle of, 38
Afonso I Henriques, king of Portugal, 221-222, 224, 226-227, 230-231, 233, 235, 237-238, 241, 254, 259, 262, 360, 533
Afonso II, king of Portugal, 247, 258, 273, 300, 310, 337, 349
Afonso III, king of Portugal, 360-361, 368, 379, 432, 434, 436, 442, 480-481
Afonso IV, king of Portugal, 404, 407, 408, 410, 413, 421, 422, 461, 500, 538, 557
Afonso V, king of Portugal, 560, 566, 568-569, 572, 574, 576-577, 583, 588, 590, 593, 597, 629, 658, 661
Afonso, count of Barcelos, duke of Bragança, 566, 592
Afonso, son of João II, 662, 674
Africa, 21, 25, 39, 95, 149, 153, 209, 216, 221, 228, 231, 293, 296, 364, 386, 413, 414, 472, 479, 484, 507, 547, 548, 556, 557, 559, 567, 569, 576, 577, 579, 580, 615, 622, 623, 628, 647, 666, 669, 671-674; North, 25, 30, 39, 42, 51, 52, 70, 92, 93, 95, 100, 127, 133, 137, 147, 154, 208, 213, 227, 232, 255, 280, 281, 286, 293, 295, 306, 324, 341, 342, 354, 374, 386, 397, 404, 412, 439, 476, 400, 514, 389, 547, 548, 604, 618, 624, 665
Agila, Visigothic king, 42
Agnes of Poitiers, 224
Agriculture, 76-77, 154-155, 300-304, 475, 615-616
Airas Nunes, 497-498
Akhbar Majmua, 115, 162
Akhila, son of Witiza, 51-52
Al-Adil, Almohad caliph, 368
Al-Andalus, 89, 91, 95-103, 105, 107, 111, 113-118, 120, 122, 124, 126, 128, 132-134, 136-138, 142-144, 148, 150, 152, 153, 155-161, 163, 174, 176, 181, 182, 184-186, 193, 204, 207-211, 216, 221, 228, 229, 233, 235-237, 241, 243, 249, 254-255, 268, 271, 276, 278, 280, 282, 285, 286, 288, 289, 290, 292-294, 297, 300-302, 304-306, 308, 313, 317, 319, 321, 324, 325, 333, 338, 339, 343-345, 348, 351-354, 364, 365, 369, 373, 488, 518; *see also* Andalusia
Al-Bayasi, Abu Muhammad, 338

707

A History of Medieval Spain

Designed by R. E. Rosenbaum.
Composed by York Composition Co., Inc.
in 12 point Intertype Weiss, 1 point leaded,
with display lines in Weiss Roman.
Printed letterpress from type by York Composition Co., Inc.
on Warren's No. 66 text, 50 pound basis,
with the Cornell University Press watermark.
Illustrations printed by Art Craft of Ithaca.
Bound by The Colonial Press, Inc.
in Holliston book cloth
and stamped in All Purpose foil.